BEST PRACTICES SERIES

Financial Services Information Systems

THE AUERBACH
BEST PRACTICES SERIES

Broadband Networking, James Trulove, Editor,
ISBN: 0-8493-9821-5

Electronic Messaging, Nancy Cox, Editor,
ISBN: 0-8493-9825-8

Financial Services Information Systems, Jessica Keyes, Editor,
ISBN: 0-8493-9834-7

Healthcare Information Systems, Phillip L. Davidson, Editor,
ISBN: 0-8493-9963-7

Internet Management, Jessica Keyes, Editor,
ISBN: 0-8493-9987-4

Multi-Operating System Networking: Living with UNIX, NetWare, and NT, Raj Rajagopal, Editor,
ISBN: 0-8493-9831-2

Network Manager's Handbook, John Lusa, Editor,
ISBN: 0-8493-9841-X

Project Management, Paul C. Tinnirello, Editor,
ISBN: 0-8493-9998-X

Server Management, Gilbert Held, Editor,
ISBN: 0-8493-9823-1

Enterprise Systems Integration, John Wyzalek, Editor,
ISBN: 0-8493-9837-1

Web-to-Host Connectivity, Lisa Lindgren and
Anura Guruge, Editors
ISBN: 0-8493-0835-6

Network Design, Gilbert Held, Editor,
ISBN: 0-8493-0859-3

AUERBACH PUBLICATIONS

www.auerbach-publications.com
TO ORDER: Call: 1-800-272-7737 • Fax: 1-800-374-3401
E-mail: orders@crcpress.com

BEST PRACTICES SERIES

Financial Services Information Systems

Editor

JESSICA KEYES

CRC Press
Taylor & Francis Group
Boca Raton London New York

CRC Press is an imprint of the
Taylor & Francis Group, an **informa** business

AN AUERBACH BOOK

CRC Press
Taylor & Francis Group
6000 Broken Sound Parkway NW, Suite 300
Boca Raton, FL 33487-2742

First issued in paperback 2019

ISBN-13: 978-0-8493-9834-6 (hbk)
ISBN-13: 978-0-367-39882-8 (pbk)

Library of Congress Cataloging-in-Publication Data

Financial services information systems / Jessica Keyes, editor. --
|2nd ed.|
    p. cm. -- (Best practices)
    Earlier ed. published under title: Handbook of technology in financial services. 1999.
    Includes bibliographical references and index.
    ISBN 0-8493-9834-7 (alk. paper)
    1. Financial services industry--Data processing Handbooks. manuals. etc.
    2. Financial services industry--Technological innovations Handbooks. manuals. etc.
    I. Keyes, Jessica. 1950- . II. Title: Handbook of technology in financial services. III Series:
Best practices series (Boca Raton. Fla.)
HG173.H343 1999b
332.1'0285—dc21
                                     99-38810
                                      CIP

Visit the Taylor & Francis Web site at
http://www.taylorandfrancis.com

and the CRC Press Web site at
http://www.crcpress.com

Contributors

DAN ADLER, *Chief Technology Officer, Inventure America, New York, NY*

ERIC APPS, *President, ANGOSS Software Corporation, Toronto, Ontario, Canada*

PHILIP BASHAM, *Strategic and Development Director, KAL, Edinburgh, Scotland*

CHARLES BASSIGNANI, *Senior Vice President, Evare, LLC, Burlington, MA*

Michael J. Best, Professor, Department of Combinatorics and Optimization, University of Waterloo, Waterloo, Ontario, Canada

KIMBERLY BETHKE, *Treasury Analyst, Amway Corporation, Ada, MI*

PAT BITTON, *Market Development Manager, Trend Micro, Inc., Cupertino, CA*

STEPHEN BLOOMER, *Deputy Managing Director, Wilco International, New York, NY*

GABRIEL BOUSBIB, *Senior Vice President & COO, Risk Management Division, Reuters America Inc., New York, NY*

TIM BROCK, *Creative Director, Sealund & Associates Corporation, Clearwater, FL*

JOHN BUCKNER, *President and CEO, IMIS Inc., San Francisco, CA*

DON CHASE, *Senior Vice President, Allenbrook, Inc., Portland, ME*

THOMAS CHESBROUGH, *President and CEO, Kapstone Systems, Inc., Kansas City, MO*

JEANNE CHINCHAR, *Executive Editor, Multex.com, Inc., New York, NY*

DONALD F. COOKE, *Founder and CEO, Medici Technology, Inc., Hanover, NH*

GREG CRANDELL, *Vice President, Marketing, Corillian Corporation, Beaverton, OR*

RICHARD K. CRONE, *Vice President and General Manager, CyberCash, Inc., Reston, VA*

JACKIE CUEVAS, *Director of Marketing, Q-UP Systems, Austin, TX*

RICHARD H. DUBOIS, *Executive Vice President, Leverage Group, Inc., Glastonbury, CT*

RHONDA R. DELMATER, *Program Manager, Computer Science Innovations, Melbourne, FL*

JIM DOUTHITT, *Director of Product Marketing, SS&C Technologies, Inc., Windsor, CT*

MYERS DUPUY, *Technical Services Department Manager, Q-UP Systems, Austin, TX*

ELY ESHEL, *CTO, MINT Communications Systems, New York, NY*

ANURA GURUGÉ, *Independent Technical Analyst Consultant, Gilford, NH*

CHRIS HAMILTON, *Marketing Director, GlobeSet, Austin, TX*

MARGARET HAMILTON, *Founder and CEO, Hamilton Technologies, Inc., Cambridge, MA*

MONTE F. HANCOCK, *Chief Scientist, Computer Science Innovations, Melbourne, FL*

KNOX HENDERSON, *Communications Specialist, NICE Systems, Richmond, British Columbia, Canada*

KIM HERREN, *Strategic Marketing Director, Output Technologies, Kansas City, MO*

MARK HILL, *President, Baker Hill, Carmel, IN*

KIM HUMPHREYS, *Vice President, nFront, Inc., Bogart, GA*

INFORMATION TECHNOLOGY ASSOCIATION OF AMERICA, *Arlington, VA*

JIVENDRA K. KALE, *Professor, School of Business, Golden Gate University, San Francisco, CA*

EVAN KAPLAN, *Founder, Aventail Corporation, Seattle, WA*

JESSICA KEYES, *President, New Art Technologies, Inc., New York, NY*

ARAVINDA KORALA, *Founder and CEO, KAL, Edinburgh, Scotland*

BERNARD LUNN, *CEO, Ionic Systems International, New York, NY*

GARY MANGUS, *Product Marketing Group Manager, Litton Network Access Systems, Roanoke, VA*

CHRIS MARINO, *Founder, Resonate, Inc., Mountain View, CA*

MICHAEL MCCAFFERY, *International Marketing Manager, Persistence Software, San Mateo, CA*

JOHN MCLEOD, *CEO, Spectra Securities Software, New York, NY*

MICHAEL A. MCNEAL, *President and CEO, Absoft, Boca Raton, FL*

C. KENNETH MILLER, *Founder, Chairman, and CTO, StarBurst Communications, Concord, MA*

RON MORITZ, *Director, Technology Office, Finjan Software, San Jose, CA*

KEN ONO, *Vice President, Technology, ANGOSS Software Corporation, Toronto, Ontario, Canada*

DAVID OOLEY, *Vice President, Sales and Marketing, NSM Jukebox, Duluth, GA*

DAVID PETERSON, *Founder, Goldleaf Technologies, Inc., Lake Mary, FL*

TIMOTHY PETERSON, *Associate Director, Performance Measurement, Portfolio Management Consultants, Inc., Denver, CO*

ART PETTY, *Vice President of Marketing, Firstlogic, Inc., La Crosse, WI*

SCOTT L. PRICE, *Senior Vice President of Agency Systems and Corporate Officer, FDP Corp., Miami, FL*

JERRY RACKLEY, *Director, Teubner & Associates, Inc., Stillwater, OK*

MARY ROSE, *Vice President, Business Development, ARKSYS, Little Rock, AR*

KENNETH E. RUSSELL, *Vice President, North American Operations, Network Controls International, Charlotte, NC*

TIM SCATLIFF, *Senior Vice President of Technology, Rescom Ventures, Winnipeg, Ontario, Canada*

BARBARA SEALUND, *President and Founder, Sealund & Associates Corporation, Clearwater, FL*

HENRY SEILER, *Founder and President, Rule Machines Corporation, Indialantic, FL*

STEVEN SEMELSBERGER, *Strategic Alliances and Market Development Manager, Acuity Corporation, Austin, TX*

JAMES SUTTIE, *President & CEO, Selkirk Financial Technologies, Vancouver, BC, Canada*

FREDERIC M. WILF, *Special Counsel, Saul, Ewing, Remick & Saul, LLP, Berwyn, PA*

DAVID WILLIAMS, *Member, Board of Directors, Corillian Corporation, Beaverton, OR*

DAVE YEWMAN, *Principal, Insync Communications, Portland, OR*

Contents

xi

Preface

WELCOME TO THE SECOND EDITION OF FINANCIAL SERVICES INFORMA-
TION SYSTEMS. Much has happened over the last year. Several of the experts who contributed to the first edition moved to other companies, some
high-tech companies folded, some were born, some even changed their
names. What is true for high-tech companies is just as true for financial services companies. The rate of consolidation has accelerated even beyond
my wildest expectations, driven by the surge of mergers in the European
markets, the accelerated customer desire for "one-stop shopping," and the
financial services mantra that "bigger is better, because competing globally requires scale and scope."[1]

However, consolidation comes in two flavors. One company acquiring
another is a purely vanilla form of consolidation. Over the last decade
mergers and acquisitions have become fairly commonplace in all industries all over the world. Consolidation becomes much more interesting
when you find that it now takes only one phone call (or Internet logon) to
buy a stock, research life insurance, and pay your mortgage. This consolidation mode of the present will only accelerate in the future.

According the Gartner Group, technology is the big driver with the proliferation of electronic delivery channels as the competitive linchpin. Bos-
ton-based Fidelity Investments exemplifies this trend. Selling a wide range
of products including life insurance and mutual funds, Fidelity is using the
Web to integrate its diverse product line. As I write the preface to this book,
Fidelity is beta testing its new Web site, which provides comprehensive information on Fidelity's product line as well as an icon to contact a telephone representative in real time. Fidelity is also piloting new software that
uses a customer's voice to authenticate these very same transactions.

This book is about the technology that has enabled Fidelity, and companies like it, to make giant strides in providing exciting products and improved services to customers. The purpose of this book, then, is to provide
a guide to the tools and techniques of technology geared specifically for
the financial services IT manager, a place where he or she can go to get the
low-down on not only the up-and-coming "hot" technologies of tomorrow
but the tried and true technologies of today. The book does this from a

GENERAL FINANCIAL SERVICES

These systems permit those in banking, insurance and securities to do such things as customer profiling, Geographic Information Systems, and Personal Financial Appliances. Computer systems exist that can even build themselves. All of these topics are covered in this section.

Jessica Keyes

Chapter 1

The "Must-Have" Guide to Total Quality for the Financial Services Manager

Jessica Keyes

IN TRACY KIDDER'S LANDMARK BOOK *SOUL OF A NEW MACHINE,* he details the riveting story of a project conducted at breakneck speed, and under incredible pressure. Driven by pure adrenaline, the team members soon became obsessed with trying to achieve the impossible. For more than a year, they gave up their nights and weekends — in the end logging nearly 100 hours a week each! Somewhere buried in the midst of Kidder's prose we find that at the end of this project the entire staff quit. Not just one or two of them, but every single one!

The Financial Services field is rife with stories such as this one. Software development projects are usually complex and often mission-critical. As a result the pressure on staff to produce is great. And sometimes, as in the Kidder example, even with success comes failure.

Successful software development projects (i.e., get the product done on time — and *not* lose staff members) have something in common. Each of these projects, in some way, shape, or form, followed one or more principles of quality and productivity. Some of these principles are clearly intuitive. But most are learned or culled from vast experience over a number of years and projects.

In today's competitive environment, Information Technology (IT) is a major partner with the business units. And because of this the push is on

0-8493-9834-7/00/$0.00+$.50
© 2000 by CRC Press LLC

for enhanced software productivity and quality. In addition, the Y2K, Dow 1000, and Eurodollar crises has put a renewed emphasis on quality and productivity — often with the legal department looking over IT's shoulder. Let's face it, intuition just won't cut the mustard any longer. Nor can an organization wait until software developers learn their quality lessons over so many projects in as many years.

This chapter has condensed several decades worth of quality studies into a few brief pages. Here you'll find everything from formulas to measure productivity to measures to take to enforce stringent quality goals. Putting some of these guidelines and techniques into your bag of tricks will improve not only the quality of your software, the productivity of your staff, but the company's bottom well too.

THE MEANING OF QUALITY

Although quality and productivity are foremost on the minds of management, few truly understand how to correlate the tenets of quality to the process of information technology.

Total Quality Management, or TQM as it has come to be known, was actually born as a result of a loss of competitive edge to countries such as Japan. In fact, the father of TQM, W. E. Deming, finding no forum for his radical new ideas on quality in the U.S., found eager listeners in Japan. Today, Deming's 14 points on quality, listed in the next section, are considered the basis for all work on quality in this country as well as Japan.

But Deming's studies were only the start of a flood of research in the field. For example, Y. K. Shetty, a professor of management at Utah State University's College of Business and the co-editor of *The Quest for Competitiveness* (Quorum Books, 1991), suggests that even though most corporate executives believe that quality and productivity are the most critical issues facing American business, many do not know how to achieve it. Shetty lists 16 organizations that have vigorously attacked this challenge: Catepillar, Dana Corp., Delta, Dow Chemical, General Electric, Hewlett-Packard, IBM, Intel, Johnson & Johnson, Marriott, Maytag, McDonald's, Procter and Gamble, Texas Instruments, 3M, and Xerox.

What Shetty found was that these organizations shared some characteristics in common. He refers to these as the Seven Principles of Quality.[1]

Principle 1 — Quality improvement requires the firm commitment of top management. All top management, including the CEO, must be personally committed to quality. The keyword here is personally. Many CEOs pay only lip service to this particular edit. Therefore, top management must be consistent and reflect its commitment through the company's philosophy, goals, policies, priorities, and executive behavior. Steps management can take to accomplish this end include: establish and communicate a

4

clear vision of corporate philosophy, principles, and objectives relevant to product and service quality; channel resources toward these objectives and define roles and responsibilities in this endeavor; invest time to learn about quality issues and monitor the progress of any initiatives; encourage communication between management and employees, among departments, and among various units of the firm and customers; and be a good role model in communication and action.

Principle 2 — Quality is a strategic issue. It must be a part of a company's goals and strategies and be consistent with and reinforce a company's other strategic objectives. It must also be integrated into budgets and plans and be a corporate mission with planned goals and strategies. Finally, quality should be at the heart of every action.

Principle 3 — Employees are the key to consistent quality. The organization must have a people-oriented philosophy. Poorly managed people convey their disdain for quality and service when they work. It is important to pay special attention to employee recruitment, selection, and socialization and to reinforce the socialization and quality process with continuous training and education. It is also a good idea to incorporate quality into performance appraisal and reward systems and to encourage employee participation and involvement. Effective communication throughout the department, between department, and throughout the organization is required to reinforce the deep commitment of management and creates an awareness and understanding of the role of quality and customer service.

Principle 4 — Quality standards and measurements must be customer driven. It can be measured by:

- Formal customer surveys
- Focus groups
- Customer complaints
- Quality audits
- Testing panels
- Statistical quality controls
- Interaction with customers

Principle 5 — Many programs and techniques can be used to improve quality, such as:

- Statistical quality control
- Quality circles
- Suggestion systems
- Quality-of-work-life projects
- Competitive benchmarking

Principle 6 — All company activities have potential for improving product quality; therefore teamwork is vital. Quality improvement requires

Software Quality Management in Today's Environment

While total quality management and software quality management (TQM/SQM) are laudable goals, most organizations realize that these are truly long-term goals. What processes, then, can be instituted on a short-term basis to provide the organization with a short-cut to quality improvement? Redmill[2] offers us a series of quick-hit tactics:

1. *Training.* Project manager and team must be trained in TQM concepts and facilities.
2. *Management Commitment.* Must always be seen to be 100%.
3. *Standards.* A comprehensive set of standards for all aspects of work should be instituted and used. The project life cycle must be covered as well as other pertinent issues.
4. *Guidelines, Procedures and Checklists.* Assist workers to meet the standards and QA agents to check the products.
5. *Quality Assurance.* Should be carried out at all stages of the life cycle and for all end-products. The QA team should be independent of the development team and audits should be carried out during the project to ensure that management and QA procedures are being adhered to. The project manager should always initiate a review of the auditors' recommendations and of all resulting corrective actions.
6. *Planning.* The project manager should be fastidious in drawing up plans and ensuring their use for control. Plans should include the project plan, stage plans, and a quality plan, which details the quality requirements of the project.
7. *Reporting.* A reporting system, to ensure that problems are quickly escalated to the management level appropriate to the action needed, should be instituted.
8. *Feedback.* Statistics that assist in project control and the improvement of quality should be collected, analyzed, and used.
9. *Continuous Review.* The whole quality system (components, mode of operation, and quality of results) should be reviewed and improved continuously.
10. *Project Manager.* Must not be too technically involved. Technical duties should be delegated to a development team manager who reports to the project manager.
11. *Nontechnical Support Team.* Should be appointed to assist in nondevelopmental matters, including coordination and interpretation of resource and time statistics, recording all expenditures, and tracking against the budget (tracking milestone). This team should report to the project manager.

The rest of this chapter is a synopsis of what I consider to be the very best of techniques and/or ideas that financial services IT managers can use for boosting quality in their development efforts. The ideas are something to mull over.

SEI'S SOFTWARE PROCESS MATURITY FRAMEWORK

The Software Engineering Institute at Carnegie-Mellon University is the bulwark of engineering productivity research. In their studies of thousands of firms they've discovered some common characteristics that can be used to pinpoint how progressive a firm is in terms of its maturity in the quest for productivity and quality.

The five levels of process maturity are outlined below.

Stage 1: Initial
Ad hoc
Little formalization
Tools informally applied to the process

Key Actions to Get to Next Step:
Initiate rigorous project management, management review, and quality assurance

Stage 2: Repeatable
Achieved a stable process with a repeatable level of statistical control

Key Actions to Get to Next Step:
Establish a process group
Establish a software development process architecture
Introduce software engineering methods and technologies

Stage 3: Defined
Achieved foundation for major and continuing progress

Key Actions to Get to Next Step:
Establish a basic set of process managements to identify quality and cost parameters
Establish a process database; gather and maintain process data
Assess relative quality of each product and inform management

Stage 4: Managed
Substantial quality improvements
Comprehensive process measurement

Key Actions to Get to Next Step:
Support automatic gathering of process data
Use data to analyze and modify the process

Stage 5: Optimized
Major quality and quantity improvements

MALCOLM BALDRIDGE QUALITY AWARD RATINGS

The Malcolm Baldridge Quality Award looks at quality from a total firm perspective — IT makes up only one component. However, since IT is but a microcosm of the whole organization, the Baldridge criteria are equally applicable to IT as to the whole organization.

Rate your organization in the space provided. The maximum points you are allowed to allocate is listed to the left of the space in which you mark your award. The section level displays the maximum number of points for the entire section. For example in Section 1.0, Leadership, the maximum is 100 points distributed across its sublevels (i.e., 1.1, 1.2, etc.).

1.0 **Leadership**   100 ___
    1.1 Senior Executive Leadership   40 ___
    1.2 Quality Values   15 ___
    1.3 Management for Quality   25 ___
    1.4 Public Responsibility   20 ___

2.0 **Information and Analysis**   70 ___
    2.1 Scope and Management of Quality Data and Information   20 ___
    2.2 Competitive Comparisons and Benchmarks   30 ___
    2.3 Analysis of Quality Data and Information   20 ___

3.0 **Strategic Quality Planning**   60 ___
    3.1 Strategic Quality Planning Process   35 ___
    3.2 Quality Goals and Plans   25 ___

4.0 **Human Resource Utilization**   150 ___
    4.1 Human Resource Management   20 ___
    4.2 Employee Involvement   40 ___
    4.3 Quality Education and Training   40 ___
    4.4 Employee Recognition and Performance Measurement   25 ___
    4.5 Employee Well-Being and Morale   25 ___

5.0 **Quality Assurance of Product and Services**   140 ___
    5.1 Design and Introduction of Quality Products and Services   35 ___
    5.2 Process Quality Control   20 ___
    5.3 Continuous Improvement of Processes   20 ___
    5.4 Quality Assessment   15 ___
    5.5 Documentation   10 ___
    5.6 Business Process and Support Service Quality   20 ___
    5.7 Supplier Quality   20 ___

6.0 **Quality Results**   180 ___
    6.1 Product and Service Quality Results   90 ___

QUICK-HIT PRODUCTIVITY RATIOS

Productivity is never easy to measure. Use the following three metrics to give you an overall feeling for productivity in your organization.

1. Raw productivity = system size/work hours
2. Delivery rate = system size/elapsed weeks
3. Defect density = number of defects/system size

Deloitte & Touche Misuses of Methodology

It probably comes as no surprise, but you can misuse as well as use any technology. The following list reflects the collected wisdom of one of the largest consulting firms.

1. "Religious Fanaticism" — This is the situation where an organization holds to the theory that there can be nothing else but the methodology. A "methodology-centric" view of the world if you'll permit the use. Such rigidity is seldom useful or productive. It also may be a symptom of other poor management practices.
2. "Bureaucracy" — Here the methodology gets wrapped up in a less-than-effective organization which adds yet another layer of protection and excuse as to why no products are produced. Using a methodology in an organization which may already have top-down communications problems and seven or more management layers between the programmers and the management will not help. It will just cause people to push more paper.
3. "The end in itself" — Very similar to (2) is the failure resulting from the total focus on the process of developing systems and not on the end results. Personnel are indoctrinated into the process and become wedded to the idea that Step "16" must come after "15" and before "17," and that every last step must be completed and documented, even when it is obvious that performing the activities

13

in a step will add no value to the result, or that what they are doing has no real business benefit.

4. "Using the wrong one" — This is rare but is sometimes seen. The few cases I have seen personally seem to arise because a methodology in place has failed to keep up with the times. For example, having no methods that focus on JAD or on structured testing or, trivially, a customer's methodology which still requires the use of a paper screen layout form when screen painters and prototyping provide far faster and more effective user interaction. A methodology incorporating no guidance in data modeling would be of little help in implementing a system using a modern relational database system.

5. "Lack of organizational penetration" — The most common problem is still lack of consistent use, starting with lack of commitment by management. Project leaders who get trained and start off by trying to conform will tend to fall by the wayside if not encouraged and coached to do better. In *Strategies for Software Engineering*, Martyn Ould identified "14 dilemmas of software engineering" that he concluded impeded the introduction of new techniques into organizations. Among the more notable examples of these "Catch 22s" are

- We can't use a new method on a project until we have seen it work on other projects.
- We could justify the use of a new method if we could quantify the costs of using it. But we use traditional methods even though we are unable to quantify the costs of using them, resulting in a continuation of the status quo and generally unreliable estimates.
- Tools that are generally applicable are generally weak. Strong tools are very specific and therefore generally inapplicable.
- An important feature of new methods is that they tend to be powerful in particular areas. This makes them generally inapplicable. The traditional methods are weak in all areas. This makes them generally inapplicable as well.

PRESSMAN'S[4] COMMON MANAGEMENT QUESTIONS

Roger Pressman is one of the luminaries in the field of IT. Here Roger poses some pertinent questions about the relationship between change and management.

1. *We are very set in our ways; is change really possible?* The *modus operandi* of every software development organization appears to be cast in concrete. The fact is that organizations change regularly: new tools, new people, new policies new products and applications, and even new organizational structures are commonplace in the software development community. Even if your organization is "set in its ways," a move toward a software engineering culture (and the changes it portends) is often essential for the continued production

of high-quality systems. Change is certainly possible, but only if both managers and technical staff take a systematic approach to it.

2. *We're going a million miles an hour, how can we make the time?* This question is often asked by managers of young, high-technology companies that are growing at a precipitous rate, or in large, well-established companies that are experiencing a significant growth in software demand. It is true that rapid growth stretches resources to their limit. But it is also true that rapid growth exacerbates any underlying software development problems that do exist. The need for change becomes more important.

3. *OK, we have to change, what do we do first?* If this question is asked, the first thing has already been done — the speaker has recognized that change is required. Once the decision to change has been made, many managers and most technical people feel that immediate action is necessary. Although a "bias for action" is commendable, the road to a new software engineering culture must be viewed as a journey with many steps. Before beginning the journey, you must understand where you are now. Understanding your current "location" is the first thing that you should do.

4. *We've worked hard to develop internal standards and procedures, isn't that enough?* Although standards and procedures can help to guide technological change, they are not enough. Many software development organizations have fallen into an "S & P trap." That is, they have expended time and resources developing voluminous standards and procedures documents that few staff members understand or use. Just because an approach to software development has been codified does not guarantee that it will be followed.

5. *Should technological change be driven from the top down or from the bottom up?* When successful technological change occurs, it usually occurs in a way that might best be called a "sandwich." Senior management establishes goals and provides resources, driving the process from the top down. At the same time, technical staff obtain education and apply methods and tools driving the process from the bottom up. Both meet in the middle.

6. *Software engineering requires a new approach and a substantial learning curve, won't this cause upheaval?* It is true that cultural change can cause upheaval if it is not managed properly. Therefore, our primary goal in implementing change is to do it in a manner that does not negatively impact the progress of ongoing projects. In a later section we discuss a strategy for implementing change that will minimize upheaval while at the same time having a reasonable likelihood of success.

7. *What about project managers, won't they resist?* If software engineering is viewed as a destabilizing influence, project managers will resist it. To gain the support of project managers, we must look at

software engineering from their point of view and ask the question: "What's in it for me?" The answer is simple — control. Software engineering procedures, methods, and tools will improve the manager's ability to control a project, something that every manager desires. Once the project manager recognizes this benefit, resistance will disappear.

8. *Money is always tight, how do I get resource commitment from management?* Too many requests for resources (to be allocated to software engineering transition) continue to use the "trust me" school of justification. That is, a request for resources attempts to sell middle and senior management on the overall qualitative benefits of new software engineering technology without translating these benefits to the bottom line. Although this approach sometimes works, it is being viewed with increasing skepticism by many senior managers. For this reason, it is necessary to develop concrete measures of the software development process and establish an historical baseline that will enable quantitative justification to be made.

9. *Why can't we just buy some good CASE (computer-aided software engineering) tools and leave the rest alone?* Any power tool can be a wonderful thing. Whether you are cutting wood, washing dishes, or building computer software, a power tool can improve the quality of your work and the productivity with which you do it. But this is true only if you understand the methods and procedures that must be applied to properly use the tool. If a power tool is used without an understanding of underlying procedures and methods, it can be both unproductive and even dangerous. Most of us wouldn't use a large chain-saw without first understanding the procedures and methods that guide its use. Few people would attempt to wash socks in a dishwasher. Yet, many software developers attempt to use sophisticated CASE tools with little more than a passing understanding of software engineering methods and procedures. Then, they wonder why "these tools don't work for us."

BOULDIN'S[5] QUESTIONS TO ASCERTAIN READINESS FOR TECHNOLOGICAL CHANGE

In *Agents of Change*, Bouldin lists the following criteria as benchmarks for readiness for technological change.

1. Is your organization newly formed?
2. Are the functions your organization performs new to your organization?
3. Is your organization growing at a reasonably rapid rate?
4. Is your organization responsible for the development of new systems?
5. Is there a general attitude of optimism, and is morale high?

6. Are your technical staff utilizing tools or methods that improve productivity?
7. Does your management support the concept of productivity in any way?
8. Is staff experiencing motivation problems?
9. Is your staff responsible for mature systems that are primarily in the maintenance mode?
10. Does your organization have a backlog of user (or customer) requests?

COOPERS & LYBRAND QUANTITATIVE MEASUREMENT SYSTEM

Coopers & Lybrand uses the following measurement system to gauge the predictability, business impact, appropriateness, reliability, and adaptability of any system.

Issue: Predictability
    Attribute: Schedule
        Metric: Deviation from estimated number of elapsed weeks
    Attribute: Effort
        Metric: Deviation from estimated number of hours per phase
        Metric: Deviation from estimated number of rework hours per phase
    Attribute: Cost
        Metric: Deviation from estimated number of hours × cost per phase
        Metric: Deviation from estimated number of rework hours × cost per phase

Issue: Business Impact
    Attribute: Time to market
        Metric: Number of elapsed weeks
        Metric: Deviation from schedule
    Attribute: Cost savings
        Metric: Personnel cost savings
        Metric: Hardware, software, and facility cost savings
        Metric: Cost of quality savings
        Metric: Turnaround time
    Attribute: Customer satisfaction
        Metric: Turnaround time
        Metric: Number of support hours
        Metric: Number of problem reports
        Metric: User satisfaction rating

Issue: Appropriateness
    Attribute: Satisfaction of system requirements
        Metric: User satisfaction rating

Metric: Percentage of requirements that can be traced to code
Metric: Number of design changes
Metric: Number of perceived goals met
Metric: Number of hours spent in requirements collection
Attribute: Fitness for use
Metric: Number of prototype iterations
Attribute: Conformance to business objectives
Metric: Percentage of business objectives that can be traced to requirements
Metric: Number of design changes

Issue: Reliability
Attribute: Correctness
Metric: Number of defects
Metric: Number of rework hours × cost
Metric: Number of rework hours per process product
Attribute: Availability
Metric: Percentage of time system is up

Issue: Adaptability
Attribute: Responsiveness to changes
Metric: Number of rework hours
Metric: Problem request completion date
Attribute: User support
Metric: Number of problem reports
Metric: Percentage of problem reports completed

DEMING'S 14 QUALITY POINTS

W. E. Deming is considered the expert who got away. Ignored in the U.S., he took his ideas and headed for Japan where he was responsible for their meteoric rise in productivity, quality and competitiveness.

1. Create constancy of purpose toward improvement of product and service, with the aim to become competitive, to stay in business, and to provide jobs.
2. Adopt a new philosophy. We are in a new economic age. Western management must awaken to the challenge, must learn its responsibilities and take on leadership for change.
3. Cease dependence on inspection to achieve quality. Eliminate the need for inspection on a mass basis by building quality into the product in the first place.
4. End the practice of awarding business on the basis of the price tag. Instead, minimize total cost. Move toward a single supplier for any one item, on a long-term relationship of loyalty and trust.

5. Improve constantly and forever the system of production and service to improve quality and productivity, and thus constantly decrease costs.
6. Institute training on the job.
7. Institute leadership (see Point 12). The aim of leadership should be to help people and machines and gadgets do a better job. Leadership of management is in need of overhaul, as well as leadership of production workers.
8. Drive out fear, so that everyone may work effectively for the company,
9. Break down barriers between departments. People in research, design, sales, and production must work as a team, to foresee problems of production and use that may be encountered with the product or service.
10. Eliminate slogans, exhortations, and targets for the work force, asking for zero defects and new levels of productivity.
11. (a) Eliminate work standard (quotas) on the factory floor. Substitute leadership. (b) Eliminate management by objective. Eliminate management by numbers, numerical goals. Substitute leadership.
12. (a) Remove barriers that rob the hourly worker of his or her right to pride of workmanship. The responsibility of supervisors must be changed from sheer numbers to quality. (b) Remove barriers that rob people in management and in engineering of their right to pride of workmanship.
13. Institute a vigorous program of education and self-improvement.
14. Put everyone in the company to work to accomplish the transformation. The transformation is everybody's job.

HUMPRHEY'S[6] PRINCIPLES OF SOFTWARE PROCESS MANAGEMENT

Watts Humphrey is the father of the concept of the "software factory." Here he elucidates on the major principles of the management of the software process.

People Management
1. The professionals are the key to the programming process, and they must be intimately involved in its development and improvement.
2. Management must focus on programming defects not as personal issues but as opportunities for process improvement.

Process Support
1. Special process groups need to be established.
2. Necessary management and professional education is provided.
3. The best tools and methods are obtained and used.

Process Methodology
1. The process is formally defined.
2. Goals and measurements are established.
3. Statistical data are analyzed to identify problems and determine causes.

Process Control
1. Management practices are established to control change.
2. Periodic process assessments are conducted to monitor effectiveness and identify necessary improvements.
3. Procedures are established to certify process quality and implement corrective actions.

MOTOROLA'S SIX SIGMA DEFECT REDUCTION EFFORT[7]

In 1987, Motorola set in motion a five-year quality improvement program. The term Six Sigma is one used by statisticians and engineers to describe a state of zero defects. The result of this program has produced productivity gains of 40% as well as winning the Malcolm Baldridge National Quality Award in 1988. Benefits include:

- Increased productivity by 40%
- Reduced backlog from years to months
- Increased customer service levels
- Shifted IS time from correcting mistakes to value-added work
- More motivated staff
- Saved $1.5 billion in reduced cost

Listed below is Motorola's quality improvement program.

1. Identify your product. Determine what is the service or product you are producing. IS must align what they do with what the customers want.
2. Identify customer requirements. Information Systems (IS) must determine what the customer perceives as a defect-free product or service. The unit of work that the user is dealing with must be considered. For example, in a general ledger system in which the user worries about defects per journal voucher and not defects per thousand lines of code.
3. Diagnose the frequency and source of errors. Four categories of metrics were established to target defect reduction:
   - New software development
   - Service delivery
   - Cycle time
   - Customer satisfaction, which is composed of a detailed service with the intent of validating the first three metrics
4. Define a process for doing the task. Motorola refers to this process as mapping but it closely aligned to the reengineering process. The

process involves using personal computer-based tools to determine flow-through of processes and answering the following questions:

- Which processes can be eliminated?
- Which processes can be simplified?

5. Mistake-proof the process. By streamlining a process and eliminating any unnecessary steps, it is possible to make the process mistake-proof. By using metrics, a process control mechanism is put into place so that problems can be addressed before they affect output.

6. Put permanent control measures in place. Once Six Sigma is reached, this level must be maintained. At this step, the Six Sigma metrics are set up to be used to continuously monitor the process: monthly quality review meetings are held where each person gets up and discusses their metric, its trend, diagnosis of source cause of errors, action plan to correct.

ERNST & YOUNG CENTER FOR INFORMATION TECHNOLOGY AND STRATEGY TQM SOLUTION

The basic tenet behind Ernst & Young's TQM consultancy is to get organizations to understand a single principle — that change is painful and lengthy. In order to effectuate any kind of change you need a 10-year plan, and management's patience is short. So, how do you motivate change over that time period? The secret is to make management extremely dissatisfied with the status quo. And to do that you need to look at the cost of the status quo. One way of accomplishing this is to examine the cost of poor quality.

By answering questions such as, "What are we spending on detecting defects?" the IT organization can begin to accumulate the statistics it needs to make the push for change. The data need not be hard to track; in most cases, they are already available through project management systems that track walkthroughs, reviews, defect rates, etc.

The following nine steps constitute Ernst & Young's quick-hit approach to tackling TQM in IT departments:

1. Create a massive discomfort with the status quo. This can be accomplished in any one of a number of ways, including using numerical data or using a customer survey.
2. Use what was found in Step 1 to get management sponsorship of the TQM process.
3. Develop a commitment to quality. Top management needs to make a visible and personal commitment to any quality program.
4. Involve others. Customers/suppliers must be involved in the TQM process.
5. Define the processes.

6. Determine value measurements. Have customers of the processes outputs determine value measurements.
7. Form teams. Form process (quality) improvement teams that use these measures.
8. Innovate/improve the process. Come up with ways to innovate or improve the process.
9. Continue to improve. Create an environment where the processes continually improve.

COOPERS & LYBRAND TQM METHODOLOGY[8]

Coopers & Lybrand have taken appropriate elements of TQM and successfully applied them to software delivery organizations. It has developed a specific four-phase methodology, dubbed Software Quality Management (SQM) which provides a framework for managing continuous improvement for software delivery.

Assessment

The purpose of the Assessment phase is to evaluate the organization's current environment and determine how well the organization meets or is likely to meet its customers' software quality requirements. In any Assessment phase, a measurement system must first be designed as a tool and to establish a quality baseline. The Goal/Question/Metric approach described below can be used to produce this measurement system.

During Assessment, it is important to understand the activities involved in the software development process as well as the organizational roles and responsibilities. The measurements currently being used by the organization must also be identified and assessed. Whenever possible, existing measures should be used as part of the quality assessment to promote familiarity and acceptance.

Nevertheless, the overall approach is to develop questions and metrics that have the greatest importance to the organization. This is achieved by focusing on the three dimensions of the goals of the Assessment: the phase under scrutiny, the relevant quality issue, and the role from which the phase and quality issue are viewed.

When conducting an Assessment, it may also be necessary to hold briefing sessions with respondents to clarify the meaning of some of the metrics. Moreover, respondents who feel that they are being imposed upon or are fearful of the measurement effort are likely to provide questionable data. It is especially important to make clear that the metrics are not being used as a mechanism for punitive actions. Since many sensitive and perhaps embarrassing issues may arise during the Assessment, it is often easier for an outside third party to manage the process and gather data.

It is also desirable to collect the data during a fixed period of time with a specific deadline. During the Assessment period, the collection team should be available to answer questions and clarify procedures. After the data are collected, they are compiled, analyzed, and translated into graphic depiction's of the major findings. The key outcome of the Assessment is the identification of opportunities for improvement by studying the consolidated findings. This resulting list of opportunities is essential for the planning and implementation of pilot improvement projects.

Getting consensus from management as to the validity of the analysis and the opportunities for improvement is also essential. Specifically, the Assessment team must be sensitive to the possible misinterpretation of the findings and conclusions which may result in assessing blame. Prior to moving on to Planning, the management sponsor must help the team identify potential trouble spots and devise methods for defusing them.

Planning

The analysis of the data collected during the Assessment provides the foundation for the quality improvement plan. The Assessment defines the organization's quality profile and identifies opportunities for improvement. The objectives of the Planning phase are to establish strategic and tactical direction, as well as consensus and commitment for improvements identified in the Assessment. A Process Improvement Plan is the final outcome of this strategic planning effort.

Typically, two different types of problems surface as a result of the Assessment: some with relatively simple, quick solutions and some more deeply rooted in organizational practices, requiring a longer period to solve. To address the first type of problem, the organization must devise short-term, measurable projects with a consistent sequence encompassing the Plan/Do/Check/Act process.[7] The second type of problem requires an effort aimed at longer-term organizational and behavioral changes. The focus of the Planning effort will be on these long-term projects.

Nevertheless, a critical success factor for any SQM project is the perception that quality improvement is attainable. The quality improvement team's ability to achieve successes on the short-term projects will help to pave the way for the entire process. Furthermore, quick management decisions on short-term projects will show the development staff that their improvement ideas have been taken seriously and that management is willing to take actions based on staff input.

Because participation and consensus of management is essential to the Planning effort, there is always considerable risk of delay. The Planning team must, therefore, conduct an intensive quality planning session with managers early in the process. Ideally, all of the planning work could be accomplished at such a session. At a minimum, the result of the meeting will be to define the "quality vision" and to establish the roles and responsibilities of the groups to be charged with the organization's quality program.

The organization's vision of what quality software means and where it expects to be must be agreed upon early in the Planning effort. Most organizations find that there are several areas where improvement efforts can be focused; however, trying to do too much at once is not a good idea. Priorities should be assigned to targets based on the following criteria:

- Criticality
- Cost
- Resources
- Timing
- Risks
- Opportunity for near-term success

The projects that are selected as top priorities will require further discussion and decisions regarding the manner in which the improvements are to be implemented. The result will be a prioritized statement of quality objectives, the process improvements to be achieved, and the measurements that will demonstrate success. In addition, each quality improvement project should have:

- A mission statement that includes improvement goals
- Schedules and resource and cost estimates for each project
- An organization structure responsible for quality management
- Measurement procedures to validate the meeting of goals

In addition to establishing procedures, it is essential that top management realize the implications of committing to SQM. It must be understood that SQM is not a pilot program but an ongoing process to enhance the way the software organization conducts business. SQM requires changing procedures, cooperating with other departments, emphasizing the process, and changing management philosophies that are ineffective yet pervasive. If senior management is not willing to commit themselves, their organization, and their people to the process, an SQM program is probably not worth starting.

Planning for software quality improvement requires more than just top management commitment and sponsorship. It also calls for attention to cultural and behavioral issues. For example, the initial reaction of staff to a measurement program may be apprehension, fear, and resistance. It must be shown that the program and data collected will be used for improvement purposes and not punishment. One or more short-term successes will demonstrate the real value of the measurement system. Also, a measurement system should indicate process and product strengths that need encouragement as well as weaknesses that need improvement.

The primary goals of the Planning phase of SQM are to define quality objectives and strategies for instituting improvement solutions. It is also important for the plan to establish the roles and responsibilities for the individuals and teams whose mission is to promote and oversee continuous quality improvements. The final product is a plan that prioritizes the quality objectives, details the means for achieving improvements in the short term, identifies and analyzes quality-related risks, and creates an agreed-upon framework to achieve long-term quality improvement objectives.

Implementation

Introducing measurement systems and the concept of continuous improvement will require far-reaching changes to an organization. During the Implementation phase, these changes begin to occur. Implementing the quality improvement plan means incorporating the measurement and improvement efforts into the organizational culture and discovering which behavioral changes need to occur. This effort, therefore, requires a corresponding change in the reward structure. A reward system should motivate the staff to change development procedures in a way that is consistent with the goals of the improvements efforts.

Once a new reward system is in place, Implementation should turn to those short-term projects that were identified in the Planning phase. These may include:

- Project tracking techniques and tools
- Formalizing reviews and walk-throughs
- Implementing Joint Application Design (JAD) sessions
- Applying new approaches to testing

Most of the efforts at improvement will require training of staff and project management in the relevant techniques and tools. These training efforts must be undertaken with the same commitment and level of support given to the entire SQM effort. If staff is not supported in its effort to change, all of the assessments and strategic planning sessions in the world will not effect change. For an SQM program to be successful, staff and management must be encouraged to experiment, take risks, and take charge of improving the process.

Once the framework of rewards, training, and empowerment is established, the long-term process improvements can be attempted. These may include:

- Implementing risk management techniques
- Introducing a structured development methodology
- Instituting Rapid Prototyping techniques
- Evaluating and implementing new CASE tools

Institutionalization

Institutionalization requires that the lessons learned during Implementation be captured and transformed into organizational assets to form the basis of a continuous improvement culture. As a first step, the experiences gained in near-term improvement projects should be analyzed, packaged, and communicated to everyone in the organization. Successes must be validated and publicized. The experience is packaged into self-contained units including approach, results, techniques, tools, manuals, and training to transform the knowledge gained into the organization's culture.

The basic techniques for institutionalizing continuous quality improvement include:

- Analyzing the results of short-term projects and comparing the results with the targets defined in Planning
- Synthesizing the experience into lessons learned, domain expertise, rules and models
- Packaging the experience as products that can be delivered to the organization

Institutionalizing SQM requires comprehensive reuse of the experience from several projects or several phases of a project. Much of the work done at this stage of the program involves educating the individuals who develop and maintain software. This education involves not only formalized training on specific process improvements, but also formal and informal quality awareness education via the promotion of quality improvement successes.

CORBIN'S METHODOLOGY FOR ESTABLISHING A SOFTWARE DEVELOPMENT ENVIRONMENT[9]

The Software Development Environment (SDE) is actually the integration of a number of processes, tools, standards, methodologies, and related elements whose purpose is to provide a framework for building quality software. This section discusses the elements of SDE and shows how to develop one.

The Elements of SDE

Project management
Business plan
Architecture
Methodologies
Techniques
Tools
Metrics
Policies and procedures

Technology platform
Support
Standards
Education and training

The Benefits of SDE

Improved problem definition
Selection of the "right" problem according to the customer
Joint customer/IS responsibility and accountability
Acknowledgment of customer ownership of system
Reduced costs of systems development and maintenance
Reusability of software, models, and data definitions
Acceptance of the disciplined approach to software engineering using a consistent methodology
Productivity improvements through team efforts and tools such as CASE

Sample Goals of SDE

Reduce systems development costs
Reduce maintenance costs
Reduce MIS turnover rate

These goals should be quantifiable wherever possible.

For example, the first goal could be stated as "reduce systems development costs by 50% over the next 5 years."

Architecture

Many organizations do not have a formal, documented architecture. There are three types:

- Business Architecture is a model of the business and identifies such things as processes and entities in the form of models.
- Computing Architecture, which at a minimum identifies hardware, software, and data communications. This breaks out into components such as operating systems, data resource management, network protocols, and user interface.
- Enterprise Architecture is a combination of the Business and Computing Architectures.

Business Plan

- Create a Steering Committee that provides direction to the MIS function.
- Translate the organization's business plan into an actionable MIS plan that supports the business' goals and objectives.

- The Steering Committee should be responsible for funding projects, setting priorities, resolving business issues, and reviewing MIS policies and procedures.

Education and Training

Make sure that analysts, programmers, and users are all trained and ready to start the development project. Training might include the following:

- Software engineering concepts
- Prototyping
- System development life cycle
- Joint application development
- Software quality assurance and testing
- Project management
- Data and process modeling
- CASE/application development toolsets

Methodologies

Whether the methodology chosen by the MIS department is a standard one, from a vendor, or developed internally, the MIS group must follow one to ensure consistency from project to project. This will enable staff to be able to move from project to project without retraining, while at the same time ensuring consistent deliverables. Questions to ask when selecting a methodology are

- Does your methodology support the entire systems development life cycle?
- Does it include maintenance?
- Is it clearly documented?
- Does it focus on deliverables instead of activities?
- Is it Application Development tool independent?
- Can you use your metrics and techniques with it?

Project Management

Questions to ask include:

- Do you have a formal project management discipline in place?
- Do you have a training program to support this?
- Is a software tool used?
- Do you have program planning and control to help manage the project?
- Do you get routine reports showing the project work breakdown structure, status reports, resource loading, and cost projections?
- Is there a formal reporting mechanism done on a timely basis to resolve problems?

Standards

Some of the areas in which standards are required are

- Systems analysis and design
- Data administration
- Database administration
- Systems testing
- Prototyping
- Documentation
- Data entry
- Systems production
- Change/configuration management

Questions to ask: "Have you identified all of the standards that are required to support your SDE? Do you have someone responsible for developing and maintaining standards?"

Support Options

- External consulting
- A sharing arrangement where you can provide services in exchange for those needed
- User groups
- Special interest groups

Automated Tool Questions

- Have you identified the tools you need in the SDE?
- Have they been approved, acquired, and installed?
- Do they support the methodologies?
- Do they support the technology platform?
- Do they support the standards?
- Is technical support available to support the tools?
- Do you have templates for use in systems development?
- Do you have a data dictionary, or repository for your data?
- Do you have tools to support each phase of the life cycle?

SIMMONS STATISTICS CONCERNING THE EFFECT THAT COMMUNICATIONS HAS ON GROUP PRODUCTIVITY[10]

This section details the many factors that dominate software group productivity. Simmons defines dominator as a single factor that causes productivity to decline tenfold. The two dominators that are discussed are communications and design partition.

What follows is a set of rules and statistics that the reader can use as a comparison in his or her own efforts to increase productivity.

1. Factors that developers must cope with in developing large systems:
   - Personnel turnover
   - Hardware/software turnover
   - Major ideas incorporate late
   - Latent bugs
2. A Delphi survey performed by Scott and Simmons to uncover factors that affect productivity found that the main factors are
   - External documentation
   - Programming language
   - Programming tools
   - Programmer experience
   - Communications
   - Independent modules for task assignment (design partition)
   - Well-defined programming practices
3. Improvement statistics:
   - Any step towards the use of structured techniques, interactive development, inspections, etc. can improve productivity by up to 25%.
   - Use of these techniques in combination could yield improvements of between 25% and 50%.
   - Change in programming language can, by itself, yield a productivity improvement of more than 50%.
   - Gains of between 50% and 75% can be achieved by single high achievers or teams of high achievers.
   - Gains of 100% can be achieved by database user languages, application generators and software reuse.
4. Dominators are factors that can suppress the effects of other factors and can reduce software group productivity by an order of magnitude.
5. Poor design partition can dominate group productivity. To obtain high productivity in the development of large software systems, the designer must break down the system into chunks that can be developed in parallel. The difference between great and average designers is an order of magnitude.
6. Communications can dominate productivity. Most project problems arise as the result of poor communications between workers. If there are n workers on the team, then there are $n(n-1)/2$ interfaces across which there may be communications problems.
7. Productivity of individual programmers varies as much as 26 to 1.
8. An individual working alone has no interruptions from fellow group members and, therefore, the productivity can be quite high for a motivated individual. It is estimated that one programmer working 60 hours a week can complete a project in the same calendar time as two others working normal hours, but at three-quarters of the cost.

9. Small groups of experienced and productive software developers can create large systems. An example is given of a company, Pyburn Systems. They scour the country for the best analytical thinkers. Its senior programmers typically earn $125,000 a year and can be paid bonuses of two to three times that amount. They work in small teams, never more than five, to produce large, complex systems. In comparison, most MIS departments produce large systems using normal development teams with developers of average ability.

10. In general, the difference between the cost to produce an individual program to be run by the program author and the cost to produce a programming system product developed by software group is at least nine times more expensive.

11. There is a point where coordination overheads outweigh any benefits that can be obtained by the addition of further staff. Statistics that support this were pioneered during the nineteenth century in work on military organization. It was noted that as the number of workers who had to communicate increased arithmetically, from 2 to 3 to 4 to 5 ..., the number of communication channels among them increased geometrically, from 1 to 3 to 6 to 10 .... From this study, it was concluded that the upper limit of effective staff size for cooperative projects is about 8.

12. In studies, it has been shown that when the number of staff increased to 12 or more, the efficiency of the group decreased to less than 30%.

13. The productive time of a typical software developer during a working day can vary from 51 to 79%. It was found that the average duration of work interruption was 5 minutes for a typical programmer. The average time to regain a train of thought after an interruption was 2 minutes. Thus, the average total time spent on an interruption was 7 minutes. If we assume five productive hours each day, then each interruption takes 2.33% of the working day, 10 interruptions would take up 23.3% of the day, and 20 interruptions would take up approximately 50%.

14. The optimum group size for a software development team is between five to eight members. The overall design should be partitioned into successively smaller chunks, until the development group has a chunk of software to develop that minimizes intragroup and intergroup communications.

BURNS' FRAMEWORK FOR BUILDING DEPENDABLE SYSTEMS[11]

The role and importance of nonfunctional requirements in the development of complex critical applications have, until now, been inadequately appreciated. It has been shown through experience that this approach fails to produce dependable systems.

Nonfunctional requirements include dependability (e.g., reliability, availability, safety, and security), timeliness (e.g., responsiveness, orderliness, freshness, temporal predictability, and temporal controllability), and dynamic change management (i.e., incorporating evolutionary changes into a nonstop system).

The purpose of the framework described in this section is to:

- Impose a design discipline that ensures that appropriate abstractions are used at each level of the design.
- Allow assertions to be developed that the nonfunctional requirements can be met by the design if implemented in a particular environment.
- Allow interactions between these nonfunctional requirements to be analyzed so that dependencies can be identified.
- Allow the nonfunctional and functional requirements to be traded off against each other.

Notes pertaining to the framework are listed below.

1. A constructive way of describing the process of system design is a progression of increasingly specific commitments which define properties of the system design which designers operating at a more detailed level are not at liberty to change. For example, early in the design there may already be commitments to the structure of a system, in terms of module definitions and relationships.

2. Those aspects of a design to which no commitment is made at some particular level in the design hierarchy are the subject of obligations that lower levels of design must address. For example, the behavior of the defined aspects committed to modules is the subject of obligations which must be met during further design and implementation.

3. The process of refining a design — transforming obligations into commitments — is often subject to constraints which are imposed primarily by the execution environment.

4. The execution environment is the set of hardware and software components on top of which a system is built. It may impose both resource constraints (e.g., processor speed) and constraints of mechanism (e.g., data locking).

5. The framework controls the introduction of necessary implementation details into the design process by distinguishing two phases in the construction of an architectural design of any application:
   - Logical architecture — embodies commitments which can be made independently of the constraints imposed by the execution environment and is aimed at satisfying the functional requirements.
   - Physical architecture — takes constraints into account and embraces the nonfunctional requirements.

6. The nonfunctional requirements of an application can be considered as projections onto the physical architecture. Distinct projects apply to timeliness, safety, and so on. The physical architecture makes it explicit where projections interact and enables criteria to be developed that cater for these interactions.

7. The framework is grounded in the object-oriented approach to system design. The object-oriented approach is widely regarded as offering a conceptual framework for mastering the complexities of the design process:
   - Objects are an adequate modeling tool for the functional requirements of the system.
   - They can be used to provide traceability through all stages of the design process.
   - They are an adequate basis for expressing nonfunctional requirements.
   - They provide an appropriate granularity for replication, checkpointing, dynamic change management, configuration, and dynamic reconfiguration.
   - They assist error containment through encapsulation.
   - They can support dynamic security by access right mechanisms on operations.
   - They can represent schedulable entities.
   - Commonly encountered standard architectures can be implemented by means of redefined classes and methods.

8. The logical architecture is concerned with defining a set of object classes, their interfaces, and relationships, which together meet all the functional requirements. In the logical architecture, communication between the classes is represented by invocation of methods.

9. The physical architecture is concerned with objects, that is, instances of the classes defined in the logical architecture. It refines the logical architecture in two ways:
   - It instantiates objects from the classes defined in the logical architecture and maps them onto the target execution environment.
   - It annotates the objects and their methods with attributes (such as deadlines) derived from the nonfunctional requirements.

FARBEY'S CONSIDERATIONS ON SOFTWARE QUALITY METRICS DURING THE REQUIREMENTS PHASE [12]

In this section Farbey expands on the general view of quality as the difference between what is expected and what is experienced:

Quality = expectations − experience

Four questions are addressed:

- Effectiveness — does the specification, considered as a solution, solve the right problem?
- Serviceability — does the specification, considered as a starting point, provide a firm basis on which to proceed?
- Prediction — does the requirement specification (together with the system test specification) provide useful measures for predicting the final quality outcome?
- Process — does the process by which the specification is produced encourage effectiveness, serviceability, and quality prediction?

1. Effectiveness. The first question concerns the quality of the specification as a solution — how well does the specification capture the problem? The ultimate effectiveness of a system depends not on the quality of software or specification, but on the degree to which the problem is correctly perceived. Focus on the specification as a product by asking questions like those that follow:
   - Is the process by which it has been produced conducive to bringing out and clarifying objectives?
   - Is it complete in that it exhausts the objectives and needs that are known?
   - Is the specification maintainable?
   - Is it readable?

   Quality attributes covered here include:
   - Functionality — does the specification capture all of the required functions.
   - Performance — does the specification meet the users' demands.
   - Usability — ease of use, learning, and relearning.

2. Serviceability. The second question concerns the quality of its content and implications for later system development. The following is a list of questions of efficiency, in this context meaning "doing things right."
   - Are the requirements consistent?
   - Are the requirements unambiguous?
   - Are the requirements compatible with the methods of later development stages?
   - Are the requirements readable?
   - Are the requirements modifiable?
   - Are the requirements traceable?
   - Are the requirements usable after implementation?
   - Are the requirements maintainable?
   - Are the requirements in compliance with documentation standards?

3. Prediction. The third question concerns the value of measures of quality that will act as predictor measurements for the eventual quality of the finished software. A predictor metric is used to predict

the value of a property of a system that will only become directly observable during a later stage of system development.

4. Process. Three processes of development are worth considering:
   - Life-cycle process such as SSADM (Structured Systems Analysis and Design), which is based on a waterfall model. In this model requirements specification occurs at an early stage and is then fixed as would be any associated metrics.
   - Prototyping approach offers an early normalization but also offers a more flexible model of system development that recognizes the problem of changing requirements.
   - Approaches that recognize specifically the social setting in which requirements specifications takes place. Control of quality during any process will probably be one of instituting checklists together with a program for completing them and acting on the results. Questions to ask at this point include (1) Is the system easy to learn? (2) Is the system easy to relearn? (3) Is there stability and maturity in the system?

HEWLETT-PACKARD'S TQC (TOTAL QUALITY CONTROL) GUIDELINES FOR SOFTWARE ENGINEERING PRODUCTIVITY[13]

Engineering productivity is extremely important to HP because they rely on new product development to maintain their competitive strength. HP introduces an average of one new product every business day; 70% of HP's engineers are involved in software development. Half of all R&D projects are exclusively devoted to software development.

It was this significant investment in software development that prompted HP's president to issue a challenge to achieve a tenfold improvement in software quality within 5 years. He also asked that new product development time be reduced by 50%.

This section points out the techniques HP utilized to meet this vast quality and productivity challenge. It's worthwhile reading for those who are responsible for spitting out new financial services products on a daily basis.

1. HP's productivity equation:

   Productivity = function of doing the right things ×
   function of doing things right

2. Cultural and organizational issues addressed to be able to motivate and support positive changes:
   - Productivity managers are used in each division to understand productivity and quality issues; evaluate, select, install CASE tools; communicate best software engineering practices; training; and establish productivity and quality metrics.

- A group productivity council is created to share the best R&D practices across divisions, metrics definition, metrics tracking, productivity councils, software quality and productivity assessment, and communication of best practices.
3. The Software Metrics Council is composed of both R&D and QA managers and engineers, whose objective is to identify key software metrics and promote their use.
4. Project/Product quality metrics used are
   - Break-even time measures return on investment, defined as time until development costs are offset by profits. The three numbers plotted are R&D investment in dollars, operating profit in dollars and time, and sales revenue in dollars and time.
   - Time-to-market measures responsiveness and competitiveness. It is defined as time from project go-ahead until release to market.
   - Kiviat diagram measures variables that affect software quality and productivity. It is a bull's-eye chart which graphs results of quality and productivity assessment.
5. Process quality metrics used are
   - Progress rate measures accuracy of schedule. It is defined as the ratio of planned to actual development time.
   - Open critical and serious KPRs measures effectiveness of support processes. It is defined as the number of service requests classified as known problems (of severity level critical or serious) that are not signed off.
   - Post-release defect density measures effectiveness of design and test processes. It is defined as the total number of defects reported during the first 12 months after product shipment.
6. People quality metrics used are
   - Turnover rate measures morale. It measures that percent of engineers leaving the company.
   - Training measures investment in career development. It is defined as the number of hours per engineer per year.
7. Basic software quality metrics used are
   - Code size (KNCSS, which is thousands of lines of noncomment source statements).
   - Number of prerelease defects requiring fix.
   - Prerelease defect density (defects/KNCSS).
   - Calendar months for prerelease QA.
   - Total prerelease QA test hours.
   - Number of postrelease defects reported after one year.
   - Postrelease defect density (defects/KNCSS).
   - Calendar months from investigation checkpoint to release.
8. Strategy for code reuse:
   - Share code (use exactly as is) whenever possible.
   - If sharing is not possible, try to leverage (minimal modifications).

- If neither sharing nor leveraging is possible, look for similar algorithms (design reuse).
- As a last resort, invent something new.
9. The Systems Software Certifications program was established to ensure measurable, consistent, high-quality software. the four metrics chosen were
  - Breadth — measures the testing coverage of user-accessible and internal functionality of the product.
  - Depth — measures the proportion of instructions or blocks of instructions executed during the testing process.
  - Reliability — measures the stability and robustness of a product and its ability to recover gracefully from error conditions.
  - Defect density — measures the quantity and severity of reported defects found and a product's readiness for use.

SPECIFICATION THOROUGHNESS SURVEY

Circle the appropriate number for each item below as it applies to your current project. For many companies surveyed, the bulk of the responses are either 1 or 2.

	Often				**Seldom**
1. Program specifications contain (hidden) errors and omissions	1	2	3	4	5
2. Design decisions are made on personal preferences	1	2	3	4	5
3. Program design process is informal	1	2	3	4	5
4. Programmers begin to code before design is complete	1	2	3	4	5
5. Inadequately defined software objectives	1	2	3	4	5
6. Programmers spend too much time correcting errors that are the result of poor specifications	1	2	3	4	5
7. Poor and inadequately enforced standards contribute to poor quality programs	1	2	3	4	5
8. Far too many omissions and errors are discovered after implementation	1	2	3	4	5
9. Inadequate commitment to quality software by management	1	2	3	4	5
10. Inadequate commitment to quality software by end users	1	2	3	4	5

CRITERIA DEFINITIONS FOR SOFTWARE QUALITY

Traceability — Those attributes of the software that provide a thread from the requirements to the implementation with respect to the specific and operational environment.

Completeness — Those attributes that provide full implementation of the functions required.

Consistency — Those attributes that provide uniform design and implementation techniques and notation.

Accuracy — Those attributes that provide the required precision in calculation and notation.

Error Tolerance — Those attributes that provide continuity of operation under nonnominal conditions.

Simplicity — Those attributes that provide implementation of functions in the most understandable manner. (Usually, avoidance of practices which increase complexity.)

Modularity — Those attributes that provide a structure of highly independent modules.

Generality — Those attributes that provide breadth to the functions performed.

Expandability — Those attributes that provide for expansion of data storage requirements or computational functions.

Instrumentation — Those attributes that provide for the measurement of usage or identification of errors.

Self-descriptiveness — Those attributes that provide explanation of a function.

Execution efficiency — Those attributes that provide for minimum processing time.

Storage efficiency — Those attributes that provide for minimum storage requirements.

Access control — Those attributes that provide for control of the access of software and data.

Access audit — Those attributes that provide for and audit the access of software and data.

Operability — Those attributes that determine operation and procedures concerned with the operation of software.

Training — Those attributes that provide transition from the current operation to initial familiarization.

Communicativeness — Those attributes that provide useful inputs and outputs that can be assimilated.

Software system independence — Those attributes that determine the software's dependency on the software environment (operating systems, utilities, input/output routines, etc.).

Machine independence — Those attributes that determine the software's dependency on the hardware system.

Communications commonality — Those attributes that provide the use of standard protocols and interface routines.

Data commonality — Those attributes that provide the use of standard data representations.

Conciseness — Those attributes that provide for implementation of a function with a minimum amount of code.

TYPICAL QUALITY FACTOR TRADE-OFFS

Integrity vs. efficiency — The additional code and processing required to control the access of the software or data usually lengthens run-time and requires additional storage.

Useability vs. efficiency — The additional code and processing required to ease an operator's tasks or provide more usable output usually lengthens run-time and increases storage.

Maintainability vs. efficiency — Optimized code increases maintainer's efforts. Using modules, instrumentation, etc.; however, increases overhead.

Testability vs. efficiency — The above applies to testing.

Portability vs. efficiency — The use of direct, optimized, or utilities decreases the portability of the system.

Flexibility vs. efficiency — Generality for a flexible system increases overhead.

Reusability vs. efficiency — The above applies to reuse.

Interoperability vs. efficiency — The added overhead for data conversion and interface routines decreases operating efficiency.

Flexibility vs. integrity — Flexibility requires very general structures. Security may be harder to insure.

Reusability vs. integrity — As above, reusable software provides severe security problems.

Interoperability vs. integrity — Coupled systems allow for more paths; that can allow either accidental or purposeful access to data.

Reusability vs. reliability — The generality required by reusable software makes providing for error tolerance and accuracy difficult.

STEPS TO REFOCUSING IT ACTIVITY

The process of squeezing extra resources from systems can be broken down into three steps, each with several components.

Step 1: Streamline the Current Systems Environment

Objectives — 15 to 20% of real cost reduction with payback in 6 to 12 months.

Activities —

1. Choose relevant organization units for analysis.
2. Allocate and costs to end products.
3. Generate ideas for streamlining costs.
4. Plan implementation.

Step 2: Focus on High-Value Priorities

Objectives — 30 to 40% reduction in current development projects, with resources reallocated to highest impact investments.

Activities —

1. Identify cost drivers and leverage points.
2. Group planned projects around leverage points.
3. Identify new opportunities and possible cutbacks.
4. Restate priorities.

Step 3: Build Ongoing Organizational Capabilities

Objectives — (1) Consolidation of gains on ongoing basis, and (2) maintenance of major improvements in organizational effectiveness.

Activities —

1. Evaluate planning and decision-making procedures.
2. Interview users and participants regarding the effectiveness of those procedures.
3. Identify weaknesses and opportunities for improvement.
4. Design procedural changes.

Notes

1. Shetty, Y. K., A point of view: seven principles of quality leaders, *Natl. Prod. Rev.*, Winter, 1991–1992, pp. 3–7.

2. Redmill, F. J., Considering quality in the management of software-based development projects, *Information and Software Technology*, Vol. 32(1), January/February, 1990, pp. 18–33.
3. Rubin, H., Rubin Associates, Pound Ridge, NY, 1991.
4. Pressman, R., *A Manager's Guide to Software Engineering*, McGraw-Hill, New York, 1993.
5. Bouldin, B., *Agents of Change*, Yourdon Press, Englewood Cliffs, NJ, 1989.
6. Humphrey, W., Software and the factory paradigm, *Softw. Eng. J.*, IEEE Publishing, Stevenage, Herts, U.K., March 1989.
7. Rifkin, G., More more defects, *Computerworld*, July 15, 1991, pp. 59–62.
8. Smillie, W., Improving the quality of software development, in *Software Engineering Productivity Handbook*, Keyes, J., Ed., McGraw-Hill, New York, 1993.
9. Corbin, D. S., Establishing the software development environment, *J. Sys. Manage.*, September, 1991, pp. 28–31.
10. Simmons, D. B., Communications: a software group productivity dominator, *Softw. Eng. J.*, November, 1991, pp. 454–462.
11. Burns, A. and Lister, A. M., A framework for building dependable systems, *Comp. J.*, Vol. 34(2), April, 1991, pp. 173–181.
12. Farbey, B., Software quality metrics: considerations about requirements and requirement specifications, *Information and Software Technology*, Vol. 32(1), January/February, 1990, pp. 60–64.
13. Anon., *Software Engineering Productivity*, Hewlett-Packard Company, Palo Alto, CA, 1989.

Author Bio

Jessica Keyes *is president of New Art Technologies, Inc., a high-technology software development firm. Prior to New Art Technologies, she was Managing Director of R&D for the New York Stock Exchange and has been an officer with the Swiss Bank Company and Banker's Trust, both in New York City.*

Keyes has a Master's Degree from New York University where she did research in the area of artificial intelligence. She has given seminars at universities such as Carnegie Mellon, Boston University, the University of Illinois, James Madison University, and San Francisco State University. She is a frequent keynote speaker on the topics of competitive strategy using information technology and marketing on the information highway, and is an advisor for DataPro, McGraw-Hill's computer research arm, as well as a member of the Sprint Business Council. She also is a founding Board of Director member of the New York Software Industry Association and has recently completed a 2-year term on the Mayor of New York City's Small Business Advisory Council.

A noted columnist and correspondent with over 150 articles published, Keyes is a publisher of the Small Business Journal *and several other computer-related publications. She also has authored and/or edited 12 books.*

Chapter 2
Distributed Integration: An Alternative to Data Warehousing

Dan Adler

DATA WAREHOUSING HAS, PERHAPS, BEEN THE MOST COSTLY systems development in the history of financial services. The concept of data warehousing grew out of regional and departmental consolidation projects in which large relational databases were used to store relatively large quantities of data and make these data available to standard query tools such as SQL and various SQL-based interfaces. These queries were very useful in helping departments track customer behavior, P&L, and, in combination with applications written in VB, C++, and S-PLUS, they helped departments and regional entities within financial institutions track market trends, manage risk, and develop predictions.

Many managers, however, when they saw the success of the special-purpose database, were inspired to take this concept to the next level. "If we can do so much with a relational database in one department, I wonder how much value we could extract by representing our entire firm in a relational database?" went the reasoning. And, for expanding global trading businesses that needed to control the risks associated with numerous local portfolios composed of complex financial instruments, the centralized data warehouse containing "everything" was particularly appealing.

At most financial institutions, however, extending numerous departmental and regional data collection projects to create a "firm-wide" data warehouse representing a firm's entire global business just did not work. Wall Street — and retail banking's Main Street — are littered with tales of multiyear, multimillion-dollar data warehousing projects that were killed

0-8493-9834-7/00/$0.00+$.50
© 2000 by CRC Press LLC

43

because they did not produce anything near what their architects promised. Problems include: transforming data stored in numerous formats, ensuring the data is "clean" and correct, developing and maintaining a firm-wide data model describing interrelationships between different types of data, managing various types of middleware to transport data from place to place, limited network resources, etc. And, of course, users became frustrated waiting for the "warehouse" and it associated promised functionality.

Still, extracting value from firm-wide information and controlling global market risk remain top priorities for financial institutions and their information technology departments, which are struggling to develop alternatives to data warehousing. One of the most promising such developments is Distributed Integration.

Distributed Integration is a new approach to integrating both firm-wide data and analytics based on Internet technologies, such as cascaded Internet servers and data caching. The "Distributed" refers to data and analytics that reside in numerous physical locations. The "Integration" refers to users' ability to access these disparate data and analytics through an *analytic browser,* which can be any application residing on any desktop which maintains an active connection to one or more *Distributed Integration servers.*

This chapter will describe how Distributed Integration solves some data integration problems that data warehousing projects do not always successfully address and show how Distributed Integration leverages existing desktop and intranet technologies to deliver this integrated data (and analytics) to large communities of internal and external users at a very reasonable price point.

THE HISTORY OF DATA WAREHOUSING

The firm-wide relational data warehouse has been proposed as a solution to numerous business issues facing financial institutions during the 1980s and 1990s.

First, in wholesale banking, per-trade margins have steadily declined in the mature foreign exchange and interest rate markets as the number of market participants increased and interest rate markets became more liquid. To respond more nimbly to market movements and to identify long-term trends, "data mining" — in which information is collected and analyzed to identify underlying patterns — became extremely popular. The data warehouse has been proposed as means of conveniently storing large quantities of historical and real-time data in order to facilitate the data mining process.

An important subset of the data mining issue for wholesale bankers and money managers is the management of time series data. These are data that are periodically collected and time stamped. This sort of data is very difficult to store in relational formats because time series records — when expressed in tabular format — are very repetitive. Likewise, time series data are collected more or less continuously. Therefore, they tend to rapidly overpopulate relational databases and reduce performance. So, time series records are more often stored in file format for convenience. Blending time series and relational data for data mining purposes has often been an objective of data warehousing initiatives.

Another trend in wholesale banking has been the development of complex derivative instruments in response to the shrinking margins described above. These more complex instruments, often developed by local trading offices in response to specific customer demands, have raised control issues highlighted by a spate of "derivatives losses" stories in the mid 1990s as banks, corporates, and investment managers recognized the importance of, first, understanding their derivatives exposures in the context of their whole portfolios and, second, keeping a close eye on rapidly expanding foreign offices. Indeed, the downside of extreme decentralization was dramatically illustrated by the failure of U.K.-based Barings Bank. In the wake of the Barings scandal, many financial institutions turned to data warehousing as a solution to their "control and security" issues.

In retail banking, the consolidation and acquisition of numerous banks meant fierce competition, and product innovation and sales became ever more critical. Data mining became very popular in the retail deposit and credit card businesses, wherein effectively dissecting the customer's spending and living habits equals better product development and sales.

Finally, both retail and wholesale financial services providers became increasingly concerned with the rapid distribution and analysis of so-called "real time" data. Indeed, the global bull market, while providing satisfying returns across the board, also makes it more difficult for investment managers to differentiate themselves from the pack or from benchmark indices. Data warehousing capable of handling real data, then, became a Holy Grail for many firms.

CHOOSE YOUR WEAPONS

While data warehousing seemed like a sound solution to many of the above-mentioned business challenges at the conceptual level, the actual implementation of data warehousing solutions did not live up to the initial promise. First, this is because of the many difficulties associated with obtaining, converting, and transporting data that effectively limit the scalability of most data warehousing solutions.

Second, if it is possible to get data into a warehouse, it is often challenging to get the data out of the warehouse and into the hands of end users who need it.

For example, traditional relational data warehouses are built in conjunction with implementation of a large, costly "enterprise" system. Such enterprise systems are typically limited to a certain number of high-priority users. Providing general access to such a system is usually too costly due to licensing fees. And, if the enterprise system performs crucial operations functions, analysts and other nonoperations staff may not be allowed to apply query tools to the data warehouse; if they did, they could slow down mission-critical processes. When general queries are permitted against the data warehouse, they are often very slow. In most cases, specialized query tools must be purchased in order to identify, copy, and manipulate the relevant portion of warehoused data.

There are three major types of data warehousing implementations, and each has different benefits and drawbacks; these are listed below. However, while all of these solutions have been successfully implemented at the local level, none has successfully scaled up to the enterprise level.

Options for Data Warehousing

Numerous Interfaces. This is the classic, old-style data warehouse in which numerous "interface" programs are developed to create even more numerous download files which, in turn, may be uploaded to a centralized data warehouse during nightly, weekly, or monthly batch processing. While the interface method does possess a certain conceptual simplicity and in fact is sometimes the only option available to handle extremely proprietary — or antiquated — bits of data, it traditionally has a low success rate. This is because the sheer number of interface programs which must be successfully run and kept in sync is usually so large. This creates problems because, first, if something goes wrong in any one of these procedures, the entire data warehouse may become inaccurate. Second, these interfaces are often difficult to fix because they are often proprietary and, wherever there is IT turnover, impenetrable and undocumented.

Replication. Data replication can be used to create both a data warehouse and numerous redundant data sources by periodically copying new records across a suitable WAN. For example, let's say bank X, headquartered in New York, has a London office and a Singapore office. Let's also say the data warehouse resides in New York. As new trades are entered in London and Singapore, they are both stored in local relational databases and copied or "replicated" and sent through the WAN to the data warehouse in New York. The same replication procedure can be used to populate a backup data warehouse located in, say, London. While this method is straightforward and has worked well for medium-sized and smaller portfolios, it also has distinct scalability problems. This is often due to excessive network traffic created by the constant copying and transmission of each and every transaction. As the network slows down, it becomes difficult to keep the data warehouse up-to-date, and network failures can result in corrupt, incorrect, or incomplete data.

Middleware. Middleware is a catch-all term referring to "plumbing" software that is typically transparent to the user and may function as an engine for any or all of the following: data transformation, data integrity checking, transaction monitoring, data transformation, data distribution, and/or object/application communication. Some financial institutions have attempted to populate large physical data warehouses through the innovative use of multiple forms of middleware. Others have attempted to link together various types of middleware in order to create their own "virtual data warehouse" in which middleware supplies applications with RAM copies of relevant data.

Regardless of which sort of warehouse one is attempting to create, managing numerous forms of middleware has some substantial drawbacks. These include the extensive effort required to ensure that different middleware packages are compatible with each other and with critical data sources, scalability limits associated with various types of middleware (particularly ORBs when used in conjunction with a "virtual" warehouse), maintenance associated with upgrades, etc.

The Data Mart Variation

In response to the limitations of data warehousing, many financial institutions have abandoned multiyear data warehousing projects in favor of what is known as the "data mart" approach. Basically, the data mart approach refers to a data warehousing projects which is based on a number of local, regional or functional implementations. The prime benefit to this approach is that, unlike the traditional "big bang" style of warehouse building, users in specific regional or functional areas can actually see results within a more predictable period of time. And, for this reason, data mart projects have found a friendlier reception in financial institutions than "old style" data warehousing.

However, the final step of a data mart project is generally to combine all the data marts into a data warehouse by periodically copying these local databases in their entirety into a centralized, relational data warehouse. Often, it is easier to create a data warehouse from data marts than to build one from scratch because data marts are usually built with consistent technology, thus avoiding the need for massive data conversions.

However, these data mart-based warehouses do not usually work well for real-time analysis, in which constant data-copying would compromise performance both at the warehouse and data mart levels. And, a data mart-driven warehouse still comes up against the challenge of distributing the contents of the warehouse in a usable format to those who need them.

DISTRIBUTED INTEGRATION: A NEW WAY

Distributed Integration is a new way to integrate global financial data, analytics, and applications and quickly distribute them to a large community of users. Unlike most traditional data warehousing solutions, this does not require all data to be physically co-located in a single huge database. Instead, the Distributed Integration architecture relies on Internet technologies to create a virtual data warehouse that is optimized for both scalability and the cost-effective delivery of critical data to large user communities.

Data and analytics residing in multiple physical locations behave like a single, integrated virtual environment through Web-enabled *Distributed Integration servers.* These servers take advantage of Internet server cluster organization and data caching techniques and thus are configured for extreme scalability.

End users access the distributed integration virtual environment through a *Distributed Integration workstation,* which simply refers to any desktop which has a direct Internet connection to one or more Distributed Integration servers.

Almost any application (such as Excel™) residing on a distributed integration workstation can be enabled to view and manipulate integrated data and analytics; such applications are referred to *analytic browsers.*

Indeed, for the numerous highly paid analysts at most financial institutions who spend the majority of their time gathering relevant information to feed into their spreadsheets and then verifying that this information is clean, consistent, and correct, the analytic browser is truly a revolutionary concept.

Exhibit 2-1 provides a quick illustration of distributed integration. It depicts a global financial organization with two or more physical locations separated by a WAN or Internet connection.

The top location, say New York, has an equities group that maintains a database of equities using Sybase. They use a distributed integration server to make the data available to their own clients. They deliver analytics to traders at home through analytic browsers. They also have a group of analysts who write specific analytics and incorporate them into the Distributed Integration server, thus making them available to other analysts and to managers for control purposes.

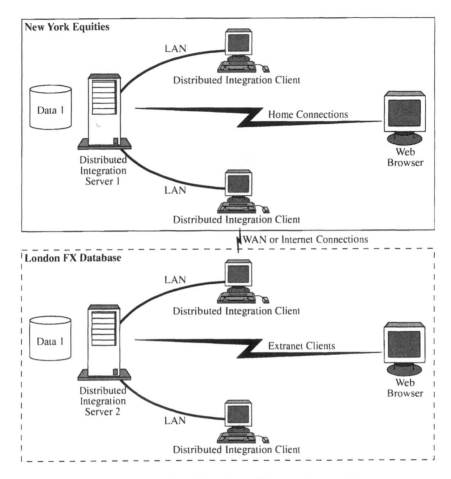

Exhibit 2-1. A sample of Distributed Integration architecture.

The bottom location, say London, has a number of other groups that maintain an FX database in FAME and a commodities database in ORACLE. They make the data available to their own traders and analysts through their own Distributed Integration server, which also includes proprietary analytics. This group is also servicing some external clients who are connected to them through the Internet, and get data, analytics, and Web-based applications from them.

LEVERAGING INTERNET/INTRANET TECHNOLOGY

Since the Distributed Integration servers in these two locations can be cascaded, as shown in Exhibit 2-2, each set of end-users can see the data in the other location. Moreover, since the Distributed Integration architecture

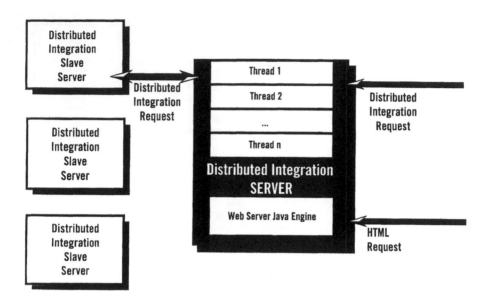

Exhibit 2-2. Distributed Integration takes advantage of cascaded server technology developed for the Internet to ensure fast and efficient management of Distributed Integration processes.

is characterized by transparent caching, the access times for local and remote data are almost identical on average. Data are transparently replicated to the location where they are used without significant IT involvement or administrative overhead; this is a far cry from the various data warehousing techniques described above, which require extensive IT resources to implement. As new locations are added with their own Distributed Integration servers, it is a simple step to make those servers known to the existing ones, thereby creating global multidirectional connectivity.

From an administrative point of view, the data, analytics, and applications are being maintained by the group that originated, and most "cares" about them, and they maintain it in whichever database they have chosen. However, because these data are integrated on the server side, local administration and autonomy does not come at the price of effective controls. This is a critical point for risk managers, HQ treasury managers, and compliance managers, who are often strong advocates of data warehousing initiatives which centralize data and in theory enhance controls.

The Distributed Integration server caching will "equalize" the access speed such that the back-end database does not become a bottleneck even if it's a small ACCESS database running on someone's desktop PC.

Distributed Integration makes it possible to then selectively share data, analytics, and applications across the entire organization without any additional integration work.

This architecture is highly scalable, since no single point can become a bottleneck as the number of locations increases. Thus, Distributed Integration avoids the scalability pitfalls associated with replication-based data warehousing solutions that tend to "clog up" a company's network.

For optimal scalability, the Distributed Integration server should be configured as a server cluster. This means it is not physically limited to a single process on a single machine. Such a server solution is implemented as a front-end multithreaded cluster manager process, with any number of symmetrical back-end servers that share the same configuration. Moreover, such clusters can always be cascaded amongst themselves, so there truly is no limit to the scalability of the Distributed Integration platform.

THE DISTRIBUTED INTEGRATION SERVER

Distributed Integration servers integrate historical and real-time data, metadata (i.e., data describing data), analytics, and applications. Because the server is capable of handling complex metadata and, by extension, almost any sort of data transformation, Distributed Integration is particularly well suited to address financial institutions' need for integrating time series and relational data.

In order to handle Web-based applications naturally and efficiently, Distributed Integration servers must also, by extension, be Internet servers. Indeed, Distributed Integration servers have been built as plug-ins to pre-existing Internet servers. As is consistent with Distributed Integration's reliance on the Web and Web-related technologies, it is most efficient to organize Distributed Integration servers as server clusters.

These Distributed Integration server clusters are stateless and connectionless, just like most Web servers, and should be capable of supporting the HTTP 1.1 keep-alive option for multiple related requests with a single connection for best utilization of network resources. This is also important from a user-functionality perspective; once data have been requested and cached, a user should be able to query that data without recopying it across the network. Likewise, incremental changes should be transmitted without the necessity of replicating the entire data set in which the changes originated.

The server cluster organization is one important reason why Distributed Integration can scale beyond traditional data warehousing solutions. As displayed in Exhibit 2-2, the front-end Distributed Integration server funnels each request to a number of preconfigured slave servers that actually handle the data and analytical requests.

Scalability is achieved by the fact that any number of slave servers can be added to a cluster, and they are automatically load-balanced by the master server. Fault tolerance is achieved by virtue of the fact that slave servers can be distributed on multiple machines, thereby reducing the chances that a single machine failure will halt the system.

A separate spool of threads handles standard Web server requests such as getting HTML pages, downloading Java applets, etc. This integrated architecture means that application, content, and data can be freely mixed to create a powerful application development and deployment model that is Web-centric and leverages the currently existing infrastructure.

Distributed Integration, it is important to note, performs best in a reasonably consistent hardware environment in which the server machines may be considered more or less interchangeable, and all the slave servers must have access to all the same data and analytics. This implies a shared configuration, as well as shared metadata and data caches. Thus, the user sees the entire cluster as a single server, with one URL address. And this URL address, then, becomes the user's gateway to the firm's total knowledge base.

The Distributed Integration server cluster architecture delivers:

- Performance — through the use of multiple machines coupled with load balancing.
- High availability — through redundancy of slave servers.
- Scalability — you can add more processes and machines as the number of users increases.

THE GATEWAY TO DISTRIBUTED INTEGRATION

Once one or more Distributed Integration servers have been configured to create a single point of integration for data and analytics, the next critical step is to cost-effectively distribute information to a large community of users. This has, in fact, been a challenge for those traditional data warehousing projects that have managed to get off the ground. A Java interface — or Distributed Integration gateway — can be used to connect desktop machines to integrated data and analytics residing on Distributed Integration servers.

When the gateway is active, a machine becomes a Distributed Integration workstation that is capable of "browsing" through all the information that is part of the Distributed Integration environment. Data and analytics can be accessed through a standard Web browser or by building software that connects existing desktop applications to the Distributed Integration environment. Applications that have access to Distributed Integration are called analytic browsers. It is possible to develop Distributed Integration add-ins capable of converting almost any application into an analytic browser.

In the financial services industry, however, one of the most useful applications of the analytic browser will be to connect spreadsheets to the Distributed Integration environment, thus allowing analysts to access integrated data without having to convert files or otherwise participate in the data-cleaning and -collection process. More advanced analytic applications will also become much more powerful when combined with Distributed Integration; indeed, one of the likely benefits of dynamically connecting end-users to an integrated environment is to speed up the pace of financial innovation.

LONG-TERM IMPLICATIONS OF DISTRIBUTED INTEGRATION

Distributed Integration, as it is implemented on a more widespread basis throughout the financial services industry, is likely to have important, even revolutionary, effects on how banks, brokerages, etc. do business in the future. And, as early adopters, the experiences of these financial services firms will serve as a model for other industries. Long-term implications of the Distributed Integration model include the following advantages.

Facilitates Financial Innovation

The desktop PC is synonymous with the modern workplace, and the PC-based spreadsheet application is synonymous with modern finance. However, the demands of today's businesses are straining the practical limits of PC-based spreadsheet analysis. A common illustration of this phenomenon is the fact that numerous highly paid financial analysts spend the majority their time gathering relevant information to feed into their spreadsheets and then verifying that this information is clean, consistent, and correct.

By providing integrated firm-wide data and analytics accessible through spreadsheets — such as Excel™ — Distributed Integration frees financial analysts from time-consuming data management duties and allows them to focus on value-added tasks. End users will also benefit from the opportunity to view and use the sum total of their firms' intellectual capital; they may combine this information in new and profitable ways.

Thus, the widespread adoption of Distributed Integration is likely to foster a new period of rapid financial and business innovation as analysts are simultaneously freed from the demands of data gathering and provided with accurate, integrated information.

Encourages a New Form of Corporate Organization: The Internet Management Model

As the number of Web-enabled workstations within corporations reach critical mass, organizations will be able to learn from the Internet and adopt new ways of managing themselves that go beyond the traditional trade-offs between centralization and decentralization. The Internet Management

Model (IMM) is one such method. It applies the Internet philosophy — that information and services are made globally available by the special interests that cherish them at low or no cost across a system which, to the customer, looks consistent, unified, and available on demand — to the corporate organization.

Distributed Integration, which allows local offices to manage and maintain their own mission-critical information while giving everyone access to the entire firm's intellectual capital, is an ideal vehicle for implementing IMM. Thus, rapid growth is sustained while top managers and business analysts have unprecedented access to the "big picture" presented by their firms' collective data and information systems. Islands of data ownership are eliminated.

By allowing firms to track individual and departmental contributions to firm-wide intellectual capital, it becomes possible to identify high- and low-performing areas. Simultaneously, IMM gives individuals and functional units much greater freedom to incorporate new data and analytics into their business activities without obtaining time-consuming approvals from central IT and business planning groups.

Allows Corporations and Financial Institutions to Manage the WHEN Dimension

As businesses' profitability becomes increasingly dependent on the timeliness and quality of the information which serves as the basis for key production, marketing, and strategic decisions, the ability to view, manipulate, and analyze data by time will become a matter of "life and death." Time-centric data, however, is often repetitive and difficult to store in conventional database formats. The Distributed Integration architecture is optimized for the rapid storage, transmission, and analysis of time-centric data as part of an integrated systems environment.

Author Bio

Dan Adler, Chief Technology Officer at Inventure America, is an authority in analytical and financial software development. From 1990-1996 he was responsible for the development of RANGER's predecessor, TicShell, at Tudor Investment Corp., as well as a system for global risk management. He also conducted research on the application of advanced statistical, neural, and genetic search algorithms to trading. In 1984, after graduating with a BS degree in Computer Engineering from the Technion, Israel Institute of Technology, he was employed by several world class organizations including Motorola, where he designed VLSI Microchips and Mentor Graphics. At Mentor Graphics, Dan led a variety of CAD projects in the areas of simulation and analysis of complex integrated circuits. In addition to his Computer Engineering degree, he also holds an MS degree in Computer and Electrical Engineering from Rutgers University. Dan has published papers in IEEE journals and conferences in the areas of CAD and Genetic Algorithms.

Chapter 3
Windows Distributed interNet Architecture for Financial Services

Dave Yewman

To COMPETE EFFECTIVELY IN THE NEXT 3 TO 5 YEARS, retail banks must migrate from monolithic core banking systems to PC-based client/server systems. To achieve this, they need low-risk ways to control costs and integrate existing legacy applications with flexible, powerful, scalable solutions that will enable the integration of multiple delivery channels.

With the recently announced Microsoft® Windows® Distributed interNet Applications (Windows DNA) architecture, the Microsoft Corporation has created a framework that allows businesses to more easily build new systems that take advantage of the capabilities of the personal computer and the opportunities presented by the Internet while integrating with existing systems. This chapter outlines how a new breed of applications can be delivered in retail banking using Windows DNA and the new Windows DNA for Financial Services (Windows DNA FS) while using existing systems and implementing "best-of-breed" solutions.

Windows DNA FS enables legacy computer systems to function in today's high-tech world. Windows DNA FS also works with powerful, scalable client/server computer systems that allow banks to use traditional delivery channels as well as Internet-oriented solutions, customer analysis tools, and load balancing.

INTRODUCING WINDOWS DNA

Windows DNA integrates the personal computer standard, the Internet, and legacy infrastructures by enabling computers to interoperate

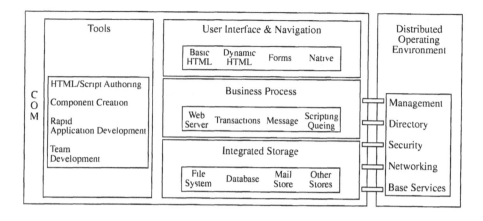

Exhibit 3-1.   Windows DNA.

and cooperate equally well across corporate and public networks. Windows DNA provides an interoperability framework based on open protocols and published interfaces that allow customers to extend existing systems with new functionality. This same open model provides extensibility "hooks," so third parties can realize new business opportunities by creating compatible products that extend the architecture (Exhibit 3-1).

Windows DNA applications use a standard set of Windows-based services that address the requirements of all tiers of modern distributed applications — user interface and navigation, business processes, and data storage. The heart of Windows DNA is the integration of the Internet and client/server application development models through the Microsoft Component Object Model (COM). Windows DNA provides a common set of services that are exposed in a unified way at all tiers of a distributed application.

By taking advantage of the capabilities in Windows DNA, developers will be able to build entirely new categories of applications, including electronic commerce and other interpersonal and intercorporate communication applications. Because they can take advantage of standard implementations of networked services and modern, component-based development methods, developers can deliver these innovative applications much more quickly than they could in the past.

These applications will have the potential for wide acceptance because Windows DNA fully embraces an open approach to distributed computing, building on standards approved by bodies such as the World Wide Web Consortium (W3C) and the Internet Engineering Task Force (IETF).

FUNDAMENTAL SERVICES

In the Windows DNA architecture, applications are built as a series of functional components. Microsoft's COM is the glue that is used to knit these components together.

Building applications based on COM components has many advantages for financial institutions. They can reuse business components they built themselves across the delivery channels. They can take advantage of the many prebuilt components available from third-party suppliers. They can tailor one of the many off-the-shelf applications that support COM interfaces to rapidly build new solutions that meet their particular business requirements.

For example, a funds transfer component built in COM can be delivered to a home banking application as an ActiveX™ Control, embedded in branch automation application for tellers to use — without programmatic change — or made available in an ATM running personal computer hardware. The user experience and branding are consistent, and clients recognize transfers in all scenarios immediately.

The net gain for the financial institution is easy to tally: one function, written once, tested once, deployed in many locations — the true promise of reusable programming.

There are currently more than 2000 vendors shipping business software products based on COM technologies. And because COM provides a language-independent component interface, financial institutions have the freedom to pick the best-of-breed suppliers, programming languages, and programming tools. The financial institution can chose a programming language based on developer experience and availability of skills rather than simply according to availability of components, technology vendors, programming tools, or environments. All Microsoft tools, applications, and systems products provide published COM-based extensibility interfaces. In fact, COM is the primary way for third parties to integrate their solutions with Microsoft products. Financial institutions can integrate existing systems through COM. Host- or UNIX-based applications are exposed to the developer in a consistent way through the COM interfaces.

WINDOWS DNA FOR FINANCIAL SERVICES

Traditionally, financial institutions have built separate IT systems and infrastructures to service different delivery channels as business opportunities and demand arose. Typically, this resulted in different IT infrastructures for different delivery channels.

Each infrastructure had its own set of hardware platforms, network protocols, middleware products, development tools, monolithic applications and data stores. Integration was typically at the data stores, leveraging the information itself but not the application logic across delivery channels. This process has resulted in longer development times, less product homogeneity and, when new banking products or services require access across the data stores, ultimately, a less satisfactory user experience — meaning that technology has helped alienate the customer from the bank rather than enhancing the relationship, which was the original intent.

Third parties that build solutions to the Windows DNA FS architecture, however, will allow financial institutions to build a reusable, reliable, scalable delivery channel infrastructure that marries the best of existing systems with the flexibility of new systems and takes advantage of the distributed services provided by the Windows NT® Server operating system and Microsoft BackOffice® family of products.

Financial institutions have long desired what Windows DNA FS promises (Exhibit 3-2). But in the past, they have had to use different client hardware platforms for each delivery channel, because of the different processing requirements of each channel and the technical limits of existing hardware.

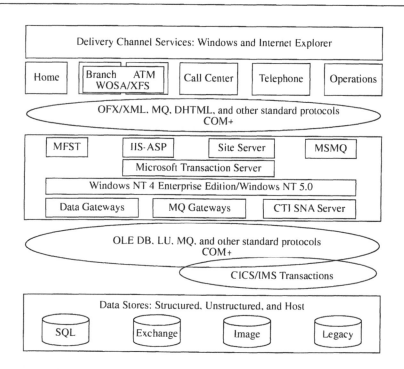

Exhibit 3-2. Windows DNA in Financial Services for Retail Banking.

For instance, a 3270 terminal connected directly to an account management application served the bank teller who needed to use only that application. However, a loan-processing officer who needed to perform word processing and spreadsheet analysis as well as account management worked with a PC, meaning that from a programmatic standpoint the bank had two incompatible infrastructures. In addition, the bank had a number of client platforms that had to be separately maintained and administered and that had to have applications developed for them. Because each of these platforms is targeted to one particular task, there is little opportunity for flexibility in deploying applications. For example, the loan calculation application that integrates Microsoft Excel and Microsoft Word cannot be used from the teller position even if business process analysis shows that the best way to service loans is through the teller. These issues lead to increased operations, development, and training costs and an inability to adapt quickly to changing business requirements.

The Microsoft Windows operating system family — Windows CE, Windows-based Terminals, Windows 95, Windows 98, and Windows NT Workstation and Windows NT Server — have a consistent user interface and programming model, enabling financial institutions to overcome the technical limitations that handicapped previous systems and to use reusable skills developed by the user, administrator, and developer.

In an integrated infrastructure, the bank teller can now use an account management application running on a Windows-based Terminal or a Windows-based Network PC (Net PC) in Task Station mode. The loans processing officer uses the loan application on a Windows-based PC in Application Station mode. This provides the bank with increased flexibility but lower administration costs. If required, the teller position can quickly and easily be reconfigured by a central administrator to run the loan application without the need for a new hardware platform and operating system. The system administrator has a consistent hardware architecture, and the developer can use a common set of services and development tools across all the delivery channels.

Within the Windows DNA FS architecture, all financial services clients — whether home banking PCs, teller positions, or self-service devices — are connected to Windows NT Server via standard IP-based protocols. This lowers infrastructure costs, decreases systems administration costs, increases reuse of administration skills, and helps lower training costs.

By rationalizing the core messaging protocols used across financial services clients, financial institutions can benefit from economies of scale by deploying one set of application components to support these core-messaging protocols. These components can be used and reused across the financial services clients.

Because of its seamless support for standard network protocols and messaging standards (such as Open Financial Exchange [OFX], XML, HTTP, and TCP/IP), Windows NT Server acts as a gateway to existing delivery channels and the corporate network. This allows financial institutions to preserve existing network investments and migrate to the new standard networking protocols in an evolutionary manner. Microsoft and other industry leaders provide many strategies for preserving investments in middle-tier transaction processing systems — including MVS, AS/400, and UNIX — by integrating them into Windows NT Server-based applications. These applications include CICS, IMS, and XA Support, Microsoft Message Queue Server, OLE DB, database replication from host databases into Microsoft SQL Server™, and Distributed COM (DCOM) support on platforms other than Microsoft.

The ability to integrate with existing systems, together with its support for new technologies such as those underlying the Internet and intranets and a wide range of high-productivity development tools, makes Windows NT a strong application development platform. Developers can produce powerful new applications that tie together existing systems and extend the reach of those systems more quickly and easily than ever.

WINDOWS DNA FOR FINANCIAL SERVICES — SERVICES DEFINITIONS

The Windows DNA for Financial Services framework defines three logical layers (Exhibit 3-3). Each layer provides the services that allow financial institutions to build the applications that meet their business requirements.

From a logical view, the three services equate to the three tiers in the Windows DNA architecture: User Interface and Navigation, Business Process, and Integrated Storage. Physical implementation of the services can be varied based on the needs of the delivery channel.

Delivery Channel Services

The IT departments of financial institutions are faced with many conflicting demands when deciding how to best serve the delivery channels. On the one hand, they need to service as many delivery channels as the business requires; on the other hand, they want to minimize the development cost of maintaining multiple heterogeneous clients.

Financial institutions can meet these requirements by taking advantage of the broad reach of the Microsoft Windows operating system family and the services provided by the Windows DNA FS architecture.

The Microsoft Windows operating system family, with its consistent user interface and programming model, allows developers to write applications that run on the broadest possible range of hardware configurations (Exhibit 3-4). From the home through the branch office and onto the

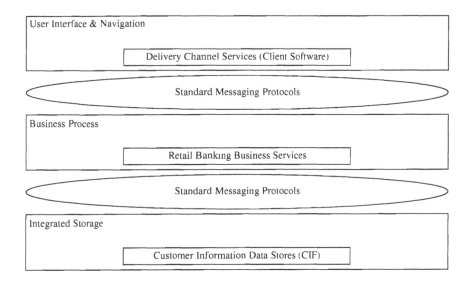

Exhibit 3-3. **Windows DNA for Financial Services.**

trading floor, there are devices based on the PC standard to suit every requirement — all running one member of the Microsoft Windows operating system family.

Financial institutions can build user interfaces using basic HTML to reach the broadest range of clients — PC, Macintosh, and UNIX — running different browsers. Financial institutions can build user interfaces using Dynamic HTML and scripting (the Visual Basic® development system

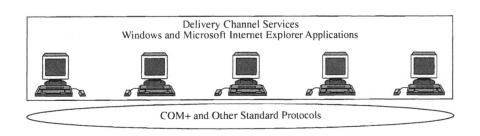

Exhibit 3-4. **Windows devices, like delivery channels, come in various shapes.**

Scripting Edition or JScript™ development software), providing the rich, flexible, and interactive experience users have come to expect from Windows-based applications. Because of the cross-platform support provided by Microsoft Internet Explorer 4.0, such user interfaces can still service a broad range of clients. Financial institutions can encapsulate business logic in scriptable components that can then be deployed on the client or on the server, depending on the client device, because COM and the scripting environment are supported at all layers of Windows DNA FS.

For instance, a home banking application may have a basic HTML user interface and a Dynamic HTML user interface; this will deliver services to all customers but offer a richer experience to customers with more advanced browser software. Microsoft Internet Information Server (IIS) and Active Server Pages (ASP) scripting technology can be used to determine the type of browser the customer is using and deliver the appropriate user interface. The components that verify user input and generate financial services requests run in Internet Explorer 4.0 either on the client or as part of an ASP on the server.

The power and flexibility of Dynamic HTML, combined with scripting and components, allow the user interface for business applications in the branch, the self-service device, the call center, and the back office to be built using this same technology. Developers can reuse business logic and user interface components across delivery channels, reducing the amount of new code they have to write. Developers can use the same tools and techniques for building all of the delivery channel applications, reducing training costs and increasing skills reuse. This reduces the cost of building a new delivery channel application as well as the time to build the application and increases the quality of the application.

For instance, a Dynamic HTML COM component that gathers the details used to transfer funds from one account to another can be used in a browser-based home banking application, in a branch-banking teller application and in a self-service device. By using a common message protocol, such as OFX, to send financial services requests from the client to the server across the delivery channels, financial institutions can reuse the cooperating components that generate those requests.

Financial institutions can use Microsoft Site Server Personalization Services to easily build user interfaces that allow customers to tailor a home banking application to reflect their particular financial needs and interests. By using advanced technologies such as Microsoft NetMeeting™ conferencing software, which allows videoconferencing over the Internet and intranets, financial institutions can offer an even richer service to their customers. For example, if a customer wants to apply for a loan but needs advice, she or he can connect directly to the call center from the home banking application to talk to a customer service representative.

By using the same Internet-based technologies to build the user interfaces for home banking and self-service devices, financial institutions can serve the customer using the same familiar user interface both at home and at a branch or in the supermarket. Not only will the customer be presented with a familiar user interface, but because services such as Personalization and NetMeeting are available, the self-service application can be tailored to reflect the customer's requirements and can offer interactive advice. Such technologies allow the financial institution to provide a wider range of tailored services to customers while reducing the customer's need to visit the branch. It increases the customer's perception of the financial institution's responsiveness and flexibility and therefore increases customer satisfaction and loyalty, while lowering costs by providing these services across the most cost-effective delivery channels.

Business Services

Financial institutions face similar challenges when building the business services that sit behind the delivery channels. They want to service as many delivery channels as the business requires, but they do not want to incur the overhead of maintaining multiple business server infrastructures (Exhibit 3-5). They want to build an application infrastructure that scales up to Internet banking and scales down to small-branch banking. They want to produce applications that deliver a single view of the customer, but they don't want to re-engineer their existing account-based transaction processing systems. They want to take advantage of the price/performance and choice advantages provided by PC-based servers, but they also want the scalability and reliability that until now have been provided only by high-cost mainframe transaction processing systems.

Financial institutions can meet all these requirements by taking advantage of the services provided by the Windows DNA architecture — Web server, transactions, messaging, and scripting.

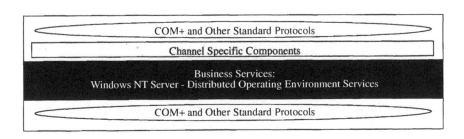

Exhibit 3-5.   Separate cooperating application logic.

Windows NT Server and the Microsoft BackOffice family of products provide the bedrock on which Windows DNA services are built. They offer integrated security and administration, fast file and print, communications, messaging and groupware, database, host connectivity, systems management, Internet, secure proxy, content creation and Web site management, and information retrieval and search services. Microsoft BackOffice server applications, with their familiar Windows-based interface, are easy to install, deploy, and administer. The use of common administration tools across the BackOffice family helps financial institutions reduce training and support needs. Integrated security means that users and their security permissions are defined only once rather than for each service, which reduces administration overhead and the possibility of errors.

Microsoft Transaction Server (MTS), now built into Windows NT Server, provides financial institutions with the services they need to more easily deliver manageable, reliable, scalable COM component-based applications that will service thousands of simultaneous users. MTS manages transaction scope across components, across databases, across machines, and even across heterogeneous systems (Windows NT, UNIX, CICS). It allows developers to build scalable solutions without having to build complex infrastructures or understand arcane programming tools and to build solutions that integrate Microsoft SQL Server, the Internet, and legacy systems via standard COM interfaces. These services allow developers to focus on building business solutions, lowering development costs substantially. In addition, using the symmetric multiprocessor capabilities of Windows NT Server, a COM component can take advantage of a powerful multiprocessor to provide functionality to hundreds or even thousands of clients.

Using the distributed services of Windows DNA FS, developers can build applications as a set of cooperating components. This allows financial institutions to build flexible applications based on components that can be used across delivery channels. For instance, in the past a home banking application and a branch banking teller application would have contained separate but almost identical business logic to transfer funds between accounts. Because this business logic was embedded in the separate applications, there was little or no chance of this logic being reused across the applications and a great chance that common business rules were implemented inconsistently. Now the business logic is encapsulated in a single "financial transaction" component that services both delivery channels, so the business logic needs to be implemented only once. This helps ensure consistent implementation, higher quality, and lower maintenance costs.

This component-based approach allows financial institutions to buy rather than build. In the past, packaged applications could save development time but were either hard to integrate with existing systems and difficult to extend or complicated to set up and deploy. By building their applications to the Windows DNA FS architecture and delivering them as a set of components, third-party developers solve the integration problem for financial institutions. With MTS taking care of transaction coordination and component isolation issues, financial institutions can integrate component-based solutions into their delivery channel infrastructure, and then make use of these same components to build new services.

Financial transaction components can be invoked via the Internet, an intranet or a LAN. Microsoft Internet Information Server and Active Server Pages scripting technology allow financial transaction components to be invoked from Web pages. The Microsoft Internet Financial Services Toolkit (MIFST) provides a framework that allows financial transaction components to be invoked based on Open Financial Exchange requests received from personal financial managers, small-business accounting packages, and browser-based home banking applications. DCOM allows financial transaction components to be invoked directly from applications such as a branch banking teller application. This flexibility gives financial institutions the opportunity to reuse financial transaction components across delivery channels — whether in the home, the branch, the supermarket, or the back office.

By taking advantage of the Windows DNA FS architecture, financial institutions can encapsulate business logic into financial transaction components. A particular component can be used for every delivery channel that needs to implement that business logic, which reduces the amount of new code developers have to write. Because developers can use the same standard tools and techniques for building components for all the delivery channel applications, training costs are lowered and skills are reused. This reduces the cost of building a new delivery channel application, as well as the time to build the application and increases the quality of the application.

By taking advantage of the legacy system integration technologies exposed through COM interfaces in MTS and Microsoft's universal data access technology, financial institutions can build components that gather information from many systems. This allows them to build delivery channel services that present a single view of the customer. The analysis tools built into Microsoft Site Server allow analysis of what pages customers visit on a Web site, how often they go there, and how much time they spend. Combining such information about customer interests with customer information held by financial institutions gives the institutions a uniquely powerful view of the customer that will allow accurately targeted sales and marketing. For example, a customer with $10,000 in her savings account who spends time online looking at information on stocks is a qualified lead for customer service representatives offering investment advice or information on money market funds.

Integrated Storage

Financial institutions need to build applications that present a unified view of customer information and associated relationship information. This unified view must transcend system boundaries whether the information lies in a legacy transaction processing system, an e-mail system, or a letter written with a word processor (Exhibit 3-6).

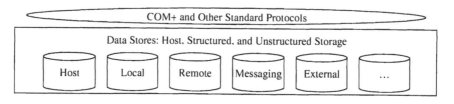

Exhibit 3-6. A unified view of customer information.

Microsoft and other industry leaders provide many tools and strategies for preserving existing investments by integrating application transactions, message queuing infrastructure, and data stores into Windows DNA applications. These tools include CICS, IMS, and XA support via COM interfaces in Microsoft Transaction Server and the Component Transaction Integrator, Microsoft Message Queue Server, and DCOM support on platforms other than Microsoft. Integration with these legacy systems preserves existing investment while using the consistent programming model of the Windows family of operating systems.

Microsoft's Universal Data Access Technology, known as OLE DB, allows access to disparate data sources through a consistent COM interface. OLE DB complements ODBC by allowing all data sources, not just relational databases, to expose their data through a common set of COM interfaces. Data from e-mail, files, spreadsheets, and documents as well as databases are accessible through OLE DB. This allows developers to access data from many sources without the overhead of using multiple proprietary data-access APIs.

On Windows NT Server, the Microsoft SQL Server database has outstanding transaction processing performance — holding the top 10 spots in the TPC-c price/performance rankings — and contains high levels of integrity and resilience, built-in data replication, and remote stored procedures. It also supports distributed transaction. Microsoft SQL Server also features intuitive graphical systems management tools that reduce training costs and administration overhead.

Data replication from host database systems into Microsoft SQL Server and distributed transactions, together with low administration overhead, allow financial institutions to distribute data where it adds the greatest value for the customer — for instance, a local branch office.

Financial institutions can use these data access services with Microsoft SQL Server to build components that present a unified view of the customer without the development overhead of using multiple proprietary data access APIs and without mandating a potentially perilous attempt to move all data into a single corporate database.

SUMMARY

Financial institutions have a vision for their future: delivering a flexible and responsive service to the customer — any service, any time, any where. Windows DNA for Financial Services is the first real solution for financial institutions that want to integrate delivery channels in both a networked and Internet-networked world. Windows DNA FS provides a consistent programming model, consistent development environment, consistent distributed services, and consistent application model to the desktop and the server. The core of these features is the Windows family of products and the distributed services built into them.

This vision needs to be supported by flexible, customer-focused IT systems that support multiple delivery channels. These IT systems must take advantage of the power of new technologies without requiring financial institutions to replace their existing transaction processing systems, and they must cost less time and effort to build than in the past. By building to this architecture, financial institutions can more quickly and easily develop delivery channel applications that integrate the new technologies with their existing systems to provide more customer service at lower cost than ever.

WHERE TO GET STARTED?

For more information on Windows DNA for Financial Services, visit the Microsoft in financial services Web site at http://www.microsoft.com/industry/finserv/.

Microsoft, Windows, ActiveX, Windows NT, BackOffice, Visual Basic, JScript and NetMeeting are either registered trademarks or trademarks of Microsoft Corporation in the U.S. and/or other countries. Other product and company names herein may be trademarks of their respective owners.

Author Bio

Dave Yewman is with Insync Communications.

Chapter 4
Evaluation of Financial Analysis and Application Prototyping Environments

Charles Bassignani

OVER THE LAST TWENTY YEARS, the emergence of relatively low-cost yet powerful desktop computers has had a profound impact on the financial services industry. The efforts of banks and money management firms to put more computing power on the desktops of traders, analysts, and quantitative researchers has led to the development of sophisticated software packages for research, analytic prototyping, and application development.

Evaluating one analytic and application prototyping environment against another is a difficult task. Diverse feature sets and scope make direct comparisons between packages difficult. The number of packages available is great and it is often difficult to discern which packages are of quality. To make the task of choosing the best environment more manageable, this chapter seeks to build a framework for the systematic evaluation of each environment by identifying the most important features for analytic prototyping and application development.

We will begin this chapter with a discussion of what we mean by the terms *analytic prototyping* and *application development*. We will then proceed with a discussion of important features in both areas. Although we will refrain from discussing particular software packages in detail, we will show examples of the tools available in some of the more common environments. It is important to point out that no single package available on

0-8493-9834-7/00/$0.00+$.50

the market today does everything. Each package has its relative strengths and weaknesses.

ANALYTIC PROTOTYPING AND APPLICATION DEVELOPMENT

Having a good analytic prototyping and application development environment is critical to the timely delivery of good software tools for end-users. The term *analytic prototyping* refers to the creation of individual tools which either embody a theoretical model in its entirety, or provide a component necessary for implementation of that theoretical model. The term *application development* refers to the act of packaging analytics, or tools, together along with an interface and some form of data connectivity to create a solution for a real-world problem. An example of application development in this context would the be the creation of a decision support system for fixed income. At a minimum, such a system would consist of a set of tools for valuing bonds, calculating yield to maturity and accrued interest, and for calculating sensitivities such as duration and convexity. This system would probably also include a Graphical User Interface (GUI) and some functionality for retrieving data from and writing data to a database. A good application development environment should support the development of all these components.

The financial application development value chain is a useful framework for understanding analytic prototyping and application development and why selection of a good environment is a critical determinant of competitive advantage in the financial services industry. This value chain consists of activities performed by academic researchers, quantitative researchers ("quants"), application developers, traders, and analysts (see Exhibit 4-1). In this framework, academics develop theoretical models in the area of fixed income, derivatives, equities, portfolio management, risk management, and foreign exchange. Quantitative researchers take these models and implement them, creating prototype analytics or tools in the process. With the help of the quants, application developers use aggregations of these analytics to create applications which are then tested by analysts and traders. Based on the results of these tests, the algorithms contained in the applications are modified and then retested. From this iterative process, emerges both a set of polished analytics and a finished end-user application. Groups of finished analytics which pertain to the same task or application area in finance are often bundled together into *modules* or *libraries*. Application developers then link these libraries together with other GUIs and an interfaces to a data sources to form even more financial applications.

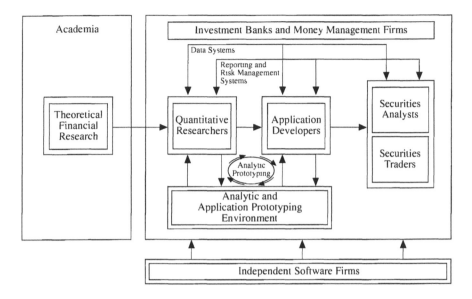

Exhibit 4-1.   The financial applications software development value chain is a useful way to see why having a good prototyping and development environment is critical to the timely delivery of good software tools.

IDENTIFYING CRITICAL FEATURES

The quality of any analytic prototyping and application development environment (hereafter "prototyping environment") can be assessed along two dimensions: core/functional analytics, and development/development support tools. The terms *core* and *functional analytics* refer to sets of tools designed for specific tasks which arise as a part of the research, prototyping, and development processes. Core analytics include tools for optimization, statistical analysis, and mathematics. Functional analytics include analytics for fixed income, equity, derivatives, portfolio optimization, risk management, and foreign exchange. Development and development support tools refer to the tools and capabilities which specifically support the development of applications from prototype analytics and research results. A good set of development tools will include support for code generation, application distribution, data connectivity, and GUI development.

CORE ANALYTICS

The availability of core analytics is an important concern in choosing a prototyping environment. Especially important are tool sets for optimization, statistics, and matrix mathematics. Tools for sophisticated statistical analysis such as GARCH and an infrastructure for financial time series analysis are desirable, as are tools for spline techniques, symbolic math, neural networks, and fuzzy logic.

Optimization Tools

Optimization involves the minimization and maximization of mathematical functions. Optimization problems frequently arise in finance, particularly in the area of asset allocation, volatility analysis for derivatives valuation, and optimal trading strategy identification and prediction. Portfolio optimization, for example, requires the application of constrained optimization to find the optimal portfolio allocation given a universe of securities to choose from, a covariance matrix for those securities, and a set of constraints, or rules, regarding how and in what quantities those securities can be held. A good feature set for optimization should include scalar minimization, linear programming, quadratic programming, functions for linear and nonlinear equation solving, and functions for least squares curve fitting.

Statistics Tools

Statistics tools are used extensively in finance, from simple descriptive statistical and regression analysis of historical data, to normal cumulative distribution-based analysis in support of Black-Scholes option pricing, to multidistribution-based approaches to Monte Carlo simulation. In addition to tools for basic descriptive statistics and regression, a good set of statistics tools should accommodate analysis based on multiple probability distributions, including normal, lognormal, t, binomial, and Poisson. For each of these distributions, the tool set should include tools for deriving and using a probability density function, cumulative distribution function and its inverse, mean and variance as a function of parameters, and random number generation.

Numerical Algorithms

Quantitative financial calculations in support of analytic prototyping requires a broad set of core mathematical functionality. From the interpolation of interest rates for the purposes of developing discount factors for a particular cash flow in time, to root-finding approaches to determining the internal rate of return on a stream of cash flows, to correlation and covariance analysis on a set of assets, to simple sorting, the availability of numerical and mathematical functionality is an important consideration in evaluating a prototyping environment.

Time Series Infrastructure

The term "time series" is widely used in many disciplines. In finance, it has a particular meaning that differs slightly from the concept in electrical engineering or other areas. A financial time series normally consists of a temporally distributed set of prices or price returns for an asset or set of assets. Financial times series will exhibit characteristics that are perhaps uniquely financial, such as data sparseness, volatility clumping, and leverage effects. Since financial time series often contain missing data, some sort of filling or interpolation is normally required as a first step in any analysis. Time series of stock prices may be missing values because trading in a stock was suspended for a particular day, because trading was suspended at midday and the prices are closing prices, or because the stocks are traded in two different geographic markets. Financial statement data, such as earnings, may also be missing values because a company failed to report earnings for one or more quarters or is in the process of restating earnings. This is especially true of publicly held companies that are very small. By contrast, in engineering, time series are normally data-complete and do not require filling or interpolation.

Financial time series analysis itself involves nearly every type of statistical analysis possible, from simple descriptive statistics to more sophisticated analytical techniques such as regression, nonstationary descriptive statistics, principal components analysis, etc. As a result, time series analytics are more an infrastructural concern than they are a set of tools and should be viewed as such.

GARCH

Generalized AutoRegressive Conditional Heteroscedascity (GARCH) modeling is a modeling approach which takes into account the existence of time dependent/conditional variance in a financial time series. In looking at the price behavior of stocks, for example, we see that volatility tends to be clustered, meaning that high price volatility tends to be followed by high price volatility and low price volatility tends to be followed by low price volatility. We also see that a return series typically exhibits "leverage effects," meaning that the impact of positive surprises tends to be less substantial than the impact of negative surprises. GARCH modeling (hereinafter GARCH) allows one to explain and model the time-varying characteristics of risk and uncertainty in a financial time series.

Many derivative securities, such as commodities futures and equity options, derive their value from some underlying asset (hence the term "derivative"). The pricing of these derivative securities depends to a great extent on the investor's estimate of volatility for the price of the underlying asset. For example, the price that one will pay for a corn futures contract which expires 3 months from now will depend on the perceived volatility of corn prices over the life of the option. The price of a call option on IBM's common stock will depend on the recent volatility of IBM's stock price, which will in turn drive investor's perceptions for price volatility over the life of the option. Prior to the advent of GARCH, financial practitioners would model volatility simply as the standard deviation of some historical time series extrapolated into the future. With GARCH, more sophisticated predictions for volatility are now possible.

In addition to standard GARCH, there are several other strains of GARCH being used in finance. Threshold GARCH, or TGARCH, looks at the leverage effect on time-varying changes in volatility above a certain threshold. Exponential GARCH, or EGARCH, gives exponential weighting to the leverage effect on time-varying volatility. Power GARCH, or PGARCH, raises the impact of leverage to a power which, in turn, is statistically estimated from the data. These four types, or strains, of GARCH are important in finance, and any good set of GARCH tools should contain at least these four models. In addition, GARCH can be segmented between univariate and bivariate types. Univariate GARCH involves the modeling of time-varying volatility for a single return series. Multivariate GARCH involves the modeling of time-varying volatility for multiple return series where the covariance of the series is considered. A good set of GARCH tools (see Exhibit 4-2) should include at least one multivariate model.

Spline Tools

Spline techniques are used extensively for fitting curves to known data points. One of the biggest areas of application for splines in finance is term structure analysis. Interest rate curves, such as zero, forward, and discount curves, are an important input to effective term structure analysis. Because of noisy and incomplete data, curves fitted to data points derived from reported market prices for fixed income securities are often very rough. As a result, these curves are often difficult to use, such as in the case where a rough zero curve leads to instances of negative rates in an implied forward curve, rates which are more an artifact of the poorly behaved zero curve than they are a result of the economic trend in the data. Cubic splines are a popular approach to fitting a "smoother" to these poorly behaved data points. These smoothed zero curves make subsequent analysis based on the information contained in or implied by the curve easier.

Symbolic Math Tools

In addition to tools for numerical analysis, the availability of symbolic mathematical tools is also an important consideration in evaluating an

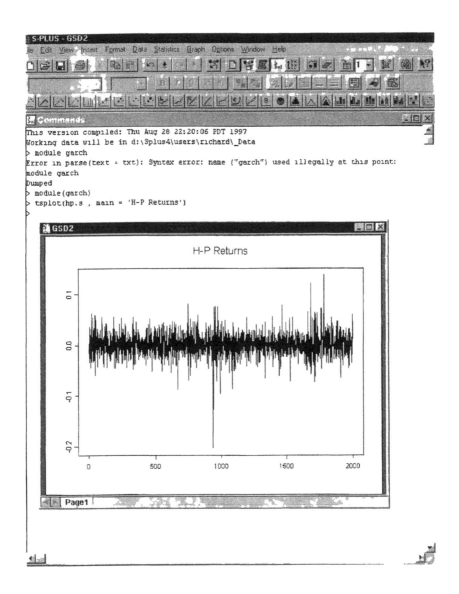

Exhibit 4-2. **MathSoft's S-Plus/S-Garch package provides a powerful platform for doing GARCH-based modeling of volatility.**

analytical environment. A good set of symbolic math tools should include tools for calculus, linear algebra, simplification, equation solving, and transformations (e.g., Fourier transforms, Z-transforms, etc.). The price

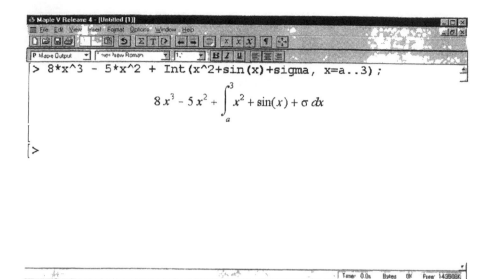

Exhibit 4-3. **Maple V provides a powerful platform for doing symbolic math computations.**

of an option is a function of the volatility of the price of the underlying asset. Because estimating volatility as an input parameter to an option-pricing model is a subjective process, analysts often would like to calculate an options price as a function of volatility without having a numeric estimate for that volatility. Symbolic math tools would make such an analysis possible (see Exhibit 4-3).

Neural Networks Tools

Neural networks refers to the application of neural net technology to real world problems. Neural networks are comprised of networks of individual elements which operate in parallel fashion to recognize patterns or systems in data. Through an iterative approach these elements make continual adjustments to weights until a pattern has been identified within the data set. These patterns are then used to make predictions with respect to future data points. Neural networks have been applied in areas including the aerospace, automotive, defense, and telecommunications industries. In finance, they have proven particularly useful for document reading, credit card application evaluation, real estate appraisal, mortgage lending, market analysis, and any area in which time series analysis is a principal activity. A good neural networks package should include predefined network architectures, like back propagation, and include algorithms for calculating network weights.

Fuzzy Logic

The term fuzzy logic refers to a mapping of an "input space" to an "output space" in which only significant information is used as a part of the mapping process. Fuzzy logic approaches to problem solving involve reducing a problem to its most basic parameters and then using expert or common sense rules for developing a system of solutions to that problem. In finance, fuzzy logic has found application in the area of market analysis and trading rule identification. A good fuzzy logic package should include an editor for creating your fuzzy system. This system editor should in turn include editors for creating membership functions and identifying rules. Finally, the fuzzy package should include a surface view for viewing the resulting fuzzy logic system.

Block-Diagramming Capabilities

Block-diagramming tools have a long history in electrical and mechanical engineering markets. In finance, these tools are gaining increasing acceptance as a means for modeling complex nonlinear securities such as mortgage and asset-backed securities. They also prove useful enabling Monte Carlo-based simulation of the nonlinear components of discounted cash flow models used for equity valuation.

In general, block diagramming enable the modeling and simulation of complex dynamic systems in a graphical manner. A good set of tools should let you build your model quickly, run the model, and make changes to the model on the fly. Since these tools are inherently graphical, the graphical user interface should be intuitive and easy to use. The tool set should include a ready-made block for all commonly used items, such as a cash flow or discount rate, or a standard stochastic process. The tools should also allow for the customization of existing block sets and for the creation of user-defined block sets (see Exhibit 4-4).

FUNCTIONAL ANALYTICS FOR FINANCE

To be an effective environment for financial analytic and application development, a package should contain functional sets of tools for the main application areas in finance. These areas included fixed income, derivatives, portfolio optimization, equities, risk management, and foreign exchange.

Fixed Income Tools

A set of fixed income tools will include tools for mapping a bond's cash flows, calculating yield and price, calculating sensitivities such as duration and convexity, and for determining total return. Whether a set of tools can accommodate bonds with abnormally short and long initial and

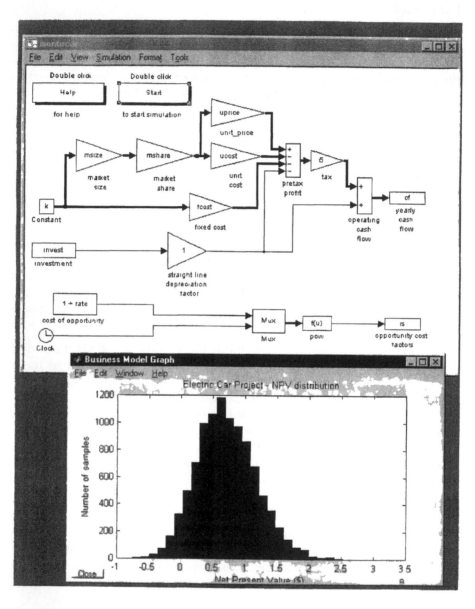

Exhibit 4-4. This MATLAB SIMULINK model contains a net present value analysis for an electric car development process. Block-diagramming models such as this make it much easier to understand the complexities surrounding a financial problem.

ending coupon periods will determine whether the tools can be used to accurately model securities being traded in the marketplace. Tools that cannot correctly model the cash flow structure of a bond in time cannot possibly return correct values for price, yield, duration, and convexity. Therefore, this should be an important consideration when evaluating an environment.

Derivatives Tools

There are many popular models for valuing derivatives (see Exhibit 4-5). Black-Scholes[1] and simple binomial tree models are common approaches to valuing equity derivatives. Black's Model[2] and Vasicek's

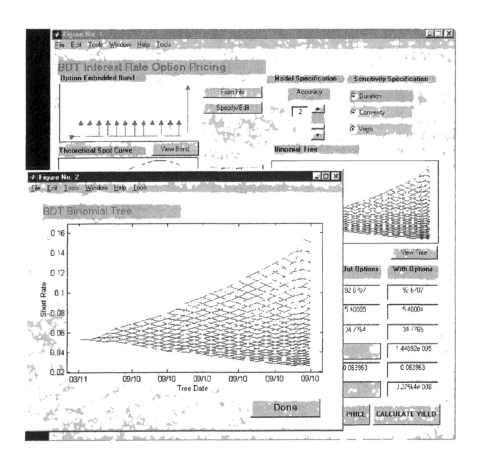

Exhibit 4-5. Black Derman Toy is a popular tree-based model for valuing interest rate derivatives. Here is an implementation of the BDT model, complete with a GUI, built entirely in MATLAB.

Model[3] are popular approaches to valuing interest rate derivatives. A set of tools for analyzing derivatives should contain at a minimum Black-Scholes, a simple binomial tree, and Black's Model approaches to valuing derivatives. In addition to these simple models, a high-quality prototyping environment will make available one or more complex tree-based models for interest rate derivatives such as the Black Derman Toy,[4] Hull White,[5] or Heath Jarrow Morton[6] model. Normally these complex models are only made available as a part of end-user decision support and trading systems costing in excess of $500,000.

Portfolio Optimization Tools

Asset allocation involves the use of portfolio optimization tools for determining which assets to hold in your portfolio and in what quantities. This is an important task for mutual fund managers looking to understand whether or not their investments are well diversified. In the case of actively managed portfolios, fund managers know that they are not holding the most diversified portfolios possible, but they still need to know what the market portfolio looks like in order to understand the nature of the "bets" they are making. Risk managers need to also understand the nature of the investments being made by these portfolio managers in terms of how risky the investments are relative to the market portfolio.

The Markowitz Portfolio Selection Model[7] and the Capital Asset Pricing Model[8] were developed in the 1950s and 1960s as means for determining how to manage asset allocation in the most efficient manner possible. These models underlie nearly all the tools which are being used to determine optimal portfolio allocation today. A good set of portfolio optimization tools should implement these models in some form and therefore should include tools for deriving an asset return time series from a price series, deriving a covariance matrix, and for determining the most efficient allocation of capital among assets. A good set of portfolio optimization tools also will allow you to specify constraints with respect to the portfolio (e.g., limitations on the types of assets or combinations of the types of assets that can be held). They should also allow you to calculate a Value-at-Risk (VAR) number for your portfolio (see Risk Management).

Equity Analytic Tools

The valuation and analysis of equity securities involve both subjective and objective components. Equity analysts spend a great deal of time talking with the management of firms and with competitor companies. They also spend a great deal of time analyzing the industries within which these firms operate. These activities lead to the development of a conceptual framework for valuing a firm. Once they develop this framework, then work begins to develop an objective, analytical framework which embodies their best estimate for intrinsic value for a company's common stock on a per-share basis. Many prototyping environments contain sets of tools for building this analytical framework. At a minimum, these sets of tools contain functions for calculating the present and future value of a stream of cash flows, for calculating the duration and convexity of those cash flows, and for calculating the internal rate of return (IRR) and net present value (NPV) of a stream of cash flows. A good set of tools will also contain functions for determining a firms weighted average cost of capital, for modeling sensitivities with respect to changes in leverage, and for modeling systematic and unsystematic risk components.

Risk Management Tools

Risk management is one of the hottest segments in the financial services industry with respect to the application of technology. Demand for tools for assessing and reporting market risk and credit risk is skyrocketing and many software vendors are scrambling to bring products to market which meet these needs. Demand is being driven by a dramatic increase in regulation both internationally and here in the U.S. with respect to the reporting of market risk exposure.[9] A continual "lowering of the compliance bar" in the area of market risk assessment and reporting and the addition of new regulation in the area of credit risk will continue to fuel demand for risk tools and applications.

In addition to standard financial tools, many prototyping packages contain tools specifically for building risk analytics and applications. These tool sets contain at a minimum tools for calculating Value at Risk (VAR), for doing "fast-valuation" of portfolios of diverse kinds of instruments, and for building the covariance matrices that are input to the VAR calculating tools. The quality of these tool sets is determined by the accuracy of their valuation analytics with respect to the accuracy of the VAR numbers generated. Quality packages will also support various types of reporting with respect to the sources of risk.

Foreign Exchange Tools

As markets become more and more global in focus the need to incorporate foreign exchange issue will continue to increase. This means, for example, that tools for calculating price, yield to maturity, and duration for bonds must now be able to treat foreign bonds and incorporate the foreign exchange rate pertaining to the market in which the security is traded. While a separate set of tools for foreign exchange is not a critical requirement for a prototyping environment, whether a package's functional tools for finance are enabled for foreign exchange (i.e., accept exchange rate data as inputs) is an important consideration. High-quality prototyping environments will have sets of tools specifically dedicated to foreign exchange analysis.

DEVELOPMENT AND RELATED ISSUES

Evaluating a prototyping environment in terms of how well it actually supports application development is, of course, important. Many packages claim to be friendly to both prototyping and application development but then fall short on the development side. To be a good application development environment there are several requirements including:

- The ability to generate stand-alone code.
- The ability to be called as an extension to another application.
- The ability to be distributed using common intranet/extranet technology.
- The ability to interact with live data sources and to interface with databases of standard type.
- The ability to generate GUIs which make other-than-command-line access to the environment possible.

Code Generation

The ability to generate stand-alone C/C++ code from tools, models, and applications built within the analysis and prototyping environment is a critical concern when evaluating prototyping environment. Many good packages include a compiler for generating C and C++ code, and many promise to soon be capable of generating Java code. These packages also make libraries containing compilable versions of core environment analytics.

CompilersThe term compiler refers not to the standard compilers available on the market for generating platform-dependent machine language code from C or C++ code, nor does it refer to the compilers which generate unibyte code from Java which is later interpreted by platform-dependent virtual machines. Instead, the term compiler refers to a tool for translating the procedural language of the analytic prototyping and application development environment into C or C++ code. These compilers also handle the issue of linking in compiled version core analytics which were used in the protoyped tools or models. Some compilers (see Exhibit 4-6) also allow for the creation of "semistand-alone" code which calls back to the application for needed core functions. Although code of this type requires that the prototyping environment be available on the local machine, it is still useful for enhancing the performance of the environment.

Math and Function Libraries When you prototype analytics or build applications in a particular technical computing environment, you use many of the core and functional analytics available as a part of the package. When it comes time to create stand-alone versions of your models, however, whether you can "include" compilable versions of these function becomes

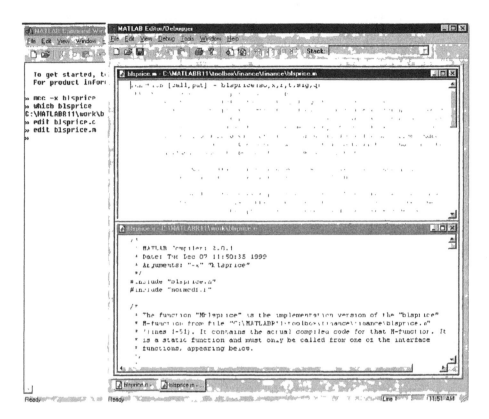

Exhibit 4-6. The MATLAB Compiler along with the C/C++ Math Library allows generation of a stand-alone C/C++ code version of MATLAB models.

an important concern. Many environments come with math libraries which can be linked into the stand-alone application when it is built. A few include other functional libraries as well, but in all cases, the user should evaluate the environment on overall library availability since this will significantly affect how friendly the environment will be to application development.

Portability

Here the term "portability" refers to whether the prototyping environment is accessible to other applications. If you choose to build an application within the environment (that is, using the environment's procedural language, core, and functional analytics, etc.) then how well the application can be made to communicate with other applications such as Microsoft Excel and other applications written in Microsoft Visual Basis, or C/C++ will be an important issue. Most applications will have one or more Application Programming Interfaces, or API's, for this purpose. An typical API will include a specification for the capabilities of data import and export as well as enabling calls to a basic environment's "engine" interface via Active X, Dynamic Data Exchange (DDE), or some other standard architecture.

Distribution

Distribution capabilities are an important consideration when developing applications for finance. Markets move quickly. Traders, analysts, and quantitative researchers' understanding of what the correct model for a particular instrument or market are often developed through an iterative process. This means that an application meant to embody those perceptions in a set of tools must also be able to be modified continually and redeployed at low cost. The emergence of intranet/extranet technology has made low-cost, rapid deployment technically feasible, and, as a result, web deployment capabilities are becoming an important quality attribute for any prototyping and application development environment. In addition, the need for rapid, low-cost deployment also has put increased emphasis on the availability of analytic libraries within an environment which can be redistributed at low or no cost.

Web Deployment The ability to develop analytical tools, models, and applications for finance in a particular prototyping environment and then deploy them over an intranet, or externally over the Internet, is becoming an important consideration in evaluating different prototyping environments. A common solution to the problem of "web distribution" consists of a server and a set of utilities for reading data contained in HTML forms and for dynamically containing HTML forms to hold output data. Functioning within a standard client-server framework, the server which resides on the server machine alongside the prototyping environment communicates with standard browsers using HTML forms. Data are sent to the server from the client machine in an HTML form. The server extracts the data and passes it to a copy of the prototyping environment for processing. Once processing is completed, the server retrieves the data package and sends it back to the client machine embedded in a standard HTML form. The benefit of distribution using this technology is that the prototyping environment need only be available on the server machine. Since many client machines can effectively use the same copy of the prototyping environment there is a significant costs savings, but this savings is limited by performance issues associated with web deployment.

Other Distribution Issues Another significant issue associated with the distribution of financial analytics, models and applications which were developed in a particular prototyping environment involves the issue of repackaging core and analytic tools. Many vendors requires that royalties be paid on any tools that are repackaged for sale to third parties. In addition, there are often restrictions on how much of a particular set of tools may be repackaged and in what fashion. Normally, vendors want to preclude you from repackaging their tools into anything that resembles a competing product. If deployment of stand-alone versions of models and applications is an important concern, then the repackaging issue should be explored up front.

Data Connectivity

Information is the lifeblood of financial markets. Since the most powerful set of analytical tools in the world is worthless without data to analyze, data connectivity is perhaps the most important characteristics to be considered in evaluating a prototyping environment. As a characteristic, data connectivity can be broken down into two areas: *data feed* connectivity and *database* connectivity.

Data Feed Connectivity The term *data feed* refers to streams of information which are made available to computing platforms over various types of public and proprietary networks. These streams of information normally contain information on security prices and other metrics, market parameters, and current events. Historically, the data feeds market has been dominated by big proprietary data networks such as Bloomberg, Bridge, and Reuters; however, with the advent of the Internet, many smaller companies have emerged which distribute information via standard intranet/extranet technology. A good prototyping environment should have the ability to import data from one or more of the major information providers who use proprietary networks, as well as import information from Internet-based information providers. These prototyping environments should also enable the packaging of these interface capabilities into applications for deployment to end-users, which means that any core functionality for interfacing with the data feeds should be made available in a compilable format.

Database Connectivity Database connectivity refers to the ability to interface with standard databases available on the market such as Oracle, Sybase, Microsoft SQL Server and Access, and Informix. Good prototyping environments will have the capability to interface with any ODBC/JDBC[10] compliant database on the market. These environments should at a minimum enable the ability to establish a connection to a database, extract data from that database, and write data to the database. Good environments will also enable database queries involving large data sets, which is an important consideration in finance. They should allow simultaneous connections to multiple databases. They should also provide some sort of graphical user interface for interacting with databases so that the user need not be fluent in Structured Query Language (SQL).

Spreadsheet Connectivity Spreadsheets are ubiquitous in finance. There are the standard data interface for many quantitative researchers, analysts, and traders. As a result, a good prototyping environment should support spreadsheet connectivity. Some products support spreadsheet connectivity via an overarching technology such as ActiveX or through a specific set of tools for linking to Microsoft Excel, Applix, or Lotus 123. Regardless off the technology involved, however, the prototyping environment should support use of a common spreadsheet as a data viewing tool (see Exhibit 4-7). A quality set of spreadsheet connectivity tools should also support use of spreadsheet package printing and report generation facilities. It should also support the calling of functions contained in the prototyping environment from within the spreadsheet itself and vice versa.

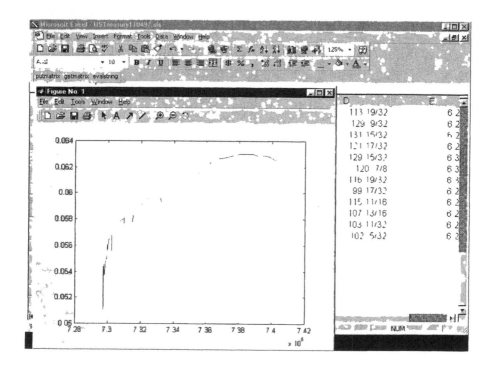

Exhibit 4-7. Excel link allows users to view MATLAB matrices in Microsoft Excel and to call MATLAB functions from within an Excel spreadsheet.

GUI Development

Developing effective Graphical User Interfaces (GUIs) is a critical activity in application development. GUIs allow users who lack the technical expertise to work in a prototyping environment from the command line the ability to still use any tools that have been built within that environment. All prototyping and application development environments should support the development of at least basic GUI components. Good environments should support the development of complex GUIs which can be built into stand-alone applications. This normally requires that a graphics library containing the environment's GUI components be available in conjunction with a compiler, math, and function libraries (see the section on Code Generation).

Report Generation

Applications are used in finance directly by traders as a part of their daily activities; however, these applications also function to support the activities of the many analysts and managers whose job it is to support and monitor the activities of these traders. As a result, report generation capabilities are an important characteristic of a prototyping and application development environment. If analysts are working in the prototyping environment directly, then it will be important to be able to generate reports which summarize their results. If analytics which were developed in the prototype environment are going to be packaged into an application which will be used by these analysts and managers, then it will also be important to be able to package the report generation capabilities of the prototyping environment into the application as well.

CONCLUSION

As we have seen, there are several characteristics to consider in comparing one analytic prototyping and application development environment to another. The core and functional analytics that are made available in the platform should be evaluated vis-a-vis the requirements of the tasks to be performed in the environment. Core optimization tools are only important if you are going to be doing research and prototyping analytics in a field were optimization problems arise, such as asset allocation. Derivative tools are only important if the goal is to build tools for valuing equity or interest rate options. Development and development support tools are an important consideration, but the sophistication required for these tools depends on the nature of the applications that will be developed within the environment. Sophisticated data connectivity is not important if the end-user application is only going to accept input typed from the keyboard. Distribution capabilities via the web are unimportant if the applications will only be deployed on the desktops of a few individuals. Evaluation of different environments should be done both to separate the quality packages from the inferior, but also to ensure that the correct package is being selected for the right area of application.

TRADEMARKS

1. Microsoft Inc. — Excel
2. The MathWorks Inc. — MATLAB, SIMULINK
3. Waterloo Maple Inc. — Maple V
4. MathSoft Inc. — S-Plus

Notes

1. This model was first introduced by Black, F. and Scholes, A., The pricing of options and corporate liabilities, *J. Pol. Econ.*, 81: 637–654, 1973.
2. Black's model was first introduced in Black, F., The pricing commodity contracts, *J. Financ. Econ.*, 3: 167–179, 1967.
3. See Vasicek, O. A., An equilibrium characterization of the term structure of interest rates, *J. Financ. Econ.*, 5: 177–188, 1977.
4. See Black, F., Derman, E., and Toy, W., A one-factor model of interest rates and its application to treasury bond options, *Financ. Anal. J.*, January–February, 1990, 33–39.
5. See Hull, J. and White, A., Pricing interest rate derivative securities, *Rev. Financ. Stud.*, 3(4): 573–592, 1990.
6. See Heath, D., Jarrow, R., and Morton, A., Bond pricing and the term structure of interest rates: a new methodology, *Econometrica*, 60(1): 77–105, 1992.
7. The Markowitz Portfolio Selection Model was introduced in two stages in the 1950s in the following article and book:
   • Markowitz, H. M., Portfolio selection, *J. Finance*, March, 1952.
   • Markowitz, H. M., *Portfolio Selection, Efficient Diversification of Investments*, John Wiley & Sons, New York, 1959.
8. The Capital Asset Pricing Model was introduced in a series of three separate articles: Sharpe, W., Capital asset prices: a theory of market equilibrium, *J. Financ*, September, 1964. Litner, J., The value of risk assets and the selection of risk investments in stock portfolios and capital budgets, *Rev. Econ. Stat.*, February, 1965. Mossin, J., Equilibrium in a capital asset market, *Econometrica*, October 1996.
9. On November 21, 1996, in response to recent ammendments to the Basle Capital Accord, a tripartite organization of the Board of Governors of the U.S. Federal Reserve, the Office of the Comptroller of the Currency, and the Federal Deposit Insurance Corporation (herein referred to as "the Agencies") issued an edict known as "The Final Rule on Market Risk." This Rule stipulates that as of January 1, 1998 financial institutions with more than 10% of their assets exposed to market risk (or trading activity in excess of $1 billion) will be required to hold an amount of capital in reserve equal to their exposure. The Final Rule stipulates that this capital charge will be determined via an assessment of value-at-risk (VAR) for the firm, using either an internal VAR model or the Standardized Approach prescribed by the Agencies. In response to the Basle Accord and to the action of the Agencies, the Securities and Exchange Commission (SEC) has also moved to issue its "Final Rules," effective January 1, 1997 require that all publicly held companies comply with their disclosure guidelines by June 15, 1997. The Final Rules require all registrant companies to disclose their exposure to market risk within the context of their financial statements.
10. The abbreviation ODBC refers to the Open Database Connectivity standard for databases. JDBC referes to the Java Database Connectivity Standard. Almost all major databases on the market are ODBC/JDBC compliant.

Author Bio

Charles Bassignani *is a senior vice president, Product Management for Evare, LLC in Burlington MA. He is also a frequent contributor to the development of tools for the MATLAB Financial Toolbox. He holds a Masters in Business Administration from Boston University's School of Management with a concentration in Finance.*

Chapter 5
Customer Profiling for Financial Services

Monte F. Hancock
Rhonda R. Delmater

DATA MINING OPPORTUNITIES IN FINANCIAL SERVICES ABOUND. As with any IT development project, executive sponsorship can be a key element in attaining the necessary resources for a successful project and the commensurate recognition, which in turn enhances opportunities to proceed with subsequent data mining activities.

ANALYSIS APPROACH

Based on conversations with financial institution executives, several areas may be identified for analysis. It is recommended that the highest priority subject area be selected as the initial focus of the data-mining project, in order to provide meaningful results from the activity. The target area could be customer acquisition profiling, customer retention, fraud detection, liability prediction, or virtually any area where sufficient historical data exist to support the analysis. If no specific goal is identified, then general data mining pertaining to a selected subject area may be conducted. The focus of this chapter is financial services customer profiling, whether for acquisition or retention purposes. Of course the target areas that are not selected initially for data mining could be the subject of studies conducted as follow-up activities.

CUSTOMER ACQUISITION PROFILING

A financial institution may select a specific loan product area and geographic region for target market penetration; for example, the commercial loan market consisting of tens of thousands of small businesses in greater Cincinnati. The size of this market is likely to preclude effective, comprehensive (one-on-one) marketing at reasonable cost.

If desirable potential customers most likely to move their business to "our" financial institution could be identified based upon available indicators, then marketing could be focused for best return-on-investment. Using advanced cognitive engineering techniques, a cognitive engine could be constructed that would

1. Use data provided by the financial institution.
2. Select from this data effective indicators of acquisition likelihood (and, possibly, customer desirability).
3. Identify those potential customers whose "acquisition profiles" indicate a higher likelihood of sale.
4. Produce a report that explains the acquisition indicators for each acquisition candidate, and gives a numeric indication of acquisition likelihood.

To support this kind of development, customer data and business history are needed for the financial institution's customers and potential customers, as well as background on the financial institution's previous marketing programs. Some of this data may be simulated or interpolated, if necessary.

CUSTOMER RETENTION PROFILING

Customer retention profiling is similar to customer acquisition profiling, as the objective is to identify predictive patterns. As with all businesses, financial institutions experience some customer turnover each year. Many departing customers do not give detailed explanations of the basis of their decision to leave. This makes it difficult to determine how to modify practices to increase retention.

If customers who are likely to move their business could be identified before a decision to leave has been made, the financial institution would have an opportunity to take action to retain their business. Similar to customer acquisition profiling, using advanced cognitive engineering techniques, a cognitive engine can be constructed which will determine effective indicators of retention likelihood and identify those customers whose "retention profile" indicates high "retention risk."

Again, to support this kind of development, customer data and business history, as well as their retention status, are required for financial institution customers.

FRAUD DETECTION

Another significant area of data mining interest throughout the spectrum of the international financial service community is fraud detection. The objective of these systems is to detect fraudulent business transactions, whether they be credit card, insurance, or domestic or international funds transfers.

Prior to automated systems of this nature, banking personnel manually reviewed thousands of transactions per day searching for fraudulent transactions. Although this labor-intensive, tedious process actually detected many fraudulent transactions, a significant number remained undetected, resulting not only in lost revenues but also in exposure for penalties such as fines, etc. Once the knowledge discovery phase of the data mining activity is completed, an unattended production system can be fielded which combines knowledge-based expert system capabilities and complex fuzzy algorithms to identify transactions of interest (concern). A confidence factor is calculated, and based on user-defined thresholds, a transaction may be allowed to be processed or rejected.

A system of this nature can significantly increase the probability of detecting fraud at the same time that it reduces the associated costs.

LIABILITY PREDICTION

Again, if an adequate base of historical information is available, a liability value can be predicted based on a new set of data. This type of analysis could be performed to predict the total liability for a population or, based on certain factors, for a specific claim. An example of each follows.

A 10-year history of hurricane claims for South Florida would provide information such as the total number of dwellings by type, the number of claims, settlement value, etc. Combining this information with the weather history and the hurricane forecast for the coming season, model(s) could be developed to predict the near-term liability.

Individual claim liability could likewise be predicted, for example, for workers compensation or other insurance claims based on feature value patterns in historical data. Information used to predict a settlement value may include age, gender, marital status, income, type of injury, attorney involvement, and so on.

GENERAL DATA MINING

Data mining is an emerging technical discipline which combines conventional decision-support methods (classical regression, statistics, modeling, procedural algorithms) with modern machine-inferencing technology (neural networks, scientific visualization, adaptive algorithms) to wade through masses of data to extract the residue of information. This marriage of "conventional wisdom" with the best of late-twentieth century computer science has produced a host of high-end tools to support experts operating in complex domains.

Intuition and utility can be preserved by the application of cognitive tools that can uncover the latent **information** embedded in the growing swell of **data.** Smart tools for making predictions from complex data are a must.

When data volume and complexity reach a certain critical level (which depends upon the domain), end users can no longer "get their arms around it." Software tools are now available to apply high-end cognitive engineering capabilities to probe effectively these complex data to pinpoint those few critical factors and their configurations, which yield market intelligence. For example, what is the predictive phenomenology of prospects who are "ready to buy?"

These cognitive tools find relationships already present, but obscure, in historical data.

THE TECHNICAL APPROACH

For effective analysis, the subject financial institution must have a substantial database of information on current and past customers. In essence, when properly organized and interpreted, these data constitute a collection of raw descriptions of historical financial institution customers, organizations that, at some time in the past, *made a buy decision* for the financial institution. These data could be collected from various operational systems or could already reside in a data mart or data warehouse.

Once the data source is identified and prepared for analysis, a collection of data mining tools can be applied to the problem of determining refined business profiles for prospects that are *ready to buy*. Once the *ready-to-buy* profiles have been generated, other cognitive engineering tools can be used to evaluate entries from a database of prospects for a marketing decision. Or the profiles may be used to manually generate a database of promising prospects. This process can be further enhanced by the inclusion of general demographic information about the regional market. Though not essential, such information can help with the refinement, interpretation, and exploitation of profiles.

Two important components of an automated decision support system's architecture are the methodology and data mining software to accomplish analyses as described below. A formal methodology and cognitive systems development tools are essential for successful implementation of a data mining application. The Cognitive Engineering Methodology (CEM) provides a structured road map for developing decision support systems.

CEM addresses both continuous and symbolic domains. Continuous domains are those in which the parameter values have continuous ranges and vary as a function of some criteria such as time or space. Examples of parameter values in the continuous domain include RF signals, temperature, voltage levels, and speed. Symbolic domains are those in which the parameter values are discrete and finite. Examples of parameter values in the symbolic domain include words, sentences, parameters, and icons. The CEM ensures the proper application of intelligent systems technology. It is a spiral process with five phases — representation, analysis, feature extraction and enhancement, prototyping, and evaluation.

- Representation establishes the form and syntax of the available information from which decisions are made.
- Analysis determines what intelligent systems paradigm(s) will be utilized when implementing the DSS. Rule-driven knowledge-based expert systems and neural networks are examples of paradigms that can be applied within specific decision support systems.
- Feature extraction and enhancement determines what measurements or other information should be used to make decisions. Measurements that serve as the basis for classification decisions are called "features." It is often the case that multiple measurements, which are known as feature vectors, are required to draw effective, consistent, and correct conclusions. Optimizing the selection of features to make decisions is of critical importance in the implementation of a DSS. In addition to the naturally occurring intuitive features that exist in a domain, nonintuitive features can be mathematically derived that simplify and speed the implementation and improve the accuracy of the DSS.
- Implementation of knowledge-based expert systems (KBES), which requires the definition of rules, demands extensive discussions with people who are intimately familiar with the problem and its solutions. Contentious issues, disagreements among experts, and addressing unexplored conditions and outcomes are hurdles that must be addressed to field an effective and reliable KBES. Use of a formal interviewing process for acquiring knowledge has successfully supported this methodology in numerous programs. This methodology takes into account aspects of the experts' organization and authority therein, in addition to employing standard knowledge engineering techniques, including stream-of-consciousness monologues, single-factor variations, and novel scenarios.
- Prototyping provides rapid feedback to the engineering staff so that changes can be made to the DSS design before any major investment is made. This mitigates risk substantially. After the first prototype is developed, the application can be reviewed and critiqued by the end user. Experience has found that spiral model-based rapid evolutionary development using "real" data is the most effective way to build decision support systems.
- Evaluation of the implemented cognitive system using blind and operational tests, as well as sensitivity, comparative, stability, and other analyses, is performed to ensure the DSS will function well under all conceivable operational situations.

The techniques that can be implemented as software routines for use in data mining can be grouped according to function. These include link analysis, classification, clustering, statistics, and prediction. These are described below, along with specific techniques that are useful in performing each function.

Link Analysis

This refers to a general collection of techniques that exploit "connections" within a data warehouse. These connections can be based upon time, cause-and-effect, or even random chance. Link analysis is also used to investigate business processes that can be represented graphically. Statistical, graph theoretic, and predictive methods are often used in link analysis. Some applicable terms follow.

Associations. These are collections of facts that occur together (e.g., buyers of product A are often homeowners). Associations are the simplest relationships in a data warehouse and are often used to suggest hypotheses for data mining: "Among the population of all prospects, are homeowners the most likely to buy?"

Sequential Patterns. These associations change in predictable ways across a population; these might involve a "time element" or might not (e.g., buyers of product A who own homes often buy product C). Sequential patterns that occur frequently constitute general "rules of thumb": "We should pitch product C to homeowners who buy product A."

Sequential Time Patterns. These are sequential patterns that have time as the central connection (e.g., "Buyers who file two complaints in a quarter have a 70 percent chance of dropping their account within the next year"). Sequential time patterns can be used to build predictive models: "Given the outstanding bids and current market, what is the likelihood that next quarter's sales will exceed $2 million?"

Classification

The function of recognizing and assigning an entity to the appropriate class based on feature attributes (i.e., data element values), dividing a set of prospects into high potential vs. others, or classifying financial transactions as potentially fraudulent is known as classification.

Neural Networks. Mathematical models of animal brains can be trained to solve difficult problems including classification.

Tree Classification. This method follows a hierarchical rule structure to determine a classification.

Simple Bayes. This is an inferencing method that uses Bayes theorem to estimate the likelihoods and probabilities of certain occurrences. This classical theory is very well developed and satisfies certain optimality conditions.

k-Nearest Neighbors. This classification method bases its decisions on how "similar" the current problem is to all of the previously solved cases: "It's most like the Smith case, so let's try what worked for Smith." The "k" refers to the number of distinct "cases" retained for matching.

Linear Discriminant Analysis (LDA). This is a classification method that creates the best decision method that is attainable by linear functions. LDA, sometimes called "linear regression," has the advantage of simplicity and ease of construction, but it is not as powerful as nonlinear decision methods.

Clustering

This involves forming subsets of the population based on cohesion .

k-Means Clustering. This method is used to recognize patterns in data based upon their population statistics. It can be used to build classifiers which are similar to k-Nearest Neighbor classifiers but match only against average "scenarios." It yields, therefore, a classification method that bases its decisions on how "similar" the current problem is to averages of previously solved cases: "It's most like the default scenario, so let's try what works for default." The "k" refers to the number of distinct "scenarios" created and/or retained for matching.

Neural Networks Clustering. Mathematical models of animal brains can be trained to solve difficult problems including clustering.

Visualization (N-dimensional graphics). Graphical plotting of feature values which enables a human analyst to see (visualize) natural groupings of the data based on future values.

Principal Component Analysis. Transforms applied to the data identify the most salient features and clusters.

Statistics — Parametric

General Statistics. Values are calculated to describe a set of data, e.g., population, sample, cluster, etc. Examples of commonly used general statistics include mean, median, mode, range, standard deviation, etc.

Linear Regression. This is a mathematical formalism for optimizing objective functions subject to linear constraints, which is used to create models for use in pattern recognition, prediction, etc.

Nonlinear Regression. This is a mathematical formalism for optimizing objective functions subject to nonlinear constraints; it is used to create models for pattern recognition, prediction, etc. It is inherently more powerful than linear regression.

Tests (T, F, Chi Square). These produce statistical values which are calculated for a set of data, often used to determine whether a sample is adequate (in size, etc.) to draw inferences for the population as a whole.

Principal Component Analysis. Transforms applied to the data identify the most salient features and clusters; this is used in parametric statistics to identify meaningful variations (statistical significance) from the norm.

Factor Analysis. This is a collection of mathematical methods (typically derived from linear algebra) for identifying and concentrating representational information in complex data sets. Sometimes called "principal component analysis" (PCA), it usually reduces the dimensionality of data and is often applied as a precursor to predictive modeling.

Statistics — Nonparametric

Knowledge-Based Training (KBT). This is the use of adaptive learning algorithms to build decision models which exploit descriptive statistics. An example is expert systems that have a learning capability.

Prediction

One of the most attractive facets of data mining is the development of insight into the business process which makes possible the development of predictive models. In competitive markets, niche selection, product release timing, and marketing focus all stand to benefit from the use of predictive models.

Predictive models can be based upon conventional methods (control charts, GANTT charts, spreadsheets, etc.), but these are largely manual. Emerging applications for high-end "cognitive engines" for predictive modeling are becoming available to commercial users. Some of these follow.

Neural Networks Prediction. This employs predictive models based upon one of the many "neural" paradigms — multilayer perceptrons, Hopfield networks, Boltzmann machines, etc.

Radial Basis Function Prediction. These predictive models are based upon one of the many RBF paradigms — partitions of unity, restricted coulomb energy (RCE) methods, adaptive taxonomic classifiers, etc.

Knowledge-Based Expert System (KBES) Prediction. KBES can be built to use heuristics obtained from human domain experts to codify expert knowledge for incorporation into predictive models. These models capture rare, perishable human expertise in executable form so that it can be

Exhibit 5-1. Cognitive Engineering Methodology

Methodology Phase	Financial Institution Project Task
Representation	Task 1: Analysis of requirements
	Task 2: Knowledge acquisition
Analysis	Task 3: Collect and organize facts and data
Feature extraction and enhancement	Task 4: Apply cognitive engineering tools to financial institution data
Prototyping	
Evaluation	Task 5: Evaluate population
	Task 6: Delivery

retained, copied, and enhanced by successive generations of human experts. This "brain power in a box" will work in any location (or *every* location), can run 24 hours a day, and never asks for a raise. If built with the ability to explain its decisions, such a system also can be used as a training tool.

Fuzzy Logic Prediction. Long popular in Japan and Europe, these systems "mathematize" soft decision-making processes. They work well when information is incomplete, partially incorrect, or imprecise.

Time Series Prediction. This is a collection of conventional and emerging techniques for predicting the next value of a time series based upon current conditions and prior history (e.g., predicting stock prices).

PROJECT APPROACH

The Cognitive Engineering Methodology described above is essentially a software industry standard "spiral" development methodology for building high-end systems. The amount of effort expended in each of the five phases depends upon the problem. The prototyping phase (the fourth phase) typically constitutes the bulk of the effort. Phases may be reordered, repeated, or eliminated, as required. Every data mining activity or problem is a little different.

This methodology facilitates a graceful, incremental development that combines substantial user input with high technology, while mitigating risk, as shown in Exhibit 5-1.

Task 1: Analysis of Requirements

Analytic staff members hold meetings and discussions with financial institution personnel to gather and define preliminary analysis requirements. The purpose of the discussions is to identify long-range program goals and immediate objectives for the current demonstration task. This includes identifying the initial profiling target area, whether targeting new

customers or enhancing customer retention. The analysis will include identification and availability of data resources, financial institution participation, and problem statement refinement.

Task 2: Knowledge Acquisition

Meetings are held with financial institution business development staff
to obtain general background information, including descriptions of marketing activities, customers, heuristics, methods, and resources. Knowledge acquisition methods are then applied, on an as-needed basis. These
include visualization exercises, standard scenarios, stream-of-consciousness monologues, etc. These exercises enhance the cognitive engineering
team's ability to quickly and reliably capture knowledge needed for the
data mining activities. Meetings also are to be held with the financial institution information technology staff to obtain detailed technical information, including database format, database access, hosting information,
policies and methods, and limitations. Implementation and design issues
will be resolved through these sessions. Timely access to the financial institution's data is of great importance, as these data serve as the basis for
all cognitive engineering work.

Task 3: Collect and Organize Facts and Data

An analysis database is then populated with the relevant data and cognitive engineering tools are applied. The analysis database serves as the
development and integration repository for all of the data mining work. It
is not essential to have a data warehouse or data mart to perform data mining, although it is imperative to have confidence that the information used
in the data mining activity is consistent and valid (cleansing, transformation), as would be expected of information of this type.

Meta data, commonly called "data about data," provide detailed definitions of data elements as they relate to specific entities. Understanding the
definition of features can aid the analysis in several ways. If data are combined from several sources, it is important that the elements be consistent
from each source in definition and in format. For assisted (interactive) data
mining, it is also important for the human analyst to understand the nature
of the data.

Task 4: Apply Cognitive Engineering Tools to Financial Institution Data

Enhancement and Data Preparation. The data are enhanced by the application of tools that find and emphasize information-bearing aspects. Data
enhancement tools allow users to determine which data items are "most
significant," to rank order data items by predictive power (salience), and to
apply transforms, which concentrate information into the smallest number

of features. This allows the development of optimized prediction engines, the creation of highly discriminating visualizations, and the suppression of irrelevant factors during data analysis. Data enhancement was applied to all of the analysis tasks in this report with great benefit.

The data are prepared for cognitive engineering through the following processes:

- Registration — proper formatting, placement of data items
- Normalization — making disparate data commensurable by suppressing irrelevant components of data items
- Feature extraction — effective representation of information within records
- Statistical analysis — analysis of data distribution in feature space
- Correlation — exploitation of similarities and differences within data
- Clustering — discrimination between disparate data items and aggregation of similar data items
- Profile generation and refinement — synthesis of information content, distribution, similarities, and differences to generate a consistent mathematical description of the commercial loan prospect population

Build Customer/Prospect Classifier. Once the data have been prepared and enhanced, classification engines are applied to create a prospect profiler. The profiler is a software routine that accepts as input a prospect record and produces as output a measure of "marketability" (likelihood of buying) for that prospect. Once the profiler has been built, it can be rapidly applied to any number of prospects.

Task 5: Evaluate Population

The profiler is applied to the prospects in a test database. Each prospect is given a numeric rating for "marketability." These ratings are compiled into a marketability roster, which will be included in the final report.

Task 6: Delivery

Final Report. A final report is prepared to describe the tools and methods applied; it will include the results of the "marketability" experiment.

Presentation. Typically, it is important to present the results of the data mining analyses to financial institution executives in order to promote the value of the activity and ensure follow-through with the application of the knowledge gleaned from the effort into a production system.

Demonstration. The presentation may include a live computer-based demonstration of the software for processing and profiling prospects.

Schedule Estimates. A project of this type typically ranges from 3 to 10 months, with check points to determine whether and how to proceed based on the "results to date."

SUMMARY

Like many businesses in the 1990s, commercial banking is becoming more competitive. Businesses grow in such an aggressive economy in two primary ways: (1) they increase existing market share, and (2) they create or penetrate new markets. Both methods are effective if good "business intelligence" is available, market information about *who is ready to buy.*

A financial institution may have limited market share in a particular loan type and geographic area and want to increase their market penetration. The market itself is likely to be large and diverse, which is both good and bad.

The opportunity is obvious. Large, diverse markets offer tremendous potential for out-year growth with many avenues for market penetration and the development of a broad, stable customer base.

The challenges are equally clear. Large diverse markets are inherently difficult to reach. Market diversity ensures that focused niche marketing techniques (journal ads, association contacts, etc.) will not have good coverage, while market size makes comprehensive marketing techniques costly and time consuming. The result is poor return-on-investment.

THE SOLUTION

A solution to this problem is to apply advanced cognitive engineering tools to help the financial institution generate "business intelligence" from its existing data. In this way, the institution can focus marketing (for reduction of expense) across all customer types (for good coverage). In other words, tools can be developed and applied that identify those customers whose backgrounds and situations indicate that they are most likely to respond favorably to a marketing contact.

Authors' Bios

Monte F. Hancock is a Chief Scientist at Computer Science Innovations (CSI) and Adjunct Professor, Computer Science and Mathematics Depts., Rollins College. He directs CSI's internal R&D with emphasis on knowledge discovery and data mining and on the application of knowledge-based expert systems and neural networks to pattern recognition. His expertise includes data visualization with n-dimensional graphics, intelligent control including simulation and classification, communications security, wavelet transforms, process optimization, and control and monitoring applications. Hancock has invented several proprietary numerical algorithms for artificial intelligence and communications security applications. These technologies have been applied in a wide range of business intelligence and scientific applications. With over 20 years of experience as a mathematician and computer scientist, Hancock's primary area of expertise is in the application of mathematics to computer engineering. His educational background includes

2 years of postgraduate work in Pure Mathematics beyond his M.S. in Mathematics from Syracuse University. His B.A. Mathematics is from Rice University.

*As Program Manager at Computer Science Innovations in Melbourne, FL, **Rhonda R. Delmater** has led several significant system development efforts for a major vendor of healthcare information content products. These include development of a classification system for hospital charge information, a data visualization workstation, and several product development efforts. Prior to joining CSI, she spent 14 years with Harris Corporation. As Senior Manager in Healthcare Systems, she was responsible for identifying and developing opportunities to apply information technology in the healthcare industry. She served as Program Manager for several projects including a Filmless Radiology Study for Health First in Melbourne, FL and a teleradiology link between a Melbourne Radiology Center and the Department of Radiology at the UCLA Medical Center. She also developed the Electronic Messaging Plan for St. John Medical Center in Tulsa, OK that encompassed both tactical and strategic solutions. She was previously the Application Development Manager for Harris Space Systems Corporation on a $1 billion pursuit at the NASA Marshall Space Flight Center in Huntsville, AL.*

Chapter 6
Business Rule Systems

Henry Seiler

THIS CHAPTER IS INTENDED FOR THE BENEFIT of financial and business analysts who may be called upon to participate in the specification and design of new business software systems or the redesign of legacy software systems. The intent is to familiarize business analysts with the new emerging software development methodologies of business rules and knowledge management, with the goal of helping them become better stewards of the business systems knowledge inherent in today's software applications.

Business rules represent the codified policies and decision-making practices of an organization. Historically, business rules have been coded directly in the program logic of an application. Today, the terms business rules and knowledge management are used to describe the isolation of business policies and decisions from application logic.

Production rule systems provide a better alternative for implementing business rules than embedding them in application logic or implementing them as database triggers. Production rule systems will allow you to achieve the benefits of business rules while avoiding the problems inherent in entwining application logic with business logic.

The processes of business rule development, knowledge management, and application development are intimately linked. They are focused on solving the problems of how to represent business knowledge and how to manage the use of this knowledge as a part of business applications. The goals of knowledge management are first, to isolate the business rules of an application into identifiable and separate components of the system rather then allowing the knowledge contained in an application to be dispersed throughout the programming of the application. And second, to represent knowledge in a fashion that is appropriate for the modeling of business decision knowledge, as opposed to program control.

0-8493-9834-7/00/$0 00+$.50
© 2000 by CRC Press LLC

Production rule systems address these goals of isolation and knowledge representation with the use of component-oriented architectures and production rule systems technologies, respectively.

PRODUCTION RULE SYSTEMS

Production rule systems differ in basic computational style from traditional procedural systems such as C++ or Basic; the main difference being the production system's use of unordered data-sensitive rules as the fundamental unit of computation. This is in stark contrast to the sequenced instructions used by traditional procedural systems. Production rule systems are most appropriate when the knowledge to be represented naturally occurs in rule form, where the relationships between rules are extremely complex, and where frequent changes in the business knowledge are anticipated. The key to production rule systems' success in modeling and processing business knowledge is in their ability to represent knowledge explicitly in chunks (i.e., rules) that are just the right size for capturing the small units or steps business analysts naturally use when solving complex problems.

Architecture of Production Rule Systems

The architecture of production rule systems is comprised of five primary components:

- Data. The facts and values of the knowledge problem.
- Rules. The If Condition-Then Action representation of the knowledge.
- Inference Engine. The underlying executor that matches data and rules.
- Knowledge Representation Language. The representation grammar for data and rules.
- Knowledge Component Objects. The packaging of rules and data into a component-reusable entity for use by an application. A package of data, rules, and inference engine is called a RuleSet.

Production System Data

The data of a knowledge problem can be considered the inputs and outputs for the set of rules used in solving the problem. Production rule systems model problem domain data as objects, which represent the things and events of the problem. The set of all data objects and their current values is collectively referred to as the context. Data values come into being in the following ways:

1. The data is statically declared in the RuleSet and initialized upon program activation of the RuleSet.
   - The data is provided to the RuleSet by the activating application.
   - The data is changed or created by the rules of the RuleSet.

- The RuleSet requests the data in an ad hoc fashion from either the controlling application or an interactive user.
2. A less obvious but most critical role that data plays in production rule systems is that it is the only means for rules to communicate with one another. The state of context data is the primary means of control of the production system. Control passes from one rule to another not by explicit linear step-wise execution or subroutine call, but by changes in the data values of the context.

Production System Rules

Rules in a production system consist of a collection of If Condition-Then Action statements. Each rule has a left-hand side, or IF part, and a right-hand side, or THEN part. The IF part of a rule comprises the conditions or antecedents of the rule. The THEN part is the action part of a rule and is often called the rule's consequent or conclusion.

The IF part of a rule is comprised of one or more clauses, or expressions, combined with the Boolean operators AND, OR, and NOT. An expression or antecedent usually is a restriction, or relational expression, on some value or attribute of some object of the context data. The object may, for example, be an object of the problem domain such as a customer or inventory item, or internal variable used for directing problem solution strategy, such as a goal.

Rules in a production system are thought of as having direction. Direction being implied by whether the IF part or the THEN part is the means by which the rule becomes active. Rules that are activated by the IF part are said to be data driven or forward chaining rules and rules that are activated by the THEN part are said to be goal driven or backward chaining rules.

Production System Inference Engine

The inference engine of production systems acts as the "unseen hand" or executor which causes processing to take place. Processing here is defined as the combining of supplied data with rules to create inferred data. It is the inferred data that is the desired end result of the production system processing.

In a RuleSet control is based on cyclical re-evaluation of the state of the context, not on any explicit ordering of instructions. There is no explicit transfer of execution control between rules as there is in traditional program statements. Rules communicate with each other only by way of the data values of the context. This complete separation of execution flow, provided by the executor from problem knowledge represented as rules, is the key to the representational and processing power of production systems. The author of a RuleSet need only be concerned with the representation of knowledge explicitly as rules, constructing the small units or steps one would naturally use when solving complex problems. The process of choosing, ordering, and connecting the steps for problem solution is carried out by the executor or inference engine.

The inference engine provides two primary problem-solving engines relevant to production systems: the forward chaining engine and the backward chaining engine. Production systems may possess additional secondary computational engines for method and command processing.

The simplest distinction that can be made between the forward and backward chaining inference engines is one of direction. The problem-solving process of a production system can be thought of as a search to find a path from an initial situation to a solution. The starting point for the search may be either the initial state or the final solution; the choice of search strategy is dependent on the nature of the problem at hand and the programmatic ease with which initial state data can be provided or final solutions can be proposed.

- Forward chaining inference processing starts from an initial data state and produces final goals or conclusions.
- Backward chaining inference processing starts from a proposed or desired goal or conclusion and proceeds to seek data in support of that goal.

These distinctions between forward and backward chaining are not mutually exclusive. It is possible, and often desirable, to use both modes of processing in a problem solution.

FORWARD CHAINING SYSTEMS

Forward chaining systems process from initial information that is provided to a final state or goal as shown in Exhibit 6-1. Sarting from an initial or current set of data, the forward chaining inference engine makes a chain

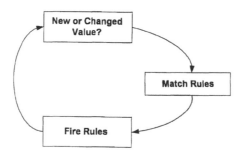

Exhibit 6-1. Forward chaining inference processing.

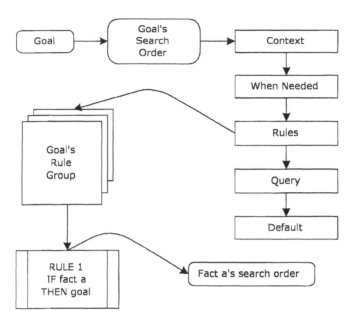

Exhibit 6-2.   Backward chaining inference processing.

of inferences until a goal is reached. In forward chaining the data values of the context are matched against the IF parts, or left-hand sides, of rules. If a rule's IF side matches the context then the inference engine executes the THEN part, or right-hand side of the rule. If the execution of the THEN part of a rule changes the data values of the context, then the inference engine repeats the entire match-execute cycle again using the new state of the context data values as a new initial set of data.

Forward chaining systems are most appropriate when the initial data are well defined by a single set of characteristics and many possible concluding goal states exists.

BACKWARD CHAINING SYSTEMS

Backward chaining systems process from a required final goal and obtain context data as needed to support that goal, as shown in Exhibit 6-2. Starting from the overall goal the inference engine breaks down the goal, into simpler subgoals. The process of subgoal decomposition continues, producing additional subgoals or context data facts for which a value can be immediately obtained. The backward chaining inference engine uses rules to facilitate the process of goal to subgoal decomposition. The THEN parts or right-hand sides of the rules are matched against currently active goals. If a rule's THEN part matches an active goal, the IF part, or left-hand side, of the rule then provides a new set of active subgoals. This process of THEN part to IF part backward chaining decomposition continues recursively until no rules can be found whose THEN part matches any of the currently active subgoals. At that point the backward chaining inference engine matches the set of currently active goals with the data values of the context. If there is a match, then the rule that provided the subgoals executes and the inference engine then uses the context data values provided by executing the rule to the next set of subgoals. This process continues until the inference engine asserts, denies, or is unable to determine the original goal.

Backward chaining systems are most appropriate for problems such as diagnostics, or categorization. These problem types share the characteristic of a single goal which can be consistently stated, in conjunction with an undetermined and/or large amount of initial information that would pose a severe burden to provide all at once, as an initial data state.

The backward chaining inference engine solves the problem of a difficult to provide complete initial data state by actively requesting context data values only when and if they are needed. In contrast the forward chaining inference engine only processes on the data values provided and never requests additional information.

PRODUCTION SYSTEM KNOWLEDGE REPRESENTATION LANGUAGE

The rule language of production systems is generally a high-level grammar for business problem representation and abstraction designed specifically for the specification and processing of business rules. A RuleSet may contain class declarations and methods, forward chaining rules, backward chaining demons, and an agenda. Thus, the major components of a production system language are

- Objects in a knowledge base are created via class declarations.
- Class declarations define the structure of the objects contained in a knowledge base. As instances, classes hold and retain the application's data values. An object's structure is defined by its class and attribute declarations.
- Rules and Demons describe the operational logic, rules-of-thumb, and cause-and-effect relationships needed to make decisions, and trigger certain events or actions during processing.
- An agenda schedules the main events and the sequences of events or procedures in pursuit of goals.

PRODUCTION SYSTEM KNOWLEDGE COMPONENT OBJECTS

For a problem-solving RuleSet to contribute effectively to a business application it must be packaged and made available to the tools being used for

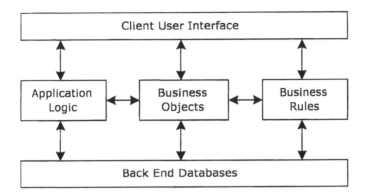

Exhibit 6-3. Business rules as part of the component development process.

creating business applications. A production system's RuleSet packages problem-solving rules by means of the industry standard Component Object Model (COM).

KNOWLEDGE MANAGEMENT

The packaging of a set of problem-solving rules into a RuleSet allows for the management and reuse of knowledge within and among software development projects. The effect of this packaging is to isolate the business rules of an application into identifiable and separate components of the system, rather than allowing the knowledge contained in an application to be dispersed throughout the programming of the application. Thus, the process of knowledge management is a cooperation of both the enabling technologies of knowledge component packages, and the design and development methodologies of business rule isolation as shown in Exhibit 6-3.

Component-oriented production systems provide, for the first time, the necessary enabling technologies for knowledge management methodologies to become an integrated part of modern business application design and development. Component-oriented production systems address each of the primary criteria of successful knowledge management.

Isolation — Production systems enforce complete isolation of business rule logic and processing from application logic processing. This allows development teams to partition design and implementation into distinct efforts for application logic vs. business logic.

Integration — Business rules are encapsulated in business objects called RuleSets. As COM Automation Servers, RuleSets achieve the highest possible degree of industry standard application and language interoperability.

Reuse — Because business policies and practices often apply to all of an organization's applications, isolated business rules can be reused. RuleSets can be reused without modification in multiple production applications.

Rapid Response to Business Change and Simplified Maintenance — Developers no longer have to review an application's lines of code to identify business rules and then change and test them. Isolated business rules can be changed very rapidly. And because they're not embedded, testing them doesn't mean retesting the entire application.

Increased Developer Productivity — Production systems are designed specifically for the specification and processing of business rules. Their use can save developers significant time and effort compared with using 3GLs and 4GLs that do not include the specialized constructs and the functionality for business rules.

APPROPRIATE USES OF PRODUCTION SYSTEMS

It is true that business rule logic can be implemented with equal process outcome in either conventional programming languages or production rule systems. The stark differences between these two means of representing and processing business logic requires the use of some discerning criteria when considering the appropriateness of one method over another. This section will discuss the types of business application problems that are best solved with production rule systems, and the further reaching benefits production rule systems bring to the life cycle of such business applications.

Background

Historically, the application of production rule systems to a problem solution was considered a high-risk, high-return endeavor. The causes of the high-risk perceptions of production rule system undertakings was not due to any intrinsic shortcoming of production rule problem representation, but rather was due to limitations imposed by the development methodologies and technologies available at the time. The key limitation was the lack of methodologies and technologies that easily enabled software interoperability.

Without any standardized methods or tools to develop applications that could share or access the capabilities of other existing applications, each program had to implement all of its required applications elements. The primary components of these application elements were user interface, database access, and client-server capabilities.

The early commercial vendors of production rule or expert system products had not only to implement their particular rule authoring, representation, and processing components, but also all the other components required to enable developers to create complete applications. The resulting products were not just production rule systems but also complete development environments for user interface, database access, and client-server applications.

The end result of expert system vendors having created complete application development environments is that prospective users of expert systems would have to choose to accept the limitations of the application development tools that housed the production rule system. The risks in using these systems were high. At a time when corporate IS was just beginning to accept the use of RAD tools from the major software vendors, choosing to use a less capable RAD tool from a not so major vendor, for the sole purpose of gaining access to the production rule system that it housed, was risky indeed. The resulting reluctance to use these tools for anything but the most complex of problems was understandable.

This legacy has left us with several misperceptions about the applicability of production rule systems in today's business applications:

- Rule system projects have a low success rate.
- Commercially available rule system tools are closed environments.
- Rule systems should only be used for extremely complex, "unsolvable" problems.

Today, packaging of rules into industry standard component reusable objects not only dispels these myths but allows us to make the following assertions regarding the appropriateness of production rule systems in today's business applications:

- Projects using component reusable production rule systems can have a higher success rate compared to projects that fail to isolate business rules.
- Component reusable rule systems are completely open and are usable by all modern RAD tools.
- Rule systems should be used for all business logic processing, regardless of the perceived simplicity or complexity of the problem.

SUITABLE PROBLEM CATEGORIES

Problems that are generally appropriate for production rule systems can be grouped into two major categories: analysis problems and synthesis problems. Naturally, the real world is never quite so black and white. It is often the case that problems contain elements of both. Nevertheless, considering them separately gives us considerable explanatory leverage.

Analysis Problems

Production rules systems are especially adept at the representation of all varieties of analysis problems. Analysis can be considered a broad umbrella term for problems categories such as diagnostics, classification, fault determination, and situation assessment. Such problems are generally solved by backward chaining systems, although forward chaining rules may be used as well. Authoring rules for analysis problems is relatively easy, since there usually is a clearly identifiable goal, e.g., a diagnosis, which yields readily to subgoal decomposition via backward chaining rules.

It is the properties of diagnostics and classification problems that make them so easily solved by production rule systems. The process of classification begins by identifying all the possible problem solutions. These become the goals of the production system. Each possible goal of the classification then becomes a relatively independent subproblem. For each subproblem, one must identify all supporting evidence necessary to assert the goal of the subproblem. The supporting evidence and associated goal are naturally modeled by the IF part and THEN part of production system rules.

Analysis systems are extremely easy to enhance and maintain. Additions or modifications to analysis systems can be localized to the set of rules associated with the subgoal of interest.

Synthesis Problems

Problem categories such as design and scheduling are considered to be synthesis problems. These problems are among the most specialized and obstinate problems known to computer science. Synthesis problems are almost exclusively solved with forward chaining production systems.

Forward chaining production systems have the ability to cyclically transform an initial context state into a series of synthesized solution steps as shown in Exhibit 6-4. The production systems for synthesis problems consist of one or more groups of rules, each of which is responsible for a given transformation of the context data to a new valid state. The new state of the context data then becomes the attention of some other set of rules which "knows" how to transform the context data into yet another valid state. Each intermediate transformed state and the temporal order in which it was generated, represents the synthesized steps for the problem solution.

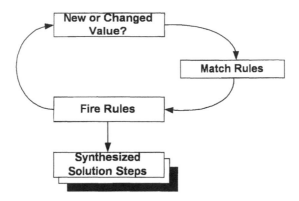

Exhibit 6-4. Forward Chaining as used in synthesis problems.

Unsuitable Problems

There are many parts of a typical business application where production rule systems should not be used. These include the application components iterated above: user interface, database access, and client-server communication. Additionally, it is undesirable to use production rule systems in the routine management of general application control. That is not to say that production rule components should not be called upon by these application components to assist in, or add intelligence to these application processes.

Another obvious category of problems unsuitable for solution by production rule systems would be mathematical or algorithmic processes that have existing and well-codified solutions. These are best solved using traditional procedural languages.

GENERAL PROBLEM CHARACTERISTICS

Whether a problem can be categorized as analysis or synthesis, it's appropriateness for solution by production rule systems should be subject to the general criteria of knowledge representation. If the problem lends itself to a representation by knowledge chunks, that is, a set of loosely coupled problem solution steps, then that logic within the overall system is best implemented by production rule systems.

A Small Example

A common business transaction is customer credit authorization. Such an application would contain the typical software elements of the presentation layer, database access layer, and physical database layer. Traditional implementations of this common business application would also contain the company's "rules" of credit authorization loosely distributed across these three layers.

Explicitly applying knowledge management discipline to the design and development methodology for our hypothetical credit authorization business application would result in the isolation of all credit decision logic in a single RuleSet.

```
!=======================================================
RULE 1 authorize against outstanding balance
IF new outstanding balance <= CreditLine OF Customer
THEN authorize outstanding balance

RULE 2 authorize against outstanding balance
IF new outstanding balance <= CreditLine OF Customer * 1.15
AND Preferred Status OF Customer IS Good
THEN authorize outstanding balance

RULE 3 authorize against outstanding balance
IF new outstanding balance > CreditLine OF Customer * 1.15
AND new outstanding balance < CreditLine OF Customer * 1.25
AND Preferred Status OF Customer IS Outstanding
THEN authorize outstanding balance
ELSE Reason OF CreditAction IS Credit Limit Exceeded
!=======================================================
RULE 1 overdue payment
IF Months Overdue OF Customer = 0
THEN authorize overdue payment

RULE 2 overdue payment
IF Months Overdue OF Customer = 1
AND new outstanding balance < profile.crline * 0.1
THEN authorize overdue payment

RULE 3 overdue payment
IF Months Overdue OF Customer >= 1
AND Months Overdue OF Customer <= 4
AND CreditLine OF Customer >= 10000
AND new outstanding balance < Bank Balance OF Customer
THEN authorize overdue payment

RULE 4 overdue payment
IF Months Overdue OF Customer > 1
AND new outstanding balance < Bank Balance OF Customer
AND Management authorization of overdue IS yes
THEN authorize overdue payment
ELSE Reason OF CreditAction IS Overdue Balance
!=======================================================
```

```
RULE 1 for authorize amount
IF PurchaseAMt OF Customer <= Order Limit OF Customer
THEN authorize amount

RULE 2 for authorize amount
IF PurchaseAMt OF Customer > Order Limit OF Customer
AND Management authorization of large amount IS yes
THEN authorize amount
ELSE Reason OF CreditAction IS Amount Too Large
!===================================================
! CreditAction Authorization  —  Main Rule
!===================================================

RULE 1 for credit authorization
IF authorize amount
AND authorize outstanding balance
AND authorize overdue payment
THEN CreditAction IS Authorized
ELSE NOT CreditAction IS Authorized
```

The backward chaining set of rules shown in Exhibit 6-5 represents the credit policies of our hypothetical company. A business application would use this RuleSet to authorize a customer's credit for a purchase transaction. The goal of this RuleSet is "CreditAction IS Authorized." Using backward chaining the inference engine would find the rule that can conclude the goal. This would cause the rule "RULE 1 for credit authorization" to be evaluated. Each of the terms of the IF part of "RULE 1 for credit authorization" would become subgoals for determining "CreditAction IS Authorized."

It is an easy exercise to follow the back chaining process through each of the subgoals: "authorize amount," authorize outstanding balance," and "authorize overdue payment."

In integrating the credit authorization RuleSet into a business application the traditional software component elements of presentation layer, database access layer, and physical database layer would be expanded to include a business layer. The business layer would gather the necessary information required, evoke the credit authorization RuleSet, and then act on the RuleSet's conclusions.

This example, though simple, exemplifies the development methodologies of business rules and knowledge management. Consolidating all the rules governing the customer credit authorization into a single component simplifies the specification as well as the ongoing revision of critical business policies.

Exhibit 6-5. Credit Authorization RuleSet

RULE 1 authorize against outstanding balance
    IF   New outstanding balance <= CreditLine OF Customer
    THEN   Authorize outstanding balance
RULE 2 authorize against outstanding balance
    IF   New outstanding balance <= CreditLine OF Customer * 1.15
    AND   Preferred Status OF Customer IS Good
    THEN   Authorize outstanding balance
RULE 3 authorize against outstanding balance
    IF   New outstanding balance > CreditLine OF Customer * 1.15
    AND   New outstanding balance < CreditLine OF Customer * 1.25
    AND   Preferred Status OF Customer IS Outstanding
    THEN   Authorize outstanding balance
    ELSE   Reason OF CreditAction IS Credit Limit Exceeded
RULE 1 overdue payment
    IF   Months Overdue OF Customer = 0
    THEN   Authorize overdue payment
RULE 2 overdue payment
    IF   Months Overdue OF Customer = 1
    AND   New outstanding balance < profile.crline * 0.1
    THEN   Authorize overdue payment
RULE 3 overdue payment
    IF   Months Overdue OF Customer >= 1
    AND   Months Overdue OF Customer <= 4
    AND   CreditLine OF Customer >= 10000
    AND   New outstanding balance < Bank Balance OF Customer
    THEN   Authorize overdue payment
RULE 4 overdue payment
    IF   Months Overdue OF Customer > 1
    AND   New outstanding balance < Bank Balance Of Customer
    AND   Management authorization of overdue IS yes
    THEN   Authorize overdue payment
    ELSE   Reason Of CreditAction IS Overdue Balance
RULE 1 for authorize amount
    IF   PurchaseAMt OF Customer <= Order Limit OF Customer
    THEN   Authorize amount
RULE 2 for authorize amount
    IF   PurchaseAMt OF Customer > Order Limit OF Customer
    AND   Management authorization of large amount IS yes
    THEN   Authorize amount
    ELSE   Reason OF CreditAction IS Amount Too Large
CreditAction Authorization – Main Rule
RULE 1 for credit authorization
    IF   Authorize amount
    AND   Authorize outstanding balance
    AND   Authorize overdue payment
    THEN   CreditAction IS Authorized
    ELSE NOT CreditAction IS Authorized

CONCLUSION

Business software systems often contain hidden knowledge about how companies do their business. Today's need for rapid adaptation and change dictates that this hidden knowledge becomes isolated, exposed, and manageable. Businesses can no longer afford to allow the rules governing their business practices to be poorly codified and hard to change. The adaptation of production rule systems, business rules, and knowledge management as a standard part of the business software life cycle will dramatically improve the ability of companies to specify, maintain, and adapt the business knowledge within their software systems. This will in turn allow companies to rapidly adapt to changing market pressures and business opportunities.

Author Bio

Henry Seiler is the founder and president of Rule Machines Corporation. He has been engaged in the design and development of expert systems and business rule systems for more than 15 years.

Chapter 7
Customer Data Quality: The Foundation for a One-to-One Customer Relationship

Art Petty

IN TODAY'S COMPETITIVE FINANCIAL MARKET, every day brings new challenges for customer acquisition and retention. To stay ahead, financial services companies are turning to decision support solutions to help identify and manage their customer relationships. Solutions such as data warehouses or data marts provide a solid foundation of accurate information upon which they can base their decisions.

Accuracy is one of the biggest obstacles blocking the success of many data warehousing projects. In fact, data quality is the No. 1 challenge facing financial institutions as they implement their data warehouses. It is not unusual to discover that as many as half the records in a database contain some type of information that needs to be corrected.

One of the most crucial areas of data quality is customer information. For the most accurate information to support your financial services business, you will need to incorporate data quality into each critical step — extraction, transformation, consolidation, and maintenance. Data quality is especially important to accurate consolidation because it allows you to recognize and understand customer relationships. As a result, you can gain

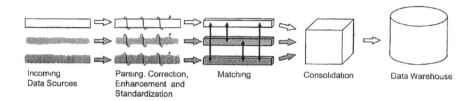

Incoming Data Sources — Parsing. Correction, Enhancement and Standardization — Matching — Consolidation — Data Warehouse

Exhibit 7-1. Data quality is achieved in three stages — cleansing, matching, and consolidation. In the data cleansing stage, the data are parsed, corrected, standardized, and enhanced for accurate matching. In the matching stage, comparisons are made within and across data sources to locate similar information. Finally, the matching data elements are consolidated and placed into a data warehouse, data mart, or other data staging area.

a clear picture of your customers, analyze their buying patterns, and predict future sales.

WHICH DATA ARE MOST IMPORTANT TO YOUR COMPANY?

Before you evaluate data quality solutions, you need to determine the type of data that are most important to your company. Will you focus primarily on customer information or are you most concerned with data such as price trends, dates, and probability scores? Once you make this decision, you can choose the data quality products most appropriate for your applications.

In either case, you will find that most data quality and consolidation products fall into one of two categories: data-referenced solutions, which combine reference tables with sophisticated algorithms, and nondata-referenced solutions, which rely on algorithms alone. In data warehouses where customer data are essential, data-referenced software is more effective. This type of software features an extensive knowledge base of empirical data, which allows you to enhance and improve the quality of your information.

Building data quality into a data warehouse involves six key elements: parsing, correction, standardization, enhancement, matching, and consolidation. This chapter will help you discover the principles and inherent problems of data quality and data consolidation, and the available solutions to help you manage them (Exhibit 7-1).

PARSING

Do You Know What Your Data Elements Are?

Parsing is the first critical component in data cleansing (Exhibit 7-2). This process locates, identifies, and isolates individual data elements in

Input Data		Parsed Data	
BETH CHRISTINE PARKER. PURCH MGR		First Name:	BETH
REGIONAL PORT AUTHORITY		Middle Name.	CHRISTINE
FEDERAL BUILDING		Last Name:	PARKER
12800 LAKE CALUMET		Title:	PURCH MGR
HEGEWISCH IL		Firm·	REGIONAL PORT AUTHORITY
		Firm Location:	FEDERAL BUILDING
		Range:	12800
		Street:	LAKE CALUMET
		City·	HEGEWISCH
		State	IL

Exhibit 7-2. Parsing is a vital step for the cleansing and matching stages. This example shows how parsing identifies and isolates the individual elements of an input record.

your customer files. These components may include such data as a customer's first name, last name, title, company name, street address, city, state, or zip code. Parsing makes it easier to correct, standardize, enhance, and match data because it allows you to compare individual components rather than long strings of data.

Parsing the Elements

There are several obstacles to parsing that may later hinder successful matching. Perhaps the most pervasive problem is discrepancies in the metadata — information about the data in your database. For example, the information in a field may not match its metadata profile. Inconsistent definitions and multiple data sources make it difficult to determine if fields possess the same characteristics from one source to the next. Other obstacles include (Exhibit 7-3):

- *"Misfielded" data* — data that are placed in the wrong field, such as name data in an address field
- *Floating data* — customer data that may be contained in different fields from record to record, resulting in data "floating" between fields

Field Format	Field data
First-middle-last-title	- - - - ▸ Juanita Alvarez, Trustee
Last-title-comma-first-middle	- - - - ▸ Alvarez Trustee. Juanita E.
Last-comma-first-middle-title	- - - - ▸ Alvarez, Juanita E. Trustee

Exhibit 7-3. Inconsistent field formats, such as the ones indicated above, present an obstacle for unparsed data, making it difficult to combine all data sources into one data warehouse.

- *Extraneous information* — data that may contain irrelevant or blank fields
- *Atypical words* — records that may include multicultural and hyphenated names, unusual titles, abbreviated business names, industry-specific acronyms, etc.
- *Inconsistent structures and formats* — operational, purchased, and exchanged data sources that may be formatted differently from each other or from the data warehouse

CORRECTION

How Do You Know Your Data Are Accurate?

Once you have parsed your data, you are ready to begin the next phase of the data cleansing process — correction. Customer information is the most difficult type of data to cleanse and validate. If your data comes from a variety of sources, you may encounter:

- Variations in abbreviations, formats, etc., because of individual preferences of the person entering the information
- Misspellings caused by phonetic similarities during telephone data entry
- Outdated information due to name and address changes
- Transpositions resulting from keying errors

Correcting the Elements

The most effective way to correct and verify your data intelligently is to use software that references a reliable secondary data source (Exhibit 7-4). In many instances, correction is used only to prepare data for matching; the original records remain unchanged.

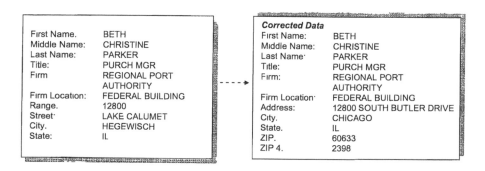

First Name.	BETH
Middle Name:	CHRISTINE
Last Name:	PARKER
Title:	PURCH MGR
Firm	REGIONAL PORT AUTHORITY
Firm Location:	FEDERAL BUILDING
Range.	12800
Street·	LAKE CALUMET
City:	HEGEWISCH
State:	IL

Corrected Data

First Name:	BETH
Middle Name:	CHRISTINE
Last Name·	PARKER
Title:	PURCH MGR
Firm:	REGIONAL PORT AUTHORITY
Firm Location·	FEDERAL BUILDING
Address:	12800 SOUTH BUTLER DRIVE
City.	CHICAGO
State.	IL
ZIP.	60633
ZIP 4.	2398

Exhibit 7-4. The record on the left contains an alias street name and a vanity city name. The record on the right shows how those elements were corrected.

For instance, some neighborhoods have "vanity" city names (i.e., Hollywood vs. Los Angeles) or "alias" street names (i.e., Valley View Mall vs. Highway 16). Some residents living there may prefer to use one city or street name over the other and, therefore, may be more likely to respond to an offer bearing the name they prefer. However, by recognizing that both names refer to the same location, you have a better chance of identifying matches.

STANDARDIZATION

Is Your Data Ready for Matching?

Standardization, the next step in data cleansing, allows you to arrange customer information into a preferred and consistent format. Some of the biggest challenges for accurate standardization of customer data include:

- Inconsistent abbreviations, such as International Investment Incorporated, Internat'l. Investmnt. Incorp., Int'l. Invstmnt. Inc.
- Unusual titles, for example, joint tenant with rights of survivorship (jt wros), power of attorney (poa), universal gift for minors act (ugma)
- Misspellings and variant spellings, i.e., Kwik, Quik, Quick

Software solutions that integrate secondary data sources perform more effective standardization and allow you to make business decisions with confidence. For example, some software is certified to standardize addresses using the most widely accepted data source, the U.S. Postal Service's National Directory. It is important to create separate fields of standardized information and not to overwrite the original data.

Standardizing the Elements

When cleansing certain types of data (names, business names, professional titles, etc.), "match standards" will facilitate more successful matching (Exhibit 7-5). Match standards — typical representations of a data element — can only be assigned by sophisticated standardization software.

Match Standards

Some software also can standardize other customer information (Exhibit 7-6), such as pre-names, post-names, titles, and business locations (Doctor to Dr., Junior to Jr., Floor to Flr., etc.). It also may identify genders, based on empirical name data, to give you a better understanding of your customers for one-to-one marketing.

ENHANCEMENT

Do You Have All the Data You Need?

Enhancement, the final step in data cleansing, adds new data and appends missing information (Exhibit 7-7). The new data provide you with

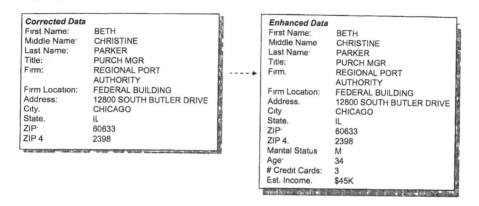

Exhibit 7-5. Once data have been corrected as in the record above, the elements undergo further cleansing. The data are standardized according to the criteria that you indicate. These same criteria will come into play again later in the matching stage.

information to help you better understand your customers and predict their buying, investing, and saving behaviors. This information may include data such as age, household income, presence of children, marital status, number and type of credit cards owned, and loan histories. Missing information that may be appended includes apartment numbers, missing address elements, telephone numbers, latitude/longitude information, county codes, and political districts.

Enhancement may be accomplished by sending your customer data to an outside firm for processing, purchasing an outside source of customer data, or surveying your customers and manually updating their information. These alternatives, however, may present some additional challenges:

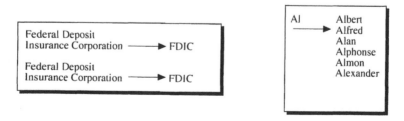

Exhibit 7-6. Sophisticated standardization software can assign match standards to facilitate more successful matching for elements such as personal and business names.

Standardized data

Pre-name:	Ms.
First name:	Beth
First name match standards:	Elizabeth. Bethany. Bethel
Middle name:	Christine
Middle name match standard:	Kristine
Last name:	Parker
Title:	Purch Mgr
Firm name:	Regional Port Authority
Firm location:	Federal Bldg.
Address:	12800 S Butler Dr
City:	Chicago
State:	IL
Zip:	60633
Zip4:	2398

Cleansed and Enhanced data

Pre-name:	Ms.
First name:	Beth
First name match standards:	Elizabeth. Bethany. Bethel
Middle name:	Christine
Middle name match standard:	Kristine
Last name:	Parker
Title:	Purch Mgr
Firm name:	Regional Port Authority
Firm location:	Federal Bldg.
Address:	12800 S Butler Dr
City:	Chicago
State:	IL
Zip:	60633
Zip4:	2398
Marital Status:	M
Age:	34
# Credit Cards:	3
Est. Income:	$45K

Exhibit 7-7. Once the data have been standardized, the record may be enhanced with additional information.

127

- External processing may be time- and cost-prohibitive
- Financial customer records may be too sensitive to send to an outside firm for processing
- Internal resources and expertise may be insufficient to integrate an external data source
- Customers may be difficult to reach or unwilling to provide additional information

There are many outside data sources available to perform enhancement. It is important to select a solution that contains the type of data best suited for predicting the behavior of your customers.

MATCHING

Can You Find the Duplicates in Your Data?

Matching allows you to identify similar data within and across your data sources (Exhibit 7-8). This is the "heart" of data warehousing. Using cleansed information and match standards, you can eliminate duplicate representations and consolidate all information about each individual customer or an entire household. This will help you to:

- Truly "see" each customer or household, and generate accurate data about them
- Enhance response rates of marketing promotions
- Reduce the risk of offending customers with repeat offers
- Identify trends and patterns to target new prospects accurately

One of the greatest challenges in matching is creating a system that incorporates your "business rules" — criteria for determining what constitutes a match. These business rules will vary from one company to another, and from one application to another.

Matching Records

In one instance, you may require that name and address information match exactly. In another, you may accept wider address variations, as long as the name and phone number match closely. Some additional challenges to matching business-to-business data include:

- Company mergers, acquisitions, or corporate name changes
- Relationships between divisions, subsidiaries, and parent corporations
- Business acronyms (i.e., NASDAQ or NYNEX)
- Initialisms — the first letter of one or more words in a title or phrase that are sounded one by one (i.e., CFO or SEC)

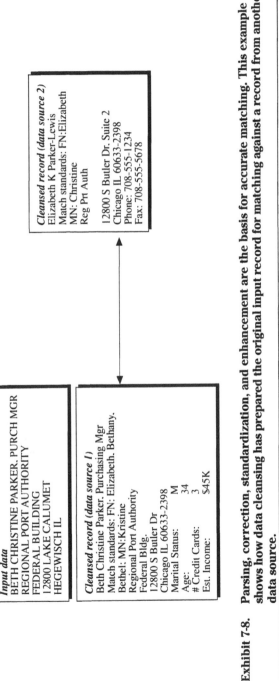

Input data
BETH CHRISTINE PARKER. PURCH MGR
REGIONAL PORT AUTHORITY
FEDERAL BUILDING
12800 LAKE CALUMET
HEGEWISCH IL

Cleansed record (data source 1)
Beth Christine Parker. Purchasing Mgr
Match standards: FN: Elizabeth. Bethany.
Bethel: MN:Kristine
Regional Port Authority
Federal Bldg.
12800 S Butler Dr
Chicago IL 60633-2398
Marital Status: M
Age: 34
Credit Cards: 3
Est. Income: $45K

Cleansed record (data source 2)
Elizabeth K Parker-Lewis
Match standards: FN:Elizabeth
MN: Christine
Reg Prt Auth

12800 S Butler Dr. Suite 2
Chicago IL 60633-2398
Phone: 708-555-1234
Fax: 708-555-5678

Exhibit 7-8. **Parsing, correction, standardization, and enhancement are the basis for accurate matching. This example shows how data cleansing has prepared the original input record for matching against a record from another data source.**

129

CONSOLIDATION

You've Matched Your Data — Now What?

Once you have located the matching records in your data, you can identify relationships between customers and build a consolidated view of each (Exhibit 7-9). This critical component of successful one-to-one marketing allows you to gain a clearer understanding of your customers. "One-to-one marketing allows organizations to better serve the customer at every point of contact," according to Tom Hurley, vice president of database marketing and research for Invesco Funds Group. When you base marketing, telemarketing, sales, customer service, and accounting decisions on clean and accurate data, you can more easily retain customers by anticipating their needs.

Consolidating Records

There are two methods for consolidation, both of which are essential for most financial services data warehousing and one-to-one marketing applications. The first consolidation process combines all of the data on any given customer using all of the available data sources. The second process, customer relationship identification, reveals links between your customers.

There are two common types of customer relationship identification, householding and business grouping. Typically, householding links consumer records that contain the same address and last name. Another type of householding identifies customers with a joint ownership or interest in an account or investment. Business grouping combines business records that share such information as company name, address, department, or title.

By identifying the characteristics and buying habits of a group or household, you can create special offers and better target direct marketing efforts. As you combine your data on each customer, you will need to determine priorities between data sources and specific data fields. For example, some records may contain more complete information but may be from an unreliable source (see "Consolidation Systems" later in this chapter).

DATA CLEANSING SOLUTIONS

What Are You Going to Do About It?

As previously mentioned, most data quality tools fall into one of two categories, data-referenced and nondata-referenced. Both systems allow you to reformat your data, but data-referenced systems go a step further.

Data-referenced solutions combine reference tables with sophisticated algorithms. In most cases, this type of solution deals better with the challenges posed by customer-centric data warehousing applications. By ac-

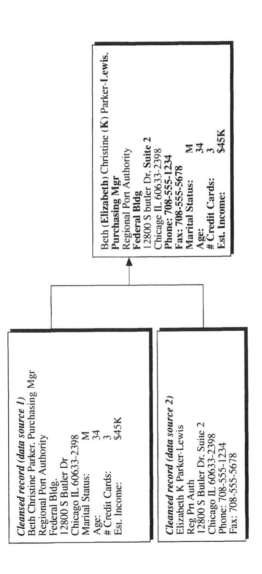

Exhibit 7-9. **Consolidation combines the elements of matching records into one complete record. The bold information in the above record was not originally contained in both cleansed records.**

cessing the empirical data in their reference tables, these solutions can intelligently parse, correct, standardize, and enhance your critical customer information, rather than simply format it.

Nondata-referenced solutions rely on algorithms alone. These solutions can handle less challenging data, such as account balances, dates, product numbers, or credit rating scores.

In either case, you should choose a data integrity solution that includes:

- Customizable standardization options
- The ability to retain original data and save corrected information
- Flexible output options

Data-Referenced Systems: Best for Customer Data. For customer-centric data warehouses, the most effective systems use empirical information. They provide the foundation for logically consolidating multiple, diverse databases.

The most proven systems for address cleansing use the National ZIP+4 Directory developed by the U.S. Postal Service (USPS). They are designed with high-speed engines that are continually certified as being 99 percent or more accurate. By leveraging the multimillion dollar, multiyear investment of the USPS, these systems offer the most comprehensive source for address parsing, correction, standardization, and enhancement.

The most effective data-integrity software can also parse names, titles, business locations, business names, and financial terms, such as trustee, retired, and deceased. By using empirical data and user-modifiable tables, these systems can more accurately locate "floating," unfielded, or incorrectly parsed data. Because they are founded on actual data, you can properly process ethnic, hyphenated, or atypical names and recognize business name and location data.

Nondata-Referenced Software vs. Data-Referenced Software

Data-referenced software also can perform enhancement for a more complete customer view (Exhibit 7-10). This information may include gender codes, salutations, geographic information (i.e., geo-census codes, county codes, and county names), and demographic data. When choosing data-referenced data-cleansing systems, look for the ability to:

- Recognize formal and informal street names, multiple addresses (reflect different addresses for account owner and beneficiary), and vanity city names
- Minimize users' learning curve using a significant base of pre-defined data; you should not need to train the product

Processing with nondata-referenced software	
JERRY BENSON, EXECUTOR	Jerry Benson, Executor
704 MARTIN LUTHER KING BOULEVARD	704 Martin Luther King Blvd.
PRINCETON FLORIDA 33031	Princeton FL 33031

Processing with data-referenced software	
Jerry Benson, Executor	**Mr.** Jerry Benson, Executor
	First Name Match Stds:
	Jerome, Jerald,
	Jeremiah, Geraldine, Jerilyn
704 MARTIN LUTHER KING BOULEVARD	**704 SW 4th St.**
PRINCETON FLORIDA 33031	**Homestead FL 33030-6914**

Exhibit 7-10. Nondata-referenced software offers limited functionality and flexibility compared to data-referenced software. The items in bold show the information that data-referenced software appends and standardizes over nondata-referenced software.

- Flag outdated or invalid address data (i.e., rural-route address converted to "9-1-1" address, or a nondeliverable address)
- Access and modify reference tables
- Assign match standards

MATCHING AND CONSOLIDATION SOLUTIONS

How Will It All Come Together?

If your data consist of unparsed data strings, you are in danger of missing many matches or of erroneously consolidating different customers. However, corrected and standardized data in discrete fields allow most matching systems to detect successfully:

- Transposed, missing, or extra characters
- Transposed words
- Phonetic errors;
- Acronyms and abbreviations

Matching Systems

There are several varieties of matching systems available, each offering a different way to arrive at a match:

- *Key-code matching* performs identical comparisons using the first few characters in one or more fields. This primitive method is rarely practiced because it uses only a small subset of the data, which can result in many false matches.
- *Soundexing* detects phonetic similarities, such as "f" and "ph" or Quick and Kwik. These errors often result from data received over the telephone, particularly with data that cannot be standardized. However,

In the address 1001 Rose St.

1001 and 101 have a similarity score of 85%
1001 and 1010 have a similarity score of 75%
1001 and 1025 have a similarity score of 50%

Exhibit 7-11. Similarity matching considers all characters in a field and their position to determine the degree of a match. In this example, the degree of the match is indicated by the similarity score.

soundexing is inadequate as a sole solution because it can only detect phonetic errors.
- *Similarity matching*, also referred to as "fuzzy matching," can identify matches by computing a degree of likeness between two discrete components. Because identical matches are not required, it can adjust for spelling, phonetic, typographical, and transpositional errors.

Similarity matching is widely considered the most effective matching method (Exhibit 7-11). It is especially valuable for data that cannot be standardized, such as last names, business names, and house numbers.

Similarity Matching.

- *Weighted matching* can be used in conjunction with soundexing or similarity matching. It allows you to indicate the relative importance of fields that determine a match.
- *Special purpose algorithms*, which are extensions of similarity matching, apply exception logic ("if/then" rules) to traditional match rules. There are four categories of special purpose algorithms.
  - *Special-case field logic* customizes matching techniques for specific fields (Exhibit 7-12). For example, these algorithms are used to identify matches between acronyms or initialisms and their full business names, or numeric components within names.
  - *General-case field logic* applies additional match logic when it encounters certain anomalies, such as blank fields. In comparing discrete components, it allows you to specify when blank fields should be considered matches against fields that contain data.
  - *Special-case multifield logic* adjusts weighting, which depends on the data found in specific sets of fields. When householding, for instance, this method would assign a higher value to the "name" field when the address is an apartment complex and the "unit number" field is blank.
  - *General-case multifield logic* performs a second match when it encounters specific anomalies, regardless of the fields in which they are found. For example, it could search for elements with low

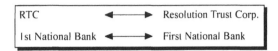

Figure 7-12. With special-case field logic, you can identify a match between a full name and its initialism or between numbers in a name and their full spelling.

parse-confidence scores, concatenate them, and compare the resulting data strings.

Combined Approach. A combined approach, incorporating similarity, weighting, and special purpose algorithms, is usually best. Multiple levels of matching may be necessary for complete data consolidation or maintenance.

When using a combined approach, you need the flexibility to modify business match rules. This is important as the reliability of certain data may vary between records and sources. For instance, people who move often have unreliable contact data. When this happens, your combined solution should provide the flexibility to use alternate fields as match criteria, such as social security number, credit card numbers, account numbers, or date of birth.

Consolidation Systems

The data cleansing and matching processes lead to one end result: accurate data consolidation. To build on this foundation, you will need a flexible consolidation solution to combine existing operational data and maintain incoming data feeds.

Some key components of proven consolidation solutions allow you to:

- *Prioritize incoming data sources.* In-house databases are usually more reliable than purchased or rented data because they tend to be more up-to-date.
- *Prioritize fields.* Fields that have been cleansed and verified tend to be more reliable than those that have not. Again, the source and recency are important considerations.
- *Maintain sources of original data.* Complete metadata allow you to trace data errors or discrepancies back to the source.
- *Identify unreliable or missing data.* Once identified, if it is economically feasible, you can request information directly from the customer or from a valid outside source.

Depending on the scope of your project, you may wish to approach consolidation one step at a time. If you do not have the resources to build an enterprise data warehouse, you may choose to start with a data mart. With each small success, you will gain expertise, confidence, and continued support for completing your data warehouse.

DON'T OVERLOOK THE FOUNDATION

As you implement your data warehouse, don't overlook its foundation, data quality, which is essential for successful matching and consolidation. It is critical first to determine which data are important and to choose the most appropriate cleansing tools. When working with customer data, a data-referenced system is the most proven solution.

With a variety of matching solutions available, look for one that combines different types of matching algorithms. This will allow you to locate, understand, and target your customers accurately.

By building parsing, correction, standardization, enhancement, matching, and consolidation into your system, you can meet your goals, which may enable you to:

- Make better and more immediate marketing decisions
- Increase market share
- Increase revenue
- Detect fraud more accurately
- Improve customer service
- Ensure clean feeds to online analytical processing (OLAP) and data-mining tools
- Implement your solution faster than building your own
- Understand your customers
- Facilitate the success of your project

The best course of action is to choose tools that offer the flexibility and accuracy your project demands. By implementing these tools, financial institutions will secure a solid foundation for building one-to-one customer relationships.

Author Bio

Art Petty, Vice President of Marketing for Firstlogic, Inc., has 14 years of experience in leading the growth, development, and management of commercial systems and technology-based business/product lines for international organizations. Petty's areas of expertise include marketing, product line, and business management; strategic planning; and marketing/business consulting. He has spoken at conferences on one-to-one marketing, along with other industry topics. He holds a Bachelor of Arts degree in Finance, as well as a Master of Business Administration degree with concentrations in Marketing and Finance.

Chapter 8
A History of Knowledge-Based Systems in Financial Services

Jessica Keyes

ONE OF THE REASONS why the computer hasn't produced the spurt of productivity that we all expected is that we are still dealing with bits and bytes of information. We still haven't learned how to turn it into certifiable knowledge. That's because most of us are still building traditional systems, that is, systems that provide merely tactical information, rather than smart systems that provide competitive advantage — systems that provide knowledge.

Financial Services has always looked beyond the ordinary toolset in an attempt to develop systems that would not only process data but turn the data into this elusive thing called knowledge. What many MIS types new to Financial Services might not realize is that the "road to smart systems" has been well traveled by the industry.

This chapter is a summary of the development of the some of the most highly publicized and eloquent knowledge-based systems of the past two decades. It's worthwhile to know where we've been in order to develop a plan to get to where we want to go.

TRANSFORMING INFORMATION INTO KNOWLEDGE

Perhaps the industry with the largest share of traditional systems is the banking industry. No one personifies banking more nor has done more for the banking industry than Citicorp's chairman emeritus Walter Wriston. In his many years as chief executive officer he revolutionized the international banking environment. And one of the tools in his toolbox of change was the computer. With over a trillion dollars a day changing hands in the New

0-8493-9834-7/00/$0.00+$.50
© 2000 by CRC Press LLC

York market alone, the banking industry has really geared up for an alliance between technology and strategy. Wriston envisioned a banking environment where the interface between man and machine permits easy access to complex information. Artificial intelligence (AI), predicts Wriston, will become the norm and not the exception. He looks forward to a day when he can walk up to a smart system in a bank lobby that will be able to answer complex questions about his account: "Can I invest in a tax-free fund? Can I do brokerage transactions?"

Quaker Oats in Chicago was one of the first consumer goods marketers to realize the potential of strategic technology. More than 15 years ago it set up its own computer program to analyze some 2 billion facts about different products and competitors. Use of this system permitted Quaker Oats to understand the data and to draw insights from it. This led it to the number one spot in such product categories as Rice-A-Roni and the ever-popular Aunt Jemima Pancakes. More recently it began to realize that new technology was making the system obsolete. So without hesitation out it went and in came a much more high-tech analytical tool. With it Quaker Oats can perform the intricate "what if" analyses that will keep it number one.

This brand of filtering methodology is a technology very much in vogue as more and more entrepreneurial start-ups compete to slay the information dragon. MIT has stepped in to become knights in shining armor when they devised a novel way to separate the e-mail wheat from the chaff. For many of us, electronic mail messages rate right up there with junk mail. The MIT system found a novel way to categorize messages as top priority if they come from certain people or if the message implies that it needs a response within a few days. Joining the Knights of The Round Table is a former LOTUS development executive. He started a company called Beyond Inc. based just on this technology. LOTUS itself has its own mail sifter. NOTES uses graphical displays to permit senders to imprint distinctive logos on their electronic missives. You can direct your mailbox to turn up its nose at certain logos and permit others access. I suppose some enterprising start-up company will find a comfortable niche in producing counterfeit logos for gate-crashing. Or will we call it logo-crashing?

Filters work for more than just turning up your nose at uninvited electronic guests. It also is a mainstay in the marketing arena. For years marketers used technology to filter relevancies out of the information glut. It started with the first totally computerized census back in 1970. The Census Bureau created demographic data on computer tapes. This provided a plethora of information on neighborhoods right down to your very own city block. By the time the 1980 census rolled around these stats had ballooned into 300,000 pages of statistics. And a whopping 10 times that amount sat patiently on computer tapes. Today the personal computer has put this same information on a desktop.

Many in the financial industry quickly followed suit. Investors Services, out of Bridgeport, CT has been collecting data for some 30 years. Today it manages Worldscope, an international database containing a wealth of information on some 5000 companies. The key here is smart filtering.

Individual Inc. sifts through full text articles and pinpoints items of interest to its subscribers. They describe themselves as operating an information refinery that takes a broad stream of raw data and turns it into actionable knowledge.

Dean LeBaron agrees to this approach. He was very much in the *avant-garde* in the middle 1970s. That's when he preached the use of computers to improve the quality of investing. Batterymarch Financial Management is one of Boston's leading money management firms with a portfolio of over $11 billion. LeBaron runs Batterymarch as one large expert system. It's "designed to operate the way an intelligent institutional investor would operate if put on a silicon substrate."

Wriston, LeBaron, and the rest of these folks recognized early on the advantages of using smarter technology. And each revels in "number one" spots in their respective marketplaces. These companies have learned to distinguish between information and knowledge. The rest of this chapter will profile several "smart systems." Hopefully the reader will begin to discern a pattern in developing these systems that can be applied to his or her own organization.

AI ON WALL STREET

What better place to start then the den of the money lions. Wall Street grabbed onto the idea of intelligent systems in a big way back in the early 1990s. Their goal? To make more money, of course. The financial markets are the most complex of systems, characterized by literally thousands of variables. While there are some shrewd wheeler-dealers around who trust their own intuition, for the most part Wall Street relies on superintelligent systems to handle and make sense out of all that chaos.

Oh, the joy of it all. To be on the floor of the New York Stock Exchange is to be at the center of the universe. The roar of the crowd and the scent of a fresh kill quickens the pulse and flushes the cheeks. But let's exit through the side door and walk down any street. Look, over there, in that tall gray limestone building, that's where all the real action is.

Behind locked doors a blinking, whirring gray box chugs away uninterrupted. A few feet away a shirt-sleeved denizen of the Wall Street canyon stands watching this magic box perform its magnus opus. Suddenly the printer began its dance and the Wall Street trading fiend scrambles to rip the report, ink still wet, from the printer. Running to the phone, our intrepid but frazzled, ivy league investment banker screams into the phone, "BUY DISNEY."

In October 1987 even the kitchen sink was in jeopardy as the market dropped over 500 points in the largest one-day decline in Wall Street's history. And now that shock wave is behind them, Wall Street has revved up spending on the iron and the stuff that goes in them. All in an often frustrating attempt to deal with market volatility, increasing globalization, and the proliferation of products that litter the market. So its no wonder that some formerly heretic disbelievers are increasingly turning to artificial intelligence to get the upper hand. Expert system applications not only will be used, but will be necessary to respond to the enormous amount of data generated by changes in the European and Asian financial markets, predict the traders who have invested lock, stock, and barrel in these technologies.

Morgan Stanley Dean Witter & Company uses an expert system on their profit and loss desk to solve what had been a costly dilemma. When a trader is busy, often the time can't be taken to review the real-time ticker and make sure that the trade just made is quoted. One of the best-known expert systems on the street, this system's goal in life is to look at all the information and figure out the likelihood that the trade hit the ticker.

Perhaps the best applications for smart systems are on the other side of the ticker. Almost every Wall Street firm has one or more projects underway to provide the trader with a toolset that will provide real-time insights and a Wall Street type of expertise. There are few people on Wall Street who don't believe that computers and automation of investing, hedging, and tracking will yield strategic leverage.

To do this, firms large and small are investing in a combination of smart systems and advanced workstation technology. Most analytics folks are looking for a minimum 50 to 100 MIPS (millions of instructions per second). Combining artificial intelligence and the speed of workstation technology gives the trading room a heady combination. Smart systems account for one out of every seven workstations sold. Citicorp, in New York, ordered 3000 DEC workstations way back in the mid-1990s. The purpose of this grand scheme was to tie its traders into a global network. This network provides each Citicorp trader with the ability to see prices on several markets. It also performs instantaneous portfolio analysis and even automatically executes orders. Yes, the integrated AI workstation approach is a potent weapon with everyone up and down the street clamoring to get a piece of the pie. Paine Webber Group's Hedging Assistant prototype made use of this strategy as does the Chicago Board of Trade's Aurora system.

Perhaps the best use of AI would be as an embedded component in a quantitative investment algorithm. This could, in fact, change the face of the street.

Fourteen years ago Charles Dym pioneered a new quantitative investment theory that butted heads with the three theories most widely held: the Modern Portfolio Theory, the Efficient Market Theory, and the Random Walk Theory. Dym's approach combined pattern recognition and probability theory. A test pilot of this theory did so well that it ranked in the second percentile of the annual Becker rankings. Fourteen years later Dym joined Larry Geisel with the goal of taking this 14-year-old theory and adding two additional components: the experience of the last decade and the ITG expert system.

Not every Wall Street smart system needs to run on a workstation or needs the power of Charles Dym's theories. The most widely used smart systems are those that come off-the-shelf and many of them run on PCs. Incline, a Nevada-based AIQ Systems company markets a trio of products — IndexExpert, StockExpert, and MarketExpert — popular with the stock-buying set.

And the list goes on. As early as 1987, Coopers & Lybrand worked with the now-defunct Drexel Burnham group to develop an expert system that would have the capability of recognizing patterns in auditing trading data. Another innovator, Manning & Napier Advisors out of Rochester, NY, long ago found a novel way to handle their ever-increasing trading volumes. Their novel approach included the use of the now-defunct Wang VS computer to build a rule-based system that guides the trader through the process of determining how many shares to buy and for what accounts. The system tracks many variables including market value, position size, and objectives of the account Not only does the system permit Manning to take advantage of smaller commissions and reduced commission rates, but it's much faster than the old way of doing business. They like to quote the statistic of the new 1.5-hour program vs. the old 7.5 hours it took to complete a trading program. Even venerable old Merrill Lynch uses an off-the-shelf expert trading package to assist in making buy/sell recommendations.

There's great potential here. From front office to back office, the expert system is being used to stem the information crunch in the same way the computer itself was used to stem the great paper crush of the early 1970s. Perhaps the most exotic use of all is on the floor of a stock exchange.

TRADING THEORIES TAKE ON A NEW ALLY — AI

"Computers Challenge the Stock Market Gurus." "Bold New Theory Could Make Investors' Day." These are headlines in the trades. Everybody, from the chairman on down to the mailboy who dabbles in securities on the side, is waiting for smart trading systems to take their bow.

Our friend Charles Dym was a pioneer 14 years ago and he's a pioneer today at the Pittsburgh-based Intelligent Technology Group. With his AI-analytic approach to trading that seems to outperform the S&P 500, AI is getting a really good name on the street.

THE WATCHDOG

Northwestern National Life Insurance Company decided to use an AI solution to solve the problem of analyzing the bond market to minimize losses and maximize revenues.

Before the decision was made to proceed with development of the system, two senior financial analysts were given a seemingly impossible task. This was to screen voluminous and quite complex financial data on individual companies of interest. This process required the use of some 15 ratios to be applied. These analysts searched out increases and decreases of these ratios in an attempt to predict future performance. They attempted to discover causes for ratio fluctuations. They then used this information in their evaluations for each company, which then led to Buy-Sell recommendations. The financial analysts really needed some tool to help them do this process faster and better.

The resulting system was developed to act as an assistant to the not-very-computer-literate financial analysts. It had to be able to access external files such as a commercially available database containing current information on over 7000 companies. It needed to have a robust form of knowledge representation and inferencing mechanisms to perform the type of financial ratio analysis that was now being set down by the expert analysts.

For each of the 7000+ companies, the user would have the option of selecting different time periods to narrow the financial analysis. At this point, the system would analyze the performance of each company using the same methodology that the human analysts had been performing for years. This in-depth financial analysis is coupled with the subjective judgment of the human analysts. This was obtained during the knowledge engineering sessions with outside consultants. In addition, the knowledge base was made even smarter by loading in the determined causes of previous ratio fluctuations. The system's output is a screening report which shows changes in performance of each company in various sort categories as well as more detailed reporting on each specific company.

The system was configured into five integrated knowledge bases. Three of the five knowledge bases contain explicit information on how the financial analysis is performed. The fourth and fifth control the user interface and the current state of the entire system, respectively.

The credit knowledge base contains information about the companies which are to be analyzed. Since an object-oriented design was used, the objects were used to great advantage by defining each company as an instance object. Each company object contains both financial and human judgment about the company.

The data knowledge base contains the specifics of the methodology of financial analysis. Showing its well-integrated nature, it is able to access the credit knowledge base to access financial data about a particular company. Once obtained, the financial analysis of the company can be performed. Here, demons are employed to activate the actual calculation of the financial ratios.

Upon completion of financial analysis the results need to be analyzed to determine a company's financial performance over time and projection of financial performance into the future. This normally human subjective analysis is performed by employing the rules knowledge base which uses production IF...THEN rules to approximate the formerly manual judgment applied by the human experts.

The development team spent under $100,000 and less than 3 months in creating a system that had immediate and enormous payback. A human analyst takes over 100 hours to perform this set of procedures for 80 companies. Watchdog takes under one hour, proving the point that a little money and a lot of expertise and creativity can go a long way.

THE BANKING CONNECTION

From Citibank's natural language money transfer system, to Chase Lincoln's financial planning system, to credit analysis, to real estate appraisal, to mortgage loan analysis, the depth and breath of these applications is staggering. That's probably because the type of work that banks do and the numbers of transactions that flitter through their systems are staggering, too.

A survey from the National Council of Savings Institutions displays some pretty interesting statistics. This survey looked into the back offices of 409 member institutions with assets between $50 million and $5 billion. It showed that the banking industry is, and has always been, very reliant on computer technology to service their vast information needs. More than 65 percent of these banks use automated teller machines. And a whopping 79 percent have automated their platform areas, showing a banking emphasis of placing smart technology within a customer's reach. In today's hostile banking environment banks are no longer assured of the profits of the past and are faced with regulatory changes, competition and unending mergers and acquisitions. Technology is needed for more than just competitive advantage — it's needed for survival.

Banks need to push away from the tactical data processing of the past. Here the emphasis is in pushing reams of paper through the bank. They need to look to strategic computing. Clark and Wolfarth[1] make recommendations to apply technology in the areas of managing customer information, developing asset-quality tracking, and in the area of expense control. Perhaps tracking asset quality will provide the biggest bang for the buck in application of technology. Here the overriding concern is to control risks and evaluate asset alternatives. Using technology for competitive advantage can also be applied in evaluating asset alternatives, monitoring non-performance, and in performing impact analyses on customer activities.

AN EXPERT FOREIGN EXCHANGE SYSTEM

Money. A delightful topic. Walking about a Foreign Exchange trading room and hearing the babble of the trading — 50 million in Deutsche Marks, 100 million Yen — makes a visitor tingle with anticipation. The amounts are so astronomical and the pace so rapid-fire the uninitiated get the distinct impression that this is just so much monopoly money.

The Foreign Exchange Environment

For the foreign exchange trader this is serious business. The world of the trader is small. Very often, a lot of people are crammed into, small dealing rooms. Shoulder to shoulder they sit, stand, and sometimes jump up and down, acting and reacting to people and blinking equipment. A stressful environment, this. Sometimes six screens are simultaneously flashing information on currency rates and other market data. Pages upon pages of information streaming by. Under the glow of these displays are the trader's connection to the outside world. Oftentimes 120 line telephone boards are not even enough so the intrepid trader installs yet new outside lines to reach clients quickly.

And it is quickly that these traders must react, for they cannot afford the luxury of deep analysis. In the bat of an eyelash they must scan and understand volumes of data, assess the historical trend of these data, discard unnecessary information, and finally reach a simple yes or no answer: to sell, to buy.

No equanimity here. Traders have been known to skip lunch, glued to their displays, eyes red and bulging, waiting for an opportunity. And when it comes they seize it and are pleased with being right somewhere around 60 percent of the time. It's the other 40 percent that's the killer, however. Traders have been known to go out for an innocent lunch to find, upon their return, that the market did a turnaround and a large amount of money was lost. So many telephones have been ripped out of trading rooms by furious traders that the telephone company has a franchise on the trading floor.

It was to this environment that Manufacturer's Hanover Trust, now part of the Chase Manhattan banking conglomerate, decided to look for technical innovation. The development of the TARA system (Technical Analysis and Reasoning Assistant) is a case study in how to do everything right in building an AI-based system.

Foreign Exchange trading is a prime banking profit center. It's a legal form of gambling in which you try to forecast which way the price of a particular currency is going. Forecasting is a tricky process. Traders have two techniques that they use to peer into the crystal ball. Using fundamental analysis, such esoteric factors as the world economy, political events, and even market psychology are studied to predict the supply and demand for a particular currency. On the flip side, technical analysis uses the techniques of charting and statistical methodologies to forecast based upon historical trend analysis. Neither method is practiced to the exclusion of the other by the trader and neither approach has any set formula and often rely on the experience and gut instinct of the individual.

It's these gut instincts that Manufacturer's Hanover wanted desperately to capture. So a team of heavy hitters was established that could bring the dream TARA to life.

The Technology

Back in the late 1980s, the trading room management team took Tom Campfield off the line. Tom, a vice-president in the investment banking sector, was one of the more senior traders at the bank. His goal was to seek out innovative

technological solutions to the problem of enhancing the trading process. This one act — taking Tom off the line — set Manufacturer's Hanover up for the success it ultimately achieved. Tom represented the highest level of knowledge in the trading area. He was a most valuable resource with his "hands-on" experience plus his academic credentials in international finance and electrical engineering.

A few miles away, the technology department at Manufacturer's Hanover offered a position to Elizabeth Byrnes. With her doctorate in clinical psychology, the bank bought themselves an expert in eliciting knowledge from human confusion. The successful development of TARA began with the joining of forces of the trading and technology departments.

The newly formed TARA team decided to do an experiment. They knew that expert systems had been developed successfully before. They had some, but not all, of the ingredients of success. They did have a recognized and willing expert in Tom. The area of knowledge they wished to capture was limited to foreign exchange trading, which was a nice narrow domain. And they possessed substantial documentation on the process of trading. What they didn't have was a manageably sized database. With live data feeds of thousands of pages a day, the problem of data access within a reasonable window of time became a *cause celebre* within the team. And what they had too much of was fuzziness. In the world of trading, no two experts often agree, each relying on his or her intuition. In fact many traders are so superstitious that the dealing room is filled with fuzzy bears, Gumbys, and the like, which are rubbed, patted, and tossed into the air for luck.

So sifting through this haze of superstition, gut instincts, and inarticulate traders was stupendously hard.

"Why did you sell Deutsche Marks?"

"Because I had the feeling it was going to depreciate."

"Why did you feel it was going to depreciate?"

"Well, I just spoke to my friend, Joe, at Solomon Brothers and he said ... and then I spoke to my friend, Mary, at Chemical who does a lot of dealings with Deutsche Marks and we just got this feeling that the DM was going to go down."

The fearless TARA team spent 3 months interviewing the traders; 3 months of pulling methods out of the words of the traders. In the year of the prototype the foreign exchange trading department had a comfortable income of $161 million. Management decided that if the system could have an impact of as little as a 1 percent increase to this income, TARA could survive. Manufacturer's Hanover also knew that virtually every foreign exchange dealing room on the street was looking into AI. So they decided to pursue TARA for two simple reasons: honest GREED and competitive advantage.

The TARA team set about looking to enhance the prototype to boost the deal success rate of the trader from the level of 60 percent it now hovered at. Their team motto was, "Maximize good trades and minimize bad trades." But the team had a problem, impatient management. They needed to install a working system by the end of the year. A very short time-frame indeed. To accomplish a very complex undertaking in a very short amount of time they needed to make quick decisions and sometimes compromise on solutions that were less than perfect.

Luck was on their side, however, during the initial prototype period. They did make the correct decisions. They had selected a high-powered and expensive Symbolics workstation. With its 19-inch monitor, TARA was able to process all of that streaming trading data in as many as 50 windows at a time. That's a lot of machine power. The psychological and technical considerations were overwhelming. Data were coming into the system in video form. Previously these data were for display only. Now they had to be captured and stored in the appropriate window so the trader could activate the screen on whim. The data also had to be made accessible to the expert programs that used these feeds as input to the "smart forecaster" that was the core of the TARA system. And all of this had to be done in a window in less than 3 seconds.

To accomplish this end the team used heavy-duty software. While most of TARA was written in LISP, Intellicorp's KEE Expert system shell was used for inferencing and knowledge representation. The knowledge representation scheme used was the rule. At the outset of the project this knowledge base consisted of some 350 rules, of which about 175 were related specifically to currency trading. The rules analyze both technical and economic factors. The technical factors can be considered the do's and don'ts of trading while economic factors use modeling algorithms. It is only after both analyses, both technical and economic, are completed that a trading recommendation is made. KEE's ability to both backward and forward chain through the rulebase is used to great advantage when the trader wants to review the rationale behind the expert system recommendation.

And sandwiched between the knock-your-socks-off workstation display and the state-of-the-art software was the trader. All dealers have their own styles. Some use the Gumby approach to trading, some use analytical methods. So TARA had to be flexible enough to open all sorts of doors and windows so the dealer could use the system in many different ways.

Using a rich graphical interface to simulate the foreign exchange trading environment, TARA can be used in two modes: as a skilled assistant and as an experienced colleague. With its knowledge base of both technical and fundamental trading strategies, TARA can assist in evaluating any of the 30-odd technical trading models stored in its innards. It tracks multiple currency, bond, and interest rates, runs algorithms, and fires rules to interpret these models. TARA makes recommendations whether to buy, sell, or hold a particular market position. As the price of a currency changes, TARA is instantly made aware of it through the diligent monitoring of the live data feed. Appropriate rules and algorithms are triggered and recommendations and alerts are flashed across the workstation display.

Like a game of tic-tac-toe, a technical model of any particular currency is composed of X's and O's. The X's representing increases in price and the O's a decrease. The model filters out insignificant price movements to permit the trader to zero in on the beginning and end of the trend. Each X or O represents a unit of price.

Manufacturer's Hanover didn't want to spend huge sums of money on just mimicking currently existing technical charting programs. They wanted to lay a foundation of knowledgeable analysis of the data by encoding technical trading rules which knew how to use these charts to trigger a Buy-Sell-Hold recommendation.

THE CITIBANK MONEY TRANSFER PARSER

Yen. Dollars. Pesos. What a nice ring to these words. And sometimes words have a way of getting all jumbled up on messages. Do you remember the movie *Close Encounters of the Third Kind*? In this classic sci-fi, the skies were darkened by the enormity of an alien spacecraft. It was kind of common as spacecraft go. You know, oval with blinking lights. What was different was its attempt to communicate with us lowly earthlings. The aliens, which turned out to be skinny little bald creatures, attempted to speak to us via blinking lights and music. This message was a sort of an intergalactic Morse code. Well, the humans on the ground looked up at this monster spaceship in awe and scratched their heads trying to figure out just what the aliens were getting at.

Getting At The Gist

Getting at the gist of the message was terribly important to our sci-fi crowd for it meant world peace and galactic harmony. Back on Earth, getting to the gist of the message means money to hundreds of banks that wire billions of dollars in the thousands of funds transfer messages that are Telexed or Swifted criss-cross the globe each day.

At Citibank the crew in the Institutional Bank International Service Management department would have done marvelously well in interpreting the musical message of our little alien visitors. Each person in this unusual entourage seems to have a musical alter ego. The lead ego plays keyboards and acts while the rest of the group either act, sing, or play the harp. This isn't as unusual as it sounds.

Expertise in the artificial intelligence branch of natural languages requires a unique perspective. After all, what kind of person likes to sit and look at a word and say to themselves, "I know that this word means these two different things in these two contexts. What are all the other contexts?"

The precision of musicianship coupled with the love of the fluidity of the human language makes for fireworks in the application of natural language. Why is natural language needed for funds transfer? In a word, the answer is marketing. A second word here is customers. Bank customers like to take the easy way out. They're paying big bucks to the banks to move money from one account to another. They want to do this transfer as easily and quickly as possible. They do not want to be encumbered with rigid formats and procedures. They just want to type an English message on a Telex and press GO.

> "Pay through Chase for the account of San Juan Bank to the account of John Doe."

> "Pay to John Doe of San Juan Bank through Chase."

There are as many ways for a message to be written as they are tentacles on aliens from Mars. Conventional programming systems, those that do Accounts Payable and Human Resources, can't cope with the vagaries of the English language. When the study of AI opened the door for use of natural languages in business, the big banks did a jump-start and forged ahead into the heady world of international funds transfer.

Citibank jumped into the deep end of the pool in the institutional banking area in the middle 1980s. The forward-thinking Citibank management decided that natural languages could be the answer to the question of how to process the thousands of garbled fund transfer messages received by the group each day. They wanted to develop a smart system that could determine who to debit, who to credit, what reference numbers to use, what account numbers to use, and all within a short period of time. So an AI project was funded.

Picking out the right city in a money transfer message is even more difficult than figuring out the right bank name. The secret of a successful money transfer is the interpretation of both bank name and city. You get a message, "Swiss Bank Zurich pay through Chase New York." A person viewing this message would immediately interpret the message as pay through the Chase New York bank which is a bank name. For the computer, it's not so easy. Remember it's looking for two banks and two cities. In this case it could interpret New York as a designation rather than as part of the bank name. And then there's the problem of messages that contain complete addresses and the street names within these addresses that contain cities. How about New York Avenue, Chicago, Illinois. As in all things automated there is a danger that this smart system is too smart and will spell-correct these addresses into something totally different from what it's supposed to be. To compensate for this, Citibank provides human staff members to verify each one.

An average money transfer message is one page long. All messages that are routed over the Telex are unstructured, free-form English of approximately one page in length. SWIFT is another method of sending instructions across the wire. The SWIFT service forces a structure on messages sent across the wire. Given the structured SWIFT format and the unstructured

Telex format, bank customers sometimes garble the two. So what you get is pseudo structure typed into the Telex. Since the SWIFT format is a bit like English Morse code, there is a great potential for system confusion. So the team wrote what they call a shunt program to determine which format the message is in and pass it to the appropriate processing program.

With all this expertise in money transfer message deciphering it's no wonder that the bank decided to expand their horizons and use natural language technology in reimbursement claims message understanding. Here the system analyzes a rather free-form message of the ilk, "I didn't get my money." The system determines whether or not this claim is a new one or old one and then routes the message to the appropriate human staff member at Citibank.

AND NOW FOR CREDIT ANALYSIS

Open any person's wallet and out will fall two American Express cards, one personal and one corporate, two Visa cards, two Mastercards, and a slew of various department store charges. Americans have taken to buying things on credit like an oinker takes to a mudbath. We revel in it.

A trillion. That's how many dollars we owe to banks, finance companies, and assorted other credit grantors. And quite a large portion of this debt can be considered deadbeat. So what's a poor financial company to do?

Banks, finance companies, and the like are in a tight bottleneck in their race to compete for mortgage, credit card, business ... ad infinitum ... credit dollars. The bottleneck occurs when the loan goes out for credit review. While these credit institutions really do want to grant you the loan, they need to be extra cautious just to whom they grant credit.

The art and science of projecting the credit worthiness of individuals and investors is called credit analysis. Here the underwriter attempts to piece together a financial puzzle consisting of many, many pieces. If it's a mortgage you're after the underwriter looks at such things as your income, debts, as well as the type of neighborhood the house or apartment is in. If you're a business the underwriter looks at revenue, assets, liabilities, cash flow, and a host of other minutia. The object here is to the grant the maximum number of loans with the minimum percentage of bad debt. This takes time and experience to accomplish. There have always been automated credit analysis systems. But now there are expert credit analysis systems.

Several vendors have jumped on the expert system bandwagon, knowing a good opportunity when they see one. First Security Bank of Idaho in beautiful downtown Boise has been innovatively using Financial Proformas' FAST credit analysis software for years. Financial Proformas, based in California, built a system revolving around 550 proprietary rules in its goal to create a system that produces historical analyses and forecast assumptions.

Another California company assists loan officers and credit analysts in assessing risk. Syntelligence's Lending Advisor was written to combat the experience void: 50 percent of the people making loans today have under 5 years of experience. Using expert products gives these 5-year-and-under babes in the woods the experience level of 30-year veterans and speeds up the process by 30 to 50 percent to boot.

How do these systems work? The secret inner workings of an expert corporate credit management system was unveiled by two professors who developed a prototype crediting granting system for a nameless Fortune 500 company.

When Venkat Srinivasan was the Joseph G. Reisman Research Professor at Northeastern University and Yong H. Kim was CBA Fellow Professor of Finance at the University of Cincinnati,[2] they set out to develop a robust, working expert credit grantor. Prototypes of this nature are often more interesting than ones in the industrial segment since academic models tend to involve leading-edge ideas. In addition, the mix of individuals involved and the numbers of reviews that this project was subjected to ensured the viability and completeness of the finished system.

Development of the system was divided into two segments. As in most expert system development projects, the first step is to elicit the knowledge from a base of one or more experts. In this case our two academics had the cooperation of a participating financial entity. A multitude of in-depth interviews of a credit management staff was performed over a period of time. To ensure that they obtained all viewpoints of the credit granting process, the team made sure that they had interviewed diverse staff members across the management hierarchy. They also did a detailed analysis of the actual decisions that were made.

Credit Granting Defined

Their analysis, which was necessarily iterative, found that the credit granting process was composed of two different processes. The granting institution must first determine a line of credit which is reviewed on an annual basis. There are always exceptions to the rule and these must be handled to the satisfaction of both the customer and the credit institution. In the Fortune 500 company that participated in the prototype the rule was that all major credit lines, defined as greater than $20,000, are to be reviewed once a year. Upon review, credit limits can be increased pending analysis of updated information on the customer. The exceptions to this rule are new customers and customers who have exceeded their credit limits.

Procedural rules for the granting of credit are heavily dependent upon the amount requested. At our friendly Fortune 500 company requests for less than $5000 are quickly approved after a cursory review of the application form, while requests for credit up to $20,000 includes review of bank references. And when more than $20,000 is requested, then watch out for that Dun & Bradstreet report.

There are so many subjective decisions to be made that it's a wonder any credit is granted at all. Let's say you stop by the friendly Moolah National Bank for a $30,000 line of credit for your new business. You sit down opposite someone in horn-rimmed glasses who grills you for over an hour on such things as, "What's the growth potential of your business?" "How are others doing in your location?" "How good is your management prowess?" "What are your bank references?" "What's your market position?" "What is your order schedule like?" "What about the other products that you market?" "What's your payment record like?" "How long have you been in business and have you ever filed for bankruptcy?" and on and on until your shirt is as wet as a sponge and your nerves turn to jelly.

The Prototype

The Srinivasan-Kim system was designed around two phases. The first is a customer evaluation phase where all of the information collected in our little scenario above would be evaluated. This entailed the design of both a database and knowledge base to support this grand plan. Once evaluated, a credit limit determination model would be deployed.

While the overall design of the system is interesting and quite insightful, as it is rare to find such a complete specification of an expert-type system, it is the rule bases that we are most interested in.

The rule base for the both the customer evaluation component and the credit line determination component is really a series of interconnected rule bases. Using 11 different classifications such as financial trend rules, business potential rules, and liquidity rules, the large rule base was able to be logically segmented. Each segment contained rules specifically for that category. The academics shared several of their rules, which are presented in Exhibit 8-1.

The judgmental conclusion of rule evaluation is ultimately passed into the credit limit model. Towards this end what is known as the AHP-based model was chosen to assist in making this all-important financial decision. The AHP model had been used in the past in areas such as predicting oil prices, planning, and marketing. AHP, based on the concept of tradeoff, works in the following way. First, the problem is broken down into a hierarchy composed of a set of elements and subelements. The very bottom level of this hierarchy is composed of the specific courses of

Exhibit 8-1.   Credit Granting Customer — Evaluation Rules

Profitability

IF	Sales trend is Improving
AND	Customer's net profit margin is greater than 5 percent
AND	Customer's net profit margin trend is improving
AND	Customer's gross margin is greater than 12 percent
AND	Customer's gross profit margin trend is improving
THEN	Customer's profitability is excellent

Liquidity

IF	Sales trend is improving
AND	Customer's current ratio is greater than 1.50
AND	Customer's current ratio trend is increasing
AND	Customer's quick ratio is greater than 0.80
AND	Customer's quick ratio trend is increasing
THEN	Customer's liquidity is excellent

Debt Management

IF	Sales trend is improving
AND	Customer's debt to net worth ratio is less than 0.30
AND	Customer's debt to net worth ratio trend is decreasing
AND	Customer's short-term debt to total debt is less than 0.40
AND	Customer's short-term debt to total debt trend is decreasing
AND	Customer's interest coverage is greater than 4.0
THEN	Customer's debt exposure is excellent

Overall Financial Health

IF	Customer's profitability is excellent
AND	Customer's liquidity is excellent
AND	Customer's debt exposure is excellent
THEN	Customer's financial health is excellent

Source: Adapted from Srinivasan, V. and Kim, Y. H., *Financial Management,* Autumn, 1988, pp. 32–43.

action or conclusions that are under consideration. Each element is assigned a relative weight using a 9-point measurement scale with 9 being of absolute importance and 1 being of equal importance. You will note that the rules in Exhibit 8-1 make frequent mention of the word excellent. For the purposes of this prototype an excellent rating was assigned a value of 9 on the 9-point measurement scale. A weight of 3 indicates weak importance of one over another, 5 indicates essential importance, and 7 indicates demonstrated importance. The in-between numbers of 2, 4, 6, and 8 are just that — intermediate values between two adjacent judgments. These pair-wise comparisons are then evaluated such that global priority levels or weights are determined. In other words, the decision-making system is required to respond to such questions as "What is the relative importance of customer background over pay habits?" What this all boils down to is a decision to either grant or deny credit.

In comparison to the nonexpert system mode of credit approval, the prototype developed in this academic exercise was deemed to be correct 97 percent of the time, which is quite impressive. Although the prototype omitted many other credit granting components such as keeping track of collateral maturities, it provides an interesting insight into the way an expert system is developed in an area of great complexity. Here, a detailed rule base was gleaned from expert users and associated with a statistical model to achieve the desired goal of accurately and consistently granting maximum credit with minimum losses.

AMERICAN EXPRESS — A GREAT EXAMPLE OF CREDIT ANALYSIS

Another company that lives by the maxim, "Max credit, Min losses" is American Express. It's hard to categorize American Express into any of the three slots that describe the financial services industry. What is American Express, anyway? For me American Express is my ticket to exotic places such as Tahiti, Paris, and China. They are better known for their unique type of credit card which is low on the credit (since you can't really carry over a balance unless you have a line of credit with an associated bank) and high on the bells and whistles, such as no preset credit limit on the gold card. This can get a body into scads of trouble in a duty-free port such as St. Thomas in the Virgin Islands, where the town is virtually littered with jewelry stores.

Why Expert Systems

Since American Express provides the most popular and prestigious of the credit cards, the gang at the home office is always on the prowl searching out the new and better.

One of the new and better tools that they discovered was a technology tool. They knew that they had a problem. This problem was not unique to the industry. Banks have dealt with this for centuries. It's call bad debt and fraud. In American Express' case, with their huge number of cardholders, it's easy to understand why their losses from bad credit authorizations and fraud would be substantial. Since conventional computer systems didn't make much of a dent in reducing this problem, the idea of an expert system became more and more appealing.

American Express began development of their expert system, to be called Authorizer's Assistant, in the early days of commercial expert system acceptance. Since few companies tread where American Express dared to go they developed new techniques which, years later, many other financial companies have endorsed in their own forays into expert systems.

One of these strategies was to create a corporate group that would coordinate this new technology among its several subsidiaries. These subsidiaries were already tackling other expert system projects in such diverse areas as trading, customer service, back-office support, and insurance underwriting. This reflects the wide variety of American Express business interests.

The Authorizer's Assistant was destined to become the *piece de resistance* of the American Express company and perhaps the single most visible expert system anywhere in the annals of financial services.

In a nutshell, the system assists operators in granting credit to cardholders based on a review of the customer's records. Since there is no preset credit limit, this process can be a bit tricky. The Authorizer usually is called into the picture if the customer is making a purchase outside of the limits of the normal computerized system. This means that small purchases can be approved by using the ubiquitous telephone automatic approval device. Here the store clerk slides your card through a slot which picks up your card number, enters the amount, and waits for an approval code. It's when the amount is over a certain level, which is different for each store, that Authorizer's Assistant goes into play.

Developing The Prototype

In developing the system, American Express choose the path of utilizing an outside consulting firm. In this case the firm was the vendor of the product that they choose to use during prototype mode. Inference Corporation sells a heavy-duty expert system shell called ART or Automated Reasoning Tool. They also sell their services as knowledge engineers. American Express took the package deal.

The goal was to build a system that would assist, but not replace, the human credit authorizer. Using the five best senior Amex credit authorizers, Inference Corp's knowledge engineers went to work at eliciting their knowledge. Their knowledge allowed them to determine whether a current transaction should be approved.

In making this determination the senior credit authorizers reviewed many items such as customer's outstanding charges, payment history, and (my favorite) buying habits. You see, the American Express philosophy is that you can charge anything as long as you pay your bills on time. Gradually, over the years that you have your credit card, you can build up the amount that you spend on your card until one day they permit you to charge a Mercedes on it. Some people have.

The system required over 4 months to prototype and consisted of about 520 decision rules. It ran on a stand-alone Symbolic workstation. Using a forward-chaining inferencing strategy, the system permitted the authorizers to speed up their review of the customer's files to grant that request faster. This assistant has the capability of guiding the authorizer through phone dialogues with merchants and cardholders. If the situation warrants, it prompts the authorizer for an appropriate inquiry to make of the customer. In addition, as is the forte of expert systems, the system can display its line of reasoning, which is a marvelous in the training of new authorizers.

While the prototype contained 520 rules, the pilot contained over 800 rules. When it came time for American Express management to review this pilot and provide a yea or a nay for wholesale deployment, they reviewed astonishing statistics. They found a 76 percent reduction in bad credit authorizations. They also found the system to be accurate 96.5 percent of the time as compared to the human rate of 85 percent. Management gave the nod and the team started to plan for deployment of this system to the 300-odd authorizers.

In order to make this system work the expert system had to be connected to the mainframe as a coprocessor. The system also had the constraint that the hardware currently used could not be changed. The original authorizer workbench consisted of a 327X IBM terminal connected to an IBM mainframe. Since American Express already had made a huge investment in this hardware, it was decided to keep it and "embed" the expert system. In embeddable expert systems the expert system component is called by the conventional mainline processor. It's not obvious to the user that this is an expert system, they just notice that extra ingredient of intelligence.

THE CITIBANK PENSION EXPERT

It's not the ides of March that scare us but the ides of April. The specter of taxes causes weak knees and fits of despair in the strongest of us. We spend the days before April 15 mired in a cocoon of pencils, calculators, and self-help tax books. Fortunately, April 15 comes but once a year for the mere mortal; but the processors of those giant pension funds are not so lucky. For these banking institutions, withholding taxes need to be calculated on a daily basis for hundreds of thousands of pensioners. For them, this is taxes with a twist.

Citibank is one of the largest banks in the world. Their data processing functions were decentralized long ago. In fact, they have more data centers and more dollars invested in technology than a fair- to middling-sized foreign country. Citibank is segmented into several diverse business lines including Individual Banking, Investment Banking, and Institutional Banking. A common thread among these three diverse areas is the Corporate Technology group. It is these gurus who set the standards and make recommendations; but it was the hot shots in the line area that really got expert systems heated up.

Pensions are big business to any bank. Hundreds of thousands of checks are processed and mailed to retirees every working day. What sounds like a simple process is complicated by the complex structure of the differing tax laws in our country. The Feds are one thing, but each state and local government is different. Any pension system must be able to process a check with the correct deductions depending on where Joe actually lives and how many exemptions he takes. If Joe lives in New York with a wife and three kids, his pension check will look different than had he moved to Kalamazoo, MI.

In 1986 Citibank realized that they had a problem. They got the news that California had passed a new tax law that was to have a profound effect on Citibank's then Cobol-based pension processing system. This Cobol system had only the capability of processing federal taxes. The specter of adding the differing, and quite complex state tax laws was quite unnerving. The Cobol system was dutifully modified. It was a 120-man-day effort for the state of California alone. The estimation for adding the remainder of the states to the system made Citibank think there had to be a better way.

Lesser men (and women) would be mortified at having to learn a new tool and new techniques as well as implement a real, not a prototype, system in a 6-month effort. The Citibank-IBM team was apparently up to the job. Citibank had one constraint, the system must be developed on their IBM 3084 MVS/XA system, forcing the developers into the untried domain of mainframe expert system shells. Around this time, the majority of expert systems were being deployed on AI workstations or personal computers. Given the hundreds of thousands of transactions and the very large databases filled with tax and pensioner information, the mainframe platform was the only game in town. The IBM mainframe expert system shell, Knowledgetool, was selected as it exhibited the richness of toolset that was necessary for the system. Using a Consulting paradigm, Knowledgetool employed forward and backward chaining as it processed each DOLS transaction by residence of the pensioner.

The Knowledgetool inference engine, written in PL/I, is touted to be a high-performance expert system shell. It uses a very efficient, but proprietary, algorithm for pattern matching. Astute users of the tool do well to employ the OS PL/I optimizing compiler on their applications as this serves to increase throughput. Citibank found that use of this tool actually enhanced the performance of the system over the more conventional Cobol approach. Remember, they already had a good benchmark completed with the Cobol system only recently redesigned for the state of California. In fact they determined that they had a decrease of 14.3 percent in clock time in the running of the expert system version of California.

How do the guts of Knowledgetool work? It processes a knowledge application in a RECOGNIZE-ACT cycle (or for you conventional programmers, loop). The inference engine matches rule conditions to existing class members and updates the conflict set with the instantiations recognized. We now have a set of rules ready to fire. This is the heart of the process and Knowledgetool uses an IBM version of the OPS5 algorithm, one of the fastest available. During the second step of this process the inference engine attempts to resolve the conflict set. Here it chooses which rule, amongst many, to fire next. Citibank took the option of controlling or predetermining the order of rules, which is a Knowledgetool feature. In the last step of the cycle, the rule selected is executed, or to use expert system parlance, fired. The rule fired is procedural and might add, change, or delete class members or might even fire a nested RECOGNIZE-ACT cycle for a nested block of rules.

Like most large MIS shops, Citibank's programming language of choice was COBOL. In fact, only one staffer had ever used PL/I. Knowledgetool, written in PL/I, had structured its development environment using a syntax similar to PL/I. So when the project was begun, Citibank was far behind the eightball. They were unfamiliar with AI, unfamiliar with Knowledgetool, and unfamiliar with PL/I. Here's where IBM stepped up to the gate. Since this was a flagship project, they supplied large doses of technical help. IBM was right there to assist with everything from installation, to knowledge engineering, to training.

The project team consisted of three full-time staff members, one consultant, and one intrepid IBMer. Since PL/I was virtually unknown at Citibank, the group spent 1 week learning the fundamentals. Another 3 days was spent in Knowledgetool training. Armed with the desire to succeed and all of this technical know-how, the team spent 2 intensive weeks on the design. At the end it took 3 months to develop the entire system, soup to nuts. They averaged five to six complex rules per day to find a total reduction of manpower usage in the range of 12 to 13 percent in comparison to the Cobol version. Since the original senior level management goal was to find tools to increase productivity, they appeared to have found a winner in Knowledgetool.

At the heart of the project was the expert and his knowledge. The system goal of this expert system was to apply the tax law at the federal, state, and local level uniformly and accurately during the processing of pension checks. The stated user goal was to automate and integrate all tax processing. The unstated goal was to eliminate the System's department interference and let the business unit run with the ball. A high-level end-user from the Pension Disbursement department at Citibank acted as disseminator of tax information. It was this person who created the rules, based on information from the Tax Department. And it was the end-user who was heavily involved in testing the accuracy of a system that would need to pass muster with the auditors.

Since this system would deal with disbursements of millions of dollars each evening, the team tested and tested and tested some more. A case history approach to validation of the system was used. This is a tried and true method of testing for expert systems as it permits a parallel test of the expert system vs. the current system or the manual method, whichever is applicable. In this case, the team jointly worked on a representative sampling of test cases. Each test case was run through the expert system and then compared with the results arrived at manually. The user painstakingly compared all test results. After all, one misguided rule could result in Grampa John in St. Petersburg receiving a surprising windfall. Testing completed, the user department gladly signed off with a flourish.

DOLS

The DOLS knowledge or rule base contains over 100 rules. Since some of these rules were generic, that is they apply to all states, the total knowledge base can be considered to contain over 200 rules. The team, practicing the "art of structured design" and having learned from the much publicized mistakes of several of our forerunner expert systems such as DEC's XCON, organized the rules by state of residence or jurisdiction. This method provides for easy maintenance. In the case of DEC's XCON, a system which assists in the configuration of DEC's one-of-a-kind computers, the knowledge base was composed of more than 10,000 rules. Rules were entered into the system in no particular order, making it a nightmare when a rule needed to be modified or erased. The new and enhanced version of XCON now contains such structure — but DEC paid dearly to have it enhanced. Fortunately for Citibank, the design team combined their conventional data processing experience, which is characterized by a love for the organized, with the new black art of expert system design to create a structured knowledge base.

DOLS can be considered a two-tier system. On the front lines is the user interface, or "Chinese menu," permitting users to modify the tax parameters in the knowledge base. Bringing up the rear is the overnight processor. Issuing hundreds of thousands of checks is by no means a real-time application. In the dead of night the conventional component of DOLS performs mundane processing routines. On ready standby is the DOLS expert system, carefully embedded into the system architecture, eager to make decisions about withholding amounts for these complex check disbursements. Pension data is stored on a standard IBM VSAM file. One of Knowledge-tool's strengths is the ability to integrate easily into the standard IBM VM or MVS batch or online environment. Interfaces exist for the IMS/VS, DB2, and SQL/DS databases as well as "hooks" for the PL/I, COBOL, FORTRAN, Pascal, and Assembler languages. This permits Knowledgetool to integrate fluidly with any existing application through one of the interfaces or hooks, as was the case with Citibank. In effect, the expert system acts similarly to any other called application, the only difference being in the sophistication of the processing.

Notes

1. Clark, C. and Wolfarth, J. H., A new era in bank data processing: managers look to DP for strategic capabilities, *Bank Adm.*, January 1989, pp. 22–28.
2. Srinivasan, V. and Kim, Y. H., Designing expert financial systems: a case study of corporate credit management, *Finan. Manage.*, Autumn 1988, pp. 32–43.

Author Bio

Jessica Keyes *is president of New Art Technologies, Inc., a high-technology software development firm. Prior to New Art Technologies, she was Managing Director of R&D for the New York Stock Exchange and has been an officer with the Swiss Bank Company and Banker's Trust, both in New York City.*

Keyes has a Master's Degree from New York University where she did research in the area of artificial intelligence. She has given seminars at universities such as Carnegie Mellon, Boston University, the University of Illinois, James Madison University, and San Francisco State University. She is a frequent keynote speaker on the topics of competitive strategy using information technology and marketing on the information highway, and is an advisor for DataPro, McGraw-Hill's computer research arm, as well as a member of the Sprint Business Council. She also is a founding Board of Director member of the New York Software Industry Association and has recently completed a 2-year term on the Mayor of New York City's Small Business Advisory Council.

A noted columnist and correspondent with over 150 articles published, Keyes is a publisher of the Small Business Journal *and several other computer-related publications. She also has authored and/or edited 12 books.*

Chapter 9

The Unfolding of Wireless Technology in the Financial Services Industry

Michael A. McNeal

HARVARD'S JOHN KENNETH GALBRAITH IS QUOTED as saying there has been no innovation in financial services in the last 500 years. Whether you can agree or not, there should be little doubt that the financial services arena needs to innovate in response to the dramatic changes in customer needs.

Certainly, the market for financial products is more competitive than ever before. This gives customers a distinct advantage to demand new and better service for less money. The resulting business environment is extremely turbulent, with hundreds of bank mergers per year, insurance industry regulation, and unforeseen shifts in the global stock market.

To add to the challenge, lines have blurred between pieces of the "financial service pie." Life insurance firms now compete against banks, brokers, and online agents. On their web sites, both American Express and Fidelity offer annuities through e-commerce, and another firm offers online quotes and applications.

All these trends boil down to one fundamental point. While financial businesses realize they have to change they don't always know how. Clearly, they will be forced to rely on technology to help them work "smarter." This includes eliminating inefficiency, reorganizing the way people work, and acting on opportunities that emerge from the technology itself.

That's where wireless computing has already gained rapid appeal in these markets. The broad genre of wireless applications and devices from simple personal digital assistants (PDAs) to advanced software for

0-8493-9834-7/00/$0.00+$.50
© 2000 by CRC Press LLC

electronic messaging will provide financial companies a special edge to compete, as well as to achieve many core objectives.

The following topics will be discussed in this chapter: the unfolding of wireless technologies in securities, insurance, and banking; the pathways to implementing a wireless infrastructure; and potential implementations in the areas of two-way paging, electronic messaging, and other future market applications.

WIRELESS AS A MEANS TO INNOVATE

Historically, new technologies tend to succeed in vertical markets first. Despite the relative youth of the wireless industry, the demand for customized solutions is strong. Banks, brokerages, and insurance companies are prepared to spend money to obtain a competitive advantage, and are willing to learn the technology from the ground up.

The mobile data market initially grew from vertical market demand. Courier, dispatch, and truck fleet companies account for an estimated 65% of this market. (*Wireless Computing,* Ira Brodsky, 1997). Federal Express and United Parcel Service, for instance, use wireless devices to dispatch trucks and to track the progress of packages from shipper to recipient.

It didn't take long for wireless computing to make its way into the financial services market. For claims adjusters, sales agents, and stockbrokers, real-time information is the key to best serving customers. In certain examples, which will be cited later, wireless can sometimes be the only answer to specific communication needs.

Today, it's no longer strange to see someone reading e-mail on a digital phone or sending messages with a two-way pager. Personal digital assistants, which fall somewhere between an electronic day planner and laptop computer, are also an effective tool for the day-to-day activities of mobile field employees.

WIRELESS COMPUTING

The following section will provide a brief overview of wireless hardware and software, with the exception of cellular, PCS, or smart phone technologies. This information should serve as a basic guide as to essential classifications regarding a broad range of wireless products, including:

- Handheld PCs (HPCs)/PDAs
- Laptop and Notebook Computers
- One- and Two-way Pagers
- Ruggedized Terminals

Wireless technology is purely a different medium through which we can push voice, data, and video transmissions. One can think of it as an invisible cable, with the potential of being stretched through increases in bandwidth and compression technologies in order to accommodate a particular application's required speed of delivery.

Handheld PCs/PDAs

Handheld PC vendors will readily admit that their devices are not meant as full-time notebook replacements. The target user is someone who needs quick access to specialized corporate data, reasonable access to e-mail, and the ability to view and edit small files.

These devices are broadly enabled computing machines of relatively limited speed, power, memory, and functionality. They are durable in nature, and offer advanced features as pen-based input, bar code scanners, and wireless modems integrated into a lightweight, sealed, and shock-resistant chassis.

Laptops and Notebooks

Such devices were also designed for field use, and feature heavy-duty cases of magnesium or high-impact plastic. They come with shockmounted circuit boards, and a minimum of connectors. They optionally support CD-PD, RAM, and ARDIS, but only one network per device. It's important to consider which designated service provider you prefer.

Full-sized laptops with integral radio modems are still scarce in the marketplace. In fact, it's very rare to find a conventional portable computer incorporating a built-in wireless modem. The only portable computers so equipped are large-format ruggedized terminals. Integral modems are popular within this category simply because outboard modems or card-mounted modems are more vulnerable to damage.

Pagers

Pagers have evolved from being a fairly generic product category to being highly differentiated in terms of capabilities and performance features. Traditional paging was designed purely to notify field professionals when a telephone call or message was waiting for them. Today, with the growth of alphanumeric, full-text paging, there is much more information being sent over paging networks.

Recent paging technologies include FLEX, ERMES, narrowband PCS, and two-way paging. Pagers have the capability to transmit e-mail, Internet information, and digital voice messages. In the future, alphanumeric pagers are expected to surpass numeric pagers in popularity as businesses demand more data-intensive features.

Two-way wireless messaging certainly represents the natural evolution of paging. Paging has actually always been two-way; until recently, the landline phone was the only practical return link. Technological progress is the key to growth. Many vendors have invested substantially in the development of cross-industry solutions. These solutions have already impacted the financial services market.

Ruggedized Terminals

Wireless-enabled ruggedized data terminals are actually specialized computers. Small, compact, and durable, these devices sport large keyboards and displays and have high-capacity batteries. Local area network (LAN) or wide area network (WAN) operation tends to define specific subtypes within this category, and relatively few devices incorporating modems are offered to the user with a choice between private and public network modems.

A ruggedized terminal should be evaluated according to the same criteria that would be applied to any portable computer. The speed, processing power, and overall system capabilities must be considered in the light of current and future applications within the enterprise, and the usefulness of the terminal must be weighed against price.

THE NEXT GENERATION OF WIRELESS SOFTWARE

Handheld PCs, laptops, and other wireless devices wouldn't be of any use unless the software to run the applications existed. In the area of paging and messaging software, one can integrate just about any office communication system with pagers. Wireless software applications allow users to be automatically paged, for instance, whenever they receive an e-mail. This type of software can also redirect coming e-mail to alpha pagers and allow users to screen incoming communications to only receive messages from certain individuals.

Other software turns pagers into a vital part of monitoring systems. Monitoring and telephony-based alerts can automatically be forwarded to the pagers of managers, technicians, and other people who need to stay informed of a system's status. Immediate pager-based alerts translate into immediate responses to malfunctioning systems and critical situations.

In wireless software applications, the term, "middleware" comes up frequently. This term simply refers to software that is intended to make a network transparent to a given application. Some wireless networks have been designed with middleware built into the transport protocols, examples being CDPD cellular and Reflex two-way paging.

An important element in wireless applications, middleware software can help to solve the idiosyncrasies of wireless transmissions. Special performance features include least-cost routing, where the middleware chooses between two or more networks, and intelligent agents, which manage the user's network by prioritizing messages. In short, this software helps to guarantee the delivery of messages and reduce redundancy.

THE CONVERGENCE OF INTERNET AND WIRELESS TECHNOLOGIES

Given the high percentage of large banks and insurance companies with sophisticated "wired" infrastructures (AS/400s, distributed computers, and networked personal computers), an optimal wireless solution should be able to bridge the gap between diverse computing environments. It should also have superior performance, reliability, and be scalable to the enterprise.

Today, there are software packages available to provide wireless communications with environments that include computing, telephony, and monitoring systems. They support the Internet (TCP/IP) protocol as an internal networking backbone; centralize users, groups and wireless carriers; and provide connectivity throughout the enterprise.

The coupling of "wired" and wireless technologies provides significant benefits to the end-users in the financial services industry. Recently, the Mutual Group (TMG) of Canada deployed a wireless solution to centralize their paging into one solution and upgrade them from numeric to alphanumeric paging. The corporate giant insures one in every 10 Canadians, with 5800 employees and 125 offices.

Another excellent example of a wireless success story occurred at one of the nation's largest banks. Every year, this bank processes 5 billion on-line transactions; produces 125 million statements and letters; issues 15 million credit cards; and responds to 200 million phone calls. To deal effectively with this volume, a sophisticated technological environment is required.

The bank recently deployed a centralized wireless messaging solution as a plug-in to their existing legacy environment. They use the software for network management, to reach their paging technicians, for general alphanumeric paging, and automated alarms from Windows NT and UNIX servers. With 545 paging users and 55 groups, their paging capabilities now allow them to send anywhere from 100 to 500 pages per hour.

In summary, the purpose of wireless software is to facilitate an individual's connectivity to necessary information at any location, whether one is on-site, down the street, or thousands of miles away. For the financial services industry, this translates into increased revenues, whether the company has local, national, or international communication needs.

WIRELESS IN THE SECURITIES INDUSTRY

In the past, brokers potentially jeopardized a client's stock position by leaving their terminals for lunch or breaking away from the office. Today, they can use wireless tools to monitor what's happening with a client's portfolio.

For the stockbroker on the trading floor, person-to-person communication is critical. There's no time to check e-mail or voicemail. Trades for thousands of dollars occur every second.

The demand for information is crucial in the securities business, and wireless data access provides the competitive edge to the demand. One of the major benefits of wireless is that it works indoors in areas lacking suitable phone jacks. In essence, it enables true peer-to-peer messaging.

As slaves to the smallest stock fluctuations, financiers can now fully capitalize on the mobility of data in fund management. In addition, using a laptop with a wireless connection to the Internet, stockbrokers can find out the latest market activities without having to be at their offices.

A Broker in Every Laptop

Wireless services in the securities industry can offer traders a combination of personalized attention of a portfolio manager with the technology necessary to keep them on track toward meeting their client's goals.

Based out of New York, a company called Wireless Financial Services offers a product called Universal Trader. It provides investors real-time prices for equities, futures, and options, and current headlines wirelessly or via the Internet. Compared to 800 numbers or cellular phones, the wireless trader dramatically reduces communications costs.

The average response time for a portfolio quote is under six seconds, and less than one second over the Internet. Some of the benefits are cross-functionality as both an order entry and quote service; freedom from client visits; the ability to send broadcast messages to clients using e-mail; and an increase in commissions by being able to serve more clients.

The Wireless Trading Floor

Few business environments are more mission-critical than those involving the flow of dollar bills. At a major stock exchange, where the flow of millions of dollars occurs per hour, the circumstances are perfect for the deployment of wireless communications. Stock exchanges are vast two-way auctions, with orders to buy and sell securities constantly flooding the trading floor.

The NYSE recently launched a $100 million integrated technology plan, designed to carry it into the next century. As part of the plan, the exchange spent $10 million on two wireless applications, after carefully evaluating all their options. They had initially considered infrared technology, but ruled it out due to the fact that infrared lacks range.

In the first application, 200 reporters were equipped with wireless touch-screen terminals. About half of all trades (stock name, price, and volume) are monitored every day by reporters. The purpose of this application was not stock comparison, but to deliver information to the outside world to facilitate further trading.

In the past, reporters used pencils with preprinted cards. Today, they are equipped with pen-based, handheld computers that have wireless LAN adapters. The adapter consists of a PC card plus a separate radio and antenna module. The unit is fastened to the EHT-30 and connected to the PC card by a short cable.

The main application equipped about 3000 brokers with wireless terminals for both data collection and comparison and settlement. The wireless LAN ensures the timely flow of information, improving the NYSE's competitive position, and eliminating deferred data entry, which reduces errors.

For wireless data users in the financial markets, new options mean more flexibility. Today, businesses can utilize the power of wireless computing to make their day-to-day activities flow much smoother.

Software developers will continue to provide niche market applications that will justify wireless technology over wire-line service. The more brokers are freed from being tethered to an office or desk, the more efficiency and productivity a securities firm will realize.

AN EFFECTIVE "FIELD PARTNER"

The major issue today for insurance companies is whether or not they will be able to compete 10 to 15 years from now. One of the keys to success will be the deployment of more efficient systems to distribute information to claims adjusters, sales agents, and other field employees.

Insurance companies were "early adapters" of wireless technology to improve their businesses. Sales agents who relied on e-mail as a means to managing customer relationships now forward their e-mail to pagers or handheld PCs. With wireless e-mail services, agents save on mobile phone costs, and keep business transactions private.

Technology for the Field

In 1995, State Farm equipped its field agents with pen-based computers to automate the processing of property claims. The hand-held PCs featured a database that allowed the company adjusters to estimate property damages and settle claims. Upon evaluating these properties, adjusters were able to wirelessly retrieve material costs for repairs, labor, and other pertinent data.

In case of disaster, mobile solutions can significantly reduce the time it takes claims adjusters to process claims. When landline communications go down, American Family Insurance rolls out a "disaster recovery trailer." Fitted with a 2.4-meter satellite dish, the trailer has 11 workstations, each with a telephone and computer, printers, copiers, and fax machine. A satellite dish links to a mainframe at company headquarters.

In the area of field sales, a London-based insurance company has had great success with mobile solutions. After equipping 1000 sales agents with laptops, they were able to have more productive client meetings. The mobile PCs allowed agents to track policy history and product preferences, as well as conduct a needs analysis on-site to determine optimal policies based on the customer's requirements.

The payback for the laptops has been reduced sales cycles. It also gives agents the ability to give policy quotes at the time of the client visit. Instead of a previous week-long process, time has been drastically cut by bypassing the need to mail in orders and signed confirmations.

REMOTE BANKING

The progress of wireless communications in banking has been mild at best. Software applications for internal use are quite common within large banks, as cited above in the section on Wireless Software.

When it comes to financial transactions with bank customers, however, possibilities for the deployment of a large-scale wireless application will be driven by strong customer demand. That's the way it's been historically, and the development of the "smart card" is a perfect example of what is to come.

An example of a potential banking application of the future is, for instance, a day when you can have your bank balance forwarded to you, wirelessly, by entering a series of numbers into your two-way, alphanumeric pager's keypad.

As a matter of fact, the basic two-way paging technology to run that application exists today. But the day when it becomes widespread is probably several years into the future. That's mainly due to the fact that software and hardware vendors are just beginning to work together on vertical solutions for the banking industry.

WET (Wireless Electronic Transactions)

With the implementation of satellite and terrestrial wireless services, electronic transactions will be conducted on a global basis. For example, if you need to use your VISA card in the Gobi Desert to pay for bottled water and a tent, in the future you will simply have your card swiped and, *voila*, you'll be able to receive your transaction approval in seconds as the whole process is wirelessly transmitted around the globe via a low-Earth-orbiting (LEO) satellite system.

The Mobile Bank Branch

By the year 2000, analysts predict that up to 75% of all routine banking will be conducted outside of the branch. Remote banking services have been around since automatic teller machines (ATMs) became widespread in the late 1980s.

The most logical extension of the ATM is (naturally) the wireless ATM. Wireless ATMs are becoming increasingly popular, because they can be placed at nontraditional locations such as cruise ships, state fairs, trade shows, and any other location where there's a need for mobility. They maintain the functionality and speed of landline-based ATMs.

It works by replacing phone links with a digital air link. The solution sends data over a CDPD network to a land-based gateway that converts the wireless data to the bank's preferred protocol, and then passes it to the processing center's host computer.

Super mobile branches will be possible with C-WAN (Cellular-Wide Area Network) technology, which enables mobile units to process transactions at a much faster rate than typical mobile units.

For Barnett Bank, while an actual branch office was being built, a "mobile branch" was deployed in a South Florida community. The mobile unit was also used to offer banking on-site at special events as well as a back-up to branches when computer lines were down.

To stay profitable, banks will have to continue to evolve their remote banking services. Joint partnerships between hardware or software vendors and large banking institutions will shape the future of banking in the year 2000. Though progress is being made, it may take years before bank customers widely accept the idea of completing account transactions via smart cards or a handheld PCs.

CONCLUSION

Wireless and mobile products are becoming an increasingly attractive option for many industries, in part because of cost reductions and continued improvements in the technology itself. The ability of wireless to allow people to move freely in their work activities will have as strong an impact on business in the future as the provision of a telephone on every desk did in the middle of the twentieth century.

Unfortunately, wireless communications won't revolutionize financial services overnight. The applications available have only scratched the surface of potential market applications for large- and medium-sized banks, insurance companies, and securities firms. The industry is still a toddler, but once it "grows up," business people in these industries will be able to capitalize on instant information to help them do their jobs even better.

Keeping up with change is paramount in the financial marketplace. We've seen automatic payroll deposits and ATM cards become ubiquitous in the space of about five years. That's what customers wanted, what they valued, and that's why it's here today.

The Future

The wireless hardware and software of the future could become one standard dataphone, as portable as your watch and as personal as your wallet. It would be able to recognize speech and convert it to text. But for now, that is still only part of a Star Trek episode.

Looking ahead, wireless technologies and applications will continue to evolve. For future generations, the one thing we will never have to replace or upgrade is the wireless medium through which information is distributed — the airwaves.

Advantages for individual financial organizations vary, but the returns are the same: gains of productivity, timely distribution of data, and improved customer service. More importantly, once wireless becomes widely accepted, the financial industry as a whole will realize tremendous gains to their own bottom lines.

Author Bio

Michael A. McNeal, President & CEO of Absoft, is a recognized leader in Internet, Java, Windows NT, and wireless communications software. He has coordinated enterprise-scale wireless projects for many corporations including EDS, IBM, MicroAge, Sensormatic, and Siemens. He is an active member of the Information Technology Forum of South Florida, and regularly speaks to key members of the high-tech industry.

McNeal graduated from the University of Florida with a B.S. in computer science and did his post-graduate work at the University of Miami. Today he is primarily involved in the development of Internet and wireless technologies, as well as business and strategic planning for Absoft. He is currently working on a project for Motorola, one of the largest wireless vendors in the industry.

Chapter 10
Personal Financial Appliances

Greg Crandell
David Williams

THE OPPORTUNITY FOR THE DEVELOPMENT OF INNOVATION in online financial services could not be better. Key standards are falling into place, and the Internet continues to grow and mature. New Internet platforms are proliferating, thus lowering the investment required for establishing a Web presence. While savvy financial service companies are offering customers more options for how service may be accessed, the challenge of providing solutions that meet the requirements of most users remains.

Most of the activity in the area of online financial services has focused on infrastructure development. This is extremely important, as the success of these services will depend on robust, scalable, and most importantly — secure solutions. But lets suppose that the infrastructure is, or soon will be, in place to enable anyone real-time access to banking, investment, and other personal financial information online. What delivery mechanism will become dominant? The options available today include browser banking, with its high availability but relatively limited functionality. These browser-based transactional Web sites don't extend the financial institution's existing delivery system. They offer little more capability differentiation than ATM or debit card access.

Existing personal finance management (PFMs) software like Quicken and Money, which combine offline financial tools with online financial support, limit the user to a single desktop. Additionally, they are "hard branded," thus subordinating the very financial institutions who will increasingly depend on this desktop presence as their primary point of contact with a growing customer segment.

Strategic differentiation will be driven by the approach the financial institution takes in investing in an innovative digital presence — a presence innovative in its value proposition for the consumer and in its integration

0-8493-9834-7/00/$0 00+$.50
© 2000 by CRC Press LLC

and presentation of the products and services offered across the financial institution.

Survey findings suggest users place a low value on the benefits of existing home banking solutions.[1] Financial institutions, looking to implement solutions for these users, are put in an interesting position. Users are not enamored with existing Web solutions and PFMs are hard to use and limit the financial institution's choices. With success hanging in the balance, these are tough issues.

The potential rewards are compelling, however. By building Internet-type distribution channels, and facilitating consumers' and merchants' entry into electronic commerce, financial institutions can place themselves in a nearly unassailable role for facilitating payment and settlement. They can open new avenues for the creation and delivery of information-rich products, and protect their role as the primary providers of financial services. In this scenario, account balances rise, transaction costs fall, and revenues grow.

What follows are some of the issues and challenges that software developers and financial institutions must face if they are to meet the needs of this rapidly evolving and increasingly "wired" customer base. Specifically, we discuss a new class of client software we have termed the Personal Financial Appliance (PFA). The readers will learn what a PFA is and how it might work for them in meeting their online financial services challenges. We believe PFAs hold the key to mass acceptance by a user audience not yet addressed by existing solutions.

INTERNET AT THE CROSSROADS

> The birth of the web marks not just another hot information technology, but the emergence of an entirely new domain of human economic life.

— Michael Rothschild, *Upside Magazine*, February, 1996.

To best understand where we are, we need to understand where we have been. Over the last 5 years the Internet has come from being a curiosity, used only by the cognoscenti, to become part of the daily activities of increasing numbers of average everyday people.[2] That the Internet has come of age is no secret, but how it will turn out in the end is anyone's guess. We are still just opening the door to what is expected to reshape the boundaries of our lives more fully than any single technology event has ever done before. While we can't say specifically what these changes will be, we can say with absolute certainty that, at least in the area of electronic financial services, things have already changed forever.

THE NEW BOSS

Today, the Internet is an amorphous collection of data sources, billboards, communities, places, people, organizations, books, libraries, newspapers, museums, stores, malls, myths, and legends. It is all of these things and more. What it will evolve into, no one knows. But, we have learned a few things about the Internet that can help us understand how and along what lines it will evolve. It is in looking at *application* development that we can learn the most about how and where the Internet is going. It is important to place application development in some larger context. The next wave can be broken down into three MegaTrends: Information Access and Management, Relationship Management, and Electronic Commerce.

Information Access and Management

No one doubts the enormous reservoir of information that is available everyday over the Internet. Consider that the earliest successful Internet entrepreneurs focused on search engines as a way to add value to a user's Internet access. Key developments to pay attention to in this area include:

- Search and retrieval engines — provide better query languages and concept extraction.
- Agent/filtering algorithms — provide better and more functional agent communities, and more precise filtering of responses.
- Web push/pull — better methods for multicasting and streaming media. Push is great; however, it suffers from poor network response and a lack of good tools for managing active content development.
- Computational media — computational media or "just-in-time" media that is rendered in real time on the user's screen. Examples include personalized news services and collaborative environments such as virtual world communities.

Relationship Management

The Internet brings relationships to a completely new level. On the Internet the notion of relationships and relationship management will need to be rethought. Key capabilities that we see users wanting include:

- Friends and family — financial institutions already view account holders in terms of households. Solutions will enable users to better manage their financial relationships with the reality of complex account ownership.
- Subscribers/customers — solutions are needed that understand the requirements of servicing online customer/subscriber communities. Financial institutions and merchants, acting as online service providers, will require new tools which enable them to nurture, grow, maintain, and *mine* their subscriber base for new business and services.

- Online financial institutions and merchants — solutions that link purchase and transaction histories to correspondence with a specific financial institution/merchant. This is critical for users to manage the various types of relationships that they may have online.

Electronic Commerce

This is the Holy Grail of the current phase of Internet development. If we can standardize the right communication and security technologies, and deliver better tools and applications for performing commerce, we believe the commercial promise of the Internet will be realized. The benefits of open access and universal availability will drive usage of the Internet for commerce precisely because it is inexpensive, always there, always open, always ready to do business. No other medium can offer this power. Key capabilities we believe users will want in this area include:

- Online banking, bill pay, and bill delivery. These are the basic capabilities that users need to automate and simplify their banking chores.
- Online investment. Trading and brokerage are considered the current instance for true empowerment. In this application, users are able to take direct control of their trading resources and make changes as required.
- Online shopping and electronic funds transfer at point of decision (EFT@POD). Online shopping is expected to grow dramatically over the next few years and lots of examples of secure credit-card transactions already exist today. But true online shopping by the masses will have to wait for a more standard method for performing it. On the other hand EFT@POD denotes a new capability which, we believe, will evolve out of online shopping. This capability gives users the ability to move funds anywhere, anytime, for any purpose the user decides.
- Online asset management. This is another new capability that we expect to become important as users develop relationships with multiple financial service providers, such as insurance companies, financial institutions, credit unions, brokers, and financial planners. They will want to consolidate these accounts into a single place where they can make decisions that could ripple through their financial world.

THE CHALLENGE

It is an indictment of the industry that the only way I can do business with Amazon.com is with my credit card.

— E. Alan Holroyde, executive vice-president, Wells Fargo & Co., as quoted in the *American Banker.*

The Internet allows financial institutions to play a larger role in point-of-sale payment initiation (EFT@POD). In the past, financial institutions have developed and/or relied upon third parties and networks to capture and initiate the payor's payment instruction, leaving the financial institution with the less attractive task of settling the payment. Financial institution-provided Internet point-of-sale services can allow financial institutions to earn more on transactions, while playing a larger role in the commerce activities of both consumer and commercial customers. This is a major opportunity for financial institutions, but one that could be lost if they don't focus on the correct battleground, i.e., if they don't start focusing on the opportunity to capture their current and prospective customers' "Internet eyeballs."

Specifically, where should financial institutions be looking? The next great steps in electronic commerce are coming through satellite, cable, and telephone company initiatives that will boost the speed and functionality of home and workplace communication devices such as telephones, televisions, and personal computers. These newly forming channels represent a genuine opportunity for financial institutions to regain the technological high ground — to lead the development of interactive commerce services, especially payment and settlement; and to lead the migration of merchants and consumers onto the information highway.

Strategically, the focus moves from service desks and sales counters to the focal points of remote electronic banking — screens and phones — where new products, new distribution channels, and new competitors converge. At these remote convergence points, value lies with information — on accounts, transactions, and services. It is here that the PFA positions the financial institution to both lead Internet commerce payment and build stronger customer relationships. Deploying PFAs will allow financial institutions to take a preeminent position in their retail and commercial customers' daily commerce activities. PFAs will open the door to direct access to demand deposit accounts, but in a way that empowers customers without risking the security of banking transactions. Exhibit 10-1 is an example of how an electronic funds transfer could transpire at the point-of-sale, allowing for real-time, guaranteed funds transactions.

If consumers use a financial institution-distributed PFA, they will be capable of purchasing online without a credit or debit card. They will be able to request payment from their financial institution, and have their checking account debited while having the merchant receive a "guaranteed funds" message, allowing for completion of the online transaction. Payment clearing and settlement can take place in a traditional fashion, but the PFA environment creates the opportunity for real-time, guaranteed funds transactions at the point-of-decision, something no other Internet commerce payment solution has successfully addressed.

FINANCIAL INSTITUTION AS AN ONLINE SERVICE: THE NEW "WIRED" CONSTITUENCY

One important legacy of the Internet will be its role in training a new class of "wired" customer. This new wired constituency is accustomed to

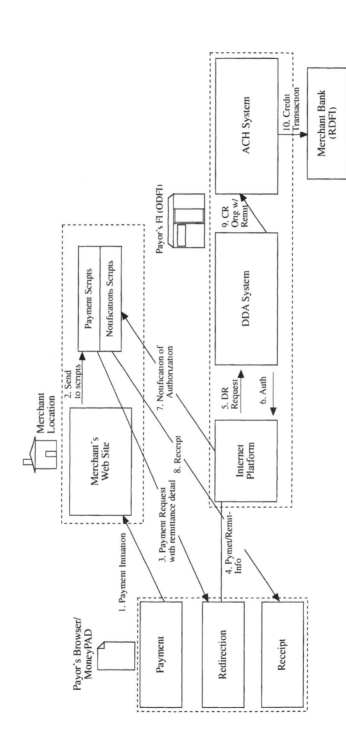

Exhibit 10-1. Internet EFT at Point-of-Decision (EFT@POD).

using the Web to select, transact, and in some instances, fulfill their requests online. These customers are demanding that their vendors offer more of their services online. This means financial institutions that are looking to grow their businesses must adopt new methods that have no precedent in existing practice.

Financial institutions need to understand their business as an online service and themselves as online service providers. That is, the financial institution is no longer just a brick and mortar establishment that occupies a specific, however elegant, space in the community. The notion of space for business in the physical world must be extended to space for business in the virtual world.

Now, financial institutions must view themselves as online service providers, and view their access points as virtual access spaces which are available 24 hours each day, 365 days per year. Users may access these services from anywhere on the net, at anytime. Continuous availability is just one of the major paradigm shifts from the traditional view of business hours.

The New Battleground: The Convergence of the Internet, the User Interface, and Payment Services

> For years bankers have said they would never allow customers to move money online, but that attitude simply leaves the door open for others to step in and serve financial institution customers. I want to be the first screen my customers see. I want to build a relationship with them that allows me to provide for all of their financial needs.
>
> — A Senior Vice-President of Internet Commerce, a $30 billion financial institution.

Financial institutions are not sitting still. They are stepping up to the challenge of providing Internet-based browser banking to their customers, both retail and commercial. The number of financial service firms offering online transactional services is growing at a rapid rate. As recently as 1994, there were only 20 banks or credit unions with Web sites, and none of them offered account access to their customers. By year-end 1998, it is estimated there will be 4800 bank/credit union Web sites, and 625 of them will offer account access. Looking to the future, the General Accounting Office (GAO) estimates 4800 financial institutions will provide online sites by year-end 1998. Separately, Online Banking Report (OBR) projects 8000 financial service institutions will provide Web sites within 4 years, and 4500 of them will offer account access to their customers.

Financial institutions entered the online remote banking space by working with technology providers to provide a link between customers' banking services and the technology providers' *client* software. It proved to be an expensive service to deploy and maintain. And rapid adoption of

Internet technologies made the financial institutions' early online efforts nearly obsolete before the programs were even in full flight.

Internet technology eliminates two parts of the home banking equation: front-end software and private network connections. While, this technology is making financial institutions' initial investments in online services look like poor ones, it has opened the playing field for financial institutions to develop branded end-user experience and to develop bank-centric payment processes, reducing the need for third-party payment processors, and increasing the opportunity for financial institutions to play a central role in online commerce.

Online Branding, Brand Control, and Other Issues Unique to Online Services

Branding over the Internet continues to be one of the most critical activities within which a Financial Service Provider can participate. Online branding, however, differs from traditional branding in interesting ways.

Online branding differs from traditional branding primarily in the methods used to implement it. Look and feel elements that people take for granted in the real world need to be specifically created in the virtual world. That is, the elements of brand in the online world need to be understood and used by the service provider to maximize the capabilities of the new medium.

In the same way, architecture, product support, and the attire of tellers contribute to the brand image of the branch financial institution, the experience of online branding is defined by the unique sights and sounds of the interaction. Online branding requires that all of the elements of the interaction be used for brand identification. Taking advantage of images, sounds, interactive dialogs, jingles, and animations as elements to be exploited by service providers seeking a differentiated experience that uniquely bonds the user to them.

Related to branding is the issue of who manages it. Who has control? Does the financial institution manage the experience of the user? Does the user's application manage the brand? Is the financial institution subordinate to the application's brand? Control of brand is a big deal as it shapes the end-user's idea of value and who is providing it. To be successful, the financial institution must grab and maintain control of its brand throughout the online financial experience. This will necessarily require the financial institution to become a more involved player in providing the online solution.

Relationships in the Screen-to-Screen World

Historically, financial institutions served their customers face to face. Personal relationships were possible and sought after as a way of better serving the customer. In the online world, of course, the face is the user interface that is presented to customer visitors. This carries tremendous responsibility on the part of the online service provider. Interfaces must be developed which communicate their function while, at the same time facilitating the brand investment necessary to retain the long-term relationship with the user. When users are a mere click away from their financial institution's most distant competitor, one must know how to keep the customer from clicking away!

Online relationships differ from standard customer relationships precisely because one may never actually meet the person with whom one is interacting. Online relationships are more like pen pals. The parties that make up an online relationship may, in fact, meet, but a strong online relationship can be developed without face to face contact. To the user the financial institution is a service, and hopefully a friend. The user is a subscriber, a visitor, a supplier, or perhaps even a competitor to the services provided by the financial institution.

Active Content (Advertising and Info Channels)

Support for advertising and access to information are often taken for granted as natural elements of online practice. However, methods differ on how this is accomplished and with what flexibility it may be used.

Active Content, or action-enabled content, refers to content the user may interact with. Trigger points in product usage, like loan retirement, should link to selling messages encouraging evaluation of new loan programs. Dynamic evaluation of competitive information available in bill payment records should drive specific related selling instances. Other examples include advertising that enables the user to seek increasingly more levels of detailed information regarding a product or service. This can also be built into the news/advertising stream that users can receive. Or, it could take the form of wizard-based help which the user can navigate to complete a task. Active content is critical to creating an engaging and memorable online experience.

Active Advertising refers to the ability for active advertising content to be broadcast to users where interaction, on the part of the user, is integral to the service offering. A desktop presence that incorporates a dynamic information/advertising channel tied to active content will be required to realize the potential of online selling. When users are informed of something that interests them, they expect to be able to interact with the message to get more information. Ultimately users expect to be able to execute a transaction.

STANDARDS CREATE OPPORTUNITY

Much has been written about the emerging standards of Open Financial Exchange (OFX) from the consortium headed by Microsoft, Checkfree, and

Intuit, and the Gold Message Standard (Gold) from the Integrion consortium, supported by IBM. We have an agnostic view of these standards, in that we believe PFAs can be supported within both.

OFX and Gold have been viewed as competing specifications, although the two are complementary in many respects. For instance, OFX focuses on *client* (front-end) *to server* messages, while Gold holds many *back-end-oriented* message sets that have no counterpart in OFX. OFX is perceived to have a PFM bias, while Gold is seen as having a thin client bias.

We fully expect these two standards to converge successfully, removing any confusion as to their uses. We believe this is a nonissue for financial institutions and fully expect the convergence of the two standards will make PFAs easier to adopt and deploy.

THE USER DILEMMA — MANAGING FINANCE CHORES

Despite all of the gains technology has contributed to the lives of its users, most individuals do not look forward to time spent reconciling financial institution accounts and paying bills. It is a chore that all must deal with and deal with on a regular basis. *Financial institutions must realize that for most people, managing finances is a drag.*

There are two categories of end-user customers: **Transactors** and **Analysts.** Each has different needs and therefore may require different solutions. **Transactors** are primarily concerned with executing transactions and include the HTML users that today make use of browser-based solutions. These solutions offer the financial institution a low cost of entry and the market is growing. These solutions, however, are poorly differentiated and do not offer much in the way of performance, richness, or interactivity.

Those who use PFMs characterize **Analysts.** These solutions are rich and offer many features for analysis. They also suffer from feature overload that is threatening to many users who are already in fear of using computers. Most users of these packages use only a small percentage of the functionality offered. While needed, these features offer a way to deal with the user's problems. When they are not needed they place a burden on the part of the user by complicating their lives with needless functionality. Increasing evidence suggests that these solutions are already slowing their penetration which, we believe, is due to adequacies in addressing the needs of the average user. This is particularly true for the wired user. Note that these solutions were originally designed for stand-alone use and only recently has Internet access been grafted on.

"After a decade of near-total failure, the online banking industry needs to begin working with innovative software developers to help make the combined online banking/money management experience less onerous and complex," stated David Fenichell, author or FIND/SVP's *Online Banking*.

The challenge for financial institutions has as much to do with *how* the customer does something, as with *what* they are doing. The task is not just home banking, *its home banking in a context and manner that best matches the customer's needs and abilities.* In the area of financial services, this is particularly difficult, as the average user already considers finance a complex subject. Thus, the financial institution must educate the customer in addition to providing a service.

Financial institutions must become online service providers, in this they have no choice. Do they also need to become software developers, thereby having to develop a new set of competencies? Current solutions do not permit a solution provider to establish a dominant brand.

The financial institution's dilemma is characterized by the need to offer a solution that gives the users a simple method for dealing with their finance chores, while growing the institution's online service offerings in a brand-managed way.

THE SW APPLIANCE PARADIGM

Enter the Software Appliance. Appliances bring convenience to user's lives by performing specific tasks exceedingly well. That is, a toaster makes toast, it does not make coffee, nor does it play your CDs. When users turn to use of appliances they do not want to think about how the appliance works; only what it can do for them and the specific task at hand.

Software appliances perform a single function, but do so far easier and more intuitively than programs that cover a broad range of functionality. Like appliances in the physical world, software appliances perform well a limited set of functions. We believe users will resonate with the appliance metaphor. The **Personal Financial Appliance** is designed specifically to mitigate the finance chores of average people. The PFA will give financial institutions the ability to deal with creeping complexity by containing the functionality their customers need most.

Reducing complexity for users interacting online has got to be a major concern for financial institutions intending to grow their businesses through online financial services. Users just want to focus on the task at hand, not the software that they need to complete the task. Our experiences in developing software for people draw heavily on the notion of appliances. We are trying to reduce the tasks of home banking to that of a simple appliance that users can quickly adapt to their needs, and that easily gives them the features they need to perform their tasks. Internet banking solutions that enable the financial institution to support existing PFM users while concurrently offering a brandable solution of their own is what the PFA is all about.

Personal Financial Appliance Solutions For FIs

A Personal Financial Appliance (PFA) can reside on a user's desktop, running as a browser plug-in or as a stand-alone object that provides interactive real-time banking functionality via the Web. Unlike traditional HTML and PFM applications, a PFA can support interactive objects, multimedia effects, and user-controllable functions. PFAs can be designed to support core banking transactions and, when bundled with an OFX-compliant server, offer financial institutions a turnkey transaction presence via the Web.

PFAs will allow graphics and information that do not require secure transmission to be directed to other server sources, increasing load ability on the active data server. Use of applets will allow the customer to view the same data in a variety of formats and combinations, thus eliminating another session to the server for reformatting of data. PFAs can be designed using an authoring tool that enables the creation of a highly customizable PFA. This tool gives the financial institution a quick and easy method of creating and protecting a brand and a proprietary customer relationship.

PFAs will support the following types of features:

- Real-time access to account information such as checking, money market, savings, line of credit, and credit card.
- Real-time intrabank funds transfers between authorized accounts.
- Ability to schedule single or recurring bill payments to any OFX-compliant bill payment provider.
- Interactive communication between the customer and the financial institution by use of e-mail messaging.
- Integrated interactive help library.
- Active content for interactive advertising control window defined by the user's placement within the control or by defined analytics on the user's data history.
- Interact with any OFX-compliant server, thereby providing the ability to route various transactions appropriately.
- Use of applets which eliminate additional server requests and enable parsing of data not requiring encryption to other sources.

ANATOMY OF AN APPLIANCE

An early version of a PFA that is available today offers five key features working together to help users manage their finances. The user interface can be customized with enhanced features, graphics, and navigation that differentiate the financial institution. The PFA can be offered for download from the financial institution's Web site and is organized in feature bundles as is compatible with other products as shown in Exhibit 10-2. The baseline transaction set offers core banking, bill payment, brokerage, and e-mail messaging. The environment features a unique look and includes an Interactive Ad Control feature.

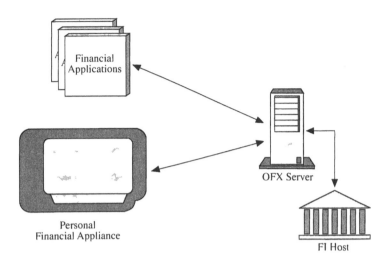

Financial
Applications

OFX Server

Personal
Financial Appliance

FI Host

Exhibit 10-2.   Personal Financial Appliance transaction set compatibility.

Exhibit 10-3 highlights some of the key areas available for branding. A description of these areas is listed below. Note that the entire look can also be changed per the requirements of the financial institution.

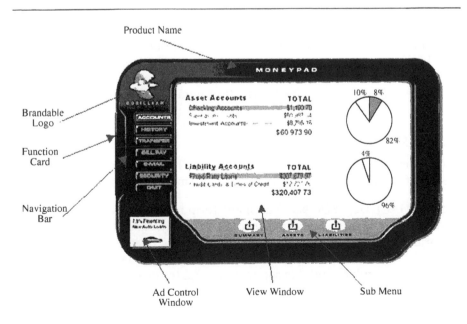

Product Name

Brandable
Logo

Function
Card

Navigation
Bar

Ad Control
Window

View Window

Sub Menu

Exhibit 10-3.   A typical Personal Financial Appliance.

1. **Product Name.** The Financial Service Provider's name or the name they give to the PFA.
2. **Brandable Logo.** The space reserved for the Financial Service Provider's logo. Note that it can be implemented as "active" giving the user the ability to link to a place of the financial institution's choosing.
3. **Function Card.** The function card defines the purpose of the appliance. Different functions can be added using the function card as the control.
4. **Navigation Bar.** The primary navigation facility with which the user interacts. It defines the key operations that the user may perform; account data, transfers, etc. It works in conjunction with the **Sub Menu.** Together, these two features guide the user through the PFAs operations.
5. **View Window.** The view window is the primary viewing window for the user. Information coming from the financial institution is displayed here. In addition, when the user interacts with the ad control, the view window can be used to display the advertising in the foreground.
6. **Ad Control.** The ad control is a special feature of the PFA. It can be used to provide real-time information, interactive advertising content, or help information to the user as part of their online experience. The authoring tool would be used to develop content for this control.

PERSONAL FINANCIAL APPLIANCES VS. BROWSER AND PFM BANKING

Exhibit 10-4 illustrates how the PFA is positioned — between existing HTML solutions on the low end and PFMs at the high end. We believe the PFA provides a good blend of functionality that includes some of the analytics of the PFM with the online transaction immediacy of standard browser banking.

Product Motivations

Many issues motivate the development of PFAs, while assuring their deployment and market success. Key among the motivations are the following:

Ease of Use (EOU). EOU is a "catch all" term referring specifically to ease of install, ease of learning, ease of using, and finally, ease of maintaining and performing a task on a computer. Ease of use has been an issue since the dawn of computers. Even sophisticated users are still daunted by computers. To better understand this aspect of computer usage lets break it down into its key facets.

Ease of Install. The installation process is the first time a user looks at a product. This is particularly true when they are selecting it from an online

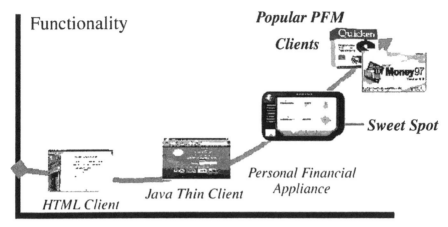

Exhibit 10-4. Personal Finance Appliance positioning.

display. There is no box to look at and no manuals to peruse, so they are at the mercy of the install program. We believe that installation is a critical time for new users and thus needs to be understood in the context of the first look.

Ease of Learning. After installation, the user must now learn how to use the application. This is where most users are at their highest state of discomfort with a new application. Is it obvious what it does from looking at it? Does the user need to configure it before use? Is there ready help for common problems? These all must be confronted.

Ease of Using. After learning the basics, is it easy to use on a daily basis? Do trade-offs made in the learning phase translate into boring usage? Many solutions that are extremely easy to learn can degrade into boring and noninteresting usage once learned. Users need to be able to tell the system whether they are new users or experienced users and the system must accommodate these usage requirements to keep it interesting for the user.

Ease of Maintaining. With the increase of Internet usage, many users are well aware that updates are a part of the software experience. That is, the application in use today will eventually need to be updated. Questions that need to be addressed include: Does the application know that an update is available? Does the service provider enable the user to upgrade at their leisure, or is it forced upon them? Can the system be updated in the background?

Ease of use and all its facets must be fully comprehended by anyone who would develop solutions for online use. PFAs can incorporate all aspects of ease of use into their design.

By engaging User Interface (UI), we are speaking of the experience provided by the application. Does the application engage the user as part of the experience of using it? The experience of an application is largely subjective. Nevertheless, there are aspects of the UI that can actively engage the user as part of the experience of using it. In an early PFA development, we took it as axiomatic that simply making the application functional was not sufficient to make it engaging.

Online Computational Media and Active Content

The Internet has opened up many new possibilities for delivering information in a way that is "just in time." That is, the user makes a request and the information is sought out and delivered in a rendered manner as if someone had actually spent time "producing" it for the user's consumption. However, it is rendered *on-the-fly* by the user's machine using conventions set by the programmer and, in some instances, by the behavior of the users themselves. We refer to information that is rendered "just in time" by the computer as computational media.

The Internet provides an excellent environment for the development and delivery of computational media. In fact, the information repository that is the Internet would not work if every request had to be produced by hand before users could access it for consumption. Computational media makes it possible for content providers to put content on the Internet without any knowledge of how it will be used or accessed. The clients and servers that make up the Internet perform this function under program control.

This distinguishes it from traditional media where the *design* and *development* of the content is separate from the *distribution* of the content. In computational media, the creation and distribution happen at the same time. Examples of the uses of computational media are to be found in many of the current personal news services like *my.yahoo.com* or *my.excite.com*. These services provide "just in time" snapshots of what's happening in the news and they can be tailored to meet specific interests and profiles of a single unique user.

Active Content is interactive in nature. Both computational media and active content are extremely useful for dynamically creating a compelling information experience for the user. An early version of a PFA incorporates computational media and Active Content specifically as a method for users to be informed of new services and for financial institutions to target specific messages for customer consumption. This feature is critical if financial institutions are to grow their service offerings within the Internet retail channel.

Asset Consolidation from Multiple Financial Institutions

Asset consolidation will become one of the key features that users require on the Internet. Asset consolidation refers to the ability to consolidate account information from multiple financial institutions for the purpose of analysis, making decisions, and taking action.

Most financial institutions today accept the fact the customer is likely to have relationships with multiple financial institutions. This stems from the fact that only recently have financial institutions been deregulated enough to give them the ability to offer the range of financial services that a user is likely to need or want. The new competitive environment of online financial services will then revolve around who or which financial institution has primacy, if not exclusivity, with the user. Asset consolidation from multiple financial institutions will then be a user requirement for some time to come.

Internet Delivered and Updated

The ability to use the Internet as a delivery mechanism is well known. It offers financial institutions the ability to proliferate changes and updates using the same medium the user uses to interact with the financial institution. Unlike PFMs, which are too large for online delivery and updates, PFAs can be easily distributed, changed, and updated over the Internet. This flexible delivery model should be considered a key requirement for Internet service solutions.

CONCLUSIONS

The world of online finance is just beginning to be realized. However, enough progress has been made for financial institutions, looking for entry into online financial services or expansion of their existing online offering, to implement solutions that will work. We have shown that the ability to meet increasing needs of online customers requires some new ways of thinking in several key areas; branding, online relationships, and simplified functionality. We believe that PFAs hold the key to growing the installed base of online customers. PFAs are simple to use, considerably more engaging for users, and can be used by the financial institution to inform and sell new services. Early versions of PFAs represent the first of a new class of software designed from the ground up as an Internet software appliance; we expect more PFA types will enter the market as financial institutions respond to the needs of their broader market base.

Notes

1. Forrester Research, Inc., Is Quicken Obsolete?, March, 1997.
2. Steve Perlman, founder of WebTV, commented that, when he saw the Campbell's Soup Company announcing its Web address in a TV commercial, he knew we had turned a corner on the Internet.

Authors' Bios

Greg Crandell is vice president, marketing for Corillian Corporation. Crandell's previous experience includes more than 14 years in financial services and Internet/Electronic commerce. He speaks and publishes frequently on the development of Internet banking and commerce, has served on the boards and committees of various payment organizations, and acted as a Contributing Editor to Online Banking Report. Crandell has earned Bachelor and Master of Arts degrees from the University of California, Santa Barbara, and a MBA in finance and marketing from The Drucker Graduate Management Center of The Claremont Graduate University in Claremont, CA. He can be contacted at gregc@corillian.com.

David Williams is a member of the Corillian Board of Directors, and a principal in DMW Ventures. Prior to joining Corillian Corporation, He was Director of Consumer Software Lab and New Media at Intel Corporation. Williams brings prior knowledge specific to managing and developing frameworks for the Intercast medium and ROSE (Rich Online Services Environment) prototypes. He has published several papers on visionary models for Online Services. He can be contacted at davew@corillian.com.

Chapter 11
Putting Inbound Fax Automation to Work in the Financial Organization

Jerry Rackley

SO MANY OF THE KEY MESSAGES AND TRANSACTIONS that drive our commerce are still conveyed on the simple yet essential piece of paper. Many of these are sent and received as faxes. Indeed, the fax machine has become the most ubiquitous printing device in the enterprise. Financial organizations and their customers favor fax transmission as a much faster way to exchange key documents: credit applications, purchase orders, invoices, credit reports, transaction confirmations, sales quotes, and many other time-sensitive documents. Not only does fax provide a faster way to distribute documents, but it provides the sender with positive confirmation of receipt. If you are a customer or consumer, fax is the easiest, fastest, and cheapest way of getting a document to its destination.

For the enterprise, the world of high technology has provided us with computer-based automated fax servers. These solutions have been around for years and are capable of accepting documents destined for printing and mailing, but instead are now transmitting them as faxes. Often the length of time required to experience return on investment in these fax servers is as little as three months. Millions of pages of faxes are reliably transmitted through fax servers every year, but until recently, computer-based fax solutions only solved half the problem associated with faxes.

The real problem with faxes is that they end up at fax machines. This is not a problem if you're dealing with the outbound side of fax distribution. But the more complex side of the fax equation is on the inbound side. How do organizations who receive hundreds or thousands of faxes a day receive them and route them to the proper recipient? For most organizations that

0-8493-9834-7/00/$0 00+$.50
© 2000 by CRC Press LLC

are buried in faxes every day, the answer is simple: in a very low-tech fashion. Until recently, technology has failed to provide a solution to automating this mission-critical inward flow of documents.

The most common approach is to maintain a sufficient number of manual fax machines to accommodate the inbound fax volume and employ "runners" to take received faxes and deliver them. In fact, some organizations have their runners on roller skates to speed up the process. While this approach can certainly be made to work, it is far from ideal. Tremendous productivity and even competitive business advantages exist for organizations who can automate this aspect of document handling. There are now commercially available solutions that solve the problems of handling high volumes of inbound faxes and route them securely to the intended recipient. In the balance of this article, the problems associated with handling inbound fax traffic and a strategy for automating it will be explored.

The sheer volume of faxes many organizations receive in the course of a day's work makes handling them difficult. Unlike a piece of mail, a fax carries with it a certain sense of urgency. Persons on the receiving end of a fax typically are not content to let it be handled like a piece of mail — they want it now! The larger the volume, the bigger the problem it is for the organization to manage. A typical scenario is a credit processing center or order processing center where applications and purchase orders are received by the thousands each day. On average, it takes 1 minute to transmit or receive 1 page of fax over a single phone line, yielding a theoretical capability to receive 480 pages over an 8-hour shift. If you have a requirement to receive 5000 faxes per day during an 8-hour period, you would need to maintain at least 11 fax machines, assuming little excess capacity.

Receiving the faxes, however, is the easy part of the process. Getting those 5000 faxes routed to where they should go within an acceptable time frame can prove more challenging. In addition to the complexity involved in managing this deludge, it doesn't scale well. Should business growth drive your inbound fax volume up, your only option is to add more phone lines and manual fax machines. One financial services organization sought an automation solution when 69 fax machines were no longer enough to allow them to receive credit applications and process them within 15 minutes. The complexity associated with managing these inbound faxes increases exponentially as the volume and number of recipients increases.

Perhaps a bigger problem than just receiving a large volume of faxes is routing them. Getting these faxed documents in-house is not enough, they must end up in the hands (or under the eye) of the persons for whom they were intended. Determining who should receive a fax is not always a straightforward affair. Processing and service centers that have heavy fax volumes don't always receive documents addressed to a specific person. They may be addressed to a department, for example. Or the correct recipient may be determined by the type of document, the time of day it was received, the location from which it was sent, or even the order in which it arrived. To compound this distribution problem further, once the fax is received in paper form, it cannot easily be routed through the organization in electronic form without rescanning it first — yet another step in an already lengthy and complicated process. It will probably have to be routed via runner or in-house courier.

Perhaps the greatest concern with manually faxed documents is security. The opportunity for the wrong eyes to see sensitive or confidential information on a manually faxed document is greater than it would be for mailed documents. In fact, the concern for security has prevented some organizations from using the fax for document exchange when otherwise it would be quite advantageous. But now there is good news: the issues of volume, routing, and security have been addressed in new, second generation fax automation solutions now in the marketplace.

Fax automation came into its own in the early 1990s. These first generation fax servers allowed a computer-generated document that ordinarily would be printed to be delivered instead as a fax. As the marketplace evolved, two strata of fax solutions emerged. The first is the familiar LAN-based solution designed to meet the needs of users generating documents from their word processors, spreadsheets, or other desktop applications. The second strata is the enterprise-wide fax server. These solutions are engineered to distribute documents generated by enterprise applications. They can handle high volumes and attach to multiple host systems simultaneously. Most also offer a LAN client solution. It was the customers of these high-end enterprise-wide fax solutions who had the need for an automated solution on the inbound side of fax. The result is AIR, or Advanced Inbound Routing. Exhibit 11-1 illustrates the possible destinations in a corporate LAN environment for a fax received by a fax server equipped with AIR.

The premise of AIR is pretty straightforward on the surface: receive high volumes of fax transmissions and route them securely through the enterprise. The receiving part is not a problem. Many vendors in this product space offer solutions capable of attaching multiple high-volume T1 (24 fax channels) communication links to their systems. What separates the best from the rest is a robust architecture to route faxes through the enterprise. Faxes can be AIR'ed based on the transmission or communications information available at the time of receipt, like ANI, DID, RSCID, DTMF, T.30 subaddressing, and other identifying data. AIR solutions can also deliver faxes based on a wide variety of attributes about the fax itself including: day of week fax was received, length of fax, time of day fax was received.

Of course, there are AIR options designed specifically for the service or processing center, like round-robin routing when it doesn't matter which processing agent handles the fax as long as it gets handled in time. You can

191

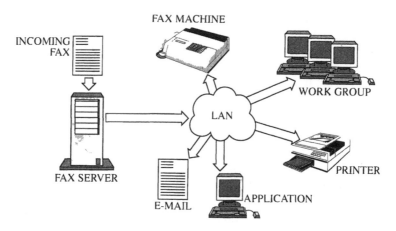

Exhibit 11-1. Destination of a fax in a corporate environment.

also exploit Optical Character Recognition (OCR) or Image Character Recognition (ICR) software to interpret recipient names, phone numbers, or other identifying information to use for routing purposes. Although this is not a 100% reliable approach with today's technology, it can still be used in certain situations.

A major benefit of AIR is security. Because faxes are received and stored as images, they may never have to appear in the form of a printed page. These faxes can be routed through the electronic infrastructure of an organization directly to the intended recipient. The most common way of doing this is through the corporate e-mail network. Faxes AIR'ed in this way appear as a normal message in the user's e-mail in-box. The fax is attached as an image file that can be viewed using the e-mail image viewer or the one supplied by the fax server vendor. More advanced implementation of AIR have faxes integrated with key business applications like order entry, often through some sort of image application. AIR provides a secure environment with many options for processing faxes.

The best way to understand the benefits of AIR is to look at examples of how companies are exploiting it. One financial services company uses AIR to receive applications for credit. Prior to automating this process, they received faxes manually and routed them via runners to their credit processing center. AIR had a significant impact on their ability to meet their target of processing credit applications within a 15-minute window. They were able to reduce their processing window from 15 to 7 minutes using AIR. A major office products retailer is using AIR to receive and route over 30,000 orders per month. The benefits are lower costs, higher productivity, but most of all a customer service advantage, all of which came with a 2-month return on investment. Insurance companies are using AIR to receive claims and commit them directly into host image applications for processing. Where organizations struggle with large volumes of inbound fax, AIR is making a big impact and providing a fast payback.

If you receive large numbers of faxed documents that must be routed and processed in a timely fashion, automated fax servers with AIR are probably in your future. Fax volumes are going nowhere but up — it is the preferred way for consumers and customers to communicate with the enterprise because it is so easy. Now, it is easy for the enterprise to automate all aspects of fax document flow, particularly the inbound side of the equation. AIR is being used as a competitive weapon by many leading-edge organizations. If you receive faxes that require some form of processing and they contain time-sensitive information or impact a customer service transaction, then its time to look at putting AIR in your arsenal.

Author Bio

Jerry Rackley is director with Teubner & Associates, Inc., a successful developer and marketer of innovative gateway software products. He can be reached by phone (405-624-8000) or email (jerry@teubner.com).

Chapter 12
Extranets for Financial Services

Evan Kaplan

THE FINANCIAL SERVICES INDUSTRY has always needed fast, reliable, and secure access to information, and that holds true today more than ever before. As we move toward a global economy, this industry grows increasingly complex, and brokerage firms, investment banks, credit card companies, insurance firms, and the like are looking for better ways to procure information. Many organizations are expecting to leverage the Internet as a means to gain a competitive advantage. However, fear of security risks and management logistics have prevented mainstream businesses from taking advantage of the Internet's potential. Extranets are rapidly eliminating that obstacle.

THE RAPID EVOLUTION OF EXTRANETS

Traditionally, companies have had to invest in expensive dedicated leased lines or direct-dial remote access software and hardware to have secure server-to-server or client-to-server communication. Solutions for internetworking over public networks have been evolving, so that corporations can now share mission-critical resources over the Internet, not just with trusted employees, but with strategic partners, customers, contractors, and suppliers. This is referred to today as an "extranet."

Extranets make use of several networking technologies, including virtual private networks. VPNs are proving to be very effective for linking branch offices and subsidiaries, yet ineffective for connecting third-party users. While VPNs provide encryption for data being transferred over the Internet, they lack adequate functionality for controlling where specific users can go and what they can do once they are on a secured network — the primary requirements of extranets. A need has surfaced within the VPN market for a solid extranet management and security platform on which nonemployee access to information and applications could be closely governed.

Like VPNs, extranets are more affordable than traditional dial-up or leased lines, but, more importantly, extranets offer the potential to generate

0-8493-9834-7/00/$0 00+$.50
© 2000 by CRC Press LLC

new business opportunities, increase partner and customer loyalty, and improve return on investment. Extranets can easily and affordably link corporations to a diverse community of users across heterogeneous borders.

The notion of using extranets to gain competitive advantage is quickly gaining momentum, as is demonstrated by the broad spectrum of vendors now claiming extranet capabilities. Few solutions today, however, truly address the unique challenges extranets present. For instance, unlike remote access and VPN scenarios, where the users are employees whose desktops and networking environments can be controlled, extranets connect partners and other outsiders who do not want another company telling them what firewall, platform, or protocol they must use. The connectivity solution has to be seamless, with minimal impact on the end user.

Extranet adoption is expected to be aggressive over the next few years, for two reasons: extranets make business sense, and partner connectivity needs to be highly secure and well managed. According to a Meta Group report released in March 1999, IT organizations may be facing an increase in external security breaches over the next year as more companies offer access to third parties. Because extranets integrate security, scalability, and management, they will enable companies to take a proactive stance against security breaches. As extranets gain popularity, they will become an integral part of every e-business plan. A July 1998 *Forrester Report* summed up the future market by saying, "Wall Street will punish customers who lack a clear extranet strategy."

HOW EXTRANETS ARE BEING USED TODAY

Financial services companies are pioneering the use of extranets to derive greater business benefits. They are being implemented in myriad ways, but in each scenario, the extranet can simplify user management and policy administration issues, reduce connectivity costs, increase scalability, leverage existing systems, and position the company to take advantage of emerging technologies.

Sample Implementation

To understand how an extranet works, imagine a full-service brokerage investment bank that makes its money from trading shares globally for hundreds of small, independent brokerage firms. The more firms who utilize their services, the more money they make. The best way to earn and retain business from these firms is to provide them with immediate, easy access to information and services. The best way to do that is by extending the investment bank's service applications to the Internet. Before that can happen, however, security must be ensured. There are extranet management and security solutions available today that can authenticate individual brokers and portfolio managers, apply granular access control based on parameters such as their association with a particular firm and department, and then encrypt all data that crosses the wire. The extranet effectively becomes the manager and conduit for secure connectivity, and the Internet becomes the private backbone.

The initial solution might look something like this:

- *Users* — 1000 customers, about 200 trading partners, and almost 500 remote employees, each with varying levels of access to information on multiple systems, including mainframes, enterprise resource planning systems, and databases accessed through a Web interface. Dozens of applications need to be secured to provide information on a self-service basis without exposing confidential data to anyone other than the intended recipients.
- *Infrastructure* — An extranet proxy server running on a UNIX machine behind the company's firewall. The client software is preconfigured and made available for download to end-users through a Web site.
- *Security options* — 128-bit SSL encryption is used, along with user-based authentication through hard token cards. Access control is defined to a very granular degree with the extranet's administration tool. The complete solution enables the company to better retain and attract customers, improve service, increase revenues, and lock in strategic partnerships.

HOW TO IMPLEMENT A SECURE EXTRANET

Historically, when people thought about securing their networks, firewall technology for "perimeter defense" came to mind. Today, with the deployment of intranets and extranets, security is not just about perimeter defense. It is about controlling individual access to many different information systems, implemented in a variety of network environments.

In this era of the extranet — in which organizations provide remote access to approved network resources for trading partners, resellers, and customers — the complexity of networking has grown exponentially, posing significant management and support challenges. Companies need a network that can survive a merger, grow to tens or even hundreds of thousands of remote users, and accommodate users with different access permissions, equipment configurations, points of network entry, and geographic locations. Managing thousands of modem banks and rooms full of networking gear is not a workable option for most network administrators in the financial industry. MIS administrators want a networking solution that simplifies configuration and management of users, regardless of location or services required.

Before beginning any serious evaluation of products and services, companies should consider the nature of the connections they will be making through the extranet, today and in the future. Having a long-term vision of the extranet will save time and money. Companies should consider the nature of those connections in terms of trust relationships. Is there a mixture of permissions required? If so, then features like tiered access control and easy management are critical. Typically, financial organizations want to connect select users from an untrusted network without connecting back to them. This requires strongly authenticating each user, not simply configuring an extranet so that anyone from a specific IP address range is allowed in. Furthermore, the extranet must have robust, user-based access control to govern strongly what the user is able to do once authenticated.

When evaluating extranet management and security solutions, be sure the following features are tightly integrated:

- *Tiered Access Control* — Once a user has been authenticated, his or her activities on the host network should be controlled based on a combination of factors. These parameters could include the user's credentials, his or her group affiliation, the port being requested, the server or subnet being requested, the time of day of the connection, or the location from which the user is connecting. Extranets that only restrict access based on source and destination cannot be as tightly controlled. The extranet should have some way to cache the user's credentials and pass them transparently with each connection to avoid basing decisions on IP addresses. More advanced extranets will also be able to modulate access privileges based on other factors, including the strength of encryption being used or the type of authentication employed. For example, a user authenticating to the extranet using a hardware token might receive an entire set of access privileges. The same user authenticating with a less robust mechanism, such as a simple password, might get only a subset of those privileges.
- *User-based authentication* — Authentication should always be done on the basis of a human rather than machine attribute. In other words, primary authentication should be based on the user coming in, not on the machine's IP address. Any solution not providing user-based authentication should be removed from consideration.
- *Strong encryption* — Encryption is one of the more complex aspects of extranet selection. Encryption standards are many and can be difficult to differentiate for even the seasoned IS professional. The best products allow organizations to use multiple methods of encryption and key management so that they can make changes and scale their system gradually over time. More sophisticated organizations will want to look for products that will allow them to embed proprietary or "homegrown" ciphers using the GSS (Generic Security Services — RFC 1961) application programming interface (API). Extranets that allow this kind of customization will provide further flexibility and potentially greater security.

- *Comprehensive auditing* — Auditing should provide the identity of the user connecting, method of authentication used, strength of encryption, IP address, identities of any accessed servers, port used, byte count, time and date of connection, and duration of connection. The extranet should also have some means of letting the administrator capture custom information through an API or management tool.
- *Easy for the end user* — Rather than users having to reauthenticate with each new connection, they should be able to sign on once and be assured that the entire session will be secure. Client software should be avoided that alters the TCP/IP stack or replaces important DLLs. This could have a negative effect on the desktop. Also, examine how the client software affects other connectivity traffic in the user's LAN and on the public Internet. Ideally, the extranet will allow all local area and Internet traffic to run as usual while maintaining a secure connection to the host network.
- *Simple, centralized systems management* — The easier it is to manage an extranet, the less chance for human error. All incoming and outgoing connection requests should go through a single point of control, just as all user records and authentication data should be controlled through one centralized database, preferably a database that is replicable. The extranet should incorporate a secure technique for accessing and monitoring the extranet and making updates as necessary. The extranet should have a method for performing load balancing, and the system should allow real-time traffic monitoring across the system.
- *Guaranteed interoperability* — The solution should be able to work with multiple standards and adapt to emerging standards. The solution should also be able to integrate with existing networking environments and leverage available systems.
- *Firewall independence* — Determine thoroughly how the extranet allows traffic to pass through multiple firewalls and, more importantly, disparate firewalls. What is required of a firewall administrator to allow traffic to pass out across the firewall? Does it entail opening ports that the administrator would prefer remain closed? Will it affect partners' firewalls? Answering these questions will determine the suitability of a given solution for servicing diverse users.
- *Value-added services* — Since an extranet manages incoming traffic from the public network, it is in a position to perform value-added services above and beyond standard security features. A well designed extranet should incorporate functions such as virus scanning, active content management (including Java and Active X), and query filtering. Virus scanning should be applied to the entire inbound data stream, not simply to select applications. Filtering should be based on specific application traffic.

- *Open APIs* — The application programming interfaces, or APIs, used in the extranet should be well documented, usable, and publicly accessible in order to allow for adaptability and customization. The extranet should be designed in such a way that it can easily service a growing and changing population of users. The system should also be able to incorporate new authentication, encryption, and filtering techniques as they become available.

PROS AND CONS OF DIFFERENT APPROACHES

The perceived lack of security associated with doing business on the Internet is the No. 1 reason financial institutions hesitate before doing mission-critical business online. Extranet management and security solutions are the key to making the networks safe for e-business applications. Many financial companies have a vested interest in taking advantage of the Internet beyond Web browsing and e-mail. They need to secure access to custom and legacy applications as well. The argument for implementing an extranet to distribute information to brokerage firms and/or clients is compelling. The remaining question is how to select the best solution.

There are numerous combinations of authentication, encryption, and authorization techniques being used to provide the necessary security for connecting people to resources. A well architected extranet will scale well, provide tiered access, and interoperate with multiple technologies, infrastructures, and applications. One fundamental aspect of an extranet management and security architecture is the OSI (Open Systems Interconnect, an international standards body) layer at which the solution operates.

Some of the core security technologies being deployed today include IPSec, PPTP, and SOCKS v5. Each technology roughly maps to a different layer of the OSI networking model, bolstering its respective layer's strengths and weaknesses. In general, higher layer solutions, as defined by the OSI model, provide greater security and access control because they have access to more information about the applications running above them than do the lower layer solutions. A simple rule of thumb is that security increases moving up the hierarchy, and performance improves moving downward.

IPSec, which is strongly supported by the router and VPN hardware vendors, is expected to be an integral component of IPv6, becoming the default standard for securing IP traffic and facilitating interoperability among routers and other internetworking devices. It does not require a client piece of software unless security needs to be extended to the desktop, so it provides appealing solutions for companies that want to extend their WAN to remote offices and subsidiaries. It is well suited for creating IP-based LAN-to-LAN VPNs, which are used most often in situations in which both sides trust each other, such as with branch offices of the same company.

Point-to-Point Tunneling Protocol, or PPTP, was initiated by Microsoft. It can support multiple, simultaneous tunnels for a single client and offer the unique capability of supporting non-IP traffic like IPX and Appletalk. The greatest benefits of PPTP are its cost and availability. It is ready-made to work with any Microsoft-centric environment, and it is virtually free because it is embedded into Windows operating systems. Because of client-side ubiquity, analysts predict that PPTP will play a dominant role in the low-security Internet-based remote access market because encryption and authentication are limited with PPTP.

SOCKS v5 is a session-layer standard that can stand alone or run on top of the other protocols, adding access control and session-layer proxying capabilities to strengthen management and security. It was originally championed through the IETF by NEC Systems Laboratory as a standard protocol for authenticated firewall traversal, but it is effectively used in an extranet context where management and security are top priorities. Unlike the tunneling protocols, SOCKS v5 uses a directed architecture, which essentially protects resources by proxying traffic between source and destination computers. It also hides the address structure of the network, making it more difficult for confidential data to be cracked. Analysts expect that, because of its firewall traversal capability, flexibility, and added security, it will be adopted by companies that need to provide highly secure, client-to-server connectivity for building supply-chain, partner, or other types of extranets. This scenario most appropriately addresses the financial services industry.

The protocols will continue to be refined and standardized, resulting in greater interoperability among products and improved communication between companies and their users. Currently, the best way to share data securely across an intranet, the Internet, or an extranet is to combine solutions that offer the best of different network layers into one management and security framework. For the financial services industry, that framework should be built around a directed architecture, which is the opposite of an encrypted tunnel, which assumes equal trust on both sides. In most cases, financial services firms should not assume two-way trust because bidirectional connections can be exploited, putting both the visitor and the host network at risk. For example, a credit card company hosting an extranet may be connected to numerous companies at once, some of whom may be in competition. It is in the interest of the visitors and the host network to avoid scenarios that allow one company to connect to the host and then exploit a connection from the host network out to a competitor — essentially to use the extranet as a "hacker's bridge." This can be avoided by implementing a solution that supports only unidirectional connections, which is possible with solutions built using the higher layer, client-server protocols like SOCKS v5.

LOOKING AHEAD

For financial companies wanting to share information globally with a variety of users, extranet-focused solutions can be used to provide powerful management and ironclad security. Financial companies can gain an immediate competitive advantage by using the Internet in a seamless and secure fashion for activities such as loan syndication and providing clients with account information and stock performance reports. By adding management and security to an extranet, companies can easily define which network resources are available to specific users. Extranet solutions that will survive the market's rapid changes will be built on open standards and a modular directed architecture that can easily incorporate the latest technologies.

In short, a top-of-the-line extranet should be easy to use and administer, highly secure, and flexible enough to work with multiple operating systems, protocols, and future markets. If the extranet solution being evaluated can pass this checklist, then the Internet can be used as a revolutionary communications medium for financial brokers, lenders, representatives of credit card companies and banks, and other professionals in every industry.

Author Bio

Evan Kaplan took his vision of a networked world and founded Aventail Corporation, a market-leading provider of Extranet Management and Security (EMS) solutions. He currently serves as the president and CEO, overseeing a company whose revenues have grown exponentially since it was started in February 1996. Prior to Aventail, Kaplan held senior management positions at WRQ, where he spearheaded the Business Development and Strategic Relations team, growing WRQ from $19 million to $111 million in sales. Prior to WRQ, Kaplan was a senior program manager for flight computers with the ELDEC Corporation. He holds an Executive MBA from the University of Washington, the youngest student to graduate from the executive program. He also holds a Master's degree in Organizational Development from Antioch and a B.S. in Environmental Science from Western Washington University.

Chapter 13
Designing a High-Performance, High-Availability Network Infrastructure

Chris Marino

As THE FINANCE INDUSTRY EXPANDS its deployment of open systems and embraces intranet/Internet-based computing, IS teams and network managers face an increasing challenge in ensuring that their company's vital information is readily and constantly available. Beginning in the 1980s through mid-1990s, enterprises have been moving from "legacy" mainframe, SNA, and similar applications to what we'll refer to as "traditional" client-server applications, in order to improve productivity, reduce administrative costs, and provide wider access to corporate data. Today, the latest network and application designs are based on a tiered server deployment which makes use of:

- Database and application servers in the back office.
- HTTP and other open systems which act as middleware to serve data to open, standards-based clients.
- End-user client applications (Exhibit 13-1).

These designs bring new customers directly to Web-based storefronts, more easily disseminate corporate information to employees, increase site performance, and reduce application development costs by adopting open, industry standards. In ensuring constant data accessibility and availability in this new model, the network administrator and CTO must be concerned with more than simple bandwidth allocation.

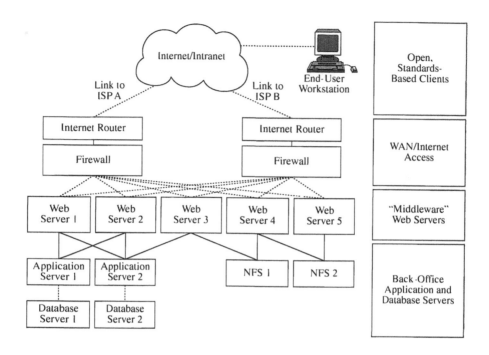

Exhibit 13-1. Areas of focus in evaluating traditional network performance.

While bandwidth is still a metric to be monitored, the more pertinent performance metrics for today's networks are application throughput and application response times.

WAN AND ISP CONSIDERATIONS: SERVICE LEVEL AGREEMENTS AND POLICY-BASED NETWORKS

In the tiered network model, each layer can be analyzed from a performance and reliability perspective. The first level to evaluate is the top level identified in Exhibit 13-1. This level provides access to and from the corporate infrastructure to the Internet or intranet. Considerations at this level involve evaluating Internet Service Provider (ISP) offerings, consideration for multiple points of presence (POPs), and evaluation of hardware solutions. As with all layers, fault tolerance is designed in by eliminating all single points of failure — this applies to Internet, as well as WAN connectivity. The network designer should strongly consider a minimum of two POPs for externally accessible data, as well as multiple access points to the Internet provided via multiple ISPs.

There have been a number of instances where an entire POP goes down due to fire, power outage, user error, or a natural disaster. Existence of a second POP in an alternate location provides enhanced system reliability, and when tied to a traffic management solution, offers the ability to load balance between POPs.

And while it is rare for a service provider to go down system-wide, the reality is that these events do happen. In addition to maintaining redundant links to the Internet via multiple POPs, the network administrator or CTO may wish to consider using multiple ISPs. If a single ISP has a major system outage and cannot route traffic to the Internet, the second POP from the alternate ISP can maintain site availability, allowing network transactions to continue as normal.

ISPs also offer various service levels to address the needs of business customers. Varying service levels can give priority to network traffic for critical applications. To accommodate service-level traffic prioritization, network equipment providers are building more intelligence into their hardware. This intelligence allows individual network components (routers, switches, etc.) to establish and enforce network policies that support the desired service levels. Service levels can be established when the network administrator classifies user groups and priorities, monitors traffic flow, changes traffic patterns to meet response requirements, and prioritizes packets (high priorities for packets involving designated users, video, and other real-time applications; low priorities for e-mail and nonurgent requests).

Establishing guaranteed service levels typically require homogeneous networks comprised of intelligent network devices from a particular vendor. These homogeneous networks, however, are often not suited or capable of optimizing application performance over the heterogeneous networks that make up today's wide-area networks and the Internet.

The answer to the problem of application performance optimization lies beyond intelligent hardware, and centers instead on building intelligence into and throughout the network. Ideally, for thorough optimization, an enterprise-wide, network traffic management solution spans all layers of the network. The solution must not be limited to just the network devices (since these approaches cannot adequately monitor application-level activity) or the application level (where it becomes impractical to incorporate intelligence about the lower levels). Independent of lower-level products and topologies, high-level traffic management tools optimize information flow and the performance of client-server applications by overseeing the entire infrastructure and intelligently allocating each request to the most appropriate resource.

Such a solution can cross over department lines to effectively manage all parts of the infrastructure, and to deliver enterprise-level performance benefits. By monitoring and adjusting overall traffic and application activity, a high-level traffic management solution optimizes corporate productivity. Reliability and high availability of corporate data services and other resources can be maximized by a traffic management solution that monitors the status of individual servers, services, or even points of presence, and reroutes to avoid any trouble spots. The solution must also scale, spanning LANs, WANs, and the Internet to keep pace with corporate growth.

HARDWARE AND APPLICATION-SPECIFIC SOLUTIONS

Today, routers (Layer 3 products) can look at packet information and provide network managers with real-time behavior information needed to enforce policy-based networks and support multiple service levels. Cisco and 3Com have extensive lines of switches, routers, and other network devices which offer various aspects of policy-based networking. Over-provisioning network bandwidth and bandwidth conservation techniques are positioned as methods for managing increasing traffic. However, since the network vendors are building in intelligence at only the device level, their policy-based solutions can not take an enterprise-wide view or include any significant intelligence for evaluating application activity; they strictly focus on packet traffic.

Some router (Layer 3 devices) manufacturers are incorporating Layer 4 functionality into intelligent routers. While this may seem advantageous, this creates a significant problem in secure environments — typical in many financial businesses. In these environments Layer 4 information maybe encrypted (IPSEC), and if routers incorporate Layer 4 functions, the protection offered by encryption is lost at every router in the network. This behavior severely compromises security and sensitive data cannot be adequately protected.

An alternative to hardware intelligence is application-specific embedded intelligence. This short-term bandaid forces application developers to become networking experts and results in less than optimal traffic management solutions. As with hardware-specific solutions, application-specific optimization cannot optimize traffic from end to end. If a POP, router, or Web server goes down, or is overburdened, application-specific optimization cannot redirect traffic, and cannot ensure that data reaches the end user. Neither network devices nor applications can communicate effectively among levels to analyze information from all three tiers and appropriately adjust all network parameters. Standard network equipment may keep traffic flowing, but it does not necessarily direct traffic to the optimal resource or server for the fastest and most reliable access.

Likewise, applications with embedded networking intelligence fail to offer an acceptable solution. Applications-based packages do not adequately consider the traffic within the entire intranet/Internet infrastructure and are not inherently compatible/testable across mixed-vendor environments.

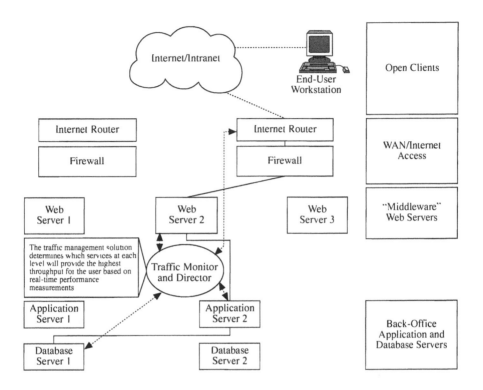

Exhibit 13-2.   Network-wide traffic management solution.

A BETTER SOLUTION

A network design based on multitiered traffic management offers the ideal solution (Exhibit 13-2) for building a high-performance Internet and intranet infrastructure. A sophisticated software-based solution can deliver traffic prioritization, load-balancing, and service-level availability, ensuring optimized end-to-end performance on a high-availability network.

Stated most simply, these software solutions optimize, coordinate, and manage TCP traffic across all three levels — WAN, server, and application. The software intelligently performs in heterogeneous environments and will accommodate the inevitable change to and growth of the infrastructure.

Solutions in this space are dominated by companies whose sole focus is on providing these capabilities. When evaluating software traffic management solutions, consider the following criteria:

WAN-based scheduling — This product or module should direct requests to the POP that offers the best performance at that time for the end user initiating the request. For optimal performance, the WAN scheduler should service requests based on at least three metrics: current client-server latencies, real-time server load, and server availability. A robust WAN scheduler lets network administrators and ISPs easily establish traffic policies and priorities, as well as guarantee high availability and high performance to users on the distributed network.

Server-level scheduling — This component of the traffic management solution lets IT organizations deploy multiserver environments that are highly responsive to client requests. Each site should appear to users as a single virtual site, even though its servers may actually be distributed across subnets and firewalls. Software-based server-level scheduling optimizes the use of server resources to respond to TCP requests. More than a simple load-balancing product, this software should provide immunity to server failure by detecting problems and redirecting traffic, without requiring dedicated hardware that would introduce a new point of failure.

Application server scheduling — Application servers deliver critical user programs such as database and other business management services. An intelligent application dispatcher can coordinate server resources to respond as efficiently as possible to client requests for applications. As with other scheduling components, the application dispatcher should be transparent to users. It should support uninterrupted service, giving priority requests the highest attention. To manage resources for the wide variety of individual application programs used throughout an enterprise, this scheduler should support all industry-standard application interfaces.

Although some vendors offer one or two of these functions, the optimal software solution integrates all three levels, providing the highest infrastructure performance possible while requiring the least amount of intervention from the IT staff. Real-time feedback from network resource monitoring should provide the basis for dynamic traffic allocation and policy updates that will help keep critical business operations running smoothly.

Exhibit 13-2 illustrates how a total traffic management solution can operate. By analyzing directly or in conjunction with server-based agents the traffic "director" determines application throughput end-to-end from the user's workstation to a database or application server and back. Based on measurable criteria including response time, CPU utilization, server availability, WAN/Internet latency, and other specified rules or policies, the director (with backup director) can ensure that data are available in the shortest time. A traditional implementation simply accounting for device "hop count" does not consider application server attributes (CPU utilization, open sessions, or server load) or rapidly changing WAN attributes (latency, response times, and POP availability).

Additionally, all software components should blend as seamlessly as possible into the existing environment. For example, traffic scheduling services should be running from any location on the network. As the network changes or grows, the software should easily scale to accommodate the changes, without requiring complex modifications or installations. A Java-based management GUI can simplify operation and reduces the requirements for special IT training.

A powerful multitiered software networking solution benefits everyone accessing data on the corporate infrastructure. The right architecture also helps IT administrators, Web masters, and CIOs tasked with creating and managing the network. Not to be overlooked, the software-based solution enables more efficient allocation of hardware assets. Rather than over-allocating hardware to ensure availability and data redundancy, IT organizations can distribute hardware in the manner best suited to the usage patterns of users.

SUMMARY

Careful consideration of the issues presented will help you design the right long-term solution and avoid some costly short-lived investments. The following four basic steps will keep you heading in the right direction:

1. Deploy or upgrade network segments and backbones to the highest-speed technologies appropriate.
2. Incorporate redundant systems at every level in the network, including Internet/WAN access, "middleware" web servers, and back-office database, file, and application servers. A single point of failure at any one level of the network obviates the benefits established by redundant systems at every other level in the network.
3. Select hardware products with embedded intelligence, which can accommodate policy-based service-level networking and work in homogeneous (mixed-vendor) environments.
4. Incorporate traffic management solutions into your infrastructure, choosing those that support the features discussed in this chapter — features that will ensure long-term solutions in a dynamic, heterogeneous environment.

By designing a network which includes the latest in traffic management solutions, the CIO and MIS department will ensure users will always have rapid access to corporate data resources, while minimizing investment in additional infrastructure purchases.

Author Bio

Chris Marino *has over 14 years experience designing, implementing, and marketing hardware and software systems. Prior to founding Resonate, Marino was the Director of Product*

Marketing at nCUBE, a manufacturer of parallel-processing video server systems. Before joining nCUBE, Marino was Product Line Manager at MIPS Computer Systems where he was responsible for the company's line of high-end multiprocessor server systems. He also held design engineering positions at Zycad and Bell Laboratories. Marino has published/presented several papers and articles on RISC technology and interactive multimedia and is a co-inventor of the company's patent-pending resource-based scheduling technology. Marino holds a B.S.E.E. from Columbia University, an MS EE/CS from the University of California at Berkeley, and an MBA from Stanford University.

Chapter 14
Applications of GIS Technology in Financial Services

Donald F. Cooke

MANY YEARS AGO, when asked why he robbed banks, Willy Sutton replied, "Because that's where the money is." Bankers and other financial services managers who deal with consumers also need to know where the money is. Do you know who your most profitable customers are? Do you know where they live? Can you locate other people like them? While you know where your branches and ATMs are, do you know where your biggest competitive threat is? How many of your customers live nearer to a competitor than one of your branches? What is the most promising location for a new ATM or branch?

GIS — the science of where — is the key to answering these questions. GIS (Geographic Information Systems) is a technology that allows computers to deal with location: where your customers are, where the competition is, and where the best prospects are located. This chapter describes how GIS works and how it can help you improve profitability and productivity.

GIS

Geographic information, which has been stored on paper maps for centuries, can be encoded and processed in computers. Since the mid-1960s GIS technology has developed from a government research tool to a maturing discipline which can have a direct, positive effect on the operations and profitability of financial institutions.

GIS works because computers can now analyze maps — stored as databases — as easily as they can compute a payroll. What makes GIS work for businesses is a detailed nationwide computer map database called TIGER, which is maintained and distributed by the Census Bureau along with census data. TIGER provides the computer with the same locational knowledge as is shown on a very detailed street map. TIGER and GIS allow the

0-8493-9834-7/00/$0 00+$.50
© 2000 by CRC Press LLC

computer to pinpoint each bank account and calculate market penetration and driving distance from each account to any bank facility.

Two decades ago, GIS was an exotic discipline reserved for hardy pioneers with big budgets for computer time and expensive plotters to display maps. Nevertheless, by the late 1970s, hundreds of large banks measured branch performance, market penetration, and customer demographics using rudimentary GIS techniques, even if the analysis only took the form of counting customers and products sold by Census Tract.

In the 1980s government regulators effectively mandated GIS use through CRA and HMDA reporting compliance requirements. CRA and HMDA reports are actually GIS applications: locating and summarizing various types of bank product use by census tract areas.

Nowadays, a $799 computer from Staples provides more power than the leading innovators had available 20 years ago. Since GIS technology can consume a lot of computing resources, the advent of powerful and inexpensive personal computers is a welcome development.

But you need more than a powerful computer to benefit from GIS. A computer doesn't do anything but consume electricity if you don't have useful software to run on it. Though you can buy wonderful GIS software packages capable of unlocking strategically useful information from operational data, it takes an experienced, technically oriented specialist to operate most of this software.

This is the state of adoption of GIS technology as the 1990s draws to a close; plenty of computing power, plenty of GIS software, lots of opportunity for benefit, but because of technical complexity, only a glimmer of true usability of GIS technology by banks. However, changes in the GIS industry will shortly make GIS an inexpensive and rewarding technology for even very small community banks.

SITUATION

Banks today operate in an environment of unprecedented threats and opportunities. Big banks can take advantage of economies of scale and expand their influence with strategic acquisitions. Small banks can use their knowledge of the community they serve, either to compete effectively against their larger competitors or to preen and position themselves for acquisition.

All banks need strategic information to operate effectively. Knowledge of many aspects of a bank's operations is essential for survival. Each bank's CEO or marketing officer should be constantly asking: Are my products priced right? Who are my most valuable customers? Where do they live? What are we doing to retain them? Can we upgrade our middle tier of customers and make them more profitable? Can we change product offerings or pricing to reduce the liability of lower-tier customers? Are our branches strategically sited relative to where our customers live and work and drive? Where should we open the next branch or ATM? Many of these questions can be answered by GIS technology.

Applying GIS technology to banking is a bit like cooking a meal: you need the right mix of ingredients and processes. The main ingredient of GIS analysis is the bank's own data. In fact, much of the value of GIS technology lies in revealing patterns of profit and opportunity from operational data. GIS works by processing routine operational data in ways that will reveal a bank's profit patterns.

The second key ingredient is the computerized street map of your area. This is essential for the "geocoding" process, for calculating driving access to banking facilities, and to permit visualization of geographic relationships in map form. While some business GIS users find the public-domain TIGER street maps sufficient, most use a privately maintained one like Dynamap/2000 from Geographic Data Technology, Lebanon, NH. Having a current and complete digital street map is especially important for processing bank customers who live on relatively new streets.

The other essential ingredients are commercially available data about households, businesses, and banking facilities:

- Household data, for example, R.L. Polk's TotaList file, are compiled from many sources such as vehicle and product warrantee registrations. TotaList serves dual purposes as a source of household prospects and the key to obtaining a demographic profile of your customers. While it's customary to profile customers by geographic areas like tracts and block-groups, it's clearly worthwhile to discriminate between the 300-odd households in a block-group by using the power of a household-level database like TotaList
- Business files, from Dun & Bradstreet (D&B) or American Business Information (ABI) provide commercial prospects and profiling information for commercial accounts. Finally, bank information, available from Thompson or Sheshunoff, is the key to analyzing competition.

THE PROCESSES

Several key processes cook these data ingredients into a nutritious strategic marketing meal.

The most important process is a well-calibrated profitability model. Good models go far beyond "Fed Functional Costs," and use all aspects of fee and interest income in balance with cost of funds and transactions of various types. It may be a surprise that the pricing model does not have to balance with the General Ledger to be useful. It is essential to be able to rank accounts from most to least profitable, based on accurate calculations.

The next essential process is householding. Householding allows the computer to pull together various different accounts for each household, based on similarities of name and address along with other clues such as social security number and telephone number. Householding allows the computer to consider all accounts owned by a household and calculate an aggregate profitability ranking at the household level.

The same householding process also matches customer households to TotaList households. This provides two benefits: customer profiling by appending TotaList's household-level demographic and lifestyle codes to customers, and identifying and tagging Totalist households which are already the bank's customers. This step automatically "merge-purges" the prospect file so you can prospect for new households excluding existing customers.

The GIS process is "geocoding," where each customer and prospect address is matched to the proper spot on the digital street map. Each address receives a unique latitude/longitude coordinate value which locks it into its place on the face of the earth. Geocoding is the foundation of GIS technology. Once all addresses have been geocoded, the power of GIS technology can be unleashed.

Finally come the GIS and analytical processes. GIS technology can show you graphically where profits are coming from and where you're losing money. GIS can define the areas of influence of your branches and those of your competitors. GIS can identify territorial advantages and weaknesses, suggesting opportunities to site new facilities or pointing out where your own branches are competing with each other. Best of all, GIS can identify areas where potentially profitable households are clustered so your marketing efforts can lure new accounts to your bank.

ACTION OR ANALYSIS?

Too often, banks and consultants use GIS technology just for analysis. While it is useful to find out about a bank through the window of GIS, if that's all that is done, the GIS becomes simply a cost burden. The analysis must lead to action if the bank is to improve its operations.

All productive use of GIS must begin with an understanding of the actions a bank can take to make changes in operations. GIS can support a wide array of decisions and actions: opening and closing branches, siting new ATMs, targeting a direct mail campaign, evaluating merger and acquisition opportunities, and selecting new prospects near a branch or in neighborhoods with high profit potential.

A banker who considers these actions in full knowledge of product profitability, cross-sell opportunity, competitive strengths and weaknesses, and other strategic factors, will outperform a banker who operates by the seat of his pants. The key is knowledgeable action, where the spatial dimension is understood and considered. Business reengineering may be necessary and it may take months to create a sales culture, but without strategic marketing knowledge, actions may just be random or futile.

Bankers should not underestimate the cost, complexity, and risks of plunging into GIS. While a fair amount of data, software, and computer power must be acquired, the main cost of a GIS operation will be staff time. Unfortunately, GIS competence is a scarce resource, and banks may have trouble recruiting or growing GIS personnel, or — worse — they may find that staff turnover gets hard to manage as GIS specialists "graduate" to higher paying jobs at other organizations.

GIS is not just another systems area that a typical IT department can acquire and master, though support of a GIS effort by IT will be essential to its success. GIS remains largely a strategic marketing function and the expertise and technology should reside there. Because of its technical nature and the day-to-day demands of running a small bank, until recently GIS has been used mainly by the largest banks, with occasional application in smaller banks through the efforts of consultants.

Everybody has seen computerized maps in various forms, from animated weather maps on TV to PC-based street maps and trip planners such as Expedia Streets '98 from Microsoft or StreetFinder from Rand-McNally. Why shouldn't GIS technology be as accessible to bankers as these mapping products are to consumers?

Geographic Information Systems is a technology that is emerging from the early adopters and is inching its way into mainstream conservative markets. Given the pressure on financial institutions of all sizes, GIS analysis leading to strategic action is likely to become a staple of bank operations in the next decade.

Author Bio

Donald F. Cooke is one of the pioneers in GIS, having been a member of the Census Bureau team that developed methodology used to computerize street maps in the 1960s. At his first company, now Harte-Hanks Data Technology, Cooke served some of the first banks that used GIS technology: Manufacturer's Hanover Trust, Wells Fargo, Bankers Trust, Security Pacific, and others. In the mid-1970s this company produced the first compliance reports, forerunners of today's HMDA and CRA work. His second company, Geographic Data Technology, is the leading supplier of premium digital street maps for GIS analysis. He is the founder and CEO of Medici, a new company concentrating on bringing GIS technology to community banks.

Chapter 15

Designing and Implementing a Virus Prevention Policy in Financial Services Organizations: Key Issues and Critical Needs

Pat Bitton

COMPUTER MANAGERS IN FINANCIAL SERVICES COMPANIES realize that computer viruses are a major threat to information security. Many have found that virus infection can be costly in time, resources, and productivity. But all too many do not know what to do about the threat of viruses. Before developing a company policy that addresses their security concerns, many computer managers want to know what questions they should be asking as well as what issues they should address.

This chapter provides a step-by-step process for developing corporate anti-virus policies by highlighting virus entry points in a company network, identifying key issues, and listing tasks. Products, people, and procedures are discussed, with an eye toward protecting companies from viruses transmitted via electronic file exchange — by far the most common method of virus distribution today. Using this chapter as a guide, computer managers in the financial services industry can tailor an anti-virus policy to their company's specific needs.

0-8493-9834-7/00/$0 00+$.50
© 2000 by CRC Press LLC

BACKGROUND

Computer viruses are a major threat to information security in all companies, but are of special concern to financial services companies. In fact, many large financial services companies based in the U.S. are currently investing heavily in reliable and secure electronic commerce and home banking applications all over the globe.

As viruses become more prevalent, the threat becomes more real, with somewhere between 8000 and 20,000 viruses existing in the world today. According to a survey released in April 1997 by the International Computer Security Association (ICSA), formerly the National Computer Security Association, almost every medium- and large-size organization in North America has experienced at least one computer virus infection firsthand. The survey also indicated that about 40 percent of all computers used in the surveyed companies would experience another virus infection within a year.[1]

Computer viruses (any program or code that replicates itself) are insidious. Without virus detection or protection, users typically do not know their systems are being infected until they see results that can range from annoying to catastrophic. And virus infection is on the rise. Despite a significant increase in the usage of anti-virus products, the incidence of computer virus infection in corporate America nearly tripled in 1996.[1]

Although several factors are behind the rise in computer virus infection, the main one is the meteoric rise in popularity and use of the Internet in business. The Internet can be thought of as an information highway — an evolving global electronic mode of communicating, providing information, and obtaining information. Two important ways of enabling this communication are e-mail for exchanging mail, and the file transfer protocol (FTP) for exchanging files. Growing at a staggering rate, the Internet is an unprecedented link between more people in more countries than ever before.

But along with these Internet capabilities comes a major problem. As the Internet becomes more popular as an e-mail and file transfer medium, users are at a growing risk from the many viruses that can be spread via e-mail attachments and FTP downloading/uploading. The ICSA survey reports that e-mail attachments as a source of infection tripled from 1996 to 1997 — from 9 percent of all infection sources to over 26 percent of infections. At the same time, virus infection via downloading of files from the Internet increased from 10 percent of all infections to 16 percent.[1]

To make matters worse, a relatively new class of viruses, called macro viruses, are now taking advantage of widespread Internet usage to spread like wildfire. In fact, these viruses are spreading faster than most anti-virus software makers can find ways to detect and remove them. Macro viruses are now the most prevalent form of computer virus in the world, representing 80 percent of all infections in North America in 1997, compared to 49 percent a year ago.[1]

This prevalence is largely due to the new way in which they spread. Because they are written in Microsoft® Visual BASIC, they can insert themselves into the macros used in word processor and spreadsheet documents, which often are transmitted as e-mail attachments. And now, a new type of malicious code, carried by ActiveX and Java controls that spice up web pages, poses the potential for PC damage simply by users browsing the web.

Before widespread Internet popularity, viruses spread slowly from one part of the world to another. For example, the Michelangelo virus that appeared in Asia in 1991 did not appear prominently in Europe until 1992 and the U.S. 1 year later. Today, viruses migrate much faster than this rate of one continent per year. The Concept macro virus that became prominent in the U.S. in August 1995 appeared in Asia only 2 months later. On the Internet, an e-mail attachment alone can transmit a virus from one country to another in less than a minute, and the number of files now transmitted through the Internet each year may number in the billions.

What this means is that if you do not have an anti-virus security policy, you need one, because inaction can be costly. Depending on the size of the infection, a virus infection incident can cost between $2000 and $500,000 in data loss and loss of productivity.[2] One study showed that the average cost of recovering from a virus infection on a network is $15,000 and that 85 percent of those sites were reinfected within 30 days.[2] You can estimate the cost of an e-mail virus infection at your company using the attached Excel worksheet.[3]

PRODUCTS, PEOPLE, AND PROCEDURES

Certainly, products such as anti-virus software are needed to thwart computer viruses. But even product vendors agree that, while a valuable part of the puzzle, products alone do not solve problems. People do. And if people understand the need for virus protection and the benefits of that protection, they are more likely to take appropriate steps. Defining these specific operational steps, "procedures" completes the triad. Through procedures, people make best use of available products to achieve the goal of comprehensive virus protection.

Exhibit 15-1 illustrates the important distinction between procedures and overall corporate policy. Charles Cresson Wood, an independent information-security consultant, defines policy as "high level statements intended to provide guidance to those who make decisions ... typically including general statements of goals, objectives, beliefs, ethics, and responsibilities."[4] Conversely, Wood defines procedures as "specific operational steps

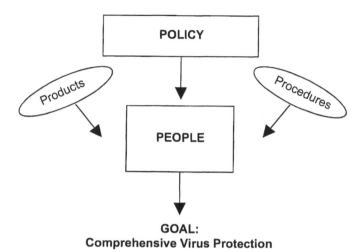

Exhibit 15-1. Products, people, and procedures are needed to thwart computer viruses.

that workers must take to achieve goals — goals which are often outlined in the policy."[4] Hence, any discussion of a corporate policy must also address procedures — the way the policy is to be implemented.

VIRUS ENTRYWAYS

The most effective way to ensure that your internal network remains virus-free is to monitor all entryways for viruses. While a detailed treatment of these entryways is beyond the scope of this chapter, Exhibit 15-2 illustrates virus entry points: through Internet gateways, groupware and intranet servers, LAN servers, and desktops.

THE HUMAN ELEMENT

The key players, and of course, the ultimate target, in an anti-virus policy are the users and managers inside the company. Understanding the attitudes of the company's staff towards information exchange and an awareness of the history of virus infection and corresponding action taken will go a long way towards enabling you to understand your organization's unique "corporate culture." And this understanding is critical to the ultimate development of a policy that is right for your company. Two companies with different corporate cultures are likely to develop different policies. And beyond policy development, these two companies may very well implement their policies in different ways.

220

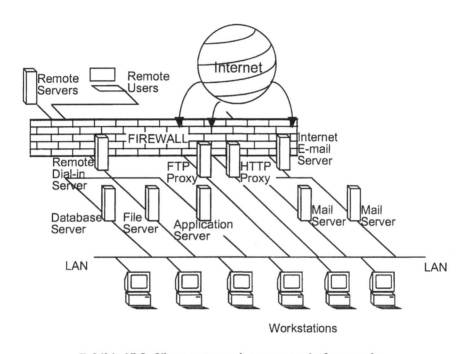

Exhibit 15-2. Virus entry points on a typical network.

Let's examine two very different company cultures and how their approaches to virus protection policies are closely linked to those cultures.

Company A, which grew quickly from a small banking firm to a medium-sized one, is quite open with its data and information. Few, if any, procedures have been established regarding information exchange, either between employees or with those outside the company. Moreover, resistance to formalized procedures is high, as the company fosters a relaxed working environment as an alternative to the typical office environment of its competitors.

So far, Company A has been lucky. Its only virus experience has been a couple of isolated run-ins with a relatively benign macro virus that was quickly eliminated from a floppy disk that had come in from an outside client. The employee had recently installed desktop anti-virus software that was able to detect the virus on the floppy before it could be copied to a hard disk. Both the employee and management reacted calmly to the virus detection, and no disciplinary action was regarded as necessary.

MIS professionals at Company A face the challenge of a workforce that is highly resistant to the kinds of procedures they view as necessary to reduce the virus threat. Employee motivation to act is low, since they have not experienced the stress and frustration of recovering from a major infection. Company A needs a campaign to promote awareness of the virus threat, reinforced by high-level corporate commitment for this endeavor. Orientations and training seminars for all employees on the virus threat and of measures to be taken to minimize it, both initially and later to remind them of the need for compliance, will go a long way toward elevating their knowledge and understanding.

Through this education process, Company A employees will learn that they can retain their relaxed working environment by taking a few simple precautions and following some procedures that require little time. Company A also needs a highly visible show of support by top management for efforts to minimize virus infection from the beginning of the policy adoption process. This can be done most easily by placing a management statement of support upfront on the anti-virus policy document.

In contrast, Company B is an established stock trading organization, with conservative employees. Company B's employees are accustomed to rules and regulations, and have come to value them for their assistance in minimizing problems. Most aspects of employee tasks are carefully organized to maximize productivity. The company has encountered macro viruses several times, without resulting in any major loss of productivity. But recently, Company B was infected by a virus received via an e-mail attachment from one of their customers that cost them considerable loss of productivity over several days. The employee who received the virus, but for whatever reason did not detect it, feared he would lose his job, and management was upset over the incident.

Company B requires less training on the need for an anti-virus policy, but more emphasis on how to implement such a policy. Less computer savvy than their counterparts in Company A, Company B employees need periodic training to learn how to combat the threat. They are already motivated to comply with procedures, given their virus encounters, and they would have no problem in adapting to the inclusion of one more set of procedures in their work environment.

PUTTING IT TOGETHER WITH PROCEDURES

While the approach taken in developing an anti-virus policy is likely to vary from company to company, some issues must be addressed in all cases — issues best addressed with a corporate policy that includes specific procedures. For example, procedures are needed for making best use of selected product and service solutions, such as how to install and set up software to take advantage of automatic configuration and deployment, how to customize the level of protection appropriately for different types of users and, most importantly, how to ensure that regular updates are obtained and deployed to all the workstations. New viruses are appearing at a rate of 250 or more every month. Operating too long without virus pattern updates unnecessarily exposes your company to new viruses "in the wild" — particularly when product families like Trend Micro's can deliver these updates to fit your schedules, in the background without interrupting work, and use a single file to update both server and workstation-based protection.

But procedures go beyond product and service solutions. Procedures must address how new behaviors can be integrated into corporate culture to replace past practices that may have exposed the company to viruses. While centralized, server-based virus protection is important, it must be supplemented by commitment from the workforce to ensure a virus-free environment.

One way to encourage this distributed responsibility is to establish a virus response team. Similar to an emergency response team or other cross-disciplinary group in an organization, a virus response team can be assembled from many different departments, then trained and empowered to deal calmly, effectively, and professionally with any virus incident. One advantage of such a team is that when an incident does occur, specific people are already selected to immediately tackle cleanup. Of equal importance, providing team members with a specific identity and status sends a message to all employees that virus protection is important and that it involves more than "the guys in MIS." Another way to draw attention to an anti-virus policy after its adoption is to periodically review and revise it to reflect changing conditions. An annual review is usually sufficient and serves to reinforce an important issue that may not have been discussed for some time.

One particularly sensitive issue is dealing with policy noncompliance. The key is to foster an environment that encourages personal (and group) responsibility and that rewards honesty. Consider, for example, an employee who promptly reports the appearance of a virus on his or her machine, probably because of downloaded unauthorized software from the Web. If this is a first-time occurrence for this individual, a formal meeting to discuss and reinforce anti-virus policy and procedures is appropriate, but further disciplinary action would discourage prompt reporting of virus incidents, allowing viruses to potentially spread unchecked through an organization. Of course, repeat offenses would call for more stringent actions. The idea is that failure to comply with anti-virus policy and procedures should be treated in a manner consistent with violations of other company policies.

Using the two hypothetical companies described in the previous section, Company A employees who detect a virus would probably not suffer an overreaction from management to a virus detection. Dismissal would not be considered for a first-time offender. Promoting awareness of the potential magnitude of the virus threat would promote understanding of the seriousness of violating anti-virus policy.

Conversely, managers at Company B might consider dismissing an employee who violated an anti-virus policy and cost the company significant loss of productivity, even if it was a first offense. At this company, taking advantage of the situation to demonstrate to others that management encourages virus reporting would reinforce anti-virus procedures and have a more positive impact than dismissing the employee.

CONCLUSIONS

It is recommended that you address a series of issues before developing an anti-virus policy. These issues can be captured in the form of questions organized in three groups — corporate culture, anti-virus product/service status and use, and virus incident history. These questions encourage you to address issues specific to your company, enabling you to tailor an anti-virus policy to meet your company's unique needs and situation, and are shown below:

Corporate Culture

1. How would you characterize the openness of information exchange in your organization?
2. Are your employees open or resistant to formalized procedures?
3. Do any formalized procedures exist that regulate information exchange in your company? If so, to what extent do they explicitly address virus protection?
4. Has management made any mention of anti-virus policy or procedures in formal announcements to employees? Any mention of other security issues?
5. Do new employees sign an agreement that includes any mention of anti-virus policy? If so, what are employees' responsibilities?
6. Does your company have a virus response team? If so, what are their responsibilities? How widely is it represented across the company? Are team members given a different status in any way?

Product/Service Status and Use

1. What anti-virus products or services does your company currently employ?
2. What virus entryways are protected with anti-virus products or services? (Refer to Exhibit 15-2 for virus entryways.)
3. Are anti-virus software products periodically updated? If so, how often?

Virus History

1. Has your company experienced any virus incidents? If so, how many in the last year?
2. What type of impact did the infection(s) have on operations?
3. How widespread within the company was knowledge of the incident(s)?
4. How did the employee(s) who reported the incident(s) react? Did they downplay its importance or were they highly concerned?
5. How did management react to the incident(s)? Was any disciplinary action taken against the employee(s)?

The policy you develop must integrate anti-virus products/services, people, and procedures in a manner consistent with your corporate culture, mission, and goals. The resulting policy must be clear, concise, and consistent with other corporate policies. Several references contain suggested outlines of security policies, which can be used as a model for your anti-virus policy.[4-6]

Exhibit 15-3 lists the steps necessary to address issues prior to policy development: develop a policy, maximize the chances of its successful implementation, and periodically review and reinforce it. After policy development, review, revision, approval, and distribution, further steps might include developing an anti-virus procedure manual, assembling and empowering a virus response team, upgrading anti-virus product/service use, and beginning an employee awareness campaign.

Anti-Virus Policy Development and Adoption Tasks

1. Assess corporate culture.
2. Evaluate current anti-virus product/service use.
3. Review corporate virus history.
4. Draft policy.
5. Review and revise draft anti-virus policy.
6. Approve and distribute anti-virus policy.
7. Draft, review, revise, approve, and distribute anti-virus procedure manual.
8. Name members of virus response team.
9. Upgrade anti-virus product/service use.
10. Begin employee awareness campaign.
11. Periodically review and revise anti-virus policy.
12. Periodically reinforce importance of policy.

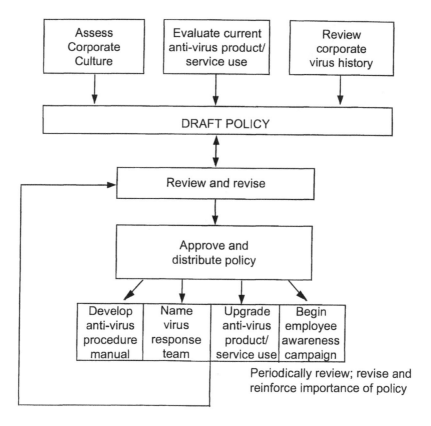

Exhibit 15-3. Effective virus prevention goes beyond anti-virus policy development.

Notes

1. ICSA(r) 1997. Computer Virus Prevalence Survey, International Computer Security Association, available at http://www.antivirus.com/corporate/white/index.htm.
2. Dataquest Survey, 1994.
3. Cost Analysis: Return on Investment, Trend Micro worksheet, www.antivirus.com/products/vcost.html.
4. Policies From the Ground Up. Charles Cresson Wood, *Infosecurity News,* March/April 1997, pp. 24–28.
5. Trend Micro Delivers the First Free On-line Virus Scanning Service, Trend Micro press release, May 7, 1997.
6. Policy Format and Structure. Gerald W. Grindler, *Infosecurity News,* March/April 1997, p. 29.

Author Bio

Pat Bitton has extensive experience in the anti-virus industry. In 1990, she joined the (then) small UK anti-virus publisher, S&S International, developers of Dr. Solomon's AntiVirus Toolkit and set up their U.K. marketing and channel programs; directed the company's international business development effort; and in 1995, led their overseas investment in sales and marketing — S&S Software International, Inc. — outside Boston, MA. In 1995 she moved to Symantec, where she was the market development manager with responsibility for strategic marketing across Symantec's anti-virus line. She has been with Trend since late 1996.

Chapter 16
Voice Over ATM

Gary Mangus

FOR ANY NATIONAL OR GLOBAL INDUSTRY dependent on quality and current communications, the push has begun to migrate to wide area networks (or WANs). The communication speed and delivery using legacy equipment is one of the keys to deploying any new network technology. Asynchronous Transfer Mode networking, or ATM, has been around about 5 years. It is gaining momentum in the present for its ability to handle large amounts of traffic and to really deliver the traffic. IP and frame relay networks have been the buzz of the communications industry, but these network protocols are revolutionary by design — there are no guarantees of service in quality of transmission or in delivery of the communication.

So the argument in new network technologies, like ATM, becomes more focused. Why migrate to a new type of network when it lessens the quality plus there are risks of losing transmitted communications? This argument becomes more heated when talking about "voice" traffic being transmitted over a data network. Most companies are accustomed to having the computer network go "down," but a voice network — no way!

This chapter will provide an overview of Voice over ATM and why this technology should be deployed today. The answer is not a technical one, but is strongly supported financially. ATM provides the quality of service like no other new network can. The financial community depends on networking much like the U.S. Government — it functions because of the information available. Financial institutions, whether a regional banking operation to a finance company or Wall Street brokerage house, have more remote sites to connect. The larger the operations center, the more likely multiple T1/E1(or even higher-speed) leased lines are involved. This chapter will discuss networks where ATM is already available for the data side of the network and the voice network has remained separate.

INTRODUCTION

If your campus or enterprise network already has an ATM network installed it may only be serving the data communications needs of your organization. Because ATM is equally adept at supporting video, voice, and data, the maximum utilization of your network can become a cost factor in today's communications decisions. Whether your ATM network is installed or simply under consideration, many vendors offer ATM network managers a unique opportunity to send voice over ATM while providing substantial savings on operational dollars through the reduction or elimination of leased lines dedicated to voice traffic.

One of the key ATM applications for an ATM switch or multiplexer is the consolidation of voice traffic over ATM by interconnecting multiple PBXs across an ATM network. To address this application, a business case is made in this chapter for using DS1/E1 Circuit Emulation — available in ATM switches as an additional module or in ATM access multiplexers, which allow for provisioning of other network interfaces.

TODAY'S ENVIRONMENT

Today's typical customer will have multiple site operations or multiple buildings on a campus. In many cases, data and voice requirements will be large enough to require more than one T1/E1 leased line between sites. These network sites can be categorized into two broad groups.

The first organization has islands of ATM networks in place for its data needs. To connect these ATM islands, it may have an ATM WAN or it may be using one or more leased lines (T1/E1 or greater) for the interconnectivity across the WAN. It may also be using additional T1/E1 leased lines for interconnecting PBXs between its sites. In other words, multiple networks may already be in place to support different services. Exhibit 16-1 is a representative example configuration.

The second organization has no ATM networks installed, but has multiple T1/E1 leased lines in place between sites to support its voice and data traffic. Exhibit 16-2 is a representative example configuration. Both organizations can be better served with a voice consolidation solution, provided there is a need for multiple site interconnection.

PBX ENVIRONMENTAL DESCRIPTION

To provide a solution for voice consolidation over ATM, the Circuit Emulation (or CE) module will interface to a PBX. A PBX, which is a small telephone switch, will have analog (or digital) connections to individual telephone handsets within a facility. These handsets are connected to the public telephone network through the PBX, via a digital trunk which is typically at the T1/E1 rate of 1.544 Mbps or E1 rate at 2.048 Mbps. Depending upon the size of the PBX and the number of calls to be supported simultaneously by the PBX, multiple T1/E1 trunks may be used to connect the PBX to the public telephone network. Exhibit 16-3 illustrates a PBX environment with one T1/E1 trunk attached to the public telephone network. If your organization has multiple sites, refer to the telephone network in Exhibit 16-4.

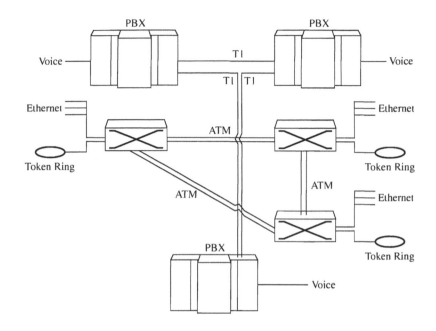

Exhibit 16-1.   Multiple ATM networks.

The ATM CE Module makes practical the transport over ATM of a class of services called Constant-Bit-Rate (CBR). CBR sources are characterized as devices which generate traffic at a constant or nonvarying rate. A typical device which requires CBR service is a PBX. Exhibit 16-4 illustrates the telephone network in an organization with multiple sites.

Other types of communications equipment which require CBR service, and therefore can benefit in the same way with ATM, are T1/E1 multiplexers and channel banks.

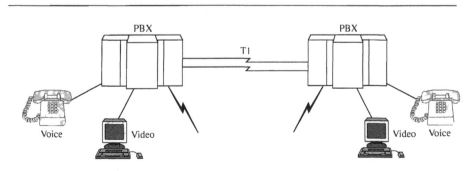

Exhibit 16-2.   No ATM networks, multiple T1/E1 leased lines.

231

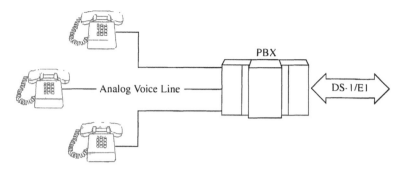

Exhibit 16-3.   PBX environment with one T1/E1 trunk.

BUSINESS CASE ANALYSIS

Exactly how much can you save by consolidating your leased lines? If you already have or are planning to use ATM for data communications, then you may save all of the costs that are now being spent on leased lines for voice. In this case, the cost for deploying ATM is already absorbed in the data communications infrastructure. By adding PBX transport for voice to your data-only network, you can further enhance the justification for the ATM network because the costs for the T1/E1 leased lines for handling the PBX traffic are eliminated. Even if you don't have an ATM network installed for data, the time is right to consider ATM for interconnecting PBXs. Voice over ATM is a solid financial business decision.

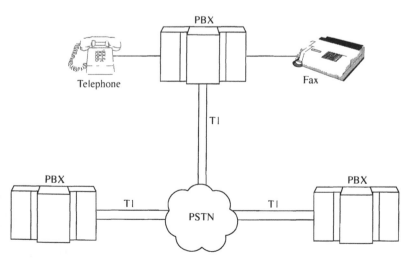

Exhibit 16-4.   PBX network with multiple sites.

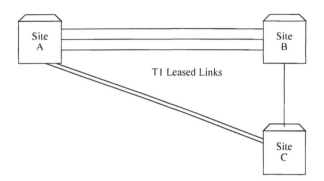

Exhibit 16-5.   Three-node leased line network.

Local service providers charge variable ATM service rates depending upon your region of the country. The financial advantage of moving to a consolidated system is based upon the difference between your current costs for existing T1/E1 leased lines and ATM implementation costs. This difference reflects your monthly operational savings achieved when you deploy an ATM network.

A simple three-node system may help to illustrate the comparative process. The example below represents a case where you may wish to eliminate costly leased lines being used for voice traffic and replace them with an ATM network. The current leased line network may look like the example in Exhibit 16-5.

Exhibit 16-6 demonstrates how the three-node network of Exhibit 16-5 may be connected over an ATM infrastructure that requires only one ATM drop per site.

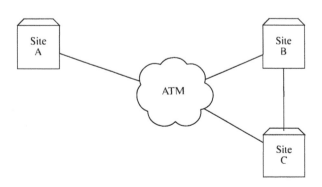

Exhibit 16-6.   One ATM drop/site network.

Exhibit 16-7. Cost of an ATM Line

Site Connection	# of T1/E1 Lines Replaced	T1/E1 Line Cost per Month	Extended Cost per Month	ATM Line Cost per Month
A-B	3	$2500	$7500	$4200
B-C	2	$2500	$5000	$4200
A-C	1	$2500	$2500	$4200
		Total	$15,000	$12,600

U.S. COST ANALYSIS

Although the specific cost for a T1/E1 leased line may vary from region to region, a typical monthly fee is $2500 per line, per month. Similarly, a typical ATM line cost for an OC-3c is $4200 per month. The financial analysis is summarized in Exhibit 16-7.

Therefore, in this analysis, it is evident that your operational cost savings per month is $2400 and you can recover the cost of the Circuit Emulation equipment in about 18 months. This example illustrates the minimal PBX interconnection network only. If you are interested in replacing more T1/E1 circuits in your network, the payback period decreases dramatically.

Exhibit 16-7 demonstrates a process to compare operational cost savings for an ATM solution that consolidates T1/E1 leased lines based on voice traffic alone. If your application uses T1/E1 leased lines to support data communications requirements, the total cost of the ATM solution would remain the same and the operational savings would increase even more substantially.

FUTURE PROOF

Without question, ATM will be the basis upon which communications will be built in the future. It represents the first practical solution for integrating voice, data, and video information onto the same network. An investment in ATM today will be an investment in tomorrow's technology.

Benefits of the Circuit Emulation for Voice over ATM

Flexibility. Structured and unstructured circuit emulation service is available from most vendors. Support for structured emulation enables users with PBXs or any other channelized services such as T1/E1 multiplexers and channel banks to be connected across PVCs on an ATM network. Unstructured services are suitable for the transport of signals from video codecs or other equipment with unchannelized interfaces where nonstandard framing is used by the end equipment.

Minimize ATM Bandwidth. Rather than sending a full T1/E1 bandwidth over the ATM network, which is the case with unstructured service, the user can save ATM bandwidth by sending only the T1/E1 time slots that are actually needed to support the desired service.

Save on Leased Line Costs. With up to 4 to 8 ports available on most modules, networks with private PBX transport between sites may be consolidated onto the ATM network. For example, the multiple T1/E1 leased lines connecting PBXs to other PBXs may now connect over a common ATM network infrastructure. This can save significant operational dollars.

Interoperability. Standards-based technology. The standards created by the ATM Forum ensure product interoperability. CE modules in ATM switches have talked to ATM access CE modules and vice versa. Nonproprietary solutions conform to the ATM Forum Circuit Emulation Service Interoperability Specification (CES-IS) version 2.0.

Quality of Service. All traffic on an ATM network is assigned to an AAL layer, or an ATM Adaptation Layer. AAL-1 receives the highest priority on the ATM network. It is transmitted first and the traffic cannot be dropped — unlike frame relay networks. Circuit Emulation for voice over ATM travels on AAL-1. The ATM Forum is preparing to release AAL-2, the greater spectrum for Voice over ATM. Today's problem lies in the recognition of AAL-2 in already installed or manufactured equipment. ATM switches and multiplexers understand AAL-1. And the circuit emulation modules understand PBXs, video conferencing equipment, and routers like CSU/DSUs, the existing equipment in the network.

SUMMARY

The concept of Voice over ATM has changed and emerged as the winner in the "voice over " networking technologies. Voice over ATM makes strong financial sense and it delivers quality voice transmissions over the network. Analyze your network today and you will see how well Voice over ATM fits into your infrastructure.

Author Bio

Gary Mangus is the Product Marketing Group Manager at Litton Network Access Systems. He has over 20 years experience in networking and fiber optic communications, the last 5 exclusively in ATM product development.

Chapter 17

Toward a More Perfect Union: The European Monetary Conversion and Its Impact on Information Technology

Information Technology Association of America

EUROPE IS BEING FACED WITH A CHALLENGE that could significantly impact its development and change the face of the global economy. Sovereign states are beginning a multifaceted process aimed at moving them into European economic and monetary union (EMU). As of May 1998, 10 countries have been confirmed in their EMU membership. On January 1, 1999, EMU member states will see the rates of their respective currencies irrevocably fixed to a new currency, the euro. On that day, the euro will become a functional legal currency within these countries. During the next 3 years, public and private sector entities will prepare for the cut over to this new currency, while conducting business in both the existing national currency (such as Deutsche Mark or Franc) and the euro. On January 1, 2002 the process of actually replacing national physical currencies with the euro will begin, with the 76 billion coins and 13 billion bills

0-8493-9834-7/00/$0 00+$.50
© 2000 by CRC Press LLC

of the old currencies being withdrawn from circulation and coins and bills of the new currency going into circulation.

The Maastricht Criteria for Admission to EMU consists of:

- Budget deficit of no greater than 3 percent of GDP
- National debt no greater than 60 percent of GDP
- Inflation no greater than 1.5 percent above the average of top performing countries
- Limits on interest rates

The move to a single currency will affect member states who join EMU immediately. It will also have a major impact for European nations which delay their entry as well as countries around the world which trade with Europe. This chapter examines the implications of this sweeping conversion for Europe's business community — a move estimated to cost in excess of $100 billion. In particular, this chapter examines the impact of EMU on the information systems which support this commerce. These implications will be explored from three principal perspectives: business strategy, information technology operational considerations, and IT supplier community concerns.

EMU and a single currency will pose difficult strategic questions for many businesses. For instance, banks realizing substantial revenue today from currency exchange operations may see this line of business diminished, perhaps even eliminated. Other firms may see traditional patterns of trade or consumer purchasing dramatically altered as price variations across national boundaries are made more transparent and potentially narrowed. In light of these new realities, information technology must be harnessed to facilitate the customer's changing business strategies; to deploy into new lines of business; to achieve a smooth transition from legacy systems, data, and operations; and to provide potential new competitive advantages.

From an operational point of view, most firms will be forced to modify or replace financial systems in order to handle the introduction of the euro. These changes will be necessary whether or not an enterprise alters its strategic course in response to the monetary conversion. Here, we will review some of the key considerations in moving to information systems with euro-enabled capabilities. Successful EMU conversion may be defined by forces external to the technical fixes involved. The Year 2000 software conversion, a process which requires extensive repairs to enable proper computer functioning after the century rollover, is being conducted in the same time frame. This head-to-head competition for corporate attention and technical resources could spell doom for organizations lacking a highly disciplined approach to the management of systems and software.

Many U.S. software firms enjoy more than 50 percent of sales from overseas markets. These software packages can be banking and finance applications, or other types of programs with finance-related features and functions. Because much of Western Europe represents a computer-intensive community, the region is an important marketplace for high-end IT consultants, system integration firms, outsourcing companies, and other value-added service providers in the U.S. Both software and services firms must have a euro strategy in place. At a minimum, this strategy must accommodate basic EMU conversion requirements as commercial products are developed or enhanced, as custom-designed systems and software are implemented, or as outsourcing workloads are processed. Savvy IT providers may find new opportunities in helping overseas clients adjust to the euro, reengineering business processes, adding new levels of integration, and containing or avoiding risks.

STRATEGIC APPROACHES TO EMU

The euro conversion may represent strategic opportunities for business development, force business process reengineering in key functional areas, require new approaches to the marketplace, and improve communication with customers, suppliers, and other trading partners. The new euro will not be just another currency, but a base currency against which all other currencies will be measured and compared. At a business level, changes in strategic direction may be needed to accommodate and leverage:

- Exchange rate stabilization
- Elimination of redundant activity (such as treasury operations)
- Price transparency
- Market expansion and improved trade opportunities
- New product and service opportunities
- New competitive pressures
- Reduced currency risk
- Simplified transaction costs
- Improved access to capital
- Greater economic stability and predictable monetary policy
- Supply chain changes
- New accounting regulations, directives, and procedures
- Shifting consumer demand patterns
- Human resources management
- Customer and employee education and training
- Electronic business and commerce opportunities and growth

In a highly fluid situation, organizations will be forced to determine which elements of the enterprise will require changes, how they will be changed, and in what time frame. Internal modifications will have external manifestations. As a result, euro conversion must be synchronized to meet the needs of both the enterprise itself and its business partners.

The 3 years between January 1, 1999 and January 1, 2002 are a "transition period," in which both national and euro currencies can be used concurrently. As a matter of strategy, an organization might elect to adopt a very aggressive approach to the euro conversion, fielding a wide array of euro-enabled products or services as quickly as possible. Companies might elect this route to demonstrate technical sophistication, to gain early market share over competitors, to acquire the longest possible learning curve, to enjoy cost efficiencies while demand is low, or to achieve other advantages. Conversely, an organization might decide to take a very conservative approach to the conversion, learning from the mistakes of others, testing the political wind, waiting for a more predictable regulatory and business environment.

The schedule of events for euro conversion is as follows:

- **May 1998:** Selection of first group of countries in compliance with Maastricht criteria to join the euro
- **1998:** Production of euro coins and currency begins
- **January 1, 1999:** Exchange rates irrevocably fixed, dual currency period begins, changeover commences, European Central Bank conducts and coordinates single monetary policy in Europe
- **January 1, 1999 to January 1, 2002:** Dual currency period
- **January 1, 2002:** Euro becomes legal tender
- **January 1 to July 1, 2002:** Euro coins and banknotes go into circulation. Old national coins and banknotes withdrawn

Each strategic approach to conversion has its attendant risks and rewards; all must be carefully considered. For instance, companies must determine how long they might support transactions in either or both national and euro denominations. Decisions must be made in terms of incoming and outgoing activity. A firm may conclude, for example, that it will only accept payments in the national currency during the transition period, while being forced by other parties to make payments in one or both currencies or to interface with systems which accept only the euro. A firm might also wish to offer its customers the choice of denomination for a transaction, and would need system changes to deal with these alternatives. Importantly, because organizations will convert systems at different times, constant communication between parties is critical to assure a smooth transition and clear identification of the denomination in use at any given time.

A "big bang" conversion — the immediate switchover of systems to euro — may mean higher risks as hidden programming errors and unforeseen integration issues emerge all at once. Organizations running behind schedule on euro conversion programs may have no alternative. More disciplined firms may take this approach to avoid the need to support both national and euro currency units in their information systems. A phased-in approach allows the enterprise to build and test on an incremental basis, containing the risks of failure. But even this strategy is not risk free. Organizations electing a phased-in strategy to euro conversion will be faced with "bridging" between converted and nonconverted systems, similar to the strategy now common in Year 2000 software programs. Bridge building requires expenditure on resources which will be discarded after the conversion is complete. Coexistence of converted and nonconverted systems also raises the possibility of data contamination, either as test data flows into production systems or as euro denominated data is mistakenly run into a production system still set for the national currency unit.

Timing and transition scheduling decisions must also factor in the organization's critical accounting and reporting requirements. For many companies, implementing the cut over from national currency to euro denomination will make most sense at fiscal year end. At this point, the enterprise is likely to be "closing the books" and going to special lengths to eliminate bookkeeping discrepancies. The year end constitutes a logical juncture for making the transition, whether in terms of a big bang or in select mission-critical systems.

Strategic decision-making goes beyond timing concerns. Some organizations may be tempted to rely heavily, perhaps even completely, on key vendors to perform the euro transition successfully. For competitive reasons, most IT vendors will view the euro as a critical customer requirement — a requirement which must be efficiently and cost-effectively addressed if that customer is to be retained. From a management perspective, however, overreliance on vendor performance is never a good idea. Even in situations where the technical work of converting information systems or software is delegated to the vendor, organizations must remain engaged with a variety of strategic considerations:

- Determining whether to replace or repair existing systems
- Deciding whether manual "patches" or parallel processing alternatives are realistic
- Assuring that euro-enabled functionality meets corporate requirements
- Mapping vendor timetables with organizational priorities and scheduling
- Providing adequate test scenarios and time frames
- Preparing contingency plans
- Monitoring vendor performance

Business processes and applicable regulations may require the use of historical data for auditing and other reasons. An abrupt break in corporate financial records from one currency to a second may potentially be unacceptable to auditors, tax officials, and others. Importantly, the conversion event will make it particularly difficult to correlate archival documents with corporate data. As a result, organizations may need to be able to express historical records in both the new and old currency. Euro conversion requires not only determining what applications must be changed, but what data — and with what functionality.

The euro conversion may place small companies with limited or no export base at a competitive disadvantage. These firms are most likely to deal in a single currency at present. As a result, such companies are the least likely to have experience developing or maintaining multicurrency systems. Such firms are also the least likely to have the "deep pockets" necessary to perform the necessary changes. Without dramatic changes in strategic marketplace approach, small companies are also the least likely to benefit from new market opportunities, risk reductions in currency fluctuation, lower transaction costs, and the like.

Vision, strategy, and strategic planning draw the best and worst from organizations. Certainly, the strategic implications of a complete transition in national currencies are profound, exceeding the bounds of a single white paper to elaborate. Common sense suggests, however, that organizations consider the strategic impact of the euro transition on existing and planned operations before launching major technical corrections to support the new currency.

THE EURO TRANSITION: IMPACTS ON INFORMATION SYSTEMS

Not every organization will elect to perform a full systems conversion to support the euro. As noted, manual workarounds or duplicate systems may be an acceptable alternative, at least in the short term. This discussion assumes, however, that the enterprise has decided to make the necessary modifications or replace existing resources with euro-enabled systems solutions.

The euro transition effectively forces financial information systems to become bilingual. Once able to operate in a single "language," now the system must be able to accept information in either (or both) the national denomination and the euro; to output in either or both; perhaps to process information in both denominations; and to interface with systems which understand only one or the other. In most systems, financial information can be input in the national currency and converted to the euro (the base unit). If required, it will be converted from euro to national currency for output. Conversion from national currency to the base unit and back again can, however, cause rounding differences. Systems able to process in two base units, both the euro and the national denomination, allow these differences to be traced and give the enterprise greater flexibility in determining when to cut over to euro operations. Such systems are apt to be more expensive, with the additional functionality relatively short-lived.

Attention to currency conversions and rounding rules are of particular importance to systems transitions. An exchange rate is computed by multiplying the euro base unit by a fixed value in national currency. To calculate amounts from one national currency to a second national currency generally requires triangulation — determining the value of the first in terms of euros, then using this amount to determine the value of the second. Other approaches should be used with caution. Regulations disallow using inverse exchange rates. The inverse exchange rate computes a conversion amount by multiplying the base unit of the national currency by its fixed value in euros. This method generates rounding differences. Even though the differences may be very small, from an accounting viewpoint system adjustments must be made to eliminate them.

Rounding errors are of special significance in dealing with historical data, particularly in cases where both detailed and aggregate data are stored. Systems in transition to the euro may pick up rounding discrepancies (and therefore performance errors) as incremental data converted to the euro no longer matches the cumulative total. Ultimately, converting all data to euro and operating in a single currency will address these issues. In the interim, this solution may be unrealistic. To avoid rounding differences and the accompanying accounting difficulties, organizations may wish to formalize a series of rules in system design:

- Agree on the number of decimals to be specified
- Anticipate discrepancies between individual and cumulative transaction amounts
- Adopt a base currency with the lowest possible increments
- Expect rounding differences and, where feasible, utilize other criteria for transaction matching
- Establish criteria for clearing rounding differences

As noted earlier, system interfaces are a key consideration. With thousands of organizations making the transition to the euro on different schedules and utilizing divergent approaches, the need for electronic bridges between enterprises is apt to be unavoidable. At the operational level, special attention must be given to coordination among electronic business partners. In short, partners must communicate on their transition strategy and modify interfaces as necessary.

Other contingencies deserve brief discussion. For instance, not all national currencies in Europe use decimals. One euro will be worth 100 cents, similar to the U.S. dollar. Information systems in countries such as Italy, without coins representing fractions of a base unit, will need to be modified to operate in at least three decimals (to support rounding). Similarly, internal controls of some information systems may need to be adjusted to support the euro. The new currency expression may trigger certain threshold actions, from running reports to denying credit requests. In many instances, dual display of currency amounts may be necessary. This capability will require attention to report formats and screen layouts. Systems must also be capable of inputting, displaying, and printing the euro currency symbol.

Not all euro impacts will occur in centralized information systems. Desktop systems such as spreadsheets and databases can be used to make important financial computations and, if left uncorrected, may be the source of conversion problems in larger corporate systems.

Software and Hardware Impacted

Enterprise Resource Planning	Electronic Data Interchange
Finance	Electronic Funds Transfer
Accounts Payable and	Shipping and Receiving
Receivable	Ordering
General Ledger	Sales Support
Point of Sale	Database Management Systems
Human Resources	Spreadsheets
Automatic Teller Machines	Operating Systems
Vending Machines	Distributed Platforms

The euro transition is often compared to the Year 2000 software conversion. In the latter situation, a *de facto* two-digit date standard for representing years in code poses a serious threat to computer operations after the century rollover. No longer able to assume a twentieth-century reference, computers may respond to these incomplete dates by computing the wrong answers or by aborting operations. In the euro vs. Year 2000 debate, discussion often focuses on which situation is bigger, more important, more costly, and other similar irrelevancies. Unfortunately, both conversions spring from real conditions and both must be addressed in a timely manner with a clear emphasis on prioritization and pragmatism.

In setting priorities and forming work plans to confront these twin issues, organizations may wish to balance the absolute completion deadline imposed by the Year 2000 rollover with the more gradual schedule offered by the euro's three-year transition period. Striking an appropriate balance will be critical because the twin conditions inevitably compete for corporate mindshare, technical staff availability, budget dollars, test facilities, and other resources.

In effect, successful euro conversion is aided by a variety of factors: European Union regulations mandate that organizations in member states have this capability; the euro conversion ties directly to the ability of organizations to conduct commerce in the European Union; and currency conversion within member states is a relatively commonplace commercial activity. Even with these forces in its favor, however, the euro transition is likely to fail if the software on which it depends cannot correctly process dates.

Organizations faced with performing the euro and Year 2000 conversions in roughly the same time frame must take a highly disciplined approach. Whether the actual conversion programs can be combined in a single enterprise-wide initiative is debatable. Regardless of whether or not this step is taken, organizations should not ignore the inherent synergies and overarching corporate considerations. These include:

- Setting program schedules which recognize internal deadlines, EU time frames, vendor compliance statements, and customer requirements
- Delaying, deferring, eliminating, or outsourcing internal projects which compete for resources and make it more difficult to test baseline configurations
- Leveraging common processes and methods to the maximum extent possible. Possible areas for productivity gains include business process analysis, inventory evaluation, configuration and program management, auditing, testing, information sharing, and external interface management
- Building common infrastructures, such as repositories for software objects, source code, software designs, test procedures, and documentation
- Coordinating on testing schedules, both internal to the enterprise and, as necessary, with industry groups
- Mission-critical system contingency planning which assumes one or both conversions fail to take place as scheduled
- Reusing successful recruitment and retention strategies for technical personnel

The euro and Year 2000 conversions are unavoidable business realities with substantial costs and risks. Failure at either task could mean drastic changes — even elimination — of the business involved. Organizations must avoid the tendency to view one as more important; rather, every enterprise with European operations, customers, or partners must tailor a management and technical approach which balances corporate resources, requirements, and opportunities.

THE EURO MARKETPLACE: CONSIDERATIONS FOR SOLUTION PROVIDERS

The euro transition represents a variety of challenges and opportunities for IT companies. Like the Year 2000 conversion, the euro situation is causing organizations to revisit certain aspects of their information systems deployments. Like Year 2000, organizations are confronted with repair, upgrade, retire, or replace decisions. Such determinations will drive new business opportunities, both for commercial software vendors, custom software developers, and systems integration firms. For instance, organizations with financial systems now capable of processing in only a single base currency may wish to upgrade and process in both euro and national currencies. Customers may demand new capabilities, such as database tools which allow easy conversion of historical data and efficient traceability back to transaction records, or new functionality for the dual currency period. And organizations may decide to achieve the new functionality by replacing legacy systems with new commercial products — a step that could directly impact vendor competition for IT budget dollars.

As in the Year 2000 situation, some IT companies will be more tactically focused, developing product and service solutions aimed primarily at getting customers over the euro hurdle. Because the euro transition is, like the century rollover, a discrete event, such IT companies may find it more difficult to demonstrate an extensive track record in the area, document success stories, generate customer references, or leverage a broad base of past experience. Other IT firms will view the euro transition in more strategic terms, looking at the situation as one more opportunity to build an ongoing relationship with the client, to better understand the customer's business processes and information systems operations, and to gain competitive advantage for downstream product and service offerings.

To be successful, IT companies will need to be acutely attuned to the customer's changed business realities. A single currency may, for instance, be the stimulus to force some firms to become pan-European or to modify transnational business and pricing strategies. Global IT firms have extensive experience helping customers identify and accommodate regional differences in business operations. Like the Year 2000 conversion, the euro will have an extensive "ripple effect" for multinational organizations, particularly in the area of supply chain management. The euro transition may represent an excellent opportunity to revisit the customer's approach to electronic commerce and supply chain interfaces, introducing business process improvements while assuring the ability of relevant systems to convert to and from euros. The ripple effect will also find its way to intranets and the Internet. Firms selling on the Internet, whether in Europe, Asia, North America, or elsewhere, may be forced to offer a payment in euros option. Likewise, multinationals may be required to insert euros into the intranets serving divisions, subsidiaries, and other business units.

Changed customer circumstances may also require IT companies to consider the downside this situation represents for some firms. As noted earlier, the euro will eliminate some business functions, particularly in areas like arbitrage and currency trading. For these customers, the euro transition comes as a two-headed hydra, bringing substantial new costs as well as lost revenue opportunities. IT consultants and systems integration firms will be challenged to help such firms redefine operations and redeploy assets to respond to the new business environment.

As with Year 2000, IT companies offering euro solutions are challenged to agree on a definition of "compliance." For a number of reasons it may be preferable to restrict any notions of "compliance" to EU-regulated matters such as precision, conversion, rounding, and triangulation rules and the euro symbol. The EU has specific regulations on rounding calculations, but other facets of euro compliance are still open to interpretation. For instance, a euro-ready solution might operate in both the national currency and in euros. Or it might operate only in euros. Similarly, a converted system may be required to show a retail customer pricing information in two currencies.

Customer expectations about euro features and benefits may vary. Some may view the introduction of euro capabilities as adding value and be willing to pay for it. Others may see it as fundamental to the operations of a software program, like offering commands in English or French. Segmenting the marketplace may also be a significant challenge. Countries are participating in the common currency on different timetables. Even those that adopt the euro in the next few years will operate in a transition period. Meanwhile, customers inside and outside the EU may realize the need to be euro enabled on schedules dictated by their own strategic business and technical considerations. Business expansions in response to a more predictable currency may trigger the need for new system architectures and new computing platforms. Such factors may leave IT vendors guessing as to when to introduce euro-capable products, to which industry sectors, on what platforms and in which countries.

Workforce availability is also a key issue for IT vendors. Unlike the Year 2000 conversion which requires more generic skill sets, the euro conversion will be performed by technical personnel with a specific understanding of financial systems. Studies suggest that most firms have difficulty recruiting appropriately trained software professionals. The schedule competition between Year 2000 and euro conversions exacerbates the problem. And in lining up the euro conversion workforce, employers may find that the talent pool is by definition smaller still.

CONCLUSION

The euro transition clearly poses a broad range of strategic and operational considerations for IT vendors and their customers. Perhaps overshadowed in North America by the Year 2000 conversion, the euro will nevertheless have major implications for organizations in and out of the EU. While the time frame for implementing the euro is more fluid than the "hard" deadline of the century rollover, fluidity poses its own problems, fostering a tendency to postpone the work and making it more difficult to determine how and when the cutover will take place.

The euro transition may cause many firms to reevaluate their approach to implementing information systems. Companies adept at strategic planning will use the technology to leverage new opportunities. This may require changes in business structure and process as well as redeployment of IT architectures and capabilities. As with the Year 2000, time is of the essence. Pragmatism will carry the day, and close attention must be paid to both business processes and their underlying and enabling information technology infrastructures. Euro-savvy IT vendors able to assist customers reach strategic goals, both in terms of technology planning and implementation of flexible solutions, will have a significant competitive advantage. Euro-savvy enterprises, similarly, will more effectively map out their post-euro business strategy and be able to enhance and create their competitive advantages.

Recommended Reading

Preparing Information Systems for the Euro, Pieter Dekker, European Commission, Directorate General XV,
http://www.ispo.cec.be/y2keuro/

KPMG Euro Overview,
http://www.kpmg.co.uk/uk/services/manage/emu01.html

The Single Currency: Everything You Ever Wanted to Know, Gillian Tett, *The Financial Times*, November 12, 1996.

Switch to Euro is Tech Challenge, Lamia Abu-Haidar, *CNET*, October 24, 1997.

Banks: Anxiety over EMU Starts to Creep In, *The Financial Times*, December 3, 1996.

Euro: Creation of a New Currency, Anne Knowles, *Datamation*, November, 1997.

Author Bio

The Information Technology Association of America (ITAA) consists of 11,000 direct and affiliate members throughout the U.S. which produce products and services in the IT industry. The Association plays a leading role in public policy issues of concern to the IT industry, including taxes, intellectual property, telecommunications law, encryption, securities litigation reform, and human resources policy. ITAA members range from the smallest IT start-ups to industry leaders in the software, services, systems integration, telecommunications, Internet, and computer consulting fields. Learn more about ITAA and its positions on the issues by connecting to its home page at http://www.itaa.org.

ITAA is committed to addressing the needs and expressing the views of the IT community, whether in the public or private sector. For this reason, projects such as this are undertaken. The Commercial Systems Integration (CSI) Committee welcomes discussion and comments on issues highlighted in this chapter.

Chapter 18

Systems that Build Themselves: Anatomy of a Development Before the Fact (DBTF) Software Engineering Methodology

Margaret Hamilton

COM.X IS A SOFTWARE DEVELOPER ORGANIZATION that develops financial and communications systems for its customers. (Com.x is a fictitious abbreviation of the name Company X.) The market leader of a rapidly growing vertical market, Com.x is at a crossroads and must decide whether to keep things the way they are now or whether it should change its way of doing business.

Even though this company is the market leader and continues to bring in new business at a startling rate, it is losing money, also at a startling rate. It could soon begin to lose market share to a company with less baggage to cope with. Com.x has difficult decisions to make, particularly regarding how to build its software.

Standards are not in common use in this company; every project does things differently. When standards are put into place, they are not necessarily standards that will benefit the company. The company is growing too fast and is having trouble delivering on time. When it does deliver, the

0-8493-9834-7/00/$0 00+$.50
© 2000 by CRC Press LLC

systems are known not to work, and it takes months longer than antici-pated to turn them into production quality for its users.

Everything depends on a handful of experts of whom there are not enough to go around. It is difficult for the company to keep its experts. They are burned out from working more than 80-hour weeks at the custom-er sites (sometimes for months) trying to put band-aids on the newly de-veloped systems and facing the onslaught of angry users.

The company violates every principle of reuse and then some. Those very same applications that were delivered when they were known not to be working were reused in order to accelerate the development of applica-tions for newer customers.

The upper management has "solved" the problem by firing the line man-agers every 2 years or so, hoping that the blame will go elsewhere. Not sur-prisingly, the problem has not gone away. Changes must be made to avoid future problems and to survive. The question is what to do and how and when to go from here to there.

In working with this company, we determined together that the first step would be to define the company just as one would any other system, such as a software cash management system or a toll booth system. This means to start by defining its goals. Then the company can define a plan that re-flects its goals. Since the company already exists, it is helpful to define it in its "as is" state before defining it in its "to be" state.

DEFINING THE COMPANY

The purpose of a business plan is to state what an organization will ac-complish over some length of time. Its operational plan states how it will be done. Before such plans are created, what is often lacking is a true un-derstanding of an organization's goals and, therefore, a means to accom-plish them (what the true business plan should be). If goals (the organization's requirements) were better defined, business plans (specifi-cations) and its associated operational plans (detailed designs) would be more realistic, and the company in question would have a much better chance to be on the right track. Otherwise, what is the system (the compa-ny) that is being developed or that is transitioning, and who are its users (the marketplace)?

The goals for Com.x were defined as part of an enterprise model using the Development Before the Fact (DBTF) formal systems theory[1-4] and a system design and development environment based on DBTF.[5] DBTF has been used to define enterprise models (including process models) for each of several organizations (including commercial organizations and govern-ment agencies). The process begins by learning about the enterprise. Part of this process is to define the organization's goals and then determine how it can best meet its goals. These goals, as well as the process needed to reach these goals, are defined as part of the enterprise model.

In defining the goals, Com.x keyed in on the things that were most important to its development, marketing, sales, and management teams based on the problems they have had to deal with in their own environment. Often these groups do not see a situation in the same way, and their ideas and wish lists have to be reconciled during this process.

Reviewing the process we went through with Com.x, the first step in preparing to transition to newer and better things is to recognize the root problems and categorize those problems in terms of how they might be prevented in the future. Deriving practical solutions comes next, and the process is repeated again and again, as we work to solve new problems with the benefit of what we know from our new solution environment. With Com.x, for example, this was accomplished by saying what is needed (defining the goals), realizing therefore what is missing, and filling in the void by satisfying the goals, including coming up with the right methods and tools.

Part of defining goals is to show how they relate to each other; for example, if a goal is not accomplished with some success, goals that depend on it have less chance of being accomplished successfully.

One output that can be obtained from such a process, particularly within a system design or software-related organization, is to understand the impact that system design and software development techniques (good or bad) have on the organization.

Interesting things surfaced during the process of working with Com.x in defining itself. For example, it quickly became clear how dependent the bottom line can be on seemingly unrelated or distantly related areas. A decision such as who is chosen to manage, build, or market the software; what software processes and methods and tools are selected; what axioms are at the very foundations of the methods selected; how one module in the organization is designed; or what a property of an object is in one of the application systems, would be taken more seriously by upper management if they realized the significance of such a decision on the bottom line.

Even before this kind of exercise, one would no doubt conclude that such decisions could impact the quality and cost of building the software. What is not so apparent is that it affects the organization in many not so obvious ways, ranging from what kind of people are attracted to your business to what kind of business you will ultimately have.

GOALS FOR COM.X

Many goals of Com.x are similar to other software development companies. One, for example, is making a profit. Other goals, in particular those at a lower level, could be quite different. One company may be interested in database-only applications, and others may be interested in the use of a specific vendor's product, such as Oracle- or Sybase-only database applications. Another may want real-time applications for manufacturing; another applications for only PC NT or only UNIX; and another, GUIs for travel agencies.

Com.x builds reasonably complex systems for its end users, which include specialized hardware and software components with a "man in the loop." These systems have both real-time-distributed and database-driven requirements to meet. Until now the company has been building systems the traditional way using a commercial GUI builder for screens, two competing database products for database portions, and handcoding in C or C++ for the rest of its software development process. These systems reside on several platforms, including UNIX, PC, and mainframes.

OPTIONS FOR COM.X

With regard to what it should do next, Com.x has several options, ranging from one extreme to the other: (1) keep things the same, (2) add tools and techniques that support business as usual but provide relief in selected areas, (3) bring in more modern but traditional tools and techniques to replace existing ones, (4) use a new paradigm with the most advanced tools and techniques that formalizes the process of software development while at the same time capitalizing on software already developed, or (5) use the same as the previous option except start over from the beginning.

Choosing an option becomes an easier task once a company's goals are understood and agreed upon. Exhibit 18-1 shows the goals that were defined for Com.x. Below is a discussion of how DBTF and an automation of it can be used to address these goals. Note that when a goal (e.g., GOAL #2) refers to another goal (e.g., GOAL #13) the goal it refers to becomes one of its reusables.

HOW THE GOALS IMPACT EACH OTHER

Each company goal is better understood if its relationships to other goals are understood. GOAL #1, to maximize short- and long-term profits, is ultimately accomplished by reaching all other goals, i.e., GOALS #2 through #13. Similarly meeting GOAL #2, to be strategic, is dependent on meeting other goals, including GOAL #9 and GOAL #13. High-level goals, such as making a profit and preparing for the future, are directly dependent on which methods and tools are used for building the company's software.

It becomes clear that GOAL #3, which is to put in place a mechanism for handling fast growth, will not be satisfied if the company keeps doing things the way it does now. Upon further analysis of this goal, to formally

Exhibit 18-1. Software Company Goals

GOAL #1: Maximize short- and long-term profits (GOALs #2–#12)

GOAL #2: Be strategic: prepare for now and the future
- Understand everything as a system (GOAL #8)
- Use strategic methods and tools (GOAL #13)
- Capitalize on reuse (GOAL #9)
- Do no more, no less (GOAL #7)
- Always apply a preventative philosophy (GOALs #3, #4)
- Eliminate problems (failure to deliver, lost profits, business lost to competitors, exit of critical personnel) before they happen

GOAL #3: Create mechanism to handle fast growth
- Cohesive plan with strategic supporting technologies (GOAL #13)
- Formally understand "as is" and "to be" states of Company X (GOAL #8).
- Hire (and keep) the best people (GOAL #5).
- Standardize throughout corporation (GOAL #6)
- Capitalize on reuse (GOAL #9)
- Transition without going backwards (GOAL #11)

GOAL #4: Prepare for the shortage of good, experienced developers and the large turnover issue that challenges our industry today
- Attract/keep good people by being the best (GOAL #5)
- Use techniques to accelerate learning
- Depend less on individuals. Replace manual with automated processes (GOAL #13). Reuse knowledge already captured (GOAL #9)
- Standardize (GOAL #6)

GOAL #5: Be the best
- Use the best methods, tools, and relationship with vendors (GOALs #9, #10, #13)
- Hire top people (incentivized with the best)
- Maintain market share and ensure lead
- Build the best systems (GOAL #12)
- Underbid the competition without sacrificing quality and profit

GOAL #6: Standardize throughout Company X, facilitating personnel to move from project to project and phase to phase. Reusables created on one project can be immediately used elsewhere and communicated on the same terms. Use same language, methods and tools (GOAL #7, GOAL #9, GOAL #13) for defining (and developing)
- Applications and reusables for all levels and layers of abstraction
- Requirements, specifications, designs, tests
- Views of development (e.g., user model)
- Hardware, software, peopleware
- Projects and project plans
- Processes of development (e.g., management, analysis, design, build, test)
- Enterprise models for Company X and its customers

GOAL #7: Apply the "no more, no less" rule to reach corporate goals
- Use true reuse: avoid reinventing the wheel over and over again (GOAL #9)
- Use true automation that does "real work" and does not propagate "make work" (GOAL #13)
- Simplify necessary tasks

Exhibit 18-1.   Software Company Goals *(Continued)*

---

* Eliminate redundant and unnecessary tasks and resources
* When possible, convert manual tasks into automation

GOAL #8: Understand everything as a system: the business, development processes, applications, reusables, user models, customer enterprises, development environment, and management
* Formally define each system with strategic methods and tools (GOAL #13)
* Formalize planning and analysis for parameters such as cost and risk
* Formalize from the beginning starting with requirements
* Trace from requirements to implementation and back again
* Requirements are implemented as a possible set of specifications, each of which is implemented as a possible set of implementations
* Everything understood in terms of its relativity

GOAL #9: Capitalize on reuse (GOAL #13). Mechanize by standardization (GOAL #6) and effective automation. Reuse only things that:
* Work
* Are inherently part of, become installed as part of, or are derived from the chosen technology
* Evolve with change
* Can be shared across projects

GOAL #10: Work with vendor(s) who understand Company X's current and future needs
* Vendor uses his own product(s) when applicable in the way that he markets it
* Is able to demonstrate highest priority lifecycle areas using Company X systems
* Can successfully support transition to new methods and tools without going backwards (GOAL #11)
* Use strategic technologies (GOAL #13)

GOAL #11: Transition to new methods and tools without going backwards (no time or money lost and less risk than before)
* Relatively fast learning curve
* Can be used to replace, evolve with, or evolve from existing technology
* Need for high productivity of new tools to make up for learning curve
* New approach should be a considerable improvement to justify its entry into Company X
* Use approach that can evolve immediately with Company X's legacy software (GOAL #9)
* Use as much as possible of what already exists to get jump started
* Use strategic technology, with features like an open architecture, to minimize risk (GOAL #13)

GOAL #12: Build better applications with faster, cheaper development
* Make prudent "make or buy" decisions for the components in the applications
* Use no more, no less rule (GOAL #7)
* Strategic technologies should be used for both make or buy applications (GOAL #13)

GOAL #13: Choose an integrated set of strategic methods and tools (only use "point" products if they can become an integral part of the strategic products) that:
* Is based on a before-the-fact philosophy that inherently avoids problems
* Inherently capitalizes on reuse (GOAL #9) and the "no more, no less" philosophy (GOAL #7)
* Treats everything as a system (GOAL #8) resulting in a system-oriented object (SOO)
* Can be used selectively on a system-wide or module basis

Exhibit 18-1. Software Company Goals *(Continued)*

- Can be used at any phase of development
- Is formal, but friendly
- Does not lock in Company X or its customers
- Can interface to other technologies and legacy code
- Evolves and provides a means to evolve a system with changing technologies and requirements
- Provides a means to reconfigure and automatically regenerate to diverse architectures from a given set of requirements
- Allows one to build in terms of it, maintaining the same formal properties
- Can integrate with old and new developments should one choose to add to the vendor's environment
- Automatically does real work (instead of supporting unnecessary manual processes which can create extra work)

understand Com.x in its "as is" and "to be" states means defining views of the company's enterprise as an evolving system. This requires methods and tools to perform such an analysis effectively (note that this part of GOAL #3 depends on GOAL #8 which depends on GOAL #13). Capitalizing on reuse (GOAL #9) also depends on GOAL #13.

In a similar way, GOAL #4, preparing for the shortage of developers, ultimately depends on the methods and tools selected. In preparing for the shortage of good developers, they must not only be attracted but also offered an incentive to stay. Good developers are attracted to companies who excel. Part of excelling means using better methods and tools. With an exciting development environment, developers and their managers are proud of their accomplishments and are more motivated, since they can deliver better systems, relieved from grinding out inaccurate code, often by hand. Managers appreciate faster throughput, reliability, and cost savings.

One way to depend less on individuals is to reuse knowledge already captured. Gone are the days when it is acceptable to have an entire organization depend on one individual to know the design of a particular component of an airplane. No matter what, developers are going to leave even when good ones are easy to find.

GOAL #5, using the best methods and tools, if they are new to the company, requires a supportive and knowledgeable vendor (GOAL #10). It also means other things, like hiring the best people, being the market leader, and building the best systems. GOAL #5 is also dependent on GOAL #13.

GOAL #6, the standardization goal, is constrained further than is immediately apparent; the same language, methods, and tools used for building all aspects of software and related systems. This means, for example, that the same language for defining the requirements for a financial system is used as that which defines its specifications or designs; this same language also could be used to define the process of developing the financial system, the enterprise of the user, and the enterprise of the project or corporation responsible for developing the software. Having the ability to successfully accomplish this depends on satisfying GOAL #13.

Coming up with an arbitrary set of standards just to have standards is not within the spirit of GOAL #6. For example, mandate a standard of using the same vendor's tools as those used by a neighboring project, when such tools do not support the project as well as other tools, is an example of not satisfying this goal. Subgoal constraints, such as using the same language, tools, etc. for all aspects of definition, help to prevent a loose and misguided interpretation of GOAL #6. This illustrates the importance of formally defining these goals.

No More, No Less

Satisfying GOAL #7 means applying the "no more, no less" rule. This means doing what is necessary to reach the company's goals but not doing anything unnecessary. Of course, the reuse goal, GOAL #9, is a key part of satisfying GOAL #7. Unnecessary work happens when meetings or paperwork are created for walk-throughs of results from manual tasks that could have been automated (such as the manual creation of code and its analysis). Other unnecessary work includes learning more than one language for different phases or for different tools when it is not necessary; doing extra work because of being locked into the wrong tool; and doing redundant work because work done to use one tool cannot be transitioned over gracefully to another tool that is needed to complete the task.

Satisfying GOAL #7 also means not making things more difficult than necessary. Most everyone learns from their own experiences — whether developing real-world systems or just getting through each day — that there are difficult (sometimes impossible) solutions to problems and very straightforward solutions to the same problem. For example, it is more difficult to perform long division with Roman numerals than with the Arabic number system.

Sometimes things can be simplified by creating solutions that will help recover from what *appears* to be the *effect* and not the *cause* of a source problem (but, in fact, is the source relative to the problem being solved). For example, dealing with a concept of recovering from the loss of computer memory is simpler than dealing separately with all of the things that might cause such a thing to happen, such as lightning, the computer being mishandled by the user, etc. Here relativity becomes a consideration in simplifying the solution. In this case, the source of the problem that is being solved resides with the computer, not the outside world which has lightning and careless users. In a sense, this is the ability of an object to have self-preservation.

Often, a solution derived for one problem solves other problems. The trick then for doing no more work than necessary is to recognize when you have solved more than one problem with a solution. For example, we developed a system that could be reconfigured in real time to more effectively respond to and recover from errors and to deal with changing priorities by going from a synchronous to an asynchronous operating system. We then realized we had also found a much better and less error-prone way to have the same kind of flexibility with the development of that system. It worked because the actual system being developed had been evolved into a more modular system to accommodate the asynchronous processes of development, where a change to a process or functional area was separate and apart from another process. This significantly accelerated the application's development and maintenance process.

Reducing unnecessary tasks not only saves time and money, but it also eliminates a dependency on processes, methods, and tools that are no longer needed. More importantly, there is no longer a dependency on armies of people (in some cases) needed to support obsolescence. And today armies of people are hard to find.

Countless systems are being tested today for Year 2000 problems. Since people were not prepared on time, this testing will no doubt continue well after the millennium sets in. It would be interesting to see how many of the systems that are being tested and maintained are systems that will no longer be used and that, therefore, could have been thrown away.

Reaching GOAL #7 and GOAL #8 (understanding everything as a system) becomes more successful when GOAL #13 is satisfied. GOAL #8 is all encompassing and cannot be satisfied overnight. Many directions can be taken, such as formally defining something from the very beginning and maintaining such formalism to its completion, or evolving the system formally throughout all of its lifetimes. Another direction could be to formally define all systems with which the target system (the application in question) has a relationship, including the business that develops it, the methods used to design and develop it, and the processes, including analysis, design, and management used to develop it.

GOAL #8, carried to its ideal, means defining systems to have a future. This means defining requirements that can be implemented in terms of a possible set of specifications or a set of specifications that can be automatically implemented in terms of a possible set of implementations (for example, to different languages, communications protocols, operations systems, databases, legacy code, etc.). These systems are all defined up front with an open architecture approach, and evolution will not become an issue later.

Everything is Relative

To truly understand a system means to understand it in terms of relativity. Everything in the world of any system is relative. One person's requirements are another's implementation; one person's application is another's operating system.

Two developers argued for weeks about which of two definitions was the correct one. Upon further analysis, they were both correct since the definitions were for different systems. One was for the end user's system. The other was for the architecture of the end user's system, a system in its own right. This is like the difference between a simulation and a simulator. Humans are destined to argue if no one bothers to define the system for which they are defining the requirements.

Reuse in the Large

To capitalize on reuse (GOAL #9) means to satisfy GOAL #13, since reuse will only work if the objects that are reused work and can evolve. Effective reuse is a possible way of alleviating a potential disaster, since it can be a powerful tool in addressing goals such as GOAL #2, which is to be strategic. Part of meeting the reuse goal is to mechanize by standardization (GOAL #6) and effective automation, both of which are inherent forms of reuse.

Reuse in the true sense of the word is a systematic process (see again GOAL #8). It starts from the beginning with requirements that allow for diverse projects with an option for different specifications, where each specification allows for different implementations (for example, one project with code generated to interface with Informix and another with Oracle; or one project with client server and another with mainframe). These different implementations can be automatically generated from each of that requirement's possible specifications.

To be successful, reuse needs to be an intelligent and formal process, under control. A mechanism can be set up by management to support all development projects in the sharing of a common set of reuse modules, itself a system. This could be a core product from which all applications could jump start their developments (what NASA refers to as reusable productization[6,7]).

Choosing the Right Vendors

Even the vendor chosen can impact a company's reuse strategy. If a vendor actually uses its own technology and products to do for itself what it is selling (in essence reusing) to the customer, this should be an excellent sign, since not only does it illustrate reuse of common experience, but it shows that the vendor really believes in what he has to sell.

It is important to work with vendors who have an understanding of the company's development needs, both for now and the future (GOAL #10). Such an understanding can be verified by having the vendor in question demonstrate its abilities by designing and developing part of a company's system with that vendor's products.

Com.x would benefit by defining for its vendors its current process of building software, starting from the definition of requirements and going all the way to final production of code and maintenance, with all of the steps and tasks that it goes through to develop an application. This would be a process model for building software, a part of the process model for the enterprise of Com.x.

The vendor can then be asked to go through the same steps with its solution (or equivalent steps to accomplish the same functionality) and demonstrate where the vendor's method is superior (or inferior). Com.x will determine if the amount of improvement justifies a transition to the vendor's methods and products and also learn what it is like to work with that vendor in the process.

Avoiding a Rocky Transition

To transition to new methods and tools without taking a step backwards (GOAL #11), with no time or money lost and less risk than before, by its very nature depends on what the new methods and tools are and how they are applied. Many things need to be taken into consideration. A learning curve that fits into a project's schedules is important, but if the benefits of using the new methods (such as productivity) is great enough to justify it, then a longer learning curve may be justifiable. To counter risk, it is also important to have a means to evolve from the existing methods to the new ones at a safe pace should it become necessary or desirable to do so. It is important, for example, that the new approach provides a means to reuse what has already been developed at Com.x. With a strategic technology, with features like an open architecture, risk is minimized (GOAL #13).

To make sure that the transition is a smooth one, it helps to start off with one or more forward-thinking technical leaders at the company. They will inspire others and can help train them as well. In addition it helps to define a process for the others that shows one way to get started, using a company project as an example of how to accomplish this.

The result of reaching GOAL #12 is better applications with faster, cheaper development. This goal will be satisfied if goals #7 and #13 are satisfied, and #7 and #13 will be satisfied if several other goals are satisfied, including #8 and #9.

The Strategic Technology Goal is the Sleeper

With the strategic technology goal (GOAL #13), "point" products and technologies are used only if they can become an integral part of the strategic product. Such a technology and products should be used only if they support the philosophy of preventing as many things as possible from going wrong that could go wrong. All objects in a system, whether they be for hardware, peopleware, or software (or some combination thereof) should be treated systematically from the start to the deployment of that system (GOAL #8). Such a technology solution inherently capitalizes on reuse (GOAL #9) and applying the "no more, no less" goal (GOAL #7), and it can be used at any phase of development.

The technology that is used should be formal, so its semantics and the semantics of the system it is used to develop are well understood. Although the properties of being formal are inherently part of the wish list for methods and associated tools, it was determined that they must also be "friendly" enough to be placed into practical use.

Often in the beginning, the durability of a technology does not surface. When considering a technnology, its ability to adapt to changing technologies, market conditions, and requirements should be taken into account. This was especially important to Com.x, since one of the major issues it had to contend with was that it was locked into a particular vendor's GUI product. In fact, when we first became involved in this process, they were about to choose a product that would have, if used, locked them in even further.

Never should a technology be adopted that locks in a corporation. The product should be able to interface to other products and provide for others to interface to it. A product that locks you in compromises choices of functionality, technology, and hardware and software products you can use (including your own reusables) both now and in the future.

With a product that locks you in, the result could be at best a significantly greater effort if you want to change your mind in the future. An example is a product that can only generate to client server applications but not to mainframe-based applications. Another is a product that can only use its own GUI environment but does not allow its users to take the advantage of additional capability from another GUI environment in the marketplace when there is a requirement to do so. Or a product that once it automatically generates its application for one database environment cannot turn around and automatically generate that same application for another database environment.

A strategic product should be able to interface to other products (call or be called by or generate to other product environments) as they come into the marketplace and to existing legacy code on an as-needed basis. It should provide a means to evolve from (and with) legacy code now and later to newer technologies and application requirements as they become available; it should provide a means to automatically generate (and then reconfigure and regenerate) diverse implementations and architectures from a given set of requirements.

A strategic product should be able to evolve and allow one to continue to build on top of it and in terms of it, maintaining the same formal properties. It should allow one to integrate with old and new developments if one should choose to add to the vendor's environment.

What is important is that the product automatically does the real work, instead of automatically supporting unnecessary manual processes, sometimes actually creating extra work. In addition, it should provide the ability to build effective reusables that will evolve with change. With properties such as these, the reliability of the software is maximized, and the cost to build it and the time to market it is minimized.

The Road to Success Exists Within Past Mistakes

Once we were well into the process of understanding more about Com.x, it was generally accepted by its management that the means to satisfying GOAL #13 could very well be found along nontraditional paths, through innovation, which means creating new methods or new environments for using new methods. In fact, the road to success may well exist within past mistakes.

As a result of this process, it was determined that DBTF was a means by which the company would meet the strategic technology goal (GOAL #13). The company for whom the goals were defined was in the right place at the right time to take advantage of such a moment.

Questions were raised. What if the company's management adopted this different kind of thinking that governed systems development? Would this kind of thinking, one that concentrated on preventing problems that surface in a typical development environment rather than fixing them after they've surfaced at the most inopportune and expensive point in time (see Exhibit 18-2) govern the company's development? Would this really significantly and positively affect the company's financial picture? How might it work? Wouldn't it require a radical revision of the way Com.x does its software?

A RADICALLY DIFFERENT APPROACH

The approach would be radical, indeed, because it would have to provide a formal framework for doing things right the first time. That is precisely Development Before the Fact (DBTF).

Too late, if at all	Compromised quality, Late to market, $$$... wasted
Integration: Mismatched methods, objects, modules, phases, application types, architectures,and products. . .	Left to devices of myriads developers. Hard to understand. Cannot trace objects. No correspondence to real world.
Elimination of errors: Methods encourage systems to be ambiguous and incorrect.	System out of control, incompatible interfaces, errors propagate throughout development.
Flexibility: Systems not defined to handle error recovery or changing requirements, architectures, users, and technologies.	Porting is new development. Maintenance is costly and risky. Critical functionality avoided for fear of the unknown. Locked in development.
Reusability: No properties in definitions to find, create, use,and ensure commonality. Focus is on implementation.	Redundancy a way of life. Errors propagate accordingly. Missed opportunities.
Automation: Supports manual process instead of doing the real work. Limited, incomplete, fragmented, disparate,and inefficient.	Most of development is manual; therefore, error prone and inefficient. Manual processes needed to complete unfinished automations.

Exhibit 18-2. Problems of traditional system engineering and software development environments.

DBTF is a new way of thinking in terms of objects as systems and systems as objects. With DBTF, each system is defined with properties that control its own destiny, including its own design and development. With this paradigm, a life cycle inherently produces reusable systems — directly or in terms of automation. Unlike before, an emphasis is placed on defining things right the first time. Problems are prevented before they happen. Each system definition not only models its application but it also models its own life cycle.

It has been our experience that the requirements definition for a software-based system determines to a great extent the degree to which the development of that system is a success. Not only should the requirements be defined to state the user's explicit intent, but they should also support the process of defining themselves and the systems implemented from them. These are underlying concepts of DBTF.

DBTF provides the means to create software that is better, faster, and cheaper; software that is reliable and affordable. With better, faster, cheaper software, the degree of failure of both the software and the process that develops it is minimized. Compared to traditional approaches, DBTF consistently has shown dramatic improvements in hitting those marks.

The DBTF paradigm is about *beginnings*. It was derived from the combination of steps taken to solve the problems of traditional systems engineering and software development. What makes DBTF radically different is that it is *preventative*˙ rather than *curative* .

Preventative Systems

We can make an analogy to a human system to explain the difference. John goes to the dentist because he has a cavity in his tooth, and the dentist determines that a root canal is needed. Had John gone sooner, the dentist might have been able simply to fill the cavity, which would have been curative with respect to the cavity and preventative with respect to the root canal. Had John eaten properly and brushed regularly, he might have prevented not only the root canal but the cavity as well.

If we add in the cost of dental care, this analogy becomes particularly instructive with respect to systems development. To treat a cavity with a root canal — that is, after the fact — is expensive. To fill a cavity on time is far less expensive. And to prevent the cavity in the first place — that is, before the fact — is far less expensive again.

Another illustration comes from our own experience in developing systems. A few years ago, one of the students in training in our group was in awe of one of the developers because he could "program so fast." But this developer's stuff was full of bugs and impossible to understand. In fact, we spent a lot of time redeveloping his application to make it work because it was not done right in the first place.

There was another developer in the group who was not nearly as fast, but almost everything he did worked and was easy to understand. The time we spent redeveloping the "fast" developer's work exceeded the time this "slower" developer spent on his stuff.

A third developer in the group got little attention from this student. He was always deep in thought. On more than one occasion, he found out that

---

˙ Preventative development technologies introduce the concept of preventing errors from entering the development process. Achieving this goal transports software development from the artistic into the engineering domain. The resulting consequences will be major increases in product life expectancy, the elimination of constant curative activities, and partial or total reusability when faced with functionality changes. The capital spent fixing errors can now be diverted to productive activities.

The wide-scale use of preventative software development technology is likely to impact world economics to an extent comparable to the appearance of the transistor. In more specific terms and on a shorter time scale, the impact of reliable corporate systems benefiting from amortization periods equal to or greater than any other item of plant and equipment would enable world economic benefits of immeasurable magnitude.

"Tools capable of achieving this formidable step will gain acceptance and forever change the software industry." *Development Before the Fact Feasibility,* Toldark Pty, 1999.

Wisdom, formally applied	Examples
Be healthy from day one.	Avoid software root canal: the system as well as its development process.
Assume everything to be relative.	One person's application is another's operating system, simulator, development environment, or architecture.
Do no more, no less.	Remove unnecessary tasks, complexity and "lock-in" tools and techniques. Inherently encapsulate in language (or automate) manual processes.
Recursively reuse.*	Intelligent from the start: formal, practical, automated, inherent, under control, flexible.
Understand everything as a system.	Formal, yet friendly means to communicate. Seamless integration from the start. Capitalize on cause and effect.
Know when to restart or fresh start.	Define the enterprise, it's goals and processes as a system. Act accordingly.*
Use process, standards, and tools that enable priorities.	Good: Solve problems as early as possible (e.g., static, not dynamic) Better: Prevent problems through definition or other form of reuse Best: Not having to deal with it at all

*A real life example

Exhibit 18-3. What does it mean to be preventative?

---

it was not necessary at all to develop the program in question because he had already created reusables.

In the end, the third developer was really the "fastest," because his approach was more "before the fact" than the others.

The first developer — the one of whom our student was in awe — might learn to develop modules for the rest of us to reuse. But what would be missing, without the benefit of the right experience or reusable knowledge, is the deep thought the third developer put into his work.

Exhibit 18-3 lists some things developers do to be preventative. The third developer understood well the first item on the list, "be healthy from day one."

The second one on the list, the acknowledgment (and, of course, follow through) that everything is relative, could very well be one of the means for getting along with others as well as a way of saving time and money. Remember the developers' project in which two people argued for weeks about what the system was to do? In this case, if members of the group had acknowledged the concept of relativity, they would have agreed on what was being defined within a defined context. This would have saved aggravation, time, and money, to say the least.

From our discussion above of GOAL #7, we know that to do "no more, no less" does not mean only that which is obvious, such as deleting things or getting rid of things no longer useful. (Certainly such an exercise is not a waste, however, since organizations spend a tremendous amount of time maintaining systems they really no longer use. Imagine how many Year 2000 efforts spent time testing systems that should have been thrown out years before. Probably more than you guessed.) It also means choosing the right tools, techniques, algorithms, and, yes, even people so that extra work is not created later because of poor choices made. For example, choosing a "lock-in" tool or technology can cause years of wasted effort later. A case in point is the poor choice of shortening the year into two digits; look at the trouble it got everyone into!

If software projects were taken as seriously by their users and managers as professional sports, you would see a different way of doing business in this arena.

A very important aspect of recursive reuse is that it be an inherent part of the language used to define your systems. It should not be up to the developer to make sure such aspects are included. It could be up to him to find a language that does this, however.

What makes DBTF be DBTF is that everything is understood as a system, no matter what it is. With such a concept, things such as reliable communication, seamless integration, and the ability to capitalize on cause-and-effect instead of being ambushed by it are not as far-fetched as before.

As they say, timing is everything. Any organization that is worth anything would like to know when to restart or fresh start its way of doing business. Such decisions make the difference between those who are successful and those who are not. Sometimes one can just "luck out," but more often than not one needs to understand the enterprise in question as a system. This begins by understanding its goals, a process which can result in the enterprise itself being defined as a formal system. Such was the case with Com.x.

The last item in this table speaks for itself from a theoretical point of view but it quickly takes on real, concrete meaning, whether at the top levels of a corporation or down at the lowest and finest grained levels of software development within that corporation. The third developer understood this concept well. Of course, the same can be said for those who appreciate his talents.

Whereas the curative approach requires continuously testing the system until the errors are eliminated, the preventative approach means not allowing

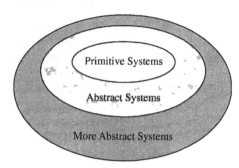

Primitive Systems

Abstract Systems

More Abstract Systems

- Use only reliable systems

- Integrate these systems with reliable systems

- The result is a system(s) which is reliable

- Use resulting reliable system(s) along with more primitive ones to build new and larger reliable systems

Exhibit 18-4. Reliable systems are defined in terms of reliable systems.

those errors to appear in the first place. Whereas accelerating a particular design and development process under the curative scenario means adding resources (be they people or processors), the preventative approach capitalizes more on reuse or eliminating parts of the process altogether.

The DBTF Philosophy

Reliability is at the heart of Development Before the Fact. DBTF treats all objects as complete systems. It provides an initial and logical framework using mathematics, within which objects, their structure, behavior, and interactions with other objects may be captured. The philosophy behind DBTF is that its objects are recursively reusable and reliable. Reliable systems are defined in terms of reliable systems (Exhibit 18-4): only reliable systems are used as building blocks, and only reliable systems are used as mechanisms to integrate these building blocks to form a new system. The new system becomes a reusable for building other systems. All levels and layers of a system have to be reliable for a system to be reliable.

DBTF is based on a set of axioms and on the assumption of a universal set of objects. Each DBTF system is defined with properties that control its own design and development throughout its life cycle(s), where the life cycle itself is an evolving system that could be defined and developed as a target system using this approach. The emphasis on defining things with the right methods the first time prevents problems before they happen. An integration of functions and object-oriented and lending itself to component-based development, DBTF is based on a unique concept of control of a system's objects (including their relationships, functionality, properties, organization, timing, priority, assignment to resources, data flow, error detection and recovery, and data).

From the very beginning, a DBTF system inherently integrates all of its own objects (all aspects, relationships, and viewpoints of these objects) and the combinations of functionality using these objects. A DBTF system maximizes its own reliability and flexibility to change, capitalizes on its own parallelism, supports its own run-time performance analysis, and maximizes the potential for its own reuse and automation. It is defined with built-in quality, built-in productivity, and built-in control.

The concept of automation is central to this whole discussion. When you think about it, automation itself is an inherently reusable process. If a system cannot be reused, it certainly cannot be automated. Consider, for example, the process of software development used within a particular organization. Were that process mechanized, it could be reused again and again. That in itself implies that the process could be automated.

DBTF is centered on doing things right in the first place by using a unique yet straightforward way of definition. A starting point is concept formulation and requirements definition, done in a way that eliminates many of the common problems of traditional software development.

This method concentrates on how one can define a system model that captures, to the greatest extent, practical goals such as reuse, portability, and interoperability. Engineering judgment is useful in determining when to use which type of modeling and how these sides of a system should play together, depending on the requirements of the target system. Under this scenario, "design" and "programming" become relative terms. Higher-level "programming" becomes design to lower layers. The focus is a system's viewpoint, keeping in mind that even lower levels of a program can be defined as a set of models.

With DBTF, we model objects from the real world with a formal but friendly graphical language and then use that model to build an implementation-independent design around those objects. We describe a set of system-oriented concepts and a modeling technique that can be used to analyze problem requirements, design a solution to the problem, and then automatically implement that solution in terms of an architecture of choice (e.g., choice of operating system, programming language, graphical user interface, communications protocol, database, or legacy code).

We see effective reuse itself as an inherently preventative concept. Reusing something that has no errors to obtain a desired functionality avoids the errors of a newly developed system. Time and money will not be wasted in developing that new system. Reuse can be successful only if the system is worth reusing. The functionality requirements of each have to be equivalent to the system being reused. This means starting from the beginning of a life cycle rather than from the end, as is typically the case with traditional methods. From there, a system can be reused for each new phase of development. No matter what kind, every 10 reuses saves 10 unnecessary developments.

The DBTF approach includes a language, an approach, and a process, all of which are based on a formal theory. The same concepts and same notation can be used throughout the entire systems design and software development process. There is no need for the software engineer to translate into a new notation at each development stage.

Formal, but Friendly Language

Once understood, the characteristics of good design can be reused by incorporating them into a language for defining systems. The DBTF language — metalanguage, really — is the key to DBTF. It can define any aspect of any system and integrate it with any other aspect, whether it is used to define highway, banking, library, missile, or enterprise systems; Internet-based, real-time, client server, or database environments; commercial, academia, or government. The same language can be used to define system requirements (where the language supports and accelerates the collective thinking process before concepts are well understood), specifications, design, and detailed design for functional, resource, and resource allocation architectures throughout all levels and layers of seamless definition, including hardware, software, and peopleware.

Although syntax independent, every syntax shares the same semantics. Overarching this is that all of these aspects are directly related to the real world and that the language inherently captures this.

DBTF's language is used to define system-oriented objects. A system-oriented object (SOO) is a system that is both object-oriented and function-oriented. Its function-oriented definitions are inherently integrated with its object-oriented definitions. With SOOs, every object is a system; every system is an object (Exhibit 18-5).

Unlike traditional approaches, DBTF concentrates on delivering formal and reliable systems as its main focus. Whereas traditional tools support a user in managing the process of developing software, DBTF's automation develops the software. In fact, it developed itself.

DBTF is used throughout a life cycle, starting with the formulation of concepts and interviewing the user and continuing with the definition of requirements, analysis, simulation, specification, design (including system architecture design), algorithm development, implementation, configuration management, testing, maintenance, and reverse engineering. Its users include end users, process modelers, managers, system engineers, software engineers, and test engineers.

MODELING A SYSTEM-ORIENTED OBJECT

Every SOO model is defined in terms of functional hierarchical networks (FMaps) to capture time characteristics and type hierarchical networks

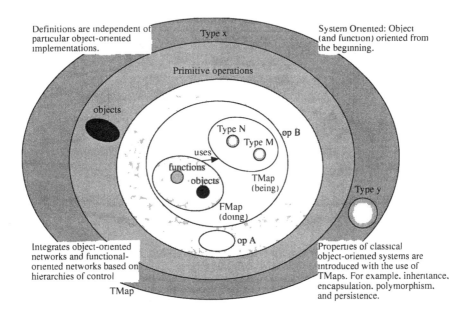

Exhibit 18-5. Every object is a system; every system is an object.

(TMaps) to capture space characteristics (Exhibit 18-6). The TMap, a static view of the structure of the objects in a system, describes the types of objects in a system and the relationships between them. The FMap describes the functions in a system and the relationships between them, including the potential interactions among objects in the system as they change state and transition from function to function. Exhibit 18-7 contains an example of a very small view of Com.x's enterprise model which has an integration of only one FMap and one TMap. In this model the TMap defines the objects having to do with kinds of employees and departments, and the FMap is used to determine if a given employee is full time or not.

This definition is complete since it has been decomposed to the bottom of both the FMap and the TMap. FMap, Is_FullTime_Employee, has been decomposed until it reaches primitive operations on types in TMap, Company X. (See, for example, Emps=Moveto:Employees (Company) where Company is of type Company X and Emps is of type Employees.) Company X has been decomposed until its leaf nodes are primitive types or defined as types that are decomposed in another TMap.

System, Is_FullTime_Employee, uses objects defined by TMap, Company X, to check to see if an employee is full or part time. First, a move is

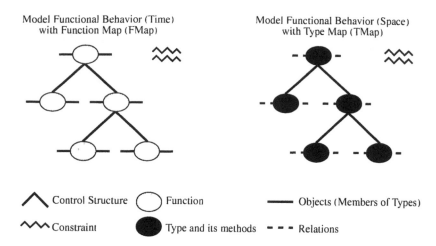

Model Functional Behavior (Time) with Function Map (FMap)

Model Functional Behavior (Space) with Type Map (TMap)

△ Control Structure ○ Function —— Objects (Members of Types)

⋀⋁ Constraint ● Type and its methods - - - Relations

All model viewpoints can be obtained from FMaps and TMaps. Maps of functions are integrated with maps of types*

A system is defined from the very beginning to inherently *integrate* and *make understandable* its own real world definition

*A map is both a control hierachy and a network of interacting objects

Exhibit 18-6. Building blocks.

made from the Company X type object, Company, to an Employees type object, Emps. The defined structure, LocateUsing:Name, finds an Employee based on a name. Once found, a move is made from Employee, Emp, to PS of type, Payscale. The primitive operation YN=is:FullTime(PS) is then used to determine from PS if Emp is full-time or part-time.

Each parameterized type assumes its own set of possible relations for its parent and children types. In this example, TMap, Company X is decomposed into Departments and Employees in terms of TupleOf. Departments is decomposed in terms of ManagementOf into Purchasing, Production, and Marketing. ManagementOf is a new parameterized type that was added by the user who defined this system. This parameterizeed type, ManagementOf, is now available as a reusable for future TMaps. Employees is decomposed in terms of OSetOf. One of the children of Employee, PayScale, is decomposed in terms of the parameterized type, OneOf.

Abstract types decomposed with the same parameterized type on a TMap inherit (or reuse) the same primitive operations and, therefore, the same behavior. So, for example, Company X and Employee inherit the same primitive operations from parameterized type, TupleOf. An example of this can be seen in the FMap where both types, Company X and Employee, use the primitive operation, MoveTo, which was inherited from TupleOf.

Type Map

Function Map

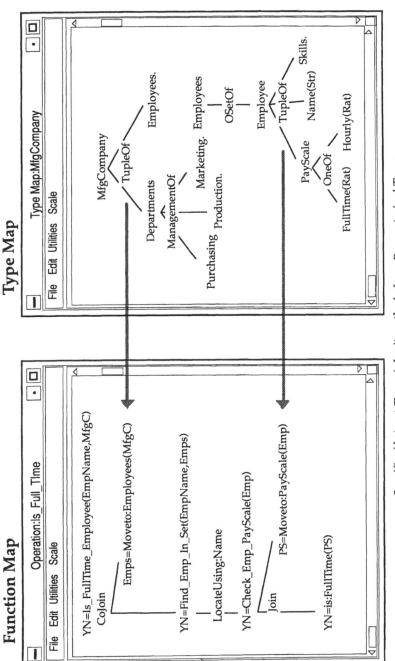

*Specific Abstract Types inherit methods from Parameterized Types
and are applied as leaf functions in FMaps*

Exhibit 18-7. A system: the integration of FMaps and TMaps.

Here each use of the MoveTo is an instantiation of the Child = Move-To:Child(Parent) operation of the TupleOf parameterized type. For example, Emps=MoveTo:Employees(Company) allows one to navigate to an employee's object from a Company X object. A type may be nonprimitive (e.g., Departments), primitive (e.g., FullTime as a rational number), or a definition that is defined in another type subtree (e.g., Employees). When a leaf node type has the name of another type subtree, either the child object will be contained in the place holder controlled by the parent object (such as with Skills.) or a reference to an external object will be contained in the child place holder controlled by the parent object (forming a relation between the parent and the external object).

With the use of mechanisms such as user-defined structures and user-defined parameterized types, a system is defined from the very beginning to inherently maximize the potential for its own reuse.

Using an FMap, the functional model describes the dynamics or aspects of a system that change over time, including data flow, control flow, and the functional mappings (data transformations) that take place within a system. An FMap is a hierarchical network, or graph, whose nodes are functions, any of which could be assigned to a process. A parent's relationship to its children is defined in terms of a function structure. A *function structure* is a type of function with unspecified function nodes in its definition, but when the structure is used, the nodes — as with the TMap — are specified or filled in.

FMaps and TMaps guide the designer in thinking through his concepts at all levels of system design. With these hierarchies, everything you need to know ("no more, no less") is available. All model viewpoints can be obtained from FMaps and TMaps, including those mentioned above: data flow, control flow, state transitions, data structure and dynamics. Maps of functions (FMaps) are inherently and naturally integrated with maps of types (TMaps).

Each function on an FMap node is defined in terms of and controls its children functions. For example, the function — build the table — could be decomposed into and control its children functions — make parts and assemble. Each function on an FMap has one or more objects as its input and one or more objects as its output. All inputs of any function in an FMap as well as all outputs are members of types in a TMap. On a TMap there is a type at each node that is defined in terms of and controls its children types. For example, type, table, could be decomposed into and control its children types, legs and top.

A TMap is a hierarchical network (control hierarchy or networked relations between objects), or graph, whose nodes are object types. Every

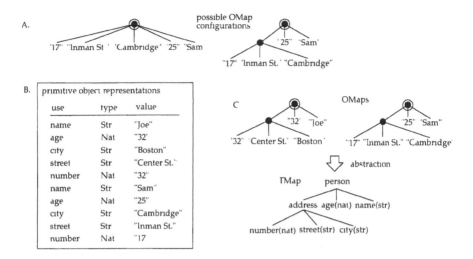

Abtracting OMaps into TMaps

Exhibit 18-8. Abstracting OMaps into TMaps.

---

type on a TMap owns a set of inherited primitive operations. For every function (operation) within an object's domain, there is an associated function control hierarchy (i.e., an FMap). Each object type node, as a parent, controls its children types; as a child, each is controlled by its parent. A parent's relationship to its children is defined in terms of a type structure. A *type structure* is a type of object with unspecified type nodes in its definition; when the structure is used, the nodes are specified or filled in.

The relationship between a parent and its children is determined by the type structure chosen to define it. A type structure encapsulates a set of operators to be applied to the relationships between the parent objects and their children objects. A type structure may also include other encapsulated object types. Every type has a set of operations associated with it.

There are other types of control hierarchies for SOOs. For example, an object map (OMap), which is an object control hierarchy, is an instance of a TMap. John's green truck represented by an OMap could, for example, be an object instance of object type, truck, represented by a TMap. In Exhibit 18-8, Joe, in one of the OMaps, is an instance of person on the TMap and Sam, on the other OMap, is an instance of the same type. Each object (a member of a type from a TMap) is an instantiation of a TMap type and resides in an object hierarchy (OMap).

273

FMaps are inherently integrated with TMaps by using these objects and their primitive operations. FMaps are used to define, integrate, and control the transformations of objects from one state to another state (for example, a table with a broken leg to a table with a fixed leg). Primitive functions corresponding to primitive operations on types defined in the TMap reside at the bottom nodes of an FMap. Primitive types reside at the bottom nodes of a TMap. Each primitive function (leaf node) on an FMap is a primitive operation of a member (object) of the TMap, a recursive function or a function that invokes another FMap to fulfill its function.

In this context, primitive does not imply low level, rather it is a term that describes the encapsulation of behavior and data behind a well-defined interface, raising the level of abstraction of a system. New primitive types are defined and recursively reused in new DBTF systems. Primitive types are also used to define boundaries between a DBTF system and other existing systems (such as database managers or existing legacy systems).

When a system has its input object states instantiated with values plugged in for a particular performance pass, it exists in the form of an execution hierarchy (EMap). An EMap is an instance of an FMap.

A way to begin designing a SOO is that an observer (or modeler) compares the behavior of real-world objects to the known tools that support the DBTF object modeling theory (see Exhibit 18-9). Objects and their behaviors are represented in the object modeling theory in terms of OMaps, each of which is an instance of a TMap, and EMaps, each of which is an instance of an FMap, as tools. An OMap is a hierarchical network of objects and their relationships. An EMap is a set of functions instances and their relationships.

A history of instances of OMap and EMap model constructions (which are really based on an underlying control theory, upon which the modeling theory is based) can be simplified by abstracting them into formal definition as TMaps and FMaps, respectively. An OMap derives the control of its objects from a TMap. Likewise, an EMap derives the control of its actions from an FMap. Once a modeler has a formal definition, it is then used to run (or regenerate the OMap and EMap instances of) the system. Since the object instantiation is to be a prediction of the original real world correspondence that was defined, it is validated by comparing it to the original real world with the object instantiation. If it matches, it is an accurate depiction of the real world, and the observer's intent has been satisfied.

Models and their Integration

Relative to OMaps and EMaps, TMaps and FMaps are reusables for capturing an object's structure and behavior. Whereas an OMap depicts an actual instance of an object's behavior, a TMap depicts one of a possible set

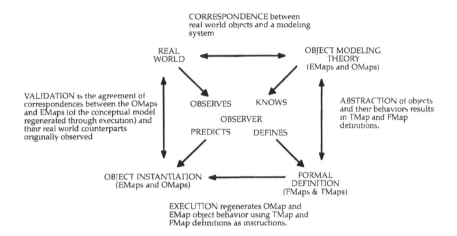

CORRESPONDENCE between real world objects and a modeling system

REAL WORLD

OBJECT MODELING THEORY
(EMaps and OMaps)

VALIDATION is the agreement of correspondences between the OMaps and EMaps (of the conceptual model regenerated through execution) and their real world counterparts originally observed

OBSERVES   KNOWS

OBSERVER

PREDICTS   DEFINES

ABSTRACTION of objects and their behaviors results in TMap and FMap definitions.

OBJECT INSTANTIATION
(EMaps and OMaps)

FORMAL DEFINITION
(FMaps & TMaps)

EXECUTION regenerates OMap and EMap object behavior using TMap and FMap definitions as instructions.

Exhibit 18-9. Modeling the real world.

of instances of an object's behavior. Whereas an EMap depicts an actual execution instance, an FMap depicts one of a possible set of execution instances. An object is an instance of a type. An action is an instance of a function.

Conversely, when one executes a definition consisting of FMaps and TMaps, the FMap abstract definition is instantiated as one or more EMaps and the TMap abstract definition is instantiated as one or more OMaps.

An FMap (Exhibit 18-10A) is a definition of a system of object events and their possible interactions. The FMap integrates with the TMap to specify the event types and the specific function (as an instance of a primitive operation of a TMap type) to be performed on each object. The FMap controls the sequencing and activation of events — the event structures — in terms of three primitive control structures (see below), which define all the possible ways in which events may functionally interact. As we discussed earlier, the concept of a structure is applied to both FMaps and TMaps.

A TMap (Exhibit 18-10B) defines the potential organization of objects for its OMap instances, the potential relations, and the interactions which an object may have with other objects. The TMap is sometimes thought of as a blueprint for object construction. These potential interactions are defined for each parent type as a set of primitive operation definitions. When used in an FMap, a primitive operation defines how the parent may interact with other objects in a particular functional context as with a primitive function.

An EMap (Exhibit 18-10C) indicates within a particular time interval the lines of active control over actions that are in force for a set of co-occurring

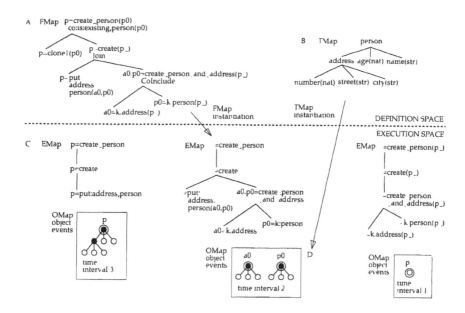

Exhibit 18-10. Relationship between definition and execution.

events and their associated OMap objects. Primitive functions of an FMap become primitive actions on an EMap. An action, once activated with its input events, transitions their associated OMap objects to output events. As new events come into existence, new lines of control are formed to bring future actions under control. When events and actions are no longer needed and they recede into the past, their lines of control are withdrawn. An EMap is always only in the present, while the FMap represents all the potential activations of the system of events and actions over all time.

An OMap (Exhibit 18-10D) indicates the current state of interrelationships of the set of objects of which it is in control. OMap objects and their relationships are subject to the actions of the EMap. As actions in response to object events are managed by the EMap, their corresponding OMap objects (referenced by an event) evolve, appear, change (having relations with other objects and severing relations), and disappear. OMap objects take on a shape or structure as constrained by the blueprint of combinations that are allowed in the TMap.

A Design Scenario

Typically, a team of designers will begin to design a system at any level (this system could be hardware, software, peopleware, or some combination) by sketching a TMap of their application. This is where they decide on

An RMap Defines the Architecture of a System
in terms of cooperating domain models and their inter-relationships

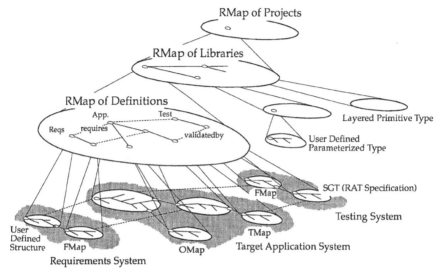

Exhibit 18-11. An RMap defines the architecture of a system.

the types of objects (and the relationships between these objects) that they will have in their system. Often a Road Map (RMap), which organizes all system objects (including FMaps, TMaps, and other RMaps), will be sketched in parallel with the TMap (Exhibit 18-11).

As we've been told by several SOO designers, "The FMaps begin almost to fall into place once a TMap(s) has been agreed upon by the design team because of the natural partitioning of functionality (or groups of functionality) provided to the designers by the TMap system." The structure of a TMap by its very nature defines several universal mechanisms that support its life cycle. For example, a TMap has an inherent way to be instantiated, to be populated using a GUI, to be stored persistently, etc.

The TMap provides the structural criteria from which to evaluate the functional partitioning of the system (for example, the shape of the structural partitioning of the FMaps is balanced against the structural organization of the shape of the objects as defined by the TMap). With FMaps and TMaps, a system (and its viewpoints) is divided into functionally natural components and groups of functional components which naturally work together; a system is defined from the very beginning to integrate inherently and make understandable its own real world definition.

277

All FMaps and TMaps are ultimately defined in terms of three primitive control structures: a parent controls its children to have a dependent relationship, an independent relationship, or a decision-making relationship. We say "ultimately" because although any system can be defined in terms of just the primitives, more abstract structures can be derived from the primitive ones. This accelerates the process of defining and understanding a system. They can be created for asynchronous, synchronous, and interrupt scenarios used in real-time, distributed systems such as those found in Internet applications. Similarly, retrieval and query structures can be defined for database management systems within a client server environment. Nonprimitive structures also can be created for more vertical market-driven reusables; for example, for a cash management or accident reporting system.

A formal set of rules is associated with each primitive structure. If these rules are followed, interface errors — which typically account for at least 75 percent of all system errors — are "removed" before the fact (that is, during the definition phase) by preventing them in the first place. In a traditional development, these errors would not even be discovered until testing. Using the primitive structures and their derivatives supports a system to be defined from the very beginning to inherently maximize its own elimination of errors.

The TMap provides universal primitive operations of type, Any, which are used for controlling objects and their object states that are inherited by all types. They create, destroy, copy, reference, move, access a value, detect and recover from errors, and access the type of an object. They provide an easy way to manipulate and think about different types of objects.

With the universal primitive operations, building systems can be accomplished in a more uniform manner. TMap and OMap are also available as types to facilitate the ability of a system to understand itself better and manipulate all objects the same way when it is beneficial to do so.

TMap properties ensure the proper use of objects in an FMap. A TMap has a corresponding set of control properties for controlling spatial relationships between objects.

Better, Faster, Cheaper Systems

The DBTF system-oriented approach has many properties required for a system to be conceptualized in terms of objects. They are discussed in terms of system-oriented objects. They serve as requirements for the analysis and design phase as well as all of the later phases, such as implementation.

Above all, a system-oriented object is about quality. Quality systems are systems that are both reliable and affordable (see Exhibit 18-12 for a listing of these properties). This table is a TMap-like definition that has a corresponding TMap sketch to go with it. Whenever a property in the table is underlined, it refers to a section that is a reusable. For example, the object "affordable" has children objects "reusable" and "optimizes resources in operation and development."

Whether a system or application is viewed as an object with its functions or as a function with its objects is not the issue. One person's object can be another person's function. Either can be viewed as a system; it is just a matter of perspective. What *does* matter is how these objects and their functions (or functions and their objects) are put together and, ultimately, how they will work together as a family of systems — both now and for future reuse.

The properties of system-oriented objects in DBTF include those which the object-oriented world has come to expect (the desirable ones, that is), and more.

The DBTF notion of system oriented objects can be represented by a simple equation.

Quality system = Reliable and affordable system =
Better, faster, and cheaper system

A *reliable* system is in control, based on a set of known axioms (i.e., assumptions), on the assumption of a universal set of objects, and it has properties of being formal, has a scientific basis, and is error-free. One can have the most beautiful theory in the world, but unless it has applicability to the problem being solved, it will be of no use. A scientific basis implies experimental results and a formal theory based on those results from which other results can be derived. An *error-free* system always gets the right answer at the right time and in the right place and satisfies the intent of the developers *and* the users.

Each axiom defines a relation of immediate domination. The union of the relations defined by the axioms is control. Among other things, the axioms establish the control relationships of an object for replacement or invocation, input and output, input and output access rights, error-detection and recovery, and ordering during its developmental and operational states of existence.

A SOO can be reliable and still *handle* the unreliable. It is predictable; yet, it can handle the unpredictable. By *predictable* it is meant that its behavior and structure can be understood in terms of its relationships without ambiguity.

Predicting the Unpredictable

To handle the *unpredictable*, an object must be able to operate under all conditions — including that which is off nominal — without affecting unintended areas, both in development and during system operation.

279

Exhibit 18-12. System-Oriented Object Properties of Development Before the Fact

Quality (better, faster, cheaper)
Reliable
Affordable

Reliable (better)
In control and under control
Based on a set of axioms
  domain identification (intended, unintended)
  ordering (priority and timing)
  access rights:incoming object (or relation), outgoing object (or relation)
  replacement
Formal
  consistent, logically complete
  necessary and sufficient
  common semantic base
  unique state identification
Error free (based on formal definition of "error")
always gets the right answer at the right time and in the right place
  satisfies users and developers intent
Handles the unpredictable
Predictable

Affordable (Faster, Cheaper)
Reusable
Optimizes resources in operation and development
  in minimum time and space
  with best fit of objects to resources

Reusable
Understandable, integratable and maintainable
Flexible
Follows standards
Automation
Common definitions
  natural modularity
    natural separation (e.g., functional architecture from its resource architectures)
    dumb modules
    an object is integrated with respect to structure, behavior, and properties of control
  integration in terms of structure and behavior
  type of mechanisms

Reusables *continued*
function maps (relate an object's function to other functions)
object type maps (relate objects to objects)
structures of functions and types
category
  relativity
    instantiation
    polymorphism
    parent/child
    being/doing
    having/not having
  abstraction
    encapsulation
    replacement
    relation including function
    typing including classification
    form including both structure and behavior (for object types and functions)
  derivation
    deduction
    inference
    inheritance

Handles the unpredictable
Throughout development and operation
  Without affecting unintended areas
Error detect and recover from the unexpected
Interface with, change and reconfigure in asynchronous, distributed, real-time environment

Flexible
Changeable without side effects
Evolvable
Durable
Reliable
Extensible
Ability to break up and put together
  one object to many: modularity, decomposition, instantiation
  many objects to one: composition, applicative operators, integration, abstraction
Portable
  secure
  diverse and changing layered developments

Exhibit 18-12. System-Oriented Object Properties of Development Before the Fact *(Continued)*

Flexible *continued*	**Understandable, Integratable, and Maintainable** *continued*
open architecture (implementation, resource allocation, and execution independence)	Provides user friendly definitions
plug-in (or be plugged into) or	recognizes that one user's friendliness is another user's nightmare
reconfiguration of different modules	hides unnecessary detail (*abstraction*)
adaptable for different organizations, applications, functionality, people, products	variable, user selected syntax
	self teaching
	derived from a common semantic base
Automation	common definition mechanisms
The ultimate form of reusable	Communicates with common semantics to all entities
Formalize, mechanize, then automate it	Defined to be simple as possible but not simpler
its development	Defined with integration of all of its objects (and all aspects of these objects)
that which automates its development	Traceability of behavior and structure and their changes (maintenance) throughout its birth, life, and death
Understandable, Integratable, and Maintainable	Knows and able to reach the state of
Reliable	completion
A measurable history	definition
Natural correspondence to real world	development of itself and that which
persistence, create, and delete	develops it
appear and disappear	analysis
accessibility	design
reference	implementation
assumes existence of objects	instantiation
real time and space constraints	testing
representation	maintenance
relativity, abstraction, derivation	

Note: All italic words point to a reusable.

Taken from Hamilton, M., Software Design and Development, *The Electronics Handbook,* CRC Press, Boca Raton, FL, 1996, Chap. 122.

This means the object must be able to change and reconfigure when necessary, as well as detect errors and recover from the unexpected. If required, the object will operate in, simulate, communicate with, respond to, and interface with other objects within an asynchronous, distributed, real-time environment.

Consistency is Critical

The formal rules behind SOOs ensure that an object is consistent and logically complete and that an object is unambiguous and there are no interface errors — that is, conflicts of timing, priority, and sharing of objects — within and between objects.

An object is *consistent* if it does not contradict any other object within its internal and external environments. Associating incorrect properties or behavior with an object is an example of an inconsistency. For instance, if John is inadvertently assigned to a mail carrier rather than a passenger aircraft for his flight home, one could conclude that the properties of mail were incorrectly assigned to John.

Timing, data, and priority conflicts are examples of inconsistencies. For example, John and Mary might be assigned to the same seat at the same time in a passenger aircraft, which would be a timing, data, *and* priority conflict all at once.

An object is logically *complete* only if it completely satisfies a set of requirements and its meaning is well understood. If an airplane's requirements are that it must fly in the air, and it has a propeller and wheels but it has no engine, then it probably does not fulfill its original requirements — unless something other than an engine will perform in an equivalent manner.

With formality comes the property of *minimality*, the ability to define necessary and sufficient information about an object. In other words, the minimality of an object refers to the ability to say everything one *needs* to say about an object to understand it but *no more* than is needed. Albert Einstein was an advocate of minimality.

The formal rules behind SOOs ensure they share a common semantic base with each other. The formal rules also ensure the property of single reference and single assignment, resulting in object states that are uniquely identifiable. This property is very important for traceability.

In and Under Control

Control is a pivotal property of system-oriented objects. A SOO is both *in* control of its children objects and *under* control of its parent object, just as objects in the real world. For instance, the CEO of a corporation is *in* control of the people who work for him but is *under* the control of the board of directors. A parent bank controls its subsidiaries but is under the control of the Federal Reserve. One could model a truck to be *in* control of the parts of which it is made and/or of the passengers and driver, which could be part of the truck as an object (depending on how the truck is modeled). The function of truck — Drive the Truck — can be modeled to be in control of its children functions — Drive Left and Drive Right — where there is a choice to drive in either of those two directions. SOOs are both in control and under control throughout all phases of their development and operation.

In DBTF, basically everything is an object, including every function. Every object has behavior (that is, function, including its dynamics), belongs to a type and has structure. Control of objects and functions is accomplished with FMaps and TMaps.

In a TMap, every object type on the hierarchy is in control of its children types and every object type on the hierarchy is controlled by its parent. For every function (operation) within an object's domain there is an associated function control hierarchy (i.e., an FMap).

We know by now that there are other types of control hierarchies for SOOs. For example, an object map (OMap), which is an object control hierarchy, is an instance of a TMap, which is an object type control hierarchy. John's green truck represented by an OMap could, for example, be an object instance of object type, truck, represented by a TMap.

As mentioned earlier, an object can be either a parent or child, depending on the role it plays. A parent object (e.g., trip) controls its children objects (e.g., plane and passengers). Each child (e.g., kind of plane) in turn is controlled by its parent (plane).

Parents can control children in different ways. A parent object might control a pair of its children to be *independent* of each other. For example, a plane would probably be modeled to be independent of passengers. Another parent can control a pair of its children to be *dependent* on each other. The morning schedule, for instance, might be modeled to be dependent on the evening schedule.

A parent can also control a pair of its children objects where one of the children is selected to *represent* that parent. In the trip system we have been discussing, there is a decision as to whether the plane chosen to represent the parent will be a mail carrier or a passenger aircraft. If, for example, the mail carrier is selected, then it will represent its parent.

Other forms of control can be derived in terms of these more primitive kinds of control. For example, there are cases in which a parent can control more than two children with combinations of independent and dependent relationships. Each parent is completely replaced by its children as we move down the hierarchy — as in the case where "trip" is replaced by "plane" or "passengers" — except that the parent always remains in control.

How Axioms Can Help Objects

We mentioned earlier that part of being reliable is being based on a known set of axioms. A SOO has these properties of control precisely because it is based on a set of control axioms.

Replacement is the ability of an object to be replaced in some manner (e.g., in terms of functionality) by one or more objects while remaining in control. In addition to having properties of control of replacement, a SOO has properties of control of access rights, ordering, and domain identification. A real-world example would be the supervisor at your job, who can turn over some of her functions to those who work under her while still remaining in control of the process.

The property of *access rights* is the ability to locate an object from a set of objects and, once it is located, the ability to reference or assign the value of that object. A parent is in control of its childrens' access rights, just as the supervisor is in control of the access rights of her workers. A password is an implementation example of a mechanism for granting such access rights. The supervisor is also responsible for providing access to objects for her workers while other things are off limits (what we call incoming objects or relations) and for providing a place for the workers to put them (outgoing objects or relations).

Ordering is the ability to establish a relation in a set of objects, with one element preceding the other element so any two object elements are comparable. Ordering includes *priority*, the ability to determine which object is more important than any other object, and *timing*. In the case of our imaginary supervisor, she would determine which worker uses a given machine first (priority) and would establish schedules and deadlines (timing). It is not unlike defining a list of things to do to make sure that they will eventually get done and prioritizing that list to make sure that the things that should get done first do get done first. Some objects' priorities are influenced by their dependencies. If, for example, it is necessary to go to the bank to get money before you eat, the bank trip is a higher priority process than eating.

With the property of *domain identification*, an object is responsible for determining whether it will be able to perform its own intended function. The object is able to identify intended from unintended phenomena as part of its domain and, therefore, is responsible for its own error-detection and recovery. As an object, the supervisor is similarly responsible for completing her own function, which is the task at hand she performs for her parent or supervisor. If the supervisor works for a bank and she handles only European transactions and if someone asks her to work on an Asian transaction, she would reject that request and send it back to where it belongs.

Having the means to define *boundary conditions* for an object provides the ability to exclude invalid states of an object safely. This provides *every* object the potential to perform its own error-detection and recovery.

Although formal, a SOO is also *practical* in that it is *affordable* to build and use. Being affordable depends on (that is, inherits the properties of) being reusable. This optimizes resources, but to optimize resources requires that an object is efficient to develop, maintain, and operate.

What do we mean by *efficient* development and maintenance? Minimum time to complete, minimum use of resources (such as people), minimum physical space of all kinds, the best fit between development functions and resources without compromising the object's integrity — all of these are indications of efficient development and maintenance.

Similarly, efficient operation means the best fit between functions and resources, as well as execution in minimum time and space.

Common definition mechanisms are also pivotal to SOOs and especially to their reuse. Just because something is *called* an object or because it follows some of the rules of object orientation does not necessarily make it a candidate for reuse. A SOO that is *reusable* depends on being flexible, understandable, integratable, and maintainable. It follows standards, is made up of common mechanisms, and the process of using it, relating to it, generating from it, inheriting it, and so on can all be automated once it has been mechanized.

Automation is the ultimate form of being reusable. The first step in the process of automation is to formalize, then to mechanize. In a SOO environment, not only the object but its development and that which automates its development should be actualized as automated SOO objects as well.

Common Definition Mechanisms

Relativity (which includes polymorphism), abstraction (which includes typing — of which classification is an example — and encapsulation), and derivation (which includes inheritance, inference, and deduction) are examples of properties of types of use of common mechanisms for a SOO. These are discussed below.

Relativity. Relativity is the ability of an object to change roles depending on such things as how, when, and with respect to what it is being used or viewed. For example, an object can be in a "being" (i.e., static) or "doing" (i.e., dynamic) state.

A dog looking at his master is in the state of "doing." A grocery store — from the "being" or static point of view — might comprise freezer cases and clerks as part of its physical make up. From the "doing" or dynamic perspective of "running the store," the object grocery store could take in customers, food, and money as input and provide profit as one of its outputs. An object can be in a "being" state and a "doing" state at the same time; for instance, the dog might be described by his master as a Shepherd that can talk (and as such the dog is in a "being" state), while at the same time the dog already is looking at his master (that is, the dog is in a "doing" state).

We could give dozens more examples of an object changing its role depending on how it is viewed. An object could be viewed as the one in control (that is, as a "parent") of another object, or that same object could be viewed as being controlled by another object (that is, as a "child"). For instance, the master as an object type is in control of the dog as an object type — the object being controlled, but the dog at the same time can be in control of the biscuit as an object.

An object also can have and not have at the same time. Again, consider the dog, which can be defined so that she is able to eat food and drink water. But at any given moment the dog might have water and not have food. Plus, depending on one's perspective, we could be referring to different dogs here. For instance, from Jane's perspective the dog being referred to is Fido. For Ron, the dog being referred to is Clark within one time frame and Rei another time. From one person's perspective the same dog could be viewed as small by John and large by Jane. It is similar to a development process, where requirements (an object) for one group are specifications for another group or even implementation by still another group. Such differences in perspective are part of the reason people fight and countries have wars. They do not realize that they can all be right and wrong or stupid and smart at the same time.

Having, which is another property of relativity, is an object's ability to have a child, a sibling, a set of proper values, and an architecture, for example. Conversely, *belonging*, another property of relativity, is an object's ability to belong to another object in terms of a defined relationship. Examples are belonging to a parent, where the relationship is one of control, or a type where the relationship is one where the object is an instance of a type.

Polymorphism. Polymorphism, which provides the ability for a particular operation to behave differently on different types of objects, is also an example of the use of the property of relativity.

The implementation selected for a given object depends on the type of object using that operation, and there can be more than one implementation for an operation. The *get* operation, for example, may behave differently on type employee than on type paragraph. A specific implementation of an operation on a type is similar to a *method* or *member function* in an object-oriented programming language. Because an operator is polymorphic, it may have more than one method implementing it. Methods should be transparent to the designer, since each object knows how to perform its own operations. The issue of methods needs to be addressed only when new operations are added to a type, or a new type is added. It should be noted that designers usually think in terms of operations rather than methods.

Abstraction. The property of abstraction is the ability to recognize commonalty among a set of objects and then identify a new object for which any of the original objects can stand. Examples of abstraction include typing, relations, encapsulation, and replacement, all of which help separate out levels of thinking.

To understand how abstraction works, think about how one designer for a given system definition might choose to focus on different parts of a problem than another designer would choose for the same application.

For example, a clock could be defined as digital or analog, with or without its hands, and whether those hands are black or white, leaving out or adding other details. Or the definition could be any device for telling time, such as a sundial with "clock" becoming a particular form of implementation for such a device. From a SOO perspective, an analog clock with hands is more general than a clock with numbers since there is no need to know how to read numbers on the analog clock.

Unlike with the use of SOOs, abstraction can potentially lead to loss of control of objects within a traditional environment. Aspects that are dealt with in an algorithm such as traceability and event priority control of ordering can inadvertently be removed during the abstraction process to make a reusable for the sake of ease of use. Such problems with events surface, for example, in applications with call backs functions, where the user is not fully in control of the priority of events. To base such abstractions on a common set of rules, which is updated to correct problems as they surface, is one way of coping after the fact. But it is far better to avoid such problems from the beginning by the very way a system is defined, where events and the rules which they abide by come built into the language used to define that system.

This abstraction process separates out the *what* from the *how* of the thinking or design process. There can be as many levels or layers as needed, depending on the different views considered desirable or necessary to define and implement an application.

Abstraction helps the designer delay decisions as long as possible or perhaps not have to deal at all with certain properties within an application. Before real operating systems became available, the details of scheduling were necessarily embedded in an application. Likewise, before GUIs were available, GUI aspects were embedded in an application. With system-oriented objects, any kind of detail (except that which is always required by the language to maintain control) can be removed from any kind of application; it is no longer necessary to embed details that can be saved as a reusable for later use. This greatly increases the potential for reuse within other architectures: the more implementation details can be removed or abstracted for a given application, the greater the potential.

If abstraction is successful, each layer lives on throughout all of its lower layers of design, with each layer containing more implementation detail than any of its higher layers. Of course, one designer's application is another's architecture or resource. One designer's design is another person's implementation.

Encapsulation. Encapsulation (or containment) allows an object to have an inside not accessible to other objects and an outside accessible to other objects. To the outside objects, the inside comprises implementation details of the object in question. From a practical view, it involves packaging related object instances and operations together. The outside view of an object may be completely replaced by the inside view of the object in question.

Encapsulation is desirable because it prevents the massive ripple effects caused by small changes to programs that are too interdependent. The implementation of an object can be changed — to fix errors, port to a new architecture, increase performance, or evolve to cleaner or better-written code — without affecting the applications that use it.

For objects, encapsulation is a natural extension of the information-hiding strategy developed in structured languages years ago. The Motif and Windows GUI environments are examples; users of Motif and Windows operations are not affected by changes in new releases of Motif or Windows since all of these changes — from the perspective of the user — are made to the inside of the objects. Operating systems, which have been around for years, are an earlier example.

Forms for Abstraction. Abstraction comes in different forms, including object behavior, object structure, functional behavior, and functional structure. *Object behavior* refers to the common relationships that hold for members of a type of object. For example, the linear ordering relationship for members of object type "time" is a behavioral characteristic of time. All derived object relationships are traced to common semantic primitives.

Object Structure. Object structure refers to the common relationships (control is such a relationship) among members of an object type. Abstraction of object structure refers to the common relationships among members of an object type without specifying particular instances that fit the pattern. As an example, a rational number can always be replaced by an object structure of two integers.

Object Types. Typing is the ability to group objects together according to common functional behavior and object structure. This means that objects with the same attributes and functions (operations) and behavior are grouped into the same object type. Money, corporation, bank, customer, engine, truck, doctor, hospital, paragraph, and book are all examples of types of objects.

A type of object is an *abstraction* of an object. For example, type "doctor" is an abstraction of Dr. Jones and Dr. Goldberg. Each object is an instance of an object type. Therefore, Dr. Jones is an instance of type "doctor."

A type describes objects important to a particular kind of application. Any choice of types is arbitrary and depends on the application. Each type describes a set of objects which could be infinite or finite. Each instance shares the same types of attributes and general behavior and has the same operations as any other instance of the same type, but it has its own values for its specific behavior and attribute. Although two banks are of type bank, one could be located in New York and another in London.

A type can be divided into subtypes, forming a type hierarchy. Every object belonging to that type (instance of that type) along with its subobjects exists as an object hierarchy and abides by the control rules of its type hierarchy. For every object there is a type, and every object knows to which type it belongs. For example, the bank in New York knows that it is a bank and what the characteristics of a bank are, such as location, owners, type, etc.

With the use of types, issues of data and behavior (i.e., dynamics and function) are combined. A modeler does not need to get involved with implementation issues, such as how an operation on an object is implemented or how many implementations exist for a particular operation. Changes made to the implementation have no effect on the modeler.

Functional Behavior. When we speak of functional behavior, we are referring to the relationship between the input and the output of an object's function. The function that states the relationship between input and output is an abstraction with respect to an algorithm for implementing such a relationship.

Whereas *object behavior* refers to the common relationships between members of a particular kind of object (green car and red car are members of a kind of object, car), *functional behavior* refers to the relationship between the input and the output of a function of an object. If a function "drive the car" takes "driver" and "car" as input and produces "driver in car" as an output, it does not matter whether the car is green or red: the function of driving either car takes in a car and a driver and ends up with a driver in the car.

Functional Structure. Functional structure refers to the relationships between functions (see above). Abstraction of functional structure refers to the ability to define common patterns between functions without specifying the particular functions that fit the patterns.

With structure, there is the ability to distinguish between relations that have properties of dependence, independence, and decision making within, between, and about objects, both in terms of types of objects and functions of types. Every relation between and among objects and between and among an object's functions and its relations is defined in terms of a structure, type structures for TMaps and function structures for FMaps.

Derivation. Reuse also can be accomplished through derivation. One form of derivation is *inheritance* — the ability of an object to derive behavior in terms of other objects. Other forms include those which are more indirect — *deduction*, the process of reasoning in which a conclusion follows necessarily from already existing premises, and *inference*, which is reasoning from the general to the specific.

Attributes, behavior, and operations are shared between types of objects based on the relationships between the types of objects as defined by a type hierarchy. A type can be defined as abstracting or as broadly as desired and then refined into successively finer and less abstract types. When an abstract type is decomposed from a parent into its children on a type hierarchy from the standpoint of a class to subclass relationship — such as that of a truck to a dump truck — each subclass may inherit all of the properties of its superclass along with its own unique properties. Not every parent-child relationship on an object type hierarchy is a class to subclass relationship. This relationship depends on how the designer designs his application.

Classification. Classification is the potential of a particular type of object to share an overlapping set of properties — that is, functional behavior and structure in common — with other objects that are subtypes of that type. A *class* is a particular kind of type, which is divided into subtypes (subclasses), each of which shares an overlapping set of properties. We refer to this as a *class hierarchy*.

The ability to share common properties among several classes within a common superclass can greatly reduce wasteful repetition within the design process. This is illustrated with the example of a dump truck. Whereas it would probably be modeled to be a subclass of class (type) truck, an engine type contained within a truck type on a type hierarchy would probably not be modeled to be a class to subclass relationship but rather a different kind of relationship on the type hierarchy. Then, the dump truck could inherit all of the properties of class "truck," such as its ability to be driven and its having an engine. But it would not make sense for the engine to be modeled to inherit its properties from a truck, or at least the same truck as the one that was the superclass of the dump truck.

Building Blocks

The use of common building blocks is important for reuse. We have discussed two kinds of common mechanisms that are needed to define and then reuse a system-oriented object, object types and object functions. They capture the properties of a definition as well as follow the path of natural modularity. A SOO *type* defines all of the relationships of an object to other objects in terms of structure and behavior. A SOO *function* defines all of the relationships of an object's function to other functions in terms of structure and behavior.

Flexibility. When an object has the property of flexibility, the user can break it up and put it together again without compromising its integrity. A flexible object is portable, extendible, evolvable, and changeable, without causing side effects. With a flexible object, one may change his or her mind both with respect to changing requirements for what the object is supposed to do as well as to where that object can reside or how it is implemented.

Portability. A portable object can work in different environments, as a layer within a changing, diverse, and multilayered system and within a secure application. *Security* is an object's ability to keep its behavior and/or structure secure from objects which do not have the "need to know."

A portable object can work within different groups of people, organizations, functionality, products, or applications. It can be a plug-in for another object, or another object can be plugged into it. It can be used for different implementations, resource allocations, or executions within sequential, multiprogrammed, or distributed environments. A portable object can be implemented with the language or operating system of choice; executed by a computer, robot, or human; and interfaced within a reactive client-server system or mainframe environment.

Breaking Objects Up and Putting Them Back Together Again. It is important to be able to combine objects with other objects to form a new object or to divide the object into a set of objects. There are many ways to break up an SOO and put it back together again.

Breaking something up and putting it back together again has an important practical use. One can use these processes to define distinct objects for the various architectures in an environment, including the functional architecture (for example, the software for the cash management system), its potential resource architectures (Windows or UNIX platform), and the mappings from the functional architecture to each of its potential resource architectures (where each mapping itself is an architecture and, therefore, represented by an object). Such flexibility makes it possible to work with each architecture and make changes to it without affecting any others.

An example of such a flexible system is an enterprise model. The functional architecture might describe a corporation's financial processes. The resource architecture includes the people (e.g., the accountants and the computers that perform financial calculations). The resource allocation architecture includes the assignment of tasks to the people and computers for performing the functions of the corporate processes.

Composition and Decomposition. Composition is the process by which a set of objects becomes a set of children to another object, their parent. Decomposition is the ability to identify one of the possible sets of subordinate objects, each set of which could replace an object in terms of its behavior. This is one of several inverse processes of abstraction. Once a set of subordinates has been chosen, the decomposition has taken place. The abstraction for this chosen set — as well as for the other possible sets — is the original before it was decomposed. The abstraction, composition, is the inverse of decomposition.

Again, take our truck type of object: it could be decomposed into wheels and engine, or it could be decomposed into a choice of a green or blue truck. In both cases, "truck" is an abstraction of each set of its decomposed objects. Similarly, the function type of object — Drive the Truck — can be decomposed into subtypes Drive to the Store and Drive Home. In both cases, the abstraction of these functions is Drive the Truck. Any object can be viewed as a "what" with respect to a set of objects into which it has been decomposed (the "how").

Integration and Modularity. Having the ability to integrate objects into larger objects (or configure a larger system out of smaller systems) is a reverse property to separating an object into smaller objects. Integration is the processing of connecting one object to another object, both statically and dynamically. Modularity is the ability to separate parts of an object in a way that allows its subparts to stand alone as objects while maintaining the same system-oriented properties (including those traditionally associated with being modular, such as portability, flexibility, and reusability).

With these mechanisms, there is *natural modularity.* Objects are "dumb" in that they do not know anything about their users or parents. Further, they provide the ability to separate parts of a system so that only those parts that need to be changed are changed when a part of the system is changed. An example is having the ability to separate a functional architecture from its resource architectures, so a change to the resource does not change the functional architecture unnecessarily, and vice versa. Another example is when an object type is changed, thus making known every impact (and only those impacts) to its functions and the functions of the objects to which it relates. With these mechanisms an object is integrated with respect to structure, behavior, and properties of control.

Just as a car does not know who is driving it, a system-oriented object does not need to know who is using it, for what purpose it is being used, or where it is going. This holds for objects as well as for functions within an object. This makes for models that are user-, intent-, and application-independent.

SOOs are also resource-independent; for example, a module does not need to know under which operating system or server it will be running. Different resources can be applied to a module depending on different constraints in the use of a module. This is important because in a given system time may be more important than space, or money may be more important than time. A module is also syntax-independent. Like the sport of orienteering, which has common semantics whether one is in Japan, Timbuktu, or Ohio, a SOO's semantics is not bound by artifacts of a particular syntax within which one chooses to state the object. A SOO is also independent of its implementation. Even in the same machine (or other kind of resource, such as a person) environment, start and stop times, for example, could vary with a multiprogramming process when one process of a higher priority interrupts another one, particularly if there are limited resources and some of them become disabled. This means that, whenever possible, the definitions themselves should have dynamic properties specified on a relative basis (as contrasted to a fixed basis).

Applicative and Computable. The property of relating one set of instances (domain) to another set of instances (range) is called *applicative*, while *computable* is the property of relating these instances one pair at a time. Applicative applies to objects when one type of object is related to another type of object. It refers to functional in the mathematical context of function; that is, the relationship of input to output. Both the input object and output object exist. The function is the relation such that each input corresponds to one output. A computation (or performance pass) is an instance of a function. An object is an instance of a type of object. For example, see the function below.

Total income = Add (salary income, consulting income) =
Salary income + consulting income

In this function there is always a unique total income for a selected combination of salary and consulting incomes.

If an object or an algorithm can be established to be allocated to each unique definition object so that it is set up to execute correctly on a resource (e.g., machine), then that definition is computable or able to be performed. *Instantiation* is the process of performing or executing a system. An object can be an instance of a type of object. An algorithm can be an instance of a function. *Timing* is the ability to instantiate an object at a given time or a given event or when an object has been given a new state.

Understandability

Fully Realize the Power of a Definition. Any system definition, if it is effective, will have the necessary and sufficient information to convey the meaning of the system to its users, its developers, and the tools that use it as input. Not only should it provide the user a means to define his needs, the developer the means to realize those needs, and the tools the means to automate the processes of development, but it should also provide a means to the user (and the tools that support him) to verify that his needs have been realized.

Many things are important if a SOO is to be *understandable*. The property of being reliable is a key. First the SOO is defined with an integration of all the objects (and all aspects of these objects) of which it is composed, each of which is a SOO and shares its same SOO properties. Relations within the structure of an object provide the ability to relate it to any other object in terms of the real world. Both its behavior and its structure are traceable everywhere and at any point in and throughout time within each phase and between and among phases, both during its development and its operation. For example, one can tell where all independencies, dependencies, and decision making takes place in every object — thus allowing a user to capitalize on these properties in making decisions (e.g., where to use distributed resources).

If a definition does not have a means to explicitly trace input access rights or output access rights for every element in a system, that system cannot be controlled, or stating it another way, that system is out of control. The same holds true for any change (and its effect) made to that definition. When, however, a definition has the property of traceability, not only is one able to trace the effect of a particular instantiation of a system, but the dynamic verification of such a system can be cut to a bare minimum, since it is no longer necessary to verify the area of the system where that particular instantiation is known to travel.

The *traceability* property provides the ability to trace the birth, life, and death of an object and its definitions, as well as its transitions between definition and instantiation; to trace changes and know the effects of an object on all other objects in a system; and to trace patterns (e.g., distributed patterns), control, and function flow (including data, priority access rights, and timing). A SOO is defined to be as simple as possible but no simpler, with "user friendly" definitions derived from a common semantic base, each of which hides unnecessary detail. One way to hide unnecessary detail is through encapsulation, a form of abstraction (discussed above).

User-Friendly Objects. One user's paradise is another's nightmare. It is therefore important that the language used for the definition of an object provide for a user-selected syntax. A SOO can be communicated in terms of common semantics to all entities, objects within and outside of its domain, all levels of users, developers, and managers as well as computing environments and automated tools.

An understandable object is defined with a natural correspondence to the real world, and it provides a history that is measurable. An understandable object also provides a means to know when it is in a state of *completion*, which is the ability to determine when an object is, for example, completely defined, developed, or instantiated.

Real-World Properties of Objects

A real-world object exists by its very nature and depends on the use of the formal mechanisms of being reliable to enable us to talk about it and understand it from all of its possible viewpoints and the possible viewpoints of its observers. Many of the real-world properties include the reusable properties such as relativity, abstraction, and derivation.

A real-world object must be *created* in order to talk about it (and relate to and represent it) and *deleted* in order to simplify a particular problem domain. To be "real world," one has to be able to *reference* and *uniquely* identify an object, as well as be able to assign properties of belonging and having to objects. The identify property is part of the property of typing under abstraction.

Persistence is another real world property. Persistence, or healthy existence, is the ability of an object, no matter how complex, to live a full life throughout all its states of being and doing. This property has definite advantages. For instance, it allows for a complex object to be found or put away at will, without having to recreate the object each time.

Identification is the ability to identify an object as a distinguishable entity with respect to its structure, its behavior, and its relationships, both in its development phases and during its operational phases.

Objects can be concrete, such as a physician or the engine in our truck, or they can be concepts, such as a management policy in a manufacturing enterprise, an idea in one's thoughts, or a value of TRUE in a Boolean. Each object has its own unique identity. Two objects are distinct, even if they have the same values: consider two people, each with the same name and birthdate.

To create a SOO means to recognize, for the first time, particular structural and behavioral properties of a real-world object as an object that exists. Deleting that object unrecognizes that object and returns the system to a new state; that is, one without that object. A SOO can be created and deleted; it has the ability for itself and all of its influences to be destroyed. It has the ability to *appear* into and *disappear* from a user's domain.

Once created, an object must be able to be referenced (the ability to use or mention that object). Because the object is unique, there is always the ability to select or find that object. With the property of *accessibility*, there is always the ability to access an object safely in all its states of existence. For example, a person object may have a name and address in one state but not a phone number. In another state, that same person object does have a phone number.

Representation is the ability of an object to have a natural correspondence to the desired aspects of the real-world object of which it is a model. Real time and space constraints provide the ability to realize an object in terms of its physical existence.

From Definition to Execution

From the perspective of relativity, the development process is an integration of many viewpoints, including an object's being, doing, controlling, and having for a particular time interval. The functional architecture as an object is a being with respect to the resource architecture as an object that it resides on for implementation and operation. From this view, the resource allocation architecture as an object is in its doing state when it maps the functional architecture to a chosen resource architecture. A TMap defines the possible states of being of an object and its relationships to other objects in terms of controlling and being controlled. An FMap defines an object in its doing state along with its relationships to other objects in their doing state in terms of controlling and being controlled. The integration of an FMap and TMap takes place when the objects in an FMap do something with objects whose being properties are defined by a TMap.

Analysis of an object is completed when all of its possible interfaces to other objects, separate and apart from its resource architecture (including being, doing, controlling, being controlled, having, and being had) are consistent and logically complete. System design of an object is completed when the process just described also includes the chosen resource architecture and implementation strategies.

Object design is the same process as system design, only with more details added to relate more directly to the object's implementation environment. *Implementation* is the process of preparing an object (and every one of its objects) for a particular execution environment to potentially have everything that belongs to it. Its implementation is completed when every object in the system is associated with an architecture of choice.

The *execution* of an object is completed when every object within its domain has everything that potentially belongs to it (throughout its past, present, and future states) as a result of its associated resource architecture(s) having references to it as part of the objects of the architecture(s) to be had.

The performance testing of a system is completed when all of the execution passes that have taken place or will potentially take place produce

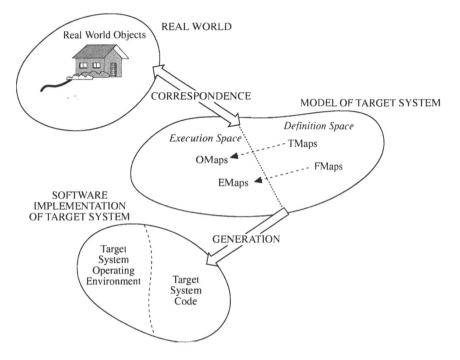

Exhibit 18-13. Representing the real world.

states of has and being had for each object that is correct according to the original requirements of the system. The maintenance of an object is another round of analysis, design, implementation, instantiation, and testing.

There is nothing magical about DBTF. It is just common sense, with a duality of control and flexibility in the process of organizing one's thoughts and recording them — so automation can take over and finish the job.

AN EMBODIMENT OF DBTF

To capitalize fully on the properties of a SOO, a suite of automated tools based on DBTF is needed for supporting its development. One such automation is a full life cycle systems design, engineering, and software development environment encompassing all phases of development starting with the definition of the meta process and the definition of requirements. Part of this environment concentrates on developing the system by working with the definition space of a system in terms of FMaps and TMaps, and the other part concentrates on understanding a system in terms of OMaps and EMaps (see Exhibit 18-13). With this environment, everything is a system. It could be an individual software module defined and automatically generated for, say, a turnpike software application or it could be a module

297

Integrated, Seamless, Configurable Environment
for Systems Engineering and Software Development
Integrates client server, data base, internet...

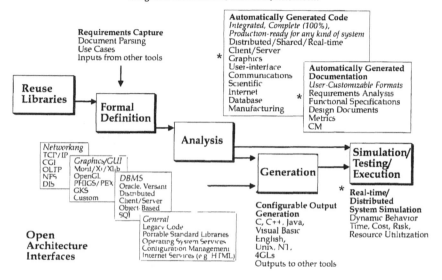

Exhibit 18-14. Engineering and software development.

defined and simulated for the requirements for the entire turnpike system, which might include, hardware, software, and operators. All of these "systems" are defined (and if software, automatically developed) as SOOs (see Exhibit 18-14).

Using FMaps and TMaps, any kind of system can be designed and any kind of software system can be automatically developed, resulting in complete, integrated, and fully production-ready code (or documentation) configured for the language and architecture of choice. Also provided is a means to observe the behavior of a system as it is being evolved and executed in terms of OMaps and EMaps.

Every system developed with this environment is a DBTF system, including itself. This is because it was used to define and generate itself. Although a full life cycle design and development environment, it can coexist and interface with other tools. It can be used to prototype a system or develop that system fully.

All models within this environment are defined with the DBTF formal systems language resulting in SOOs. This modeling process could be in any phase of the life cycle, including problem analysis, operational scenarios, and design. Models are submitted to a data flow structure calculator to provide automatically the structures of control for every nodal family (every parent and its children), with an analysis of the local data flow for a given model. The analyzer can then be used to ensure that each model or set of models was defined properly. This includes static analysis for preventative properties and dynamic analysis for user intent properties.

Once a model has been decomposed to the level of objects designated as primitive and analyzed successfully, it can be handed to the generator. The generator automatically generates a fully production-ready and fully integrated software implementation for any kind of application, consistent with the model, for a selected target environment in the language and architecture of choice.

The generator is generic: it can be configured to interface with language, database, graphics, client/server, legacy code, operating system, communications systems, Internet-based systems, and machine environments of choice. If the selected environment has already been configured, the generator selects that environment directly; otherwise, the generator is first configured for a new language and architecture.

The type part of the generator generates object type templates for a particular application domain from one or more TMaps. The code generated by the functional part of the generator is automatically connected to the code generated from the TMap and code for the primitive types in the core library, as well as (if desired) libraries developed from other environments.

Once the generator is configured for a new environment, a system can be automatically regenerated to reside on that environment. This open architecture approach provides more flexibility to the user when moving from an older technology to a newer one. For example, one system automatically generated C code for part of an application, Ada for another part, and FORTRAN for another. The system was then executed with executables generated from three different languages all executing concurrently, communicating via TCP/IP protocol to perform a coordinated multiprocessing task. The user-configurable generator has been configured for several languages, including C, FORTRAN, COBOL, Ada, and English, and soon will be configured for Java and Visual Basic.

The DBTF environment has a completely open architecture that allows a user to put wrappers around a set of capabilities so that it can be configured to generate automatically to an architecture of choice. It can be configured to interface to a system at all levels, from high levels, such as a DBMS API, to low levels, such as operating system calls (e.g., POSIX). With a user-configurable open architecture for interfacing to databases (e.g., Oracle, SQL Server), operating systems (e.g., UNIX, NT, OpenNT), user interface (e.g., Motif, Windows), communication protocols (e.g., TCP/IP, SNMP, SNA), Web packages such as Front Page, and legacy code of choice, there is no need to lose time to market and spend unnecessary resources to port to a new environment.

Examples of interfaces currently available are UNIX, Motif, and TCP/IP as well as cross-targeting from UNIX to Windows console applications. With this facility, there is a choice of code generation using a single solution specification (also user configurable). There is no need to port to a new environment. Once the generator is configured for a new environment, it will automatically regenerate the new system to reside on that environment. Thus, the generator becomes an agent of reuse across its target code implementations.

The generated code can be compiled and executed on the machine, where the DBTF environment resides where those platforms have been configured or can be ported to other machines for subsequent compilation and execution. User-tailored documents and metrics — with selectable portions of a system definition, implementation, description, and projections such as parallel patterns, decision trees, and priority maps — also can be configured to be generated automatically by the generator. Once a system has been generated, it is ready to be compiled, linked, and executed.

To maintain traceability, the source code generated by the generator has the same name as the FMaps and TMaps from which it was generated. Once generated, a system is ready to be executed. If it is software, the system can undergo testing for further user intent errors. It becomes operational after testing.

As part of the execution and testing phase, an OMap editor is provided, a run-time system which automatically creates a user interface based on the data description in the TMap.

Run-time constraint tests that validate correct object manipulation and construction as well as unit test harnesses for testing each object and its relationships are automatically generated. The automatic user interface is provided with the OMap editor for populating and manipulating complex objects, including storage and retrieval for persistent objects. This provides the ability to test the target system at any input-output interface with predefined object test data sets.

In addition the generator automatically generates test code that finds an additional set of errors dynamically. For example, it would not allow an engine to be put into a truck that already had one nor allow an engine to be removed from a truck with no engine.

To support testing further, the developer is notified of the impact in his system of any changes; those areas that are affected (for example, all FMaps that are affected by a change to a TMap) are demoted.

The GUI environment (as well as its interface to the Internet) is tightly integrated with the development of an application. The user interface is graphical and displayed in terms of RMaps, FMaps, and TMaps (using a tree-like representation of models). RMaps at a library and project level are used as a high level organizational tool to support user coordination and support user understanding of the organization of the system.

GUI (e.g., Motif) support is provided while preserving traceability, interface integrity, and control seamlessly between the GUI part of the application and the other parts of the application. Its automatic data-driven interface generator supports rapid program evolution. Layers of loosely to tightly coupled GUI integration are provided. At the lowest level of integration, a set of primitive data types is provided to access the power of Xlib, Xt, and the Motif windowing system. Each of these layers is defined with primitive operators and types that match the API for that layer. At this layer, all of the raw power of the windowing system may be accessed.

An intermediate layer above these base level APIs (called GUI and GUIELEMENT) is provided that encapsulates most of the repetitive operational aspects of Widget management and construction of X widgets. Since this layer was defined as SOOs, its object editor can be used to specify and view information about the window hierarchy. In addition, the GUI objects may be stored persistently as OMaps to be used during the initialization, modification, or analysis stages of GUI development.

The highest layer is tightly integrated with the TMap system. It is at this layer that the object editor is always available to an application to populate and manipulate objects based on the TMap. The object editor has standard default presentations as well as a set of primitive operators that allow a user to use the OMap editor presentation features to develop interactive GUIs that are tightly coupled to the TMap (e.g., automatic generation of a system of menus from a TMap description).

Other screen description technologies (e.g., WYSIWYG GUI builders) may also be used in conjunction with a translator of their export capabilities to a DBTF GUI specification. An example translator was developed to go from Motif UIL as an output of ICS's Builder Xcessory product.

In addition to the above GUI layers, users can define their own primitive type interfaces to user-chosen APIs, providing the end user with freedom and flexibility of choice. Throughout all of these choices, the APIs are integrated with the use of FMaps and TMaps, a part of DBTF's systems language.

In addition to generating production-ready code from FMaps and TMaps with the generator, FMaps and TMaps can be executed directly by a system analysis component that operates as a run-time executive, as an emulator, or as a simulation executive. A SOO definition is an executable specification in that it has information in it for its simulator to understand its behavior and dynamically analyze it for things such as risk, timing, and cost, and a higher layer operating system to execute it. For software that same definition can be used as input to the automatic code generator. The result is a rapid prototype for a system designer or a production-ready system for a software developer. That which is simulated by the DBTF simulator can be integrated with that which is automatically generated by the generator to a very fine or loosely grained level.

As an executive, resources are scheduled and allocated by the systems component to activate primitive operations. As an emulator of an operating system, it dispatches dynamically bound executable functions at appropriate places in the specification. As a simulator, it records and displays information. It understands the real-time semantics embedded in a SOO definition by executing or simulating a system before implementation to observe characteristics such as timing, cost, and risk based on a particular allocation of resources. If the model being simulated has been designed to be a production software system, then the same FMaps and TMaps can be generated automatically for production.

The analysis component can be used to analyze processes such as those in a business environment (enterprise model) or a manufacturing or software development environment (process model), as well as detailed algorithms (e.g., searching for parallelism).

The documentation environment is integrated tightly with the definition of the system. In fact, documentation can be generated automatically from a SOO definition by the generator, wrapping in the user's own comments should it be desirable to do so; and that same definition can itself become part of that same generated document. Documentation from the various model viewpoints of a system can be collected and integrated into the documentation of the system. This means, for example, that a resulting document could also include descriptions of the requirements, the testing, developer's issues, and the developer's decisions made about a definition of a system.

The baseliner facility provides version control and baselining for all RMaps, FMaps, TMaps, and user-defined reusables, including defined structures. The build manager configuration control facility's primary role is to manage all entities used in the construction of an executable. This includes source files, header files, and context information about the steps taken to produce the executable. This facility also provides options for controlling the optimization level, debugging information, and profiling information of the compiled code.

The requirements component, provides users with more control over their own requirements process. In addition to generating metrics, it allows users to enter requirements into the system and trace between those requirements and corresponding FMaps and TMaps (and corresponding generated code) throughout system specification, detailed design, implementation, and final documentation.

With the requirements component, a user can define any relationship between objects and describe the complex dependencies between these objects. This allows the user to query on, for example, the relationships between a set of requirements and its supporting specifications and implementations.

A session manager component is provided for managing all sessions, the project manager component for managing all projects, the library manager component for managing libraries within one project, and the definition manager component for managing definitions within a library.

The project manager component is the system management interface for all projects and users. It lets the user create, enter, and delete projects, and it maintains a list of file system mount points on which projects may reside, watching them for adequate space. For each project, the project manager component also maintains a list of users who may access the project and enforces these access privileges.

The library manager component is the system management interface for a single project, where each object it manages is a library. The library manager allows the user to create, enter, and delete libraries within that project. Libraries may also be linked together into subtrees; this enables one library to use the definitions in another. Library utilities work on the currently selected library to provide error recovery, environment configuration, searching, and other useful support.

The definition manager component is the system management interface for a library, where each object it manages is a definition. Maps may be created, edited, and deleted, as well as taken through their respective life cycles.

The definition editor component of the definition manager component is used to define FMaps and TMaps in either graphical or textual form. Each manager manages an RMap (Road Map) of objects, including other managers, to be managed (refer again to Exhibit 18-11). An RMap provides an index or table of contents to the user's system of definitions; it also supports the managers in the management of these definitions, including those for FMaps, TMaps, defined structures, primitive data types, objects brought in from other environments, as well as other RMaps. Managers use the RMap to coordinate multiuser access to the definitions of the system being developed. Each RMap in a system is an OMap of the objects in the system used to develop that system within each particular manager's domain. The Road Map editor is used to define RMap hierarchies.

The Process in Action

Using the DBTF automated environment, an organization can select a management process that works for its type of environment. For example, some projects may wish to manage the process of managing the development of a system by following the traditional waterfall model. Others may choose a spiral development model. Below we discuss some aspects of a system design and software development process which can be applied in either type of management model.

Requirements Capturing

A typical development process begins with the capturing of requirements which are usually in the form of a customer-supplied English document. As part of this process, the requirements component is used to parse automatically a requirements document. Key expressions (for example, "cash management system") and key words (for example, "shall") are then filtered from the requirements.

An RMap is then automatically generated, which essentially is an outline of the sections in the requirements document. Each node in the RMap corresponds to an FMap and its automatically generated functions, which continue to outline the paragraphs of a section of the requirements document. An FMap leaf node function under a parent function associated with a paragraph is associated with a requirements sentence. Each requirements sentence is uniquely identified and is numbered with a requirements identifier used to make correspondences to the target system, which will be defined by the user during the design process. Each FMap corresponds to a requirement based on keyword/key phrase matching of sentences in the requirements document.

Those statements with the key words and expressions (i.e., the requirements statements) are attached to functions in an FMap belonging to a node in the RMap (which corresponds to a section in the original requirements document), along with information the user chose for the purpose of establishing traceability and gathering metrics throughout the life cycle. As part of the design process, reusables can be used to fulfill some of the requirements associated with the nodes on the RMap. For others, some FMaps and TMaps may already have been defined for this system. Others are yet to be defined.

A requirement in a definition (e.g., the currently selected requirement in an FMap or a TMap) can be connected graphically (via RMap model relationship connectors) by the system designer to other definition nodes (e.g., another set of requirements or a target system model) for the purpose of tracing requirements to testing and target system functions. A traceability matrix is generated automatically based on traceability between different model types information classifications.

The requirements editor allows the user to specify, query, and report on a database of information about a model and its relationships. This information, together with its formal definition, is used for gathering metrics about the system and its development (such as who is responsible for the object in question, constraints, TBDs, requirements from the user, etc.), providing a mechanism to trace from requirements to code and back again, ensuring that the implemented system meets the requirements. The generator can use this information to generate reports on the progress or state of the development of the current target system and its relation to the original requirements. This includes information about the development process, issues, and information about the contents of the model object itself.

The requirements are modeled by the development of FMaps and TMaps to match a user's initial set of English requirements. The automatic import facility reads a user's requirements document and builds an RMap of FMaps matching the requirements it used to get a head start on the development of these FMaps and TMaps. Changes to the requirements could then made to the FMaps and TMaps, which are a formal and consistent representation for the requirements.

Once the requirements are in this form, the analyzer is able to determine automatically if all of the requirements are consistent and logically complete and traceable. If a user makes incremental changes to the requirements document and then reimports it by generating a new RMap of FMaps for those requirements, the requirements component will allow for requirements document changes and then reimport those requirements with a minimum of disturbance to the established RMap of FMap requirements models and their associated links to other models (e.g., testing systems or the target system under development).

Following is an RMap excerpt taken from the system, agent001db (Exhibit 18-15). agent001db is used to manage the interaction of agents and objects being traded between them. Within this system there are producers and consumers. Consumers can specify objects (and their characteristics) that they need and producers can identify objects (and their characteristics) that they can provide. The agent database automatically provides a trading service that matches supply and demand. When a producer specifies the items that can provide, a listing of all potential consumers is provided to the producer so that he may have the the option of selecting the consumer. The agent001db automatically selects a consumer for the producer, if he does not select one. In addition to providing trading services, agent001db provides general purpose search and presentation services.

Requirements Tracing

For requirements tracing, RMap relations are drawn automatically and visually between model types on the RMap, which is then printable as an

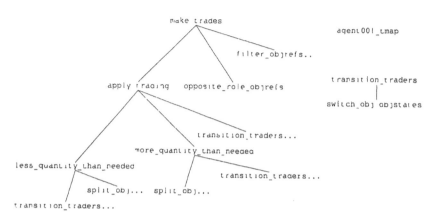

Exhibit 18-15. RMap sample from agent001db.1

RMap diagram. A traceability matrix can be generated automatically for any combination of RMap model relationships to provide traceability information.

Code Coverage

The need for code coverage testing is minimized with the use of SOOs. The use of the formal language for defining the system ensures no interface errors, which means that there will be no logic in danger of not being used properly due to interface problems in the models since the model, if it had an interface error, would be caught by the SOO analyzer before the code was generated automatically from that model. This eliminates the need for wire-tracing-oriented tests for analyzing generated code.

Since all of the code is automatically generated from the FMaps and TMaps of the target system by the generator, the chance for a human to miss either creating the code for part of a model or interface incorrectly to the other code in the system is eliminated.

Additional test coverage analysis can be performed by configuration of the generator to generate coverage analysis FMap calls to provide user definable monitors in generated code (e.g., C). Decision information inherent within FMaps and TMaps can be used for test case initialization for these numbers.

Software Design Modeling

With this development environment, complete life cycle development is based on formal methods using a formal language from requirements to code generation.

Following are excerpts of FMaps, TMaps, and OMaps taken from the agent001db system, as well as an excerpt of C code that was automatically generated by the generator from the set of FMaps and TMaps that these were taken from (Exhibits 18-16, 18-17, 18-18, and 18-19). Notice that the FMap, apply_trading , is an FMap node on the excerpted RMap.

Debugging

We have already discussed how run-time constraint tests that validate correct object manipulation and construction, as well as unit test harnesses (at the granularity of an FMap) or testing each object and its relationships are automatically generated by the generator. An automatic user interface is provided with an object editor for populating and manipulating complex objects, including storage and retrieval for persistent objects. This provides the ability to test the target system at any input-output interface with predefined object test data sets.

Debugging is also done at the code level with the user's native debugger. The code is generated with variable and function names that match closely to their corresponding names in the design specification of FMaps and TMaps. The debugger is used to set breakpoints and examine values of simple object variables. The OMap editor (with a Motif windowing interface) is used to examine complex OMap objects (from within the debugger) and to modify their values or load other OMaps having test values. Testing is also supported by ASCII output generation of OMap objects from the debugger.

In addition, code regression testing can be defined in FMaps to perform comprehensive analysis of any subsystem portion of the system at the granularity of an FMap model. A unit test harness interface is generated automatically upon request for any FMap operation in the system. This test harness provides access to data sets corresponding to the inputs of the FMap in order to drive the regression testing. The resulting outputs of these test data sets can then be validated for correctness.

Much of the testing is no longer needed when using this environment since the semantics of the formal systems language not only supports the user to think, design, and analyze his system's requirements in an organized manner but also eliminates errors from the very beginning; its analyzer automatically ensures that the language was used correctly so that such errors are indeed eliminated. Systems are defined to handle safely changes both during development and operation, increasing flexibility and reducing unpredictability.

All interface errors are found automatically, starting with the definition of a system (up to 75 percent of all errors found in a traditional environment at testing time, after implementation, are found before implementation with the DBTF approach, and more are found automatically by tests

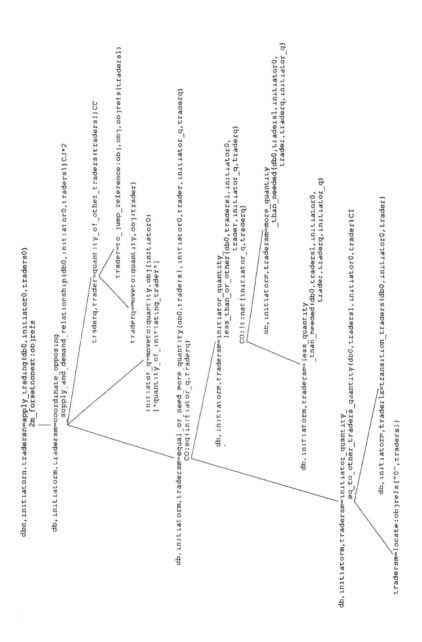

Exhibit 18-16. Excerpted from agent001db FMaps.

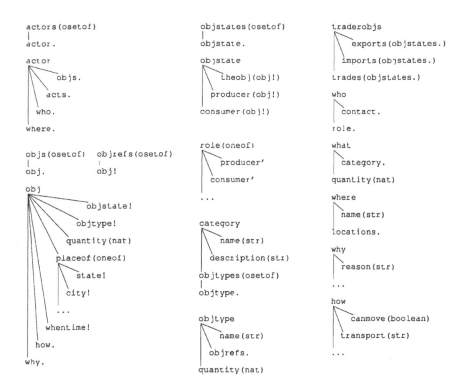

Exhibit 18-17. Excerpted from agent001db TMaps.

generated by the DBTF generator). All objects in a system are under control and traceable, again, obviating the need for another set of tests that are needed in a more traditional setting.

Code Generation

Code is generated automatically (or regenerated) for any part or type of model in a system (and for any part of the system that has been changed, obsolete code is replaced automatically and integrated into the new and changed code) whether it be GUI, database, Internet based, communications, real time, distributed, client server, multiuser, or mathematical algorithms. There is no manual work to be done to finish the coding task. The generator is accessible to a user to tailor it for his own brand of generated code, if needed. This generator can be used to provide output information that can be used as input by other tools or as output for testing (such as showing all of the decision points in the system). This feature can also be used as another means of rapid prototyping for systems design studies.

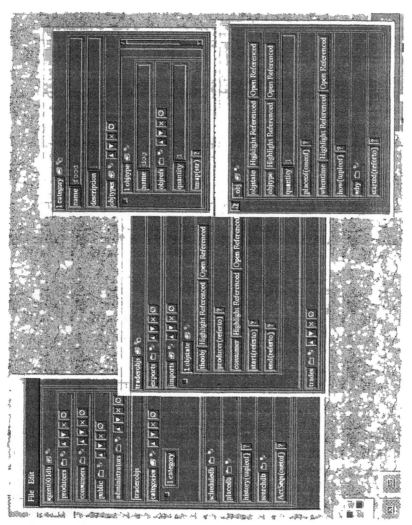

Exhibit 18-18. Excerpted from agent001db OMaps.

```
/*  001-Generated C code for functional specification 'APPLY_TRADING'
        VERSION: 3.2.3.9 C-RAT
         AUTHOR: Hamilton Technologies Inc. Copyright 1991.
      OPERATION: APPLY_TRADING
      GENERATED: Wed May 27 15:58:38 1998
         SCCSID: @(#) %M% %I% of %G%.
*/
#include "AGENT001DB.h"
...

fAPPLY_TRADING(V0DB0,V0INITIATOR0,V0TRADERS0,
               V0DBN,V0INITIATORN,V0TRADERSN)
IDECLARE_AGENT001DB(V0DB0)
...
{                    /* __LOCAL_VARIABLE_DECLARATIONS__  */
DECLARE_NAT(C1)
...
                     /* __FUNCTION_SOURCE_CODE_BEGINNING__  */
...
rec1_0REPEAT=1;
while(rec1_0REPEAT--){
   ATNULL_OBJREFS(V0TRADERS1,V1_0ATN)
   COPY_BOOLEAN(V1_0ATN,D1_D10)
     if(D1_D10<1)
  {if(D1_D10 == REJECT_BOOLEAN) {REJECT_TEST_BOOLEAN()}
   MOVETO_OBJ_OBJREFS(V0TRADERS1,V2_PO)
   CONVERT_OMAP_OBJ(V2_PO,V2_POOM)
   JUMP_REFERTO_OMAP(V2_POOM,V2_OBJOM)
   CONVERT_OBJ_OMAP(V2_OBJOM,V0TRADER)
   MOVETO_QUANTITY_OBJ(V0TRADER,V0TRADERQ)
   MOVETO_QUANTITY_OBJ(V0INITIATOR0,V0INITIATOR_Q)
   EQ_NAT(V0INITIATOR_Q,V0TRADERQ,D0D7)
     if(D0D7<1)
  {if(D0D7 == REJECT_BOOLEAN) {REJECT_TEST_BOOLEAN()}
   LT_NAT(V0INITIATOR_Q,V0TRADERQ,D0D8)
     if(D0D8<1)
  {if(D0D8 == REJECT_BOOLEAN) {REJECT_TEST_BOOLEAN()}
   fMORE_QUANTITY_THAN_NEEDED(V0DB0,V0TRADERS1,V0INITIATOR0,
                              V0TRADER,V0TRADERQ,V0INITIATOR_Q,
                              &V0DB,&V0INITIATORM,&V0TRADERSM);
}/*FALSE*/
else{/*LESS_QUANTITY_THAN_NEEDED*/
...
}/*FALSE*/
else{/*0INITIATOR_QUANTITY_EQ_TO_OTHER_TRADERS_QUANTITY*/
   fTRANSITION_TRADERS(V0DB0,V0INITIATOR0,V0TRADER,
   &V0DB,&V0INITIATORM,&V0TRADER1X);
   LOCATE_OBJREFS(C1,V0TRADERS1,V0TRADERSM)
...
return;
}
/*  -------------- end of source -------------------*/
```

Exhibit 18-19. Excerpted from code automatically generated from agent001db FMaps and Tmaps.

The quality of the generated code has been given high marks by its users since it inherits all of the SOO qualities, including interface correctness and traceability, from and to the requirements and design from whence it came and within the code layer itself.

While the task of configuring the generator is in process, the user can develop his systems using a current generator configuration to automatically generate his applications. Once the new configuration of the generator is prepared, the user can regenerate his system automatically for the newly configured architecture. Once this new configuration is completed, it can be used over and over again as a reusable for other projects.

Detailed Design Document Generation

A change in a DBTF specification is followed by an automatic regeneration of the code that has been impacted with the change, using the generator in order to guarantee that the code matches the integrity of the specification. Because DBTF's documentation environment is tightly integrated with the definition of the system, a new document or portion of a document can be generated automatically by the generator from a specification that has changed. Documentation (e.g., detailed design documents generated from the SOO models) can be generated automatically (when analysis is completed or when needed) from those same specifications, making them always consistent with the generated code.

Documents can be generated to match document templates or document artifacts corresponding to those for other phases. This documentation (partial or complete) can then be imported into, for example, MS Word for processing and/or direct incorporation into the other phases.

In the DBTF development process, changes to the requirements are made in the requirements FMaps and TMaps. Any relationship connections between models are maintained automatically. For example, if a requirement FMap has a dependency relation to a supporting target system (software) model and the requirement FMap is deleted, then the dependency relation is removed. Test models can be evolved as needed and regression tests performed as needed. The design information is extracted and put into the document based on a document configuration of the generator .

A definition can have additional information about it and its relationships provided by the user. This information, together with its formal definition, is used for gathering metrics about the system and its development, providing a mechanism to trace from requirements to code and back again, ensuring that the implemented system meets the requirements. The generator can use this information to automatically generate reports on the progress or state of the development of the current target system and its relation to the original requirements.

Mapping Changes to Code

With DBTF, maintenance is performed at the specification model level. Target changes are made to the definition or model rather than to the code. Target architecture changes are made to the configuration of the generator environment rather than to the code. All changes are traceable. If, for example, a TMap is changed, all of the FMaps impacted by that change are demoted. With traditional products, after the shell code or partial code has been generated, it is necessary for programmers to add or change code manually; as more code is written, it becomes less possible to regenerate the shell or partial code from changes in the requirements, because the manual code would be destroyed or made obsolete. The maintenance process using traditional products becomes increasingly manual and therefore error prone as the software evolves. With the DBTF approach, the user does not ever need to change the generated code, only the specification, and then regenerates (automatically) only that part of the system that has changed. Once again the system is automatically compiled, linked, and executed without manual intervention.

Integration with Legacy Systems

Because the architecture of the DBTF environment is open, it allows for interfacing to existing or future legacy code. Several options exist for such an interface. Wrappers can be placed around existing or legacy code to create primitives for the generation environment to automatically interface to; systems can be defined to have FMaps that directly call legacy code, and legacy code can send input to DBTF generated code at execution time; the generator can be configured to generate language-specific statements that interface to the legacy code; or shell scripts within the environment are open to end-user modification (e.g., modification of link and compile scripts).

Prototyping

A DBTF system can be presented before the fact to end users as a rapid and evolving prototype, starting with a skeleton "show and tell" or "mock up" of what is to come for the user. DBTF enables design and modeling of any concept that humans can envision. It could be, for example, the target system, the testing system (including the operational model), a model of the development process for building target systems, a model of the end users's enterprise or the enterprise of the developer organization itself.

FMaps and TMaps are used to model regression tests that are used in the testing system. These test cases are stored as OMap files, and then code is automatically generated from the test system models by the generator. The regression tests are then ready to run. The results are captured as OMap files. Regression testing is related to coverage analysis by a test case.[8] Regression testing includes the use of the generator code generated for coverage analysis. In addition, any special analysis functions can be developed as a part of the test system to analyze the results (i.e., output objects) of a test case with the input objects for that test case.

Fully Integrated Life Cycle

As these scenarios illustrate, the DBTF environment automates the development process within each phase and between phases, beginning when the user first inputs his thoughts and ending when testing his ideas. The same language and the same tools can be used throughout all phases, levels, and layers of design and development. There are no other languages or tools to learn. Each development phase is implementation-independent. The system can be generated automatically to various alternative implementations without changing its original definition.

Traceability is backwards and forwards from the beginning of the life cycle to implementation to operation and back again (for example, the generated code has names corresponding to the original requirements). There is also traceability upwards and downwards, since it is a seamless process from requirements to specification to design to detailed design. A primitive in one phase — say, requirements — becomes the top node for a module in the next lower-level phase, specifications. The environment takes advantage of the fact that a system is defined from the very beginning to inherently maximize the potential for its own automation.

If the real system is hardware or peopleware, the software system serves as a simulation upon which the real system can be based. Once a system has been developed, the system and the process used to develop it are analyzed with tools such as simulation, together with metrics to understand how to improve the next round of system development.

A new set of alternatives is provided by this approach for the different disciplines associated with the traditional development process. Take, for example, reverse engineering. Redevelopment is a more viable option, since a system can be developed with higher reliability and productivity than before. Another alternative is to develop main portions of the system with this approach but hook into existing libraries at the core primitive level and reuse portions of existing legacy code that are worth reusing, at least to get started. In the future, for those systems developed within the DBTF environment, reverse engineering becomes a matter of selecting the appropriate generator configuration or of configuring the generator environment of choice and then generating to the new environment.

The DBTF system engineering and software development environment can serve more than one purpose for Com.x. It can be used to define and simulate Com.x's enterprise, and it can be used to satisfy its strategic technologies goal (GOAL #13).

MEETING COM.X'S GOALS WITH DBTF

Exhibit 18-20 contains a preliminary TMap sketch of the goals as types of objects in Com.x's enterprise model. Among other things, this model shows the goals discussed above and their relationships, including dependencies. In this sketch the goals are presented with a slightly different view than in Exhibit 18-1. Here the relationships in the TMap are more explicitly shown in terms of being direct or indirect. In addition, we begin to make more use of reusables to express the goals (for example, Be the Best, a goal itself, and Depend Less on Individuals). These goals are defined with a partially filled in Type Map (TMap), and the models are created with the use of the DBTF systems design and development environment.

In this TMap sketch, the top node type is Maximize Profit (see upper left hand corner). This sketch has been decomposed a few levels in order to illustrate some of the types of relationships in this system. The types on all of the other nodes are needed in this definition to define how to Maximize Profit. Several other TMap sketches are contained in this model, each of which is a reusable for at least one TMap. See, for example, TMap, Be the Best, which is used in Maximize Profit, Handles Fast Growth and Prepare for the Shortage of Good People.

One of the interesting findings in examining this model is that every goal, if you drive it down to a low enough level, is dependent on GOAL #13, including GOAL #13 itself, since it is recursive. Similarly, all of the goals are dependent on GOAL #9, including GOAL #9 itself. Clearly, if they are not already, the reuse and technologies strategies used within the corporation should take on the highest of priorities in determining whether the company is in fact meeting the requirements that are important for all of its goals. This includes maximizing short- and long-term profits for the corporation.

We have already concluded that we will go a long way towards maximizing profits (GOAL #1) if we address the other goals successfully. In a similar way the other goals depend to a large extent on meeting still other goals, each of which, if it is addressed, helps to address the goal in question.

The fact that a SOO definition can describe any kind of system and not just a computer-based target system is a valuable consideration for both GOAL #6 and GOAL #8. It could be any system, for example, a human-based system such as a development work plan. In this case the functions are implemented by people as resources and the simulation analyzes the system behavior in terms of how they would execute the plan. It also could be the testing system (including the operational model or user model), a model of

Exhibit 18-20. TMap sketch of goals.

316

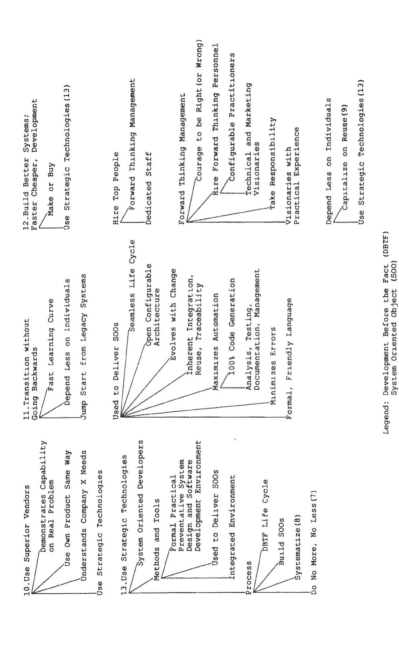

10. Use Superior Vendors
   Demonstrates Capability on Real Problem
   Use Own Product Same Way
   Understands Company X Needs
   Use Strategic Technologies

11. Transition without Going Backwards
   Fast Learning Curve
   Depend Less on Individuals
   Jump Start from Legacy Systems

12. Build Better Systems: Faster Cheaper, Development
   Make or Buy
   Use Strategic Technologies (13)

13. Use Strategic Technologies
   System Oriented Developers
   Methods and Tools
      Formal Practical Preventative System Design and Software Development Environment
      Used to Deliver SOOs
   Integrated Environment
   Process
      DBTF Life Cycle
      Build SOOs
      Systematize (8)
   Do No More, No Less (7)

Used to Deliver SOOs
   Seamless Life Cycle
   Open Configurable Architecture
   Evolves with Change
   Inherent Integration, Reuse, Traceability
   Maximizes Automation
   100% Code Generation
   Analysis, Testing, Documentation, Management
   Minimizes Errors
   Formal, Friendly Language

Hire Top People
   Forward Thinking Management
   Dedicated Staff

Forward Thinking Management
   Courage to be Right (or Wrong)
   Hire Forward Thinking Personnel
   Configurable Practitioners
   Technical and Marketing Visionaries
   Take Responsibility
   Visionaries with Practical Experience

Depend Less on Individuals
   Capitalize on Reuse (9)
   Use Strategic Technologies (13)

Legend: Development BeFore the Fact (DBTF)
System Oriented Object (SOO)

Exhibit 18-20. *Continued.*

the development process for building target systems, a model of the end user's enterprise or the enterprise of Com.x. Working together with Com.x we defined part of their project's work plan with FMaps and TMaps as well as other models.

Motivating the Staff

With a DBTF environment, both developers and managers can be proud of their accomplishments and more motivated, since they can deliver. With the current critical programmer shortage affecting our industry today, it is clear that Com.x is not as dependent on individuals with an environment such as this at their disposal, particularly since it can be set up not only to do a major part of the programmer's work (for example, generate 100 percent of the code), but to make it reliable and straightforward to reuse. These are additional contributing factors for reaching GOAL #4 and GOAL #5.

Although meeting GOAL #13 can support GOAL #8 in many ways, it is important that Com.x take the initiative to use a strategic technology that will, for example, trace its own requirements as a company to its evolving implementations (the company as it operates on a day-to-day basis) in order to understand itself better as an organization. The DBTF environment's ability to trace from requirements to design code and back again in fulfilling GOAL #13 can be used directly to fulfill GOAL #8.

Following the No More, No Less Path (GOAL #7)

The formalism behind DBTF enforces a major part of the "no more, no less" rule, a prime example of which is reuse. The fact that DBTF-developed systems will not lock an organization in means that unnecessary work can be avoided. DBTF systems incorporate a structure and process for the continuous evolution of any or all parts of a system. Not only can the models as well as their automatically generated implementations be reused, but new implementations can be regenerated from any model, and this can be done by using reusable architecture configurations.

The fact that the DBTF approach does not lock an organization in to process, architecture, design, or implementation with today's rapidly changing technologies was especially appealing to Com.x, since this was a main problem area for them. The user has designer freedom without compromising integrity of the system. In fact, the designer can abstract to as high (or as low) a level as he would like. The only constraints imposed are those that support the designer in making systems with properties of preventative systems, such as having no interface errors.

Following the "no more, no less" path means getting rid of everything that is truly no longer needed, but it does not mean getting rid of things that are needed just to show that money is being "saved." With strategic methods and tools that follow the "no more, no less" path, a multitude of processes, methods, and tools are truly no longer needed.

With one formal semantic language to define and integrate all aspects of a system, diverse modeling languages (and methodologies for using them), each of which defines only part of a system, are no longer necessary. Learning is minimized. Why, for example, learn C, followed by a replacement of C with a more modern C++ followed by a replacement of C++ with Java? Each is a major step that requires significant training and reverse engineering. One could instead use — and continue to use — a single definition language and automatically generate the latest implementation environment.

No longer is there a need to reconcile multiple techniques with semantics that interfere with each other. This was of great interest to Com.x since there were too many mixed messages in the company. The right hand never knew what the left hand was doing, up and down and across the corporation.

Techniques and tools for transitioning from one phase of the life cycle to another become obsolete. Dealing with all of the paperwork that is either manually or automatically generated to support the manual processes of development when they could be automatically developed can be eliminated. Techniques for maintaining source code as a separate process are no longer needed, since the source is automatically generated from the system specification.

Verification also becomes obsolete. Techniques for managing other paper documents give way to entering requirements and their changes directly into the requirements specification database. Testing procedures and tools for finding most errors are no longer needed because those errors no longer exist. Tools developed to support programming as a manual process are no longer needed when programming is automatic.

No longer needed are tools that focus on the measurement of complexity. Instead of measuring it, it becomes minimized. Complexity does not increase with the size of the system, since more reuse is possible and all objects are under control, integrated, and traceable.

No longer is it necessary to do what is unnecessary over and over again or to keep adding on after the fact when there is a way to do it right the first time.

Inherent Reuse

The reuse goal (GOAL #9) is a natural and inherent part of the DBTF life cycle. Every SOO is a candidate for reuse. Objects, no matter how complex, can be reused and integrated, creating new and evolving candidates for reuse. Environment configurations for different kinds of architectures can be reused. A newly developed system can be safely reused to increase even further the productivity of the systems developed with it.

Configurations for different kinds of architectures can be reused to the extent that a system never has to be retired for reasons such as a new implementation language, operating system, or hardware architecture. A system would be a candidate for retirement only if there was no need for its type of functionality (for example, if a company retired all of its missile systems and decided to build toll booth systems instead).

Even then, with such a drastic change, there are reusables that can be generic enough to be reused on toll booth systems or missile systems if they were originally developed for banking systems and vice versa. Inherent reuse with SOOs recursively and safely raises objects to a new and higher level, seamlessly integrating aspects such as the GUI, database, and communications side of a system with all of its other parts. This is something Com.x never had the chance to do before, since its GUIs could not be integrated with its other applications.

Reuse succeeds only if what is reused works and is under control. Such is the case with SOOs. Every defined model becomes inherently a candidate for reuse. Reuse is supported in FMaps by abstract functions using a set of pre-defined or user-defined structures, operations, universal operations (those containing polymorphism) and user-defined FMap structures (functional templates with or without polymorphism). Reuse in TMaps is supported by abstract types using a set of pre-defined or user-defined parameterized types (i.e., type templates); leaf types referencing other abstract types, relations (pointer-like), or recursive types; user-defined primitive types (at code level or layered onto FMaps and TMaps); user-defined layered types and user-defined parameterized types.

Learning from history is a form of reuse. Software fails because of what we do not learn from history. DBTF succeeds because of what has been learned from history.

Getting the Right Vendor

With respect to GOAL #10, we mentioned above how a vendor's understanding of the company's environment can be verified by having the vendor in question demonstrate its abilities on real systems. Initially, our staff defined a portion of Com.x's requirements for one of its projects and simulated them; designed and developed to operational status a part of one of their target applications with our environment; defined formally the process (itself as a system) of developing a Com.x system in a scenario where the company and we would work together. The output of this process was a developed module for Com.x's customer. Com.x personnel were trained in the technology, and a set of reusables was developed that could be used in common on company projects.

FMaps and TMaps were used throughout for all steps, from formally defining parts of the target application to formally defining the steps of developing it as well, in order to illustrate how all of these processes can be viewed and developed as formal systems.

The fact that the vendor actually uses his own technology and products to do for himself what it was selling to the vendor was a big plus for the customer. The fact that the DBTF environment was used to completely define and generate itself was also of significance because it means that its developer is its own user (or customer). Over eight million lines of code have been generated by the DBTF environment to generate its own major versions. It has been important to us that we use our own methods and tools in the same ways we have our customers use them. We would not have the environment we have today if we had not upheld this ground rule for ourselves.

From "As Is" to "To Be"

The learning curve of DBTF is relatively short. A week's introductory course proves sufficient to start using its environment. Internships are used typically to teach in-depth techniques that are applied to solving problems in a particular application area. Internships reinforce that which is taught in the introductory course. One can become quite productive after a month of regular use. This is because the process is intuitive, there is only one language and only one set of integrated tools to learn for the life cycle, and it is straightforward. Also, everything else is derivable from the initial concepts, its formalism enforces the "no more, no less" rule, and the modeler concentrates on the objects in a system and how to relate and use them, not on how to make them be object oriented. All of these aspects contribute to meeting the transition goal, GOAL #11.

Another aspect of GOAL #11, transitioning from another environment to a new one, can be done, for example, by using the DBTF environment for creating wrappers around legacy code, including code generated by other tools, and turning it into DBTF primitives, which can then be generated automatically to by the generator. If other chosen tools support openness, the code generated by the generator can be integrated with (or accessed by) these other tools.

To make sure that the transition was a smooth one, our staff defined the process of working together with the company, formally, with FMaps and TMaps. Such a plan was defined (and parts of the system simulated) to show how the organization will not lose time but gain, even though this would be a transition to a new, more formal and systematic way of doing things.

Integrating the Parts

One of the problems that can occur with traditional systems, including object-oriented ones, is the difficulty in integrating the parts. The process is error prone and time consuming. This is not the case with DBTF since all of its parts are by their very nature formally integrated. The result is an integrated, seamless design and development environment. There is no longer an additional expense for integrating diverse products for developing different parts of a system or phases of the system, or for integrating the modules or views (e.g., data flow, timing, state transition, and object types) of a module created with or resulting from these disparate products.

DBTF systems are defined to handle changes during development, operation, and evolution since all objects are system oriented, integrated, under control, and traceable. All aspects of system design and development are integrated with one system's language and its associated automation.

With respect to choosing a strategic technology (GOAL #13), integration in all forms is key. One of the most severe problems that occurred with Com.x's software was its integration or lack thereof. This included their more recently developed object-oriented based applications.

Real World Experience

Many systems have been developed with the DBTF development environment. Countless evaluations have been performed where DBTF and its environment were compared to other approaches. These evaluations have taken place within government, industry, and university environments; within database and real-time distributed environments; within domain analysis, process modeling, requirements definition, testing and software development environments; and within banking, software tool building, Internet, avionics, missile, manufacturing, and nuclear environments to name a few. In every comparison, the DBTF environment has finished first — no matter how large or complex the system being developed. No doubt this was because each of those other approaches was after the fact.

One example was the experiment performed by the National Test Bed.[9] The NTB provided the same problem to each of three contractor/vendor teams. The application was real-time, distributed, multiuser, client/server, and had to be defined and developed under U.S. Government 2167A guidelines. While all three teams successfully completed the definition of preliminary requirements, only two teams continued on to complete detailed design successfully. One team, the DBTF team, continued on to generate complete and fully production-ready code automatically. Both C and Ada were generated from the same definitions, and at the completion of the experiment a major portion of this code was running in both languages.

Several systems have been analyzed by users of the DBTF environment on an ongoing basis in order to understand more fully the impact properties of a system's definition have on productivity in its development. Collective experience strongly and consistently confirms that quality is maximized and cost and time to market are minimized with the increased use of DBTF's properties and its automation (GOAL #12).[8-14] We learned that a system's productivity, for example, increases with an increase in quality and flexibility in that system and in the system which develops that system. In fact, the earlier such properties exist, the higher the productivity.

Exhibit 18-21 contains a summary of how DBTF compares with traditional, after the fact methods. DBTF's preventative philosophy, to solve a given problem as early as possible, means finding a problem statically is better than finding it dynamically. Preventing it by the way a system is defined is even better. Better yet is not having to define (and build) it at all. Only then have we satisfied the reuse goal, the other one (in addition to the strategic technology goal) that needs to be satisfied to successfully achieve all of the other goals in the business.

In Boehm, the highest percent of life cycle cost of a traditional system was attributed to maintenance.[15] What this suggests is that the impact of a change in the systems that were studied was difficult to track and test since traceability is all but nonexistent in these environments. This is consistent with our own findings that the productivity of a system development process increases with the degree of quality of that system's definition. Further, Boehm showed that the longer it takes to find an error, the more expensive it becomes. That is, it costs much less to find it in the requirements phase than the design phase, less to find it in the design phase than the coding phase, etc. Yet most errors that occur in large systems already exist in early stages. What this means is that the earlier the quality of a system is established in that system's development, the more the productivity of that system's development increases.

It should be no surprise that the results of using the DBTF environment from the perspective of productivity were consistent with many of Boehm's findings. For example, since errors are dealt with before the fact, the productivity would be expected to increase dramatically with the use of this environment over traditional methods, and it did. Maintenance, however, is no longer the time sync that it was within a traditional environment. This is in major part because all SOOs are traceable and candidates for reuse.

One cannot make a one-to-one correlation when comparing life-cycle phases in DBTF to traditional life-cycle phases, such as allocating percentages of time to these phases. In Roetzeim, the life cycle is broken down into management (20 percent), documentation (12 percent), System Design (13 percent), detailed design (12 percent), coding (13 percent), unit testing (10

A Comparison

Traditional (After the Fact)	Before the Fact
75% interface errors ~Most found after implementation ~Some found manually ~Some found by dynamic runs analysis ~Some never found	*No interface errors* ~All found before implementation ~All found by automatic and static analysis ~Always found
Ambiguous requirements ~Informal or semi-formal language ~Different phases, different languages and tools ~Different language for systems than for software	*Unambiguous requirements* ~Formal, but friendly language ~All phases, same language and tools ~Same language for software, hardware and any other system
Automation supports manual process ~Documentation, programming, test generation, traceability, etc, are mostly manual	*Automation does real work* ~Documentation, programming, test generation, traceability, etc. are automatic ~100% code generation for any kind of software
No guarantee of function integrity after implementation	*Guarantee of function integrity after implementation*
Systems not traceable or evolvable ~Locked in products, architectures, etc. ~Painful transition from legacy ~Maintenance performed at code level	*Systems traceable and evolvable* ~Open architecture ~Smooth transition from legacy ~Maintenance performed at spec level
Reuse not inherent ~Reuse is adhoc	*Inherent reuse* ~Every object a candidate for reuse
Mismatched objects, phases, products, architectectures and environment ~System not integrated with software ~Function oriented <u>or</u> object oriented ~GUI not integrated with application	*Integrated & seamless objects, phases, products, architectures and environment* ~System integrated with software ~System oriented objects:integration of function oriented <u>and</u> object oriented ~GUI integrated with application ~Simulation integrated with software code
Product x not defined and developed with itself	*DBTF's automation is defined with and generated by itself*
Dollars wasted, error prone systems ~Not cost effective ~Difficult to meet schedules ~Less of what you need and more of what you don't need	*Better, faster, cheaper systems* ~Maximum dollars saved ~Minimum time to complete ~No more, no less of what you need

Exhibit 18-21.

percent), integration testing (17.5 percent), and configuration management (2.5 percent). These percentages would be quite different with a preventative approach.

Management, for example, has less to do on a relative basis, since so much of it becomes inherent or automated; integration takes up a relatively small percentage of time since it, too, is inherently accommodated; maintenance for reasons such as those discussed above is reduced considerably on a relative scale; coding is reduced significantly since while it is automated, a good part of the documentation process is automated as well; and because of results such as these and others such as those discussed above, testing becomes minimized.

The focus is now on areas such as analysis and design, which is as it should be; there is still a requirement for a human to input his thoughts. Reuse has a major part to play in savings during these phases as well, because of the added power that a designer has with object thinking and designing in terms of SOOs.

Return on Investment

The DBTF environment has been shown to significantly cut expenses and time to market while building better systems, resulting in unprecedented productivity savings (GOAL #12). Money and time saved by users of the DBTF environment are not insignificant. With each new experience, more is learned about the implications of DBTF. The goal is to be able to measure the degree to which DBTF impacts productivity under various scenarios in order to understand how to capitalize on it even more. The more we learn, the better estimates will be for future DBTF systems.

The Bottom Line

Compared to a traditional C development, the productivity of DBTF-developed systems was from 10 to 100 times greater than if they had been developed with traditional approaches (see Exhibit 18-22). According to these results if a system is estimated to cost, say, $60 million using traditional approaches, a 10 to 1 savings (at the lower end of the spectrum) would cost at most $6 million with a preventative approach. Upon further analysis, it was discovered that the productivity was higher the larger and more complex the system — the opposite of what one finds with traditional systems development. This is due in part because of the high degree of DBTF's support of reuse. The larger a system, the more it has the opportunity to capitalize on reuse.

But there are other reasons for this higher productivity as well, such as the savings realized and time saved due to tasks and processes that are no longer necessary with the use of this approach.

There is less to learn and less to do — less analysis, little or no implementation, less testing, less to manage, less to document, less to maintain, and less to integrate. This is because a major part of these areas has been automated or things inherently take place because of the nature of DBTF's formal systems language.

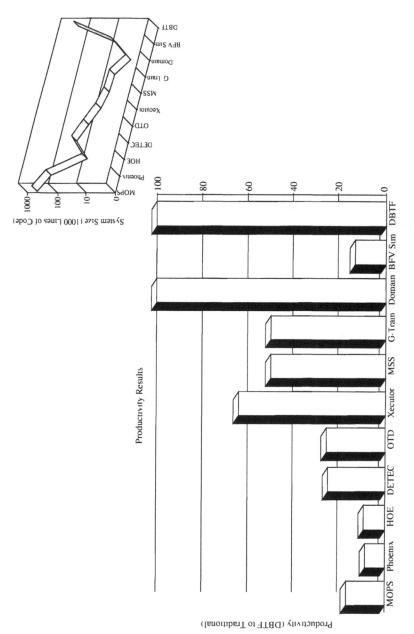

Exhibit 18-22. Productivity results.

Not only does the DBTF approach significantly increase productivity, but as more reuse is employed, productivity continues to increase. Measuring productivity becomes a process of relativity — that is, relative to the last system developed. Older methods for measuring productivity are no longer applicable.

Towards this end, an area of great interest with users has been that of capitalizing on the power of reuse within DBTF environments. Take, for example, an SOO as a reusable. It can be categorized in many ways. One is according to the manner in which its use saves time (which translates to how it impacts cost and schedules). More intelligent tradeoffs can then be made. The more we know about how some kinds of reusables are used (for example, particular FMap and TMap User Defined Structures which are FMaps with variable functions and TMaps with variable types, respectively), the more information we have on estimating costs for the overall system.

Exhibit 18-23 illustrates what can be saved with the additional use of just a couple of user-defined structures in FMaps or TMaps which have certain attributes. Here, if it takes 40 nodes on a map to define a user-defined structure (see lower left-hand corner in table) and it takes 3 nodes to use it, then if there were 1000 uses of the structure, there would be 3040 nodes used (statements to write as part of a definition) with the use of the structure and 40,000 nodes (statements to write) without it. If productivity is measured in terms of statements, say, for requirements or test cases (software is often measured in terms of lines of code), then with the use of these structures in the manner described, the productivity would be increased by approximately 13 to 1 (productivity using these structures over not using them). This is in addition to what is already saved by transitioning from a traditional approach to DBTF.

Since DBTF is a systems theory for defining, designing, and developing software systems in terms of SOOs, it can become part of the specification for meeting the strategic technology goal of any company that develops software. The goals defined for a company are the requirements for its enterprise as a target system.

THE RIGHT OPTION FOR COM.X

Analysis of Com.x's goals shows a strong dependency between all of them and the software approach it uses, or, putting it in another way, a strong dependency on the properties in the software it develops. Decisions made today about the company's software methods and tools could be the deciding factor as to whether its business will succeed.

Once organizations like Com.x begin to understand the degree to which a technology affects them, software will be given its due respect. The right strategic approach and the technology that executes it forms the foundation

Exhibit 18-23. Analysis of End User Work Characteristics (Cost Benefits Analysis with User-Defined Reusables)

Kind of Structure	Number of Nodes		Number of Uses of Structure	Number of Nodes with Structure Capability	Number of Nodes without Structure Capability
	Definition	Each Use			
Structure with one plug-in node	10	2	10	30	100
			100	210	1000
			1000	2010	10,000
	40	2	10	60	400
			100	240	4000
			1000	2040	40,000
Structure with two plug-in nodes	10	3	10	40	100
			100	310	1000
			1000	3010	10,000
	40	3	10	70	400
			100	340	4000
			1000	3040	40,000

Note: A function is at the node for an FMap structure, a type for a TMap structure.

for better, faster, cheaper software, the answer to success in business, certainly in a business which delivers software.

It is high risk for Com.x to keep doing things the way it has been. As with any organization, change is not easy, but Com.x knows that change will be necessary in order to save itself. Option 1, therefore, would not be an option. To do so would compromise reaching the company's highest priority goals. The second option of applying a more or less quick fix would at best address only some of the problem areas and then only on a temporary basis. Maybe worse yet is bringing in an entirely "new" but traditional approach. Not only does it take the time and effort to transition from one approach to another, but the new approach still suffers from the basic core problems of the one being used by the company today.

In order to reach the goals as defined above, the company would need to choose the fourth or fifth option of evolving to the use of tools and techniques that formalize, preventatively, the company's process of software engineering. The fourth option is probably most practical in a short-term consideration. The fifth option, although most desirable from a long-term view, would take more time and should be chosen if such time, including lead time, is available on the project that will first apply the new technology.

DBTF and its automation address in major part the subgoals defined for the strategic technologies goal (GOAL #13). Should it not have all of the components desired by Com.x's developers either now or in the future, it has an environment that is completely open, open to interface to other products or to be interfaced to by other products, and open to allow for enhancements to be developed, brought in from the company's existing or future legacy code and interfaced and/or added to the DBTF environment by the company itself. Not only can it be configured to generate to any language, architecture, OS, communications, database, etc., but it could be configured as well to generate automatically to a special purpose environment (such as a language of another product or specialized embedded code).

In today's market it becomes increasingly important for a product to be able to interface to others and for others to interface to that product. A lock-in product compromises the ability to make choices in the future. The result is limited functionality, technology, and architectures — hardware and software products that can be used (including legacy software) both now and in the future.

It may not always be considered realistic for a project to develop a particular application from the standpoint of a pure systems viewpoint where in the ideal world the requirements are understood first as a system before later phases of development. Should this be the case, the DBTF approach has the flexibility of either supporting its users in defining such an application from its beginning or in starting to use it in defining such an application in a later phase of development, such as with one of its software module subsystems (for example, the host software) in a detailed design phase. The software implementation would then be automatically generated from the design of this subsystem.

It becomes evident that what is really needed for Com.x is a way to create *durable* systems — durable because they incorporate a structure and process for the continuous evolution of any or all parts of a system and durable because they provide a way to productively, instead of destructively, manage change to a system — change in the businesses they support and change in the technologies used to implement them. Once durable systems are developed, the company will be free to safely make the key decision of when and how it transitions what it has today to what it needs tomorrow.

Such a transition as would take place with the fourth or fifth option presents a major opportunity to take a step back and examine the underlying process used to design, build, and deploy software and examine where the next introduction of modern (in the real sense) technologies and products truly fit within the company's systems development framework.

Despite everything, two things remain constant at Com.x. Its systems and software fail often, and change is inevitable. This is only compounded in an atmosphere of rapid growth. Change in the software industry needs no introduction. But it is this facet of our industry that has provided at best a foundation of quicksand for the systems deployed to date. We cannot do anything about changing change, but we can do something about dealing with it. A transition from the old to the new, which uses a formal, before the fact systems approach, will go a long way towards addressing this issue.

CONCLUSION

Within today's commercial enterprise, users demand much more functionality and flexibility (which includes durability) in their systems than before. Models are distributed, including Internet models which are a popular form of distribution in use today. And given the nature of many of the problems to be solved, their systems must be error-free. These environments and object-oriented projects begin to sound like the earlier days of real-time, distributed environments, where complexity gave rise to new kinds of problems, including those having to do with interface and integration issues. The issue should not be, for example, whether an approach is object-oriented or component-based or one that the competitor is using, but rather whether it will be what is needed to meet the highest priority goals of the organization.

Although change is difficult for any organization, changing from a traditional environment to an environment like Development Before the Fact is like transitioning from the typewriter to the word processor. There is certainly the need for the initial overhead for learning the new way of doing things, but once having used word processors, would we ever go back to the typewriter?

Following the "no more, no less" rule, for example, becomes one of the deciding factors. Yet, if we think about it, it is a matter of common sense. Not only does it result in using the best strategic technologies, but it makes sure that they are used the way they should be, capitalizing, for example, on reuse and treating everything systematically. One result is that of removing the need for armies of people that are no longer needed to support obsolescence. This brings freedom, both for the people who should not be locked into using obsolete methods and to the corporation who should not be losing profits by doing unnecessary work. At the end of the day, freedom is the most valuable commodity of them all, for without it we lose control of our destiny.

True, many software companies today are doing quite well using traditional, informal, and after-the-fact development techniques — relatively speaking, that is, when it comes to making a profit. But how long will this last? As with anything, it is usually a matter of time and timing. And as we said earlier, every system is relative. What works for success today may not work tomorrow, especially if there are known weaknesses in the system.

Others will catch on and realize that there is a better way to do business after all, especially those who have less to lose. They could well leave the so-called successful ones behind in the dust.

[001, 001 Tool Suite, Function Map, FMap, Type Map, TMap, Object Map, OMap, Execution Map, EMap, Road Map, RMap, Xecutor, OMap Editor, 001 Analyzer, SOO, System Oriented Object, Resource Allocation Tool, RAT, AntiRAT, Object Editor, Primitive Control Structures, Development Before the Fact, DBTF, RT(x), 001 AXES, agent 001db are all trademarks of Hamilton Technologies, Inc.]

Notes

1. Hamilton, M. Development Before the Fact in Action, *Electron. Design,* June 13, 1994.
2. Hamilton, M. Inside Development Before the Fact, *Electron. Design,* April 4, 1994.
3. Hamilton, M., Zero-defect software: the elusive goal, *IEEE Spec.* 23(No. 3), 48, March, 1986.
4. Hamilton, M. and Hackler, W.R., *Object Thinking,* McGraw-Hill, New York, 1999.
5. *The 001 Tool Suite Reference Manual, Version 3,* Hamilton Technologies, Inc., Cambridge, MA, 1993–1999.
6. Hornstein, R., Willoughby, J., Hamilton, M., Heuser, W., LoPinto, F., and Hawkins, F., From Space Systems R&D to Commercial Products: Technology Transfer Initiatives to Benefit Small Satellite Missions, NASA Headquarters, Fall, 1997.
7. Hornstein, R.S., A Cross-Cutting Agenda for Achieving a Faster, Better, Cheaper Space Operations Infrastructure, AIAA Workshop on Reducing the Costs of Space Operations, Arlington, VA, 1995.
8. Ouyang, M. and Golay, M.W., An Integrated Formal Approach for Developing High Quality Software of Safety-Critical Systems, Massachusetts Institute of Technology, Cambridge, MA, Report No. MIT-ANP-TR-035.

9. Software Engineering Tools Experiment-Final Report, Vol. 1, Experiment Summary, Table 1, Page 9, Department of Defense, Strategic Defense Initiative, Washington, D.C., 20301-7100.
10. Keyes, J., *Data Casting: How to Stream Data Bases Over the Web*, McGraw-Hill, New York, 1988.
11. Krut, B., Jr., Integrating 001 Tool Support in the Feature-Oriented Domain Analysis Methodology (CMU/SEI-93-TR-11, ESC-TR-93-188), Software Engineering Institute, Carnegie-Mellon University, Pittsburgh, PA, 1993.
12. Huang, M., The Comparison of 001 to Java, Ariel Technologies Technical Demo, September, 1998.
13. Hamilton Technologies, Inc., What Others Say about 001, Evolving Documented Testimonials Received from Customer Base.
14. Hamilton Technologies, Inc. Customer Profiles, Evolving Documented Interviews from Customer Base.
15. Boehm, B., Software Engineering, IEEE Trans. Computers, December, 1996.
16. Roetzeim, W.H., *Developing Software to Government Standards*, Prentice Hall, New York, 1991.

Author Bio

Margaret Hamilton (mhh@htius.com) is the founder and CEO of Hamilton Technologies, Inc. (HTI), based in Cambridge, MA. She is a pioneer in the systems engineering and software development industry. Hamilton's mission has been to bring to market a completely integrated and robust tool suite that is based on the unique systems theory paradigm, which she created, called Development Before the Fact (DBTF). In bringing her product to market, her company leveraged the power of reusability and the reliability of seamless integration to provide a tool that sharply decreases errors while simultaneously increasing productivity. The result is an ultrareliable system at a fraction of the cost of conventional systems. Hamilton's goal was to embed this formal and completely systems-oriented object (SOO) framework into a highly efficient, high performance, completely graphical, portable workbench of smart tools which the systems engineer and software developer could use throughout the entire design and development life cycle. Today this ideal has been surpassed with the 001 Tool Suite.

Earlier in her career, as the leader of the Software Engineering Division at MIT's Charles Stark Draper Laboratory, Hamilton was the director of the Apollo on-board flight software project and created Higher Order Software (HOS), a formal systems design theory based on empirical studies of Apollo.

After this, Hamilton founded and was CEO of Higher Order Software, where she was responsible for the development of the first comprehensive CASE tool in the industry. This tool, called USE.IT, was based on her formal design theory, HOS.

Chapter 19
Multimedia-Based Training (MBT) for Financial Services

Barbara Sealund
Tim Brock

WHEN THINKING OF MULTIMEDIA, one often associates it with slick interfaces, interactive widgetry, hyperlinking, branching, and a plethora of user access and controls. Multimedia-Based Training (MBT) can also use a multiplicity of media: text, image, audio, video, and animation. Media can be used simultaneously, sequentially, and interactively to train users on systems as well as to convey conceptual information. MBT can support conventional instructional strategies ranging from guided tours, matching exercises, drill and practice, questions and answers, to simulation, scenarios, games, and more.

WHY MBT?

Numerous studies have proven that the more senses activated during a learning session, the greater the retention. In addition, if the media is merged to create a believable "virtual" environment — a learning environment that conjures a kind of theater of the mind — then a greater opportunity for "mental practice" can improve performance. The idea of electronic performance-based training is certainly not new, but the use of multimedia to enhance the user experience — creating a more realistic or engaging performance environment — is just beginning to be fully developed.

Multimedia can be used to create interfaces that suspend disbelief so that users are motivated to try things over and over until mastery is achieved. When talking to professional athletes or musicians about their skill, many say it is 80 to 90percent mental. For the football player, the ability to mentally previsualize a physical response to the coming play is the key to his success. Proper mental rehearsing is fundamental. For the musician, mentally hearing and anticipating the note before it actually happens is often

0-8493-98 34- 7/00/$0 00+$ 50
© 2000 by CRC Press LLC

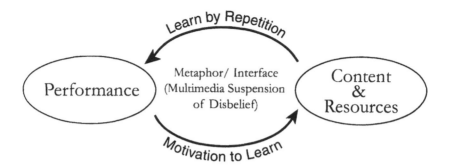

Exhibit 19-1. MTB can provide the focus and motivation for repetition of a job function by creating a "virtual rehearsal place."

90 percent of the effective act. One Los Angeles-based concert violinist will not perform a concerto in public without first "playing" the piece several times in her mind without the instrument. Good mental rehearsal habits for both the athlete and the musician are fundamental to professional quality performance. MBT can provide the focus and motivation for repetition of a job function by creating a "virtual rehearsal place" (Exhibit 19-1).

DEVELOPMENT ISSUES: EXAMPLES IN FINANCIAL SERVICES INDUSTRY

The onset of rapid application systems development brings with it many challenges for training. MBT is one answer to the challenge of "how can we train the multitudes of people globally who need to use our new online banking application?"

Bank executives today face the new challenge of being able to effectively and successfully implement new application systems, which seem to roll out more frequently than ever before. In addition to rapid application systems development, technical teams are becoming more sophisticated in developing systems that meet the specifications of their user. These systems often impact not only an employee base, but the bank's customer base as well. To add to the complexity of implementation, often the systems will be rolled out globally across multilingual and multicultural environments. All too often, training is not considered an integral part of the initial deployment, thus failure of a well-designed application system becomes imminent.

It is important to acknowledge that training will make a significant impact on the successful implementation of new application systems and that the earlier the involvement of the training team, the better. In fact, a well-designed training solution will run parallel with the application development, even to the point of common deliverables. For example, a thorough analysis of the new application should be completed with the first deliverable, which is a Project Analysis Report for the training project plan.

It is from this analysis phase that the training team along with the systems deployment team can make the best decision for an effective training solution. Without this critical phase of the project plan, you will begin the journey without a road map and perhaps with an undetermined destination.

The good news is that with appropriate analysis and planning of the training, the training team can become a dynamic and motivational part of the project team as well as bring value to the successful implementation of the application system.

While MBT is one of the most instructionally dynamic media, it is not always the best training solution. Each individual implementation and environment needs to be carefully reviewed before decisions can be made on the most appropriate training media for the specific application. Again, the due diligence spent at the analysis phase will save volumes in time and dollar savings at the implementation phase.

A high end Custom Training Team tends to view each project at the level of:

- What is the training issue/problem/challenge
- What can we do to help
- What will we do to support

Oversimplified:

- Business Need
- Business Solution

The following examples illustrate various business challenges that customers have been faced with, and how a selected Custom Training Team supported the business need with a successful training solution.

Case Study A: System Conversion Affecting 38,000 Employees

Business Need. One of the largest financial organizations in the West was converting 990 branches to an integrated banking application system. The conversion would affect 38,000 employees, all of whom would require training to perform their job function. Accomplishing the task with classroom training was virtually impossible considering the size of the audience, geographic location throughout the U.S., the aggressive schedule, and the lack of expertise.

Business Solution. The Custom Training Team had the systems conversion experience, training experience, and the systems expertise that would ensure a successful conversion and implementation of the training materials. The Training Team designed and developed a Total Training Solution which encompassed 27 fully-integrated Computer-Based Training (CBT) courses totaling 43 hours of instruction, 7 days of Classroom Training for Train-the-Trainer, including Leader and Student Guides, Self-Study Workbooks, Job Aids and Pre/Post-Test and Scenario Handbook utilizing Computer-Managed Instruction. The training materials provided step-by-step instructions on how to perform system functions and emulated the system so learners could practice in a nonthreatening environment. The implementation of the training materials was a tremendous success.

Case Study B: Market Terminology for Global Audience

Business Need. One of the world's largest banks required training for a very large and diverse audience. The training would need to familiarize the audience with market terminology covering areas such as securities, buzzwords, and accounting/taxation.

Business Solution. The Custom Training Team designed a menu-driven CBT course to allow students to select areas of terminology relevant to their job function. The course contained four main categories: buzzwords, markets, securities, and miscellaneous. Within each category terms were listed in alphabetical order and were accessed via a sub-menu. Upon selection of a term, a tutorial would appear along with an example. At the end of each category the student could select a testing segment to ensure their knowledge of the terminology presented. The course was highly successful and used worldwide.

Case Study C: Standardization for Bank Card Division

Business Need. One of the nation's largest banks, located in the northeast, desired to standardize training for its three geographically dispersed training sites. The training sites conducted intense three-week courses to train customer service representatives on their role and responsibilities within the bank card division, as well as how to use the division's computer system. At the time, the training varied not only from site to site, but from trainer to trainer. Standardization was a major goal for the bank card division, not just in training, but in all aspects of the business.

Business Solution. The Custom Training Team conducted in-depth training analysis with all three sites to reach a consensus of the topics to be covered as well as the best training approach. The Training Team then designed a 3-hour CBT course which provided instruction relative to the organization, the bank card industry, and the customer service representative's role and responsibilities.

Included in the customer service representative's role and responsibilities was product knowledge, calculations such as average daily balance, minimum monthly payments, finance charges, and ensuring customer satisfaction. The trainers could then concentrate on systems training and role-playing. The CBT course was a big success and helped give the customer service representatives a positive self-image related to their role within the organization.

Case Study D: Major HR System Impacting Over 500 HR Managers

Business Need. More than 500 Human Resources managers and input clerks in a major bank were being prepared to convert to computerization of all personnel records. The system would cover inquiries, updating personnel records, payroll, and changes to the bank's personnel records. Generic software was to be customized for the massive, 2-year project.

Business Solution. The Custom Training Team stepped in at the start to develop custom computer-based training for each unit. The CBT was ready at least 4 weeks before the new software was to go online, so that employees had ample time to learn the system before implementation. Records on more than 30,000 employees were computerized in the ongoing project, which continues today.

Case Study E: 800 Relationship Managers Selling Bank Services

Business Need. Managing the relationships between a major travel and entertainment credit card company and its corporate clients was the job of more than 800 relationship managers who received computer-based training created by the Custom Training Team.

Business Solution. The 1-hour training explained the benefits of the credit card marketing program, enabling them to sell their package to major clients.

Case Study F: Graphical Interface Increases Retention

Business Need. One of the nation's largest insurance companies was trying to find an efficient method of disseminating information with respect to a business resumption policy that was being implemented. An additional goal was that those employees to whom the information was distributed be able to "try out" the new mechanisms: first to see how the new plan would work, and second to ensure that they understood the new policies and procedures.

Business Solution. The Custom Training Team studied the plan, analyzed the client's goals, and developed a highly interactive Multimedia-Based Training module. Users were given an overview of the plan and specific procedures for completion of the necessary paperwork. Throughout the module, users were required to answer questions to test retention of the material. Finally, the user was given an opportunity to practice "filling in" the forms on the computer screen. The module would then inform the user as to the correctness of their work. Graphics and animation were used consistently throughout the module to maintain user interest.

MBT APPLIED TO FINANCIAL SERVICES

Interface Issues

Analysis is vital for creating an effective MBT interface. Analysis reveals the business needs for training. Those needs then direct the development of an effective metaphor/interface. Below is a general synopsis of the corporate banking learning environment, including a brief analysis of corporate culture, the audience, and performance tasks.

Corporate Culture Analysis

The corporate banking culture is changing quickly. These changes are happening on global and local levels. Banking applications are merging and moving online. Employee time is precious. The training paradigm is changing from instructor-led to user independence — online, just right and just in time. As currencies begin to merge, questions arise within the corporate culture about these trends and their future impact on banking. In short, the culture is changing rapidly and customers as well as employees are looking with some uncertainty to the future.

Audience Analysis

The training audience in banking includes internal and external customers from around the world. They range from high level decision makers to end users. The internal/external clients may be senior managers (decision makers), security managers, information technologists, sales representatives, and end users. Computer experience and subject familiarity encompass a wide range. End users for example may have a high level of exposure to systems. In summary, the banking audience requires a fast, global, modular training solution with a broad-based appeal.

Task Analysis

Task analysis is crucial for defining the MBT interface requirements. This is where the core performance skills are clarified and from which scenarios are created. Performance tasks are either based on using an existing system or are based on mastery of conceptual content.

APPLYING AN MBT INTERFACE

These two mastery types have different interface requirements. If performance on an application system is needed, then the interface requirements could be minimal, since using the system is the instructional focus. If mastery of specific conceptual information is needed, then the interface could be more robust, but should serve the need of those conceptual requirements.

In addition, the business need could require both systems and conceptual skills. A sales manager may be required to know the global features of a new banking application as well as know how to use the system. For example, this new banking application may feature online banking anywhere, anytime, just enough, and just in time. It may have certain online performance standards that would require "hands-on" scenario practice. The MBT interface solution for this training need could be a virtual internet "palm-top" Personal Digital Assistant (PDA) with real-time access to assets, foreign exchange, and settlement functions — demonstrating a "hands-on" modular, online banking experience — from anywhere in the world.

CREATING A REALISTIC INTERFACE

Interfaces really are the machines that make MBT work. The more consistent and believable the machine, the greater the suspension of disbelief and the more engaging the training. If the interface simulates a chest of drawers or a filing cabinet for example, then the drawers should open like drawers, they should sound like drawers sliding on wood or steel. If the interface metaphor is based on a particular Picasso painting, then buttons should appear and function in a cubist multiple-view style. If the interface is a walkie-talkie or cell phone, then the Liquid Crystal Display (LCD) panel should light up with green upper-case san serif letters and the audio should sound like its coming through the phone's speaker. In other words, realism helps bring the interface to life — all for the purpose of engaging the user.

There are numerous ways to create immersive interfaces, but one of the most powerful tools is 3D animation. Three-dimensional (3D) modeling and animation can greatly support MBT interface realism. Information in the "real world" is rarely conveyed in two dimensions (2D) only — even paper has a thin 3D quality. If interfaces are to be realistic, evoking an immersive "theater of the mind" quality, then 3D modeling and animation can help add this 3D value to MBT.

PUSHING THE "Z" (DEPTH) AXIS

Most users and some designers see a blank screen as a 2D flat surface with only an X and Y (cross) axis. Some perceive paintings as 2D shapes and colors and most people perceive text as flat 2D strokes and shapes. However, if those 2D letters extrude and become 3D objects then the Z (depth) axis is now active. With the activation of the "Z" axis, designers have a powerful metaphor for building not only two-dimensional shapes but 3D forms such as cubes, spheres, or cylinders. These 3D forms can become extended surfaces for organization of information. Text can be "mapped" not only onto the front plane of a cube, but also can be mapped onto to the side, back, top, or bottom of the cube. The 2D surface expands to 3D for organizing more information on multiple surfaces within a 3D multimedia space.

PUSHING THE "T" (TIME) AXIS

If a 3D space can draw one into a static "mindscape" of information, animation can cause that landscape to come alive and can be used to actually transport users to other "information objects," rooms, or "mindscapes." Also, animation can further economize the use of space and help imprint a lasting impression on the mind. Gravity and time can be manipulated to simulate the desired effect. Reality can be "changed" to economize space and kinetic objects can be "loaded" with content.

Movement involves time and sequencing. Nothing draws attention like movement. This is a TV/film-saturated culture. This cultural immersion in the language of movement can provide an incredible reference for interface designers who wish to attach information and content, not only to static objects, but to kinetic objects as well.

AUGMENTING REALITY

Once an interface is plausible, effectively engaging the user, the next stage of development can be very exciting: augmenting or exaggerating portions of reality. Just like in motion pictures or in cartoon animation, the exaggeration or augmentation of reality can take us somewhere. Disney's flying elephant Dumbo, for example, has enough reality to draw us into the story, but when the little elephant's ears fill with air and Dumbo flies — reality is exaggerated. Augmenting reality can evoke our imaginations and help greatly with retention and motivation. Other forms of augmentation may include humor, the miraculous, time travel, and futurism.

FUTURISM — PUSHING THE INTERFACE PARADIGM

Futurism can be great fodder for augmenting reality in MBT. Believable interfaces in a virtual multimedia environment can easily shift into the next paradigm. Future trends in technology can be experienced through simulation, exaggerating reality to engage users. For example, in online banking MBT, realistic interfaces could project future applications of personal real-time banking transactions between individuals and institutions across the globe. Just think of it, real-time currency foreign exchange transactions between hometown, U.S.A. and Peking, China. These extensions of reality can be a form of "intertrainment." In short, just like cinema, MBT interfaces should take us to a place we've never been.

TRUSTEE TRANSFER - PARTIAL
EXERCISE FLOW CHART

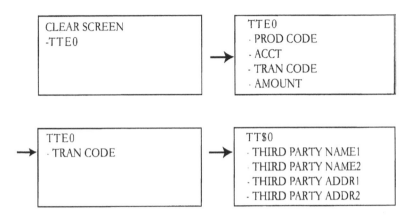

Exhibit 19-2. A simple example of a transactional task in banking — a trustee transfer transaction.

ONLINE BANKING: MBT INTERFACE SCENARIO EXAMPLE

To bring all this back to financial services, the following flowchart (Exhibit 19-2) is a simple example of a transactional task in banking — a trustee transfer transaction. The current task is expanded to a typical scenario practice exercise (Exhibit 19-3). The original computer-based training screen (Exhibit 19-4) shows the original mainframe systems environment where the scenario exercise was to be practiced by an end user. The original computer-based training (CBT) interface simulates the systems application environment, which is purely text-based. The user is prompted to enter a transaction code, select the transaction function, and enter another code to select a third-party beneficiary.

Practice Exercise

Osama Suliman has decided to transfer part of REA
473023689432165 to Got Rocks National Bank, P. O.
Box 99999 Littleton, CO 80120. You are responsible
for transferring the $10,000.00.

Exhibit 19-3. The current task is expanded to a typical scenario practice exercise.

```
                        TTEO 3 IDS  REA TRUSTEE TRANSFER INQ   95/04/19 08.55.40
APMU        CO  9999 OP               MS       ACTION SUCCESSFUL
ACTION          COID
PROD CODE       ACCT                     SHORT NAME


TRAN CODE                        CURRENCY
AMOUNT
EFFECTIVE DATE                             ENTER TRAN CODE FOR INQUIRY
                                             6627 - WITH PENALTY
PAYMENT AMOUNT              .00              6628 - WITHOUT PENALTY
WITHHELD AMOUNT            .00
ACCRUED INTEREST          .00            ENTER TRAN CODE TO POST
PENALTY AMOUNT           .00               6593 - WITH PENALTY
                                           3085 - WITHOUT PENALTY
PROJECTED LEDGER BALANCE                .00

AIP MADE     AIP ADJ AMT                 .00
          +----------------------------------------------------+
          | Complete the required fields on TTEO to            |
          | determine the effect of the partial                |
          | withdrawal on Dr. Suliman's account balance.       |
PF:       +----------------------------------------------------+
```

Exhibit 19-4. The original computer-based training screen shows the original mainframe systems environment where the scenario exercise was practiced by an end user.

The following screens (Exhibits 19-5 through 19-8) apply an MBT interface to the same scenario exercise, providing a "virtual rehearsal place" for user performance.

The MBT interface reflects a corporate bank environment with marble pillars and a surreal 3D representation of time (Exhibit 19-5). It features a global "hand-held" device with a futuristic twist, displaying an imbedded screen (Exhibit 19-6) suggesting online Internet/global access. The interface is dimensional, and combines present-day familiar browser elements within a futuristic "palm-top" globe-like device.

Within the interface, the scenario exercise is represented as if it is an online transaction (Exhibit 19-7) — possibly a real-time event. Osama Suliman is signed on and engaged in a trustee transfer to a third-party person. As the scenario plays out, the user is taken to the next screen (Exhibit 19-8) showing the third-party beneficiary, Gozde Kucuk — either a video representation or a real-time telepresence representation — an individual touched by the transaction. The scenario is applied in an exaggerated reality. The user is immersed and transported to the world of "online" banking.

MBT for Financial Services. Who says training for banking has to be boring?

Exhibit 19-5. Providing a "virtual rehearsal place" for user performance scene 1.

Exhibit 19-6. Providing a "virtual rehearsal place" for user performance scene 2.

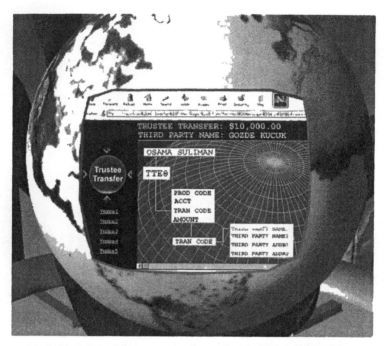

Exhibit 19-7. Providing a "virtual rehearsal place" for user performance scene 3.

Exhibit 19-8. Providing a "virtual rehearsal place" for user performance scene 4.

Authors' Bios

Barbara Sealund is President and Founder of Sealund & Associates Corporation the country's leading training development company utilizing multimedia and Web-based technologies. Sealund has managed multimillion-dollar training projects for Fortune 500 companies such as Chase Manhattan Bank, Lehman, Citibank, and IBM. Tapping into her experience in the banking industry, Sealund built a reputation as a systems-training expert. The company began designing and building computer-based training (CBT) for mainframe systems such as Hogan, M+I, and IBA during the mid-80s. Sealund founded the company in 1985 recognizing the need for corporations to move toward a more technological-based training solution for major conversions to new software application systems. She has been selected as a finalist for the "Entrepreneur of the Year," a nationwide competition sponsored by INC. Magazine, Merrill Lynch and Ernst & Young, and has received an award from IBM for the delivery of "The Americans With Disabilities Act Compliance Training" using OS/2 and CD-ROM. Sealund has Master's in Business and Adult Education from the University of South Florida and a Bachelor of Arts degree in English and Business Education from the University of Florida.

Tim Brock is the Creative Director for Sealund & Associates Corporation and manages the artistic direction of all custom interactive and documentation projects. He has developed interface designs for clients such as Citibank and Eckerd Corporation. Before joining S&A, Brock spent 5 years at the St. Petersburg Junior College as both an Instructor in Charge and computer graphics specialist. While there he was the Art Director and Interface Designer for the award winning Basic Enforcement Academy Training (BEAT) courseware project, a collaborative effort between SPJC and Sealund & Associates to design interactive training for "X-Generation Cops". This interactive courseware is currently used to train cadets for the St. Petersburg Police Department. The project won the Technology Research Award by the Tampa Bay Regional Planning Council and was featured in The Ultimate Multimedia Handbook (Revised, McGraw-Hill 1997). Brock's background also includes 2 years at the Banff Centre for the Arts in Alberta, Canada. As a Media Arts Computer Graphics Associate, he taught and collaborated with artists from around the world. He is a graduate of the Pratt Institute in Brooklyn, N.Y., with a Master's degree in Communications.

Chapter 20
Law (or the Lack of It) on the Web: A Primer for Financial Services Technology Managers

Federic M. Wilf

THE INTERNET APPEARS TO BE A "WILD WEST" circus that is above or unconnected to the law. The reality is that the Internet is pretty wild, but the law of each and every country, state, province, county, municipality, town, and borough applies to the Internet, and its most-famous aspect, the World Wide Web ("Web"). Web site developers, programmers, users, and others (this chapter uses the term "webmaster" for convenience) all need to be aware of the mechanisms of the law so as to get the maximum amount of protection for her work, while making sure that she does not trip over someone else's rights by mistake.

WHY THE WEB IS DIFFERENT FROM A LEGAL PERSPECTIVE

The law responds to each new technological challenge by first studying it, and then, if appropriate, doing something about it. For example, the Copyright Office started accepting copyright registrations for computer programs as early as 1964, but it was not until 1980 that Congress amended the U.S. Copyright Act to explicitly protect computer programs. Moreover, when the law initially confronts an issue, it usually does so in fits and starts.

The law tends to pigeon-hole issues. The Internet breaks all of the pigeon holes as it is a different form of communication that, in itself, can carry virtually all prior forms of communication. Distinctions that make sense in hard copy or on television may be irrelevant on the Internet, while the technology of the Internet creates new distinctions that do not apply to any other media. A single Web site may contain text, photographs, artwork (two-dimensional and three-dimensional), music and sound recordings, video, software, scripts, databases, and so on, all of which have been altered and arranged to form a single integrated work.

The law deals with Internet legal issues by analyzing each element that goes into a Web site as if the element were by itself. An element-by-element analysis may take a little more time to complete, but, as you will see, you do not need a lawyer to conduct this analysis. Much of this you can do yourself.

WHAT THIS CHAPTER COVERS

This chapter discusses legal issues that webmasters should be aware of under U.S. law. For example, if a webmaster would like to copy and use a photograph from another Web site, and there is no copyright notice, can the webmaster do this legally?

Suppose a webmaster has completed a Web site that consists of text, video, and sound, as well as searching software. How can the webmaster protect the work, or at least have the right to sue anyone who pirates the work?

There are fairly simple techniques to protect what the webmaster has created, as well as methods to enforce that protection. The other side of the coin is that the webmaster does not want to unwittingly infringe the rights of others, so a basic understanding of common legal problems can be helpful.

This chapter briefly discusses copyright, privacy and contract law as they apply to Web sites.

WHAT THIS CHAPTER DOES NOT COVER

This chapter discusses a number of legal issues that webmasters face, but it does not cover every legal issue. Nor does it say everything that needs to be said for each issue that it does cover.

This chapter discusses the law in the U.S. Except for a few brief references, it does not discuss international law or the law in any other country. More importantly, many issues in U.S. law (such as contract law) are a subject of state law, which means that the law will be different from one state to the next.

This chapter does not provide the "final word" on the state of the law. The law continues to change. One example is the U.S. Copyright Act, which was completely rewritten in 1976. However, Congress has seen fit to amend the Copyright Act several times each year since then. All of the areas of law discussed in this chapter are also subject to constant change.

Finally, this chapter does not provide legal, accounting, or other professional advice. If legal advice or other expert assistance is required, the services of a competent professional should be retained.

DO'S AND DON'TS

Normally, a list of do's and don'ts would be placed at the end of a chapter. We place it at the beginning, so that you have the answers while you read the details.

Do

- Consider patents.
- Use "SM" (service mark) and "TM" (trademark) for your marks for services and goods.
- Consider filing trademark applications with the state, federal, or foreign governments.
- Place copyright notices.
- File copyright applications for your Web sites.
- When multiple companies or parties work on a Web site, agree beforehand in a written document who will own the copyright and other rights.
- Review contracts with your attorney before signing them, and use an attorney to develop written agreements with your customers.
- Investigate the law of every country in which your Web site is used to provide services or sell goods.

Don't

- Mail HTML or software files, or other works, to yourself to secure rights (it's an urban myth).
- Wait until after signing an agreement to call your attorney.
- Assume the law doesn't apply to you because you're on the Internet.
- Assume the First Amendment protects you throughout the world (as one pundit likes to say, the U.S. Constitution is a local ordinance in cyberspace).
- Assume that the law in other countries is like that of the U.S.

COPYRIGHT LAW

Copyright law is the primary means to protect Web sites. Copyright law is designed to protect "expressions" of ideas, while making available to others the underlying ideas, facts, and information. Copyright law defines what is and is not protected, as well the methods by which protection is enforced.

Owning a Copyright as Opposed to Owning an Object

When a person buys a book or a record, that person then owns the physical object — the book or record. Owning the book or record does not give the purchaser the right to copy the book or record, or make new versions of the book or record.

So, if you purchase a videotape of a 10-year-old movie, you can watch that movie and show it to your friends. However, you cannot copy scenes from the movie into your Web site that is your guide to cinema without the permission of the person or company that owns the copyright to the movie.

As for the videotape, you can also sell it to another person (so long as you don't keep any copies for yourself). In copyright law, this is called the "first sale doctrine." Once the physical copy embodying the copyrighted work is sold, the purchaser can use or dispose of that copy any way she likes, so long as she does not make copies of the work (or portions of it).

Source of Law

The United States Copyright Act is the sole copyright statute in the U.S. This has been so since Congress pre-empted the field with the Copyright Act of 1976, which became effective on January 1, 1978.

No state is allowed to legislate in the area of copyright law, so there is no state copyright law. Nor is there a "common law" (judge-made) copyright law, so that judges will not create new rights or responsibilities, as they can in other areas of the law. Judges may interpret the U.S. Copyright Act, which means that a judge can create explanations and structures for resolving disputes where the Copyright Act is ambiguous, unclear, or incomplete.

For those who have access to federal statutes, the Copyright Act may be found in Title 17 of the United States Code. When this chapter refers to a section number, it will be to a section number of Title 17. For example, the definitions of copyright terms are found at Section 101 of the Copyright Act.

Definitions of Key Copyright Terms

Copyright law is whatever Congress says it is. Key to an understanding of copyright law is the terms that Congress uses in the Copyright Act. The definitions are important because a particular term will have one meaning in copyright law and a different meaning in a different area of the law. For example, the term "publication" in copyright law means dissemination to the general public; while "publication" in libel law means any dissemination of libelous matter to any other person, in public or private.

The following are key terms defined in Section 101 of the Copyright Act.

"Work". A "work" in the copyright lingo is any embodiment that contains expression that may be protected under the copyright law. Works include building designs, drawings, books, or any kind of text, two-dimensional and three-dimensional art, computer programs, movies, etc. All of the things protected by copyright law and discussed in this chapter are called "works."

"Audiovisual Works". An audiovisual work is a series of related images and any accompanying sounds that are intended to be shown by the use of machines, such as projectors or electronic equipment, including computers and televisions. It does not matter whether the audiovisual work is embodied in tape, on film, on floppy or CD-ROM, or in an MPEG file.

"Derivative Work". A derivative work is a work that is based upon one or more preexisting works, regardless of the type of preexisting work. The derivative work can be in any form in which a work may be recast, transformed, or adapted. Digitizing a photograph creates a derivative work (the digital version) of a preexisting work (the film-based or analog photograph). A derivative work can constitute an original work of authorship that is separate and distinct from the preexisting work. As noted above, however, the copyright owner can control whether a person is allowed to make derivative works of the copyright owner's work.

One key issue involving derivative works is the point at which a derivative work is no longer considered derivative. For example, if you digitize a photograph, that creates a derivative work that can be recognized as a copy of the original. If you then alter the digitized version to the point where it is no longer recognizable in any way as a derivative of the original, then you have created a new work.

Think of it as melting down a bronze statue. If you melt it down partially, and part of the original is still recognizable (even a small part), then you have a derivative work. However, if the bronze is melted completely into a liquid and then poured into a new mold, an original work is created that no longer owes anything to the prior work, except for the raw material.

Thus, if you take a photograph on print film of the White House, that is an original work. If you digitize the print, you have created a derivative work. If you then use the digital version (the first derivative work) of the White House photograph to create new images, such as a Blue House, a Pink House, a Green House, a Fuchsia House, each of these variations would be a separate derivative work, owing to the original print-based work. However, if you so changed the digital version of the photograph that none of the original work is recognizable, then the newest version is no longer a derivative work of the original work.

"Fixed in a Tangible Medium of Expression". The Copyright Act automatically protects all works — including Web sites — as soon as they are written on paper, stored on a disk, or saved in some other medium. As an example, if one person talks to another person face-to-face, no copyrighted work is created. However, if one person records the conversation on audiotape or videotape, or in an MPEG or WAV file, then a copyrighted work is created.

"Copyright Exclusive Rights". The Copyright Act grants five exclusive rights to a copyright owner, who may: (1) copy or reproduce the work, (2) prepare derivative works, (3) distribute copies, (4) perform the work, and (5) display the work. Thus, the owner of the copyright can control who copies the work, who can make new versions of the work, who can distribute copies of the work by hard copy, mail, or e-mail, who can perform the work on stage or screen, and who can display the work on the walls or monitors of an art gallery.

"Author" and "Owner". The "author" is the person who creates a work. The creator of the work is called an "author" even though the creator may be creating a photograph, a videotape, a sound recording, or a Web site.

The "owner" is the owner of the copyright at any given time. Initially, the author and the owner are the same person, because the author is the initial owner of the copyright. Then, the author may transfer the copyright to another person, who becomes the owner. Often, the terms "copyright owner" and "copyright holder" are used interchangeably.

"License". A "license" is a contract by which the copyright owner allows another person to exercise any one or more of the five exclusive rights. An "exclusive license" means that only the licensee can exercise the licensed rights. A "nonexclusive license" means that the owner is free to allow people other than the licensee to exercise the licensed rights.

"Assignment". A document by which the copyright owner transfers all of the exclusive rights to another person, who then becomes the copyright owner.

"Publication". Distribution of a work by sale, rent, or lending copies of the work. Generally speaking, any distribution of a copyrighted work to the general public is deemed a publication of the work, regardless of whether copies the work are sold by mail order, door-to-door, or while standing on a street corner. As soon as a Web site is publicly available on the Web, it is "published" for the purpose of copyright law.

WHEN COPYRIGHT ATTACHES

Copyright law automatically protects any copyrightable work that is "fixed in a tangible medium of expression" (see above). Another way to think of it is that copyright law protects any work that has some physical embodiment, even if it is only a series of magnetic blips on a tape or disk.

You do not have to register your copyright, although registration is recommended for most works that can be copied and which are worth more than the few dollars it costs to register the copyright with the Copyright Office. (See Copyright Registration later in the chapter.)

WHAT COPYRIGHT PROTECTS

At its most basic form, a copyright is a right to copy. The owner of the copyright can control who can have a copy and what can be done with it.

The copyright owner can allow one person to have five copies, another person to have three copies, and refuse to allow a third person to have any copies.

The copyright owner of a photograph can allow one person to make a copy of the photograph and incorporate it into a Web site, allow another person to use the same photograph for advertising purposes only, while licensing a third person for the sole purpose of distributing e-mail copies of the photograph to Internet addresses that begin with the letter "q."

The Idea/Expression Dichotomy

Copyright law does not protect ideas, but only expressions of ideas. If there are many ways to express an idea, then copyright law will protect one expression from being copied or incorporated into another expression without the permission of the copyright owner. In copyright lingo, this separation of ideas and expressions is called the "idea/expression dichotomy."

If there is only one way, or just a handful of ways to express an idea, then the Copyright Act may not be used to protect that idea, and other people may use any expression of that idea.

The problem with drawing a line between ideas and expressions is that the line is drawn at a different place for each work. Thus, for one computer program, the line may be drawn in one place, while in another computer the line is drawn in a different place. Moreover, since most copyrightable works contain many elements and pieces, each element is separately evaluated for the purpose of drawing the line between idea and expression.

So, if a brochure contains photographs, text, and drawings, then each photograph, each paragraph of text, and each drawing constitute a separate element that must be evaluated to determine where the line is drawn between idea and expression. Is one photograph an unadorned picture of a man in a business suit? If so, then anyone can use the idea of photographing a man in a business suit, but this particular photograph cannot be copied or reproduced without the permission of the copyright owner.

WHO IS THE COPYRIGHT OWNER

Under Section 201 of the Copyright Act, ownership of the copyright goes to the person or persons who created the work (the "authors" of the work). Thereafter, the copyright owner may transfer ownership to another person, partnership, corporation, or other entity that can own property.

The exception to this general rule is "work for hire," which has two distinct and different definitions found in Section 101 of the Copyright Act.

Work for Hire in Employment Relationships

Under the first definition of "works made for hire," an employer is deemed to be the "author" of all works created by an employee within the scope of his or her employment.

It does not matter whether the work was created at the office or at the employee's home, and it does not matter whether the work was created when the employee was being paid, or was on a lunch break. As long as the type of work created falls within the broad boundaries of the tasks the employee performs, then the employer automatically owns the copyright to that work. No written documents are necessary.

As an example, if a person who works as an accountant as an employee of a large accounting firm creates a rock video Web site at night, then that accountant would personally own the copyright to the Web site. Creating Web sites is not within the "scope of employment" of the accountant.

By contrast, if a person is employed to create Web sites of all types by day, then her employer may own the copyright to any rock video Web site she creates at night.

Work for Hire in Independent Contractor Relationships

The first definition of "works made for hire" is limited to employment relationships. By contrast, the second definition of "works made for hire" is completely different in that it applies to independent contractors who create certain types of copyrightable works, and requires that each contributor sign a written document.

The second definition of "works made for hire" states that the copyright in specially ordered or commissioned works will be owned by one party where all the parties expressly agree in a written document or documents signed by all of them that the work to be created is a work for hire.

This definition is limited to (1) contributions to collective works, (2) parts of a motion picture or audiovisual work, (3) translations, (4) supplementary works, (5) compilations, (6) instructional texts, (7) tests, (8) answers to tests, and (9) atlases. These nine classes of works may be thought of as "commissioned work for hire." This definition of work for hire does not apply to any other type of work. A Web site can be a "work made for hire" under this legal definition if the Web site is instructional, and if the contributors agree in writing beforehand that the Web site is a work for hire.

Where Work for Hire Does Not Attach

Work for hire does not apply to self-employed individuals who are creating copyrightable works by themselves. A person working alone (and not as an employee of anybody else or of any partnership or corporation) will own the copyright and will be called the "author" of the work.

Work for hire does not apply to independent contractors creating works that are not commissioned works for hire (see above). So, a photographer who takes photographs of a product for an advertising campaign does not come under either definition of work for hire, and the photographer will own the copyright for each photograph. Photographs are not one of the nine types of commissioned work for hire discussed in the Copyright Act, even though the photographer was commissioned by someone else.

Work for hire does not apply to independent contractors creating commissioned works for hire where there is no written agreement. If 10 people agree to contribute to the making of a film, but there is no written document signed by them, then the film is not a work for hire. Instead, all 10 people who contribute will be joint owners of the copyright in the film.

How to Ensure that Only One Person or Company Owns the Copyright

The Copyright Act defines who will own the copyright by default. However, the default may be changed at any time by use of a written document signed by the parties.

Regardless of whether either definition of "work for hire" applies to a type of work, you can always write and sign an agreement among those who contribute to a work that one person or company owns the copyright. Thus, an independent Web site developer can assign her copyright to her client in writing. An employee and an employer can even agree in writing that the employee will own the copyright to everything she creates, regardless of whether it is within the scope of her employment.

COPYRIGHT NOTICE

Section 401 states that copyright notices are optional, but, if you are going to use them, then the notice should consist of three parts: (1) "Copyright," "Copr." or "©"; (2) if the work is "published" (see above), then include the year of first publication; and (3) the name of the copyright owner. Copyright notices are still strongly recommended, but are no longer required.

355

Under the Copyright Act, if the author places a copyright notice on a work, and then later sues an infringer, the infringer cannot claim in court that she did not know the work was protected by the author's copyright.

Prior to 1989, any work published without a copyright notice ran the risk of losing its copyright protection. This approach allowed readers and users to assume that any published work that did not bear a copyright notice was in the public domain, and thus available for re-use by everyone else. Now that the law has been changed, you must assume that all works are protected under copyright law, regardless of whether or not the work bears a copyright notice. The good news is that it is tougher to lose a copyright, but the bad news is that you must assume that everything is protected by copyright law, unless you are told otherwise.

COPYRIGHT REGISTRATION

The first thing that you should know about copyright registration is that it is optional, but recommended for many works. Section 408 will tell you that. The second thing that you should know about copyright registration is that you do not need a lawyer to do it for you. The Copyright Act does not say that, so I will. Registering a copyright is a fairly simple and painless process.

Congress uses a "carrot and stick" approach to copyright registration. The "carrot" is that if you file the copyright application early enough, you get additional rights should you need to go to court and sue an infringer. The "stick" is that you cannot file a copyright infringement lawsuit unless you have received the certificate of registration, or at least have filed the copyright application.

Why You Should Register Your Copyright Early and Often

Copyright registration is recommended for any work worth more than the filing fee (presently $20), and for any work that may be stolen or otherwise infringed. If the work is worth less than the filing fee, why bother? If the work cannot be stolen or infringed (which is not the case for most works), then there is no need to bother.

There are several reasons why early registration of copyrights is recommended. First, under Section 411, you need to have a certificate that shows the copyright is registered before you can sue anyone for infringement (although Congress has been debating removing this requirement). Since it normally takes several months to receive the certificate of registration, you would have to wait several months before suing an infringer, or you would have to pay an additional fee to get the certificate of registration back in a week. By filing early, you will already have the certificate of registration in hand in case you have to sue someone.

Second, in a copyright infringement suit, under Section 412, the copyright owner may get attorney's fees and additional types of damages if the copyright application was filed prior to the start of the infringement, or shortly after publication (i.e., within 3 months of the date of first publication). If the copyright is registered after the infringement begins, then the copyright owner cannot ask for attorney's fees or additional types of damages called "statutory damages" (see Damages and Remedies, below). Congress has been debating removing the filing of a copyright application as a prerequisite for attorney's fees and statutory damages, but Congress had not passed a bill changing this part of the law as this book went to press.

How to Get and File an Application for Copyright Registration

You should not need a lawyer to file a copyright registration. Unlike federal trademark and patent applications, the process is simple.

Call the Copyright Office at (202) 707-3000 for free copyright application forms and instructions, or download them in Adobe Acrobat (.pdf) format from <http://lcweb.loc.gov/copyright>. The telephone number currently is an extensive voice-mail system that will allow you to leave your name and address, and the Copyright Office will mail you forms and instructions on how to fill them out. It usually takes 4 to 6 weeks to receive the forms. Once you have the forms, you can always make more forms for yourself by photocopying the hard copy forms onto a good quality white bond paper. This will make the Copyright Office happy because they don't want to mail out any more forms than they have to. Of course, if you download the forms and instructions, you will not need to wait 4 to 6 weeks to receive them and you can print an unlimited number of copies without having to photocopy them.

To register a copyright, you need to send the completed application (two sides of one piece of paper), a check for the filing fee (presently $20), and a copy or other specimen of the work. Different forms are used for different types of works, and the specimen will also be different from one type of work to another. For most Web sites, the specimen of the work is one copy of the site printed on paper, plus up to 50 pages of code or scripts used on the site.

Once you file the application, it often takes 3 to 8 months to receive the certificate of copyright registration. Neatness counts on the application because the Copyright Office will make a few marks on the application, and then photocopy the application onto a nicer piece of paper to create the certificate of copyright registration. If you can't easily read the application, neither will anyone else, least of all a judge who is trying to enforce the registration as shown on the certificate. If you later lose or misplace the certificate that you receive, you can always get another from the Copyright Office for a small fee.

TRANSFER OF COPYRIGHT

A copyright owner may transfer all or part of a copyright by a written document, or by bequeathing the copyright in a will like any other family heirloom. A copyright may not be transferred by an oral agreement, although the parties can make an oral agreement effective by following it up with a written document.

If the copyright is transferred by a written document, the person transferring the copyright needs to sign the document. The person receiving the copyright may sign the document, but it is not effective unless the person transferring the copyright signs the document.

A copyright is "divisible" which means that the owner of all five exclusive rights can transfer one of the five rights to one person, another of the rights to a second person, and the rest of the rights to a third person. This often makes it difficult to track down who owns which rights when the copyright has been parceled out among several owners.

COPYRIGHT TERM

Knowing the copyright term is useful, since it allows you to plan how long you will have rights to your own work, as well as help you determine whether another person's copyright has expired.

Works Created Since 1978

Under Section 302, for all works created by individuals since 1978, the copyright is good for the life of the author, plus 50 years. If two or more individuals are the creators of a work, then the copyright expires 50 years after the last author dies. Thus, if a particular work is created by a webmaster in 1999, and the webmaster dies in the year 2030, the copyright will be good until the year 2080.

For all anonymous works, pseudonymous works, and works made for hire, the copyright is good for 75 years from the date of first publication, or 100 years from the creation of the work, whichever occurs first.

Thus, for a Web site where all the contributors signed "work for hire" agreements, the copyright will last for 100 years from the date that it is created, or 75 years from the date that it is first made available to the public, whichever term is shorter. Another example is where an employee creates an intranet Web site for her employer in 1999, and the work is not made available outside the company, the copyright will be good until the year 2099.

This assumes that the Copyright Act is not changed again in the interim; however, the Copyright Act will likely be changed on this issue. It seems likely that Congress will change the length of copyright protection for individuals from life-plus-50-years to life-plus-70-years. The term for anonymous works, pseudonymous works, and works made for hire would be extended to 95 years from the date of first publication, or 120 years from the creation of the work, whichever occurs first.

Works Created Before 1978

During the period 1909 through 1977, the copyright on a published work was good for 28 years, and then had to be renewed (by filing a paper with the Copyright Office) for another 28 years. Unpublished works received unlimited protection. Just to complicate things, Congress wrote in Section 304 that the copyright in any work published prior to 1978, but still protected as of 1978, would be protected for up to 75 years. As you might expect, this led to confusion that made a lot of work for copyright attorneys.

Unpublished works under prior law were protected so long as they were not published. Thus, a personal diary written in the 1860s would be protected from copying forever under prior law, so long as the diary remained unpublished. However, under Section 303, all works not published by 1978 remain protected under the Copyright Act, but that protection would terminate no later than 2002 if the work remains unpublished, or no later than 2027 if the work is published between 1978 and 2002.

As a rule of thumb, you "should" assume that any work published before about 1922 is in the public domain (which means that anyone can use it), and that any work created (published or not) in or after 1922 is protected by the Copyright Act, unless proven otherwise.

THE REAL MEANING OF "PUBLIC DOMAIN"

In the copyright context, the term "public domain" means that nobody owns or has a claim to a particular copyrightable work. Thus, anyone can use, copy, or make derivative works of a public domain work. Some people confuse the "public domain" with "published work" or "publication." A work that is publicly available or published via the Web or otherwise is not necessarily in the public domain.

When a copyrightable work enters the public domain, it never leaves the public domain. However, anyone can take a public domain work, add new expression to it, and claim a copyright in the new work. However, the copyright in that circumstance covers only the new expression (the aspects that were added), so the original work will continue to be in the public domain for anyone else to use.

As an example, the stories of the Brothers Grimm are now in the public domain because they were published well before 1922. Anyone can copy the original stories, translate them into English, edit them, add new art work and video, and publish the result on a Web site. Copyright law will protect the new art work, the video, the new translation (translations of human languages are considered derivative works), as well the editing if the editing is more than trivial. If anyone does copy the Web site or protected elements of the Web site, then that person can be sued for copyright infringement. However, copyright law will not prevent anyone else from going back to the original stories, making their own translation, and publishing them with other art work on their own Web site.

INFRINGEMENT OF COPYRIGHTS

Once you have a copyright, you may need to sue a pirate. On the other hand, you may need to know what you face if someone accuses you of being a copyright pirate.

Filing a Copyright Infringement Action

As noted above, U.S. citizens cannot file a copyright infringement action unless they have received a certificate of copyright registration from the Copyright Office. Although Congress has debated removing this requirement, it was still in effect when this book went to press.

By contrast, a French citizen who created a Web site in Germany for a Japanese company that hosts his Web site in Sri Lanka can file a copyright infringement suit in Peoria, Illinois without first obtaining a U.S. copyright registration.

You should always have an experienced attorney represent you in court. Like the television commercials that show professional race car drivers on race tracks, you should not try litigating a copyright infringement case by yourself.

Damages and Remedies that a Court May Award

Under Section 504 of the Copyright Act, the copyright owner asks the judge to award either "actual damages" or "statutory damages." Actual damages is measured by taking the money lost by the copyright owner and adding to that the amount of money made by the infringer as a result of the infringement.

Statutory damages means that the judge picks a number in a range (presently $500 to $20,000) per work infringed and awards that amount as damages. Moreover, if the judge finds that the infringement was committed "willfully," then judge picks a number from a larger range (presently $500 to $100,000) per work infringed. Statutory damages are usually chosen when the infringer has not lost much money as a result of the infringement, yet needs to teach the infringer a lesson by making the damage award much higher. Unfortunately, statutory damages are available to copyright owners only when the copyright is registered prior to the beginning of the infringement, or shortly after the work is first published.

The judge can always assess court costs and order the seizure and destruction of all infringing copies. The judge can also issue injunctions. Under Section 505, if the copyright was registered prior to the infringement, the judge has the option of making the infringer pay the attorney's fees and expenses of the copyright owner, which can total tens or hundreds of thousands of dollars.

FAIR USE OF COPYRIGHTED WORKS

Certain uses of a copyrighted work may not be prosecuted. One set of uses is called "fair use," which is defined in Section 107 of the Copyright Act. Fair use is not a magic formula that instantly turns copying into a permitted use. Rather, it is a set of guidelines that balance the rights of the copyright owner with other rights and needs, including First Amendment concerns and the need to give students and teachers additional leeway for educational purposes.

Fair use is limited to a handful of certain types of uses, mostly related to teaching, comment, and criticism. Four factors are weighed to determine whether a particular circumstance is a fair use or an infringement.

In one case, several publishers sued a nationwide chain of copy shops located on college campuses. College professors assembled copies of articles from magazines and journals into a sort of text book, and left the copies at the copy shop. The professors then told their students to go to the copy shop and pay for one copy of the hand-made textbook. When the publishers sued the copy shop, the copy shop claimed that it is allowed to make copies as a fair use because the professors wanted the copies for teaching purposes. The courts sided with the publishers because the professors did not bother to ask permission from the copyright owners before copying the articles, and because the hand-made text books competed with text books sold by the publishers. Similarly, if the professors had posted the same text on a Web site for reading by their students, the outcome would likely have been the same.

Types of Uses Recognized as Fair Uses

The making of copies without permission is excused as a fair use only when the purpose of the use is criticism, comment, news reporting, teaching (including multiple copies for classroom use), scholarship, or research.

The purposes are fairly narrowly constrained. So, teachers can invoke fair use when they make copies for their classroom, but publishers of classroom books cannot claim fair use, because the book publishers are not directly teaching students.

First Factor: Purpose and Character of the Use

The first factor weighed is the purpose and character of the use, including whether such use is of a commercial nature or is for nonprofit educational purposes. Thus, if the person making the copies is doing so for a profit, that weighs against fair use. However, if the person is making copies for teaching at church, this factor will weigh in favor of fair use.

Second Factor: Nature of the Copyrighted Work

If the copyrighted work is one that generates large amounts of money, such as advertisement-funded Web sites that receive a great deal of traffic, popular books, records, or movies, then any copying will be closely scrutinized. If the copyrighted work is not a money-maker, then fair use is easier to prove.

Third Factor: Amount Used

It is an axiom of copyright law that an infringement occurs when even a small part of a work is copied, especially if the portion copied is of high quality or is important to the rest of the work.

The third fair use factor recognizes that by weighing the amount and substantiality of the portion copied in relation to the copyrighted work as a whole. If one paragraph is copied from the text of a large Web site, then the portion is not substantial. However, if 20 seconds are sampled from a two-minute song, that is substantial, especially if the 20 seconds contains the chorus of the song.

Fourth Factor: Effect on the Market

One of the primary purposes of the Copyright Act is to ensure that authors of copyrighted works are compensated. So it is not surprising that the fourth factor of fair use is the effect of the copying on the potential market or value of the original, copyrighted work. If each copy made without permission replaces a copy that would have been sold, then that weighs against fair use. If the copies made do not affect the sales of the original, then this factor weighs in favor of fair use.

Application of Fair Use

Initially, the use of the copy should fit into one of the categories (criticism, comment, etc.) stated above. Then, all four of the factors are weighed together. Some factors can be more important than others. There is no mechanical application of "three-out-of-four factors wins."

For example, what happens when a publisher creates a Web site containing the copyrighted works of a living playwright without the playwright's permission? The Web site contains all of the text of all of the playwright's plays, plus full-motion video of one play that the publisher captured off a television rebroadcasting an old movie version. The Web site is intended for students who pay $2 each time they access the Web site. Is this a fair use?

First, you must consider the type of work. Teaching, scholarship, and research are all included as fair use purposes, so the Web site should be weighed under the four factors. The first factor cuts against a fair use. The publisher is making money in this venture, even though the purchasers may be nonprofit educational users. Second, the nature of the copyrighted work consists of highly profitable works (plays and movies, which are subject to video rental income and broadcast royalties), even though the sales of texts of plays probably do not generate large amounts of income for playwrights or other copyright owners (since the producer of the movie may own the copyright to that production).

The third factor also cuts against fair use because the Web site contains an entire movie and the entire text of each play. Finally, the fourth factor also cuts against fair use since each access to the Web site potentially replaces one copy of each play manuscript that could have been sold, as well as one copy of the movie that could have been sold. So, this is not a fair use, and the publisher should seek licenses from the playwright and the owner of the copyright in the movie.

INTERNATIONAL COPYRIGHT LAW

The U.S. has signed a number of treaties over the years that grants protection of U.S. copyrights in other countries, while protecting in the U.S. copyrighted works created in other countries. At this time, the number of countries that are not a party to a copyright treaty to which the U.S. also belongs is fairly small. Accordingly, you must assume that works created outside the U.S. are as well protected as works created inside the U.S. Similarly, works that are created in the U.S. are protected outside the U.S.

Most of the better-known copyright treaties use "national" treatment, which means that Web sites created in Germany are protected in the U.S. as if they had been created in the U.S. by U.S. citizens, while U.S. Web sites are treated in Germany as if they had been created by German citizens in Germany. The details of the laws do change from one country to another, so caution is urged before marketing your products in any country that does not have a tradition of protecting copyrighted works.

COPYRIGHT COLLECTIVES, STOCK HOUSES, AND AGENCIES

You should consider what permissions, if any, you need for a Web site long before you begin development. You may find that a piece of music or a video clip is either unavailable for licensing, or is so expensive that it may as well be unavailable. License fees are negotiated based on the type of use, the market that you are selling to, and the number of years you expect to use it.

You can license the use of copyrighted works from others by using stock houses, copyright collectives, and other agencies. Each agency has the right to license the use of copyrighted works to others on the basis of a set scale of fees, or they have the power to negotiate fees with you on behalf of the copyright owner.

The agencies provide a large selection of works to choose from, which makes it easier to conduct one-stop shopping for licenses to use copyrighted works in your Web sites presentations. If your work needs only one or two permissions, for example to use the music and lyrics of a few popular songs, which you are personally performing for inclusion on your Web site, then you should contact the copyright owner or collective agency yourself and negotiate the transaction. By contrast, if you need permissions to use dozens of works, and you intend to sell your work commercially around the world, then you should consider hiring a permissions company to track down the permissions and negotiate on your behalf.

There are hundreds of agencies from which to choose. Several agencies have offices around the country. The names and principal addresses of several of the better-known agencies follow.

PERMISSIONS AGENTS

A Web site is at its best when different types of elements are juxtaposed. However, using preexisting elements requires that you seek and obtain all necessary permissions. A permissions agent or company can do the work for you, and probably be more efficient, which helps your budget. One of the better-known permissions companies is

BZ/Rights & Permissions, Inc.
125 West 72nd Street
New York, NY 10023
(212) 580-0615

TEXT

Most text can be licensed directly from the author or the publisher. Terms are generally negotiable, although the license fees vary widely. The Copyright Clearance Center was formed to help collect royalties on a variety of journals and other hard copy publications, and more recently has started licensing online rights. The Center may be reached as follows:

Copyright Clearance Center, Inc.
222 Rosewood Drive
Danvers, MA 01923
(978) 750-8400
http://www.copyright.com

Licensing of Original Music Compositions

The licensing of music is broken down into several categories based on the type of music-related work, and the type of license sought.

Web sites works may need (1) an original composition license if the final product includes covers of original compositions not previously recorded, (2) a mechanical license to cover a previously recorded song, and (3) a synchronization license where music is combined with video.

Original compositions are the sheet music and lyrics written by composers and lyricists. Anyone who wants to record or perform an original composition should contact the appropriate rights organization for this purpose. Two of the best known are

American Society of Composers, Authors and Publishers (ASCAP)
One Lincoln Plaza
New York, NY 10023
(212) 621-6000
http://www.ascap.com

Broadcast Music, Inc. (BMI)
320 West 57th Street
New York, NY 10019
800/366-4264
(212) 586-2000
http://www.bmi.com

Mechanical and Synchronization Rights

Once a music record or CD is made available to the public for private home use, any song (original composition) on that record or CD can be recorded by another webmaster or group. This is required pursuant to Section 115 of the U.S. Copyright Act. The type of license is called a "mechanical license" (because records used to be considered "mechanical" reproductions) or a "compulsory license" (because the Copyright Act makes it difficult for the copyright owner to refuse permission). Mechanical licenses do not apply to music used for movies, television, or other visual images.

"Synchronization licenses" are licenses to use music in combination with visual images in movies, television or home video. Synchronization licenses are negotiated on a case-by-case basis, and are not subject to compulsory license rates.

The agency best known for mechanical, synchronization, and related licenses is

The Harry Fox Agency, Inc.
National Music Publishers' Association, Inc.
711 Third Avenue
New York, NY 10017
(212) 370-5330
http://www.harryfox.com

PHOTOGRAPHY

Photography is often licensed through stock photography agencies, one of which can be found in virtually every city, and many large towns (check the phone book).

Almost all of the stock agencies are aware of digital uses, and many offer images in digital form in popular binary formats. License rates depend on the type of use and how many people are likely to see the photo or other image.

One agency on the cutting edge of digital uses of images is

Media Photographers Copyright Agency (http://www.mpca.com)
American Society of Media Photographers, Inc. (http://www.asmp.org)
Washington Park, Suite 502
14 Washington Road
Princeton Junction, NJ 08550-1033
(609) 799-8300

MOVIES AND VIDEO

Several stock houses that handle still photography also license video stock. Movies and television video can be licensed directly from the copyright owners (usually the production firms) or their distributors.

You have to be careful about using movies and television, because like other audio-visual work, they incorporate the copyrighted works of others, including music and still photographs. The copyright owners of the movies may not have the right to license to you the background music or other pre-existing works incorporated into the movies. In those cases, ask the copyright owners for their licensing information so that you can get all of the permission that you need in writing.

TRADEMARK LAW

A trademark is anything that designates the source of goods or services, including words or terms, drawings, graphics, sounds, and even colors in some cases. Certainly, domain names can serve as trademarks. In creating your Web sites, you must be careful not to infringe someone else's trademark by associating your Web site with the other person's trademark.

Trademark law is a matter of commerce. Trademark law is not concerned so much with originality as with the commercial impression created by the trademark owner. If you place on your home page a roaring lion above the phrase, *Ars Gratia Artis,* then MGM's present owner may sue for infringement of their trademarks, which includes both the roaring lion and the Latin phrase.

SOURCES OF TRADEMARK LAW

Unlike copyright law, there are several levels of trademark law in the U.S. A "common law" trademark is one that accrues rights merely through use. If you adopt a distinctive term for your business and promote it, then you gain common law trademark rights on a "use it or lose it" basis. Your rights do not begin until you start using it, and are limited to the goods you sell or services you provide, in the geographic area in which you provide them, and last only so long as you continue to provide them. The price is reasonable, however, since there is no application and no filing fee.

Each of the states has adopted a trademark law. Any trademark registered with a state agency receives additional rights within that state, but those rights do not extend outside the state of registration. State trademark registrations are useful for marks used within only one state, and which are not worth the additional cost of filing a federal application for registration. Most states use simple application forms, and the filing fees tend to be between $50 and $150.

The third source of trademark law is Congress, which in 1988 substantially revised the federal Trademark Law (also known as the "Lanham Act" after Rep. Walter Lanham). A federal trademark registration provides the trademark owner with the right to sue any infringer in federal courts throughout the U.S., and provides substantial remedies in favor of the trademark owner against infringers.

Unlike common law trademarks, where rights do not accrue without use, an application for a federal trademark registration can be filed without any use of the mark. Called an "intent to use" or "ITU" application, the ITU application allows the trademark owner to gain a reservation on the trademark long before the goods are ready for market, but the registration does not issue unless and until the applicant files another document stating that

367

the applicant has begun use of the mark on goods or in connection with services in some form of commerce that Congress can regulate, usually by selling goods from one state to another. Applications can also be filed on an "actual use" basis, which means that the goods or services have been sold across state lines, or between the U.S. and another country.

Federal trademark applications are more extensive than state applications, and the filing fee is, as this book went to press, $245 per class of goods and services. Web sites are in one class, while packaged software is in another class. Unlike copyright applications, trademark applications are difficult enough that you should consider retaining an attorney to file and prosecute the application.

STRENGTH OF A TRADEMARK

The more distinctive a trademark, the "stronger" it is. Trademarks are characterized by their strength. Stronger marks provide better protection and can be enforced against a wider range of other marks for different goods or services. Weaker marks can only be enforced against virtually the same mark for virtually the same goods or services. The spectrum of trademark strength follows.

Generic Terms

A generic term or design is one that is used for a category of goods or services. A generic term cannot be protected as a trademark, because it is needed for the purpose of classification. The term "Web site" is generic.

Descriptive Terms

A descriptive term or design is one that describes the goods or services but is not generic for the goods or services. A descriptive term cannot be used as a trademark unless it gains a "secondary meaning," which means that when people hear the term, they think of a particular source or set of goods, rather than all goods with that characteristic. The term "WINDOWS" is descriptive of all software that uses windowing technology, but the term "WINDOWS" has gained a secondary meaning, that of Microsoft's operating environment, "Microsoft Windows."

Suggestive Marks

A suggestive term or design suggests what the goods or services may be, but is not descriptive of them. The term "MICROSOFT" suggests microcomputer software, but the term does not describes the products of Microsoft Corporation. Suggestive trademarks are protectable and make for good trademarks.

Arbitrary Marks

An arbitrary term or design has a real meaning to most people, but the meaning is different from the goods or services it is associated with. The term "APPLE" by Apple Computer Corp. is a good example of an arbitrary mark because most computers are not made of apples. Arbitrary terms and designs make for excellent trademarks.

Coined Marks

A coined term is one that has no meaning except that it is associated with the goods or services. The term "BORLAND" is a good example of a coined term as the term has no meaning outside of the fact that Borland International uses the term on its software. Coined marks are on the opposite side of the spectrum from generic terms.

TRADEMARK NOTICES

Any good you sell or service you provide can bear a notice in the form of "TM" ("trademark") or "SM" ("service mark"). It doesn't cost anything, but it puts the world on notice that you claim your trademark rights.

The circle-R character ("®") is reserved for owners of current federal trademark registrations. It cannot be used by owners of state registrations (unless they also have a current federal registration). Similarly, filing a federal application is not sufficient to use the "®" symbol; a federal certificate of trademark registration must first be issued.

Each of your works may also contain a notice that "[your trademark] is a trademark of [name of your company]." If you have a current federal registration, you can state that "[your trademark] is a registered trademark of [name of your company]."

If you are properly using the trademarks of another, then you should include a trademark notice. For example, if you prepare a training CD-ROM called "How to Use Microsoft Windows," then you should include the trademark notice that "'MICROSOFT' and 'WINDOWS' are registered trademarks of Microsoft Corporation." You can use the approach for each trademark of which you are aware. Many works also bear a catch-all trademark notice; "[your trademark] is a [registered] trademark of [name of your company]. All other trademarks are trademarks or registered trademarks of their respective owners."

LIKELIHOOD OF CONFUSION

Trademark infringement is generally a matter of determining whether the consumers of the trademark owner are "likely to be confused" by a trademark used by another. In determining "likelihood of confusion," a court will consider how close the marks are in sound (since trademarks are often passed from person to person by word of mouth), how close the goods or services are, and whether the goods or services are provided in the same way or in the same "channels of commerce."

For example, the trademark "EXCEL" is a good one for both Hyundai and Microsoft. However, there is no likelihood of confusion, because consumers will not mistake a Hyundai Excel car with a Microsoft Excel spreadsheet.

TRADE DRESS

In addition to the protection trademark laws provide to names and logos, the law also protects the distinctive nonfunctional packaging of a product. The totality of a distinctive product's packaging is known as trade dress.

This total package includes the look of the product, the packaging, and can even include the design and shape of the product and its packaging. Trade dress can be protected by two different methods: (1) if distinct enough it can be registered on the Principal Register of the U.S. Patent and Trademark Office; and (2) if it has achieved a secondary meaning in the marketplace it can be protected under the guise of unfair competition.

CHARACTERS

Trademark law will protect the use of two-dimensional and three-dimensional characters, and terms associated with the characters, so long as they are associated with goods (such as videos, T-shirts and other clothing, lunch boxes) and services (e.g., cable services).

A well-designed character such as Mickey Mouse can be protected under trademark law indefinitely, so long as the character continues to be used on goods and associated with services. With the power of Web technology, it is tempting to copy well-known characters from cartoons, animation, and toys. However, almost all such characters are trademarks of their owners, and their use without permission from their owners is to invite a trademark infringement suit. The Walt Disney Co. and the rights owners of children's cartoons have been especially active in policing their marks against infringement.

TRADEMARKS ON WEB PAGES

Trademarks are part and parcel of a company's marketing and advertising efforts. The World Wide Web has proven to be one of the most effective communication mediums since the invention of television. So it's no surprise that many companies are using the World Wide Web to advertise their wares and display their trademarks.

There is little doubt that the use of a trademark on a Web Page connected to the Internet is used in interstate commerce for the purpose of advertising services to generate goodwill. As noted above, use of a mark in connection with a service generally means that the mark is placed on advertising or marketing materials, or other materials that may be associated with the provision of services, such as letterheads and invoices. Use of a service mark on a Web Page will also qualify as a service mark for use in interstate commerce so long as the Web site is associated with the provision of services. Even the simplest of "brochureware" Web sites that contain service marks will be deemed to be a good use of the service mark in interstate commerce.

Use of a mark for goods on a Web site is generally unlikely to be deemed use of that mark in interstate or other commerce. Marks for goods (unlike marks for services) must be placed on the goods or packaging for the goods. Even in the case of packaged software (which is considered a goods, not a service) sold via Web site by downloads to users, the placement of a mark on the Web site will not be a good use in commerce. Instead, the mark should be in the software itself (e.g., on a boot-up or "splash" screen) since software downloaded from a Web site will not have any hard copy packaging.

TRADEMARKS UNDER WEB PAGES

Search engines on the Web, such as Yahoo!, AltaVista, Lycos, Webcrawler, and HotBot, do not actually search the Web each time that a user enters a query. Instead, each search engines create an index of Web sites by reviewing each Web site that it finds or is told about, and then builds an index of terms that it deems relevant. Most search engines look at keyword meta tags to help create the index, because keyword meta tags indicate what the author of the Web page considers important.

Of course, some Web page authors fill the keyword meta tags with terms that they consider important to attract the type of users they would like, as well as repeating certain key words dozens of times in the hope that the search engines will rank their page as more "relevant" than those of their competitors. And then there are the Web pages in which the keywords in a Web page will include terms and trademarks of the author's competitors in the hopes of attracting users away from the competitors' Web pages. This has led to several law suits.

There have been several cases in which the author or owner of a Web page placed trademarks belonging to others in the keyword meta tags of the page in the hopes of attracting users who are interested in the trademarks. In each of the cases so far (as of this printing), some or all of the defendants consented to removing the plaintiff's trademarks, and notifying the search engines to re-index the defendant's Web site, so as to remove the plaintiff's trademarks from each search engine's index of the defendant's Web site.

TRADEMARKS ON SOMEONE ELSE'S WEB PAGES: LINKING AND FRAMING

In several cases, the owner of one Web site has sued the owner of another Web site because the first Web site includes links to the second Web site. Generally, the allegation is that the link on the first Web site associates the contents of the second Web site with the goods or services offered by the first Web site, especially when the link is not clearly marked to show that the user will be obtaining a document from a different Web site.

For example, one newspaper in the Shetland Islands sued and obtained a preliminary injunction against another newspaper in the Shetland Islands on the allegation that the defendant's Web site misled users into thinking that the defendant was the source of the some of the articles accessed from the defendant's Web site, when, in fact, the defendant was linking to discrete articles on the plaintiff's Web site. Although initially couched in terms of copyright law, the claim sounds better in trademark law as a claim that the defendant was passing off plaintiff's information reportage as its own. The parties subsequently settled.

In another case filed and subsequently settled, *The Washington Post* and several other large news organizations sued a small Web site owned by a company called Total News with numerous allegations of trademark infringement and unfair competition. A user who surfed on over to the site would receive a frame that contained the first site's own content and advertising in several windows, plus buttons that served as links to *The Washington Post* Web site, CNN Web site, Fox News Web site, and so on. A user who clicked one of the buttons would receive the content of *The Washington Post* or other Web site in one large window of the frame on the user's screen, but the first site's buttons and advertising would remain in the other windows of the frame. Unfortunately, the first site had never asked for permission from any of the news organizations because it believed that it did not need permission. After all, all that the first site did — so it argued — was to establish the frame and the buttons, and it was the user who downloaded the content of the other Web sites by clicking on a button. The parties settled, and the first site as of this writing is still linking to some news organizations, presumably with their express permission.

DOMAIN NAMES AS TRADEMARKS

A domain name can serve as a trademark for the goods or services provided or advertised by a company on the Internet at its domain name, so long as the domain name is used as more than just the computer address for a Web or other Internet site.

A domain name can be registered as a trademark, so long as it used as more than "just" an Internet address or URL. Since each domain name (usually a combination of top-level domain and second-level domain) must be unique for the domain naming system to work, domain names are generally issued on a first-come, first-served basis. The result is a number of lawsuits filed by plaintiffs who claim that they should have the sole right to use a domain name registered by the defendant.

To illustrate the connection between domain names and trademarks, a writer by the name of Josh Quittner registered the domain name "mcdonalds.com" and established an e-mail address for himself as "ronald@mcdonalds.com." His article, Billions Registered (*Wired*, October 1994, at page 50) sounded the charge for others to register trademarks they did not own as their domain names in the hope that the trademark owner would then ransom the domain name. Quittner's own demands were relatively modest; McDonald's complied with Quittner's demand that it pay to have one public school in New York City connected to the Internet.

Many who followed Quittner's lead did so by registering large numbers of domain names incorporating the trade names and trademarks of well-known companies. Unlike Quittner, they did not offer to turn over the domain name in response to an act of charity, but sought payments of large sums of money. Called "domain name arbitrage," "cybersquatting," "domain piracy," "domain grabbing," and any number of other terms, the practice has led to many suits against domain name owners by trademark owners claiming that the domain name infringes or dilutes a trademark. Several of these cases have alleged dilution of famous trademarks under the federal and state dilution statutes.

In cases where the domain owner does not compete in any way with the trademark owner, the dilution claims have been more successful, although the courts have strived mightily to find that a plaintiff's trademark is "well-known" to fulfill the condition precedent of the dilution statutes. In what appears to be a self-fulfilling prophecy, if not a matter of circular logic, the courts note that the domain name owner had hoped to sell the domain name to the trademark owner, thus suggesting that the mark must be sufficiently "well known" to attract this unwanted attention.

The use of a domain name can also lead to a tarnishment claim. Thus, the use of a domain can reduce the value of the trademark owner's right in its trademark. In one case, the owners of the TOYS 'R' US trademark sued the owners of the "adultsrus.com" domain name on the grounds that the domain name was associated with the advertising and sale of sex-related products on a World Wide Web site at <http://www.adultsrus.com>. The court expressly held that defendant's use of the second-level domain name "adultsrus" for sex-related products tarnished the rights of plaintiffs in the 'R' US family of marks for children's toys and clothing.

PRIVACY AND PUBLICITY LAW

The rights of privacy and publicity are two sides of the same coin. The rights of privacy and publicity apply even if you photograph or record (video, audio, or both) a person out-of-doors in a public location, such as a park, town square, or walking down the street. The law deems that a person has the right to control how her image is used.

This is a growing area of law that is more closely related to trademark law. California and New York have passed statutes that protect privacy, and other states are likely to follow.

DON'T MAKE PRIVATE PEOPLE "PUBLIC" WITHOUT THEIR PERMISSION

If the person is a private person, then she may prohibit the use of her image for your profit or gain. A private person has the right to remain private.

CELEBRITIES HAVE THE RIGHT TO CONTROL THEIR PUBLICITY

If the person is a public person or celebrity, she may be able to prohibit your use of her image without proper compensation, primarily because she is deemed to have a property interest in her image. In other words, she can make money from her status as a celebrity, so you cannot use her status to help sell your product without her permission.

One good example of the right of publicity is the Bette Midler case. A car manufacturer wanted to run a series of commercials that featured Ms. Midler's singing. Ms. Midler decided not to participate, so the car manufacturer hired someone else who sang just like Bette Midler. Ms. Midler sued and won about $400,000 because people who listened to the commercials thought that she was singing in the commercial. Even though no image of Ms. Midler was used, her vocal style was sufficiently distinctive to serve as her trademark. Since everyone agreed that Ms. Midler's vocal style helped sell cars, Ms. Midler was held by the court to have the right to control when her voice and vocal style could be used to help sell cars.

RELEASES

There is no better way to ensure that you have all the rights that you need to use a person's image or other distinctive features than to get a release. Professional photographers use releases all of the time. You may need to consult an attorney to ensure that the release you would like to use is enforceable under the law of the states in which you will use the release, and to make sure that the release covers every type of use that you contemplate.

WHEN YOU CAN USE THE WORKS OF ANOTHER PERSON

There are several ways in which you can use and incorporate the works of others into your Web sites. Ask yourself a few questions.

First, is the work in the public domain? As discussed above, public domain means that nobody owns the copyright or other rights to the work. If you have access to an original Leonardo da Vinci painting or manuscript of a Mozart concerto, then make your own copies without fear of copyright violation.

Second, if the work is not in the public domain, can you get a license to use or copy the work? The saying goes that "it is easier to beg forgiveness afterwards than to ask for permission beforehand." However, for copyrighted works, permission is often easy to get and costs very little, while forgiveness is very expensive. At the very least, forgiveness (including legal fees, court costs, and damages) costs a great deal more than permission.

Third, will any original work that you copy be recognizable as a derivative work? As noted above, a derivative work remains a derivative work only so long as any part of it is still recognizable as originating with its predecessor.

Fourth, does the work affect anyone else's privacy or publicity rights? If a person can be recognized by her looks, voice, or other distinctive attributes, that person can request compensation. So long as you have appropriate releases from each individual, or the person that you have licensed the work has the appropriate releases, then this will not be an issue.

Author Bio

Frederic M. Wilf *is special counsel with the law firm of Saul, Ewing, Remick & Saul LLP, where he chairs the firm's Technology Group. Wilf is resident in the firm's Berwyn office, where he practices technology and intellectual property law, with an emphasis on the Internet, telecommunications, and computer industries. His clients include Internet service providers, Web site and software developers, vendors and consultants, as well as companies of all sizes that use technology. Wilf may be reached via the Internet at fwilf@saul.com or fwilf@compuserve.com, and at the following address: Saul, Ewing, Remick & Saul LLP, 1055 Westlakes Drive, Suite 150, Berwyn, PA 19312, U.S.A. Saul Ewing's home page on the World Wide Web is at <http://www.saul.com> and Wilf's listing appears at <http://www.saul.com/lawyers/5082.html>.*

Chapter 21

Using Net-Based Interactive Technology for Online Marketing, Sales, and Support of Financial Services Firms

Steven Semelsberger

We're going to integrate the Internet completely into the Schwab organization.

— *Charles Schwab*, Chairman and Co-CEO, Charles Schwab & Co.

THE IMPORTANCE OF IMPLEMENTING SOFTWARE SOLUTIONS to improve customer service and provide operational efficiency has been well documented. Most likely, you've already experienced several waves of euphoria as vendors have promised significant returns on investment from the latest in software gadgetry. From the mainframe boom of the 1970s through the UNIX and client/server explosion of the late 1980s to the "thin client is in," multitiered approach to computing in the 1990s, solutions have come and gone as application writers and software manufacturers have pushed each other to develop robust, easy to implement, highly scalable solutions for critical business functions.

0-8493-9834-7/00/$0 00+$.50
© 2000 by CRC Press LLC

While applications from currency exchange, to account maintenance, to options pricing have all become automated and computerized, most leading investment banks, brokerage houses, and diversified financial institutions have yet to move beyond the branch or the telephone as a means to actually interact with their customers. A few companies have adopted online banking services to allow customers to perform simple tasks, such as pay bills or check balances, over the Internet. Many have established a marketing presence on the Web, utilizing the easy access of the Internet to hawk products and services. Others, spurned into action by up and comers like e*Trade, have invested heavily in the infrastructure needed to carry out online trades.

Still, actual Web-based customer interaction has been limited to a few basic frequently asked question (FAQ) sections and an occasional "e-mail for more information" link. Only a few visionaries in the financial services industry have truly embraced the Internet's potential for a complete array of interactive services.

When one examines the usual customer life cycle, it becomes evident that the rise of the Web offers companies an unsurpassed opportunity for efficient, effective, and personalized interactive service. The Internet provides a significant opportunity for four key functions:

1. Community building. The interactive nature of the Web enables companies to give their customers a global forum to express ideas, concerns, thoughts, and demands, both with each other and with company representatives. While the idea of these "many-to-many" forums can be daunting for some, as Hagel & Armstrong noted in their 1996 manifesto on virtual communities, *NetGain,* interactivity is the most proven means to develop a sense of allegiance to an online destination or brand. Ongoing threaded discussions and interactive chats are two proven methods to bring customers together around a concept, product, or service. Each will be discussed in detail below.
2. Marketing events. The Web also creates new opportunities for financial service providers to hold interactive events in a "one-to-many" manner. Individual customers, spread across boundless geographies, can now have access to high-ranking company officials who may have never been reachable through traditional communication channels. Video streaming in conjunction with moderated chats has given rise to a new era in communication and will be explored below.
3. E-Commerce. With Forrester's prediction for Internet commerce to rise to $327 billion by 2001, most organizations are scrambling to unlock how they can utilize the Web to efficiently and effectively increase top line revenue. While specific e-commerce payment and tracking systems are discussed elsewhere in this book, this chapter

will focus on how interactive communication mechanisms can be utilized to increase purchase conversion rates and enable cross-selling and up-selling. Specifically, live interaction, offered as a main component of a corporation's Web site, (through interactive text conferencing, screen synchronization, telephone callback, and even voice and video over IP), provides the human touch that is often needed to encourage a purchase decision.

4. Customer support. Once an individual has become a customer, it is critical that he or she receives an appropriate level of service and support. The Internet offers a multitude of new, efficient, interactive support channels, ranging from self-service options all the way through a multitude of live communication channels. The Internet-enabled customer support process will be explained in an upcoming section.

The four pillars of Web-based customer interaction can be summed up in the diagram shown in Exhibit 21-1.

This chapter will focus on describing applications to enable organizations to effectively build Internet communities, market to their customers, interact with prospects to sell products and services online, and finally, provide efficient customer service and support. It will also serve

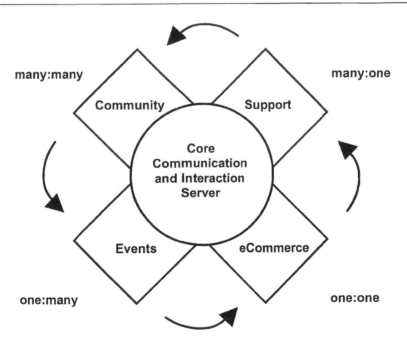

Exhibit 21-1. The four pillars of Web-based customer interaction.

as an introduction to specific software vendors and to set basic expectations for technical and human resource requirements to implement and maintain interactive forums.

BUILDING AN INTERNET COMMUNITY: MANY-TO-MANY DISCUSSIONS

At this point, many Web sites are vast arrays of "brochureware," or jumbles of pages of marketing materials. However, analysts and executives alike have realized the need to improve both information and interaction if they are to fully realize the potential of the Internet. John McCarthy, an analyst at Forrester, says that corporations need to be thinking about how to provide a compelling experience for their customers. "Static Web pages that you have to go and fetch just aren't going to make it," says McCarthy. McCarthy stresses that the next wave of Web sites will focus on "intelligent interactivity." These effective applications will draw customers in with engaging content, collect information, and use the information to direct clients to products and services of targeted interest.

A major component of these intelligent sites will be the use of interactive, threaded discussions and live chat. Both offer compelling advantages and can be used as stand-alone solutions or as an integrated system.

THREADED DISCUSSION SERVERS

Users of Usenet servers are quite familiar with the concept of threaded, topical discussions. The idea is simple: a customer, community member or corporate representative initiates a thread with a question or statement posted in an online "bulletin board" accessible by other community members. Individuals who visit the thread can then post follow-up statements and replies, or initiate new conversation threads.

An example of a threaded discussion (also frequently called message board) environment is shown in Exhibit 21-2.

In this instance, iBank, a fictional Internet financial services corporation, has set up a threaded discussion environment to provide user forums where individuals can search for information, browse, and post questions about various topics of interest such as car loans and online banking. Threaded discussion servers have several key benefits:

- Information posted is accessible by all future users, increasing knowledge transfer.
- Website visitors can view information in a self-service mode, decreasing their reliance on live bank representatives for information.
- Threaded discussions can be viewed from within the browser, allowing easy integration into existing Web sites or corporate intranets.

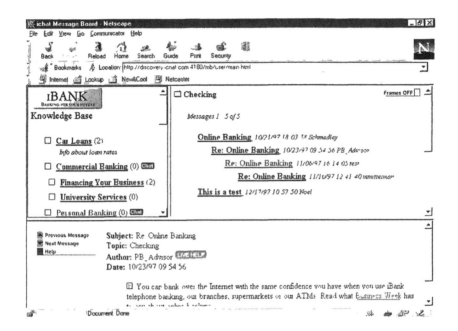

Exhibit 21-2. A threaded discussion group.

- A sense of community can be quickly established without having the constant site traffic that chat requires (see below for information on text-based chat).
- Users can visit and post messages and replies at their convenience, without having to meet at predetermined times.

THREADED DISCUSSION REQUIREMENTS

Generally, threaded discussion servers are fairly quick and easy to set up. The majority of the effort can be in maintaining and monitoring threaded discussion topics. Depending on the level of human filtering, threads and posts can be monitored by a single individual on a daily basis, or could become a multiperson full-time task.

Most message board applications work with major Web servers (Microsoft IIS, Apache, and Netscape Enterprise Server), post information in straight HTML (meaning that firewalls shouldn't pose a problem), and support numerous databases, including SQL, LDAP, and ODBC compliant storage applications. Windows NT 4.0 and Sun Solaris 2.x are by far the most popular operating system versions available.

While vendors have a variety of requirements for system memory, 32 MB should get you started. Plan on setting aside plenty of disk space (100 MB just to get off the ground) as growth in message posts can quickly fill up a hard drive.

CHAT SERVERS

Long a key "late night" component of proprietary online offerings such as CompuServe and America Online, chat exploded onto the Web in early 1996. Since then, chat has become a must-have for major Internet destination sites. Initially, text-based chat was seen as a gimmick to draw traffic to a Web site and allow users to banter about frivolous topics of discussion.

However, the rise of several prominent discussion areas on the Web quickly ended any preconceived notions about the application of chat to the financial services arena. The Motley Fool and Yahoo!'s financial forums (shown in Exhibit 21-3) have drawn substantial attention, serious, worthwhile discussions, and even advertisers' dollars.

As the Yahoo! screen shot exemplifies, text-based chat is a simple, flowing process that entails users entering into conversations in an open forum.

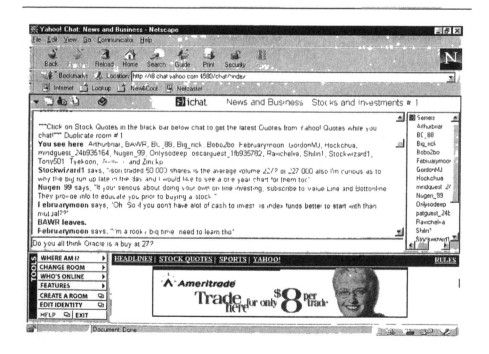

Exhibit 21-3.   Sample financial forum on the Web.

Conversations are often dynamic and spontaneous, and regular users are quite often outspoken and critical. Yet no other application has demonstrated to have as effective a draw for Web users: *Business Week* estimates that chatters stay on Web sites for up to three times the 10-minute average and chat-enabled Web sites report up to 50% increases in traffic.

For financial services corporations, open chat rooms can also be utilized as ad hoc meeting areas, enabling distributed teams to collaborate on problems, discuss market trends, and work on projects — all in real time.

The major benefits of adding chat capabilities to your Web site include:

- Increased user loyalty — users who develop a community perspective around your Web site have a significant probability of returning to your online forum.
- Immediate information exchange — sites have the ability to find out issues of importance and major customer concerns immediately.
- Logging user feedback — information exchanged in chats can be stored for future reference.
- Captured eyeballs for advertising — chat rooms, with their long, average visit times, provide an excellent forum for advertisers.

Chat Server Requirements

Most chat servers handle both administrative functions and user sessions from within a standard browser environment. Setup and configuration time is generally minimal, but can become quite lengthy, requiring up to a few days if user loads are anticipated to go above 1000 concurrent chatters, the company has an extensive firewall setup, or the site desires extensive user interface customization.

Most chat servers work with major Web servers (Microsoft IIS, Apache, and Netscape Enterprise Server). Firewalls can be tricky, since the chat information is often passed through a port other than the standard :80 port open for HTML transfer. To counteract these concerns, major chat vendors have developed firewall proxy servers to encapsulate chat text in straight HTTP.

Various chat servers come with proprietary user information databases or support standard apps, including SQL, LDAP, and ODBC compliant storage databases. As with threaded discussion servers, Windows NT 4.0 and Sun Solaris 2.x are by far the most popular operating systems available.

While vendors have a variety of requirements for system memory, 32 MB should get you going. Storage requirements are not as great as needed as message boards, since (unless you leave logging options on) information transmitted is not stored. Plan on a minimum of 20 MB to get started.

Case Study: Citicorp (www.citibank.com)

Citicorp firmly believes in offering user forums to build a sense of community around its products and services. The bank has added both threaded discussion and real-time chat capabilities to provide customers with an interactive resource to learn about investment options and bank services from company representatives and other users. Additionally, the Web site utilizes guides who host financial subject areas such as mortgages, credit cards, and pension plans. At each customer information section, the guides answer questions, steer users to information, write columns, and moderate chats.

The bank's embrace of real-time, interactive communication software represents a paradigm shift in the corporate approach to the Web, says Forrester analyst Emily Green. "Service companies are starting to grasp the intimacy aspects of the Web," she says. "With the size of the investments that they make online, [banks] need to make sure people stick around."

ONLINE EVENTS: ONE-TO-MANY DISCUSSIONS

While threaded discussion boards and open chat rooms create community forums that encourage users to return to share information on their latest and greatest investment recommendation, moderated online events are an excellent means to bring targeted customers together to exchange information in a controlled manner.

Internet events are the "Larry King Shows" of the Web — users have an opportunity to submit questions directly to the individuals running the event. Usually, a group of screeners will filter and edit incoming questions. Appropriate and interesting inquiries are then presented to the speaker and to the audience as a whole — to be answered in real-time. Exhibit 21-4 demonstrates the normal flow of an Internet event.

While Internet events are typically run using special moderating add-ins to leading text chat software packages, many organizations have turned to a blended multimedia offering for their online discussions. For example, using video-streaming technology, an investment bank could bring one of their sector analysts online to present his or her conclusions about a specific investment vehicle or market trend.

During the course of the presentation, the analyst could also present slides, graphics, and charts to the audience. Since the entire event is pushed out to the users' browser (generally by breaking the browser into frames for text content, video, and presentation graphics), the attendee won't need any additional software or hardware (such as microphones, Internet phones, or video cameras) to receive a multimedia-rich experience. Although outside of the scope of the financial services industry, the screen shot shown in Exhibit 21-5 demonstrates an online event that was held by

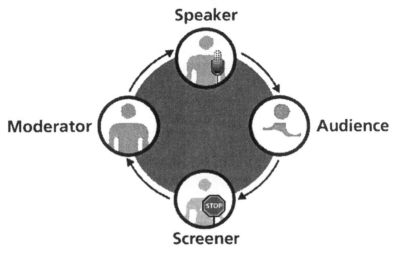

Exhibit 21-4. The normal flow of an Internet event.

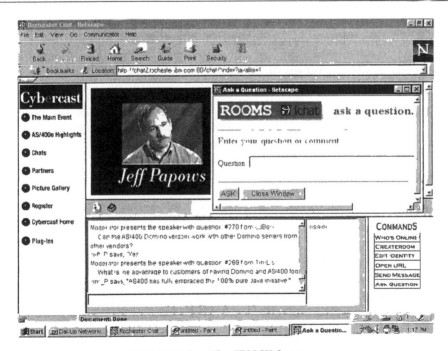

Exhibit 21-5. The IBM Web event.

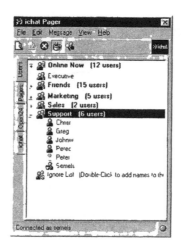

Exhibit 21-6. Instant messaging.

Jeff Papows, president and CEO of Lotus, to introduce the new IBM AS400e server.

One of the major challenges of running online events is actually communicating to the targeted audience the location, time, and content of the event in a manner that draws significant attention and ensures participation by audience members. Instant messages, generally text-based announcements that pop up in the forefront of open windows on users' computers, are a great way to invite targeted participants to online forums.

Using instant messaging technology, clients can be notified the second that critical new investment information is available. They can then join a real-time, interactive discussion in a moderated chat environment. For instance, as Federal Reserve Board chairman Alan Greenspan is testifying, a broker can send instant messages to her clients, inviting them into a closed session with leading analysts and company economists who offer insight and advice into appropriate market plays. An example of an instant message is shown in Exhibit 21-6.

Online Events Requirements

Hosting online events requires more human intervention and thought than merely providing an open chat forum. Still, most event moderating tools are quite simple to use and can be installed and running in a few hours. Systems and technical requirements are comparable to the chat server section discussed above.

Case Study: Merrill Lynch

With nearly $1 trillion under management, Merrill Lynch realizes the importance of providing exceptional services that will enable them to continue to strengthen their customer relationships. For example, they were one of the first major financial services organizations to utilize e-mail for more efficient client interaction.

During the fall of 1996, Merrill Lynch began to look for a software solution that would allow them to hold moderated events where their technical and financial experts could conduct online seminars. After reviewing various products and considering proprietary, online service companies, they chose an open, Internet solution. Joe Corriero, director of interactive technology, summed it up this way: "After we experimented with events on America Online, we realized that we would never reach our targeted customer base through AOL's closed community business model. We clearly saw the Web as the future for our customer interaction needs."

Online events represent a logical progression of the use of Internet technology and mark an exciting new opportunity for Merrill Lynch customers to interact directly with leading company minds. Merrill Lynch actually holds three types of online events:

- Public events — industry luminaries present their predictions on market trends and technological innovations.
- Private events — financial consultants interface with their key clients over the Web to discuss investment strategies and appropriate market moves.
- Financial consultant-only events — financial consultants gather together for training and focused discussions.

E-COMMERCE: ONE-TO-ONE DISCUSSIONS

With Web-based transactions expected to grow to more than U.S.$220 billion by 2000 (source: International Data Corp), the returns for investments in technology that provide the means for customers to gather information and make informed purchases will be enormous.

With extended economic prosperity, the opportunities for financial services organizations that provide investment services to high net worth individuals are exceptional. As John F. Snyder, portfolio manager of the John Hancock Sovereign Investors Fund, puts it: "We're in the seventh year of an economic expansion and inflation is 2% and falling. Things really are different."

Additionally, the extended bull market has increased assets in 401(k) plans — at a compounded annual rate of 18% over the past decade — to around $810 billion, according to Access Research Inc. in Windsor, CT.

With equity markets on a run that has no foreseeable end in sight and average customers with 65% of their financial investments allocated to equities, communication between high net worth individuals and their financial consultants is of the utmost of importance.

The Internet is an exciting new communication channel for e-commerce-motivated interaction. Where companies and customers were once locked to the phone or face-to-face meetings to correspond, the Internet enables customers to set up accounts, monitor market activity in real-time from their office or home, and research and conduct trades.

What's been missing until recently has been a means to actually communicate with a company representative online for advice during the course of a purchase evaluation. Many would-be buyers have left very slick Web sites in disgust after they've been unable to find the answer to an elusive question. To make sure that prospects receive information without having to suffer through a tedious phone call or wait for an e-mail response, several new solutions are being offered.

Text-Based Conferencing, Screen Synchronization, and Web ACDs

Chat solutions, either in open forums or in specific one-to-one, channeled environments, create the capacity for instant correspondence. Upon clicking on a "live help" button, a prospect can be given the opportunity to enter into a text dialogue with a sales rep who can then push information such as investment portfolio charts, diagrams, and product/service descriptions (through browser screen synchronization) directly to the customer. Exhibit 21-7 represents one potential application for text-based conferencing.

While several stand-alone chat applications can function for basic live support, the integration of a Web-automated call distributor (ACD) to route requests for help to appropriate agents based on customer attributes, work flow rules, and agent availability will be needed to handle heavily trafficked call centers that wish to complement their telephony commerce efforts with Internet-based, e-commerce support.

CTI CallBack

Offering a callback mechanism for customers is another option for live correspondence. While a button that allows a customer to submit a request for a phone call brings one close to true Internet interactivity, the delays inherent in actually routing a call to the appropriate agent in conjunction with the limits for customers with a single phone line (such as an investor dialing in from a hotel room) make CTI callback a secondary option at this point.

Voice and Video Conferencing

H.323-based voice and video transmissions have been heralded as major new breakthroughs in Internet telephony and conferencing. However, the bandwidth, processing power, and hardware requirements to actually run

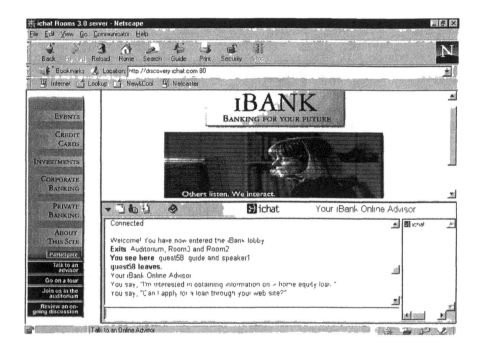

Exhibit 21-7.   An example of text-based conferencing.

a video transmission, and the limited quality still inherent in live, packet-switched communications, make this option one to consider on a limited basis.

BENEFITS OF LIVE INTERACTION

Live interaction, through singular applications of the technology described above or through a multioption, mutlichannel communication center, offers several benefits to e-commerce efforts, including:

- Higher closure rates.
- Higher average sales prices due to agent cross-selling and up-selling activity.
- Improved customer satisfaction due to live human availability.

Live Interaction Requirements

Each of the applications described above requires a variety of hardware and software depending on the scope of the project and the integration into telephony support processes. In most cases, it is recommended to work with the vendor and a leading e-commerce and/or call center system integrator such as Cambridge Technology or TSC to develop the optimum solution for your efforts.

Once launched, live Internet interaction can be run as a stand-alone environment, or integrated into telephone-based sales efforts. Human requirements can range from a single, part-time agent to monitor activities all the way through, to a multihundred rep call center to handle thousands of concurrent transactions. An additional benefit to consider with text-based conferencing is the multitasking capabilities and voice breaks that text correspondence enables agents to experience.

Case Study: Pristine Capital Management

Pristine Capital Management (PCM) was named Baron's number one day trading site on the Web for 1997 and is an outstanding example of a start-up Internet company that has successfully utilized chat to create an e-commerce-driven business model. PCM believes that their short-term trading style (2 to 5 day holding period) takes advantage of a very profitable market niche overlooked by most active investors. Too brief for large institutional concerns to take advantage of and, at the same time, too lengthy for floor traders (who typically don't hold positions overnight) to be comfortable with, this time frame offers the perfect opportunity for independent traders who possess the expertise necessary to profitably exploit it.

In June 1997, Pristine launched a real-time trading room on the Web — revolutionizing the financial trading industry. This virtual trading room, using interactive text-based conferencing technology, provides live, ongoing stock recommendations and market commentary throughout the trading day, effectively bypassing end-of-day services and cumbersome intra-day phone messages.

Members with access receive a steady flow of real-time trading ideas, just as if they were sitting in the private trading room of the editors. Breakouts and stocks that are on the verge of exploding to the upside are recognized in a matter of seconds, allowing users to act quickly. Subscribers also get pre-market commentary moments before the markets open, and informative post-market remarks are made to summarize each day's events.

By charging a monthly membership fee of $525, Pristine has seen a dramatic return on their investment in live, text-based conferencing technology. "Within 1 month of launch, we signed up over 150 customers," Tony Nunes, Director of Technology for Pristine stated. "Real-time, Web-based text conferencing has provided the means for us to launch an extremely profitable service."

CUSTOMER SUPPORT

As discussed thus far, Internet-based interactive technology can be used to bring a prospect to a company's Web site to participate in ongoing discussions and debates over various investment instruments. It can also be used to hold major online events, further closing the gap between an individual's transition from prospect to customer. Live interaction then can be the critical element in e-commerce initiatives, as customers seek to buy everything from specific equities to new insurance plans online, and often need assistance before actually conducting a transaction.

The final piece of the customer life cycle arises from the support side of the equation. Customer service is at the forefront of most organizations' concerns. With support labor costs escalating and customer expectations for immediate, personalized attention rising, financial services innovators are turning to the Internet to serve as a new channel for customer correspondence.

Through both interactive self-service and live help, organizations hope to reduce their share of the $60 billion that Brean Murray Institutional Research estimates is spent on support labor costs. According to Forrester Research, increased self-service, better distribution of information, and more efficient agent utilization can enable organizations to experience a 43% decrease in labor cost per customer contact through deployment of Web-based customer interaction solutions.

Internet-Based Customer Support in Action

One easy method to envision Web-based customer interaction is through a description of a customer's experience on a major financial services site. Research indicates that over 80% of customer call center inquiries are routine questions, so the support process starts by giving customers easy self-help options, allowing valuable support agents to focus on more complicated inquiries, premium customers, and sales opportunities. Browsable and searchable self-help options including dynamic frequently asked question (FAQ) and knowledge base searching capabilities where customers can easily find answers to investment questions, account status, or portfolio position.

If they are unable to locate the support information required, customers can then have the option to send an e-mail inquiry or enter into a live help mode. Automated e-mail routing and response capabilities ensure a timely response in conjunction with escalation to a live agent if the question is unrecognized.

Should the customer request live help, dynamic queuing mechanisms route the request to the appropriate agent or group, based on customizable business rules and attributes such as customer profile, question urgency, and agent availability. Ideally, the agent and customer will have multiple options for live interaction, including text-based conferencing, synchronized browser screens, phone callback, and voice and video conferencing (see the

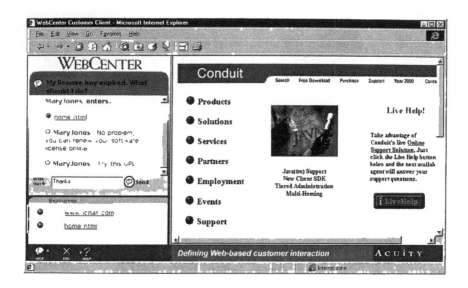

Exhibit 21-8. Text-based customer interaction.

e-commerce section above for descriptions of each). Exhibits 21-8 and 21-9 demonstrate a text-based interaction session from both a customer and agent perspective.

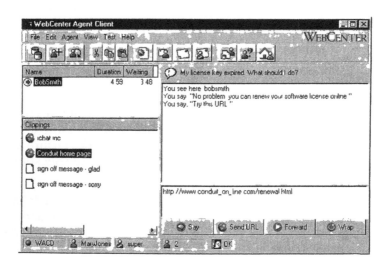

Exhibit 21-9. Text-based agent interaction.

Following the live help session, customer and session data can be automatically stored in a third-party customer management system, posted in the organization's knowledge base for future self-service sessions, and when requested, e-mailed directly to the customer. With the live help option, customers can be guaranteed a response in real time, without having to log off from a company's Web site to pick up the telephone.

Customer Support Requirements

As with major e-commerce undertakings, each of the applications described above requires a variety of hardware and software, depending on the scope of the project and the integration into telephony support processes. In most cases, it is recommended to work with the software vendor and a leading customer support and/or call center system integrator such as Cambridge Technology or TSC to develop the optimum solution for your efforts.

Case Study: Charles Schwab & Co.

Schwab's help desk group, responsible for supporting 700 distributed financial executives, uses Web-based, interactive technology for self-service and live help. At Schwab, employees are given the option to search and browse various online FAQs and knowledge bases to discover new investment vehicles, analyst recommendations, and HR information. They also have the ability to receive technical support online in a self-service mode. If the employee wishes to click into a live help session, Schwab's interactive, net-based system enables text conferencing and browser screen synchronization. "Web-based customer interaction is the foundation of Schwab's leadership position," says Rick Washburn, VP Customer Technology, Charles Schwab & Co. "Our vision for delivering an outstanding client experience through efficient self-service, online delivery and personalized, real-time, interactive support, has created an excellent environment for efficient, effective service."

CONCLUSIONS

As described in the opening section, Web-based interactive software enables financial services organizations to effectively build communities, hold online events, assist their customers during the purchase decision process, and provide appropriate levels of support ranging from self-service through to live assistance.

With Forrester's claims that Web-based customer interaction software can lead to a 43% decrease in labor cost per customer contact, and vendor claims that live help on a Web site can increase sales margins by 15 to 25% through up-selling, cross-selling, and efficient content distribution, the return on investment (ROI) for interactive initiatives can be substantial.

Pristine Capital Management, as described above, experienced an ROI of several hundred percent during 1997. Forrester envisions that a $650 million company will save approximately $1 million through the deployment of interactive customer support software.

With these types of figures and a new array of outstanding products from a multitude of vendors, now is the time to turn your static Web site into a major interactive marketing, sales, and support system.

Author Bio

Steven Semelsberger is the Strategic Alliances and Market Development Manager for Acuity Corporation, the leading provider of Web-based customer interaction solutions. With over 1300 customers including top financial institutions such as Merrill Lynch, Charles Schwab & Co., Citicorp, Janus Funds, and Dow Jones, Acuity has gathered extensive expertise in developing net-based applications for marketing, e-commerce, customer service, and support. Semelsberger has worked with leading NYC investment banks, brokerage houses, and commercial lenders in various software sales and marketing roles. He holds an MBA in high-technology marketing and finance from Duke University's Fuqua School of Business and a B.S. in management from Binghamton University.

Chapter 22
Internet Security Analysis Report: An Executive Overview

Mary Rose

THE RAPID GROWTH OF THE INTERNET has prompted companies in all industries to look closely at the significance of the Internet and question if a presence should be developed, and if one is developed, what it should be. One of the key issues surrounding an open system like the Internet is security: security of data, e-mail, and financial transactions. Some business managers troubled by recently publicized security breaches have decided to take a wait-and-see approach.

While this reaction is understandable, the major drawback is the loss of a window of opportunity, a key competitive edge. Although the Internet may seem intimidating, it can be a marketing advantage in that it offers equal footing on which to compete. Smaller community financial institutions can effectively compete with the larger national players via the Internet the world over. Security is a valid concern, but many of the risks are viewed as greatly overrated by some industry analysts. In addition, there are software programs and hardware systems to reduce the risk.

However, in spite of this concern, the financial services industry is experiencing rapid growth on the Internet. Nontraditional competitors are continuing to take market share. Financial institutions who do not offer PC-based online services are consistently reporting losing customers. It is imperative that financial institutions become quickly educated with the Internet possibilities. Those who do and develop a viable presence will remain competitive and be seen as players who intend to stay around. Financial institutions have historically maintained carefully controlled and audited systems. The idea of an open system is in direct conflict with fiduciary relationships. However, the possible enormous gain can far outweigh the risks. It is our opinion that if certain precautions are taken, the risks can be minimal.

0-8493-9834-7/00/$0.00+$.50
© 2000 by CRC Press LLC

Most financial institutions have found that internal theft by employees constitutes the majority of losses. Thus, secure systems must have internal and external controls. Education is the key to understanding and controlling potential exposure.

INTERNET VS. INTRANET

An increasing number of corporations and financial institutions are installing Web servers on internal corporate networks (intranets) for private purposes such as human resources information and internal databases. In this case, the server is not attached to the Internet. As the applications are increasing in diversity, access by nonemployees such as bank clients are continually being added.

Web servers on the Internet are considered to be much more vulnerable because of the worldwide access to them. Thus, software that provides security or as it is commonly referred to, fire wall software, should be considered essential when placing a Web server on the Internet (see Exhibit 22-1).

Internet/Intranet Choice

Financial institutions have the choice of installing banking software products on the Internet, an open system, or on a proprietary, closed, intranet system. If an institution chooses not to offer Internet access to client accounts, the system can be installed as an intranet where clients dial a private phone number to connect to the Web server, as shown in Exhibit 22-2. This option allows a financial institution to provide remote client account access with the option of migrating to Internet access at any point in the future.

SECURITY DESIGN

Basic security measures should be used for intranet installations. For Internet installations, fire wall software and a router are used for additional security.

Basic Security Measures

Security should consist of multiple layers of protection. Basic security design is broken into five categories described below.

For Client Security. Financial institution customers are required to have secure browsing software such as Netscape or Microsoft Internet Explorer. Attempts to connect with a nonsecure browser will be rejected. These clients are provided with an Identification Code and a Password that are required to successfully connect to the system. Financial institutions must carefully instruct their customers on the importance of protecting their

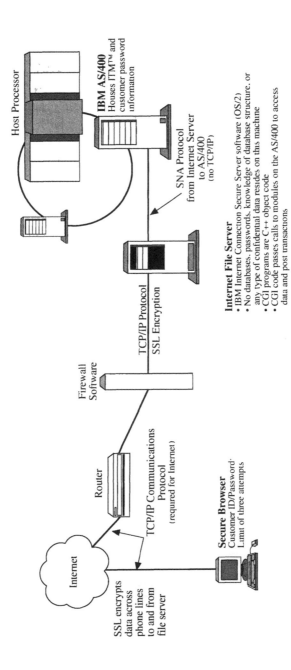

Exhibit 22-1. Fire wall software.

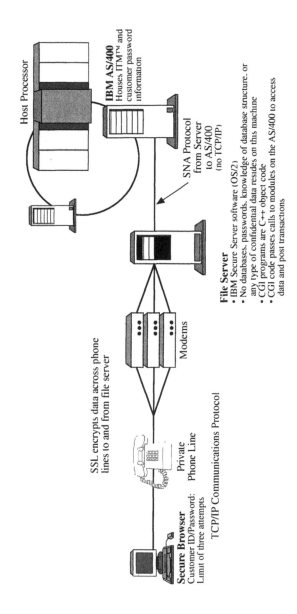

Host Processor

IBM AS/400
Houses ITM™ and
customer password
information

SNA Protocol
from Server
to AS/400
(no TCP/IP)

File Server
• IBM Secure Server software (OS/2)
• No databases, passwords, knowledge of database structure, or
  any type of confidential data resides on this machine
• CGI programs are C++ object code
• CGI code passes calls to modules on the AS/400 to access
  data and post transactions

Modems

SSL encrypts data across phone
lines to and from file server

Private
Phone Line

TCP/IP Communications Protocol

Secure Browser
Customer ID/Password:
Limit of three attempts

TCP/IP Communications Protocol

Exhibit 22-2. The system can be installed as an intranet; clients dial a private phone number to connect with the Web server.

sign-on security information. Both identification code and password will be designed to be difficult to access randomly, and will contain a combination of letters and numbers.

There is protection against repeated unsuccessful attempts to sign in to the system. Three unsuccessful attempts will lock the customer out of the system, requiring contact with the financial institution to reestablish service. This is for the obvious protection of both parties. Audit reports of these incidents are printed for review. When a customer has successfully signed on, the request received by the server is checked to ensure the customer has signed into the system, thus making it difficult for an intruder to masquerade as a customer by attempting to bypass the security screens.

For Phone Line Security. All transactions that are passed across phone lines are encrypted using SSL (secure sockets layer). Therefore, customers must use a secure browser to successfully connect to the system. Encryption prevents eavesdropping on phone lines to obtain information.

For Web Server Security. Banks will be required to place the server in a secure physical location that prevents unauthorized access to it. A password will be required to access the server console. All unnecessary TCP/IP services are disabled on the Web server, such as login and Telnet. [Financial institutions should disable the capability to FTP (upload files) to the server.] Virus detection software will be installed on the server to minimize the risk of infection and its potential damaging consequences. Audit files are backed up daily.

The Web server houses absolutely no identification/password information or customer account data. There is no information on the server that can provide any degree of insight into the customer information which resides on the AS/400 or other host processor.

For Host Data Security. Databases on the host processor are accessed only by call modules requiring specific parameters and called by a program on the Web server. The module performs additional integrity checks such as ensuring all account numbers involved in the request belong to the client.

In many cases, all transactions are memo posted to host databases so that clients have up-to-date account information. Transactions can be posted online if the financial institution prefers. The host should have additional checks that can limit the number of fund transfers and limit the total amount of funds transferred in a 24-hour period. Evening processing could provide audit and balancing reports prior to posting the transactions to the host databases (memo posting only). Any suspect transactions would then be held and examined prior to posting.

For Internal Network Security. TCP/IP protocol is the favorite and most powerful tool used by intruders to break into a network. TCP/IP must be used between the client and the Web server. Financial institutions should not use TCP/IP between the Web server and the AS/400. SNA should be used instead. The typical intruder who may manage a connection to the Web server will have a tremendous challenge in reaching the AS/400.

Beyond the AS/400, there are additional internal security measures a financial institution has the option of implementing. As previously stated, internal theft/fraud by employees constitutes a major percentage of losses by financial institutions. There are software applications that encrypt all data traveling across internal networks. Access by each individual workstation and/or employee can be carefully defined. Thus, internal theft/fraud can be greatly reduced, if not eliminated.

FIRE WALL SOFTWARE FOR INTERNET IMPLEMENTATIONS

Because definitions of a fire wall vary, the concept is initially confusing. The term fire wall is sometimes used in reference to fire wall software, but such software is only one piece of an overall fire wall system. *For the purposes of this chapter a "fire wall" is defined as all techniques utilized to prevent unauthorized traffic from moving through a Web server.* The objective is to present multiple and difficult obstacles for confronting potential intruders. It is important to note that fire wall software cannot protect a site from all forms of intrusion, specifically:

- Viruses which can't be detected by fire wall software. Virus software is available.
- Internal attacks that are on the other side of the fire wall and inside the financial institution.
- Back doors into the network such as dial-in connections that do not pass through the fire wall.

For financial institutions or enterprises who choose to implement products on the Internet, using highly rated fire wall software is imperative. When a Web server is attached to the Internet without security, literally anyone in the world can access it. It is important to offer customers the choice of a Unix or Windows NT fire wall platform for several reasons:

- Many financial institutions do not have in-house Unix expertise. Windows NT is a common and popular operating system.
- Unix-based fire wall packages cost more and require more expensive hardware.
- Some financial institutions have Unix expertise and prefer to use it despite the cost and skill required.

SUMMARY

An Internet presence must not be ignored by the financial services industry. While the Internet is an intimidating concept, it offers the opportunity to compete with other financial services providers on equal footing. Benefits of acting now outweigh the concerns of security risks.

Many industry analysts believe that Internet security concerns are greatly overrated. While security issues must be taken seriously and safety measures must be investigated and implemented, financial institutions should not postpone Internet development plans due to these fears. Secure account access can be provided for customers.

Security should be designed in layers to present multiple, difficult obstacles for a possible intruder. Categories of security include customer security, encryption of data over phone lines, Web server security measures, host data protection, and internal network techniques.

Financial institutions who do not offer customers the ability to offer PC-based online account access in an intranet or Internet environment (or both) are losing customers to those institutions who do.

Author Bio

Mary Rose serves as vice president of Business Development with ARKSYS, an international payment systems software company. She has over 12 years of experience in tactical planning with 6 years involving the information technology industry.

Chapter 23
Multicast Applications and Technology for the Financial Services Industry

C. Kenneth Miller

MULTICAST NETWORKING TECHNOLOGY and applications can greatly benefit the financial services industry. Unlike other vertical markets for multicast technology and applications, there are clear compelling reasons in the financial services sector for all of the multicast categories of applications.

There is a wide variety of multicast applications as shown in Exhibit 23-1. Many associate real-time multimedia synonymously with multicast; in reality, there is a whole spectrum of multicast applications as Exhibit 23-1 displays. With the exception of the top left quadrant, real-time multimedia, virtually all of the applications above require reliability, i.e., data must be complete at the receiver to be useful. This is in contrast to real-time multimedia delivery, where the loss of some data is acceptable.

With multimedia delivery, timeliness is the important parameter; the multimedia flow must come with minimal timing variation, which is called *jitter*. Some loss of data is acceptable as long as the flow of data is constant. The killer one-to-many multimedia applications for businesses are remote training and multimedia events which would most often use a corporate intranet rather than the public Internet as the underlying network infrastructure. Video conferencing is an important many-to-many multimedia application.

0-8493-9834-7/00/$0.00+$.50
© 2000 by CRC Press LLC

	Real-time	Nonreal-time

Multimedia	• Video server
	• Video conferencing
	• Internet audio
	• Multimedia events
		• Replication:
		  – Video & web servers
		  – Kiosks
		• Content delivery
		  – Intranet & Internet

Data-only	• Stock quotes
	• News feeds
	• White boarding
	• Interactive gaming
		• Data delivery
		  – Server-server
		  – Server-desktop
		• DB replication
		• SW distribution

Exhibit 23-1. Multicast applications.

With the rush of technology overwhelming us, training becomes more and more important, and it is not always convenient to be trained in the same location. Similarly, multimedia events are looked at as being an important new tool to facilitate communications between management and employees in large organizations.

The financial industry has been one of the early adopters to embrace the use of multimedia to view events over networks in real time; they wish to know of business news such as mergers and acquisitions as well as other fast-breaking business news as soon as it happens, while observing the body language of the presenter as well as the words associated with the event. For them, there could be much money to be made by correctly judging the real message of the event. To be able to do this, you need high quality video and audio, which means bandwidths of at least 1.5 Mbps. Starlight Networks, an early multimedia solution provider, is targeting the financial industry to provide high quality multicast multimedia streaming solutions.

The set of reliable multicast applications has widely varying requirements. The two non-real-time quadrants contain applications where timeliness is not very important. Additionally, these applications are typically one to many rather than many to many. Data-only real-time applications (the bottom left quadrant) have two basic types of application; collaboration, such as network gaming and data conferencing which are many to many, and data streams, such as ticker tape and news feeds which are one to many.

The data-only real-time applications have a sense of timeliness, i.e., the amount of latency allowed is relatively small. For example, a collaborative game or data conference cannot afford to have a latency that exceeds the tolerance of the human being playing the game or participating in the conference. Ticker tape feeds also have data that need to be delivered within a small time window as the data are quite volatile.

These applications also have different scaling requirements. Collaborative applications have modest scaling requirements, usually involving 100 or less in the group. In contrast, one to many applications can have very large scaling requirements of thousands, or even possibly millions of simultaneous recipients.

The data-only real-time application that is most interesting to the financial industry is ticker tape streams. There are different requirements for the ticker tape stream depending on the consumer of the information. If it is a casual user, the stream does not need to be absolutely reliable, as the stream is continually refreshed by updated trades. However, if the consumer of the stream is an actual trader, the requirements are very stringent; reliability, timeliness, and concurrency are all needed.

The simultaneous requirements of reliability, timeliness, and concurrency cannot be satisfied without resorting to an over-designed network which is guaranteed to not be congested and has redundancy built in. This is in fact how this is accomplished today. Most of these "feeds" have not been designed using reliable multicast, but reliable multicast and multicast IP networks could be used to advantage in this application.

There are a number of non-real-time multicast applications that are of interest to the financial industry. The financial industry is characterized by many remote offices to whom information needs to be disseminated rapidly. It is also desirable to have the information disseminated to these offices relatively concurrently, so that all offices are synchronized, i.e., are dealing with the same up-to-date information.

The same thing can be said for the software running on the computer resources at the remote offices. Not only is it desirable to have all computer systems in synchronization with the latest software, but also it is cost effective to have centralized management of computer resources in many cases. Both of these can be accomplished by the ability to reliably multicast software and business information to these remote offices.

Download of multimedia files for replay off a local server may also be desirable in some instances. In this case, the multimedia content is sent as a file via reliable multicast to a local server for replay later.

TECHNOLOGY

The TCP/IP protocol suite is shown in Exhibit 23-2. TCP/IP provides two choices for the transport layer (layer 4), TCP and UDP. The transport layer is responsible for end-to-end delivery of data from one host to another.

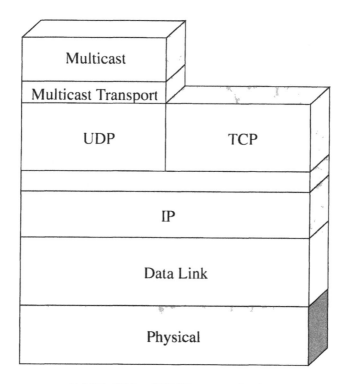

Exhibit 23-2. TCP/IP protocol suite.

Most applications, e.g., File Transfer Protocol (FTP) and HyperText Transport Protocol (HTTP), operate over TCP because of the rich services provided: error correction, packet ordering, congestion control, and port multiplexing. UDP, in contrast, provides minimal services; only error detection and port multiplexing. If a UDP packet is detected in error, it is simply discarded.

However, TCP operates only in a point-to-point (unicast) manner from one host to another host. Thus, most multicast applications operate over UDP as shown in Exhibit 23-2 and provide their own specialized transport in the application. Additionally, multimedia applications cannot use TCP in any situation, as TCP is designed for data and is not capable of delivering the constant flow required.

Multimedia applications have settled on the Real Time Protocol (RTP) and it's companion Real Time Control Protocol (RTCP) to be the transport of choice for multimedia transport. RTP is a simple protocol framework, and there are a number of companion specifications for carrying different payloads, e.g., MPEG (Motion Picture Experts Group) for high-quality video, H.261 and H.263 for video conferencing quality, and a variety of audio formats. Given that the financial industry wants high quality for media events, the MPEG payloads are most important.

Unlike the case where multimedia streaming has standardized on RTP/RTCP as a specialized transport, no such protocol or protocols have been standardized for reliable multicast. The subject is now being studied in the Internet Research Task Force (IRTF). The decision to have the subject of reliable multicast be studied in the IRTF rather than the Internet Engineering Task Force (IETF), the body that works on Internet standards, was that the technical issues are complex and basic techniques should be recommended before standardization.

Nevertheless, there are a number of commercially available reliable multicast products available — tool kits from Globalcast supporting Scalable Reliable Multicast (SRM), Reliable Multicast Transport Protocol (RMTP), and Reliable Multicast Protocol (RMP), and application products and tool kits from StarBurst Communications which support the Multicast File Transfer Protocol (MFTP). MFTP also includes a mechanism for setting up groups, as well as providing a reliable transport protocol.

Additionally, Cisco announced at the IP Multicast Summit in February, 1998 support for Pretty Good Multicast (PGM). PGM is a reliable multicast protocol that supports all multicast applications and thus can act as a multicast equivalent of TCP. PGM gains scaling by assistance of network elements, i.e., routers in the network infrastructure. PGM was first publicly documented in an Internet Draft in January, 1998 and products incorporating PGM along with Cisco routers with PGM code for scaling will likely be available in 1999. PGM looks to be a significant offering in land-line networks with Cisco routers in the infrastructure. However, alternative network infrastructures such as satellite will not benefit from this scaling.

Additionally, TIBCO is a company that provides messaging middleware software, called TIB/Rendezvous, targeted to the brokerage sector of financial services. This software includes a proprietary reliable multicast protocol that is not publicly described. However, this proprietary protocol is not that scalable, and has therefore primarily been implemented over LANs. TIBCO is heavily embracing PGM to be its underlying reliable multicast protocol for the future that scales to the wide area network.

Two concepts have been heavily promoted by TIBCO, *publish/subscribe* and *subject-based addressing*. Both are relevant to brokerage applications. Publish/subscribe is really synonymous with send and receive. Subject-based addressing provides a mechanism to identify content in a message stream based on subject. This can, for example, be used to pick out particular types of stocks in a ticker tape feed and even redirect a piece of a ticker feed to consumers desiring it, based on subject.

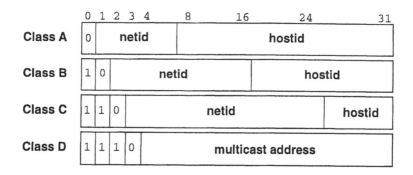

Exhibit 23-3.   IP address types.

IP MULTICAST NETWORKING

Multicast IP uses different IP addresses than are used for point-to-point communications, as shown in Exhibit 23-3. Class A, B, and C IP addresses used for point-to-point communications have a host and network component; in contrast, Class D IP addresses used for multicast transmission to a group simply have one address space indicating the multicast group.

Class D addresses also differ in that often the address is only used on a session by session basis, as opposed to the semipermanent nature of Class A, B, and C addresses.

The multicast address space occupies the range from 224.0.0.0 to 239.255.255.255. The Internet Assigned Numbers Authority (IANA) maintains lists of registered users and assigns new numbers for new uses. The range from 224.0.0.0 to 224.0.0.255 is reserved for permanent assignment for various uses, including for use by routing protocols.

Joining particular multicast groups is receiver initiated using the Internet Group Management Protocol (IGMP). IGMPv1 (the version most implemented) is specified in RFC 1112,[1] and defines a dialog that occurs between routers supporting multicast routing and hosts on a subnet attached to that router. IGMP has since been upgraded twice, and IGMPv2 is specified in RFC 2236.[2] IGMPv2 has, as its primary enhancement, facility to reduce group leave latency. IGMPv2 is now starting to be implemented in new versions of operating systems and in routers, but remains backward compatible with IGMPv1. IGMPv3 is still a work in progress.

IGMP

IGMPv1 is defined in RFC 1112. This defines the protocol and the dialog that occurs between a host in a multicast group and the nearest router supporting multicast, as shown in Exhibit 23-4. Multicast routers that are

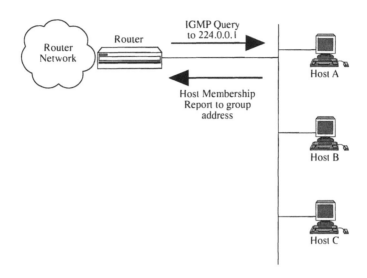

Exhibit 23-4.   IGMP dialog.

chosen to be the *designated router* (DR) for a subnetwork periodically transmit Host Membership Query messages to determine which host groups have members on their directly attached subnetwork. Host Membership Query messages are sent to the "all hosts group" (224.0.0.1) and have an IP time-to-live (TTL) of one. This means these messages are confined to the directly attached subnetwork and are not forwarded by any other multicast routers.

When a host receives an IGMP Query message, it responds with a Host Membership Report for each group to which it belongs. These messages are sent to the group address to which it belongs. Thus, if a host belongs to multiple groups simultaneously, it must send multiple Host Membership Reports to each group. Host Membership Reports likewise have an IP TTL = 1 and are thus confined to the local subnetwork.

Host Membership Reports suppress redundant messages by means of random backoff timers. Each host generates a random backoff time, after which it sends the Host Membership Report(s). If, during the timeout period, a host hears a Host Membership Report identical with one it was about to send, it suppresses its response. Multicast routers do not need to know the exact host in the group in that subnetwork; it only needs to know that there is at least one host in that group on that subnetwork. This feature serves to reduce the traffic required to be sent on that subnetwork.

Even though the nearest multicast router is not in the host group being reported, all multicast addresses must be received promiscuously by all of their interfaces. The sending of the Host Membership Report on its group address also is a convenient mechanism to allow other hosts in that group on that subnetwork to listen and suppress identical Host Membership Reports from other hosts on that subnetwork.

Multicast routers periodically transmit IGMP Queries to the subgroups to which they are attached. Hosts do not send Host Membership Reports except when queried by a router with one exception; when a host first joins a group. At this time, a host sends a Host Membership Report without waiting for an IGMP Query. Thus, joins to a group are immediately reported to the nearest DR multicast router, whereas leaves from a group are only determined by a timeout, i.e., no response to an IGMP Query. Polling intervals for IGMP Queries and timeout to declare a leave are both configurable parameters.

The total latency in setting up a group is dependent on the sum of the time to notify the nearest router of the join, plus the time to set up the multicast routing by the routers in the network. Typically, this is seconds. The latency to leave a group is longer, as the timeout needs to expire based on no response from an IGMP Query to declare a leave. Then that leaf of the multicast tree needs to be torn down by the routers. This total time may approach a minute for typical configurations. IGMPv2, as its primary enhancement, adds explicit leave messages so as to reduce the leave latency and make it closer to the join latency.

MULTICAST ROUTING PROTOCOLS

Multicast routing protocols are used by routers in a network or internetwork to optimally route multicast packets through the network or internetwork from the source to the multiple destinations that consist of the members of the multicast group. This is analogous to the unicast (point-to-point) routing protocols that are the backbone of operation in all TCP/IP networks including the Internet.

Unicast routing protocols use two basic techniques: *distance vector* or *link state*. Earlier routing protocols were distance vector, such as Routing Information Protocol (RIP) and IGRP (Cisco proprietary). Open Shortest Path First (OSPF) became the dominant link state routing protocol. Link state routing protocols converge quicker, important considerations for networks that may change dynamically.

Some multicast routing protocols are derived from distance vector or link state unicast routing protocols. However, a new category of *shared tree* protocols has also been introduced for multicast. Thus, multicast routing protocols come in three basic flavors; distance vector, link state, and

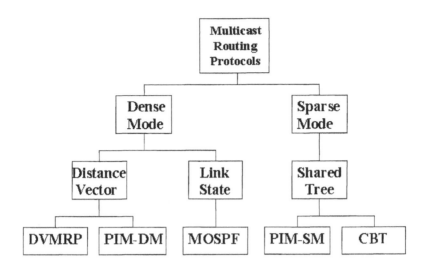

Exhibit 23-5.   Multicast routing protocol family tree.

shared trees. Distance Vector Multicast Routing Protocol (DVMRP)[3] and Protocol Independent Multicast — Dense Mode (PIM-DM)[4] are distance vector based, Multicast Open Shortest Path First (MOSPF)[5] is link state based, and Protocol Independent Multicast — Sparse Mode (PIM-SM)[6] and Core Based Trees (CBT)[7] are shared tree based.

DVMRP, PIM-DM, and MOSPF have been called *dense mode* multicast routing protocols, as they require some form of flooding of datagrams to the network to find multicast routes and this is most suitable for areas with dense concentrations of group members, such as campus networks. In contrast, the shared tree protocols, PIM-SM and CBT have been called *sparse mode* multicast routing protocols, as they are best suited for widely dispersed group members in a wide area network. The family tree of multicast routing protocols is shown in Exhibit 23-5.

All multicast routing protocols need to set up *distribution trees* to route datagrams to the members of the group in an optimal way. The challenge is to create multicast routing protocols that can set up these distribution trees quickly, efficiently, and without excessive network traffic. The different multicast routing protocols each have their strengths and weaknesses, as discussed further below.

The *dense* mode protocols, DVMRP and PIM-DM, are relatively simple in concept and create optimal source-rooted trees for distribution of data from the source. DVMRP and PIM-DM are both independent of the unicast routing protocols used in the network; DVMRP includes its own unicast routing protocol and PIM-DM uses the routing tables from whichever unicast routing

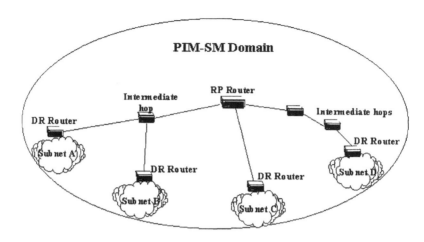

Exhibit 23-6. PIM-SM showing RP.

protocol is being used. These unicast routing protocols help the multicast routing protocol figure out the optimal routes.

MOSPF is also a dense mode routing protocol, but it is an extension of the popular OSPF unicast routing protocol and as such is dependent on it being the underlying unicast routing infrastructure. MOSPF, like DVMRP and PIM-DM, calculates optimal multicast distribution trees rooted at the source.

All of the dense mode routing protocols depend on periodic flooding of packets to determine routes. As such, they are viewed as being most appropriate for networks where the group members are densely packed in the network, such as in a campus network.

The *sparse* mode protocols, PIM-SM and CBT, create shared trees based on selection of a *rendezvous point* (RP) in PIM-SM or a *core* in CBT. This is illustrated in Exhibit 23-6 for PIM-SM.

The *designated router* (DR) for each subnet determines which rendezvous point (RP) or core should be selected for a particular multicast address and joins to that RP or core. All traffic to the group then passes through the RP or core. No flooding to determine routes is performed and the same shared tree is used, independent of the source of traffic. Additionally, much less state is required of the routers to keep track of multicast routes. The only negative is that the tree is not optimal from the point of view of number of hops. The RP or core can be located far from the bulk of the members of the group. PIM-SM has the optional facility to switch to a source-routed tree based on some criterion, such as overload of the RP, to help gain the best of both worlds.

All of the major router vendors support one or more of these multicast routing protocols in their most recent software releases. DVMRP is the earliest multicast routing protocol, and is also supported in a program called *mrouted* which is available in many Unix host platforms.

All of the above multicast routing protocols are *interior gateway* protocols, i.e., they are used within one *autonomous system* which is a routing domain under one administrative authority. A major hole is the lack of a standardized *exterior gateway* multicast routing protocol, which would be used for multicast routing between autonomous systems in similar fashion as the Border Gateway Protocol (BGP) is used to route between autonomous systems with unicast routing.

The InterDomain Multicast Routing (IDMR) working group of the Internet Engineering Task Force (IETF) is working on this problem and presented the first proposal for an interdomain multicast routing protocol, to be called Border Gateway Multicast Protocol (BGMP),[8] at the December, 1997 IETF meeting. Thus, this problem is on the way to be solved, but is still work in progress.

All of these multicast routing protocols were developed assuming a mesh-like land-line network infrastructure, such as is present in today's Internet. However, a second alternative networking infrastructure is being proposed by many as a risk averse way to gain high-speed multicast services. This approach is a hybrid satellite/land-line network as shown in Exhibit 23-7. The satellite is inherently a broadcast medium, and multicast is therefore a subset. The satellite is also a one-hop network that can be delivered anywhere without having to string cable.

This approach is also very cost effective if the number of remotes is large, as the recurring charges are typically independent of the number of remotes. For example, one satellite carrier has tariffs for satellite coverage in the U.S. shown in Exhibit 23-8.

Additionally, remote equipment needed is on the order of $1000 per remote receive site. Since the tariffs are fixed, this provides a very cost-effective solution if the number of remotes becomes large.

However, a low-speed land-line connection to the sender is needed to insure reliability. This can be very inexpensive; zero if there is already an Internet connection in place and on the order of about $70 per month for zero CIR frame relay service. Additionally, a dial modem connection or ISDN connection could be used whose tariff would consist of a monthly charge plus a usage charge.

There is an issue with this scenario, however. Static routing is needed as standard routing protocols do not automatically work with this network

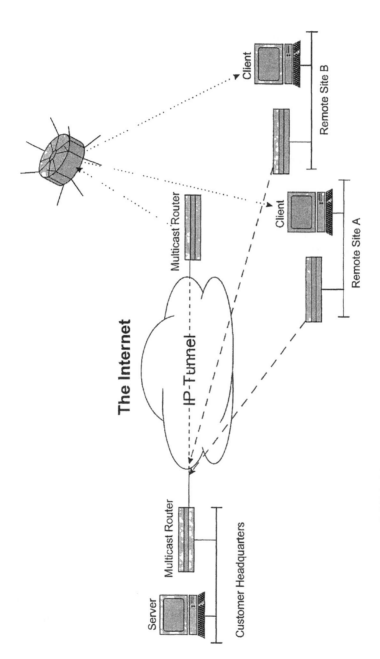

Exhibit 23-7. Hybrid satellite/land-line network infrastructure.

Exhibit 23-8.   One-Way Satellite Tariffs

Date Rate	Price/Month	Price/Receiver (100)	Price/Receiver (1000)
38.4 Kbps	$8746	$87.46	$8.75
56 Kbps	$9546	$95.46	$9.55
64 Kbps	$9746	$97.46	$9.75
128 Kbps	$10,746	$107.46	$10.75
256 Kbps	$13,746	$137.46	$13.75
512 Kbps	$16.746	$167.46	$16.75
1.0 Mbps	$22,246	$222.46	$22.25
1.5 Mbps	$33,846	$338.46	$33.85
2 Mbps	$42,846	$428.46	$42.85

Source: Microspace Communications Corporation. Raleigh, NC.

infrastructure. The UniDirectional Link Routing (UDLR) working group in the Internet Engineering Task Force (IETF) is working to correct this deficiency.

The digital satellite broadcast industry is also viewing the ability to provide high-speed one-way multicast data services as a new opportunity, and tariffs could be even lower in future.

MULTICAST APPLICATIONS TARGETED TO THE FINANCIAL INDUSTRY

As mentioned earlier, the financial services industry has a need for all classes of multicast applications as shown in Exhibit 23-1.

Multimedia Applications and Associated Protocols

In the real-time multimedia class (upper left quadrant of Exhibit 23-1), multimedia events are of particular interest. The Real Time Protocol (RTP) documented in RFC 1889[9] is the protocol that has been created to transport multimedia streams over IP networks. It's companion, the Real Time Control Protocol (RTCP), is used to monitor and control RTP sessions. RTP is on standards track in the IETF.

RTP operates over UDP, as shown in Exhibit 23-9. The multimedia stream file format (e.g., QuickTime or Microsoft's ASF) and the Codec, e.g., MPEG, and the actual application operates over RTP.

RTP is a protocol framework that is deliberately not complete; companion "profiles" need to be specified to completely document how a specific application will be handled within RTP. The MPEG1/MPEG2 profile was first documented in RFC 2038 and was recently updated in RFC 2250[10] and is the one that would be most important to the financial industry in being able to deliver high-quality video and audio for events. MPEG streams typically need to flow at data rates of 1.5 Mbps or higher.

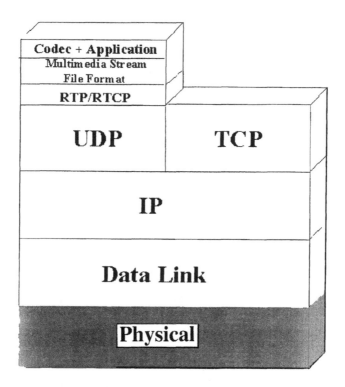

Exhibit 23-9.   RTP in TCP/IP protocol suite.

Multimedia streams (also called "flows") need to recover their time relationship at the receiver, i.e., jitter needs to be removed to be coherently received. This is accomplished by buffering real-time data at the receiver for a sufficient time to remove the jitter added by the network and recover the original timing relationships between the media data. In order to know how long to buffer to achieve synchronization, each packet must carry a time stamp which gives the time at the sender when the data was captured.

Each RTP flow is supplemented by Real-Time Control Protocol (RTCP) packets. There are a number of different RTCP packet types. RTCP packets provide the relationship between the real-time clock at a sender and the RTP media time stamps, and provide textual information to identify a sender in a conference from the source ID. RTCP session messages are restricted in rate, so that as a group grows in membership, the rate of session messages remains constant, and each receiver reports less often. A member of the group can never know exactly who is present at a particular time from RTCP reports, but does have a good approximation of group membership.

QUALITY OF SERVICE (QOS) AND THE RESOURCE RESERVATION PROTOCOL (RSVP)

Multimedia streaming applications require a minimum bandwidth for the stream or "flow." The Resource ReSerVation Protocol (RSVP) was created to allow a flow to reserve bandwidth, hop by hop, from the receiver back to the source, i.e., provide a quality of service (QoS) for the flow. Note that receiver initiation is the same methodology as that of joining a multicast group, which is also receiver initiated. RSVP is documented in RFC 2205[11] and is now on standards track within IETF.

Multimedia flows must be delivered on a certain schedule (rate) or the data become useless. If delivered too late, multimedia traffic is worse than useless, as it impedes delivery of later multimedia data. QoS techniques have been proposed to reserve bandwidth for multimedia flows, as the best effort characteristic of TCP/IP networks otherwise makes multimedia viewing quality poor, especially when the flow is at a high speed as would be expected with MPEG flows.

RSVP is the first documented specification to address QoS needs for real-time multimedia traffic, where the host application requests the QoS from the network. A number of router vendors, including Cisco Systems, are supporting RSVP in their router products.

Reservation requests are originated at receiving hosts and passed upstream to the sender(s). Reservation requests are unidirectional, i.e., from sender to receivers. At each hop upstream to the sender, reservation requests are made. The RSVP process passes the request to *admission* control and *policy* control, both of which are local decision modules. Admission control determines if the node has sufficient resources to supply the requested QoS. Policy control determines if the requester has the administrative permission to make the reservation. If either test fails, the reservation is rejected and suitable error messages are sent to the receiver(s). If both succeed, the node is set to select the data packets defined by the reservation request and interacts with the appropriate link layer to obtain the desired QoS. As flows hit a replication point at a network node, they are merged together as one flow to proceed with reservation requests back to the source.

There are a number of issues with RSVP. As it now stands, admission control and policy control are both locally administered. This means that there is not any coordination between routing nodes in the network (unless performed manually), increasing the probability that a reservation request at one of the hops upstream to the source may refuse the request. If this happens, there is no mechanism to try to find another route back to the source that can accept the request, meaning the application could get shut out and not get any service. This problem was discussed in a Data Communications article last year. A recent Internet Draft[12] discussed scaling issues of RSVP and questioned its use in high-speed backbones.

These issues are less important in Intranet or private network scenarios, where one network manager can set QoS policies uniformly in the routing nodes throughout the network and can work to insure that there is sufficient resource allocated for multimedia flows. Scalability is also less of an issue in these environments.

An adjunct protocol used with multimedia streaming applications is the Real-Time Streaming Protocol (RTSP) as defined in a recent Internet Draft.[13] RTSP is a control protocol very similar to HTTP/1.1 that is used to establish and control either a single or several time-synchronized streams of continuous media such as audio and video. It does not typically deliver the continuous streams itself, although interleaving of the continuous media stream with the control stream is possible. Essentially, RTSP acts as a "network remote control" for multimedia servers, similar to a VCR control for television.

A number of companies offer multicast multimedia streaming applications based on RTP and a number of multimedia profiles, including StarLight Networks, Precept, Icast, RealNetworks, and Microsoft in their NetShow application, which is included in Internet Explorer, Microsoft's Internet browser. Many of them also support RSVP. StarLight has targeted the financial industry as one of its key markets.

More information on these companies may be found at their Web sites as follows:

StarLight Networks:	www.starlight.com
Precept Software:	www.precept.com
Icast:	www.icast.com
RealNetworks:	www.real.com
Microsoft:	www.microsoft.com

RELIABLE MULTICAST APPLICATIONS AND ASSOCIATED PROTOCOLS

Unlike multimedia streaming applications, reliable multicast protocols are not yet standardized nor are any on a standards track as of yet. It is being studied in the Internet Research Task Force (IRTF) which is tasked to recommend techniques to be used by a working group in the Internet Engineering Task Force (IETF) to create a standards track reliable multicast protocol.

The issues viewed as most difficult by Internet researchers are those of congestion control and "fairness" to TCP traffic. Most Internet traffic is TCP, as it provides for error correction and packet ordering and thus ensures that the data received for an application is correct. TCP combines four different algorithms; slow start, congestion avoidance, fast retransmit, and fast recovery. Slow start and congestion avoidance are the two properties that are most relevant to determining behavior of a reliable multicast protocol so as to be "fair" to TCP.

However, that does not mean there are no reliable multicast products or protocols available commercially. There are a number of research protocols, and a number of products and toolkits available commercially. The protocols used, however, are not viewed by the Internet research community to be sufficiently able to handle congestion and fairness in the global Internet, but are very suitable for use on private networks and intranets over which most data in financial organizations traverse.

There is a wide range of reliable multicast applications with different requirements for transport, as can be seen from Exhibit 23-1. The real-time applications in the lower left quadrant are also varied in themselves. Data conferencing and network-based games, which are many to many collaborative applications, have low latency requirements along with small group sizes. Data streaming applications such as ticker tape and news feeds, which are one to many, need only semireliability sometimes and group sizes can be large — in the tens of thousands or even millions.

The non-real-time applications depicted in the right half of Exhibit 23-1 all involve delivery of data where low latency is not important. This is often described as *file transfer*, where the data to be transferred reside on a hard disk or other permanent memory and is delivered to another host and written on another hard disk or permanent memory. The data to be sent can be of any form; multimedia, software executables, documents, or images.

There are three primary companies that offer reliable multicast software products that reside in hosts: Globalcast Communications, TIBCO, and StarBurst Communications.

Globalcast offers protocol toolkits to allow application software vendors or IS departments to incorporate reliable multicast capability into their product or application. Globalcast offers three different protocols as follows:

Reliable Multicast Protocol (RMP)
Scalable Reliable Multicast (SRM)
Reliable Multicast Transport Protocol (RMTP)

RMP has the oldest origins and has limited scaling capabilities, so is probably of least interest to the financial community. SRM[14] is the darling of the Internet researchers and was originally designed to operate with the wb whiteboarding data conferencing tool that was created by researchers at Lawrence B. Livermore Laboratories. SRM is set up to be a framework protocol much like RTP is in the multimedia world. Neither of these has been deployed to any great extent in commercial applications.

RMTP[15] was originally developed by Bell Laboratories researchers who became a part of Lucent Technologies when Lucent was divested from AT&T. Lucent licensed RMTP to Globalcast which is offering it as a toolkit.

RMTP has not had much commercial deployment as yet either, but has been implemented for a message billing application inside a major carrier. RMTP supports both data streaming applications and file transfer and gains scaling in routed networks by adding hierarchy.

TIBCO and StarBurst Communications both offer applications as well as an underlying reliable multicast protocol. TIBCO has specialized in reliable message streaming applications with its TIB/Rendezvous software. The current reliable multicast protocol used in TIB/Rendezvous is proprietary, and not publicly documented. It is thought to not scale very well over wide area networks, with the result that TIBCO products today have been mostly installed on local campus networks. However, they have participated with Cisco Systems in the creation of a new reliable multicast protocol just documented in an Internet Draft in January, 1998 called Pretty Good Multicast (PGM).[16] PGM appears to be the protocol of choice for TIBCO in the future. PGM depends on assistance from routers in the network infrastructure to achieve scaling.

TIBCO has heavily marketed two intertwined concepts, *subject-based addressing* and *publish/subscribe*. Information is sent (published) on a subject name. Interested parties listen for (subscribe to) specific subject names. This has been used to benefit in financial trading systems. For example, securities data feed handlers can "publish" the latest stock prices to hundreds of traders on a trading floor simultaneously using TIBCO technology.

StarBurst Communications specializes in multicast file transfer with software that can provide centralized multicast group setup and control as well as reliable delivery to up to tens of thousands of receivers. The protocol used is the Multicast File Transfer Protocol (MFTP) documented as an Internet Draft[17] originally in February, 1997 and updated in March, 1998. MFTP was created by StarBurst Communications and refined with the help of Cisco Systems.

MFTP is more than just a reliable multicast protocol, as it is also a group setup and management protocol. Groups can be set up at a central location and critical information can then be "pushed" to the group members that have been set up.

Recall that joining a multicast group using IGMP is receiver initiated. This has resulted in most group setup procedures occurring similar to broadcast television; content is advertised somehow about its availability and receivers "tune" in, similar to the way television watchers tune their TV to desired programming. The sender has no knowledge of who is listening. This model is satisfactory for the sending of noncritical information but is not very satisfactory for the delivery of critical information, where the sender wants confirmation of delivery.

StarBurst created a "Closed Group" model as a part of MFTP. A group is created at the sender. At the start of a session, the sender directs the group members to join using "Announce" messages. Those directed to join respond with "Registrations" to tell the sender they are available. After all register or after a user-defined timeout, transmission of the file(s) commences. At completion, all receivers confirm delivery with essentially one positive acknowledgment called a "Done" message, which is confirmed.

This model has proven attractive to the financial industry. Financial Publishing/Thomson Financial uses an "Extranet" to deliver daily 40 to 60 Mbytes of derivative financial information for a fee via the network to their customers. Their customers are paying for this information, so it is essential that there is a record of delivery at the central site. The Ohio Company delivers the company's 300- to 400-Mbyte electronic financial database of financial properties to its 200 investment executives at 50 offices in 5 states. This database is updated immediately as inventory changes to make sure that all investment executives have up to date information.

Exhibit 23-10 summarizes the reliable multicast applications and the companies that can provide solutions. GlobalCast does not have application products, but have underlying reliable multicast toolkits, hence is

	Real-time	Nonreal-time
Multimedia		Delivery of multimedia content as files StarBurst (GlobalCast)
Data-only	Message streaming apps., e.g., tickertape TIBCO (GlobalCast)	Critical data delivery, e.g., databases, sw StarBurst (GlobalCast)

Exhibit 23-10. Reliable multicast applications and companies with products.

shown in Exhibit 23-10 in parentheses. More information on these companies may be found at their Web sites as follows:

StarBurst Communications: www.starburstcom.com
GlobalCast: www.gcast.com
TIBCO: www.tibco.com

SUMMARY AND CONCLUSIONS

Multicast IP as a networking technology and the various applications and associated protocols can provide very valuable tools for productivity for financial organizations. The applications are very varied from multimedia events to ticker tape and news message streams to critical information update to multiple remote offices. In all cases, IP multicast technology can save money over alternative solutions in its ability to conserve both server and network resources. In other cases, the application cannot even be applied without using multicast technology.

Historically, many financial technology solutions have been customized, leading to expensive solutions. Multicast IP and the protocols associated with the applications are either standardized or are publicly documented and available for support by multiple organizations. Early financial organizations who are pioneers have started to use multicast IP technology to benefit in their organizations. All financial organizations should at least investigate it to see how it can benefit their enterprise.

Notes

1. Deering, S., Host Extensions for IP Multicasting, RFC 1112, August, 1989.
2. Fenner, W., Internet Group Management Protocol, Version 2, RFC 2236, November, 1997.
3. Waitzman, D., Partridge, C., and Deering, S., Distance Vector Multicast Routing Protocol, RFC 1075, November, 1988.
4. Deering, S., Estrin, D., Farinacci, D., Jacobson, V., Helmy, A., and Wei, L., Protocol Independent Multicast Version 2, Dense Mode Specification, Work in Progress, Internet Draft, *draft-ietf-idmr-pim-dm-05.txt*, May 21, 1997.
5. Moy, J., Multicast Extensions to OSPF, RFC 1584, March 1994.
6. Estrin, D., Farinacci, D., Deering, S., Thaler, D., and Helmy, A., Protocol Independent Multicast — Sparse Mode (PIM-SM): Protocol Specification, Work in Progress, Internet Draft, *draft-ietf-idmr-pim-sm-specv2-00.txt*, September 11, 1997.
7. Ballardie, T., Core Based Trees (CBT version 2) Multicast Routing, RFC 2189, September, 1997.
8. Estrin, D., Meyer, D., and Thaler, D., Border Gateway Multicast Protocol (BGMP): Protocol Specification, Work in Progress, Internet Draft, *draft-ietf-idmr-gum-01.txt*, October 31, 1997.
9. Schulzrinne, H., Casner, S., Frederick, R., and Jacobson, V., RTP: A Transport Protocol for Real-Time Applications, RFC 1889, January, 1996.
10. Freed, N. and Kille, S., RTP Payload Format for MPEG1/MPEG2 Video, RFC 2250, January, 1998.
11. Braden, R., Zhang, L., Berson, S., Herzog, S., and Jamin, S., Resource ReSerVation Protocol (RSVP) — Version 1 Functional Specification, RFC 2205, September, 1997.
12. Mankin, A., Baker, F., Braden, B., Bradner, S., Romanow, A., Weinrib, A., and Zhang, L., Resource ReSerVation Protocol (RSVP) — Version 1 Applicability Statement Some Guidelines on Deployment, RFC 2208, September, 1997.

13. Schulzrinne, H., Rao, A., and Lanphier, R., Real Time Streaming Protocol (RTSP), Work in Progress, Internet Draft, *draft-ietf-mmusic-rtsp-09.txt,* February 2, 1998.
14. Floyd, S., Jacobson, V., Liu, C., McCanne, S., and Zhang, L., A Reliable Multicast Framework for Light-weight Sessions and Application Level Framing, ACM Transactions on Networking, November, 1996.
15. Paul, S., Sabnani, K. K., Lin, J. C., and Bhattacharyya, S., Reliable Multicast Transport Protocol (RMTP), *IEEE J. Sel. Areas Comm.,* April, 1997.
16. Farinacci, D., Lin, A., Speakman, T., and Tweedly, A., PGM Reliable Transport Protocol Specification, Work in Progress, Internet Draft, *draft-speakman-pgm-spec-01.txt,* January 29, 1998.
17. Miller, K., Robertson, K., Tweedly, A., and White, M., StarBurst Multicast File Transfer Protocol (MFTP) Specification, Work in Progress, Internet Draft, *draft-miller-mftp-spec-02.txt,* February 13, 1997.

Author Bio

C. Kenneth Miller is the founder, Chairman, and Chief Technology Officer of StarBurst Communications. StarBurst Communications is the leading company providing reliable multicast solutions for commercial applications with such corporate customers as GM, Ford, Chrysler, Toys 'R Us, Thomson Financial, and many others.

Miller has been in the data communications industry since 1972. He founded Concord Data Systems in late 1980 and served as its president and CEO until 1986. Concord Data Systems was a pioneer in high speed dial modems and was the author of the IEEE 802.4 LAN standard, which became the lower layer for the MAP factory LAN standard.

Miller was a regular columnist in Data Communications Magazine *from 1992 to 1994. He has also published numerous articles and participated in many panels at trade show and other industry events. He wrote a book entitled* Multicast Networking and Applications *published in 1998 by Addison-Wesley.*

He received a BEE degree from Rensselaer Polytechnic Institute and a MSEE degree from the University of Pennsylvania specializing in communications.

Chapter 24
An Introduction to the Internet for Financial Services Developers

Jessica Keyes

BEFORE THE "INFORMATION HIGHWAY" BECAME SYNONYMOUS with the brave new world of video-on-demand, high-powered multimedia, and 24-hour home shopping, it was a road well traveled by those needing an efficient and productive way to keep on top of their business.

For those in the financial services area, the information highway, or information services as it was known pre-Al Gore, offers a wealth of information that will help you do your job faster, better, and smarter. And in spite of all the hubbub about it, it has been easily accessible for more than a decade.

The difference is that today it's no secret anymore. While not everyone knows how to get to it, everyone at least knows it's out there. Most organizations are quickly realizing that they simply don't have a choice any longer. Not hitching a ride on the information highway (IH) is becoming a distinct competitive disadvantage.

The IH is really a misnomer (at least for now). Look at a map of the U.S. and you'll see what I mean. While there are some major arteries criss-crossing the country, the map is really a spider's web of roads all connected together to enable you to go from any one point in the U.S. to any other point in the U.S. It's the same with the IH — really a collection of interconnected networks. Understanding how to navigate it enables you to get from any one point in the IH to any other point in the IH.

While the IH probably has more information nuggets tucked into its hard disks than the New York Public Library, for some strange reason it's e-mail that seems to have captured everyone's attention. The ability to communicate with millions of people across thousands of computers across seven continents is no mean feat. It's also a productivity booster.

Of course, the IH is far more than e-mail. It's also a series of databases and bulletin boards. Both provide sources of information that are worth looking into. Bulletin boards are exactly what they sound like, places to post information. Public forums are open to anyone who has a urge to take a look-see. For example, many of the software companies have bulletin boards that enable users to file trouble reports and/or download "fixes" to those troubles.

The most interesting of bulletin boards are those that are maintained by the various special interest groups that have sprung up on the IH. Sometimes referred to as forums, these are veritable goldmines of camaraderie and information. For example CompuServe, now a part of America Online, has a Legal forum where I've been able to get assistance that would have cost me thousands of dollars if I had spoken to a nondigitized attorney.

CompuServe's Finance forums are similarly well endowed. The Investors Forum's libraries, for example, include such esoteric items of interest as stocks/bonds, fixed income, option trading, futures, commodities, newsletters, theories, charting, and technical analysis.

There's also all that shareware. CompuServers are a "sharing" lot so there's quite a bit of "free" software. (Shareware is, for all intents and purposes, free. However, you are often asked to make a donation of a rather nominal sum for the care and feeding of the developer of the program you are using. Payment is optional, but always appreciated.) If you were to access the charting and technical analysis library of the aforementioned Investors Forum, you could download QCharter 1.3, which is a shareware program for historical quote charting. Similarly, you could download useful ratios, macros, and text files such as an index of the SEC's EDGAR database.

While shareware software and databases dominate the forums, the database research services of the IH are the real prize here. Knowledge-Index (KI), the night-owl version of Dialog's very expensive professional research database service, is a veritable gold-mine of financial information. For a paltry $16 an hour (after 6 p.m. and all weekend), you get access to dozens of databases including: Books in Print, Business Dateline, BusinessWire, Pr NewsWire, Harvard Business Review, practically all of the computer news and business publications (including Pravda), as well as Standard & Poor's Daily News and Corporate Descriptions.

If you recall our earlier discussion comparing the IH to a network of interconnected roads, you'll begin to understand how it works in relation to the services on CompuServe. When you sign on to CompuServe you log on to CompuServe's computers, but when you request access to KI, CompuServe actually passes your request across a bridge to Dialog's own computer — hence the accurate analogy of a series of connecting roadways.

CompuServe offers numerous other financially oriented services (i.e., bridges). Basic Quotes provides delayed quotes for items such as stocks, options, indexes, exchange rates, and mutual funds. Citibank's Global Report, which happens to be the primary information resource for many large corporations, integrates and organizes news and financial data including real-time foreign exchange rates, spot commodity prices, and industry news. Commodity Markets and Pricing offers exactly what its title says it offers.

Company Analyzer provides public company information including income statement, balance sheet, and ownership information from Disclosure (which is also available) and an S&P estimate on future earnings. All you need is the company name, ticker symbol or CUSIP number.

It wouldn't be feasible to describe the myriad other services offered on CompuServe. They run the gamut from D&B's Business Directory to FundWatch Online to Thomas Register Online to TRW Business Profiles to Investext, which is a full-text online version of all the research reports done in the last 2 years.

America Online and MSN all offer commensurate services. Of course, Financial Services firms will benefit from providing information on services such as American Online and its rivals. As shown, Citibank, S&P, D&B, and a host of others have already made an investment in just such an undertaking. Today it is possible to use these non-Internet service providers to provide services to existing customers, to market to prospective customers, and to even provide information for a fee to whoever wants it.

For the most part, systems development in this venue is surprisingly easy and affordable. For example, CompuServe provides free access to an online area where the organization can develop its service as well as access documentation for software with which to build the service. The developing organization is merely responsible for the time and labor necessary for creating, maintaining, and promoting its database, including transmitting and reformatting the product during the developmental stages.

CompuServe, and its parent, America Online, approach all Information provider relationships as a partnership. They provide sufficient training, documentation, connect time, and disk storage for product development at no cost. They also provide the full support of their marketing and technical staff to assist in development of the organization's product to its full potential.

Interestingly, programming knowledge is not necessary, though it is helpful to be familiar with videotext services and menu-driven formats.

The actual format for the product will depend upon the nature of the information. CompuServe makes available, at their cost, several programs to facilitate the service's delivery:

Menu-driven display — This program can be likened to an electronic magazine, whereby menus serve as the "table of contents" and lead the user to articles of information. This works well for concise factual information.

Keyword search — This program enables the developer to assign keywords to each entry and allows the user to enter the word(s) he or she wants to find. It is particularly appropriate for dictionaries, access to information by state, date, or special interest, and other reference material.

Gateway arrangement — This is where information resides on the organization's host computer and the user is "transferred" to the host computer to access the information. This is particularly appropriate for information that requires immediate responses or minute to minute updating, such as stock prices.

Wire service — This CompuServe program gathers a continuous stream of information and makes the information available to users as soon as it is received. Information is dynamically added to menus in reverse chronological order. This continuous updating is typically used for news wires which require timely processing of large amounts of data.

Developers can transmit information to CompuServe by various means. With a terminal and a modem the developer can dial CompuServe's network and directly type the information into a CompuServe database using a CompuServe word processing program. Other means available are uploading and submission of diskettes and tapes to CompuServe's computer center.

A host of savvy financial services organizations have been using these Information Superhighway service providers for years for definite competitive advantage. But with the thousands of articles and growing interest in the Internet, most of these organizations are looking to the Net as well. But what they're finding is that the Internet is as different from the proprietary service providers as night is from day from a development perspective.

Where CompuServe works as a partner to help the organization deploy its service — going as far as providing access time and disk space — development on the Internet means going it alone. As you'll see in the rest of this chapter, there are many choices as well as issues that need to be grappled with if the financial services organization is to use the Internet successfully.

USING THE INTERNET

A commonly asked question is "What is the Internet?" The reason such a question gets asked so often is because there's no agreed-upon answer that neatly sums up the Internet. The Internet can be thought about in relation to its common protocols, as a physical collection of routers and circuits, as a set of shared resources, or even as an attitude about interconnecting and intercommunication. Some common definitions given in the past include:

- A network of networks based on the TCP/IP protocols.
- A community of people who use and develop those networks.
- A collection of resources that can be reached from those networks.

Today's Internet is a global resource connecting millions of users that began as an experiment over 20 years ago by the U.S. Department of Defense. While the networks that make up the Internet are based on a standard set of protocols (a mutually agreed upon method of communication between parties), the Internet also has gateways to networks and services that are based on other protocols.

In many ways the Internet is like a church: it has its council of elders, every member has an opinion about how things should work, and you can either take part or not. It's your choice. The Internet has no president, chief operating officer, or Pope. The constituent networks may have presidents and CEOs, but that's a different issue; there's no single authority figure for the Internet as a whole.

The ultimate authority for where the Internet is going rests with the Internet Society, or ISOC. ISOC is a voluntary membership organization whose purpose is to promote global information exchange through Internet technology.

The council of elders is a group of invited volunteers called the Internet Architecture Board, or the IAB. The IAB meets regularly to "bless" standards and allocate resources, like addresses. The Internet works because there are standard ways for computers and software applications to talk to each other. This allows computers from different vendors to communicate without problems. It's not an IBM-only or Sun-only or Macintosh-only network. The IAB is responsible for these standards; it decides when a standard is necessary, and what the standard should be. When a standard is required, it considers the problem, adopts a standard, and announces it via the network.

No one pays for the Internet. Instead, everyone pays for their part. The National Science Foundation pays for NSFNET. NASA pays for the NASA Science Internet. Networks get together and decide how to connect themselves together and fund these interconnections. A college or corporation pays for their connection to some regional network, which in turn pays a national provider for its access.

Many big corporations have been on the Internet for years. Up until now, their participation has been limited to their research and engineering departments. Businesses are just now discovering that the Internet can provide many advantages to their bottom line:

1. Providing information to end-users is less expensive than with the proprietary networks such as CompuServe which normally charge a royalty on profits made.
2. There are many more users of the Internet than on all the proprietary networks combined. At last count there are were 22 million users of the Internet compared to less than 5 million on proprietary networks.
3. Advances in technology have provided the ability to build visual storefronts which include liberal use of images and even video and sound. This is made possible through deployment of the browser graphical user interface and use of the Hypertext Markup Language (HTML) which has quickly become an Internet standard.

Perusing the glossary at the end of this article demonstrates the great variety of capabilities that the Internet provides organizations looking to it to provide information. Although browser interfaces currently dominate the press, the readers should be aware that the Internet was successfully disseminating information long before Netscape Navigator or Microsoft Internet Explorer was ever developed.

Essentially the Internet is being used by organizations in five venues:

1. E-mail — Organizations are making good use of e-mail to correspond to clients and staff members. Updates and notices can be inexpensively and quickly routed to all four corners of the world.
2. FTP — One of the oldest of the Internet technologies, File Transfer Protocol, enables organizations to provide databases of files (i.e., text files or programs) that others may download to their personal computers.
3. Gopher — A distributed information service that makes available hierarchical collections of information across the Internet. This service uses a simple protocol that allows a single Gopher client to access information from any accessible Gopher server, providing the user with a single "Gopher space" of information. Public domain versions of the client and server are available.
4. Telnet — This technology enables those outside of the organization to remotely log in to a host computer as a guest to access information that resides on that host.
5. World Wide Web — The newest of Internet technologies, when used in conjunction with the browser graphical interfaces provides the ability to store hypertext and images for use by current and future customers.

Financial Services firms are using all of these technologies to take advantage of what is, for now at least, a practically free worldwide network.

Using FTP and E-Mail for Support

Network Software Associates (NSA) is a consulting firm that supports the government and industry — including financial services. With offices on the West and East coasts, NSA needed to find a way to better support their customer base. For NSA, the solution turned out to be the Internet.

NSA found that a large percentage of customer support traffic comes from the user requesting help in locating information or help in performing a certain function. The other important task in customer support was in providing timely software updates and fixes.

If the request is not time-critical, the user can be trained to e-mail a request for help to the customer service group or, alternatively, to other users. This second option is a form of e-mail known as Usenet.

Both the IS organization and the user community can greatly benefit from setting up Usenet discussion groups. In essence, Usenet is Internet e-mail with a twist: It is a mailing list to which users subscribe where a message is sent not to one individual, but to the entire mailing list of individuals.

Starting a Usenet. NSA is one of many who have opted to start its own Usenet group on the Internet. Although an organization doesn't require permission to start a discussion group, it does require some special intelligence and some computer resources.

In the tradition of the Internet, the software to manage the Usenet mailing list is provided on the Internet itself. The software, known as Listserv, can be downloaded free of charge using the Internet's File Transmission Protocol (FTP).

Usenet enables NSA customers to solve some of their own problems. Responding to questions and problems from the user community is only half of NSA's customer support problem the other is providing fixes, patches, and software updates. NSA feels there is no reason to use sneakernet anymore when you can distribute software to users through the network. (Sneakernet is the network created by physically walking from location to location to deliver software to users.)

Using FTP. To accomplish this, NSA decided to implement an FTP server. The support of NSA users is handled using FTP for file transfers. NSA places the files in a common access location and then sends users an e-mail to inform them of the latest release, thereby giving them the option to obtain it or not.

According to NSA, becoming an FTP server is not as straightforward as it would be if one were dealing with a centralized organization complete with tech support personnel. Connecting to the net is no easy task and requires developing a careful plan (see below). NSA didn't, and, as a result, suffered from it. For example, NSA did not accurately predict the high level of customer usage of its Internet-based services. As a result, they had to increase capacity by installing a higher-speed line.

That this was so difficult a task is the result of the Internet relying on physical numerical addresses called IP addresses. IP, or Internet Protocol, is the network layer for the TCP/IP Protocol Suite. It is a connectionless, best-effort packet-switching protocol. For example, a server that we know as ns.uu.net has a physical address of 137.39.1.3. Since getting a higher speed line also requires a new address, there is a big conversion effort that must be undertaken to change the mapping between logical and physical addresses.

Implementation Consideration

There are a plethora of implementation issues that the NSA had to consider when opting to create an FTP server.

Hardware. The first decision was to consider the type of hardware to be used as the FTP server. Most organizations opt for high-powered, Unix-based workstations since they understand that the higher the number of users the more powerful the machine must be.

NSA opted for a Sparcstation and the Unix operating system since the number of users was large. However, most companies starting out can get by with a 486-based IBM PC-compatible.

Software. Unix is the operating system of choice for most servers since most of the software running on the net (i.e., FTP itself) is Unix based. In addition, of all the server-based operating systems, Unix is the most robust in the client/server arena.

In addition to the operating system, the organization must also ensure that telnet and FTP software is available on that server. While telnet is your basic remote telecommunications software readily available from a variety of sources, FTP comes in a couple of flavors. The traditional flavor of FTP is simply a series of Unix commands. This can be confusing to non-Unix users. Vendors have recently come out with a more graphical form of FTP, but there is a high financial cost associated with it. So instead NSA decided that, although difficult to use, a bit of training and support would go a long way towards alleviating the problem of dealing with the Unix shell.

Phone Line. The organization must order, install, and test the circuit or phone line that is connected to the server. Before this can be accomplished, however, a model of the expected usage of the Internet must be developed to accurately determine line capacity. Model variables include number of users, number and type of services being used, and amount of data being uploaded and downloaded.

NSA uses a dedicated connection to hook the FTP server to the Internet. This requires a dedicated, point-to-point telecommunications circuit and an IP router, which is a dedicated networking device, linking the organization to the Internet. Line speeds usually range from 9.6 kb to 45 Mb, with the most common connection speeds being 56 kb and 1.54 Mb. NSA ultimately required a 65-kb line to assure good response time for its users.

An alternative is to use a dial-up connection. This method uses a regular phone line and a workstation. When a network connection is needed, the workstation is used to establish a connection over the modem and phone line. At the end of use, the connection is broken. Line speeds range from 9.6 kb to 56 kb, with lower speeds being most common. Obviously slower than a dedicated connection, this solution is used by organizations which have fewer users dialing into the network. The trade-off here is increased response time vs. lower costs.

Costs. Depending upon the number of users and the hardware configuration, the cost of implementing an FTP server ranges from $1000 to $5000 per month with a one-time hardware and phone line installation cost averaging $13,000.

What you will wind up paying is really dependent upon the number of servers you use, the number of customers you have, what they're doing and the amount of time they spend on the net, the type of software you're running, and the speed of your line.

INTERNET SECURITY CONSIDERATIONS

Ten of the largest buy- and sell-side firms, including Scudder, Salomon Brothers, and Goldman Sachs & Co., have joined together to establish the Financial Information Exchange or FIX for short. FIX is a common protocol for sending and receiving equity trading information including orders, execution details, fill reports, and account allocations.

With the goal of eliminating the proliferation of proprietary order routing systems, one standard industry protocol means that brokers will be able to reach multiple clients while buy-side traders can reach multiple brokers.

Since April of 1994, Fidelity has been communicating with Goldman Sachs & Co. and Salomon Brothers using the FIX protocol. According to all indications, these firms are experiencing a tremendous surge in productivity

433

because these brokers no longer have to manually key in the information. From a liquidity point of view, sells and buys can be more quickly matched.

FIX allows customers to see on-screen multiple inbound indications from different brokers on the same stock, and fill information coming back on multiple orders. The most intriguing aspect of FIX is that the protocol to enable open communication between firms has been written to allow messages — including equity trade orders — to be sent over the Internet.

Security Risks

Wary of Internet hackers, those participating in FIX over the Internet have deployed stringent security measures including data encryption as well as strong fire walls. Internet subscribers can receive FIX information over the Net at fix@world.std.com. Included are the FIX protocol specification, FIX committee meeting minutes, application notes, and FAQ (frequently asked questions).

The Internet poses a particularly high level of security risk. Few need to be reminded of the case of Cornell University graduate student Robert Morris, Jr., who programmed an Internet worm that single-handedly brought down 6000 machines. In November of 1991, the U.S. General Accounting Office reported that computer hackers from the Netherlands broke into military computers. More recently a group of students known by the name The Posse have been taking down systems just for the thrill of it.

Setting security policies and procedures really means developing a plan for how to deal with computer security. A procedure for creating a security plan includes the following steps:

- Look at what you are trying to protect.
- Look at what you need to protect it from.
- Determine how likely the threats are.
- Implement measures which will protect your assets in a cost-effective manner.
- Review the process continuously, and improve things every time a weakness is found.

Most organizations utilize several of the following methods to ensure security.

Passwords. Many organizations are lax in enforcing password assignment and maintenance for users of their mainframes and other in-house servers. Shadow passwords, which means that no public password files are available for the casual browser, is the preferred method.

Of course, all of this is worth nothing if security isn't an intrinsic part of the corporate mind-set. Security begins with the individual. There has been more than one instance of employees giving out Internet IDs and passwords to friends — incidents usually immediately followed by a few break-in attempts.

Data Encryption. Encryption is perhaps the most popular method of security for financial firms using the Internet. But it comes with its own set of problems.

Other than a lack of standards in the industry, there remains the problem that people need to have some way of decrypting the message. If the messaging is done internally (i.e., over the organization's own network), or between two or more cooperating organizations (e.g., securities firms transmitting buy and sell information between each others' computers), then a private encryption key can be used. But if you're messaging on the Internet and a customer needs to transmit private financial information, a public key needs to be sent along with the message. The problem is that this public key needs to be decrypted at the receiving end of the message.

Fire Walls. The hardware and software that sits between the computer operation and the Internet is colloquially known as a fire wall. Its specific mission is to examine Internet traffic and allow only approved data to pass through. One type of fire wall is a software-driven filter in the network connection. An organization may have 60 machines handling Internet e-mail; however the use a software filter makes it appear to the outside world that they only have one. It is also a good idea to strip the organization's host address. In this way it is possible to lock out those who would attempt to get into a system through e-mail.

A second approach to building a fire wall is to use computers as routers or gateways. The main thrust of this solution is to route all Internet traffic through what is sometimes referred to as a bastion (i.e., bastion meaning wall, as in a wall between the main computer and the Internet) host. Essentially, this technique is simple. The bastion host is a server which is connected both to the Internet and the organization's main computer installation. Only users and/or information with the proper security clearance are routed through the bastion host to the organization's computers.

USING THE BROWSER

A variety of organizations are using a combination of the World Wide Web and a browser-type interface — in the guise of either Netscape Navigator or Microsoft Internet Explorer — to do everything from providing information to enabling catalog shopping.

The World Wide Web is a hypertext-based, distributed information system created by researchers at CERN in Switzerland. Users may create, edit, or browse hypertext documents — either in a text-based format or using a graphical user interface. As with most Internet technologies, software to run a Web site as well as develop graphical user interfaces is freely available on the Internet itself.

First Union Corporation, with headquarters in Charlotte, NC, is a bank holding company made up of eight financial institutions that is seriously interested in contributing to the free flow of information on the Internet.

First Union's vision of the future lies in its commitment to the delivery of what they refer to as Cyberbanking^{SM} to its customers and strategic partners. Although, like most financial services firms First Union is just getting started, they plan to enable their customers to buy products and services over the Web without worrying about security issues and having the money directly debited from the customer's checking or credit card account.

First Union has created what they call the First Access Network. Although today it contains information solely about the bank, First Union soon hopes to provide its commercial customers with the ability to build virtual storefronts. Even without these virtual storefronts, First Union's Web network is impressive for the amount of information it provides. This includes:

Corporate Mission	Relocation Services
History of First Union Corporation	Investing for the Future
Financial Information	Brokerage Services
Investor Relations	Estate Planning
Stockholder Account	Retirement Services
Stock Listings	Insurance Services
News Media Contact	Business Services
Career Opportunities	Consumer Reference Library
Products and Services	Career Opportunities
Checking Accounts	The Consumer's Guide to Credit
Savings Accounts	Using Credit
24-Hour Service	Basics of Credit
Credit Solutions	What Every Consumer Needs to
Loans and Leasing	Know about Credit Cards
Buying and Refinancing	VISA Home Page
Your Home	History of the Credit Card
Mortgages	History of the Banking Industry
Equity Loans	First Union and the Community

Each of these items, which appears on First Union's Home Page, is a link to a separate hypertext document which contains information about the titled subject.

Creating a Web document requires marketing and artistic skills as well as technical skills. Since an HTML (hypertext markup language) document is hypertext-linked, developers often have to draw a storyboard to keep track of where there are going.

Web document designers really have to understand the ramifications of designing a document that will be displayed in a networked environment. The general rule of thumb is to keep documents relatively small, and relatively uncluttered. Don't put large images in the document because it would take a long time to download these images over a slow link although the text comes very fast.

The major impediment to using the Web is speed. Most users of the Internet are accessing it using fairly slow 28,000 bps modems, so downloading images that are typically 200 kb can be painstakingly slow. The point here for developers is to be well aware of what your prospective users will be using as their graphical user interface.

Most developers limit their use of graphics to thumbnail images with the ability for the user to request a full screen image. Since these images are stored on the organization's host (unless this work is contracted out to one of the many Internet service providers), careful deployment of imagery will prevent a network disaster. If you have a large document with many, many images, you can take a major hit on the net by requesting these images all at once.

Programming the Web is really a misnomer. Developing an HTML document is more akin to word processing than programming. And, in fact, major vendors such as Microsoft have provided HTML extensions to their word processing packages at no additional cost.

HTML (Hypertext Markup Language) is really a rich text formatted document which looks like the example below (from First Union):

```
<ul>
<li> <a href="#mission">Corporate Mission</a>
<li> <a href="history.html">History of First Union Corporation</a>
<li> <a href="financial.html">Financial Information</a>
<li> <a href="financial.html#investor">Investor Relations</a>
<li> <a href="financial.html#account">Stockholder Account</a>
<li> <a href="financial.html#stock">Stock Listings</a>
<li> <a href="financial.html#media">News Media Contact</a>
<li> <a href="careers.html">Career Opportunities</a>
```

HTML enables the developer to embed images as well as provide for hypertext links to other documents and even other Web sites such as the Visa Home Page.

There are really two halves to creating an online presence on the World Wide Web. You have to create one or more documents using HTML and then you have to develop a way to present those documents to someone looking for them on the Internet. In other words, you have to become a Web server.

Becoming a Web server requires some careful planning. Additional software, itself available free on the Internet, needs to be obtained and configured. In addition, the organization needs to estimate the bandwidth of the telecommunications line as well as the required capacity of the hardware. This is all dependent upon the amount of information to be disseminated and the number and workload of the users using the system.

Internet Users' Glossary

Address. There are three types of addresses in common use within the Internet. They are e-mail address; IP, internet, or Internet address; and hardware or MAC address.

Anonymous FTP. Anonymous FTP allows a user to retrieve documents, files, programs, and other archived data from anywhere in the Internet without having to establish a user ID and password. By using the special user ID of "anonymous" the network user will bypass local security checks and will have access to publicly accessible files on the remote system.

Archie. A system to automatically gather, index, and serve information on the Internet. The initial implementation of archie provided an indexed directory of filenames from all anonymous FTP archives on the Internet.

Archive Site. A machine that provides access to a collection of files across the Internet. An "anonymous FTP archive site," for example, provides access to this material via the FTP protocol.

Cyberspace. A term coined by William Gibson in his fantasy novel *Neuromancer* to describe the "world" of computers, and the society that gathers around them.

Dial-up. A temporary, as opposed to dedicated, connection between machines established over a standard phone line.

Electronic Mail (e-mail). A system whereby a computer user can exchange messages with other computer users (or groups of users) via a communications network.

E-mail Address. The domain-based or UUCP address that is used to send electronic mail to a specified destination.

Encryption. Encryption is the manipulation of a packet's data in order to prevent any but the intended recipient from reading the data. There are many types of data encryption, and they are the basis of network security.

File Transfer Protocol (FTP). A protocol which allows a user on one host to access and transfer files to and from another host over a network. Also, FTP is usually the name of the program the user invokes to execute the protocol.

Gopher. A distributed information service that makes available hierarchical collections of information across the Internet. Gopher uses a simple protocol that allows a single Gopher client to access information from any accessible Gopher server, providing the user with a single "Gopher space" of information.

Internet. While an internet is a network, the term "internet" is usually used to refer to a collection of networks interconnected with routers.

Internet. The Internet (note the capital "I") is the largest internet in the world. Is a three-level hierarchy composed of backbone networks (e.g., NS-FNET, MILNET), mid-level networks, and stub networks. The Internet is a multiprotocol internet.

Internet Relay Chat (IRC). A worldwide "party line" protocol that allows a person to converse with others in real time.

Internet Society (ISOC). The Internet Society is a nonprofit, professional membership organization which facilitates and supports the technical evolution of the Internet, stimulates interest in and educates the scientific and academic communities, industry, and the public about the technology, uses, and applications of the Internet, and promotes the development of new applications for the system. The Society provides a forum for discussion and collaboration in the operation and use of the global Internet infrastructure. The Internet Society publishes a quarterly newsletter, the Internet Society News, and holds an annual conference, INET.

Point-to-Point Protocol (PPP). The Point-to-Point Protocol provides a method for transmitting packets over serial point-to-point links.

Serial Line IP (SLIP). A protocol used to run IP over serial lines, such as telephone circuits or RS-232 cables, interconnecting two systems.

Telnet. Telnet is the Internet standard protocol for remote terminal connection service.

Wide Area Information Servers (WAIS). A distributed information service which offers simple natural language input, indexed searching for fast retrieval, and a "relevance feedback" mechanism which allows the results of initial searches to influence future searches.

World Wide Web (WWW or W3). A hypertext-based, distributed information system created by researchers at CERN in Switzerland. Users may create, edit, or browse hypertext documents.

Author Bio

Jessica Keyes is president of New Art Technologies, Inc., a high-technology software development firm. Prior to New Art Technologies, she was Managing Director of R&D for the New York Stock Exchange and has been an officer with the Swiss Bank Company and Banker's Trust, both in New York City.

Keyes has a Master's Degree from New York University where she did research in the area of artificial intelligence. She has given seminars at universities such as Carnegie Mellon, Boston University, the University of Illinois, James Madison University, and San Francisco State University. She is a frequent keynote speaker on the topics of competitive strategy using information technology and marketing on the information highway, and is an advisor for DataPro, McGraw-Hill's computer research arm, as well as a member of the Sprint Business Council. She also is a founding Board of Director member of the New York Software Industry Association and has recently completed a 2-year term on the Mayor of New York City's Small Business Advisory Council.

A noted columnist and correspondent with over 150 articles published, Keyes is a publisher of the Small Business Journal and several other computer-related publications. She also has authored and/or edited 12 books.

Chapter 25
Introduction to E-commerce

David Peterson

ANOTHER MONDAY MORNING ARRIVES. You quickly make a list of the things you have to do today. The list includes buying a gift for your nephew and having it delivered, checking on airline reservations for a trip the following month, and making a change in your 401k deductions. You want to get the latest novel by Tom Clancy. You need to scan your checking account balance and transfer funds from savings to cover a check you will write today. You want to check the latest stock quotes for your held securities portfolio. You need to send a note to your brother who lives in an adjoining state regarding the upcoming family reunion. If you have access to the Internet and World Wide Web, all of these tasks can be accomplished from the comfort of your home in a fraction of the time it would require otherwise.

Welcome to the bold, new world of electronic commerce. Today anybody can access the ever-growing world of online information, transactions, and purchasing. This introductory chapter shows you, the financial institution, how to identify opportunities in the electronic access market, capitalize on those opportunities, and develop a strategy for providing solutions to current and future customers.

For the purposes of this chapter, electronic commerce is defined as your customers' ability to access your institution remotely to (1) get information, (2) perform transactions on existing accounts, and (3) sign up for additional services. While many banks are rapidly expanding their online offerings to include insurance, brokerage, trust, and other financially related services, these are merely other types of activities to which the ensuing discussion may also be applied.

Today's customer is faced with many challenges. The amount of time that individuals have to take care of their personal finances is severely limited. Today it is common for both parents to work. To accommodate the resulting limitation on families' time, financial institutions now provide access to services at nontraditional times and places.

0-8493-9834-7/00/$0 00+$.50
© 2000 by CRC Press LLC

Banks are usually open only when most people are at work. Therefore, typical bank operating hours are not convenient for most banking customers. With the proliferation of the personal computer and other electronic channels, however, banks may make their services available whenever and wherever it is convenient to the customer.

More checkbooks are balanced at 10 p.m. than 10 a.m. Late at night, when a customer discovers a missing check item, and therefore cannot balance her checkbook, the bank's access and delivery channels, or lack thereof, become most real to her. When earlier surveyed, this very customer may not have indicated a desire for accessing the bank via electronic channels, but now having experienced the need for late-night access, that desire materializes. Some customers are so accustomed to their financial institution's limited accessibility that they are not aware other means of access exist. The simple act of balancing the checkbook, however, may feed the customer's need for electronic access more than any other.

The typical business customer's needs differ from those of the typical consumer. Businesses want to know what's happening with their accounts on a daily basis. Almost all small businesses today operate on a cash basis. From this standpoint, businesses need to know exactly what items hit their accounts from the previous day's work. They maintain a list of their issued items, and, once the items have cleared the bank businesses know exactly which outstanding items may post against their accounts in the future.

Regardless of whether we are talking about late-night access for the retail customer or daily access for the business customer, customers today have wants and needs that require more than traditional banking hours and access can accommodate.

So, is the brick and mortar bank branch an endangered species? No. The bank lobby is there to sell other products and services, such as individual retirement accounts, trust services, specialized lending services, and so forth. The "lobby" has tremendous value as a service delivery channel. But for traditional "bank lobby" questions, such as balance inquiries, account transfers, loan payments, year-to-date interest inquiries, etc., electronic channels provide a higher level of service than is delivered when the customer comes in the bank, sits, and waits for the next available bank representative.

THE "PROFITABLE" CUSTOMER

Banks are increasingly focused on the profitability of their customers. Profitability studies indicate that the most profitable relationships, both personal and business, are those with customers who are looking for online services. In general, profitable customers represent 20 to 25% of your total customer base. These are the customers on which your financial institution must remain fiercely focused, and these are generally the customers who are most interested in electronic commerce and electronic banking.

TYPES OF ELECTRONIC DELIVERY SYSTEMS

There are differences between providing customers electronic access via a private network vs. an open network such as the Internet. Private network access provides a direct connection between a customer's access device, such as touch-tone telephone or PC, and the financial institution. The Internet, however, is an open network. The Internet was originally designed to prevent a foreign enemy from being able to knock out U.S. computer networks by creating an extensive web of telecommunications routes and connections over which information may be routed. It was created to facilitate the free flow of information between numerous PCs and mainframes. Therefore, information flowing over the Internet is accessible to everyone connected to it.

Which kind of delivery system do financial institutions need? It depends on the financial institution, the sensitivity of the information being delivered, and the security (or perception of security) being implemented. For example, if a wire transfer instruction is sent to the bank via a private network, that instruction travels directly through a connection from the customer's access device to the bank, without travelling through any other system. If, however, the wire transfer instruction is routed through the Internet, the connection to the financial institution is not direct. The instruction can and is routed through several different PC servers on its way to the bank.

Today, the Internet's ability to provide secure information sessions has greatly improved. In fact, there is very little evidence to suggest that a transaction performed during a secure session over the Internet is substantially less secure than a transaction performed over a private network. But the perception of a lack of security still exists, and customers who are not accustomed to the Internet may still prefer private networks. This perception is changing rapidly.

Realize that the bank already has multiple delivery systems in place. Branches are delivery systems where customers come in, buy products, and execute transactions. The ATM is another delivery system. Many banks now participate in credit and debit card programs that provide yet another delivery system. Rather than treating each individual access channel or delivery system as a separate product, these channels and systems should be evaluated together to determine how successful they are in luring and retaining profitable customers.

If a customer desires to use online systems, then that customer will gravitate to the type of financial institution that provides such systems.

The issue then is not whether a particular product is profitable, but whether the institution is meeting its most profitable customers' needs. What happens when those needs are not met? Generally, if one institution does not meet a customer's need, there is another institution ready, able, and willing to do so.

ONLINE VS. OFFLINE ACCESS AND DATA CENTER VS. IN-HOUSE PROCESSING.

As you investigate various electronic banking services, you must address whether a new service should be online with your current host system. Your host system, whether an in-house system or one processed by a third-party service bureau, houses most of the information your customers want and need. Many customer requests are processed on that host system. Smaller financial institutions who are not online post their transactions at the end of the day in a batch mode, and information is then made available the following day. This can lead to "untimely" information for the customer. It is important for banks to clearly disclose any aspects of their technology that affect its customers. Customers must be aware of any time lapses between when requests are submitted and when they are performed on the host system. Depending on the access device, a disclosure to this effect may be played or displayed automatically to prevent any confusion.

Other issues also arise with offline services. For systems that are solely dependent on online information, the customer's offline request cannot be fielded, and the financial institution must communicate, in an appropriate way, that the information is not currently available. Also, if a financial institution offers online services, there must be a mechanism for information delivery at times when the host system is not available. This can be achieved by downloading information from the host system and populating a database at the electronic delivery channel level. This database may be updated on a regular basis so that information is available to the customer at all times, even when the host isn't available.

SHOULD A BANK HOST ITS OWN SYSTEM?

Security concerns, one of the biggest reasons banks do not host their own systems, are slowly diminishing as security devices called routers and fire walls make the Internet a safer place to conduct business.

Additional security issues arise when a bank installs its own access to the Internet. For this reason, and the increased expense of maintaining and securing such access, many financial institutions have found it prudent to have third parties provide the Internet access.

Should financial institutions then choose an in-house or hosted processing option? It really depends on whether they have the interest and expertise required to provide Internet access themselves. In many cases, the decision is based on which type of Internet access the institution wants to provide its in-house staff, and other activities in which the financial institution may be engaged.

PLANNING AND IMPLEMENTATION CONSIDERATIONS

Another important consideration when implementing an electronic banking system is the attitude of senior management. It is important that the decision makers be literate when it comes to electronic commerce. Often, the Internet and the speed at which electronic commerce is progressing may go unnoticed by senior management.

The Anti-Mirage

Why does it go unnoticed? You might call this the "anti-mirage" effect. A mirage is something that you can clearly see but that is not real. As you get closer and closer to it, it disappears. An anti-mirage is something that you don't see or can't see but that is very real. It's there, but it's invisible.

The electronic community is an "anti-mirage." A bank executive might see traditional development, construction projects, and a growing commerce base. Because these are visible, the executive can assimilate the information and assess whether each may be an area worthy of a branch or other access device. The same philosophy should be applied to electronic commerce.

Senior management must be challenged to go out and explore these systems and virtual communities for themselves. Every financial institution should have at least one PC connected to the Internet, and this PC should be made accessible to all employees, if for nothing more than to conduct research and foster awareness. At a minimum, both management and staff should have the opportunity to experience the information and communities of interest and commerce that now exist on the Internet.

Once senior management understands — once they have realized that the Internet is something real and vital to the bank's future growth — the financial institution — from top to bottom — will ultimately embrace the idea.

THE IMPLEMENTATION TEAM

Once the financial institution has decided to pursue electronic commerce options, the next step will be to involve individuals from the various sectors of the financial institution. These individuals will form the implementation team.

This team should address all areas of the bank, concentrating on the operations area where the actual computer systems will be implemented. A member of the senior management team, a member of the client services team (such as a customer service representative), and most importantly, a member of the marketing department should be involved. Good communication must be established so that as the project moves forward all of these individuals move in sync. At the time the product or service is ready to be rolled out, a well-organized team will ensure that the implementation is smooth.

Choosing a Good Technology Partner

One of the keys to entering e-commerce successfully is selecting a good technology partner. It is a given that most financial institutions cannot, and should not, implement these systems on their own. Even in the area of the Internet, where it is presumedly simple to create a Web site, it is prudent to have professional assistance.

The technology partner should be rooted in the knowledge of electronic access. The institution would do well to find a technology partner that can provide multiple pieces of the puzzle, even if it is not going to implement everything at once. In the future, when the financial institution wants to incorporate additional pieces of the technology pie, it will want to go back to the same vendor and have a continuity relative to the implementation and performance of the system.

The bank needs a technology partner that is going to provide multiple device access. It should use a vendor that can, for example, process both business and retail customers through the touch-tone telephone, through direct PC access, and through the Internet. All of these access channels may not be needed initially. A good first step is touch-tone telephone access and direct PC access for performing basic banking functions. The institution should ensure that the vendor also has an Internet product available so that when the institution is ready to implement Internet access, it can get it from the same vendor. That vendor should be able to provide a sound technology plan that gives the financial institution a blueprint for long-term implementation.

Education and Training

One thing that cannot be overemphasized in rolling out any type of electronic banking initiative is the education and training necessary for both staff and customers. Staff education is something most banks have on their "to do" list, but often never get to it even though it is invaluable.

Consider the analogy of the farmer. One of the greatest assets the farmer has is the farm equipment he utilizes. If the farmer leaves his equipment sitting in the field and never performs even the most rudimentary maintenance, his equipment will certainly deteriorate. To safeguard his investment, the farmer must ensure his equipment is regularly maintained and in prime condition to harvest his crops. It isn't any different for a bank and its employees. Employees are the bank's most important assets. Training employees is the basic maintenance that ensures the bank will advance technologically and operationally.

What are the best ways to train? First, every employee should have a PC on which they may install and use the bank's software products and access the Internet. Many employees do not have access to this type of technology at home. One way to change this is for the bank to subsidize and/or facilitate its employees' purchase of home PCs. Providing employees with ready and regular access to a PC can dramatically impact their technical literacy and ability to understand and sell PC-based services. It also says a lot about the commitment of the financial institution to its employees.

The bottom line is that if a bank employee feels comfortable and competent speaking about electronic banking with your customers, your customers will feel more comfortable and excited about accessing your institution electronically. If someone comes to your bank and asks an employee about a new Web site, think of the positive impact on the customer when that employee can answer the question immediately without referring the customer to another employee. A confident response is a confidence builder. Employees who stumble when answering customer questions plant a seed of doubt about the institution's ability to deliver quality products and services.

In many cases, customers are willing to participate in electronic banking initiatives but aren't, themselves, up to speed on electronic commerce. Some studies suggest that as few as 7% of any given bank's customers are technophiles, or people who are technologically advanced. However, if the 25% of the customers who provide your institution's profit base are generally open to new and better ways of banking, a little bit of technical education may go a long way.

A GREAT TRAINING TOOL

Put an Internet-connected PC in your lobby and make it available to customers. By doing this you are "training" your customers to feel comfortable with computers and, more importantly, to associate computers and electronic access with your financial institution. Giving your customers a PC to 'experiment' on will make them more comfortable with and interested in the electronic services you offer.

Another opportunity is customer training sessions. The best times for such sessions are immediately after working hours. At these sessions, you can address viable issues in a comfortable, nonthreatening environment. Invite some select customers to speak specifically about their experience with the product or service. Include bank employees who can answer questions. In addition to providing information about electronic banking, you

447

can also use this opportunity to discuss other kinds of issues that may be very valuable to you and your customers from an investment or regulatory standpoint.

You can provide education and training for both your employees and your customers through a local college, university, or tech school. These sessions are extremely valuable and demonstrate to both your employees and your customers that your financial institution is interested in education and is willing to make the extra effort to help.

MARKETING

A financial institution can decide to purchase the equipment, secure a great vendor, and train employees; but without marketing it's "all dressed up with no place to go." Regardless of how good the product is, people won't use it if they don't know about it.

One of the biggest problems with financial institutions today is a lack of enthusiasm for the products and services they roll out. Most products and services today are very generic and difficult to differentiate from the products and services of other financial institutions.

Proper marketing then begins with the attitudes and enthusiasm of your institution's personnel. Internal staff "buy-in" is a crucial and necessary step before a media plan is developed, brochures are printed, and the product or service is rolled out.

When the staff feel good about a product or service, it sends a clear signal to the customer. It says "we're confident you are being served well at this bank." Most financial institutions' lobbies are not customer friendly. They often feel like a library, a place where people feel inhibited from speaking up, much less free to ask questions. Financial institutions cannot afford to create such environments for their customers, particularly when rolling out an electronic banking initiative. The concept is too new, the questions too many. The lobby should be abuzz with activity, excitement, and vigorous Q&A.

If the institution's attitude about electronic banking is "Well, we have to do this because everyone else is," or "We don't really think it's a good idea, but we have to do it," this attitude will permeate every employee's attitude and effectively disable any marketing effort. Internal enthusiasm for any new product or service is essential for its success.

From a traditional marketing standpoint, the institution should evaluate all media opportunities, possibly with the aid of a professional marketing organization if the bank does not have an experienced in-house marketing team. Brochures, signage, advertising, and public relations activities are as important to launching an electronic banking initiative as to launching any other product or service. The difference with marketing electronic banking is that you reach the type of individual who would seek this type of product.

It is crucial that the financial institution market the product through its Web site. One of the most effective marketing tools is an individual's ability to download a product directly from a Web site. While this does create some security concerns, which can be overcome, it constitutes a marketing coupe. Partnering with other area organizations in joint marketing programs is another way to market a new service, especially if the partner has ties to your target market, such as a local Internet Service Provider (ISP). A financial institution and an ISP can join forces so that the ISP offers a low introductory rate for people who are not Internet-ready but who want to be if the price is low enough.

There may also be opportunities with local computer stores who may agree to pre-load the financial institution's software onto PCs before delivering them to customers. This is a common practice with larger companies such as Microsoft. Today's computer comes equipped with a myriad software options. Adding your product to the mix, and marketing the concept on a local basis, can prove very effective. Many of these relationships may be simple to establish if these vendors are already customers of your financial institution. It certainly makes sense to take advantage of any local relationships you already have.

BEYOND THE INITIAL PUSH

Perseverance is key to marketing any electronic banking product or service. No matter how much enthusiasm is mustered initially, no matter how well the bank trains, no matter how engaging the marketing material, if an institution stops the push after the initial roll-out, the product or service will not succeed in the long run.

The marketing plan must be part of the bank's broader long-term strategic plan, not something that is seen as a novelty product that might succeed or fail on its own. There has to be an ongoing marketing program, combined with ongoing education and training. The financial institution will be releasing upgrades of its electronic service offerings, so it must persistently communicate the evolution and improvement of its products and services.

An ongoing marketing program is particularly important for reaching people who are not psychologically and/or technologically ready at the first roll-out. In 1, 2, or even 6 months after the initial push, another cycle of advertising and marketing should take place that will move to action the person who is then ready to purchase the service.

Again, the key is enthusiasm for the program. Enthusiasm cannot be taught, but it can be caught. Senior management's enthusiasm should infect the rank and file. The vendor or vendors that you work with can often be very helpful in this regard.

Communicate that electronic banking is not a passing fad. This whole issue of electronic access to a financial institution is the future, and it is moving faster than we ever imagined. Just 2 years ago, who would have thought we would be conducting the level of e-commerce we are today.

Electronic banking is the future. It does not matter where your financial institution is physically located. Sooner or later, you will have to reckon with electronic banking. In fact, electronic banking makes geography and location even less an issue. Your electronic location will soon become as important, if not more important, than your physical location. Your electronic location is your institution's on-ramp to the information highway, the world of electronic commerce.

Author Bio

David Peterson is founder of Goldleaf Technologies, Inc., an Equifax company. In 1988, Peterson took his experience of helping independent banks and, along with two partners, created Legend Technologies. In a joint venture with DCR out of Colorado, the two companies developed a system known as "TREEV," which enabled banks to store documents on laser optical discs. Peterson played a key role in introducing the product to new markets as well as educating the financial world on other technical breakthroughs.

Peterson is recognized nationally as an industry leader and expert on electronic banking and consulting. He frequently conducts seminars and workshops designed to help banks embrace technology. He has written numerous articles, and is a frequent speaker at events sponsored by banking organizations such as IBAA, NACHA, Community Bankers Association, MICROBanker, and IBM Common.

Chapter 26
Transactional Application Servers: Providing the Scalability for Global Electronic Business

Michael McCaffery

THIS CHAPTER WILL TAKE A DETAILED LOOK AT THE LATEST PARADIGM in distributed computing, transactional application servers, in an effort to demonstrate a technology capable of providing a proper infrastructure for Internet electronic business applications. It will explore the evolution of various distributed technologies and explain how simply having a scalable Web server is not sufficient to bring back end systems to the Internet. The right distributed architecture is essential; more machines and more hardware do not necessarily equate to better scalability and higher throughput. When competitors are a mere mouse click away, a highly optimized infrastructure is absolutely critical to providing the speed and service required by today's consumers.

THE NEED FOR DISTRIBUTION

With the advent of the personal computer (PC) and the Internet, virtually all corporate computing infrastructures have made the transition from a highly centralized mainframe environment to a highly decentralized distributed environment. This migration was largely due to the fact that mainframes were becoming increasingly expensive to maintain, while smaller workstations and PCs began to enter the market with increasingly faster processors and lower prices. As the majority of new software products and tools shifted to the workstation and PC markets, it became cost prohibitive for companies to add any additional systems to the mainframe. However, this new decentralization from the mainframe introduced a whole new range of issues in terms of interoperability of the hardware and software packages purchased. In attempting to understand the real value presented by today's transactional application servers, it is important first to understand some of the deficiencies in previous enterprise architectures.

THE MAINFRAME: USER INTERFACE, BUSINESS LOGIC, AND DATA ACCESS ALL ONE PHYSICAL MACHINE

True enterprise computing began on large mainframes. At the time these were the only types of computers that could support multiple users, support many different simultaneous applications, and provide data storage and security. This was an era long before the rise of the personal computer.

The architecture of the mainframe was very simple. Users interacted with "dumb terminals," which interacted over a local private network to the large mainframe. They are known as dumb terminals because they had no local processing power, no graphics, and no local storage. Ironically, the dumb terminals of the mainframe era are really no different than the modern Web portals and network computers (NCs), with the exception of the powerful graphic capabilities of modern browsers and NCs. Note the similarities in the dumb terminal/mainframe environment and that of the current Web browser/server environment as shown in Exhibit 26-1.

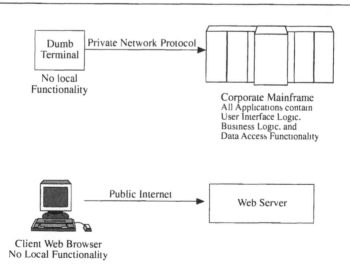

Exhibit 26-1. The early one-tier mainframe model and its similarities to the current Web browser client architecture.

Thus, since the local dumb terminals had no processing ability, it was up to the mainframe applications to do all the processing. All mainframe applications had to have presentation logic, business logic, and data access logic together in the same executable program. Each program had to write logic to accept the user input from the dumb terminals, the processing logic to analyze the input, and the logic to get data from data sources. Each program contained all three logical tiers, and they all ran on one physical tier, the large mainframe.

In a similar fashion, Internet-based architectures are very similar, each trying to keep as "thin" a client as possible. The obvious difference is that Internet architectures make use of Web browser clients, which do allow for graphical interfaces and can perform some local processing. However, in an effort to ensure that an Internet client can run in virtually any Web portal, it is necessary to limit the functionality of the client application to simply providing an appealing user interface. Thus, the role of a transactional application server is to fulfill the business logic processing and data access functionality as done previously by the mainframe. However, the application server overcomes many of the problems with the mainframe architecture, as described in detail in the following paragraphs.

The "one-tier" mainframe approach presents many architecture deficiencies. There is only one machine, the mainframe, to support every user. This is an obvious performance bottleneck, with all work being done on a single machine, regardless of the size of the machine. The only way to overcome this problem is to upgrade and enhance the mainframe with additional resources; however, this solution is far too expensive for most companies and does not provide a long-term strategic solution. Moreover, these upgrades are major undertakings, which are extremely disruptive, forcing the entire mainframe to go down, leaving all users unable to work. Mainframe dumb terminals have no graphical capabilities, so users require extensive training to learn new applications. With specific regard to applications, because all of the presentation, business, and data access logic is coded in each individual program, any slight change requires the entire program to be shutdown and changed, again leaving users unable to work.

It is clear why mainframes and the "one-tier" model have been phased out. There still exists a significant investment in these applications and this hardware, so it is not feasible to simply throw out the mainframe. Rather, companies are trying to find new ways to leverage their investment while phasing these applications on to a more cost-efficient computing platform.

THE CLIENT/SERVER REVOLUTION

The first attempt to overcome the deficiencies of the "one-tier" mainframe architecture was brought forth by the many hardware vendors. The

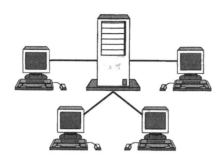

Exhibit 26-2. The early client/server architecture, Client PCs connecting via local area network to a File Server.

early client/server architecture was sparked by the introduction of the PC and the development of low-cost high-performance multiuser server machines. With the introduction of the PC, users could suddenly be empowered to work on their own outside of the corporate mainframe. They had their own desktop applications, so they were not as reliant on the mainframe for all its services. Further, the servers could be used for services such as file sharing, data storage, and printing. Thus evolved what is now commonly referred to as "clients" and "servers." Clients were the PCs on every desk connecting via a local network to a shared hardware server. Client/server in its infancy simply reflected the physical PCs and servers, the hardware rather than the software.

As this "two-tier" hardware paradigm began to become more popular, software packages and implementations were designed to fit this model. Using one of these tools, developers would create desktop applications containing both the presentation logic (using their graphical tools to paint screens) and business logic written in the programming language provided by the tool. The data access would typically be included in the business logic as either embedded SQL or using the open database connectivity (ODBC) application programming interface (API) in order to access relational databases. The actual data resides in a relational database on the server. Thus, all three logical tiers are in the client program, making it "fat," relying almost exclusively on the processing capabilities of the client PC. All the processing in this architecture is done on the small desktop PCs, thus losing all the benefits of high-end multiprocessor server machines. The client/server architecture is shown in Exhibit 26-2.

An advantage of the client/server model is that it minimizes but does not eliminate, the bottleneck at the server, by distributing processing between the PC client and the server. Unfortunately, this architecture still suffers from many of the same flaws as the mainframe.

- *No Reusable Components.* Any modification of any of the presentation interface, business logic, and data access functionality has major impact on the others. Since the user interface presentation logic has business logic and data logic embedded in it, small changes to just one button on a screen can cause huge amounts of reprogramming.
- *Inefficient Fourth Generation Programming Languages.* Moreover, the 4GLs used to program these applications are proprietary and are not efficient for complex programming.
- *Poor Performance.* Performance also becomes a consideration as the application is extended to additional users across larger networks because the application is completely relying on the processing power of the small desktop PC.
- *Maintenance and Software Distribution.* Any small change to this desktop application requires an entirely new executable program to be created, and this must be distributed to every client. In a small LAN this may not appear to be an issue, but over a WAN this could be very hard to manage.

An alternative approach at this time was to attempt to take advantage of the increased processing power and speed of the multiprocessor server machines rather than relying on the smaller client PCs. Moving business logic and data access to the back-end server became a priority of the database vendors. Their solution was to have developers develop all of the business logic and data access within their relational database management systems (RDBMS), as triggers and stored procedures. In this model, the client applications would simply make requests to the RDBMS; all business logic and data access would take place within the RDBMS on the single server machine.

This approach solves many of the problems with the "fat client" model. Presentation logic is now physically separated from the business logic and data access. If changes are made to the client GUI, these changes have no effect on the server functionality, making maintenance significantly easier. Programming can now begin to be done in parallel between those developing GUIs and those writing business logic and data access.

Fundamental problems still render this architecture unsuitable. There is limited scalability because the model relies on the one centralized RDBMS on the one physical server machine. As the number of clients grows, having only a single database on a single machine becomes a tremendous bottleneck. Similar to the mainframe, the only way to solve this is to upgrade the database and add more hardware resources to the server. Similar to the mainframe, this does not present a strategic long-term solution. This model also requires developers to become reliant on proprietary stored procedure languages for writing business logic and proprietary data access protocols.

ENTERPRISE MIDDLEWARE AND MULTITIER ARCHITECTURE

After it was clear that for client/server to move beyond addressing departmental solutions and toward global enterprise solutions, architectures had to eliminate the early correlation to physical PC client machines and server machines and focus on software distribution. It became clear that presentation interfaces, business logic components, and data access functionality had to be separate within applications and distributed over different physical hardware servers to maximize the processing efficiency and scalability. This is a drastically different programming paradigm and requires a "middleware" infrastructure to support it. For an application to be broken into separate modular programs running on separate hardware, we now must address how these programs find each other and communicate with each other. The notion of distributing the three logical software tiers now presents implementation dilemmas not seen before. Issues such as the following have emerged:

- *Communications Infrastructure.* In a global corporation there will be a complex environment of heterogeneous hardware platforms. Regardless of the differences in each of these PCs, servers, and mainframes, there must exist a common communications network and protocol which will allow connectivity within this environment. Further, this issue must be expanded to consider remote users, dial-up connections, mobile computing, and the ubiquitous connectivity of the Internet.
- *Application Partitioning.* There must exist a clearly defined mechanism for separating applications into a presentation component, a business logic component, and a data access component. This must be a standard with which corporations can standardize development in an effort to have parallel distributed development. In this manner, one group of developers can focus on creating the visual user interface, while another group writes application logic, and another separate group creates data access components. The partitioning must allow for each separate group to build and test their respective components without affecting the other development groups.
- *Distributed Security.* Now that the application will be run across several platforms and allow a wide variety of users, security becomes an issue. Security must address the issues of authentication, authorization, and encryption. Authentication verifies that the user is not an imposter and will continue to verify the user for each separate component to which it makes requests. Once a user has been authenticated, it is important to determine if the user has the authority to

perform the operation requested. After a user is authorized to connect to a particular service, encryption will ensure the integrity of
the message, guaranteeing that the contents have not been read or
altered.
- *Directory Services.* Having services distributed across multiple hardware server machines requires some type of naming or directory service for programs to find the remote services they require. In a
multitier environment, programs register their service and location
with a network directory service. Clients will use this directory service to locate the business logic and data access services they require.

Several different distributed multitier architectures emerged to address
these concerns.

Remote Procedure Calls and Transaction Processing Monitors

One of the first distributed architectures was that of remote procedure
calls. This allowed developers to write business logic functionality as a series of separate C programming language function routines. Developers
would define the interface of the C function routines in some type of interface definition language (IDL) and then use a vendor tool to generate client
and server side code to link the components together, as shown in Exhibit
26-3.

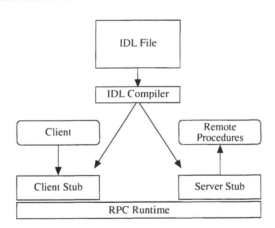

**Exhibit 26-3. An example of the RPC programming model. Developers de-
fine C-language functions in interface definition language
and use a tool to generate client and server "stubs." This generated code is compiled into the client code and server code,
respectively.**

The RPC model was significantly more scalable than the previous "two-tier" model in several ways. It allowed applications to run multiple instances of business logic and data access functions across different hardware platforms to scale to a large number of clients. It provided a standard mechanism for partitioning applications between the presentation and business logic layers, IDL. Using IDL, client developers could focus on developing user interfaces while server developers could write implementations for the business logic functions. It provided a standard directory and security service for client programs and server programs to utilize. Finally, it provided the first ability to "reuse" components. Common business logic functions could be reused in multiple applications because they were written in such a modular fashion.

Although RPC did begin to address many of the deficiencies in the "two-tier" model, it did not provide the best overall solution. Most RPC implementations only supported the C programming language, a very difficult programming language to work with, on a limited number of platforms. This prevented easy integration with popular desktop GUI applications. Further, there was no defined interface mechanism for writing data access components. Developers were forced to write complex code to interact with the naming and security services and to make use of multithreading. However, one of the major reasons why the RPC model was not used more widely was the fact it was not object oriented; it was purely function based.

Transactional processing monitors (TP monitors) extend the functionality of the RPC model to allow developers to write data access components involving transactions with the DBMS. This integration allows data access components to be written to begin a transaction in the DBMS, make updates to data, and either commit or rollback the changes.

While these conventional TP monitors are very powerful in their ability to provide atomic, consistent, isolated, and durable transactions, there are several drawbacks. TP monitors are quite expensive and typically involve a great deal of customization. Interfaces for each vendor are different and quite complex to use.

Object Request Brokers and the Object Transaction Service

Object request brokers build off of the model started by RPCs. Both ORBs and RPCs make use of the interface definition language, although they are slightly different. In the ORB model, developers build server side objects, not functions, using IDL to define their interfaces. Similar to the RPC model, the ORB IDL is then used to generate client and server side code to facilitate network communication between the separate programs. Thus, instead of making remote procedure calls, the ORB model provides for remote method invocations. The ORB model allows business

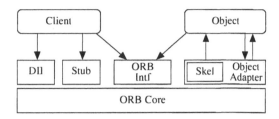

Exhibit 26-4. The CORBA communication model.

logic components to be built as a series of reusable objects, which can then be distributed across multiple platforms.

The advantage of the ORB model is that there is an industry standard put forth by the object management group (OMG) called the *common object request broker architecture* (CORBA). CORBA defines standard mappings for using a variety of programming languages such as C, C++, Java, Smalltalk, and COBOL. Further, it defines interoperability with the Microsoft Distributed Common Object Model (DCOM) to allow interoperability with a wide variety of different software applications. Further, the CORBA specification defines a standard network protocol, the Internet inter-ORB protocol (IIOP) to allow different products from different vendors to interoperate. The CORBA model is very similar to that of the RPC model as shown in Exhibit 26-4.

Sun also has introduced a Java-based ORB referred to as remote method invocation (RMI). RMI has also adopted IIOP as the underlying network protocol, allowing interoperability and communication among the widest array of possible software and hardware.

While CORBA, DCOM, and RMI have been widely accepted and used, they still do not address all of the issues required for global enterprise applications. Each of these ORB solutions is stateless; there is no defined mechanism for providing persistent storage for the private data within the business logic objects. Moreover, developers are still forced to write too much complex code dealing with directory services, transaction services, multithreading, and concurrency.

Similar to the role of conventional TP monitors with the RPC model, the OMG's object transactions service (OTS) is designed to provide an ability for data access ORB components to utilize transactions with a DBMS. The OTS itself is not a commercial product; rather, it is a specification that provides a standard object-oriented interface to existing TP monitors. Thus, applications can be coded with the standard OTS interface for beginning and committing transactions, regardless of how the OTS is implemented.

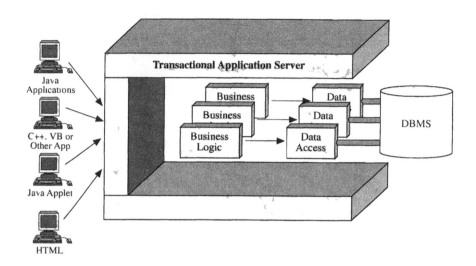

Exhibit 26-5. The application server model, demonstrating a "container" architecture, allowing developers to focus on building components to be executed and managed by the container.

While this overcomes the issue of having proprietary TP interfaces in the application, it still requires the developer to be aware of complex transaction and concurrency issues when writing business logic and data access.

Transactional application servers

Transactional application servers have attempted to address many of the gaps in the various distributed paradigms previously discussed. The architecture behind a transactional application server is to provide a developer "container" with which developers build standard business logic and data access components. By using the advanced functionality of the specialized container, developers can finally focus exclusively on business logic components without being burdened with a specific low-level understanding of threads, transactions, and concurrency. This is because the container will provide implementations for each of these advanced services. The architecture of the application server is shown in Exhibit 26-5.

While the term "application server" has come to mean different things to different people, the majority of commercial implementations share some common functionality.

Support for Standard Internet Protocols, HTTP, HTTPS, IIOP, SSL, and Providing Session Management. Application servers actually started in an effort to quickly "Web-enable" critical back end business systems. Early client/server

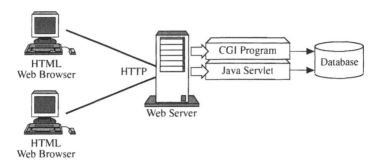

Exhibit 26-6. The first generation of Web-enabled applications had HTML presentation logic connecting via HTTP to a Web server, which passed the request to either CGI programs or Java Servlets, which implemented the business logic and data access functionality.

architectures were a nightmare to manage because each end user had to have custom software installed and configured locally on his or her PC. This PC was then connected via a private network to the server. This architecture is not dynamic and does not allow business-to-business solutions, as everything is isolated within a single corporate network. With the rise of the public Internet, corporate information systems are being challenged to break away from private corporate networks and allow users to access this functionality from any Web browser. Applications built for Web access thus far have been built using one of two protocol solutions, either a combination of HTTP and HTTPS or IIOP and SSL.

The Hypertext Transfer Protocol (HTTP) and Secure Hypertext Transfer Protocol (HTTPS) represent the majority of Internet applications today. Client interfaces are built in combinations of HTML and various scripting technologies and communicate via HTTP to corporate Web servers, which utilize the Common Gateway Interface (CGI) for building business logic components. An alternative to CGI is to build these server business logic components as Java Servlets. In either case, the architecture is the same, as shown in Exhibit 26-6.

This overcomes the software distribution problem, as client machines need only a generic Web browser and an Internet connection. They no longer need to install and configure custom applications on their desktop for connecting to corporate resources. However, this does represent a challenge, as HTTP is a stateless protocol. Every time a user downloads a new screen, she must establish a new connection to the Web server. Thus, in order to develop Internet "transaction"-oriented applications (i.e., banking, E-commerce, etc.), developers using this model would have to develop their own methods to guarantee session identity and transaction integrity. Application servers are designed to provide robust session tracking for Web clients.

461

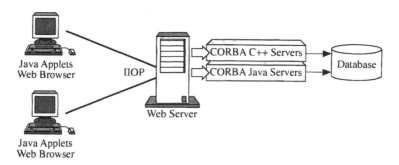

Exhibit 26-7. Users download Java Applets containing all necessary client interface code. Nothing needs to be preinstalled on the client.

A more recent protocol for Web applications is the Internet inter-ORB protocol (IIOP). This protocol was introduced with the OMG CORBA specification and has been widely adopted for developing transaction-oriented applications. IIOP provides a standard format for the existing protocol of the Internet, TCP/IP. In this model, client applications are built as Java Applets, small Java programs dynamically downloaded to run in the local Web browser. This has tremendous value as it allows heterogeneous environments to be able to interoperate quickly if they are each built on top of the same network transport. There also exists a standard mapping of IIOP to the secure sockets layer (SSL) protocol to allow for encrypted transactions over the Internet.

Similar to the HTTP/CGI/Java Servlet approach, using CORBA and IIOP over the Internet allows a "zero-administration" client. No custom client application needs to be preinstalled on the client PC. The end user will simply use any Web browser as a client and connect to the corporate Web server. The Web server will then pass the request off to either a CGI application, to service HTTP clients, or to a CORBA application, for Java Applets as shown in Exhibit 26-7. Application servers facilitate this integration with commercial Web servers and provide enhanced development environments to build these business logic components.

The zero-administration client is perhaps one of the most significant enablers of business-to-business solutions. By standardizing on Web interfaces and Web protocols for all client access, the definition of a "user" changes. A user is no longer limited to an end user in your company. With the ubiquity of the Internet and Web browsers, users can now be partners, distributors, and suppliers.

A Component or Container Development Environment. As previously mentioned, part of the reason RPC, CORBA, and RMI have never dominated enterprise development is because all paradigms required too much low-level

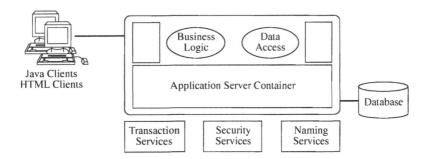

**Exhibit 26-8. application server "container" architecture, designed to
shield the developer from low-level complexities and focus
exclusively on the business logic and data access.**

coding by the developer. The developer had to explicitly write complex code
to deal with directory, transaction, and security services, to deal with operating system threads and network socket connections, and to deal with load
balancing and failover. Thus, many middleware projects were either unsuccessful or over budget; too many coding resources were spent focusing on
infrastructure rather than on application logic.

Application servers focus on the notion that CORBA and RMI are necessary technologies for the transport of messages but should be transparent
to corporate developers. Thus, there should exist a higher level "container," which shields the developer from having to worry about any low-level
network and system issues. Therefore, an application developer can spend
time focusing on writing business logic and data access components that
are then run within the context of a container. This architecture is shown
in Exhibit 26-8. Currently, there are two competing standards for application server containers, Sun's Enterprise Java Beans (EJB) and Microsoft's
Transaction Server (MTS).

EJB defines a container model by which vendors provide tools to automatically generate the complex container code for the developer. This allows developers to use specialized tools to model and build business logic
and data access "Java Beans," which are portable and reusable. EJB application servers are built on top of an ORB protocol, RMI, IIOP, CORBA; however,
the developer never need be aware of this underlying functionality. This provides tremendous flexibility in combining application servers with existing
CORBA or RMI applications. EJB application servers are also built with the
Java transaction service (JTS), which is a Java implementation of the CORBA
OTS, providing EJB application servers a standard interface to provide transactional capabilities. Again, this is all transparent to the developer. Thus, EJB
application servers provide the standard directory, communications, security, and transaction services available in the previous distributed paradigms;

however, the developer does not need to write any code to make use of these services. It is all provided by the container.

The Microsoft solution provides a similar environment for reducing the complexity of code required by business logic developers. It is built on top of the DCOM proprietary Microsoft protocol rather than EJB's RMI/IIOP solution, reducing some of its capabilities over the Internet. The advantages with MTS is that it is free, built into Windows NT, and has been a commercially available solution much longer than any EJB application servers. However the Microsoft solution works only on Microsoft NT Server machines, whereas EJB application servers are being supported by a wide range of vendors on multiple hardware platforms.

An effective container model is critical for the time to market need in electronic business applications. Companies on the Internet distinguish themselves by the services they can provide, and as new services are available, the infrastructure must be highly flexible and adaptable to add new functionality. This is what a container model provides, an environment where developers can add reusable components as needs and requirements change, allowing the application server to handle the low-level complexities. Traditional IT development cycles are not feasible in Internet applications, as companies cannot afford to wait.

Database Connection Pooling and Caching. The most common bottleneck in all of the distributed paradigms is inefficient data access. Although separating business logic from data access makes for easier development and maintenance, this often presents inefficiency and redundancy, as commonly requested data will always require new connections and requests to the back-end DBMS. Since a DBMS can only handle a finite number of concurrent client connections, it is not uncommon for applications to have slow performance, regardless of running multiple business logic and data access server objects, running parallel hardware CPUs, and running multiple operating system threads. Providing transparent connectivity to back-end data sources and efficiently managing those resources are critical functionality in any application server.

Establishing connections to data sources presents one of the most resource-intensive and time-intensive operations in distributed computing. The process of opening a socket connection to the database, logging in, logging out, and closing the socket connection are tasks that become increasingly repetitive and very resource intensive. This problem is exacerbated by the potentially high volume of requests for data from incoming clients. Thus, a common pattern for overcoming this issue is to create a database connection pool. In this model, the application server will establish a predefined number of connections to the database at server startup. As new clients make requests for data, the application server will simply select an available database connection from the pool and instantly pass the query to the database. When the client has finished its request, the application server will return the request back to the connection pool for future requests from future clients.

Database connection pools also can be combined with various threading models to increase performance. Separate threads can be established for each incoming client connection to allow for a maximum number of incoming client requests. As each client request is dispatched to a separate thread of execution, that thread can then utilize an available database connection from the pool. An alternative approach is to use a thread pool, which can be established to maintain separate database connections on separate operating system threads. This will have a tremendous impact on maximizing the total overall efficiency of the application server.

While connection and thread pooling greatly enhance the speed of access to the database, a common reason why distributed architectures fail is because of stateless business logic components constantly accessing the same data. Thus, although connections are easily taken from the pool, they are used over and over to get the same data. Application servers overcome this redundancy and inefficiency by making use of middle-tier caching. This is a very different model presented by application servers, providing significant functionality over that supplied only by the RPC and ORB communication layers. The idea behind caching is to take the data access objects developed, and rather than maintain these as stateless entities as CORBA and RMI provide, make them stateful. In this new paradigm, the data access objects represent data contained in the back-end database. Thus, as client programs make requests for data, rather than having to communicate via network connection to the database, a local in-process call is made to the data access object in the cache, as shown in Exhibit 26-9.

The application server takes care of any synchronization with the database and handles transaction integrity when changes are made. Intelligent caching is a critical element in application server optimization, significantly reducing network traffic to the database and providing significantly faster performance. Moreover, it shields the developer from having to write any of the low-level logic dealing with database connections and data access.

Efficient data management and access are essential to a strategic electronic business application. In the Internet application paradigm, customer service and responsiveness are crucial. Companies moving to the Web are often slashing prices below cost in an effort to attract and keep users loyal to their site. The only way to keep consumers coming back is to be able to offer custom services based on demographics, buying patterns, targeted promotions, etc. These services can only be effective through highly optimized data access and analysis provided through middle-tier data caching.

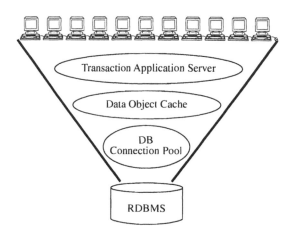

Exhibit 26-9. Transactional application server's use of caching and database pooling for optimum data access.

Every second saved by obtaining information from the middle-tier cache instead of having to make remote calls across the network to the DBMS means the difference between retaining loyal customers and having impatient customers who will simply click elsewhere.

High Availability, Load Balancing, and Automatic Failover. While middle-tier caching is powerful, in a global infrastructure it becomes increasingly important to have multiple application servers to handle the heavy client volumes. This requires resolution of the following issues.

Distributed and Synchronized Cache. Having multiple application servers available to handle incoming clients is not sufficient; they must be distributed. An update made to a middle-tier cache in one application server must be replicated globally to other application servers. Application servers must be distributed and support a cache synchronization technique. In this case, an update to the cache in Tokyo will replicate this change transparently to the cache in London. This is absolutely critical in global electronic business systems where customer orders can be placed with any application server cache, which will affect inventory and sales data in other remote application servers. Single changes need to be propagated automatically; human users need not be involved.

Load Balancing. Distributed application servers must transparently route requests to the least utilized resources for maximum throughput. This is typically implemented as a feature of the application server's naming and directory service. A client will make an invocation to the naming and directory service to request the network location of a certain service. The naming and directory service will then perform some type of load balancing algorithm in order to determine which application server can supply the requested service the fastest. The client will be automatically connected to that application server in order to service the request. Business over the Internet forces little barrier to entry, so if a site is not responsive even for only a few minutes, customers can easily click to a competitor's site to browse their services, making effective load balancing mandatory.

High Availability and Fail-over. Electronic Business Systems must be available 100 percent of the time, 24 hours a day, 7 days a week, with no exception. As such, it is absolutely essential that a distributed application server have automatic fail-over and recovery built in. In this manner if the local application server crashes or suffers from a hardware failure, clients can automatically be rerouted to another application server. Because distributed cache synchronization is an absolute requirement in this model, clients can be assured that although they are now connecting to another application server, it will have the most updated information. In the Internet paradigm, during the time in which your application server is down and unable to service incoming customers, those customers are placing orders with your competitors.

Transaction Support. To expand on the data access functionality provided by the application server, it should provide support for distributed transactions. The actual resources involved and the interaction with the database should be a function of the application server, not of the developer. The application server should provide the developer with a simple interface for beginning, committing, and rolling back transactions. Beyond this, the application server should provide the low-level code to coordinate these with the database. In the case of a middle-tier cache architecture, the application server is responsible for providing the necessary optimistic controls to guarantee the integrity of transactions with data in the cache and coordinating these changes with the database.

SUMMARY

As businesses are constantly moving toward providing services to their customers, distributors, and partners over the Internet, there must be an infrastructure to support this. The solution must be HTML- and Java-enabled to support a wide variety of Web browser and portal clients, using the ubiquitous Internet as a standard transport. The solution must work easily with industry standard Web servers, to enable the largest number of concurrent users to access the information over the Web. The solution must provide optimized data access and transaction support and provide a reusable programming architecture. Finally, it must be built for global use, providing distributed functionality, caching, load balancing, and automatic fail-over. This infrastructure is available through transactional application servers.

Transactional application servers have been able to overcome the deficiencies with previous distributed architectures to provide a complete solution for the rigorous requirements of electronic business applications. Although this technology is relatively new, it is poised to become the leading development model for Internet-based applications for the next several years.

Author Bio

Michael McCaffery is currently the International Marketing Manager at Persistence Software in San Mateo, CA. He works directly with international partners and distributors to help promote Persistence and Enterprise Java Beans. He can often be found speaking in the areas of application servers, EJB, and CORBA.

Prior to his work at Persistence, McCaffery spent several years with Visigenic Software, developing and conducting training courses in both VisiBroker for C++ and VisiBroker for Java, as well as developing sales training material. He worked in Visigenic's European facilities in Paris and London, in sales, sales support, training, and consulting, in VisiBroker for C++ and Java. He is the author of The Official VisiBroker for Java Handbook, *from McMillan Publishing.*

Michael started his software career in Boston at Open Environment Corporation (purchased by Borland International, in 1994), working in Technical Support, Consulting, Training, and Account Management. He holds a Bachelor's Degree in Business Administration, with a concentration in Management Information Systems from Boston University.

Chapter 27

Enterprise Application Integration in Financial Services

Ely Eshel

THE FINANCIAL INDUSTRY HAS ALWAYS BEEN AT THE CUTTING EDGE OF IN-FORMATION TECHNOLOGY, and is now at the frontier of enterprise application integration (EAI). This chapter examines the drivers for EAI in the financial industry, describes why and how middleware should be applied to implement solutions, analyze various middleware technologies available to address EAI requirements, and discusses the criteria for selecting the appropriate middleware. Specific case studies illustrate different styles of implemented solutions.

INTRODUCTION

From the early days of information technology, the financial industry has been on its cutting edge. The rigorous requirements of financial transactions, from payments to trades, were always a little more than off-the-shelf software could provide, and developers of applications in this industry needed to create their own proprietary solutions. Interfacing those applications, in the infrequent situation where it was required, was implemented on a case-by-case basis, following the same paradigm which was employed for their development.

The recent advances in information technology, the evolution of highly capable off-the-shelf software, and various business drivers stemming from the changing landscape of data processing are all now dictating a different approach to application integration. As the requirements for enterprise application integration grew, so did the technologies addressing them, as well as our understanding of the technologies best suited for these tasks.

In the following sections we will undertake a review and an evaluation of the current status (and future directions) of EAI in the financial industry. This will be presented in three parts:

- A review of the most prominent business drivers and technology issues for EAI in the financial industry.
- An analysis of the middleware technologies applied to deliver financial services EAI today, with a glimpse into some future trends.
- A few case studies of EAI implementations in the financial industry.

Please keep in mind that this is not a product review and, even though the information presented is based on specific products, none will be mentioned explicitly, and discussions will revolve around *classes* of products rather than specific brands.

CHALLENGES

Users and developers of enterprise application integration in the financial industry face many challenges. Some of these challenges may be faced by other industries as well, but most are unique to this industry or at least particularly noticeable.

We divide the challenges into two categories:

- Business drivers: trends, developments or situations relating to the business activities and goals of financial services organizations.
- Technology issues: current availability of technologies and their utilization.

Business Drivers

In the following sections, business issues that are driving EAI in the financial industry are reviewed. Many financial institutions face more than one of the challenges described below, and in most cases EAI is driven by more than a single business need.

Mergers and Acquisitions. Recent years have witnessed significant activity of mergers and acquisitions in the financial industry. These events span the gamut from the consolidation of institutions of similar types, through the acquisitions of competitors, to the conglomeration of corporations providing diverse services. Two traits are common to most of these events:

- They aim to expand the range of provided services or the geographical coverage (domestic or international) of these services, or both.
- They strive to reduce costs by eliminating redundancy, consolidating services, and streamlining operations.

Both goals face the challenges of connecting diverse multiple applications — proprietary or not, in one or more locations — to create seamless information flow throughout the enterprise.

Transaction Volumes. The volume of financial transaction is growing at a high pace, both within and between organizations. Some of the reasons for this growth are the following:

- Expansion of services by the financial industry.
- Improved automation of previously manual procedures.
- Increased number of financially savvy investors and traders.
- Easy Internet access.
- Stronger need to disseminate and correlate information within organizations.

No matter what the reasons are, the volume increase imposes a significant challenge — how to be able to cost-effectively sustain these volumes and scale the systems for even higher volumes.

Settlement Time. As more and more financial activities rely on electronic means, the demand to reduce settlement times is increasing. It becomes more and more difficult to accept settlements taking more than a few minutes. After all, the transactions are entered and performed electronically. Even as regulators are pressuring the industry to reduce settlement time, participants are putting an even stronger pressure on their counter-parties. The challenge in accomplishing this goal is primarily that of performance, which requires removing as many barriers to settlement as possible. This is reflected in the push for STP and ZLE (see below).

Risk Management. While volumes are expanding and settlement times are shrinking, the challenge of risk management is increasing. It is no longer possible to evaluate risk as a back-end task. Large numbers of transactions are flowing in real-time, to be settled quickly, and risk evaluation requires consolidating information from multiple sources, now in real-time. Employing electronic techniques to evaluate risk only solves part of the problem, that of the need for human intervention. The challenge of information retrieval from multiple sources in real-time is still not completely resolved.

Internet and Web-to-Legacy Integration. One of the factors exacerbating the EAI challenges mentioned above is the explosion of the Internet and the usage of the World Wide Web. Volumes are higher, settlement times are shorter, and risk management is more complicated because more numerous participants are introduced into the financial community, many of whom are private citizens or nonfinancial organizations. At the same time, many of the systems currently in use were never designed to interface with the "outside world" or to support the volumes and performance now demanded; these require face-lifting and perhaps much more serious modifications.

Rapid Deployment. Competition in the financial industry is fierce. In order to stay competitive, new and improved services must be offered continuously. The time from conception to deployment is now measured in weeks rather than in years. Many of the newly conceived services must rely on information already available within the organization, but interfaces to retrieve it are hard to develop, costly, and time consuming.

Another aspect of the need to rapidly deploy new services is the requirement to quickly integrate services, particularly following a merger or an acquisition. A customer of the financial organization may be identified not as a single customer but as many different ones, causing undue hardship when one's information needs to be reviewed, consolidated, or updated. This situation also prevents the organization from leveraging the knowledge it accumulated regarding its customer base in order to offer better, more competitive services.

Straight-Through Processing (STP). The primary goal of Straight-Through-Processing is to improve the responsiveness of financial organizations to financial activities, from transaction execution to customer service. This can be accomplished by automating as many steps as possible in the processing chain of activities, in particular minimizing human intervention. The difficulty lies in the need to hand over activities between disparate systems while ensuring that the information transferred is valid. Otherwise, the receiving application would require human intervention to analyze and repair the information before acting upon it, slowing down the processing sequence.

The Zero-Latency Enterprise (ZLE). An even stronger perspective relating to streamlined processing is the Zero-Latency Enterprise, which emphasizes the need to eliminate all processing delays in order to get as "instantaneous" a response as possible. Even though this term is more applicable to enterprise resource planning (ERP) applications, the basic concept it embodies applies to the financial industry as well and is strongly related to STP.

Technology Issues

The technologies available today often fall short of adequately addressing the business needs. These technological hurdles, and their impact on EAI, are reviewed in the following sections.

The Interface Tangle. As the number of applications that need to be integrated grows, so does the number of point-to-point interfaces that must be developed. This presents EAI efforts with multiple challenges:

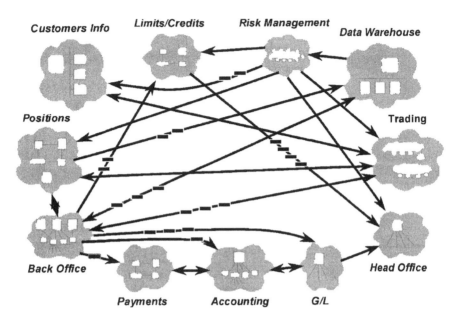

Exhibit 27-1. Multiple communicating applications requiring a large number of interfaces.

- The development cost of each interface is high, both in resources and in time.
- The large number of interfaces makes information flow complex, contributing heavily to maintenance costs.
- A large number of interfaces is a significant factor in impeding the accommodation of change, due to the potentially prohibitive number of components that must be modified.

Exhibit 27-1 depicts an environment where many applications, some internal to the financial institution and some external, need to communicate. It demonstrates the large number of interfaces, by no means all possible combinations, required to facilitate these information flows.

Business Logic Localization. Most of the applications in use today incorporate all the business logic within themselves, thus producing two challenges to face EAI:

- Any change in business rules requires modifications of the application code, with all associated procedures and costs.
- Business logic is not reusable, requiring repeated development of the same rules and replicated maintenance.

The combination of these two aspects also means that there is no mechanism to modify a rule once and have this change automatically propagate throughout all the applications.

The Development Bottleneck. The interface tangle and business logic localization both require the employment of programming, which is the cause of a serious bottleneck in the ability of financial services firms to bring new products and services to market quickly and cost-effectively. As long as there is such a need for programming and as long as most development efforts continue to depend on programming resources, this bottleneck is obstructing any effort to address effectively the EAI business drivers discussed above.

TECHNOLOGIES

In spite of the technology issues reviewed above, technologies that address at least some of the business drivers do exist. They all fall into one category of software, middleware. In the following sections, these middleware technologies are reviewed, pointing out their positive and negative aspects relative to the technology issues presented in the previous sections. These technologies are mostly generic, but some products possess more knowledge of the financial industry and, therefore, are more appropriate for delivering EAI solutions in this particular industry. Exhibit 27-2 illustrates the three layers of middleware. Their primary functions are explained below.

- *Transport* provides the transport of data with the appropriate quality-of-service. The better products are based on message queuing or message bus technologies, but remote procedure calls are still available. Choices of delivery options include synchronous or asynchronous modes, with or without store-and-forward. The high-end products provide all these capabilities.
- *Distribution* is responsible for information distribution, generally in one of two modes, request/response or publish/subscribe. Most products providing services at this layer also include the transport layer.
- *Intelligence* performs contents-based and context-base activities, such as validations, transformations, routing, and enrichment. The more capabilities a product provides, the higher its usefulness is. Products at this layer either include the lower layers or rely on other products to provide the lower-layer services.

Communication Middleware

Message Delivery. There are several products on the market today that provide message delivery at varying quality-of-service levels or distribution architectures, covering the bottom two layers described above. A review of

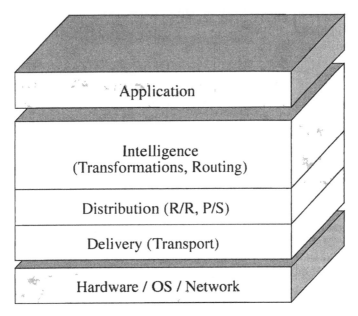

Exhibit 27-2. The three layers of middleware.

these products is outside the scope of this discussion, and much has been written about it already. Regardless of features, all products operate at a low level, only slightly above network protocols. Thus, as much as they make the programming phase of application development easier than it was a few years ago, they still are programming tools and do not eliminate the bottleneck described above. The major limitations of this class of products are as follows:

- They are geared for the use of technical experts and not business users.
- They address only transport and distribution issues and not application interfacing issues.
- Their intelligence relative to the context and contents of the information, as described above, is rather limited.
- They require significant programming efforts, localized to the applications utilizing them. Therefore, the business logic remains encapsulated within each application, preventing the reuse of business knowledge and causing duplication of development and maintenance efforts.

Point-to-Point Interfaces. Relying on message delivery products, with their lack of intelligence regarding the context and contents of the information they deliver, dictates that interfaces would be point-to-point, with all the disadvantages created by the interface tangle and contributing to the development bottleneck, both of which were described above.

Integration Brokers

At the top layer of middleware reside integration brokers, also known as message brokers. Their particular characteristics, and their contribution to financial services EAI, are described below.

Message Delivery. In general, integration brokers rely on message delivery products to transport the information. These products may be included within the integration broker, or be external third-party products. The message delivery functions are usually completely hidden from the user of the broker, helping to alleviate some of the development bottleneck.

Message Repository. A critical component of a high-end integration broker is a message repository. Since message delivery products usually do not retain messages after they have been retrieved once, a repository of messages is needed to store them safely as they are processed within the broker. This repository provides for audit trail, archiving, play-back. enrichment, consolidation, and workflow management capabilities. Message repositories, just like message delivery products, are rarely exposed to the user of the integration broker.

Adapters. From a functional perspective, adapters are the elements of the integration broker in which its knowledge of its business environment is encapsulated. Adapters can serve in two capacities:

- *Formatters*, where they provide validation and transformation services relating to specific industry standard or proprietary message formats,
- *Gateways* to private and public networks, where they provide support for the specific protocols of these networks as well as the networks' specific message formats.

As a rule, the more industry-specific knowledge an integration broker possesses (embodied in its adapters), the better its suitability to the EAI task. Brokers that command knowledge of most of the standards in the financial industry are more valuable for EAI efforts in this industry. Adapters serve a major function in addressing the technology issues reviewed above. They allow for reusability of knowledge by centralizing formats and reduce programming requirements by allowing this knowledge to be maintained by business people.

Rules-Based Engines. The most important feature of an integration broker, that which distinguishes it from a message delivery mechanism, is its ability to process messages based on rules. This is usually accomplished by a rules-based engine, one that can accept processing rules and apply them to messages as they flow through the broker. Rules engines will, in most cases, rely on formatters to provide the format knowledge of the messages they need to process.

Several architectures can be employed to implement this capability, from interpreted, mostly proprietary, fourth generation languages to code generation. These architectural choices have important implications on the broker's performance and flexibility: interpretive implementations can accommodate more dynamic rule changes, while generated code provides higher performance.

Similar to adapters, rules engines are the most critical contributors to knowledge reusability and reduction in programming.

Hub-and-Spokes Topology. Integration brokers utilize a hub-and-spokes topology, where all traffic goes through the broker in order to be safely stored, analyzed, validated, transformed, enriched, and routed. This topology is the single most important factor in eliminating the need for point-to-point interfaces: only interfaces between applications and the broker need to be specified, rather than between each application pair. Exhibit 27-3 shows how the hub-and-spokes topology reduces the number of interfaces in the same environment presented in Exhibit 27-1.

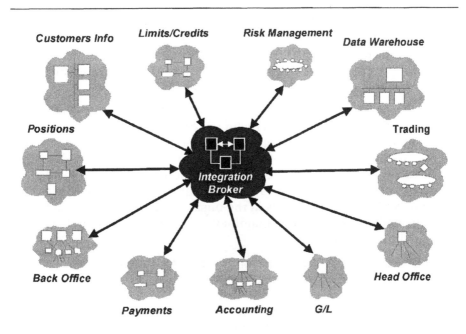

Exhibit 27-3. Hub-and-spikes topology reduces the number of interfaces.

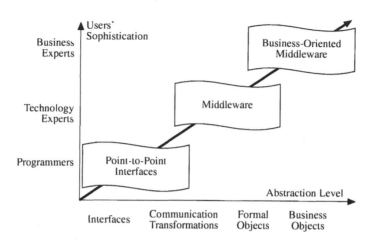

Exhibit 27-4. Level of sophistication vs. level of abstraction.

Another advantage of this topology is centralized management and control, but the potential for a single point of failure needs to be addressed by stand-by and disaster recovery mechanisms.

Business-Oriented Middleware

As much as integration brokers contribute to addressing the business requirements, often they do not address all the technological issues. The main aspect at which integration brokers fall short is the question of usability: who is the actual user of EAI technology ?

Even the high-level integration brokers expect the rules to be defined by an information technology expert who understands the business and not by a true business expert. Integration brokers model primarily message formats and routing and do not do an adequate job of modeling business activities. Exhibit 27-4 charts the relationship between the users level of sophistication and the technologies level of abstraction. It demonstrates that the more sophisticated a user is in the business, and thus potentially less sophisticated in information technology, the higher the technology's abstraction level need to be.

The goal of innovative and state-of-the-art EAI technologies is to provide the business user with as high a level of abstraction as possible, aiming to model the complete business process as accurately as feasible. This modeling can take many forms, but common to all is the ability to model the actual business activity in terms familiar to the business user, using tools common to the business environment. Details of specific applications and formats are hidden by establishing these capabilities as low-level services defined once, and only once, by information technology personnel. Business users are then able to create, modify, and maintain business rules regarding information flow without any technical knowledge.

By delivering this level of abstraction, business users will be freed from their dependency on information technology to support business rules and information flows, which will allow information technology organizations to concentrate on technical infrastructures rather than business issues.

At this point in time, truly business-oriented middleware does not yet exist. Some integration brokers, however, are well on that path, and future directions in this area should be a factor in evaluating middleware for EAI.

SOLUTIONS

The case studies below present several EAI implementations, with varying degrees of complexity and sophistication. The following aspects of each implementation are described:

- Business problem
- Solution architecture
- Business benefits

Private Banking Trading System

Problem. A private banking institution wanted a system that would act as a centralized switching platform between different applications and networks (such as SWIFT, SIC, SECOM, Telex, and Fax) and its trading application, increasing the bank's control and management of the information flow for its trading activities. The goal was to reduce manual intervention and increase the efficiency of the operations department. The bank had multiple connections to external networks and applications and needed to connect multiple environments while reducing high running costs and overhead.

Solution. A message broker was employed, providing data connectivity across the large-scale, heterogeneous applications and network environment. With its intelligent processing capabilities, the bank could easily add new interfaces and functionality according to business needs and convert messages from proprietary trading systems to clearing networks and settlements centers. All of the bank's communication services are handled through one integrated platform, allowing data flow between the bank's back office client/server and mainframe applications and external networks. The broker's ability to interface directly with the various networks was a critical factor in the selection of this architecture. Exhibit 27-5 depicts this solution.

Trading Application

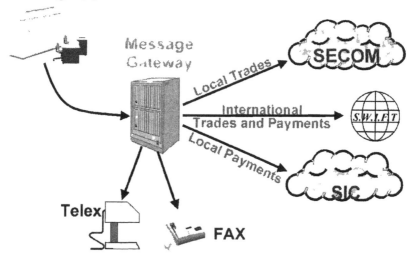

Exhibit 27-5. Using a message broker.

Benefits. The IT team looked for state-of-the-art products that would give the bank an added advantage. The message broker provided the bank cost-effective operations by reducing the processing cost per transaction and enabling a shortened and secure settlement cycle time.

Broker/Dealer Electronic Trade Confirmation (ETC) System

Problem. As part of their internal standardization effort, a large broker/dealer decided to use the Financial Information eXchange (FIX) protocol exclusively for all internal communications. As much as this decision simplified the interfacing of internal applications, it presented a challenge in interfacing those applications with external ones that do not support the selected format. In particular, the Electronic Trade Confirmation (ETC) application needed to communicate with the Oasis Global Direct (OGD) clearing network, using that network's format. Part of the challenge was the need to implement the translations in a flexible manner, allowing for proprietary enrichments to both protocols.

Solution. The implementation of this solution was relatively simple: a single message broker, possessing the knowledge of both formats, was installed. Internal applications only use the FIX format, never seeing messages in the OGD format. The broker serves as a gateway between the internal environment and the OGD network. The flexibility inherent in the process of defining the participating message formats as well as the ease

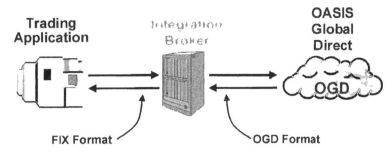

Exhibit 27-6. A single broker acting as a gateway.

of enriching them were the major criteria in the selection of this solution. Exhibit 27-6 depicts this solution.

Benefits. The benefits reaped from using the message broker for transformations were as follows:

- Adherence to internal standard with no ill-effects on internal applications
- Shortened development time

Custody Management System

Problem. In order to support its growing business, a custodian wanted to shorten the time and lower the cost required to support new customers, thus allowing the institution to lower its fees and acquire new customers quickly. In addition, by automating as much of the process as possible, human intervention, and thus human errors, could be substantially decreased. In order to facilitate this, the need arose for a system that would enable the introduction of new customers, with the associated complexities of supporting both standard and proprietary information formats and their translation into and from in-house legacy formats, in a timely and cost-effective manner. The goal was to reduce the required time from months to weeks.

Solution. The installation of an intelligent message broker, one capable of supporting both standard and proprietary formats and transforming between them, was the primary component of the solution. Having built-in knowledge of the required standard information formats, as well as the capability to quickly introduce proprietary formats without any programming, was the key factor in the success of this solution. Thus, the institution was able to accept a new customer and quickly accommodate its information formats with minimal effort. Providing the necessary processing with a very high degree of automation also reduced the cost and improved the service to its customers. Exhibit 27-7 depicts this solution.

481

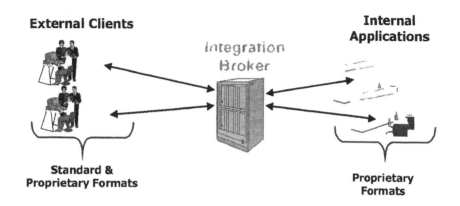

Exhibit 27-7. An intelligent message broker.

Benefits. The message broker implementation provided the custodian with the following benefits, all of which deliver bottom-line advantages:

- Shorter and less expensive time to market with its new service
- Timely and cost-effective cycle for the introduction of new customers
- Improved STP service to customers
- Reduced operational costs
- Lower fees to customers
- Better customer retention

International Bank Payment System

Problem. One of the largest banks in the world, with branches and subsidiaries on all continents, needed to streamline and reduce its expenses in handling electronic payments. The bank was using the SWIFT network for all payment transactions, not only between itself and other institutions but also within its branches and subsidiaries, and had 17 operation centers with connections into that network. At the same time, the bank already had a global communication network of its own, but it was not utilized for this service. In addition, applications were required to generate payment instructions in the SWIFT format, adding complexity to these applications and increasing the rate of errors requiring manual intervention.

Solution. Because of the global nature of the bank's operation, a network of message brokers was deployed, reducing the number of operation centers to four (each with a backup site). The message brokers are connected using the bank's private network, routing transactions among themselves, minimizing SWIFT network access to interbank payments only. The brokers also serve as connection points for the bank's internal applications, accepting messages in the applications' proprietary formats and transforming

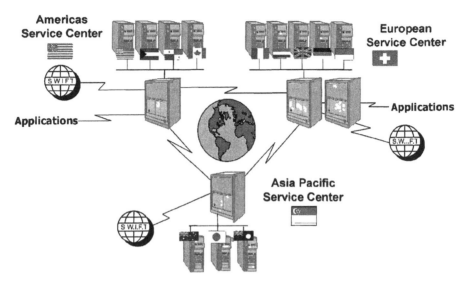

Exhibit 27-8. A network of message brokers.

them to the SWIFT format for transmission. The message broker's ability to validate messages prior to their delivery to the SWIFT network, as well as its ability to communicate with this network directly, were primary criteria in this implementation. Exhibit 27-8 depicts this solution.

Benefits. Several benefits were obtained with the architecture described above, translating directly to bottom-line benefits:

- Consolidation of operation centers, significantly reducing operating costs.
- Reduction of SWIFT traffic, lowering transaction payments.
- Simplification of application interfaces, lowering cost and reducing development time.
- Higher degree of automation, reducing error rates and improving STP.

Author Bio

Ely Eshel is CTO of MINT Communication Systems, a leading provider of EAI solutions for the financial services industry, and founder and former CTO of Momentum Software, a leading provider of Message-Oriented Middleware which was acquired by Level 8 Systems. He has 26 years of software industry experience, dedicating the last 12 to middleware technologies and products, their development and successful incorporation in enterprise-scale mission-critical distributed applications. Prior to this, he held project management positions in the defense industry and key financial services providers, responsible for the development of many real-time and online applications. His expertise is in software products and development tools, with emphasis on applying software technology to solving business problems.

Chapter 28
Spreadsheets as Containers of Malicious Payloads
Ron Moritz

IN JANUARY 1999, FINJAN SOFTWARE DISCLOSED THE RUSSIAN NEW YEAR EXPLOITATION. The Russian New Year demonstrated how easy it is to move spreadsheet files to desktop computers and showed how such spreadsheets can contain a malicious payload. In effect, Russian New Year solved that age-old problem faced by attackers: "How do I deliver my malicious code to the desktop?" Russian New Year is a vehicle to enable the delivery of code over the open network, and it is, therefore, a demonstration of the danger associated with mobile code.

Russian New Year (Exhibit 28-1) is a vulnerability in that it exploits two legitimate features in order to introduce an attack onto the user's desktop without the user's involvement. When used together, these two features enable an attacker to introduce high-risk program code onto the desktop by moving an Excel spreadsheet source document from a Web server to a Web browser. The spreadsheet serves as an initiator or launching point for a malicious program. The malicious program can do things like create and write data to a file on the hard disk, close that file, and then execute it. Using the CALL function, an attacker can locate and steal key files and data that are available and accessible to the user, no matter where those files reside. Since the electronic spreadsheets are so critical to the technology landscape of modern financial services entities, the risk associated with mobile code must be understood.

Monday, December 21, 1998, 6:36 p.m. Israel time. Four days before Christmas. The countdown has begun and the western world is winding down. It should prove to be an easy week. Time to catch up on the technical journals that have been neglected in weeks past. The telephone rings. My San Jose office is on the line. A respected computer security guru, one of the old timers that everyone knows by reputation, name, and attitude,

Russian New Year Exploit
s'Novim Godom

Exhibit 28-1. Russian New Year.

wants to talk. There is a sense of urgency that sends electricity along the spine. The three-way call is established, and a stream-of-conscious flow of words is sent along the trans-Atlantic copper wire.

This is serious. My eccentric "deep throat" source who is affiliated with a U.S. defense contractor claims that *his source* in Russia has discovered a way to combine legitimate functions and services in order to deliver a stealthy electronic attack through a simple Web transaction. "It's so obvious!" I scream, as I hit my head with the palm of my right hand. How is it possible that all the brilliant minds working on information security problems have not put the pieces of *this* puzzle together? Needing more information, the following email message is sent:

> I have a DSS/Diffie-Hellman 1024/2048 key registered at the MIT server <pgpkeys.mit.edu>. The fingerprint for that key is:
>
> 36BE DB15 4F1F 110A 23B0 6167 C454 0848 8657 11C3
>
> — Ron

Shortly thereafter I receive an encrypted package over email:

> Found it — was the second valid one. Enclosed is the sample set I sent to CERT [the quasi-government Computer Emergency Response Team based at Carnegie Mellon University in Pittsburgh, Pennsylvania]. Please do not allow it to be circulated beyond your group. As I mentioned it works with W95/98/NT 4.0 (workstation or server) and Office 95/97. The SMTP portion works with Outlook98 while the HTML works with IE 4.0, 4.01, 4.01 SP1 (latest) and Netscape 3.01, 4.04, 4.06 (what I have tried) and does not work under Netscape 4.5 (latest).

Opening the package with my private key using a pass-phrase that I am certain is not crackable, I discover sample code that confirms the tingle I felt in my spine earlier in the evening. Audit antennae are now fully active and, despite the late hour, I begin searching the Web for clues. It is difficult to imagine that something so obvious has been so well concealed. Was the problem simply ignored or is the software industry unable to envision scenarios where a series of legitimate operations are used together to breach functional computer security controls?

Monday, December 21, 1998, 11:21 p.m. Israel time. I send back the following response to my "deep throat" source:

> Wow! Document received. I visited both
>
> http://www.microsoft.com/security/bulletins/ms98-018.asp and
> http://www.w3.org/TR/REC-html40/present/frames.html#h-16.5
>
> With your sample the threat is extremely clear.
>
> I'll get back to you with some results following our internal research.
>
> — Ron

Tuesday, December 22, 1998, 1:19 a.m. Israel time. I wake my R&D director; this is no time for sleep. I send the following e-mail to greet the engineers in the morning:

> I spoke with Aviv. He's in class Tuesday morning but wants Alex 1 or Alex 2 to take a look at our HTML scanner to estimate how much work will be required to enhance it to parse the <IFRAME> tag info to "find" *.XLS source files being moved to the desktop.
>
> — Ron

And so began the end of 1998 and the start of 1999. Many hours of research will be invested to understand this new vulnerability. Many people will lose their year-end holidays. So much for the vacation I had planned at the Sea of Galilee.

THE RUSSIAN NEW YEAR

The "Russian New Year" exploitation is a new type of mobile code attack that clearly illustrates the latent security threats on the Internet and the importance of inspecting any type of code that is downloaded onto a personal computer. By definition, mobile code is any program that can be downloaded to and installed and executed on a remote machine without user interaction. A concept introduced by Java™ in 1995, mobile code is used to build and deliver applications across different computers using the

487

Exhibit 28-2. The Russian New Year exploit.

Internet, as well as for sharing software functions across the Web. But when mobile, code including Java, ActiveX™, JavaScript™, and VisualBasic™ Script, is exploited, it becomes one of the top five Internet security concerns facing corporations today.

The ease with which a maliciously coded program can be designed, assembled, and scattered across the Internet makes mobile code a high-risk issue. According to the Hurwitz Group, 90 percent of electronic commerce applications are written using mobile code. Zona Research notes that 80 percent of Web sites use mobile code in their programming. While 72 percent of respondents in a recent ICSA survey said mobile code is a high to moderate security risk, only 27 percent of those same corporate customers surveyed say they have established a corporate mobile code security policy.

The genius of the Russian New Year exploit (Exhibit 28-2) is in taking two legitimate functions normally used separately and combining them to deliver an attack that can be extremely malicious and damaging. One of the functions is found in HTML, the programming language of the Web. The other function is found in Microsoft Excel™. With this combination an attacker could secure access to a desktop with the same rights and privileges granted to the desktop's owner. This includes access to steal or copy private files without user knowledge.

While the exploit requires that the Excel application be installed on the desktop, Excel does not have to be running for the exploit to succeed. Moreover, no interaction on the part of the desktop user is required. As an

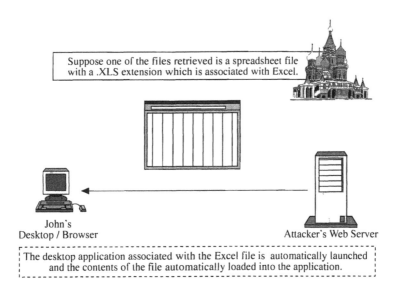

Exhibit 28-3. Malicious code can be delivered within an Excel spreadsheet.

innocent Internet user visits a Web site, the user's browser can be instruct-ed to request a spreadsheet file from the Web server. When the spread-sheet file arrives, the browser will automatically pass control to and launch the desktop application associated with the passed file, in this case, Excel. Malicious code can be delivered in the payload of the Excel spreadsheet (Exhibit 28-3). Normal Excel operations can be used to save such payload data onto a drive accessible to the local system and the CALL function, de-scribed in more detail below, can then be used to launch or execute the re-cently saved malicious code. The Russian New Year exploit is this combination of these features and events.

What is important to note is that this exploit may not be visible to the computer user; therefore, it may not be possible to tell if you have been the victim of an attack delivered through the Russian New Year. Has high-risk program code been introduced onto your desktop simply by moving an Ex-cel spreadsheet source document from a Web server to a Web browser?

TECHNICAL DISCUSSION OF HOW THE RUSSIAN NEW YEAR EXPLOIT WORKS

Several years ago, Microsoft introduced a very useful service in their Office products, macros. Using macros to automate repetitive tasks and to make spreadsheets and documents more dynamic is now common-place, despite the security risk presented by macro viruses. Today it is well understood that macros in an untrusted document or spreadsheet may have malicious consequences and such files should be loaded with caution. Antivirus software routinely scans for Office macro viruses.

Less well known is a feature of Microsoft Excel (both the Office 95 and Office 97 versions) called "CALL," which allows a call statement to be issued from inside a spreadsheet cell. The call statement enables "certain types of executables," like an external DLL (dynamic link library), to be run from within a spreadsheet without a warning to the user. Such statements can do things like create and write data to a file on the hard disk, close that file, and then execute it.

Call statements included in macros or as functions in cells are executed on the opening of the spreadsheet file. Excel spreadsheet files are usually denoted with the extension ".XLS." According to Microsoft, "If the executable called by the function is of a malicious nature, a worksheet containing this function could represent a security risk to customers." You can read more about the security issues associated with the CALL function at http://www.microsoft.com/security/bulletins/ms98-018.asp.

HTML, the programming language of the World Wide Web, is a set of statements or functions that can be interpreted by a Web browser to cause a Web server to provide some service. Several HTML statements enable the transfer of various source files from a remote Web server to a client Web browser (Exhibit 28-4). This feature can be used, for example, to allow Web pages to be included inside other Web pages or to enable multiple application support for more robust Web interaction.

Web programmers have many tools available to enable them to move various types of files from a Web server to a Web browser. One such capability may be found in "floating" or inline HTML frames (IFRAME). The IFRAME element allows Web authors to insert an inline frame within a block of text, that is, to insert one HTML document in the middle of another HTML document. Information to be inserted inline is designated by the IFRAME <src> or source attribute. More information about IFRAME can be found at http://www.w3.org/TR/REC-html40/present/frames.html#h-16.5.

Now, suppose that the source of the frame content for an inline HTML frame is not a Web programming language file, normally denoted with the HTM or HTML extension, but a file of type XLS, usually indicating an Excel spreadsheet file. The example HTML code may look like this:

```
<IFRAME WIDTH="0%" HEIGHT="0%" NAME="fnam" SRC="
<location>/file.xls">
    <FRAME NAME="fnam" SRC="<location/file.xls" width="0%"
    height="0%">
      Message</FRAME>
```

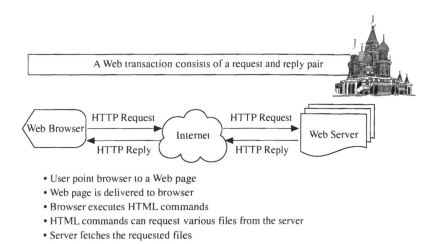

• User point browser to a Web page
• Web page is delivered to browser
• Browser executes HTML commands
• HTML commands can request various files from the server
• Server fetches the requested files
• Server sends the requested files to the browser

(Same concept with HTML aware / enabled e-mail client:
The Web page with HTML is delivered as body of e-mail.)

Exhibit 28-4. A Web transaction consists of a request and a reply pair.

<EMBED NAME="enam" SRC="<location>/file.xls" width="0%"
height="0%">
</IFRAME>

Combining the Excel CALL function with the ability to transport files over an open network, that is, over the Web, results in an exploitation that is significant. Specifically, since the XLS extension is registered (by the Windows registry) as associated with (referenced by) the Excel program, then XLS files transferred to the browser through IFRAME and related HTML commands are immediately passed to and processed by the referenced application, Excel.

When Excel starts, it executes functions in cells of the spreadsheet. If one of the functions is a maliciously coded CALL function, then it is possible that the Excel spreadsheet can be used to copy an executable program (for example, executable ASCII) to the hard disk and execute it. In fact, the executable ASCII could be self-extracting UUEncode (UUE) file. UUE is a popular utility for encoding and decoding files exchanged between users or systems in a network. Basically, what UUE does is to translate or convert a file (it can be an image, a text file, or a program) from its binary or bit-stream representation into the 7-bit ASCII set of text characters. The text characters can then be stored and carried as the content in a spreadsheet cell. Once delivered onto the desktop, it can be converted back to its binary form and executed; anything is possible (Exhibit 28-5).

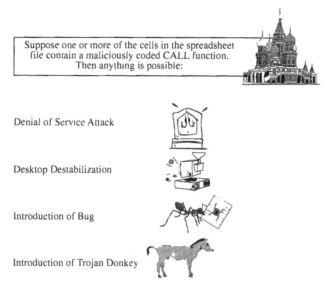

Suppose one or more of the cells in the spreadsheet file contain a maliciously coded CALL function. Then anything is possible:

Denial of Service Attack

Desktop Destabilization

Introduction of Bug

Introduction of Trojan Donkey

Exhibit 28-5. Anything is possible once content is delivered to the desktop.

SUMMARY

Call statements may be included in macros or as functions in cells. They are executed on the opening of the spreadsheet (e.g., XLS) file. An attacker could exploit this functionality by embedding a CALL function within an Excel spreadsheet and sending it to an unwary user as an e-mail attachment or simply during the user's interaction with the attacker's Web page.

Combine this vulnerability with services provided in HTML to move source files from a Web server to a Web browser. At the desktop, source files may be linked or associated with a variety of desktop applications. For example, the XLS extension is normally associated with the Microsoft Excel application. If the source file downloaded includes an XLS extension, then it may be immediately passed to and processed by the referenced Excel application.

It is worth noting that the Excel application does not have to be running. When the malicious spreadsheet file arrives at the desktop, the browser will automatically transfer it to the associated application. If the application, Excel, is not running, it will be launched by the Windows operating system.

When Excel starts, it automatically executes functions in cells of the spreadsheet. If one of the functions is a maliciously coded CALL function, then it is possible that the Excel spreadsheet can be used to deliver an attack onto the local hard disk or a networked drive and execute it (Exhibit 28-6). The attack will have access to any service or capability that the desk-

This spreadsheet just copied one of your
document files to a remote FTP site.

Exhibit 28-6. It is even possible to steal your data files.

top user has access to, without restriction. Theft of files, for example, will not be a problem.

What is Affected?

Microsoft Excel (both the Office 95 and Office 97 versions) includes the function, CALL, which enables "certain types of executables" to be run from within a spreadsheet without a warning to the user. Such "executables" can include external dynamic link library (DLL) programs, MS-DOS batch (BAT) files, or code resources. The CALL function can serve as an initiator or launching point for a malicious DLL or other program. The malicious program can do things like create and write data to a file on the hard disk, close that file, and then execute it. Using the CALL function, an attacker can locate and steal key files and data that are available and accessible to the user, no matter where those files reside.

All 3.x and 4.x versions of both the Microsoft and Netscape browsers (except Navigator 4.5) are vulnerable. HTML-aware e-mail readers, such as Microsoft Outlook 98, are also vulnerable since such programs can read and process HTML in message bodies.

Solutions

The Microsoft patch for Excel 97, which can be applied only after installing the Office 97 Service Release 2, disables (removes) the CALL function from Excel. Microsoft's patch eliminates the vulnerability by disabling the CALL function in worksheets; however, it does not disable the CALL function when used within macros. Nevertheless, it is recommended that users who do not require the CALL function apply this patch. Localized or language-specific versions of Office 97 Service Release 2 were not available as of March 1999. And, although the bug also affects Excel 95, at present there also is no patch for that version. (The reader is advised to consult with Microsoft regarding patch release schedules.)

Users of Netscape Navigator 4.5 do not appear to be vulnerable. However, our testing was not exhaustive, and one should consider that the exploit still may be possible through as yet undiscovered means. Users of other versions of the Netscape browser can "disassociate" the Excel application from various MIME content types (extensions) by removing the association reference in the browser's properties.

Users of Microsoft Internet Explorer 4.x browsers can prevent the Russian New Year exploit by setting the security preference to HIGH. However, this setting is frequently too restrictive in that it also prevents other types of mobile code from reaching the desktop.

A noteworthy concern: it is insufficient to rely on blocking of files with the .XLS extension. Using CGI (and other) scripts, an attacker can associate nonstandard source file extensions (content types) with desktop applications such as Excel. This "hiding" technique can be used to deliver hostile code in a file with any extension, .RANDOM for example, which the attacker could also associate with the Excel application. By adding a single line to the HTTP header, the Excel application would be automatically launched upon receipt of a file with a non-XLS extension.

As with any security strategy, it is recommended that corporations deploy multiple lines of defense ("security by depth") to reduce risks associated with the Russian New Year exploit. Several third party solutions were introduced to address the implied risks posed by combining the Excel CALL function with the HTML source file transport feature. The first came from Finjan, who provided a patch to its SurfinGate content inspection server. SurfinGate's advanced, high-speed HTML scanning engine can block high-risk file and content types from moving from a Web server to a Web browser over HTTP. SurfinGate can even respond to CGI (and other) scripts that can specify the content-type of a file with a variable (file extension) in the HTTP header.

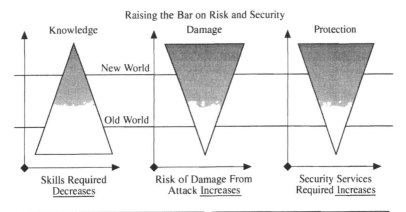

Exhibit 28-7. Raising the bar on security.

What Should You Do?

In today's world, fewer skills are required to inflict greater damage to systems than ever before. Raising the bar on risk and security (Exhibit 28-7) requires both knowledge and diverse solutions and strategies.

First, be aware of mobile code and the category of attacks and the types of dangerous activity that could be delivered through mobile code. Second, Excel users who do not have a need to execute DLL procedures via the CALL worksheet function are encouraged to apply the Microsoft patch, if possible, to disable the function. The patch is applied onto Office 97 Service Release 2 and available via the Office Update Web site at http://office-update.microsoft.com/downloadDetails/xl97cfp.htm.

As discussed above, the patch works by disabling the CALL worksheet function, but DOES NOT disable the CALL function from within macros. Also, the patch is (currently) available only for English and International English versions of Office 97 that have been patched through Service Release 2; and it is not available for users of Office 95. Therefore, the third step is to install a third party mobile code security product, such as Finjan's SurfinGate content inspection server, at key network interconnect points.

ASSOCIATED ARTICLES AND KEY LINKS

On January 5, 1999, *The Wall Street Journal* ran a key article on the Russian New Year entitled "Computer Experts to Disclose Discovery Of Potentially

Serious Web-Security Gap." This article can be accessed through the following link: http://www.finjan.com/wsj2.cfm. Free links with access to information about the Russian New Year include:

http://www.msnbc.com/news/229187.asp
http://www.news.com/News/Item/0,4,30521,00.html
http://more.abcnews.go.com/sections/tech/DailyNews/
    excelwoes990106.html
http://www.infoworld.com/cgi-bin/displayStory.pl?99015.wnfinjan.htm
http://www.infoworld.com/cgi-bin/displayArchive.pl?/99/02/
    n09-02.47.htm
http://www.computerworld.com/home/print.nsf/all/9901118886

Author Bio

Ron Moritz is Director of the Technology Office at Finjan Software, where he serves as primary technology visionary. As a key member of the senior management team interfacing between sales, marketing, product management, and product development, Ron helps establish and maintain the company's technological standards and preserve the company's leadership role as a developer of advanced Internet security solutions. Ron was instrumental in the organization of Finjan's Java Security Alliance and established and chairs Finjan's Technical Advisory Board. He is currently chairing the industry standards initiative to develop a Common Content Inspection API specification.

Ron is one of a select group of Certified Information Systems Security Professionals. He earned his M.S.E., M.B.A., and B.A. from Case Western Reserve University in Cleveland, OH and he has served in various capacities, including president, with both the north coast chapter of the Information Systems Security Association and the Northeast Ohio chapter of the Information Systems Audit and Control Association. He has lectured on Web security, mobile code security, computer ethics, intellectual property rights, and business continuity and resumption planning.

Chapter 29

Growth Optimal Asset Allocation Strategies With Downside Protection

Jivendra K. Kale

MULTIPERIOD PORTFOLIO THEORY PROVIDES A DESIRABLE ALTERNATIVE to mean-variance and mean-semivariance analysis for portfolio selection application systems. It targets long-term portfolio growth explicitly as the criterion for portfolio selection, while mean-variance analysis and mean-semivariance analysis are single-period modeling techniques. It is particularly appropriate for the vast majority of investors saving money in their pension plans, since their goal is high long-term portfolio growth. Maximizing long-term portfolio growth leads to an optimization technique where the expected utility of the portfolio is maximized using the log utility function. The portfolios produced by this method are known as growth optimal portfolios, but they are typically riskier than investors would like. The expected utility maximization method for generating growth optimal portfolios can be extended to add downside protection to portfolios. The resulting portfolios maintain the goal of achieving high long-term growth but conform more closely to an investor's risk preferences when downside protection is added to the portfolio to the extent desired by the investor. The amount of downside protection added corresponds to the investor's Degree of loss aversion. This technique has the added benefit of using all the moments of the asset return distribution, while the mean-variance and mean-semivariance techniques use only the first two moments. As a result, this technique is superior for portfolio selection, when asset return distributions are asymmetric or fat-tailed. This article demonstrates the long-term growth with downside protection technique with portfolios constructed from stocks, and U.S. treasuries of different maturities. The growth optimal portfolio contains stocks only

0-8493-9834-7/00/$0 00+$ 50

and is appropriate for an aggressive investor. As downside protection is increased, the portfolio composition shifts from stocks to 1-year and intermediate-term treasuries, the two fixed income asset classes that have the most positively skewed return distributions. As the portfolio composition shifts from stocks to 1-year and intermediate-term treasuries, the skewedness of the portfolio's return distribution also moves in the positive direction, making the portfolio more desirable for investors with greater loss aversion. Overall, the long-term growth with downside protection technique provides the power and flexibility to select the best portfolios of all types of assets, for investors with vastly different levels of loss aversion, thus making it a desirable alternative to the traditional portfolio selection methods.

INTRODUCTION

Mean-variance analysis combined with quadratic optimization is currently the most common way to construct portfolios of individual securities and asset classes. This technique was pioneered by Markowitz (1959), who put forth the notion of a mean-variance efficient portfolio. It works best when the asset return distributions are approximately normal. Since stock return distributions are approximately normal, mean-variance analysis combined with quadratic optimization is an effective method for constructing stock portfolios. Markowitz also proposed using mean-semivariance analysis, suggesting that the technique produces efficient portfolios "somewhat preferable," to those produced by mean-variance analysis when asset return distributions are asymmetric. Return distributions for bonds and options are asymmetric and deviate significantly from normality. Semivariance is a measure of dispersion of downside returns, and as a measure of risk for portfolio selection it has sparked some recent interest. See Fishburn (1977), Sortino and v.d. Meer (1991), Harlow (1991), and Rom and Ferguson (1991). Both the mean-variance and mean-semivariance methods are single period modeling techniques, and neither addresses the issue of long-term growth over multiple time periods.

Multiperiod portfolio theory offers an alternative approach to portfolio construction by explicitly targeting long-term growth as the criterion for portfolio selection. This approach to portfolio construction leads to portfolios that are different from those obtained by either mean-variance or mean-semivariance techniques. The work by Mossin (1968), Hakansson (1971, 1974), Leland (1972), Ross (1974), Huberman and Ross (1980), and Grauer and Hakansson (1982, 1985, and 1993) in this field applies the expected utility criterion of Von Neumann and Morgenstern (1953) for choice under uncertainty to portfolio selection. Kale (1998, 1999) demonstrates an expected utility based portfolio selection technique that optimizes growth with downside protection, in studies that examine the effect of differences in loss aversion between investors. The expected utility maximization techniques work well with all types of asset return distributions, including skewed and fat-tailed distributions. This article draws on the theoretical and empirical research in multiperiod portfolio theory to describe its major concepts, their application to practical portfolio selection, and the benefits of taking the long-term perspective.

METHODOLOGY

Capital growth in an investment portfolio will follow a compounding process during the T future time periods that the portfolio will be held.

$$W_T = W_0(1 + r_{P1})(1 + r_{P2}) \dots (1 + r_{PT})$$

where:

W_T = ending wealth after T time periods
W_0 = beginning wealth at time 0, i.e., today
r_{PT} = portfolio return in time period t, a random variable

Portfolio growth, or compounded portfolio return over the T time periods, R_{PT} is defined as

$$R_{PT} = \{(1 + r_{P1})(1 + r_{P2}) \dots (1 + r_{PT})\} - 1$$

The ending wealth W_T can be written as

$$W_T = W_0(1 + R_{PT})$$

The goal for most investors is to maximize the ending wealth, W_T. This is certainly true for investors saving over the long term for their retirement. This form of savings represents the largest proportion of savings in the U.S. It is also likely to be true in Europe and other parts of the world, as they move away from state-sponsored pension plans to those that are modeled after the U.S. pension plans. Maximizing long-term wealth is quite different from the type of investment objective used in mean-variance and mean-semivariance analysis, where the efficient portfolios considered for selection have a life of one period only.

The ending wealth, W_T, would be maximized if portfolio growth, R_{PT}, over the T time periods is maximized. Maximizing portfolio growth leads to selecting investment weights in each period to maximize the expected utility of the portfolio, where the utility function is the log of one plus the portfolio return in that period (Luenberger 1998). Putting it another way, the log utility function is the "derived" utility function, whose expected value should be maximized in each period without regard to the other periods, in order to maximize long-term growth. The portfolios selected by this procedure are known as "growth optimal." The expected utility criterion for choice under uncertainty that is used in this method of portfolio selection was developed by Von Neumann and Morgenstern (1953), where the utility function used with the expected utility criterion should reflect the preferences of the investor. The log utility function reflects the risk and return preferences for an investor who wants to maximize long-term portfolio growth.

For each future period the growth maximizing utility function is

$$U = \ln(1 + r_P)$$

where:

    U = portfolio utility for the period, a random variable
    $\ln$ = the natural logarithm function
    r_P = portfolio return for the period, a random variable

The portfolio return can be written as a function of the asset weights and returns,

$$r_p = \sum_{i=1}^{N} w_i r_i$$

where:

    w_i = investment weight for asset i
    r_i = return for asset i for the period, a random variable
    N = number of assets in the portfolio

When the investor's goal is to maximize portfolio growth, the expected utility criterion leads to the following optimization problem for each future period:

Maximize

$$E(U) = \sum_{S} p_S \ln(1 + r_{PS})$$

where:

    S = scenario, and the summation is over all scenarios
    p_S = probability of scenario S occurring
    $\ln$ = the natural log function
    r_{PS} = portfolio return in scenario
and,

$$r_{PS} = \sum_{i=1}^{N} w_i r_{iS}$$

where:

    r_{iS} = return for asset i in scenario

This expected utility maximization procedure produces growth optimal portfolios. In practice, growth optimal portfolios are riskier than investors would like, since they can incur significant losses in some periods; see Grauer and Hakansson (1985). The growth optimal portfolio selection procedure can be modified to account for differences between the risk preferences of different investors. Kale (1998, 1999) demonstrates a portfolio selection technique using growth optimization with downside protection developed recently by Financiometrics Inc., in studies that examine the effect of differences in loss aversion between investors. This approach treats losses and gains differently and penalizes losses only. The portfolios in Kale's studies were constructed from selected asset classes. The portfolio selection technique is an extension of the expected utility maximization approach used for selecting growth optimal portfolios and conforms to the requirements of the Von Neumann and Morgenstern expected utility criterion. The technique starts with a growth optimal portfolio and adds downside protection to it. The amount of downside protection added depends on the "degree of loss aversion" specified for the investor. Setting the degree of loss aversion to zero generates the growth optimal portfolio. The larger the degree of loss aversion specified, the greater the downside protection added to the portfolio. When the degree of loss aversion is set to a number greater than zero, the resulting portfolio will no longer be growth optimal, but it will have the desired level of downside protection for a given investor. Thus, it will reflect the risk preferences of the investor more closely than the growth optimal portfolio.

The long-term growth with downside protection technique has another advantage over mean-variance and mean-semivariance analysis, in that it uses all the moments of the joint distribution of asset returns for portfolio construction. In contrast, the other two techniques focus on just the first two moments of the distributions. The semivariance technique does emphasize downside protection, but it ignores the potential for large gains on the upside. Historical returns for fixed income securities show a marked positive skewedness, which is picked up by the long-term growth with downside protection technique but is missed entirely by mean-variance analysis and is only partially captured by the mean-semivariance approach. In addition, the long-term growth with downside protection technique deals very effectively with the prevalence of large positive and negative stock returns described by Mandelbrot (1997) that make stock return distributions fat-tailed. It accounts properly for the contribution of large positive returns to long-term growth and the contribution of large negative returns to downside risk. The portfolios constructed with this technique show a definite positive skewedness in their return distributions, in line with the preferences of most investors for large positive returns but no large negative returns.

The following sections describe the data and show some of the results obtained by Kale (1999). To study the effect of different types of risk preferences, three different values of the degree of loss aversion were used to construct the portfolios. The first value was zero, which created growth optimal portfolios that would be appropriate for an aggressive investor. The second value was set to 15, to represent an average investor. This value would result in a 60:40 mix of stocks and long-term government bonds, if these securities were the only two types of assets allowed in the portfolio. The third value was set to 80, to represent a conservative investor. This value would result in a portfolio with one third of the assets invested in stocks and two thirds invested in long-term government bonds, if these were the only two types of assets allowed in the portfolio. Data from 1983 through 1998 for the S&P500 index and long-term U.S. treasuries were used to calibrate these values for the degree of loss aversion.

DATA

The asset classes from which the portfolios were selected in Kale (1999) were stocks represented by the S&P500 index, 1-month treasuries, 1-year treasuries, intermediate-term treasuries, and long-term treasuries. Monthly returns data from 1926 through 1998 were contributed by Ibbotson Associates for these asset classes. The returns include dividends and coupon payments. All the portfolios were constructed at the end of 1998. They represent portfolios that investors would hold for 1999 and into the future. Deciding on an appropriate time period for the data history to be used in portfolio construction is always difficult, so three different base sample periods were chosen from the period spanning 1926 through 1998. They represent different economic environments. The first base sample period was 1983 through 1998, which represents the recent experience, after the late 1970s and early 1980s era of high short-term rates and inflation was over. The second base sample period was 1946 through 1998, the post-war period, and the third base sample period was 1926 through 1998, the entire available data history.

The monthly returns were compounded to generate a time series of quarterly joint returns for the five asset classes. Exhibit 29-1 shows the summary statistics for these returns for the three base sample periods. This exhibit and all the exhibits that follow show quarterly returns that are not annualized.

The 1983 through 1998 period is characterized by much higher mean return and average growth rates across the board for all asset classes, when compared to the other two periods that contain much longer histories. The "average growth" is defined as the geometric average quarterly return for the period. It reflects the effect of compounding the returns. The difference between the average growth and mean return is greater

	A	B	C	D	E	F	G	H
7								
8					Asset			
9								
10			U.S. 30 Day	U.S. 1 Yr	U.S. IT	U.S. LT	S&P500	
11			T-Bills	Gvt.	Gvt.	Gvt.		
12								
13								
14								
15					1983 through 1998			
16								
17	Maximum		2.53	4 73	8 78	19 73	21 33	
18	Minimum		0.70	0 31	-3 78	-6 96	-22 63	
19	Median		1.39	1 71	1 92	2 03	5.10	
20	Mean		1.49	1 79	2 38	3 07	4.27	
21	Std. Dev.		0 47	0 82	2 82	5 38	7 14	
22	Skewness		0 24	1 10	0 18	0 50	0 84	
23								
24	Avg. Growth		1 49	1 79	2 34	2 94	4 02	
25								
26								
27								

	A	B	C	D	E	F	G	H
7								
8					Asset			
9								
10			U.S. 30 Day	U.S. 1 Yr	U.S. IT	U.S. LT	S&P500	
11			T-Bills	Gvt.	Gvt.	Gvt.		
12								
13								
14								
15					1946 through 1998			
16								
17								
18								
19	Maximum		3 81	9 37	16 57	24 36	22 94	
20	Minimum		0 09	-1 05	-6 35	-14 51	-25 16	
21	Median		1 17	1 16	0 87	0 88	3 86	
22	Mean		1 19	1 41	1 50	1 49	3 26	
23	Std. Dev.		0 75	1 21	2 83	4 84	7 42	
24	Skewness		0 85	2 34	1 39	1 07	0 68	
25								
26	Avg. Growth		1 18	1 40	1 46	1 38	2 98	
27								

Exhibit 29-1. Summary statistics for quarterly joint returns.

	A	B	C	D	E	F	G	H
7					Asset			
8								
9								
10			U.S. 30 Day	U.S. 1 Yr	U.S. IT	U.S. LT	S&P500	
11			T-Bills	Gvt.	Gvt.	Gvt.		
12								
13								
14								
15					1926 through 1998			
16								
17								
18								
19	Maximum		3 81	9 37	16 57	24 36	88 84	
20	Minimum		-0 05	-1 25	-6 35	-14 51	-37 68	
21	Median		0.82	0.94	0 87	0 97	3 92	
22	Mean		0 93	1 16	1 34	1 40	3 24	
23	Std. Dev.		0 78	1 15	2 54	4 29	11 62	
24	Skewness		0 93	2 29	1 50	1 12	2 10	
25								
26	Avg. Growth		0.93	1.15	1 31	1 32	2 64	
27								

Exhibit 29-1. *Continued.*

when the magnitudes of the quarterly returns are higher and their standard deviation is higher. Another interesting observation is that the skewedness of the returns to all the fixed income securities is positive for all three base sample periods, while it is negative for the S&P500 index for both the post-war periods. Among the fixed income securities, the 1-year treasuries stand out in their consistently and substantially higher positive skewedness, as compared to the other fixed income securities.

RESULTS

The results described here are from Kale (1999). Exhibit 29-2 shows the compositions of the optimal portfolios for the three types of investors by column. The three panels contain portfolios constructed using data from the three base sample periods. The aggressive investor's portfolio is the growth optimal portfolio, and it is 100 percent invested in stocks, regardless of the base sample period used to construct the portfolio. This consistency of the portfolio composition, when different base sample periods are used, is an important result for strategic asset allocation. It suggests that aggressive investors with long horizons should be invested 100 percent in stocks at all times, when the choices are limited to stocks and U.S. treasuries. The shift from stocks to treasuries as loss aversion grows is predictable, and it is evident in the compositions of the portfolios of the average

	Aggressive Investor	Average Investor	Conservative Investor
Base Sample Period: 1983 through 1998			
1 Month T-Bills	0 00	0 00	0 00
1 Year Treasuries	0 00	0 00	13 42
Intermediate Term Treasuries	0 00	0 00	27 79
Long Term Treasuries	0 00	39 83	30 00
Stocks (S&P500)	100 00	60 17	28 79

	Aggressive Investor	Average Investor	Conservative Investor
Base Sample Period: 1946 through 1998			
1 Month T-Bills	0.00	0 00	0 00
1 Year Treasuries	0.00	15 05	71 83
Intermediate Term Treasuries	0 00	24 05	7 44
Long Term Treasuries	0 00	0 00	0 00
Stocks (S&P500)	100 00	60 90	20 74

	Aggressive Investor	Average Investor	Conservative Investor
Base Sample Period: 1926 through 1998			
1 Month T-Bills	0 00	0 00	0 00
1 Year Treasuries	0 00	0 00	50 80
Intermediate Term Treasuries	0 00	62.63	36 91
Long Term Treasuries	0 00	0 00	0 00
Stocks (S&P500)	100 00	37.37	12 30

Exhibit 29-2. Compositions of the optimal portfolios for the three types of investors by column. Optimal portfolio holdings in percent.

investor and the conservative investor. Except for portfolios constructed from data from the 1983 through 1998 base sample period, the shift from stocks to bonds is to the intermediate-term treasuries and 1-year treasuries, not long-term treasuries. The large weights assigned to the 1-year treasuries are a reflection of the consistently high positive skewedness of the returns to these securities relative to the other fixed income instruments. The 30 percent plus weighting assigned to long-term treasuries in the average and conservative investors' portfolios constructed with data from the 1983 through 1998 base sample period is a result of the huge gains made by the long-term treasuries from the big decline in long-term interest rates during this period. This appears to be a temporary phenomenon, since the portfolios constructed from the data from the longer base sample periods do not support this large weighting for long-term bonds. The results in Exhibit 29-2 suggest that the highest portfolio growth rate will be obtained with stocks alone and that the best way to add downside protection to this investment strategy is to reduce the investment in stocks and replace it with 1-year treasuries and intermediate-term treasuries. Interestingly, neither T-bills nor long-term treasuries were as useful as 1-year treasuries and intermediate-term treasuries in reducing downside risk while maintaining long-term growth as a goal.

The compositions of the portfolios will determine their future performance and the level of growth potential and downside protection that can be associated with them. Even though past performance is not an infallible guide for future performance, it is always interesting to look at the simulated past performance of portfolios constructed using different types of strategies. Exhibits 29-3 through 29-6 show the performance for 1983 through 1998 for the portfolios of the three types of investors, which were constructed using data from the 1946 through 1998 base sample period. These portfolios are shown in the middle panel of Exhibit 29-2 for the three types of investors. Each portfolio was assumed to be held unchanged for the entire 1983 through 1998 period. The 1946 through 1998 base sample period was selected since it contains a sufficiently long history that is relevant to today's markets. There is an overlap of 16 years between the 1983 through 1998 period used for calculating performance and the 53-year 1946 through 1998 period, used for constructing the portfolios. This is not a problem, since the purpose of examining the performance is to demonstrate the differences in the nature of portfolios constructed for different types of investors.

Exhibit 29-3 shows the summary statistics for quarterly returns for the portfolios of the three types of investors. Exhibit 29-4 shows the corresponding frequency distributions of quarterly returns.

	Aggressive Investor	Average Investor	Conservative Investor
	Summary Statistics		
Maximum	21 33	13 51	5.70
Minimum	-22 63	-12 29	-2.71
Median	5 10	3 55	2.16
Mean	4 27	3 44	2.35
Std. Dev.	7 14	4 54	1.75
Skewness	-0 84	-0 60	-0 18
Avg. Growth	4 02	3 34	2 33

Exhibit 29-3. Quarterly portfolio returns 1983 through 1998. Returns are in percent and are not annualized.

The notable change from the aggressive investor's performance to the more conservative investors' performances is the elimination of large negative returns. The minimum quarterly return went up from –22.63 percent for the aggressive investor, to –12.29 percent for the average investor, to –2.71 percent for the conservative investor. These increases are 10.34 percent and 19.92 percent, respectively, from the aggressive investor's minimum. The cost of eliminating this downside risk was the scaling back of some of the large positive returns. The maximum quarterly return went down from 21.33 percent for the aggressive investor to 13.51 percent for the average investor to 5.70 percent for the conservative investor. These decreases are 7.82 percent and 15.63 percent respectively, from the aggressive investor's maximum. For the average investor, the increase in the minimum, 10.34 percent, is greater than the decrease in the maximum, 7.82 percent. For the conservative investor the increase in the minimum, 19.92 percent, is greater than the decrease in the maximum, 15.63 percent. In contrast to the aggressive investor, the magnitude of the maximum is greater than the magnitude of the minimum for both the average and conservative investors. The net result is a change in the nature of the distributions of quarterly returns, from one that has a large negative skewedness of –0.84 for the aggressive investor, to ones that have a smaller negative skewedness, –0.60 for the average investor and –0.18 for the conservative investor.

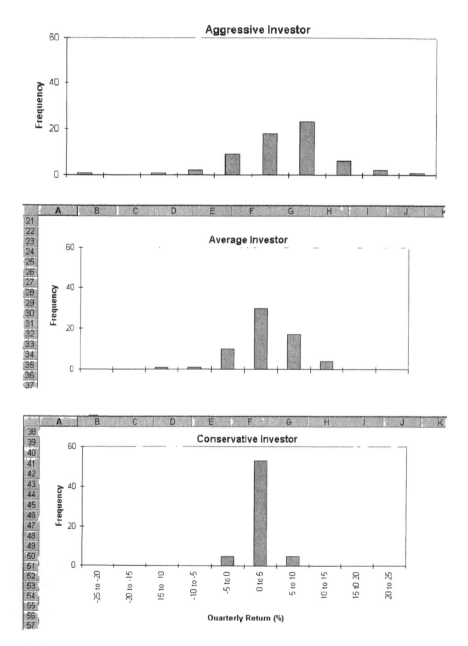

Exhibit 29-4. Quarterly portfolio return frequency distributions for 1983 to 1998. Base sample period: 1946 to 1998.

The standard deviation of quarterly return also dropped substantially from 7.14 percent for the aggressive investor to 4.54 percent for the average investor to 1.75 percent for the conservative investor. These numbers for the standard deviation of quarterly return correspond to annualized equivalents of 14.28 percent, 9.08 percent, and 3.50 percent, respectively. Clearly, the conservative investor is extremely conservative.

Adding downside protection to the growth optimal portfolio required giving up some of the upside return, which cuts back on portfolio growth for the average and conservative investors. The average quarterly growth rate dropped from 4.02 percent for the aggressive investor to 3.34 percent for the average investor to 2.33 percent for the conservative investor. The corresponding annualized growth rates are 17.08 percent, 14.04 percent, and 9.65 percent, respectively.

Exhibit 29-5 charts the performance history for the aggressive and average investors' portfolios for 1983 through 1998, while Exhibit 29-6 does the same for the aggressive and conservative investors' portfolios. The two exhibits show a consistent pattern of change in portfolio returns as the degree of loss aversion increases from the aggressive investor to the average investor and finally to the conservative investor. Both charts show that the magnitude of the decrease in losses is greater than the magnitude of the decrease in gains, which skews portfolio returns in the positive direction as loss aversion increases.

CONCLUSION

The technique of selecting portfolios for high long-term growth with downside protection is a desirable alternative to mean-variance and mean-semivariance analysis. It is based on multiperiod portfolio theory and has

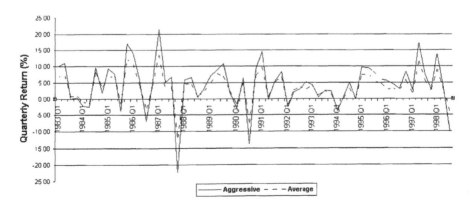

Exhibit 29-5. Quarterly portfolio returns history for 1983 through 1998 base sample period: 1946 through 1998.

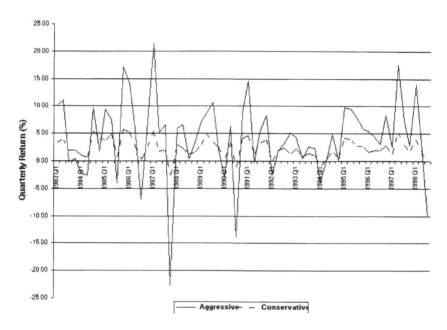

Exhibit 29-6. Quarterly portfolio returns history for 1983 through 1998 base sample period: 1946 through 1998.

the power and the flexibility to produce a whole range of portfolios from an aggressive growth optimal portfolio to more conservative portfolios that conform more closely to investor preferences for high long-term growth tempered with the desired level of downside protection. The amount of downside protection added to the growth optimal portfolio depends on the degree of loss aversion specified; the larger the degree of loss aversion, the greater the amount of downside protection added. This was observed in portfolios constructed from stocks and U.S. treasuries. Regardless of the sample period of the data used in constructing the portfolios, the growth optimal portfolio consisted of stocks only. As the degree of loss aversion specified for the investor was increased, the investment in stocks was steadily replaced with 1-year and intermediate-term treasuries. The losses suffered by the resulting portfolios declined more than the drop in gains, which made the skewedness of the portfolio return distributions more positive. The standard deviation of portfolio returns, which is the traditional measure of risk, also declined. This process of portfolio optimization accounts properly for gains that contribute to long-term growth and for the losses that contribute to downside risk. The changes in the characteristics of the portfolio as the degree of loss aversion increases follows a pattern that is more desirable than a reduction in variance or semivariance alone.

The results shown here are limited to stocks and U.S. treasuries, but the long-term growth with downside protection technique can be extended to all types of assets.

ACKNOWLEDGMENTS

The author thanks Financiometrics Inc. for access to its Growth Optimization System, and Ibbotson Associates for its data history.

References

Fishburn, P. C., Mean risk analysis with risk associated with below-target variance, *Am. Econ. Rev.*, March 1977.

Grauer, R. R. and Hakansson, N. H., Higher return, lower risk: historical returns on long-run, actively managed portfolios of stocks, bonds and bills, 1936–1978, *Fin. Anal. J.*, March–April 1982.

Grauer, R. R. and Hakansson, N., H., Returns on levered, actively managed long-run portfolios of stocks, bonds and bills, 1934–1983, *Fin. Anal. J.*, September–October 1985.

Grauer, R. R. and Hakansson, N. H., On the use of mean-variance and quadratic approximations in implementing dynamic investment strategies: a comparison of returns and investment policies, *Manage. Sci.*, 39(7), July 1993.

Hakansson, N. H., On optimal myopic portfolio policies, with and without serial correlation of yields, *J. Bus.*, 44, 1971.

Hakansson, N. H., Convergence to isoelastic utility and policy in multiperiod portfolio choice, *J. Fin. Econ.*, 1, 1974.

Harlow, W. V., Asset allocation in a downside risk framework, *Fin. Anal. J.*, September–October, 1991.

Huberman, G. and Ross, S., *Portfolio Turnpike Theorems, Risk Aversion and Regularly Varying Utility Functions*, Yale University, 1980.

Kale, J. K., Asset Allocation Strategies for Long-Term Growth with Downside Protection, for All Types of Asset Return Distributions (working paper), Golden Gate University, San Francisco, 1998.

Kale, J. K., Stocks, Bonds and Bills in Asset Allocation Strategies for Long-Term Growth with Downside Protection (working paper), Golden Gate University, San Francisco, 1999.

Leland, H., On turnpike portfolios, in *Mathematical Methods in Investment and Finance*, Shell, K. and Szego, G. P., Eds., North-Holland, Amsterdam, 1972.

Luenberger, D. G., *Investment Science*, Oxford University Press, New York, 1998.

Mandelbrot, B. B., *Fractals and Scaling in Finance: Discontinuity, Concentration, Risk*, Springer-Verlag, Berlin, 1997.

Markowitz, H. M., *Portfolio Selection*, Blackwell, Oxford, 1991.

Mossin, J., Optimal multiperiod portfolio policies, *J. Bus.*, 41, 1968.

Rom, B. M. and Ferguson, K. W., Post-modern portfolio theory comes of age, *J. Inv.*, Fall 1994.

Ross, S., Portfolio turnpike theorems for constant policies, *J. Fin. Econ.*, 1, 1974.

Sortino, F. and v.d. Meer, R., Downside risk: capturing what's at stake, *J. Portfol. Manage.*, Summer 1991.

Von Neumann, J. and Morgenstern, O., *Theory of Games and Economic Behavior*, 3rd ed., Princeton University Press, Princeton, NJ, 1953.

Author Bio

Jivendra K. Kale is on the faculty of the School of Business at Golden Gate University in San Francisco and is a Principal at Financiometrics Inc. He has a Ph. D. in Finance from the University of California, Berkeley, and has worked as a senior consultant at BARRA and Gifford Fong Associates. He has written several articles in the areas of market microstructure, equity risk models and portfolio optimization, and his consulting work includes portfolio optimization and performance attribution for money management applications.

Chapter 30
Quadratic Programming for Large-Scale Portfolio Optimization

Michael J. Best
Jivendra K. Kale

QUADRATIC PROGRAMMING (QP) IS THE MOST WIDELY USED METHOD for portfolio construction. It is most effective when the assert return distributions are approximately normal. This method works particularly well for large stock and bond portfolios which can contain several thousand assets and where risk is typically measured relative to a benchmark. The requirements for portfolio constructions can be quite complex. In addition to the usual budget constraint, a portfolio may be required to have upper and lower bounds on all assets. The portfolio may be required to satisfy constraints such as limits on industry holdings, beta, or dividend yield for stock portfolios, and limit on issuers holdings, duration, and convexity for bond portfolios. Accounting for the transactions costs of trading is necessary where these costs increase with the size of the transaction because of the price impact of trades. Incorporation of some, or all of these features, can result in a quadratic programming (QP) problem which is simply too large for practical use with a general purpose quadratic programming method. However, general purpose QP algorithms can be specialized to take account of the particular structure of portfolio problems enabling large problems to be solved in a practical way. Here, we give an overview of three things: (1) formulation of the portfolio optimization problem as a QP, (2) QP solution methods, and (3) specialization of QP algorithms to solve large-scale portfolio optimization problems.

Portfolio optimization is the technique for finding the best portfolio for the investor, given the available set of portfolios and the investor's

0-8493-9834-7/00/$0 00+$.50
© 2000 by CRC Press LLC

tolerance for risk. The investor's risk tolerance defines the trade-off between the expected return on the portfolio and its risk. In his original formulation of the portfolio optimization problem, Markowitz (1952) defined portfolio risk as the variance of the portfolio return. This approach to portfolio selection is known as mean-variance analysis, and it works well when the asset return distributions are approximately normal. Optimization is used widely for the management of investment portfolios throughout the world. Money managers use it for a variety of applications. Among them are (1) asset allocation, for calculating the optimal investment in asset categories such as stocks, bonds and cash, or the optimal investment in different countries; (2) stock portfolio optimization, for calculating the optimal investment in different stocks for a given risk tolerance or maximizing expected portfolio return for a given level of risk, or for tracking a stock index; (3) bond portfolio optimization, for calculating the optimal investment in different bonds for a given risk tolerance, cash flow matching, portfolio immunization, or for tracking a bond index.

Portfolio optimization problems have linear and quadratic terms in the objective function and are subject to a set of linear constraints. The constraints can be on individual asset holdings, asset group holdings such as industry and issuer constraints, portfolio characteristics such as beta, dividend yield, or duration and convexity. In addition, transactions costs must be paid for trades that are necessary to change the existing portfolio to an optimal one. These transactions costs typically vary with the size of the trade. Larger trades have a larger price impact on the market price of a security, resulting in higher transactions costs. The price impact of large trades is particularly important for portfolios of small company stocks, where it can be as high as 1000 basis points (Sinquefield, 1995).

Portfolio optimization problems can be formulated as Quadratic Programming (QP) problems when risk is measured as the variance of return. For a stock or bond portfolio optimization where the number of assets in the universe may be in the thousands, these problems become very large when constraints and variable transaction costs are introduced into the QP formulation. To solve these problems quickly, particularly on a workstation, requires specialized techniques that take advantage of the structure of the problem. The following sections lay out problem formulation, describe the different types of algorithms that may be used to solve the problem, and describe the specialized techniques that can be used to solve the large-scale portfolio optimization problems quickly on a workstation.

PORTFOLIO OPTIMIZATION AS A QP

The Basic Markowitz Model

Consider a universe of n assets. Assume the data

$$\mu = (\mu_1, ..., \mu_n)' \quad \text{and} \quad \Sigma = [\sigma_{ij}]$$

are known, where μ_i is the expected return for asset i and σ_{ij} is the covariance of returns for assets i and j. Thus, μ is the vector of expected returns and Σ is the (n, n) variance-covariance matrix of asset returns. Let $x = (x_1, ..., x_n)'$ denote the (as yet unknown) holdings vector; i.e., x_i denotes the investment weight for asset i, $i = 1, ..., n$. In terms of x, the expected return of the portfolio μ_p and its variance σ_p^2 are

$$\mu_p = \mu'x \quad \text{and} \quad \sigma_p^2 = x'\Sigma x.$$

Markowitz's seminal idea (Markowitz, 1952) is to define a portfolio to be efficient if for some fixed level of portfolio expected return no other portfolio gives a smaller portfolio variance. Thus, an efficient portfolio is the solution to the optimization problem

$$\min\left\{\frac{1}{2}x'\Sigma x \,\middle|\, \mu'x = \mu_p, l'x = 1\right\}, \tag{30.1}$$

where l is a vector of ones. The constraint $l'x = 1$, called the budget constraint, requires the investment weights to sum to 1. The set of all efficient portfolios is generated as the expected portfolio return, μ_p, is varied in (30.1).

Equivalently, one can define an efficient portfolio as one for which at some fixed level of portfolio variance no other portfolio gives a larger portfolio expected return. This results in the optimization problem

$$\max\left\{\mu'x \,\middle|\, x'\Sigma x = \sigma_p^2, l'x = 1\right\}. \tag{30.2}$$

Again, the efficient portfolios are generated as the variance of portfolio return, σ_p^2, is varied in (30.2).

A mathematically equivalent formulation of (30.1) and (30.2) is

$$\max\left\{t\mu'x - \frac{1}{2}x'\Sigma x \,\middle|\, l'x = 1\right\}, \tag{30.3}$$

where t is a non-negative scalar parameter. t can be thought of as a risk-tolerance parameter. When t = 0, indicating a low tolerance for risk, the solution of (30.3) is the minimum variance portfolio. When t is large, indicating a high tolerance for risk, the solution to (30.3) will emphasize the maximization of the expected portfolio return, μ_p, and put little weight on the minimization of the variance of portfolio return, σ_p^2.

Problems (30.1), (30.2), and (30.3) are equivalent. For our purposes, it is convenient to work with (30.3). If Σ is positive definite (so that it is invertible), the solution for (30.3) may be written in closed form. Indeed, denoting the optimal solution by $x(t)$ to emphasize its dependence on t, it may be shown that

$$x(t) = h_0 + th_1 ,\qquad (30.4)$$

where

$$h_0 = \left(l'\Sigma^{-1}l\right)^{-1}\Sigma^{-1}l, \quad h_1 = \Sigma^{-1}\left(\mu - \left(l'\Sigma^{-1}l\right)^{-1}\left(l'\Sigma^{-1}\mu\right)l\right).$$

Note that from (30.4), $x(t)$ is a linear function of t.

It is important to realize that the simple model (30.3) can be solved using only matrix multiplication and matrix inversion to calculate Σ^{-1}. No QP algorithm is required. The expected return and variance of efficient portfolios may be calculated in terms of t using (30.4). Doing so and eliminating t gives the relationship between σ_p^2 and μ_p for efficient portfolios:

$$\left(\mu_p - \mu'h_0\right)^2 = \mu'h_1\left(\sigma_p^2 - h_0'\Sigma h_0\right).\qquad (30.5)$$

This is the well-known efficient frontier, a parabola in mean-variance space.

Short Sales Restrictions

The computational complexity of the optimization problem (30.3) increases dramatically when bounds on asset holdings are added to the problem formulation. Asset bounds may be restrictions on short sales or legal and institutional restrictions on large holdings in individual stocks and bonds. Short sales may be precluded by adding nonnegativity constraints (i.e., $x \geq 0$) to (30.3), to give

$$max\left\{t\mu'x - \frac{1}{2}x'\Sigma x \mid l'x = 1, x \geq 0\right\}\qquad (30.6)$$

The computational difficult in (30.6) stems from the nonnegativity constraints. It is not at all clear which constraints will be *active*, i.e., which holdings will be zero, in the optimal solution. At first, this may seem like a fairly simple problem, but it is not. Since each holding may be zero or positive, there are two possibilities for each. With n assets, there are 2^n possibilities. For a medium-sized portfolio having $n = 500$ assets, there are $2^{500} \approx$

3.27×10^{150} possibilities. Obviously, enumeration of all possibilities is not practical for other than problems having a very small number of assets.

What is required for the solution of (30.6) is a QP algorithm. An algorithm in this context is a precise set of instructions that will construct a better portfolio from an existing one. The instructions are then repeated with the new portfolio replacing the previous one, until an optimal solution is obtained. Virtually all QP algorithms have the property that the optimal solution will be obtained in a *finite* number of steps. The execution of a single repetition of the instructions is called an *iteration* of the algorithm. The reader may be familiar with the Simplex Method for Linear Programming (LP). QP algorithms will be discussed in more detail in a later section.

The inclusion of nonnegativity constraints (or any *inequality* constraints) in (30.6) changes the character of the optimal solution for (30.6). Rather than being linear for all t, the efficient portfolios are now *piece-wise linear* in *t*. This means there are a finite set of numbers $0 \le t_1 \le \dots \le t_s$ such that the efficient portfolios are given by

$$x_i(t) = h_{0i} + th_{1i}$$

for all *t* with $t_i \le t \le t_{i.1}$, and for $i = 0, \dots, s-1$. This means that the efficient portfolios are still linear functions of *t* but the coefficients differ in each interval $(t_i, t_{i.1})$. The efficient frontier (30.5) now becomes a piece-wise parabola.

The number of intervals, *s*, depends on the problem data in (30.6), and there is no way of determining it *a priori*. It could be very large. Each interval differs from the previous in that an assets holding is either reduced from a positive value to zero, or some other assets holding moves from zero to a positive value, or both. That is, each interval corresponds to a change from an adjacent interval of at most two asset holdings in the active constraint set, which is the set of constraints where the asset holdings are zero in (30.6).

To solve (30.6) for all *t* and thus generate all of the parametric intervals, the appropriate computational tool is a *parametric* QP algorithm (the parameter being *t*).

Fixed Transaction Costs and Asset Bounds

Fixed transactions costs are costs that do not change with transaction size. These costs can be incorporated into the model (30.6). Suppose x_0 is the vector of holdings in the initial portfolio. Let $x^{\cdot}$ denote the vector of asset purchases and x^{-} denote the vector of asset sales. Then the new asset holding vector x satisfies

$$x = x_0 + x^{\cdot} - x^{\cdot}, \quad 0 \le x^{\cdot} \le d, \quad 0 \le x^{\cdot} \le e,$$

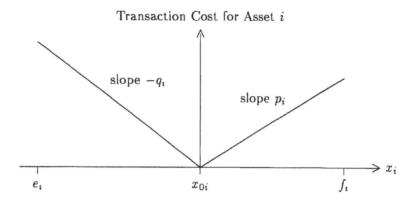

Exhibit 30-1. Fixed transactions costs.

where d and e are vectors of upper bounds on scales and purchases, respectively. The upper bounds on purchases and sales are equivalent to bounds on asset holdings, assuming that the initial holdings satisfy the asset bounds. The new variables $x^{\cdot}$ and x^{-} have to be included in the problem formulation. One way to incorporate fixed transaction costs is to use a linear cost function. For asset i, letting p_i and q_i denote the percentage transactions costs on the buy and sell sides, respectively, the transactions cost represents a reduction in expected return. The total transactions cost for an asset is (see Exhibit 30.1)

$$p_i x_i^{\cdot} + q_i x_i^{-} ,$$

and the transactions cost for the portfolio is

$$p'x^{\cdot} + q'x^{-} .$$

Assembling these features into (30.6), the fixed transaction cost QP formulation becomes

$$
\left.
\begin{aligned}
\text{maximize: } & t\left(\mu'x - p'x^{\cdot} - q'x^{-}\right) - \tfrac{1}{2}x'\Sigma x \\
\text{subject to: } \quad l'x \quad\quad\quad &= 1, \\
x - x^{\cdot} + x^{-} \quad &= x_0, \\
0 \le x^{-} \le d, & \\
0 \le x^{\cdot} \le e. &
\end{aligned}
\right\}
\tag{30.7}
$$

Note that for n assets, the problem formulation (30.7) has $3n$ variables (n each for x, $x^{\cdot}$, and x^{-}), and $5n + 1$ constraints (n equality constraints $x - x^{\cdot}$

$+ x^- = x_0$, $2n$ lower and upper bounds on x^-, $2n$ lower and upper bounds on x^- and 1 budget constraint). Incorporation of upper and lower bounds on all assets as well as transaction cost results in a much larger and more complicated QP problem, with three times as many variables as the original QP problem.

Variable Transaction Costs

The fixed transactions costs model assumes that the cost of transacting is the same for all sizes of trades. Allowing transactions costs to vary with the size of the trade to account for the price impact of a trade, is a more accurate representation of securities markets. This approach divides up the range of trading each asset into a number of intervals and assigns a particular cost to each range. Thus, a small trade may have a small transaction cost, whereas a large trade may have a comparatively large transaction cost since the price impact of the trade will be larger. Accounting for this is particularly important when the market for an asset is thin, which is typical for small company stocks and many international assets. Rex Sinquefield (1995) of Dimensional Asset Advisors, who specializes in small stock funds, remarked that the price impact of trades in small stocks can be as high as 1000 basis points. Loeb (1983) provides more evidence of the price impact of trades.

The vector of asset holdings, x, is defined in terms of its deviation from the initial portfolio x_0.

$$x = x_0 + x^{\cdot} - x^{\cdot},$$

and each of $x^{\cdot}$ and x^- is expressed as the sum of holdings in each of k intervals:

$$x^{\cdot} = x_1^{\cdot} + x_2^{\cdot} + \cdots + x_k^{\cdot},$$

$$x^- = x_1^- + x_2^- + \cdots + x_k^-,$$

where

$$0 \le x_i^- \le d_i, \quad 0 \le x_i^{\cdot} \le e_i, \quad i = 1, \ldots, k.$$

The purchase transaction cost for the first interval x_0 to $x_0 + e_1$ is $p_1'x_1^{\cdot}$. If trading continues to the second interval $x_0 + e_1$ to $x_0 + e_1 + e_2$, the transaction cost is $p_1'x_1^{\cdot} + p_2'x_2^{\cdot}$. This model of stepped transactions costs corresponds to the execution of limit orders in the specialist's limit order book. Exhibit 30.2 shows transactions costs for $k = 3$ intervals.

In general, the total transaction cost is

$$p_1'x_1^{\cdot} + \cdots + p_k'x_k^{\cdot} + q_1'x_1^- + \cdots + q_k'x_k^- .$$

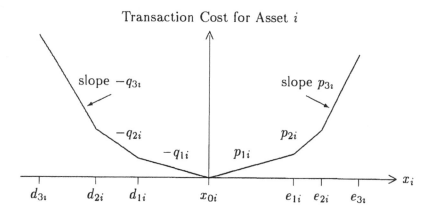

Exhibit 30-2. Variable transactions costs.

Note that this formulation is incremental. It implies an upper bound on total asset holdings of $x_0 + e_1 + \cdots + e_k$ and a lower bound on asset holdings of $x_0 - d_1 - \cdots - d_k$.

It may be important to allow for linear constraints in addition to the budget constraint. Accordingly, we replace $1'x = 1$ with $Ax - b$, where A is an (m, n) matrix. These constraints may include a budget constraint and other constraints, such as group constraints, constraints on beta, or company size. Although the linear constraints have been defined as equality constraints, this formulation allows for inequality constraints, which are converted to equality constraints by the inclusion of slack or surplus variables.

Incorporating these features into (30.7), the variable transactions costs QP formulation of the portfolio optimization problem becomes

$$
\begin{aligned}
\text{maximize: } & t\left(\mu'x - p_1'x_1^+ - \cdots - p_k'x_k^+ - q_1'x_1^- - \cdots - q_k'x_k^-\right) - \tfrac{1}{2}x'\Sigma x \\
\text{subject to: } \quad & Ax = b, \\
& x - x_1^+ - \cdots - x_k^+ + x_1^- + \cdots + x_k^- = x_0, \\
& 0 \le x_i^+ \le d_i, \quad i = 1,\ldots,k, \\
& 0 \le x_i^- \le e_i, \quad i = 1,\ldots,k.
\end{aligned}
\tag{30.8}
$$

Note that for n assets, the problem formulation (30.8) now has $(2k + 1)n$ variables and $(4k + 1)n + m$ constraints. For a problem with $n = 2000$ assets, $m = 1$ equality constraint, and $k = 3$ variable transactions costs, (30.8) is a QP with 14,000 variables and 26,001 constraints.

OVERVIEW OF QP ALGORITHMS

In this section we will argue that general purpose or off the shelf QP algorithms are unsuitable for all but very small portfolio optimization problems. This is because general purpose QP algorithms do not take advantage of the algebraic structure inherent in the portfolio optimization problem.

The earliest QP algorithm is that of Beale (1955, 1959). This algorithm has the basic property that it will solve a concave QP in a *finite* number of steps. More recent algorithms also possess this finiteness property but are preferred because they require considerably fewer iterations. Some methods are parametric. These methods introduce a scalar parameter into the QP such that when the parameter has a large value, an optimal solution for the parameterized problem is evident. The parameter is iteratively reduced to zero, whereupon the original QP is solved. Methods of this type are Wolfe (1959), Markowitz (1956), and the Complementary Pivot Method of Lemke and Howsen (1968). Markowitz's method is particularly noteworthy because it is designed specifically for portfolio optimization and generates the entire efficient frontier. In contrast, general purpose QP algorithms solve the problem formulated in (30.8) directly, to get the single optimal portfolio, given the value of the investor's risk tolerance parameter t. For problems with many asset bounds (such as problems with variable transactions costs), the direct method used by the general purpose algorithms can save a tremendous amount of computational time when compared with the parametric approach.

Most recent general purpose QP algorithms solve problems in exactly the same way. Indeed it has been demonstrated in Best (1984) that many QP algorithms will generate the same sequence of points when applied to the same problem and using the identical starting point. These algorithms include those of van de Panne and Whinston (1969), Fletcher (1971), Gill and Murray (1978) and, Best and Ritter (1988). They differ outwardly because of the different methods they use to solve linear equations or because they assume different model problems.

One parametric quadratic programming algorithm developed specifically for portfolio optimization is due to Perold (1984). This method is a generalization of Markowitz's (1956) parametric method which allows the covariance matrix to be semidefinite. In addition, Perold's method uses sparse matrix technology to solve the Karush-Kuhn-Tucker system for each parametric interval. The goal is to reduce the computation time of the algorithm as well as the workspace required by it. Although using sparse matrix factorization techniques is in general a good idea, we argue that it is far more effective to use such techniques *after* full advantage has been taken of the algebraic structure of the problem, as our method does.

We give a more detailed comparison of Perold's method to ours in a later section.

In order to explain some of the basic principles of QP algorithms, consider the model problem:

$$\max\left\{c'x + \frac{1}{2}x'Cx \,\middle|\, a_i'x \le b_i, \quad i = 1, \cdots, m\right\}, \tag{30.9}$$

where x is a vector of dimension n. This is a *general* problem, in that no assumptions are made concerning the structure of the m linear constraints. It is assumed that a feasible point x_0 is known. Constraint i is *active* at x_0 if $a_i x_0 = b_i$ and *inactive* otherwise. Let these active constraints be accumulated in a matrix A_0 with corresponding right hand-side b_0. Then $A_0 x_0 = b_0$. Most QP algorithms maximize the objective function for (30.9) in the intersection of the active constraints; i.e., they solve

$$\max\left\{c'x + \frac{1}{2}x'Cx \,\middle|\, A_0 x = b_0\right\}. \tag{30.10}$$

This is equivalent to solving the linear equations

$$\begin{bmatrix} C & A_0' \\ A_0 & 0 \end{bmatrix}\begin{bmatrix} x \\ u \end{bmatrix} = \begin{bmatrix} -c \\ b_0 \end{bmatrix}. \tag{30.11}$$

The system of equations (30.11) is called the *Karush-Kuhn-Tucker* system for the active set. In moving to a better point, a previously inactive constraint may become active. If so, its gradient is added to the rows of A_0 and (30.11) is resolved. The number of active constraints may increase for many iterations until the optimal solution for (30.11) is feasible for (30.9). At this point, the Karush-Kuhn-Tucker multipliers, u are examined. If all are nonnegative, the QP is solved. Otherwise, some active constraint with a negative multiplier is allowed to become inactive. This means that a row of A_0 will be deleted.

In general, the number of rows of A_0 will increase or decrease by 1 at each iteration of a QP algorithm. The dimension of the coefficient matrix of (30.11) will vary between (n, n) and $(2n, 2n)$. Various QP algorithms solve these equations using matrices of different types and sizes. One could, in fact, explicitly compute the inverse of

$$\begin{bmatrix} C & A_0' \\ A_0 & 0 \end{bmatrix}$$

and then the solution of (30.11) is

$$\begin{bmatrix} x \\ u \end{bmatrix} = \begin{bmatrix} C & A_0' \\ A_0 & 0 \end{bmatrix}^{-1}\begin{bmatrix} -c \\ b_0 \end{bmatrix}.$$

Exhibit 30-3.   Execution Requirements for a General Purpose QP Algorithm

Portfolio Model	Storage (MBytes)	Operations per Iteration (Millions)	Exec Time (Hrs:Min:Sec)
Restricted short sales	32	4	0:5:4
Fixed transactions Costs andbounds	288	36	0:45:36
Variable transactions Costs and bounds ($k = 3$)	1568	196	4:8:16

The various QP algorithm utilize different linear equation solving methods and matrices to solve (30.10). The sizes of these matrix structures varies between (n, n) and $(2n, 2n)$, depending on the number of active constraints and is a feature of the particular algorithm. The smallest of these is the Best and Ritter method, which requires the use of only an (n, n) matrix, independent of the number of active constraints.

To get a rough feel for the execution times required to solve the QP, suppose we apply this algorithm to a portfolio optimization problem with $n = 2000$ assets. To update a matrix of dimension (n, n) requires approximately n^2 arithmetic operations. Now there is no known way to estimate the total number of iterations required by the QP algorithm: it may be just a few or it may be extremely large. Nonetheless, let us imagine the algorithm takes n iterations. To estimate the total time required by the algorithm, we need to know the speed of the computer we are using. One of the authors who uses a Pentium processor-based workstation running at 60 MHz performed the following experiment. A small program was written to multiply 10^9 pairs of floating point numbers. When run, this required 38 seconds of computing time. Consequently, a single floating point operation required 3.8×10^{-8} seconds. This figure was used to compute the estimated computation time of a general purpose QP algorithm for each of our portfolio models as shown in Exhibit 30.3.

For the Restricted Short Sales model, a storage requirement of 32MB may not be too demanding for a workstation, and the 5 minutes execution time is probably acceptable. However, the computing demands for the Fixed Transactions Costs and Bounds model are excessive, while the Variable Transactions Costs and Bounds model has impractical computational requirements. In the next section we show how an efficient, special purpose QP algorithm can be developed for portfolio optimization problems. One final note: the estimated execution times in Exhibit 30.3 are quite fictitious since they are based on the assumption of n iterations of the QP algorithm. They would be multiplied by 1000 if it turned out that $1000n$ iterations were required.

A SPECIALIZED QP ALGORITHM FOR LARGE-SCALE PORTFOLIO OPTIMIZATION

The specialization of the QP algorithm for large-scale portfolio optimization consists of three innovations: (1) determination of a good starting point for the QP algorithm, (2) efficient solution of the Karush-Kuhn-Tucker system for the active constraints using a small kernel matrix, and (3) handling of all upper and lower bounds as well as break points for variable transactions costs *implicitly* rather than explicitly. Incorporation of these three innovations produces a specialized QP algorithm, which requires a small number of iterations, requires a small workspace, performs a small amount of computational work per iteration, and, consequently, can solve large-scale portfolio optimization problems very quickly on a workstation.

Solving a QP is equivalent to determining the indices of those constraints which are active at the optimal solution. Let us call this the *optimal active set*. Once the optimal active set is known, the optimal solution can be obtained by solving the linear equations (30.11) for the problem formulation (30.10). If we start the QP algorithm with an active set that is close to the optimal active set, then relatively few QP iterations will be required to solve the problem. This is to be compared with a general purpose QP algorithm which would begin with an arbitrary feasible point.

For a portfolio that is optimized regularly, one would expect that the active set for the initial portfolio x_0 would be quite close to the optimal active set, and so x_0 is an excellent candidate with which to initiate the QP algorithm. However, x_0 may not be feasible for (30.8). In this case, we can use a variant of the Upper Bounded Simplex Method (see for example Best and Ritter, 1985) to solve a Phase 1 problem for the constraints

$$Ax = b, \quad d \leq x \leq e.$$

The modification simply keeps nonbasic variables at their corresponding component of x_0 unless forced to a bound.

The Karush-Kuhn-Tucker system for (30.8) will be extremely large because it has $2(k+1)n$ variables, the equality constraint relating x to x_0 will always be active, and many variables will be at a bound. If the benefit of moving an asset away from its initial holding is smaller than its transaction cost, then it is implicitly considered to be at a bound. The critical information for the Karush-Kuhn-Tucker system may be obtained by solving a much smaller system than (30.8). The constraints of (30.10) temporarily force the many variables that are at their bounds to remain at their bounds. Let B denote a sub matrix of columns of A corresponding to variables *not* at a bound. B is analogous to the basis matrix for the simplex method of linear programming. In the LP case B is square, whereas here it will generally have more columns than rows. Let x_B denote the sub vector of variables not at a bound. The components of x_B are called *basic* variables. The remaining variables are called *nonbasic* and are denoted by x_{NB}. By substituting x_{NB} into (30.11) and rearranging terms, we have the linear system

$$\begin{bmatrix} \Sigma_{BB} & B' \\ B & 0 \end{bmatrix} \begin{bmatrix} x_B \\ u \end{bmatrix} = \begin{bmatrix} c_1 \\ b \end{bmatrix}, \tag{30.12}$$

where

Σ_{BB} is the sub matrix of Σ corresponding to x_B,
c_1 is computed from the problem data and x_{NB},
and u are the multipliers associated with the constraints $Ax = b$.

We call (30.12) and its coefficient matrix the *kernel system* and *kernel matrix*, respectively.

Our algorithm is a specialization of the general purpose Algorithm A described in Best (1985). As such, it proceeds first by minimizing the objective function in the intersection of the active constraints. As the current kernel equations are solved, feasibility is accounted for. An asset may be moved to a bound or an asset may be moved to the end of an interval corresponding to the current Variable Transactions Costs. This is treated as a new active constraint, and the corresponding row and column of the kernel matrix are deleted. The inverse of the kernel matrix, or a factorization of it, is then updated. As the algorithm continues, other new constraints become active, and the size of the kernel matrix continues to decrease. Eventually, a quasistationary point will be determined. (See Best [1985] for details.) Note that the kernel matrix can never be smaller than $(2m, 2m)$ since this would mean an extreme point for (30.8) has been obtained, and an extreme point is a quasistationary point.

Once a quasistationary point has been determined, the algorithm tests for optimality. This requires the calculation of the Karush-Kuhn-Tucker multipliers for all of the active constraints. Since (30.8) has $4nk$ inequality constraints, there are potentially this many multipliers to compute. However, each asset holding can only be either in the interior of a Variable Transactions Costs interval or at an end point of it. In the latter case, two multipliers must be computed; one for an increase into the next interval and one for a decrease into the previous interval. Of course, when the asset holding is at either its lower or upper bound, only one multiplier is computed. The various multipliers can be obtained by substituting u from the solution of (30.12) into the dual feasibility conditions for the problem and utilizing complementary slackness. The smallest multiplier associated with an active inequality constraint is then selected. If it is nonnegative, then all optimality conditions for the problem have been satisfied, and an optional solution thus has been obtained. If it is indeed strictly negative, then the corresponding constraint is dropped from the active set. This means that the data for the new basic variable are added as a new row and column to the coefficient matrix for the kernel problem. The algorithm then proceeds by seeking a new quasistationary point, and the process is repeated. The optimal solution obtained by this method is a true global optimum.

The variance-covariance matrix Σ may not be positive definite. It is possible for it to be positive semidefinite. This would be the case if there were dependencies among the assets, or if one or more risk free assets were included in the model. Some QP algorithms explicitly exclude the semidefinite case. Markowitz's (1956) method is restrictive in this way. Wolfe's (1959) method has two variations, one for the positive definite case (the "short form") and one for the semidefinite case (the "long form"). Our method allows for both the positive definite and positive semidefinite cases in a single unified framework. Positive semidefiniteness, or singularity of Σ, comes into play at just one point in our algorithm. After a quasi-stationary point has been obtained and a previously active constraint is being dropped, then a new variable becomes basic, and its associated data are added as a new row and column to the coefficient matrix of the new kernel problem. If Σ is positive definite, the new coefficient matrix will be non-singular. If Σ is only positive semidefinite, the coefficient matrix may be singular. In this latter case, a vector in the null space of the kernel matrix leads to a new nonbasic variable. The net effect is a switch of nonbasic and basic variables, or a switch of row and column of the kernel matrix. It has been shown in Best (1985) that after the switch, the modified kernel matrix is nonsingular. Note that if Σ were the zero matrix (and thus our model problem were an LP, a perfectly legitimate special case), then the switching would occur at each and every iteration.

We are now in a position to expand the comparison of our method with that of Perold. Suppose both methods are applied to the model problem (30.9) and that the constraints of (30.9) include upper and lower bounds on all assets. Then the coefficient matrix (call it H) of the linear system to be solved at each iteration, namely (30.11), will contain many unit vectors and thus be sparse. Perold's method uses a LU sparse matrix decomposition of H. However, H can be quite large; at least (n, n) and at most $(2n, 2n)$, where n is the number of assets, and there is no guarantee on the size of the factor matrices L and U. By contrast, our method solves the linear system (30.12) at each iteration. Let H_B denote the coefficient matrix for (30.12), i.e., the kernel matrix. The number of rows of the submatrix B is precisely the number of linear equality constraints in the given problem. This number is usually quite small. Indeed, it could represent just the budget constraint. Therefore, the dimension of H_B is close to that of Σ_{BB}, namely, the number of assets, not at a bound, and for many problems this number will be quite small. The situation is similar for variable transactions costs.

If our method were applied to an LP ($\Sigma = 0$), then the kernel matrix would have constant dimension $(2m, 2m)$ at each iteration, and it would be of the form

$$\begin{bmatrix} 0 & B' \\ B & 0 \end{bmatrix},$$

where B is the basis matrix for applying the Upper Bounded Revised Simplex Method [see Best and Ritter (1985)], and the Variable Transactions Costs are handled in a suitable manner.

For Variable Transactions Costs, if an asset holding is at an end point of its interval, the situation is essentially the same as if the holding were at a bound. Our experience has been that only a small proportion of asset holdings tend to differ from their bounds, where transactions costs create implicit bounds. For a 2000 asset problem, there may be 10 percent, or 200 such assets. Usually the number of rows of A is quite small, so let us ignore it for purposes of comparison. The kernel matrix for (30.12) is then at most (200,200). Exhibit 30.4 shows the storage requirements and execution times for the specialized QP algorithm. Comparison of these figures with those of Exhibit 30.4 shows quite dramatically the importance of a specialized QP algorithm for portfolio optimization.

We conclude this section by giving actual execution times for our QP algorithm applied to four problems. Exhibit 30.5 summarizes the results of four portfolio optimizations with Financiometrics, Inc.'s Quadratic Optimization System, which implements the Best-Kale algorithm. The optimization was done on a PC with a 400-Megahertz Pentium II processor. From Exhibit 30.5 the first test problem has 500 assets and a single linear constraint and the number of basic variables (n_B) at each iteration varied between 1 and 6. The dimension of the kernel matrix for (30.12) is thus between (1,1) and (6,6), and the number of arithmetic operations to update the kernel matrix at each iteration varies between 1^2 and 6^2. By contrast, a general purpose QP algorithm would be updating a coefficient matrix like that for (30.11), the dimension of which would vary between (n, n) and $(2n, 2n)$. For the first problem, a general purpose QP algorithm would be updating a (500, 500) to (1000, 1000) matrix at a computational cost of between 500^2 to 1000^2 arithmetic operations per iteration. It is the dramatically smaller number of arithmetic operations per iteration that results in very small execution times for the Best-Kale algorithm.

The situation is similar for the second test problem. This problem has 70 linear equality constraints, and each one of them will have an associated basic variable. For the Best-Kale algorithm, the computational work at each iteration is proportional to between 70^2 and 75^2 operations, whereas a general purpose QP algorithm would require between 570^2 to 1000^2 operations per iteration. The situation is similar for the third and fourth prob-

Exhibit 30-4. Execution Requirements for a Specialized QP Algorithm

Portfolio Model	Storage (MBytes)	Operations per Iteration (Millions)	Exec Time (Hrs:Min:Sec)
Restricted Short Sales	.32	.04	0:0:30
Fixed Transactions Costs and Bounds	.32	.04	0:0:30
Variable Transactions Costs and Bounds	.32	.04	0:0:30

Exhibit 30-5. Execution Requirements for a Specialized QP Algorithm

Problem Number	Number of Linear Constraints	Number of Assets	Computation Time (Seconds)	n_B
1	1	500	2	1 to 6
2	70	500	5	70 to 75
3	1	1000	11	1 to 32
4	70	1000	26	70 to 88

lems and is even more favorable to the Best-Kale algorithm because the number of basic variables remains very small compared to the total number of assets.

CONCLUSION

Specialization of quadratic programming techniques for the purpose of solving large-scale portfolio optimization problems by taking advantage of the algebraic structure of these problems can yield dramatic improvements in computer memory requirements and execution times. The innovations we have introduced can produce improvements of over 1000 times in execution times for the optimization of large portfolios. These innovations make it practical to solve large-scale portfolio optimization problems on a workstation.

Notes

Beale, E.M.L., On minimizing a convex function subject to linear inequalities, *J. R. Stat. Soc.* (B), 17, 173, 1955.

Beale, E.M.L., On quadratic programming, *Nav. Res. Log. Q.*, 6, 227, 1959.

Best, M.J., Equivalence of some quadratic programming algorithms. *Math. Prog.*, 30, 71, 1984.

Best, M.J. and Grauer, R.R., The analytics of sensitivity analysis for mean-variance portfolio problems. *Int. Rev. Fin. Anal.*, 1(1), 17, 1992.

Best, M.J. and Ritter, K., *Linear Programming: Active Set Analysis and Computer Programs,* Prentice-Hall, Englewood Cliffs, NJ 1985.

Best, M.J. and Ritter, K., An effective algorithm for quadratic minimization problems, *Z. Op. Res.*, 32(5), 271, 1988.

Fletcher, R., A general quadratic programming algorithm, *J. Inst. Math. Applic.* 7, 76, 1971.

Gill, P.E. and Murray W., Numerically stable methods for quadratic programming, *Math. Prog.*, 14, 349, 1978.

Lemke, C.E., On complementary pivot theory, in *Mathematics of the Decision Sciences, Part I*, Dantzig, G.B. and Veinott, A.F., Jr., Eds., American Mathematical Society, 1968, 95-114.

Loeb, T.F., Trading cost: the critical link between investment information and results, *Fin. Anal. J.*, 39(3), 39, 1983.

Markowitz, H., Portfolio selection, *J. Fin.*, 77, March 1952.

Markowitz, H., The optimization of a quadratic function subject to linear constraints, *Nav. Res. Log. Q.*, III, 111, 1956.

van de Panne, C. and Whinston A., The symmetric formulation of the simplex method for quadratic programming, *Econometrica*, 37, 507, 1969.

Perold, A. F., Large-scale portfolio optimization, *Manage. Sci.*, 30(10), 1143, 1984.

Sinquefield, R.A., Value and Size Factors in Balanced Portfolios, Ibbotson Associates' 1995 Institutional Software and Data User Conference.

Wolfe, P., The simplex method for quadratic programming, *Econometrica*, 27, 382, 1959.

Authors' Bios

Michael J. Best *is on the faculty of the Department of Optimization and Combinatorics at the University of Waterloo, and is a principal at Financiometrics Inc. He has a Ph. D. in Operations Research from the University of California, Berkeley, and is a leading authority in the field of quadratic programming. He has written several articles and a book on mathematical programming, and his consulting work includes optimization applications in banking and portfolio management.*

Jivendra K. Kale *is on the faculty of the School of Business at Golden Gate University in San Francisco, and is a Principal at Financiometrics Inc. He has a Ph. D. in Finance from the University of California, Berkeley, and has worked as a senior consultant at BARRA and Gifford Fong Associates. He has written several articles in the areas of market microstructure, equity risk models, and portfolio optimization, and his consulting work includes portfolio optimization and performance attribution for money management applications.*

Chapter 31

Risk Management Meets Customer Relationship Management: Closing the Data Mining Loop with DCOM and Visual Basic

Eric Apps
Ken Ono

RISK MANAGEMENT IS A CORE COMPETENCY OF GROWING IMPORTANCE FOR BUSINESS ENTERPRISES. Failing to effectively manage risk negatively impacts on performance, occasionally in dramatic fashion. Conversely, improving the effectiveness of risk management procedures and systems can generate significant improvements in operating performance and results, not a trivial outcome in the increasingly competitive and uncertain environment confronting most businesses.

When risk management systems are more closely integrated with other enterprise applications and when risk managers work collaboratively with other lines of business professionals, these improvements can become exponential, transforming risks into identified, actionable corporate opportunities. Data mining, already an important part of the risk management process, has an important role to play in facilitating tighter integration of risk management and other key corporate functions, at both technical and operational levels.

In this article, we review this role — in the context of the relationship between risk management and customer relationship management — and look forward to the "next steps" in the evolution of the data mining industry. We examine how improvements in data mining technology, notably through the adoption of Microsoft's DCOM (Distributed Component Object Model) and VB (Visual Basic) technologies, can enable risk managers and their line of business peers to "close the loop," technically and operationally, combining and integrating improved risk management processes with more effective line of business enterprise applications.

RISK MANAGEMENT AT THE MILLENIUM

Risk managers are gatekeepers, responsible for identifying, quantifying, and managing corporate risk exposures. Over the past decade, technology has played an important role in this process, as well as in developing, testing, and implementing risk management strategies. Improved and more timely access to relevant data and the emergence of a variety of statistical, analytical, and visualization tools promoting data exploration and knowledge acquisition have facilitated improvements in the risk management process.

As always, however, technology is a double-edged sword. As we move into the twenty-first century, the advent of the "e-corporation" with its "digital nervous system" has substantially raised the stakes of the risk management game, from an organizational perspective and for risk managers in particular. Enterprises are increasingly dependent on electronic intermediation in their commercial relationships with customers, suppliers and partners. In this environment both event-related and transactional data volumes are growing exponentially, and decision timeframes are being correspondingly compressed. Risk managers require more effective means to identify, assess, and manage risk — quickly.

Enterprises are also concurrently deploying more sophisticated knowledge discovery technologies to monitor, evaluate, and "learn" from the myriad electronic interactions created by accelerating technology innovation. Customer relationship management (CRM) systems, which are designed to promote a greater understanding and awareness of customer needs and related business opportunities, are one popular example of this trend.

Despite the fact that risk managers and other managers, such as CRM adopters, are often exploring the same data elements, their objectives and often their agendas remain distinct. This operational dichotomy is suboptimal (and therefore creates unnecessary risk exposure) for both operational and technical reasons. The CRM arena is illustrative. Operationally, effective "customer relationship management" implies (among other things) that appropriate risk/return profiles are devised and assigned (explicitly or implicitly) for customer types and ideally individual customers, and that corporate interactions are reoriented around the opportunity sets these assigned profiles reveal. From a technical perspective, the process of exploring data and acquiring knowledge in risk management and CRM contexts are also closely related and share common features.

DATA MINING IN RISK MANAGEMENT

The process of applying data mining and knowledge discovery analytical tools and methodologies to corporate data assets already plays an important role in the overall analytical tool kit used by enterprises to assess, evaluate, and manage the myriad factors that impact on risk. Most innovative enterprises have come to realize that their data assets are their largest "off balance sheet item," with all the consequences this entails in terms of unlocking asset value.

Data mining is an inherently horizontal or "infrastructure" technology. It applies across industries and, within each enterprise, has relevance in a wide variety of contexts. From a pure risk management perspective, data mining can facilitate the process of managing and reducing risk by identifying and assessing the significance of large volumes of enterprise data which may impact on risk and by modeling the risk exposures resulting from the presence or absence of these identified variables. For example, data mining can be used to model, through exploration, analysis, categorization, reporting, and rules generation, the factors that impact on numerous areas of risk exposure, such as incidence of fraud, creditworthiness, payment and default risk, collections management, production risk, or litigation risk.

The fundamental traditional goals of the data mining process, using automated exploration and analytical techniques to uncover actionable business information, which can be used to achieve the objectives of risk management and reduction, continue to be relevant. Data mining tools have become increasingly important in assisting risk managers in responding to the time and productivity pressures they face getting to "end of job." And they continue to improve. Data mining tools are becoming increasingly sophisticated, powerful, and accessible to a wider range of business users for risk analysis.

These improvements are important for risk managers because they achieve two important objectives: (1) enabling more rapid, productive, and effective completion of risk management modeling analysis and (2) enabling a broader range of users to participate in the analytical process.

These improvements enhance productivity at two levels — by permitting more comprehensive and timely assessments of all relevant risk factors and by enabling a more efficient division of labor among those involved in the risk assessment process.

But performance enhancements — the ability to effectively explore and rapidly evaluate ever-growing volumes of data in the search for knowledge — tell only a small and entirely expected part of the story. Software is always supposed to get better! More fundamentally, certain data mining technologies now make it possible for enterprises to more easily implement predictive models which impact on risk in a number of operational contexts and to readily integrate these technologies with other operational systems. To see the "next step" in data mining for risk management requires an understanding of Microsoft's DCOM and VB technologies and how they can promote more effective integration of risk management, technically and operationally, with other business operations.

COM — MICROSOFT'S OBJECT FRAMEWORK

Most Windows users are familiar with OLE (Object Linking and Embedding). You unconsciously use it for everyday operations such as inserting pictures into documents. At the heart of OLE is COM (Component Object Model). COM essentially allows two arbitrary software components to talk to each other. COM has recently been extended to Distributed COM (or DCOM). DCOM works just like COM but facilitates a broader range of connectivity and deployment options by permitting communication among software components on remote machines. DCOM is shipped as a standard part of the current Microsoft operating system. One of the fundamental advantages of COM/DCOM is that it facilitates interoperability by enabling any DCOM-compliant software application to be readily integrated with or communicate to any other similarly designed application.

The only significant competitor to COM/DCOM is currently CORBA (Common Object Request Broker Architecture), which is promoted, with varying degrees of enthusiasm, by other hardware and software vendors such as Sun, Oracle, and IBM. While CORBA has its own technical strengths, Microsoft's overwhelming dominance in the operating system environment, its looming presence in the database management systems environment, and the extensive third party customization, systems integration, and enterprise application domains which revolve around Microsoft-based standards make the outlook for CORBA an open issue. These factors, combined with the fact that numerous software development tools vendors are releasing connectivity tools that allow DCOM- and CORBA-based systems to interoperate, suggest that DCOM is likely to be the predominant deployment paradigm for business applications, including those in the risk management domain, over at least the next two technology development cycles.

Visual Basic

As a second tool in its well-stocked strategic arsenal, Microsoft has developed and actively promotes Visual Basic (VB) as a programming language and software development environment, particularly for enterprise applications. VB is unremarkable and, in some respects, the "same old, same old" that has been around for decades. However, it is particularly effective at very quickly and conveniently producing and using COM components and ActiveX controls. Developers can knock out applications and components remarkably quickly using precoded DCOM compliant wizards and code generators. And where Microsoft stops, hundreds of other software development companies start by offering a dizzying array of additional add-ons and components, many of which are free or virtually so.

Any COM object exposes all the methods, properties, and events that make up its interface. Development environments such as VB can understand these interfaces. Using COM, a developer can create objects that seamlessly integrate into any COM-enabled Windows development environment. Delphi, PowerBuilder, and J++ all support COM. One the most significant aspects of VB is not the program itself but its prevalence and the legions of developers who live, breathe, and use it. Microsoft dominates the development tools market like no other company.

USING DCOM AND VISUAL BASIC TO CLOSE THE LOOP BETWEEN RISK MANAGEMENT AND CRM

The combination of DCOM and VB provides a powerful framework for the integration of the data mining and modeling process with both risk management and other line of business operations. Using data mining components, for example, developers can create applications that tightly integrate predictive modeling as an integral step of any business process where data mining is relevant to business outcomes. In a risk management context, these predictive models can then be implemented — in simple to develop and deploy applications — to monitor, identify, and initiate appropriate responses to any identified event or transaction-related activity that impacts on risk.

As powerful as it has been to date, data mining remains used as a relatively "blunt" instrument — predominantly for "understanding" data through exploration and high level modeling; it is less frequently used for interactive strategic business planning or continuous outcome improvement. Specific predictive modeling activities — segmenting markets, identifying customer attributes, building risk profiles, and the like — have focused on relatively simple tasks, such as to score datasets, to support strategic business plans, or to guide and refine specific marketing campaigns. Often the modeling effort itself has been, by and large, the "end of job" and the modeling analysis has been largely the preserve of the quantitative expert.

With the advent of DCOM/VB, a new vista of possibilities is presented to those who truly understand their data and wish to maximize their competitive advantage, in risk management as well as other contexts. Integration of risk management systems and customer relationship management systems through data mining-driven processes, for example, can "close the loop," enabling sales representatives in the field to run data collected during their initial customer interaction (in real time, instantaneously as received) against one or many predictive models. They can immediately understand and assign, for example, the risk profile associated with the particular customer, turning what might otherwise be a riskier interaction for the enterprise into a product or service sales opportunity tailored and priced specifically for their needs, while also being profitable to (or at least less risky for) the enterprise.

Predictive models (covering such risks as fraud, customer default, collection and loss recovery, or attrition) developed through the application of data mining technology can also be operationalized and deployed — embedded in useful and easy to understand applications — with relevant line of business personnel across the enterprise. Call centers and customer service and support bureaus are obvious examples in the CRM context. These deployed applications focus on the end result — prompt and appropriate intervention action in response to targeted/tested behaviors manifested through the myriad customer interactions an enterprise's personnel confront each working day. Those involved have only the vaguest notion, if any, that data mining has played a role in shaping the interaction; they are simply doing their job.

As complex as this sounds, the complexities are largely organizational ones ,and the implementation is relatively trivial, involving the use of VB to quickly and cost-effectively establish the connectivity bridges.

CONCLUSION

COM is universal glue for software. Using COM-enabled data mining technology can be a highly strategic technique for incorporating more robust knowledge discovery into the risk management process and integrating the risk management process more tightly with other operational systems and business applications, such as customer relationship management solutions. The results: more improved risk profiles; more effectively managed outcomes; and improvements in key operating performance indicators, such as revenue growth, cost reduction, and profitability.

Authors' Bios

Eric Apps and *Ken Ono* are the President and Vice-President, Technology, respectively, of AN-GOSS Software Corporation, a Toronto, Canada-based developer and publisher of advanced data mining software.

Chapter 32
Java-Based Application Servers for the Financial Sector

Anura Gurugé

ONCE Y2K BECOMES HISTORY, the most pressing challenge facing MIS professionals in the financial sector will be that of persuasively leveraging the popularity and the reach of the Web to enhance corporate revenues, market share, and profitability. Indubitably, the Web will have to be gainfully harnessed to dramatically increase corporate earnings via electronic commerce transactions, to expedite customer interactions via automated "Internet Call Center" and, in general, to enhance overall competitiveness through new, innovative electronic services (e.g., home-banking, "instantaneous" loan approvals, etc.) Though Web-based, online investing has only been around since around 1996 and security concerns still abound, a May 1999 report from Dataquest shows that 15 million people in North America alone were using the Web on a regular basis to track their investment portfolios, while 4.5 million were already buying and selling shares and mutual funds online. Charles Schwab, one of the pioneers in Web-based trading, claims that it has 2.2 million online customers — and that 61 percent of their trades, totaling nearly $7 billion a week, are now conducted securely and expeditiously over the Internet without any intervention by customer service representatives or brokers. Web-based trading, Home Banking, and Internet Call Centers by 2001 will be indelible, integral, and strategic features of the financial sector landscape.

Established, successful financial institutes will invariably discover that they do not have the luxury of time, resources, or latitude to develop brand new systems from scratch just to address the burgeoning Web opportunities. Instead, they will have no choice but to extend their existing, highly proven information systems, replete with mission-critical applications and diverse databases, to incorporate Web-based transactions. Java application servers are rapidly gaining a stellar reputation as very powerful, flexible, strategic, cost-effective, and platform-independent means of synergistically integrating existing information systems with the Web. Java application servers, in essence, enable existing information systems, applications, databases, and processes to be reused in the context of the Web.

WHAT IS A JAVA APPLICATION SERVER?

A Java application server is a server resident, middleware component. It is written and developed using the highly acclaimed and now widely popular Java programming language that was introduced by Sun Microsystems in 1995 to explicitly address the needs of Web-oriented applications and the creation of truly interactive Web pages. A Java application server sits between a standard Web server and the existing information systems — where the existing information systems are likely to consist of a mix of mainframes, minicomputers, UNIX systems, and NT servers.

Java application servers utilize a classic three-tier architecture, where the existing information systems act as data servers and the clients are PC or workstation users connected to the Web or an intranet. Within this three-tier configuration, the Java application server, true to its name, acts as the "application server component" between the data servers and the clients. Exhibit 32-1 shows the three-tier architecture of a Java application server.

Java application servers will enable financial institutions to readily and cost-effectively implement a new genre of object-oriented applications specifically targeted at Web users. These new, Web-centric applications, however, will be able to adroitly access, manipulate, synthesize, and above all reuse any and all forms of existing corporate data and business logic — irrespective of their nature, location, or vintage. This "reusability" aspect is the primary lure and justification for this type of application server vis-à-vis Web integration. These application servers enable corporations to maximize and extrapolate the significant investments that they already have in terms of computing platforms, mission-critical applications, and databases to address their emerging Web requirements — obviating the need to recreate or replicate resources purely for Web use.

Feature-rich and proven Java application servers are now readily available from a variety of different companies — including some big names such as Netscape and Sun. Some of the better known Java application servers now available include: BEA's WebLogic, Sun's NetDynamics, Bluestone's Sapphire/Web, Novera's jBusiness, Netscape's application server, and Inprise's application server.

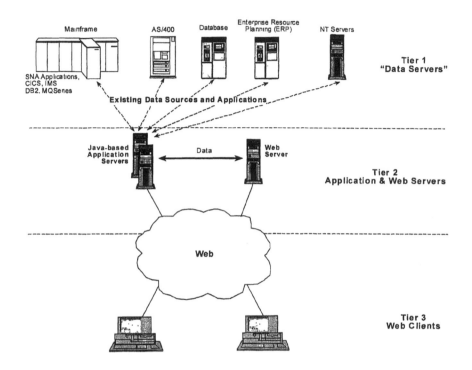

Exhibit 32-1. The three-tier client-server architecture of Java-based application servers.

WHY JAVA?

Middleware solutions that enable existing information systems to be extended to incorporate Web-based applications do not necessarily have to be Java based, and there are indeed many non-Java application server offerings on the market today, with IBM's well-known MQseries family being but one example. There are, however, definite tangible advantages for opting for a Java application server. Key among these advantages are the following.

Platform Independence

"Write once; run anywhere" is Java's overriding and now substantiated value-proposition. Consequently a Java application server is not tied to a particular computing platform such as UNIX or NT. Instead, Java application servers can be deployed on a range of platforms that, in addition to UNIX and NT, include HP 3000s, IBM AS/400s, and even IBM (or compatible) mainframes. This platform independence eliminates concerns related to scalability and platform obsolescence. Scalability, in particular, is a major concern when it comes to developing Web applications, given the huge pool of potential users on the Internet. Thus, in many instances, corporations have to envision the need to accommodate thousands of concurrent Web users per application. Having the flexibility of being able to change platforms easily, without having to change application servers, mitigates scalability concerns, since one is not locked into one particular platform technology, operating system (e.g., NT), or vendor.

Effortless Extensibility Thanks to Enterprise JavaBeans

Java, true to contemporary programming philosophy, is inherently object oriented. In addition, there is a widely endorsed standard for server side Java object development and integration, specified by Sun in 1997, known as Enterprise JavaBeans (EJBs). Today most of the major Java application servers include comprehensive support for EJBs. With this EJB support, the functionality of a Java application server can be readily enhanced and extended using different EJB-based components from different vendors. Thus, EJBs elevate Java's trademark platform independence to the next logical level, software vendor independence. Given the support for EJBs, one is no longer locked into one particular software vendor when it comes to Java application servers. A Java application server from one vendor can be enhanced using EJBs from another vendor. It is even possible to mix-and-match EJB components from different Java application servers and from different vendors. This is particularly germane when it comes to back-end connectivity options to existing systems. A corporation might select a Java application server based on its prowess in the areas of directory services, object integration, load-balancing, and database access, only to discover that this particular product currently does not offer 5250 access to IBM AS/400 systems. Such an omission is no longer a show-stopper. It would, in general, be possible to get the necessary connectivity option, in this example a 5250 access module, in the form of an EJB component from another vendor.

Standardization on Java for Web Applications

Applets written in Java and dynamically downloaded from a Web server on demand are by far the most widely used mechanism to extend the functionality of Web pages by transparently adding interactive intelligence at the client side. Today it is difficult to spend any time surfing the Web without encountering a Web page that will automatically download a Java applet to bolster the capability of the Web page or in some cases even the Web Browser being used. Savvy Web designers no longer think of Web pages consisting entirely of HyperText Markup Language (HTML)-based content. Instead, they think of Web pages as an amalgamation of HTML and Java applets. Consequently, corporations will inevitably end up with in-house Java programming expertise and experience as they start to venture into Web-based applications. Furthermore, given its Web orientation and platform-independent ubiquity, Java is rapidly becoming the programming language of choice among the software development community. The legions of COBOL programmers that have gamely sustained financial sector applications for the last 3 decades will over the next decade be replaced by Java programmers. Of that there can be no doubt or debate. Given that Java will invariably play a key role in the development of future Web applications and that corporations will end up with a growing pool of Java aficionados, it makes strategic sense to standardize on Java application servers as well. It should also be noted that Java application servers do support applications written in Java. Thus, new Web applications as well as applications to integrate existing data sources with Web page content can be written in Java and executed within the context of a Java application server.

Architected Robustness

Java is typically an interpreted language that runs within a program execution environment known as a Java Virtual Machine (JVM). JVMs are architected with comprehensive memory protection and validation to obviate any type of failures due to one program violating the memory space of another component. The interpretive nature of Java coupled with this memory protection ensures that Java applications in general enjoy exceptional "up-time" and resilience. A Java application server, which is but a Java application, should thus prove to be a robust and reliable server-side mission-critical offering capable of delivering the high availability vital for most financial sector applications.

A PLETHORA OF CLIENTS — SOME THIN, SOME SOPHISTICATED

Most Web applications are targeted at Web Browser users. Data exchange with these users will be via Web pages, augmented with Java applets where necessary. HTML-based Web pages and applets will be downloaded to the Web Browser, from a standard Web Server, using the HyperText Transfer Protocol (HTTP). Security in the form of user authentication and end-to-end data encryption between the browser and the server will be realized using either secure sockets layer (SSL) technology or secure HTTP (HTTPS), which is essentially a form of short-duration, per-transaction SSL.

These applications that rely purely on HTML-based Web pages and Java for their data interchange are known as "Thin Client" Web applications. The term "Thin Client" alludes to the fact that the only software required at the client is a basic operating system (e.g., Windows 95) plus a standard Web Browser à la Netscape Navigator or Microsoft's Internet Explorer. No additional software is required to support any dynamically downloaded Java applets, since modern Browsers now include a built-in, full-function JVM to execute Java applets. Such Web applications can also be accessed from network computers (NCs), in addition to PCs, Apple Macs, and UNIX workstations.

All Java application servers support this type of "Browser Only" Web applications that rely purely on HTML, HTTP, and Java applets for all of their data interchange. The applications server, true to the conventions of the Web, will, however, work in tandem with a standard Web server to download the application specific Web pages and applets required by the browser users. Security across the Web will usually be handled using standard SSL or HTTPS between the browser and the Web server — in the same manner as if there was no application server involved.

Some Web-oriented financial applications may, however, require more local processing at the PC/workstation than is feasible with just a "thin client" approach. In such situations it would be normal to have an application program that will execute on the client machine in conjunction with a server component. These client applications, where necessary, will execute alongside a browser — rather than within the browser per se as is the case with Java applets invoked through a Web page. Such client applications could be written in C, Visual Basic, C++ or Java. Java application servers will typically support such "sophisticated" (or "fat") clients, in addition to, and concurrently, with conventional "thin clients." Thus, corporations can enjoy total flexibility when it comes to the design and implementation of their new "client-server," Web-centric applications.

The client application could use any Internet Protocol (IP)-based mechanism, including Transmission Control Protocol (TCP), User Datagram Protocol, or HTTP, to interact with its companion server component executing on the Java application server. It would also be possible to use an application-specific protocol, on top of IP, or even TCP/IP, to realize the client-server communications. This client-server communication would not occur through a Web server and would take place directly between the client and the server across the Web or an intranet. Consequently, the application, rather than the Java application server or a Web server, will be responsible for any and all security, such as end-to-end data encryption. While Java application servers do support client-server applications that rely on this type of nonobject-oriented communication, it is not the approach they advocate. Java application servers promote and encourage object-oriented program development.

With Java application servers it is possible to use standards-based object invocation and interaction between the client and the server. Today, objects created by different groups or vendors can be uniformly invoked and integrated, irrespective of differences in platform type between the object's source and its destination, using a methodology known as an "Object Request Broker" (ORB). The industry standard for ORB is the "Common Object Request Broker Architecture" (CORBA) that was developed by the Object Management Group (OMG). Java application servers support CORBA at the server level for server-side applications, as well as CORBA-based object manipulation across the network between clients and a server. The standard for performing CORBA across IP networks such as the Internet and intranets is known as "Internet Inter-ORB Protocol" (IIOP). Java application servers support IIOP for object-based client-server interactions.

The native Java scheme for ORB is known as "remote method invocation" (RMI). Most Java application servers also support RMI. RMI will be used when the client application is an object-oriented application written in Java. A client-side Java application differs from a Java applet in that it is not dynamically downloaded from a Web server as a part of a Web page-related operation. Instead, a Java application is a traditional application that is written in Java. Whereas Java applets execute in the JVM provided by Web browsers, Java applications run on a JVM provided by the operating system. Thus, Java applications are not tied to Web browsers or Web servers. Java applications can, however, run alongside an active browser.

IIOP- and RMI-based interactions occur directly between the server component running on a Java application server and the relevant clients. These interactions do not go through a Web server. When using IIOP or RMI, the security measures used between the client and the server will again be the responsibility of the actual application, rather than that of the application server or a Web server.

The types of clients that can be supported with a Java application server can thus be summarized as follows in Exhibit 32-2.

THE ANATOMY OF A JAVA APPLICATION SERVER

A typical Java application server, as shown in Exhibit 32-3, can be thought of as consisting of the following key components:

Integration Engine

This is the heart of the application server and the execution environment in which the Web applications will run. The integration engine will be highly object-oriented and support EJBs, CORBA, and RMI to facilitate industry standards-based object invocation, manipulation, and integration. With scalability being a perennial issue vis-à-vis Web applications, nearly all Java application servers provide a built-in scheme for load-balancing, whereby multiple instances of the Java application server, each on a separate platform, can work together, in parallel, dynamically servicing a large

Exhibit 32-2. Types of Clients Supported with a Java application server

Client Type	Client Software	Protocol	Object-Oriented	Web Server Involved	Client Application Written In
Thin client	Web browser	HTML/Java over HTTP	No	Yes	N/A
Traditional client	Client application	Application specific over IP	No	No	C, Visual Basic …
Object-oriented client	Object-oriented client application	IIOP	Yes	No	C, C++, Visual Basic, Java …
Java client	Object-oriented Java client app.	RMI or IIOP	Yes	No	Java

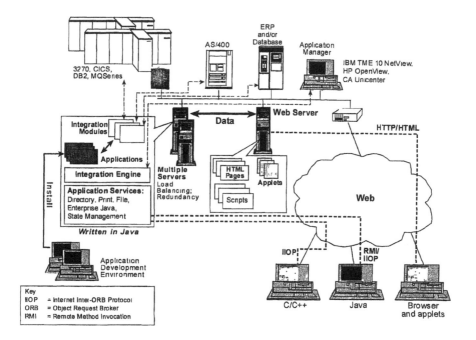

Exhibit 32-3. The generic architecture of Java-based application servers.

pool of Web users. In some instances, individual components of the application server may be distributed across multiple servers to realize the desired processing and memory requirements. Most offerings will support load-balancing using a least-used, first-available, or random allocation mechanism to distribute new users across the multiple servers. In some instances, the Java application server may provide a load-balancing agent, in the form of a "script," that works directly with a Web server. With such a scheme, new user requests for the application server will automatically be directed to the "next-in-line" server by the Web server. The load-balancing mechanism will also provide fault-tolerance in the form of "fail-over" protection. Thus, in the event of a server failure, the user "sessions" being serviced by that server will be transferred over, automatically, to another server.

Application Services

These will be a set of core services for the Web applications, such as directory, print, file, time, and state management. These days directory services will invariably include support for the de facto industry standard Lightweight Directory Access Protocol (LDAP) and also possibly for the widely used and endorsed Novell Directory Services (NDS). State management helps applications keep track of various events and process these events asynchronously. Some application servers will also provide security functions, such as SSL, for use by the Web applications.

Integration Modules or Backend "Hooks"

These are the modules that enable the new Web applications to adroitly interact with existing data sources and applications. The common integration modules available with most Java application servers include:

- Open Database Connectivity (ODBC) and Java Database Connectivity (JDBC) for accessing relational databases
- 3270 and 5250 to enable access to mainframe or AS/400 resident SNA mission-critical applications using terminal emulation
- VT220-type asynchronous terminal mode access to applications running on minicomputers and UNIX machines
- Specific interfaces to Enterprise Resource Planning (ERP) applications such as those from SAP, PeopleSoft, and BAAN
- CICS interface, typically via the client-server-oriented CICS External Call Interface (ECI), to the widely used IBM Transaction Processing subsystem that runs on mainframes, AS/400s, HP Systems, UNIX machines, and even NT servers
- MQSeries interface to IBM's message queuing-based middleware offering that is now being increasingly used to develop new client-server applications in IBM environments
- Specific security server interfaces to enable Web applications to avail themselves of security services, such as user authentication

Application Manager

This component will typically work in conjunction with a popular network management platform such as IBM's TME 10 NetView, HP's OpenView, or Computer Associate's Unicenter and enable administrators to monitor and manage the ongoing operation of the Web applications, the integration modules, as well as the Java application server itself. Given that the Java application server and the Web applications will become key mission-critical resources at most financial institutions, this management capability is crucial to ensuring smooth, trouble-free, high-availability operations.

Application Development Environment

This component facilitates the development of the Web applications that will run on the Java application server. There are, however, two very different schools of thought as to how this key function should be provided vis-à-vis a Java application server. Some application servers, such as the Bluestone Sapphire/Web, provide an integrated development environment

(IDE), replete with development expediting software development kits (SDKs), as a part of the application server. Such IDEs, consistent with current program development ideology, tend to be highly visual à la the paradigm popularized by Visual Basic. They support program construction via components that can be "dragged-and-dropped" on a screen using a mouse. Other Java application server vendors, on the other hand, advocate the notion that there are already plenty of very good Java application development products on the market and that there is no point in trying to reinvent the wheel. BEA Weblogic and Novera's jBusiness fall into this category. Thus, rather than providing their own IDE, they recommend that corporations use any of the popular Java development tools such as Symantec's Visual Café, Inprise's Jbuilder, IBM's VisualAge for Java, or Microsoft's InterDev.

PLATFORMS FOR JAVA APPLICATION SERVERS

An underlying premise and value proposition of a Java-based application server is platform independence. In theory one can run a Java application server on any system that has a full-function implementation of a JVM. Nonetheless, most Java application servers today run on UNIX systems and NT servers. This is mainly because Java application server vendors find that these are the most readily accessible boxes for testing and "certifying" their software.

Customers are also buying into this NT- and Unix-oriented thinking, at least for the time being, in order to validate and gain experience with this new technology. With Y2K issues still abounding, most do not want to experiment with larger boxes, such as mainframes. Scalability and reliability tend to be the main concerns in selecting the appropriate platform for Java application servers. Unix systems scale better and are typically more robust than NT servers but on the other hand tend to be more costly. Given that all application servers support load-balancing and fault-tolerance, it makes sense in many instances to deploy multiple servers, typically NT servers.

The beauty of Java application servers is that they are not restricted to NT or UNIX. Full-function, up-to-date JVMs are now available on IBM mainframes (including those running the VM operating system) and AS/400s. A few of the Java application server vendors, such as BEA Weblogic, are now promoting the AS/400 as a viable and attractive platform. Some list mainframes as a potential platform in their marketing collateral but do not pursue this claim much further. This has mainly to do with testing and support. Most Java application server vendors do not have a background that involves mainframe-based solutions. Neither do they have ready access to mainframes. Thus, testing and supporting their product in a mainframe environment is a real issue. In terms of scalability and reliability, mainframes are in an exceptional class of their own. Financial institutions know this, and to be fair, so do the application server vendors. So the current climate will change in the near future, especially once the dust has settled after Y2K. At that point, most likely led by IBM, many vendors will start supporting their Java application servers on mainframes.

BOTTOM LINE

Web-enabling existing financial applications as well as developing new Web-specific applications will become the number one challenge for most financial institutions as soon as they have successfully overcome their Y2K hurdles. Java application servers are an optimum, strategic, and cost-effective means for implementing new applications, reusing existing resources, and Web-enabling existing applications. Platform-independent Java is rapidly becoming the programming language of choice for the twenty-first century, and Java application servers leverage the power and popularity of Java to facilitate Web integration. Proven and feature-rich Java application servers are now available from a variety of vendors. Moreover, the EJB capability of these application servers ensure that one can build a customized, best-of-breed Java application server using components from different vendors. Financial institutions that are now in the process of evaluating options for Web integration really have no choice but to seriously consider Java application servers as a very strong contender that is likely to meet, if not exceed, all of their current and future requirements relative to the Web.

Author Bio

Anura ("SNA") Gurugé *is an Independent Technical Analyst Consultant who specializes in all aspects of contemporary IBM networking. He has first-hand, in-depth experience in SNA-Capable i•nets, SNA/APPN/HPR/AnyNet, Frame Relay, Token-Ring switching, ATM, System Management, and xDSL technologies. He was actively involved with the Token-Ring switching pioneer Nashoba Networks.*

Over the last 7 years, he has worked closely with most of the leading bridge/router, intelligent hub, FRAD, Token-Ring Switching, and Gateway vendors, and has designed many of the SNA-related features now found on bridge/routers and "gateways." He has also helped large IBM customers to re-engineer and totally overhaul their old SNA-only networks. He is the founder and chairman of the SNA-Capable i•net Forum (www.sna-inets.com).

He is the author of Reengineering IBM Networks, SNA: Theory and Practice, *as well as several other books on SNA, APPN, and SAA. His latest book* Integrating TCP/IP i•nets with IBM Data Centers, *was published in August 1999. He also is the Editor of Auerbach's* Handbook of Communications Systems Management.

In a career spanning 24 years, Gurugé has held senior technical and marketing roles in IBM, ITT, Northern Telecom, Wang, and BBN.

Section II
Banking Trends in Technology

BANKING HAS CHANGED A LOT since I was a manager for Bankers Trust back in the 1980s. Then the state-of-the-art was CICS running on a 3270 terminal. But even then there were signs of momentous things to come. I remember ordering one of those "portable" terminals that were so nouveau back then. It weighed in at about 40 pounds but did manage to have a built-in coupler (remember that word?). I may have been one of the very first telecommuters as I sat on my terrace laboring over a hot program at the rapid pace of 300 baud while my peers back at the office sat hunched over their 3270s envying my experiment with the great outdoors.

Things obviously have speeded up a lot since then. In fact, the very core of banking has been altered radically by the rapid technological development of every facet of the banking process. One need only look at the headlines over the past few years to see what I mean.

Chicago-based Northern Trust Co., working with Sun Microsystems and Open Business Systems, is testing a Web-based bill presentment application for the business-to-business market.

NationsBank, Charlotte, N.C., has launched an Internet-based corporate transaction and delivery service. The offering, called NationsBank Direct, enables corporate customers to access a full range of services via the Web, including U.S. dollar and foreign currency payments, receipts, treasury management and foreign exchange.

Chase Manhattan Bank, New York, has developed a Web browser-based platform to give corporate treasury and investment professionals integrated access to account data plus let them conduct financial transactions from one application.

Compass Bank, Birmingham, AL has rolled out a virtual brokerage as a complement to its CompassPC Banking home banking program. CompassWeb Brokerage enables customers of the $12.9 billion bank to perform online trading of stocks, options, and load/no-load mutual funds, as well as access up-to-date financial market information and research.

In mid-January of 1998, NationsBank became the first U.S. bank to perform a transaction using SET 1.0, the initial "production" version of the platform, which is based on encryption and bank-issued digital certificates that authenticate cardholders and merchants in an online transaction. Bank of America, First Union Corp., Wells Fargo, Royal Bank of Canada, and Mellon Bank also are moving full steam ahead with SET.

Visa International has announced plans to join Sun Microsystems and other key players in the development and promotion of a Java-based smart card microprocessor core, using the Java Card application program interface (API).

According to a study by Mentis Corp., Durham, NC, by early 1999, roughly half of all multibranch banks will provide home banking access via a direct-dial PC modem connection or the Internet. Of banks with at least $250 million in deposits, 48 percent will offer online banking by the close of this year, compared with 28 percent that offered it at the end of the third quarter in 1997.

Smart cards are beginning to catch on in a big way. A number of big U.S. banks — including First Union Corp., Wells Fargo, U.S. Bancorp, Bank of America, First Chicago NBD, NationsBank, and Fleet Bank — have kicked off smart card pilots. Chase Manhattan Bank and Citibank have issued Mondex and Visa Cash cards to customers to use for purchases at participating merchants on Manhattan's Upper West Side.

All in all, total information technology spending by U.S. retail banks is expected to rise nearly 6 percent annually over the next 5 years, lifting industry expenditures by about $7 billion, said a survey by Datamonitor, New York. Reaching $23.49 billion last year, overall bank IT spending stands to swell to almost $31 billion by 2002, according to the study, "IT in U.S. Retail Banking."

While technological advancement is certainly a key factor in this flurry of banking activity, market forces play a key role, too. Since the late 1990s, with the advent of NAFTA and the impending deadline of the Euro, business borders have all but disappeared. Banks, which have always had an international bent, are even more aggressively pursuing the global market. But if technology plays an important role in satisfying business requirements at home, it plays a critical role in satisfying business requirements abroad. Without technology, in other words, going global just is not possible.

In this section some of the best of the best wax eloquent about some of the banking technologies that spring hot from today's headlines — check imaging, Internet Banking, SET, Kiosks.

Today's banking community, like most other business communities, is seeing a radical shift in its most fundamental technological principals.

Those of you reading this book cover-to-cover will find me repeating this again and again in each of the section introductions. To put it simply, the Internet is taking over. Starting with Marc Andreessen's development of Mosaic, the world's first Web browser, while he was still a student at the University of Illinois, its new incarnations in the form of Netscape Navigator and Microsoft's Internet Explorer have become the new technological architecture of business.

From home-banking via the Internet to Internet billing. From online investment services to paperless checking, to Windows 98, whose primary interface is the Web browser, the Internet is the face of all things to come.

Jessica Keyes

Chapter 33
Grab a Ringside Seat for the Best of Banking Technology

Mark Hill

THE "PAPERLESS SOCIETY" has not developed as quickly as computer gurus had anticipated. When technology is used, accessing specific information from electronic filing systems can prove even more daunting than searching through stacks of paper files. Information is continually rekeyed for different purposes — at times, incorrectly — misplaced, not updated, and so on. However, within technology lies the centerpiece of productivity — a system that produces a single electronic file of all information needed to respond quickly and effectively to customer and bank needs, as shown in Exhibit 33-1.

Not many banks would jump at the chance to create a time-intensive, mistake-ridden, cumbersome customer information management system that sheds new business opportunities faster than a tree drops leaves in the fall. Not many would hasten to send a relationship manager to call on a customer knowing someone else from another department in the bank had just been there the day before. Probably not too many would opt to spend more than $600 on a sales call when $300 would do the trick. But it's happening at bank after bank in which tradition and function win out over change and process. Something different is happening at banks where change is not a bad word and a single electronic file opens the door to seamless and ongoing productivity.

The time has never been riper to chip away the walls of traditional kingdoms of sales, credit, collateral, document preparation, etc. Improvements in technology — particularly computer networks and the ability to share information — are enabling stronger sales cultures, better customer service, and streamlined staffing. By allowing employees to operate as members of a team rather than as functionaries and by transforming a hundred bits of information into a dynamic sales strategy, the bank in effect takes a

0-8493-9834-7/00/$0.00+$.50
© 2000 by CRC Press LLC

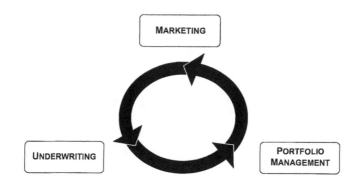

Exhibit 33-1.   Lending as a process.

series of roadblocks in a congested city and creates a virtually limitless freeway.

Yet all too often, banks install new software expecting automatic entrance to the autobahn. Only when software is considered as part of the entire change process can significant benefits be realized. Many times managers consider automation as "automating the current process." The freeway comes when technology is considered along with relevant business issues such as standardization, centralization, and staffing, as shown in Exhibit 33-2.

Competition in lending is well documented. At times, it appears that credit products are used as loss leaders. Consider a recent Business Banking Board study that compared underwriting costs for small business lending. Basis points per dollar of principal were 340 for average performers and fewer than 60 for "best-in-class" performers. If the

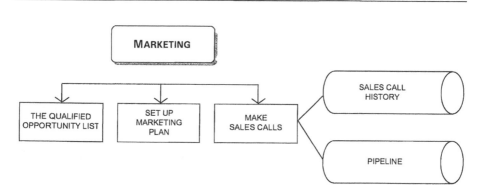

Exhibit 33-2.   Information flows through the sales process.

competition is enjoying this type of advantage, making money in small business lending will be an uphill battle.

The single-source information system can be thought of as an electronic credit file with the added information of business development activities. It supports flexibility in the deployment and structure of assets. By using centralization to eliminate the handoff of data from one functional area to another, the flow of information is complete and no time is wasted tracking down answers. Rekeying errors are eliminated, and there's a great competitive advantage in having the entire bank team see what products a customer has — credit, deposits, trust, cash management, leasing, or other. Moving from function to process is, well, a process.

IMPROVING BUSINESS DEVELOPMENT

Relationship managers begin the effort with a qualified list of the most profitable opportunities that will take the least amount of effort to bring to fruition. Interestingly, a very important part of this list if going to come from previous processes and from information already available within the bank. The list is not really a list in the set of opportunities that is managed by the process. A qualified list offers two key advantages:

1. Sales efforts are focused on profitable opportunities that are likely to be approved.
2. Relationship managers do not waste time (nor do they make the bank look foolish) by calling on businesses that another relationship manager in the bank has already approached.

Information to build the list comes from two places: current and prospective customers. The lender's current customers are the most likely primary source of new business. The information should indicate what products a customer has and does not have and reveal what cross-selling opportunities exist. For example, users will have the ability to identify customers with loan relationships greater than $1 million and who do not presently use deposit or cash management services.

However, market share eventually will decline if relationship managers do not go outside the customer base for new business. A systematic approach to identifying new customers can be realized by using a data provider, such as Dun & Bradstreet, to acquire generic demographic information for all businesses in the area. Those businesses must be qualified based on various criteria such as credit, before putting forth sales efforts. D&B information also can support the qualification process. For example, a lender with expertise in a particular line of business can focus on a particular standard industry classification code with proper credit characteristics.

$700

$636

$600

$500

$400 $338

$300

$200

$100
       BEST   AVERAGE

Source: The Advisory Board Company

Exhibit 33-3.   Cost per sales call.

CONTROLLING SALES CALL COSTS

A sales call on a prospect is an expensive proposition, as shown in Exhibit 33-3. Using a conservative approach, each call costs more than $100 and possibly costs closer to $400. In a market in which sales calls are required to cultivate new business, it makes sense to give relationship managers easy access to information for sales call preparation.

In another Business Banking Board study on small-business lending, total annual sales costs for the most profitable teams were $166,000 per officer. Costs included compensation, management, entertainment, and administration. Each officer made an average of 231 calls per year — including 77 calls on prospects. If only 25 percent of the expense was allocated to calling, then the average call cost close to $200. It pays to plan.

Once the data are merged and the list is created, a detailed sales plan can be developed to determine who needs to be called on and when. This plan should be integrated into the previously collected customer and prospect information profiles and be centrally located so that any team member can view and coordinate tasks with others.

Many relationship managers simply do not like to make sales calls. A sales plan can help systematize the prospecting effort; rather than a one-time "blitz," calls can be made in a logical and systematic way to help make them part of the bank's "sales culture." The system simply provides the structure.

As sales calls are accomplished, a record should be kept to maintain a history of sales efforts to particular customers and prospects. By integrating this record into previously collected information, less effort is required in recording the call — much of the information relating to the call is already set up. Integration also centralizes access to a history of sales efforts.

The process step of recording sales calls also is a good time to update information about the business activity pipeline. The update would include information such as proposed products that may be coming up for approval and information about products offered by a competitor that the customer or prospect uses. Again, this information should be added to previously captured information, in addition to correspondence between customers and relationship managers throughout the process.

MOVING THE BUSINESS THROUGH UNDERWRITING

Once an opportunity is identified, information previously developed in the pipeline can be used to complete an application, credit summary, or credit memo. Depending on the size, type, and complexity of the credit, the application will go to credit scoring or through a manual approval process.

With so much data already collected, underwriting can be streamlined as shown in Exhibit 33-4. Data concerning marketing activities and related comments are now easily available to credit analysts. Current product and relationship information are already part of the database — correspondence, D&B business information, previous credit memos, and principal information are all there. Electronically recorded loan review comments on

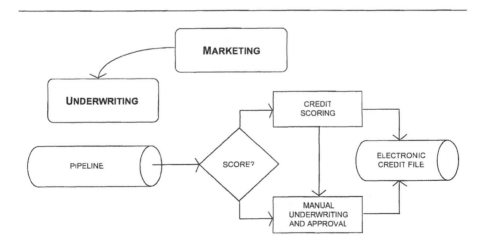

Exhibit 33-4.   Information flows through underwriting.

existing relationships can be viewed and distributed with ease to staff involved in the underwriting process.

Lenders considering scoring should do so by using an empirically derived scorecard, not a "home-grown" or "subjectively derived" methodology. While a scorecard is a relatively simple concept, the development of the proper characteristics and weighting is complex. It is also important not to rekey all the information into a scoring system. Because no one vendor can provide everything, it's essential for vendors to agree to work together to design a system that easily moves data between areas of the scorecard and prevents the need to rekey.

The pipeline contains information traditionally considered part of an application. Credit applications that fall within predetermined criteria for scoring are passed to the scoring system. Scores will fall in a range for pass, fail, or manual review. Applications not appropriate for scoring go through a manual approval process. All activities relating to the underwriting process are stored in the electronic credit file. Spreadsheets, credit memos, D&B information, covenants, collateral, related entities, and credit scores should all be stored in a central, easy-to-access system.

Credit scoring allows for an objective measure of risk and can be used to modify pricing. With integrated information about the credit and the relationship, projected pricing and profitability take very little time to determine and become a systematic part of the process. There are significant benefits in reviewing the profitability of relationships before "matching the competition." Weeding out marginally profitable and riskier accounts is one of those benefits.

BOOKING THE LOAN

Once the bank and the customer approve the transaction, all the previously entered information needs to flow to a document preparation system to complete the required documentation, as shown in Exhibit 33-5. Any vendor under consideration should be committed to both importing and exporting information. While vendors often indicate they can interface with a given system, it is helpful if the chosen vendors guarantee it. The chosen system should also load the necessary information to the mainframe without rekeying. Exceptions and new product data will flow from the document preparation system to the database for ongoing follow-up.

ONGOING MONITORING AND SERVICING OF THE PORTFOLIO

In a property constructed system, the portfolio information will be systematically updated — on a daily basis if desired — from the mainframe or other product systems, keeping product information current. This update

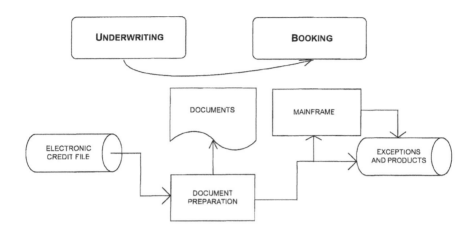

Exhibit 33-5.   Information flows through booking.

is actually a feed to the beginning of the entire process in which business opportunities are identified, as shown in Exhibit 33-6.

Watch lists and loan review comments should be part of the information contained in the single electronic database. In addition, as mentioned previously, all correspondence with a customer can be maintained in the data-

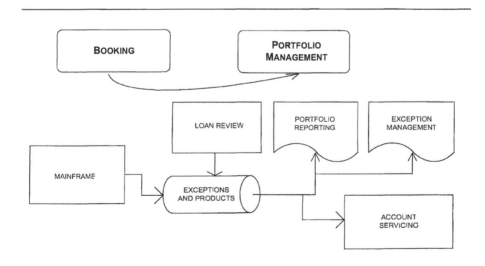

Exhibit 33-6.   Information flows through portfolio management.

base. Integration of Microsoft® Word allows documents to be created using a familiar tool and stored in the security of the database.

Ongoing exception tracking activities should be kept to a minimum. While there has been some consideration going to completely eliminating these activities to conserve expenses, the tracking of exceptions based on exposure can provide a payback, particularly if there is a downturn in economic activity. For example, a follow-up on uniform commercial code or insurance exceptions may be warranted only if the exposure is more than $75,000.

Account maintenance activities can be documented in the database to keep the team apprised of customer status. An informed team member will quickly be able to assist a customer with any questions.

Automated portfolio reviews, using products similar to D&B's Alert Services™, can cut down on the manual effort required to continually monitor the credit strength of the portfolio. The ability to integrate such services into the centralized database eliminates the need to build yet another external interface.

SUMMARY

Technology is changing the ability of commercial lenders to serve small- and middle-market businesses. Those institutions that use technology effectively will have several advantages over their competition. Their relationship managers will:

Be able to cover more ground in their sales efforts.
Be better positioned to service their customers.
Experience lower overall costs.

The most effective employment of technology is to view lending as a process and thereby eliminate the inefficiencies associated with multiple systems in multiple departments with manual handoff of data between them. Rekeying is time-consuming, often inaccurate, and often incomplete. Just as important, an integrated database facilitates communication between members of the team.

In considering methods of using technology to change the way a bank operates, the bank can look at centralization, standardization, scoring, and staffing. Tasks should not be automated based on the way they have been carried out in the past.

When reviewing new software for use in a bank, the lender must be sure that the software fits within the framework of the entire lending process. In today's environment, software that addresses only one function will have a limited life. Software that pulls all the information together into one place and is integrated with other lending systems provides a competitive advantage by enabling greater efficiency, service, and productivity.

Note

This chapter excerpted with permission from *The Journal of Lending and Credit Risk Management,* 23:12, December 1996.

Author Bio

Mark Hill serves as President of Baker Hill, where he exercises primary responsibility for strategic marketing, product development, sales and support. He maintains an active role in sales and marketing, frequently participating in sales presentations to clients. He has overseen the development of Baker Hill's OnePoint® suite of integrated, Windows-based lending products and its newest offering, OnePath®, a loan application automation system.

Hill joined Baker Hill in 1985, 2 years after its founding. Under his energetic leadership, the company has increased its staff tenfold in less than 7 years and revenue growth has grown by 354 percent since 1997.

Prior to joining Baker Hill, Hill has served as an auditor with Grant Thornton and a marketing representative for IBM. He holds a bachelor's degree in Accounting from the University of Notre Dame and an MBA in Management Information Systems from Indiana University, Bloomington. He is also a Certified Public Accountant.

Chapter 34

Banking Technology in Emerging Markets

Bernard Lunn

THE *ECONOMIST* MAGAZINE publishes a weekly "Emerging Market Indicators." There are 25 countries covered. They range from the obvious countries like China, India, Indonesia, Brazil, and Russia (the "Big Emerging Markets") to those countries that would now prefer to see themselves in the developed markets category such as Hong Kong, Singapore, and Israel. This list does not include all the countries that might be classified as "submerged" or "preemerging" and this list would cover most of Africa, Cuba, Indochina, the Balkans, and Central Asia.

Taken together, these countries represent the vast majority of the world's population and the growth markets of the next century. Banking is the essential lubricant to these new economies, first helping them make the initial transition from subsistence farming and then helping their companies to trade with the world; and technology is the essential lubricant of banking.

So how much time do bank technology developers spend thinking about the specific requirements of these markets? Not a lot. The assumption is usually "whatever works in America will have to work in these emerging markets." Faced with price sensitivity in these markets, the vendor's usual response is to reach for "last year's model." The vendor's local branch office or distributor receives reams of marketing literature from the head office that seems to bear little or no resemblance to the day-to-day ground realities of the market that he or she is operating in. Let us look at some of the ground realities of banking technology in emerging markets.

Telecommunications are usually unreliable and prohibitively expensive — Getting a leased line installed takes the patience of Job and the reliability is likely to be patchy at best. In India, for example, a long-distance telephone call costs about four times more than in America. At the same time the labor cost is about four times less than in America. You can see how this will make you think differently about the cost justification of wide

0-8493-9834-7/00/$0.00+$.50
© 2000 by CRC Press LLC

area networks. Weak telecommunications means that the classic centralized mainframe approach is unlikely to be viable.

Labor costs are much lower — This changes the cost justification arguments. In America it is clearly more effective for customers to use ATMs rather than human tellers, but this is much less clear-cut in emerging markets. Often, a solution that is high on labor content and low on capital cost is most appropriate. It may also be worth remembering that the $1000-per-day consultant staying at a four-star hotel for a couple of weeks will be costing the same as the annual salary of the person that is receiving the advice. A system that demands a large amount of external consultancy is unlikely to be viable.

Layoffs are politically unacceptable — Many banks are still government owned and union dominated. Automation is allowed as long as it does not involve layoffs. Simple downsizing as practiced in the West is not viable. Emerging-market banks have to manage the much more difficult feat of downsizing and growing at the same time. This is viable as long as banking markets are growing (as opposed to contracting in the overly banked West), but there are daunting retraining and human resources issues.

English is not the first language for most people — Bank staff are unlikely to have grown up using PCs. "Ease of use" is not just a marketing buzzword; it is the critical success factor.

The scale can be daunting — India has over 80,000 bank branches. One bank alone, State Bank of India, accounts for over 10,000 branches. Solutions that may work well in hundreds of branches may simply not work when stretched to thousands of branches.

Trade finance instruments — Bills and letters of credit are an integral part of everyday business. You cannot easily run a credit check, so these instruments are used for domestic as well as international business. In America, Trade Finance is viewed as a specialized activity for the international department. In emerging markets these instruments are a normal part of everyday retail banking.

These are all major issues. However there are silver linings in the clouds. For example, banks do not have to deal with a large number of legacy systems. Vendors selling the delights of data warehousing get little reaction in emerging markets. The banks do not have multiple incompatible data sources that need to be cleansed and integrated into one big warehouse.

Most core banking systems were designed in the 1970s. Remember the 1970s? Flared trousers, bad haircuts, and Saturday Night Fever; also batch processing, dumb terminals, flat files, telex, and COBOL. While we may have gotten rid of the embarrassing fashions, the legacy of the core banking systems is still very much with us. Nor do banks in the West seem in any hurry to replace these dinosaurs. Concerned with immediate problems such as Y2K and Euro, the temptation is to simply patch up and surround the old core systems with more modern client-server applications.

So what does a bank in the emerging markets do? It can stick with primitive branch-based "islands automation" or it can install a 1970s-era mainframe solution. Neither is attractive. What is needed is a new generation of core banking systems that fully exploits the technology potential of the 1990s.

Banks have an opportunity to "leapfrog" and bypass a whole generation of technology. Emerging-market banks also have one major benefit over their American or European counterparts — growth. With strong growth in population and GDP, and with weak telecommunications, there is plenty of room for growth in good, old-fashioned, branch-based retail banking.

So, what do emerging-market banks look for from their core banking systems?

Easy to customize — Emerging markets have different requirements, so customization is unavoidable. Software will need to be adapted. Can a local team make these changes? Or do you have to send in those $1000-per-day gurus? Software must be as easy to install, customize, and use as mass-market "shrink-wrapped" software. Setting parameters should be done using "Wizards," requiring no more skills than, say, creating an address book in MS Access.

Easy to learn — If you install a new system in the West, you can be pretty confident that the end users will have used computers before. At worst, you can expect to provide training in the nuances of the application or in the differences between Windows 3.1 and Windows 98. Do not make this assumption in emerging markets. It is very likely that many of the end users have never used a computer before. It is likely that English is not their first language. The "fear, uncertainty, and doubt" factor will be very high. So new systems have to be very easy to learn, with a simple, consistent GUI and context-sensitive help.

Distributed processing — The centralized mainframe model won't work in these markets due to the cost and unreliability of wide-area telecommunications. The reality today is that most systems operate as stand-alone branch automation systems. Each branch is an "island automation." Banks are moving towards a distributed processing architecture, where key branches in major regional cities act as "regional processing hubs." These hubs are connected to head office by VSAT (satellite). Smaller local branches can connect to the hub via local leased lines. More remote branches will still operate stand-alone, maybe sending data by dial-up modem or diskette. Most European or U.S. banking systems are not built to manage this level of distributed architecture, as they rely on mature networks.

Integrated all-in-one rather than many different best-of-breed solutions — Banking systems in America have evolved. This means that there are many different subsystems, all of which have to be interfaced. A major bank may literally have hundreds of such separate applications. These systems may be built and maintained by specialist vendors. Each vendor specializes and aims to offer "best-of-breed" in his or her area. This approach won't work in emerging-market banks. The specialist packages are usually not supported in these countries and the cost of integration would be prohibitive. Emerging-market banks may not need great functional depth in each area, but they do need a very broad spread of functionality in a single integrated package.

Low-cost mass-market components — Systems must run on open systems platforms such as NT and UNIX, typically on Intel-based platforms.

Some vendors may take the simple view that it is only a matter of waiting for these markets to catch up and then they will deploy the same technology they use in America and Europe. There are certainly some banks, often those which have recently been formed, which seem to differ very little from their developed-market counterparts. Also, every seminar on new technology is very well attended, as bankers aim to learn more about what is happening elsewhere, but there is a big difference between window shopping at a seminar and spending precious foreign currency. The emerging banks are looking to learn not just what the West did right, they also want to learn from the mistakes. They want to use the latest technology in ways that are genuinely appropriate to their real needs.

Emerging-market banks have an opportunity to leapfrog their developed-country counterparts by investing in core banking systems that are based on modern technology. They can move directly from simple branch automation systems to a distributed "banking information architecture" thus bypassing the 1970s-era centralized mainframe systems.

What is wrong with these legacy core systems? Some people would tell you that the problem is that they run on proprietary mainframes. The solution would then seem to be to simply replace these old dinosaurs with some up-to-date UNIX or NT boxes in a client-server configuration. This is a superficial analysis and misses the real problem. There is nothing wrong with the mainframe per se. It is a good box for handling large volumes of transactions securely and reliably. Mainframes also manage batch processing exceptionally well and, yes, batch is still very much a reality in banking systems. IBM has done a great job of repositioning the mainframe as a large server, indeed it is the only server tough enough for the really demanding jobs.

No, there is nothing wrong with the hardware architecture. It is the software architecture that is the problem. It is all very well saying that the mainframe is a modern server in a client-server system, but this is a bit weak when the only software on the mainframe looks like it came out of the ark.

So how does this old software architecture create a problem? One glaring example today is the Year 2000 bug. Large sums are being spent to solve this problem in legacy banking systems. Clearly, any modern system will use four digits for dates so that they are Y2K compliant. If the system is object oriented it may have only one date "object" that is called whenever an application requires a date. Think how much easier that makes maintenance.

Easier maintenance does not sound like a big advantage, but look again and you may see that "maintainability" (or "enhanceability") is the most important criteria for a system. Any system has to change with the times (Y2K being just one obvious example). If you can do this more quickly than your competitors, you have a major strategic advantage.

You might think: "well, just solve the Y2K problem" and all will be well with that old legacy system. However anybody who actually has to maintain these old systems will tell you that Y2K is only the tip of the iceberg. One example will illustrate what lies below the tip. A major U.S. bank found it had a problem with its international banking system due to the declining value of the Italian lira. The lira had declined to a level where an additional digit was needed. Does this sound like a small problem? Only if Y2K is a small problem. The number of places in the system where the currency field had to be amended, and all the "ripple through" effects, meant that the bank needed a major project. This project lasted many months, took a sizable chunk out of the budget, and distracted IS management from more strategic projects.

So "maintainability" is a major strategic advantage. In business terms it translates into how quickly the bank can take advantage of changes in the market. However "fixing the plumbing" usually takes a back seat to more glamorous projects with a more obvious ROI. So banks keep plastering over the cracks.

Emerging-market banks do not have this legacy to contend with. They can invest today in systems that will enable them to grow over the years. These modern, maintainable systems should have the following key attributes.

Object oriented — An object-oriented system does not mean faster initial development — usually this will take much longer. The big payoff comes when you want to make changes, because the object paradigm isolates a particular function that needs changing (say, date or currency or interest calculation) in one place.

Layered — A layered architecture isolates "Presentation" and "Business Rules" and "Data" into separate layers. You can make changes in one layer without affecting the other layers. For example, you can change the user interface without affecting the core processing in the business layer.

Message based — Those 1970s-era legacy systems assumed that the only device that would interface with the system would be a dumb terminal green screen. That hardly works in the 1990s when the application needs to interface to Windows® PCs, Web browsers, SWIFT, interactive voice response, ATMs, and much more; and in the coming decade the application will have to interface to devices we have not even thought of today. All of these devices communicate through some form of "messaging protocol." Thus, a modern system has to communicate easily through messaging systems (via a messaging layer that translates messages from the external format into the internal messaging protocol).

A system built on an object-oriented, layered, and messaging architecture provides the foundation (or "plumbing") that will enable the bank to compete in a fast-changing environment. Emerging-market banks have the opportunity to put such systems into place today and thus leapfrog their competitors that are saddled with old legacy systems.

Author Bio

Bernard Lunn *is Chief Executive Officer of Ionic Systems International Limited, based in New York. Ionic develops and markets a multicurrency, multibranch core banking system known as The Banking Engine™. Ionic is specifically focused on the needs of emerging markets. Ionic software is designed, developed, and maintained in Pune, India.*

Prior to starting Ionic in 1996, Lunn has worked for international banking software companies such as Midas-Kapiti International. His experience in banking systems spans the globe. During the 1980s he worked throughout Europe from a base in London. In 1989 he moved to New York and then in 1994, he moved to Singapore .

Chapter 35
Going Global — Systems Issues for Servicing a Global Business*

Stephen Bloomer

THE STARTING POINT WHEN SELECTING A SYSTEM to support a global trading and settlement operation is to realize that such a system does not, and probably cannot, exist. There is no single system from one vendor that fully supports the complex varieties of trading which exist. The development risks and time needed to make any existing system truly global in function are too great. What can be built is an architecture which will efficiently integrate a variety of solutions into what can loosely be described as a system. Once this is understood it is then possible to start looking into the issues involved in selecting and implementing a system.

It is no coincidence that a number of the largest international investment banks are currently developing or seeking to develop systems to support their global securities trading activities. There are a number of commercial pressures which are driving the banks to undertake this task, and it is worth considering what these are as a first step to understanding the issues facing development of, and the requirements for, such a system.

The trend to deregulate the activities that financial institutions can undertake has led most banks to adopt the one-stop shop approach to providing services. The aim is not only to earn additional profit by providing more services, but to ensure that the bank retains the important high-revenue customers who demand a full range of services, and who often prefer

---

*"Going Global — Systems Issues for Servicing a Global Business" © Armstrong International, Ltd. Reprinted with permission from *Back Office Focus*, March 1998.

to use a single trusted supplier. So wherever a customer wants to trade, the bank needs to have some presence and expertise.

The customers have grown more sophisticated and international in their outlook. Rationalization into larger pan-national companies offering a greater range of products and services has occurred across the financial services industry. Companies that traditionally offered only pensions, mortgages, or insurance services within a single country may now be part of a corporate structure offering all these services across a number of countries. This trend has been boosted by the relaxation of restrictions on movement of capital internationally and of trade restrictions in general.

The continual growth of capital available to fund pensions, the burgeoning personal finance market, high levels of government borrowings, and the relative maturity of the developed capital markets have pushed the investing institutions to consider new products and new markets for investment — the so-called emerging markets. This has created an increased volume of trades and, hence, strain on systems and operations.

By definition, many of the new markets and products carry a higher level of risk — not an endearing concept to fund managers. Risk can be minimized by spreading investments across regions as well as countries, markets, and instrument types. The recent Asian economic downturn serves as a reminder of the dangers of overspecialization. However, a market downturn does not mean disaster for everyone; markets in heavily devalued currencies represent a new opportunity to some.

Information Technology (IT) is partly responsible for introducing global trading. The hugely improved performance of networks and the adoption of communications protocols by software vendors are the main factors enabling books to be passed round the time zones, so maximizing opportunities in all markets. Although 24-hour book trading has not been widely adopted in practice, efficient networks make the work of some specialized trading, like arbitrage, simpler.

All these pressures have pushed the top tier of investment banks to set up a truly global presence for trading and settlement. Having assessed what's driving these banks to set up global operations, the next stage is to look at how operations can be structured.

To be able to trade in multiple markets in a cost-effective manner, many of the major players are adopting a similar model for the structure of their operations, as illustrated in Exhibit 35-1. Typically, to serve clients from one country who are trading in securities in a second country, the investment banks maintain a local client-facing entity to provide a "personal" service to the client. To provide a quality service they need expertise in the market in which the security is traded, so that the clients'

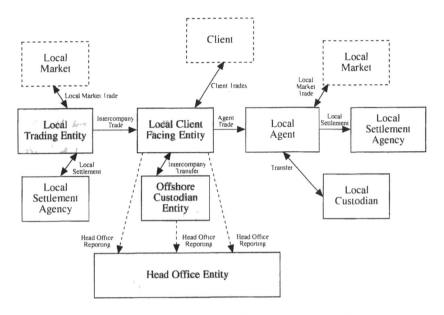

Exhibit 35-1.   The business model most often preferred.

international orders can be satisfied by using one of two routes. If a bank has a trading entity in the relevant market it will rely on its local traders, who usually are backed up by a local settlement operation. Complications may be added if the stock and cash are to be held in custody offshore for tax reasons, possibly involving another entity of the parent bank. However, where there is no in-house local trading entity, then the bank makes use of local agents, with the stock and cash settlement being handled locally and held in custody locally.

This generates a complex web of inter-entity transactions involving a client-facing entity, an entity which executed the trade (either on its own books or with a counterparty), and possibly a separate custodian entity. This is potentially an administrative nightmare, particularly when foreign exchange deals, market, or national regulatory reporting and head office reporting requirements are added in.

Adopting this multi-entity structure can have the benefit of opening up otherwise restricted markets to overseas entities. By trading via a locally regulated and approved entity, an entity based in a different country can trade in a market from which it would otherwise be barred. If the IT infrastructure can support this type of complex intercompany trading, it can enable much higher levels of international trading, expanding the international services provided.

With the business structure of the participating companies established, one final area worth investigating, before looking at the challenges for a multi-entity system, is to look at the problems encountered in operating the current systems. Put bluntly, is a new system really needed for global trading?

Supporting a global operation presents a number of problems for the systems currently used. Obvious pressures include the higher volumes of trades being transacted and the universal commercial drive to minimize labor costs by using new technology, in this context straight-through processing.

Round-the-clock trading and settlement eliminates the possibility of running many system processes heavy on resources as overnight batches. This, coupled with the relentless shortening of settlement periods, and the difficulty of performing any end-of-day processing for a 24-hour operation, make the requirement one for a largely real-time system. Overnight batch runs of certain processes are simply not quick enough for current business needs. For example, to take advantage of excess collateral held at Euroclear by repoing it out relies on knowing today's positions today. This will only be intensified as settlement periods get even shorter.

With a number of high-profile, high-value failures of banks' risk management operations over the last few years, it is unsurprising that there is demand for enhanced risk management tools, particularly for assessing global risk. It is not just a case of local branches or specialist operations monitoring their exposure; the cumulative picture could be where the real danger lies. The speed at which high-value, highly geared positions (particularly in derivatives) can be built up demands protection way beyond a traditional reporting system. Sophisticated analytical tools linked to all the main processes working with real-time data are needed.

One strategy adopted by banks for attracting and retaining customers is to offer different products to those offered by the opposition. So, a myriad new financial products have been devised. The acceleration of the creation of new financial products means that the systems need to be easily adapted for new products and processes. Straightforward capitalized interest bonds can now be processed on some back-office systems, but now there is a need to process the Russian Prins securities for which part of the interest is capitalized into a new instrument. This kind of functional change is needed more often, and so the task of changing the system must be easy and straightforward. Difficulty in making this type of change can mean that the system is dictating the level at which a firm can operate in a new market.

The traditional mainframe is notoriously time-consuming to code. This is exacerbated by the likelihood that by now the system has been tweaked beyond recognition, employing many add-ons and work-arounds, making the effects of any change extremely difficult to predict. The other problem of coding for older systems is the scarcity of programmers with the right skills. A scarce resource has a tendency to become an expensive resource. The time and cost of updating and maintaining mainframes are forcing banks to move from more traditional forms of system architecture and coding to newer, more flexible approaches like component-based and object-oriented programming, with a modular structure in a client/server environment.

Two other well-publicized factors highlight the need for system adaptability and may be sounding the death knell for many current banking systems — the millennium date problem and the introduction of the Euro currency. As both these projects will take a lot of IT and business resources to solve, they might appear at first sight to be reasons to delay the start of implementing a replacement system globally. However, the scale of work needed to enable existing systems to deal with four-digit dates and the new currency running in tandem with existing currencies is forcing many IT strategists to recommend implementation of new systems. This can be the most cost-effective way, or even the only possible way, to meet the deadlines for these events.

If the system can open new business opportunities or offer a faster or cheaper service, that makes it easier to convince the business management to back it. An example of this occurred in the currency warrants market in Hong Kong. By moving decisively into the new market, one of the large Swiss investment banks established a dominant market share. This move was only possible because the bank had a flexible system capable of being set up quickly for settlement in a new instrument type.

So, for many investment banks there is a strong business and technical case for replacing their existing systems. If the need is for an integrated system to support a global operation then a number of considerations above the usual ones for sourcing any system come into play.

One way of achieving the flexibility required by today's environment is to use a highly modular structure for the system, of the type illustrated in Exhibit 35-2. This greatly enhances the ability to make quick and easily managed changes and eases the job of linking products from more than one supplier when building a global system. This opportunity to select and link the best-of-breed solutions should deliver the most functionally rich and efficient system.

Any new global system must support a network of devolved corporate entities who regularly transact between themselves, but it must also be capable of producing the consolidated picture for global position-keeping, risk management, and management reporting.

All of this demands that a system must be capable of handling complex inter-entity trading. At its most extreme, it is possible to construct realistic scenarios in which there can be a chain of six or seven legal entities of the

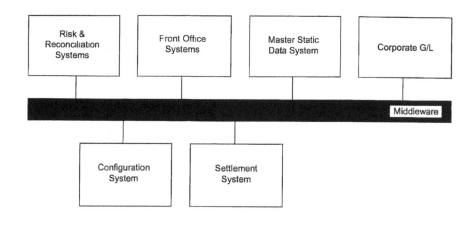

Exhibit 35-2.   The IT model is growing in popularity.

---

one parent company involved in a single client trade. The main challenge is to ensure accurate position-keeping across entities and possibly systems. Some form of double-entry bookkeeping using inter-entity accounts is a solution which, while not requiring cutting-edge technology, does require considerable investment in business modeling and system configuration. What is needed is sophisticated message routing capabilities in the system, with the efficiency of the middleware being vital.

None of what has been outlined so far has touched on a major issue in the specification of a global system — where are the data to be stored? Do you adopt a central data depository which feeds out to the local sites or a localized one with consolidation at a global level? There is no one answer to this.

The tendency to centralize brings cost savings and makes the resourcing of skilled systems staff easier, whereas if every global site has its own system to maintain there are obvious cost implications. However, overcentralization can result in recreating many of the problems of performance and inflexibility to local needs associated with mainframe systems.

One approach is to divide data processing into real-time transactional and batched processing for record keeping. The transactional processes like trade enrichment, trade confirmation, and settlement instruction generation, and the steps involved in settlement management, require real-time processing and so may be more suited to local data storage and processing for purposes of speed. Processes which can be run as batches, such as position accruals, can take advantage of a more centralized model. A limiting factor on the level of this centralization is the difficulty of defining an end-of-day for a global 24-hour system. A regional day-end may prove to be the top level of data centralization for this type of processing.

The extreme poles in the centralized vs. distributed data repository landscape are rarely seen. Some data appear to be more suited to being centralized from an operational point of view. Local data management of specialized instruments and clients would appear best left to those with local knowledge. When needed centrally, for example to calculate global exposure to clients, this can be consolidated. However, client, counterparty, depot/nostro, and security details are static data which may be needed across several entities and systems, particularly if there is a large proportion of inter-entity trading. Therefore, it can be more efficient and lessen the risk of failures due to incorrect static data to maintain these data centrally and make them available using publish and subscribe technology.

Another useful guide as to where to place data on the centralized/distributed axis is to look at the starting point of the legacy systems. It seems curious to take the history of the legacy systems into account when replacing it, but few IT professionals would advocate a big-bang approach to implementing a global system. The complexity of the task and the investment and operational risks of this approach rule it out. So the task is how to replace the legacy systems in a phased way.

The method by which the global business was built up can be highly significant in the way a supporting system can be developed. The most frequent method of business expansion internationally is acquisition of local firms, which usually brings a developed system specific to the local needs. The alternative is to set up a new start operation where there is the option of developing a specific local system or adapting a system which exists elsewhere in the global business. Typically, the inheritance or development of a local system presents a problem with the consistency of IT products for the global operator — staff need extensive retraining to move between sites, and each site needs its own system training, support, and development resources.

If you are replacing systems which support an international operation which has grown up organically, i.e., by setting up new start offices, there is a good chance that there is a common core to the systems which can take advantage of having a centralized approach. However, the more common method of expansion is by acquisition of smaller local companies, which invariably means a mixed bag of legacy systems. This will steer the design towards a more distributed data model, with consolidation through interfaces where needed.

Once an inventory of existing systems has been taken and a data model has emerged from a study of this, there remains the thorny question of how to prioritize the replacement of the legacy systems. The deciding factors may include identifying legacy systems which are limiting the business growth, or which are particularly expensive to maintain. However, there may be overriding outside factors which dictate the order for the replacement program. If part of the current systems will not be able to handle trading in Euro-denominated securities, or if there are excessive costs required to solve any Year 2000 date problems in the legacy systems, this may prove decisive in prioritizing replacement.

One irony when replacing legacy systems is that those banks which already have legacy systems with a high level of commonality and integration are likely to find the transition period more problematic than those who are replacing a system with little or no common core. There is often a problem in phasing the switch to the new system as it is difficult to identify discrete areas of functionality for switching. Once switching starts, the existing level of integration takes a step backwards. In the medium to long term, the benefits of the new system will be felt as higher levels of integration are regained.

What should never be overlooked is the need for active and enthusiastic participation by the business users in a major IT project. The desire to show benefits to users early in the project can shape priorities. You might choose to replace a part of the system which is very visible to the end user in order to promote a positive view of the project, rather than a "black box" system with which the user is unfamiliar. For a major IT project, there is a strong case for bringing in specialists to manage the project who are used to factoring in the less obvious but very important human factor.

When a first phase of implementation has been selected detailed planning for it can commence. That is probably as much detailed planning as should be undertaken at this stage. There will undoubtedly be lessons to be learned from phase one to be used for subsequent phases. Just as importantly, new business opportunities may arise, changes in the corporate structure of the bank may occur, market conditions may change significantly, and new IT solutions may evolve, any of which may require a rethink of the subsequent phases.

Changes like these may even affect the global strategy. The key is to plan in detail for the current phase only and review the strategy on a regular basis, perhaps annually. Adherence to some rigid 5-year master plan is very unlikely to deliver a good system. It's not just the opposition pack who keep moving — the landscape itself is shifting. To be able to change fast and keep ahead relies on pragmatism and agility. For any system large enough to support a global operation, this agility must be factored into the design of the system selected. It must be capable of changing quickly to support the business, otherwise the user will always be left playing a clumsy and increasingly expensive game of catch-up.

Author Bio

Stephen Bloomer *is Deputy Managing Director at Wilco International. He is responsible for the strategic direction of Wilco's products, both through broadening the coverage of existing products and by strategic partnerships with other vendors. He also has global responsibility for sales. Bloomer joined Wilco in 1987 as a programmer/designer, working initially on Wilco's communications products. He subsequently co-designed Wilco's Gloss trading and settlement system which is now used by over 40 prominent firms in the U.K., Europe, U.S. and Asia Pacific. The success of Gloss led directly to Bloomer's promotion to the Wilco Board as Technical Director. Bloomer graduated from Cambridge University where he studied the natural sciences.*

Chapter 36
A Brief Case History in Internet Banking*
Myers Dupuy

THE STATE NATIONAL BANK OF BIG SPRING, TEXAS is a pioneer among community banks. From running an enterprise-wide LAN (local area network) to being the first Texas-area community bank to offer check imaging, from selling stamps in ATM machines to connecting every desktop in the office to the Internet and e-mail, State National has earned a reputation as a technology leader in the community banking industry.

It is no surprise, therefore, that as the industry's decision makers are just warming up to the growing consumer demand to have secured account access over the Internet, State National found and successfully implemented a solution for Internet banking and electronic bill payment before most of the bigger banks even thought of the idea. To date, the bank reports that everyone is happy: the local ISP (Internet Service Provider), the customers, and especially the bank.

State National's senior vice president, Robert Buckner, headed the Internet banking project from developing the Web site, selecting the Internet banking vendor and software package, dealing with the security issue and, finally, marketing the product to SNB's customers.

Operations staff across the nation will be dealing with these new issues in the not-to-distant future as banks begin to seek an answer to the Internet banking question. Let us use State National as a test case for community banks and see what lessons can be learned from their experiences with Internet banking.

THE WEB SITE: POSTCARD VS. INTERACTIVE

To begin with, your bank will need a Web site. Web sites can typically be classified by one of two general types: the postcard or the interactive. The

---

*"A Brief Case History in Internet Banking" © Independent Bankers Association of Texas. Reprinted with permission from *The Texas Independent Banker,* September 1997.

581

postcard site is essentially your brochure on the Internet. It offers no more information or services than if someone sat down in your lobby for 5 minutes and browsed the available literature. People may visit once for novelty's sake. But you can bet that if you don't change your site frequently it will collect dust in cyberspace. In short, the postcard site is not worth your time or your money.

The interactive site, on the other hand, has tools that offer real value to the customer. Can someone go to your Web site, for instance, to order checks, buy movie tickets, see the school calendar, trade securities, get stock quotes, or buy insurance? With all of the new Web sites out there competing for attention, customers probably won't continue visiting your site if they are under the impression that it never changes. It's not enough to show up at the ball well-dressed; you're going to have to dance a little to get noticed.

Robert Buckner and State National were determined to build an interactive Web site. "Why spend the money for a site that is only a billboard? No one is going to spend the download time to read your site more than once if they don't think they'll get anything new for it. I wanted something out there that was always changing and had something new all the time, for people to continually come back to the site."

If you visit *www.statenb.com* (Exhibit 36-1) you will see that State National succeeded in creating the quintessential interactive site. It recently was named by *The Money Page (www.moneypage.com)* one of the Top Ten Internet Banking sites in Cyberspace.

What makes *www.statenb.com* so great? Well, it's got the basics: a page about the bank history, products, and services, the "e-mail us" page. But beyond these standard postcard features, it has these valuable tools:

Weather — Up-to-the-minute weather reports that include time, temperature, heat index, wind speed, humidity, barometer, and rainfall data; it's even got a Nexrad radar map and a colorful graphic of the next 4 day's forecast for the Midland/Odessa area.

Stock quotes — 15-minute delayed stock quotes, commodity quotes, and real-time quotes on indices and foreign exchange, real-time and historical news headlines, and portfolio tracking.

Securities trading — Soon to have online order entries for stocks and options, real time order status, and portfolio information, real-time and delayed stock quotes, access to no-load mutual funds, direct telephone access with a licensed representative, and downloading of customer securities agreements.

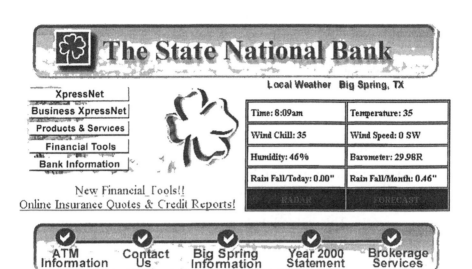

The State National Bank

XpressNet

Business XpressNet

Products & Services

Financial Tools

Bank Information

New Financial Tools!!
Online Insurance Quotes & Credit Reports!

Local Weather   Big Spring, TX

Time: 8:09am	Temperature: 35
Wind Chill: 35	Wind Speed: 0 SW
Humidity: 46%	Barometer: 29.98R
Rain Fall/Today: 0.00"	Rain Fall/Month: 0.46"

RADAR   FORECAST

ATM Information   Contact Us   Big Spring Information   Year 2000 Statement   Brokerage Services

I Bank Information I Products & Services I XpressNet IBusiness XpressNet I
Financial Tools I ATM Information I Contact Us I Year 2000 Statement I
I Brokerage Services I Privacy Statement I

EQUAL HOUSING
LENDER

Thank you for visiting The State National Bank. For more information on our
products and services please email, fax or phone us at the following
email team.info@statnb.com
phone (915) 264-2100
fax (915) 267-1553

Another site by

Exhibit 36-1.   The State National Bank Web site.

Financial calculators — Amortization tables and other statistics for loans; also helps you to determine the savings you need to buy a particular home or retire by a certain age.

Currency conversion — Allows you to determine the value of currency when it is changed from one denomination to another.

Extensive community information — Provides comprehensive Big Spring history and statistics and acts as a community information center by posting upcoming civic events.

On choosing a Web site, Buckner commented, "I encourage people to shop around before committing to a Web site developer. Because this is a fairly new market, Web site design rates can vary greatly between design firms. I liked the design firm we went with because they allow us to make our own changes. We needed that freedom because we change our site at least once a week, often more than that." Some firms will require that you use their updating services to change your Web site, which has the potential to make the cost of updating an interactive site prohibitive. "We were also able to get all of our interactive products — the stock quotes, online

583

trading, calculators, etc. — through our designers in a package which made it easier and more cost-effective," Buckner said.

INTERNET BANKING SOFTWARE

The main consideration for State National, as a home-owned community bank, was to find Internet banking software that could be customized and integrated into their local business community. Buckner said, "For some people who aren't used to it, the Internet can have a tendency to sound hi-tech and impersonal, so we were looking for software that would allow us to keep giving our customers a personal touch even on the Internet."

The bank runs the system on their own computers. "We wanted to keep control of [Internet banking] in-house since we already had the hardware and the personnel we needed to support it. We really didn't need a service bureau scenario. This helped us keep the on-going monthly costs quite low," said Buckner. Running the system in-house also means that changes, such as adding new customer accounts, take effect immediately instead of the next day which is usually the case in the service bureau environment.

Bill Payment

The system uses a nationally based electronic payment processor that provides the ability to pay most national retailers in a true electronic environment. The payment processor can handle payment requests for retailers who are not set up to receive electronic payment by receiving the bank's requests and routing a paper-drawn check to the retailer on behalf of the bank.

One part of State National's bill payment system provides State National with a very strong marketing tool in the local business community. This component is an electronic payment method that takes place when the company receiving payment has an account at State National. The system internally routes the payment from the specified account of the customer who is paying the bill to the receiving company's account. This ACH transfer is the fastest of the available electronic payment methods and doesn't incur a fee for the bank. "We think the system will provide a strong incentive for businesses to open an account with us," said Buckner.

Security

Security is across the board the biggest issue for the decision makers. Robert Buckner commented on what he and his bank did for security: "We looked at the relative risk associated with accessing a copy of our batch data over the Internet. When all of the security technology we use was laid out on the table we were confident that we had taken the necessary precautions to ensure that the risk incurred is within acceptable parameters. We do this through, among other things, firewall technology and staying current with the latest security patches for our Web server provided by Microsoft™."

In addition, the customer must call the bank to set up an Internet account, which gives State National the opportunity to educate its customers on the significant importance of password and account privacy.

Bottom Line

In the 8 months State National has had Internet banking, what has it done for the bank? The Web site *(www.statenb.com)* received national acclaim as one of the Top Ten Internet banking sites in America and it has become widely regarded in the Big Spring community as *the* local information center. Buckner commented that people who don't bank with State National regularly go to *www.statenb.com* for its information and services.

The bank receives about one e-mail a day from customers who want to open an account using the electronic applications and from noncustomers who were surfing the site and want to open some type of account. The bank also receives several e-mails a week from overseas individuals and companies wanting to open an international account.

There are currently 379 customers using the bank's Internet systems. Aside from customers who simply aren't sure how to operate the Internet, State National reports minimal customer service calls. Buckner mentioned with a hint of pleasant surprise that the bank's senior-citizen customers, who have typically been perceived as non-Internet users, have been the most vocal and supportive of the new service. The advantage for senior citizens, said Buckner, is that Internet banking "allows people to see their statement or account information at any time of the day without any time constraints."

CONCLUSION

Buckner and State National are confident about their choice to implement Internet banking and they see the advantages growing. "We are pleased with community support we have received. This Internet product has helped to reinforce our image as a customer service organization and that will help us tremendously in both the short and the long run."

Author Bio

Myers Dupuy manages the Technical Services Department at Q-UP Systems in Austin, TX. Myers received his degree in Philosophy with an emphasis on legal ethics at the University of Texas at Austin. He entered the electronic commerce industry by becoming the second full-time employee at Q-UP Systems, which has grown considerably in the past 2 years and has become a player in the Internet Banking market.

Chapter 37

How "Internet Bill Presentment" Changes the Deployment Strategy of Home Banking and Online Payment

Richard K. Crone

AS A BUSINESS TOOL, the Internet is rapidly transforming the world of commerce and banking — making us faster and more efficient and allowing us to provide more personalized services to the end user or customer. As a result, financial service providers now have a battery of completely new ways to add value and distinguish themselves from the previous generation of commoditized financial transactions.

The advantage of the Internet compared to existing proprietary online connections and banking services is that the Net allows financial institutions to combine "content" from multiple sources onto "one" computer desktop. This capability is now considered one of the key enablers for accelerating the use of home banking programs. By delivering billing content, namely statements, remittance notices, and other recurring bills directly to consumers, banks can attract more electronic consumers to their virtual banking storefronts.

Internet bill presentment and payment does indeed change the value proposition for home banking and supports customer movement from physical branches and paper transactions to electronics. In the bill payment world, if you present a bill in paper, you get paid with a paper check.

0-8493-9834-7/00/$0 00+$.50

Thus, it stands to reason that if you present your bill electronically, you will most likely get paid electronically. Purveyors of home banking programs know that if they are to achieve the exponential increases projected for home banking they must get the "billing content" incorporated into the bill payment and home banking services.

It's the biller's bills, and they own the content. All this is very good news, but there is an important caveat. One of the realities that banks must face in the pursuit of bill presentment services is that it's the biller's bills. Billers generate and own the billing content. Similarly, consumers don't owe the money to the bank; they owe it to the biller. And it's unlikely that billers are going to easily let go of their billing content without clearly understanding how such an action will impact their own relationships with their customers. After all, the billing touchpoint is one of the most guarded and protected assets of a business, primarily because brand reinforcement is at its most critical point when the customer pays. For most service companies, "the bill is the brand" — as consumers, we don't think "Ah, PG&E or ConEd" each time we snap on a light, but we sure do when we pay our electrical bill and thus guarantee service for the coming month.

The billing touchpoint not only maintains a customer's ongoing commitment to the biller's service, but also sets the stage for cross-selling more services that can be used to deepen the customer relationship. This creates what strategist and author Michael Porter calls a "barrier to exit." No wonder savvy billers look at billing as a sales- and customer-bonding opportunity, not just the mere collection of receivables. And the Internet takes this a step further because an Internet-presented bill can be used as content to draw a customer into a regular interactive electronic dialog.

In certain electronic billing scenarios, competitors are trying to break into this touchpoint as customers contemplate either extending their commitment or ending it with the original service provider (OSP). To maximize the benefits of this precious touchpoint, billers are looking to craft their electronic billing and payment receipt process in a way that enhances their own branded, one-to-one, direct interaction with their customers. The introduction of a competitor's offering or interloping agent can dilute the direct interaction and leave the OSP vulnerable to losing this customer to a competitor.

How does this impact financial institutions? We know that having access to billing content is critical to catapulting home banking programs into exponential growth. So how does a bank ride the Internet billing tide and expand the use of its home banking program without appearing to be poaching the content of billers?

A new point of collection appears on the biller's bill, regardless of where it is presented. The answer is relatively simple. The emerging new point of

Internet bill collection requires the cooperation and collaboration of billers, and it just so happens that the wholesale side of banking has the perfect processing model waiting in the wings. This is the unbranded lockbox and cash management services now provided to billers. It is the wholesale bank's existing relationship with billers that can be used as a new leverage point to extend the payment system franchise beyond the retail bank's current home banking customer base.

Essentially, the wholesale bank needs to get its payment service embedded on the biller's online statement, and by doing so it will create a new acquisition channel for the retail side of the bank. Both sides of banking have much to gain from this. For example, the wholesale bank not only serves billers, but it also does so anonymously by not putting its brand on a bill or on the remittance processing service. There's no need to because wholesale banks are well compensated through serving the biller as the repository and cash management solution. As wholesale banking's single largest customer segment — accounting for as much as 50% of some banks' profits — major billers have a lot of weight to throw around and it is a good idea for banks to remember their heritage of serving billers anonymously.

Home banking, on the other hand, is viewed as a retail banking initiative. It hinges on gaining a commitment from consumers for a bank-sponsored service that may include, among other things, electronic bill payment. Internet bill presentment and payment involves consumers, billers, and their respective banks. And, first and foremost, it requires the development of a new delivery channel and a new customer service interface point for billers. Bankers, armed with an understanding of what billers must do to "electrify" the billing and collection process, can begin to objectively analyze the various business models offered for Internet bill presentment and payment.

THREE Ps OF INTERNET BILLING

To achieve the benefits of Internet billing, billers must invest in the development of their own interactive billing and online payment capabilities whether they outsource the function or develop the capabilities in-house. In either case, billers will be obliged to address the three Ps of interactive billing: presentment, payment, and posting.

Presentment: Added Value for Customers Builds Better Barriers to Exit

The presentment component involves taking static statement data, which are now directed to printers, and hosting that information on an interactive Web-based bill presentment server. With the Web, billers can customize the user interface to each individual customer. It is the user interface, custom layout, and navigational components that billers build into their interactive sites that can be used to differentiate them from the competition and leverage the billing touchpoint.

For example, the interactive presentment function has spawned a whole new form of billing functionality that can be called "statement analytics." Statement analytics are Web-based functions that can be used by individual consumers to analyze their billing data in ways that are personally meaningful to them. For example, a consultancy may wish to arrange its phone bill by phone numbers in order to analyze how many calls were made to a particular location. Providing this capability via the Web can be a true added value for a telephone company's customers. Along the same lines, American Express' small-business customers are using its credit card interactive billing capabilities as a cash management tool, creating highly individualized review processes for themselves. In this way, American Express has turned the interactive statement into a daily touchpoint that didn't exist before (building loyalty not only before and during the purchase, but after the sale, too).

Linking Presentment and Payment: Cost Savings and Instantaneous Settlement

Internet billing also provides billers with direct cost savings and cash management benefits. The critical assumption for the second P of interactive billing is that once customers have reviewed their bills online they can also pay online, thus fulfilling their financial obligations to the OSP. Linking presentment and payment is a critical component, not only for deepening a biller's customer relationships, but also for realizing the cost reductions originally promised to billers by home banking.

It is estimated that the fully bundled costs to the biller averages between $0.75 to $1.50 per retail remittance. The major components in the fully bundled costs include the computer production runs, statement rendering, printing, statement stuffing, mailing, mail receipt from customers, envelope extraction, sorting by payment type (full, partial, multiple, white mail), workstation processing (assuming OCR stub and check), data entry, reject handling, balancing, posting, and account update. Billers driving customers to their own Web site and securing online payment can cut their costs by approximately 50% even if they continue to send out paper statements. Obviously, if they can eliminate the distribution of paper statements, billers' costs can be reduced even more dramatically.

Role of Electronic Checks in Securing Electronic Payment

The key to Internet payment is providing a cost-effective payment mechanism that can be securely implemented and easily used by a biller's customers. Consumers are used to fulfilling recurring payment obligations with checks while billers prefer this form of payment because it is the least expensive form of remittance.

The equivalent of a paper check now exists on the Internet in the form of electronic checks. Subscribing to an electronic check service allows the biller to securely accept and process these electronic checks on their own Web site. Cash register software provides a connection' to the biller's bank for depositing and settling electronic checks while providing the electronic payment information needed to update the biller's accounts receivable system.

Electronic checks provide consumers with the benefits of convenience and safety while allowing billers to maintain their existing depository relationships with their banks. Unlike many home banking programs, the consumer and the biller can initiate the electronic check directly to the bank without third-party intermediation. This, in turn, lets the biller control the other key component of interactive billing, which is posting.

Posting: Maximizing Cash Management Benefits

The final P of interactive billing is posting. Once the statement is presented and payment is secured the biller must post to their accounts receivable system and update the customer's account. Unlike the manual check and list process or the proprietary connections that characterize many home banking services, this is an automated connection that the biller can control and maintain for its own gain, without any dependency on a third party. Because the biller is making the connection itself to its own accounts receivable systems, it can do so without having to make changes or conforming to someone else's presentment, payment, or posting standard. Additionally, because the biller is not dependent on an outside third-party processor, the biller can establish its own posting algorithms for providing credit to its customer accounts. The biller can also maximize the cash management benefits of accelerating electronic check deposits directly to its depository institution.

Three Ways to Present and Pay Bills Via the Internet. Using the three Ps framework as a backdrop, bankers can more easily evaluate the pros, cons, risks, and costs of each of the various approaches to Internet bill presentment and payment. There are essentially three ways to present and pay bills using the Internet:

1. **Directly on the biller's Web site.** Biller registers its own customers to come to its Web site to view and pay bills. This is known as "biller-direct."

'Rather than delivering cash and check deposits to a physical bank branch, an electronic check service uses advanced encryption to securely deliver EFT requests directly to a bank's systems for processing.

2. **Billers deliver their bills to a third-party concentrator.** Biller sends all its statement and remittance detail to a service bureau that present bills on behalf of many different billers. This is known as a "closed delivery" concentrator.
3. **Links to consumer magnets.** Using the full power of hypertext links, billers maintain billing detail on their sites but cooperate with consumer magnet sites that provide directional pointers for consumers to retrieve, view, and pay their bills online. This is known as a "shared link" concentrator.

None of these approaches are mutually exclusive. However, the economic model and fees charged by the purveyors of each approach will most definitely affect how fast each achieves critical mass and break-even processing volumes. For example, the biller-direct approach is generally approached from an in-house processing standpoint, thus the marginal cost for making all the billing records available on the site is relatively small. This is in sharp contrast to the "closed delivery" concentrator model that charges anywhere between $0.32 to $0.60 per presented bill. The concentrator's pricing model sets the marginal cost for presenting each new bill at a very high level. This motivates billers to minimize and limit the bills presented through this proprietary channel to those customers that request to see their bills at a location other than the biller's own site.

Banks must be sensitive to the decision-making process that billers go through in selecting and timing the deployment of each of the various bill presentment channels. Just as banks had to make a decision in selecting which channel to deliver home banking services, so too with billers. Whether it's a bank selecting a home banking channel or a biller selecting a bill presentment channel, the same criteria are used in the decision to select an information-based electronic distribution channel:

- Access and reach to the target markets and customer segments of the financial institution or biller.
- Ability to enhance, manipulate, and personalize the informational content for the financial institution customer or biller.
- Point of presence processing (POPP) capabilities and statement analytics that allow value creation to occur when the customer is interacting with the institution's system or the biller's bill or statement.
- Connection effort, speed of accessing information, and overall ease of use from the consumer's perspective.
- Integration cost with existing data processing systems, especially the biller's accounts receivable systems.
- Security, privacy, and control of data flows.

Again, these were the criteria that many banks applied to their home banking decisions and the formulation of their electronic retail delivery strategies. Many of those decisions focused on selecting between proprietary and nonproprietary electronic connections with customers.

Obviously, the best channel combination maximizes access to the greatest number of desired customer segments at the least cost, and with the greatest branding and control at the faceplate (computer screen) level. In considering electronic banking options, banks chose primarily between proprietary (private) and nonproprietary network (Internet) connections. Billers will face the same decisions — choosing between connections that are closed and controlled by third-party providers vs. open and direct interfaces with consumers on their own Web sites.

BILLER-DIRECT: THE NEW POINT OF COLLECTION

One the easiest decisions a biller can make regarding Internet bill presentment and payment is to host the bills on its own Web site. It offers the simplest way to regain customer touchpoints lost to other payment methods offered by home banking services and captures the cross-sell opportunities by leveraging the one-to-one interaction power of the Internet. Billing and payment can be used to reinforce the relationship with the original service provider through the biller's own site, e-mail, and "subscribe" technology. In each of these approaches customers are allowed to view billing obligations online and authorize payment directly over the Internet securely from their checking accounts. Examples of this service in operation today can be found at the Internet Web sites of NUI Corporation (www.nui.com), Kansas City Power & Light (www.kcpl.com), and American Express (www.americanexpress.com).

The biller-direct route empowers billers to use their own customer statement data as compelling content to drive traffic to their own storefronts and service displays. An electronic cash register service allows the biller to accept and track all three forms of electronic payment: electronic cash, credit card, and electronic checks. Billers are able to genuinely reduce their back-end processing costs since all of the functions are under the control of the OSP and its bank.

In addition, the biller-direct model enables one-to-one communications for mass customization of client messages. This important capability allows billers to deepen their customer relationships through personalized electronic dialogs, weaving the billing process into the other cross-sell content on their Web site.

Electronic presentment and payment also provides billers with a new way to distinguish themselves competitively by packing valuable new information-based or statement analytic services into their customer interactions. For example, account history, item sorting, and instantaneous answers to customer questions can be integrated into the interactive billing and payment process, further reinforcing the relationship between the biller and its customers. The key benefit is that this can all be accomplished without being disconnected from the biller's proprietary account statement nor relying on or being intermediated by third parties.

View from the Webtop

Critics of this approach cite the drawback of having to go to several individual Web sites to view and pay bills. However, features in the leading browsers, such as bookmarks, make it very easy for consumers to accumulate their payment obligations on their own computer desktops, or "Webtops," as opposed to relying on a third-party service. When it is time to pay some bills, it is simply a matter of going to the "bill payment folder" and opening the obligations the consumer wants to meet at that time. Even newer technology allows Web users to "subscribe" to specific Web sites. Once subscribed, specified information such as bills can be downloaded at predetermined intervals so consumers can automatically receive and review all their bills once a day, once a week, once a month, or whenever they specify. In this way, credit card and cellular phone bills can, for example, appear every Friday morning as you prepare your weekly expense report.

In this manner consumers can now participate in home banking, one biller and one payment at a time, without the disturbance of changing bill paying habits and without investing time in learning a third-party software package or incurring the ongoing cost of a home banking service. You have the immediacy and security of making an electronic payment without giving up the control to someone else. For many consumers — perhaps the vast majority — Internet bill presentment and payment at the biller's own Web site makes optimum sense. From the consumer's point of view, it certainly represents another avenue of customer service and convenience, unburdened by the shackles of paper and free from the timing and lack of control issues that plague other bill delivery channels. Not to provide the biller-direct option to that segment of consumers that value convenience, timing, and control leaves the door dangerously open to competitors that do — just as banks that didn't jump on the ATM or debit card bandwagons early on soon regretted their lack of competitive advantage.

PRIVACY MATTERS: WHO'S LOOKING AT THE BILLS?

Internet billing also presents a major privacy challenge. As billers assess the value they place on their customers they need to also assess the value of ensuring customer privacy. Consumers expect billers to maintain the confidentiality of their statement data and payment obligations. The current paper-based method of paying recurring bills supports the preexisting covenant of trust between biller and consumer. For example, consumers expect billers to send the "sealed" envelope to only them for opening. The only thing viewed by anyone else is the address in the window envelope that the Postal Service uses to deliver the mail. When it is opened, consumers are not watched as they review the bill or statement stuffers and they fill out their checks in complete privacy. The privacy covenant is further maintained in the consumer's mind when the sealed envelope is returned via the Postal Service directly to the biller. Why should it be any different on the Internet? Consumers are going to expect, and even demand, that billers honor the privacy covenant on the Internet — that their bills are delivered only to them and that their payments go directly to the biller.

The biller-direct model comes closest to emulating the existing paper-based billing world that consumers experience today, but without the paper. In the biller-direct model, billing information is controlled and secured by the biller. This makes it fairly easy for the biller to self-regulate while deploying its own verified security measures to guard against misappropriation of information, mishap, and mischief. It is also relatively easily to verify and enforce the integrity of the billing data throughout the payment process.

CONCENTRATOR: SENDING THE CUSTOMER SOMEWHERE ELSE TO PAY

With billers moving quickly towards the Internet for presentment and payment, it is certain that *some* entity, either a bank or a third party, is going to reap the payment processing rewards. Billers interested in interactive billing and payment are already falling into two camps (those whose banks can support them with direct billing and payment services, and those that are looking towards third-party payment concentrators. In the first instance, the biller is empowered to accept payment directly at its own Web site. Those that fall into the concentrator camp, on the other hand, delegate their direct billing opportunity to become ciphers on another company's bill payment list. Lumped together with a consumer's other payment obligations, they have little or no opportunity to strengthen customer bonds. In fact, it is typically the intermediating party's logo and corporate identity that is reinforced.

However, some billers will be tempted to achieve the cost savings without considering the important customer relationship issue discussed above. As a result, they will delegate the customer interaction function to a concentrator that aggregates the billing obligations of many different billers on one site. The other billers aggregated on the site may be both friend and foe. To understand the magnitude of the risk, we need to compare the communication touchpoints of the both the biller-controlled and concentrator models, as shown in Exhibit 37-1.

The items on the left-hand side of Exhibit 37-1 are functions primarily under the control of the biller, including the customer interaction and branding of the billing process, payment, and other ancillary services. The items

Exhibit 37-1.   Biller-Controlled Vs. Concentrator Model of Bill Payment

Biller-Controlled Billing Chain	Concentrator Billing Chain
Biller prepares electronic statement and sends electronic notice directly to customer	* Biller prepares electronic statement and sends directly to concentrator
Consumer uses PC to access the Internet and securely enters biller's Web site	> Consumer securely enters concentrator's Web site or uses a Microsoft, Intuit, or bank-branded interface to retrieve bills
Consumers review custom presentment of their entire statement with analytics including a rich array of cross-sell content completely controlled by the biller	* Consumer reviews only the "amount due" portion of the bill or statistic statement
	* Concentrator charges biller to present banner advertisements on their own bill
Consumer writes an electronic check directly to the biller for BOTH bill and cross-sell content: sale and collection complete	> Consumer authorizes third party to make payment to the biller which may or may not include payment for the items promoted through banner advertisements
Customer service: biller	> Concentrator injects their own cross sell messages and can consummate sale online
	> Bill payment processed by third party
	> Check and list or electronic remittance submitted to biller by concentrator
	* Customer service: biller, processor, or bank

shown with a greater-than sign (>) are new functions introduced by the concentrator into the billing and remittance process and are controlled and branded by outside third parties. The items shown with an asterisk (*) represent either the negotiated or unconscious sharing of the customer interface and branding by the biller with third parties. Remember, you are looking for the items on the left side of Exhibit 37-1. As you can see, the concentrator model portends forced co-branding and minimal biller control of the customer interaction session.

Banks must realize that if a biller sends its customers to a concentrator to pay, the biller's bank loses the opportunity to be the depository institution and processing entity for the bills being presented. Even if the bank is hosting bill concentrating services, if they are relying on a third-party service bureau to operate the service they are truly not the one garnering the fee income, advertising revenues, and other benefits that come from serving billers — that has now been delegated to the third-party service bureau. The information learned from tracking consumers is gained by the concentrator, not the bank or the biller, since the concentrator is the entity tracking the cookies planted on the consumer's PC.

Banks should look back on how bankcard draft processing evolved to clearly see that the strategy is completely the same for payment concentrators in the Internet billing market. Compared to when banks received the physical bankcard draft, electronic draft capture made it much more difficult for banks to maintain their customer relationships. Instead, billers could shop nationally for processing and no longer had to interact with their local bank when depositing bankcard drafts. As a result, non-banks now process 75% of all bankcard transactions. And when banks gave up the customer contact and allowed their merchants to deposit electronically to non-bank third-party concentrators, they gave up the depository relationship by default.

With Internet billing and payment, the peril is even more profound. We are not talking about ancillary credit services, we are talking about the lifeblood of the bank: demand deposit accounts. Standing by while third parties inject themselves into this picture will lead not just to a strategic retreat, but to a total rout that jeopardizes a bank's profitable DDA customer relationships while leaving the lucrative Internet field to the non-bank victors, perhaps for good.

CONSUMER MAGNETS AT HIGH TRAFFIC SITES

The third method of bill presentment is a hybrid of the first two models. In the third approach, content aggregators merely provide navigational services for finding, grouping, and viewing various billing obligations. Instead of requiring billers to ship all of their billing data and service content to a third-party service bureau for publication and distribution, they point customers back to the individual Web sites of the original service providers. This model offers the best of both worlds, providing customers with a single site for the identification and aggregation of billing obligations without intermediating the content of the biller.

One example of this is the bill presentment and payment offering of Intuit in their latest release of Quicken and Quicken.com. In each case the biller registers with Intuit. Then, using the point-to-point connection capabilities of the Internet, Quicken relies on the biller to display billing detail directly to the Quicken user through the use of an embedded browser inside of the Quicken software.

Banks can follow suit by providing biller identification and "pointing" services as well. What this portends, however, is that the battle for home banking shifts from the banks to the billers. This realization dramatizes the need for collaboration between the wholesale and retail sides of the bank.

SERVING THE BILLERS

In most banks, there is a longstanding wall between wholesale and retail banking. Now is the time for banks to tear it down. It's incumbent on the wholesale side of the bank to take the leadership role and show the retail side how to deal with billers. Implicit in this is helping billers register consumers to pay their bills directly over the Internet at a biller's own Web site in the same way they signed up the biller's customers to direct debit services and other Automated Clearing House Pre-authorized Payment or Deposit (ACH PPD) services.

By offering billers electronic lock box services, not only at a bank site but also at the biller's own Web site, banks can now provide a new cash management service without intensive capital investment, labor, or the logistically bound infrastructure inherent in the paper-based remittance process. Plus, banks can do it as anonymously as their billers' desire, and without the costly check and list remittances that characterize traditional home banking programs. A bank can even offer a managed ACH PPD service for a premium, warehousing the PPDs using an electronic cash register service and providing yet another value-add to the biller's business.

Taking this approach has huge implications for the DDA base of retail banks. For example, DDA customers that have at least one ACH PPD link to their account maintain higher idle balances, making ACH PPDs the single greatest contributor to the increasing profitability of demand deposit accounts. Banks also immediately inherit quasi-DDA relationships with every Internet bill-paying consumer and can thus extend their reach far beyond their traditional boundaries by capitalizing on these potential new retail customer touchpoints. It doesn't matter if the bill-paying consumers are retail customers of the bank or not. And it doesn't matter where they live. Thus, taking an aggressive stance with Internet bill presentment and payment can open new doors for a bank, even as it deepens a bank's existing DDA relationships with its most prized depositors: billers and electronic consumers.

How Does the Bank Maximize Its Involvement at Each New Point of Collection?

The key strategy is embedding the electronic lockbox service not just at the biller level but at the individual statement level. Banks must link their wholesale payment services to each electronically presented statement, regardless of where the electronic statement is rendered or delivered, in order to protect and extend a new retail relationship with the bill-paying consumer.

By the same token, banks providing direct debit programs to billers sit in the enviable position of being able to provide billers with the lowest-cost form of remittance over all other forms of payment. It is from this launch pad that banks possess a competitive advantage. Internet billing and payment, combined with "customer-initiated direct debit" or electronic checks, extends this competitive advantage to the Internet bill presentment and payment arena. But it does so only as long as the bank can embed its electronic check capability on each electronic bill. As long as the bank has woven its electronic check capability into each electronically presented bill, the bank can be assured of participating in and adding value to the bill payment process, regardless where the bill is presented and paid. By embedding payment one biller and one payment at a time will ensure that the bank protects its prized commercial depository relationship with its billers, regardless of whether the biller collects payment directly on its own Web site, customer magnet site, or through a "closed delivery," third-party concentrator.

This said, banks must recognize that it is in the biller's best interest to quickly provide a biller-direct option at its own Web site, no matter what other channels it eventually employs. This allows the biller to realize maximum value from customer-initiated direct debit, while fully leveraging the interactive one-to-one marketing capabilities inherent to the Web. Once established on the Internet with a biller-direct capability at its own Web site, a biller is in the optimal position to extend the number of its electronic channels or connections and thus capture more low-cost, high-value online payments. Implementing a biller-direct model is a step that can be taken *now* while payment concentrators, which rely on critical mass and standards to attract consumers to deliver a meaningful ROI, ramp up and come on-stream.

IMPLEMENTING AN INTERNET BILL PRESENTMENT AND PAYMENT STRATEGY

Here is a suggested roadmap that banks can follow when establishing an electronic lockbox service that will maximize the value of Internet bill presentment and payment for both banks and their billers.

1. **Develop the solution** — As discussed above, the first step to establishing an electronic lockbox service is to determine whether to offer just payment and posting, and thus leave the choice of presentment solutions to the billers, or to offer a complete presentment, payment, and posting solution. It is possible to do both by selecting partners to recommend to billers for the presentment piece. As the solutions are rolled out, the bank will gain experience integrating these partners and will then have multiple complete solutions.
2. **Create the business model** — There are many ways to package and price an Internet bill presentment and payment solution. These should be evaluated and the chosen one(s) carefully outlined so the sales force can articulate the benefits to the customer. Sales targets, incentives, and profit and loss goals should be set.

3. **Develop the sales message** — A bank's message to its biller customers will be a simple one. As the bank is already the biller's trusted custodian of the cash management, physical lockbox, and A/R service relationships, it should be the automatic choice for operating and consolidating the electronic lockbox relationship. A bank's sales point should be that no matter where the biller goes to find partners for its electronic bill presentment initiatives, the bank's electronic lockbox solution should be used to consolidate and enable payments to the biller (and thus directly to the bank). Additionally, this service will enable the biller to create a *totally* electronic back-end posting system in conjunction with bank services already being provided. This should set the expectation in the biller's mind that when dealing with any bill-presentment vendor, they should bring their bank in on any meetings as the payment and lockbox provider.

4. **Train the sales force** — For the biller, the Internet bill presentment and payment decision involves strategic decisions about customer relationships, as well as issues surrounding marketing, customer service and support, cash management, and information systems. As such, it can be a long and complex sell. It can take up to 1 year for a biller to choose a solution. Much of the sale process is education about alternatives. Bank sales personnel need to be trained in the benefits of the solution, the pitfalls, and the overall process. Banks have a significant advantage in this arena; they are currently a trusted agent carrying out lockbox services. Banks should leverage this advantage by beginning to sell to current customers and then branch out to non-bank billers.

5. **Set goals and establish a measurement process** — Internet billing and payment is not for every biller initially. Early adopters can by identified relatively easily. They are usually early adopters of other types of technology and pride themselves on being first in their industry. They should have a relatively "wired" customer base. Certain areas of the country, such as the East and West coasts are further along the online curve. The current account manager will be able to assess the predilection of a particular biller to consider Internet bill presentment and payment. Initially, a bank's sales force will learn a great deal about the sales process. Feedback loops need to be in place to disseminate this information rapidly to other calling officers. This is an emerging market and it changes very quickly.

6. **Identify early adopters among current customers** — Pick several good customers with the right attributes. Price the solution so they receive an advantage for being first.

7. **Conduct several pilots** — Develop a test site, which can also serve as a demonstration site for customers. Pilot several different customer types to ensure that the software is completely exercised. If

multiple presentment solutions are to be integrated, try to pilot one of each.

8. **Launch** — Like any new product or service launch, Internet bill presentment and payment requires visibility, marketing support, and so on. Electronic billing is a hot topic. Visibility is relatively easy to come by and most of the nation's billers are evaluating it in some way, shape, or form.

MANY HAPPY RETURNS ON INVESTMENT

As we've seen, Internet bill presentment and payment offers a significant opportunity for a bank to enhance its current cash management services, decrease its costs, and develop new revenue streams while deepening its relationship with its wholesale and retail customers. Additionally, this increased functionality helps create higher barriers to exit.

How does one go about projecting a return on investment from Internet billing? To begin with, creating an electronic lockbox service opens a new point of collection for the bank. The bank is no longer geographically restricted to offering lockbox services only where it maintains locations. Additionally, with electronic lockbox, profitability can be achieved with low volumes because there is little capital investment required.

Banks taking such a course can expect higher profit margins due to reduced paper processing, with cost savings somewhere between $0.75 and $1.25 for each paper check that is eliminated, according to the National Automated Clearing House Association (NACHA).

Additionally, an electronic lockbox service can represent a new source of fee (non-interest) income from billers. These fees can supplement current fee income. There are also one-time revenue opportunities. An electronic lockbox service allows a bank to create a further revenue stream by marking up a third-party electronic check service upon resale to a biller.

Branding opportunities are also available by co-opting the biller as a value-added reseller (VAR) of bank services and generating new customer touchpoints for retail customer acquisition. A consumer paying his or her bill on the biller's Web site through a bank's electronic lockbox creates a new touchpoint, which can bring in new retail customers.

For the first time, the wholesale side of the bank can create a competitive advantage by tracking new retail accounts. The opportunity exists to use the accounts registered with billers to expand home banking services. A bank could even issue a digital debit card against registered accounts held by other banks and start garnering new fees.

FINANCIAL BENEFITS OF INTERNET BILL PRESENTMENT AND PAYMENT

Potential Hard Dollar Benefits to Banks

Increase bank's deposit base
Decrease processing costs
Increase fee income
Increase number and diversity of services offered to retain customers
Increase bank's earning capability
Decrease clearing and settlement costs
Increase click stream revenues
Increase access to funds
Increased one-time revenue opportunities in the resale of the electronic
   check services to billers

Potential Soft Dollar Benefits to Banks

Increase new customer acquisition opportunities
Increase issuance of bank-branded digital debit cards
Increase brand positioning
Increase market penetration
Increase perception in the marketplace as an industry leader in service
   and innovative service technologies
Increase point-of-collection channels to expand collection bandwidth
Decrease geographical dependence of paper-based lockbox services
Increase customer loyalty

CONCLUSIONS

Electronic bill presentment and payment is here to stay. Industry projections indicate that 10% of all bills will be paid via the Internet by 2003 (source: MSFDC). This translates to approximately 2.5 billion electronically submitted lockbox items.

Every bank has a choice. A bank can leverage its current trusted relationships with billers to take ownership of the emerging bill presentment and electronic lockbox to protect its commercial deposit base. Or it can wait for non-bank entities to intermediate its relationship with it most profitable customers — billers.

Deploying a secure electronic check service to enable biller-direct bill payments creates an electronic lockbox that has several significant benefits for any bank:

Extend existing services to new markets — Enhance current lockbox and cash management services without adding processing facilities, equipment, and operations. This is accomplished by embedding a bank's payment capabilities on every statement generated by a biller over the Internet.

Create a defensible perimeter by protecting a bank's depository relationship with billers at the electronic remittance level — By providing this service, a bank is assured of processing the payments regardless of where the bill is rendered or presented electronically on the Internet. This approach protects the depository relationship at the originating point, namely the electronic remittance statement.

Establishes the bank as the payment vehicle of choice, regardless of where the bill is presented — Billers will present bills at multiple Web sites to reach their consumers. A bank's wholesale banking services group runs the risk of being intermediated by third-party payment concentrators in the same way that banks were intermediated by credit card processors more than a decade ago. Embedding online payment in the online bill ensures that all funds flow to the bank directly, not via a third party that may or may not be another financial institution.

Create a tool for the retail home banking market — When retail customers pay a bill on a biller's Web site, they will, if the enabling bank wishes, always see the bank's brand. This provides additional visibility and cross-selling opportunity for the retail side of the house.

Positions the bank as a biller-centric solution — Billers are a bank's natural wholesale customers. The electronic lockbox is bought and paid for by billers. An aggressive approach to Internet billing allows a bank to retain its place in the payments business.

Finally, by empowering billers to accept payments directly at their own Web sites, and directly on their own bill for that matter, a bank doesn't have to wait for new retail customers to walk into its branches, visit its ATMs, or sign up to its home banking programs anymore. Instead, a bank gains the universal Internet as a channel into a new customer base, courtesy of its billers utilizing its electronic lockbox services.

There's not a lot of time for hesitation. Both billers and non-banks are moving quickly. Banks still have the inside track with their existing biller relationships. By not moving resolutely, a bank runs a major risk of being disassociated from its billers — its bread and butter clientele — and of being edged out of much of the emerging electronic bill payment process. By the same token, billers stand to lose the marketing benefits inherent to Internet billing as they become disassociated from their own clientele to whom they act as the original service provider. Will they thank their bank for allowing that to happen? Doubtful. It's up to bankers to take the lead, in order to preserve and extend their bill payments leadership.

BANKING TRENDS IN TECHNOLOGY

Author Bio

Richard K. Crone *is Vice President and General Manager at CyberCash, Inc. He is responsible for the development and release of the PayNow* ᵗᵐ *Secure Electronic Check Service. He organized a software development effort that produced a commercial grade prototype for transferring funds electronically over the Internet using bank checking accounts. His team secured several numerous strategic alliances with other service providers, giving CyberCash a lunching pad for releasing its new service and access to a sales force with existing relationships in nearly 100 percent of the accounts targeted for the new PayNow™ service.*

Prior to joining CyberCash, Crone was with Home Savings of America, as Senior Vice President and Co-Director of Electronic Banking, during its successful launch of online banking with Microsoft Money and Intuit's Quicken.

Crone spent 8 years with KPMG Peat Marwick's Financial Services Consulting Practice, leaving as a Senior Manager and director of the Firm's Center for Electronic Banking. He played an instrumental advisory role in the formation of business plans for both private and public funding of several Internet-based new ventures.

Crone has published over 100 articles, including authoring the "Notes From the Infobahn" column in the Management Strategies Magazine *of the American Banker. His most recent publication appears in the* Billing World Magazine *titled "Advantages of Having Bills Paid at Your Own Web Site."*

Chapter 38

The Self-Service Revolution: Harnessing the Power of Kiosks and ATMs

Aravinda Korala
Philip Basham

TWENTY-FIVE YEARS AGO, the very idea of going to a machine in order to withdraw money from a bank seemed outlandishly fanciful. Yet, with the rapidity so often associated with technological change, it soon became just another part of everyday life. To those cash withdrawal functions were soon added account management and bill payment facilities; then came product promotion as banks began to market broader financial services to their captive audience of ATM users. Such facilities have now contributed, along with home banking, phone banking, and changing consumer behavior to the steady demise of branch networks, with fewer and fewer transactions being conducted across a counter with a fellow human being.

According to figures from Retail Banking Research, there were 600,000 ATMs installed worldwide at the beginning of 1997. More than U.S.$20 billion was invested simply in the purchase of these machines, a sum which is greater than the investment in all other self service channels put together. The largest number of machines, about 34% of the total, are installed in the Asia Pacific region, though Japan alone accounts for most of them. Europe had 31% of the installed base and North America had 26.5%. In Europe, there was one ATM for every 2400 people.

The world's leading ATM manufacturer, by some margin, is NCR, which has almost half the global market; IBM/Interbold, Siemens Nixdorf, and

0-8493-9834-7/00/$0 00+$ 50
© 2000 by CRC Press LLC

605

Olivetti share another third of the market, with the other vendors vying for the remaining sixth. In 1997, NCR delivered a record 42,440 ATMs world-wide (excluding Japan), a remarkable 37% increase over 1996 deliveries. One important part of this growth was in what NCR terms off-premises installations: typically, ATMs placed in convenience stores, retail malls, and gas stations. "There's still plenty of growth in the off-premise arena," says NCR's Andy Orent, the vice-president for self service in the U.S. He also believes there will be more innovative solutions, such as the Financial Service Centers NCR has designed and built for the 7-Eleven chain.

This form of extended functionality is indeed vital to the continuing growth of the ATM market. The number of cash transactions per ATM is actually decreasing, reflecting the fact that increased availability is not generating proportionally additional use. This decrease is also attributable to the reduced reliance upon cash in the modern world, with security fears and a simple desire for greater convenience fueling a steady growth in the use of noncash media, such as credit cards and e-cash. ATMs are, therefore, evolving to meet these new demands, particularly with facilities to enable the recharging of smart-card-based cyberpurses. Some, including those for use by 7-Eleven, also encompass check cashing, a facility which is of special use to those receiving government benefits but who do not have bank accounts.

Buoyancy in the ATM market is now mirrored by what has traditionally been seen as its younger brother — kiosks. Delegates at a recent KioskCom conference heard a prediction that the kiosk market would grow to almost $3 billion by 2003. For some time now, it has been possible to use kiosks for specialist applications, such as information enquiry, but there has been a recent and significant increase in the volume of transactional facilities made available through such devices. Notable amongst these is e-ticketing by a number of airlines, who are also using kiosks to speed up check-in and reduce the number of manned check-in desks. From simple touch-screen enquiry kiosks, the technology has developed such that additional devices like credit/smart card readers, statement and receipt printers, tickets dispensers and audio speakers, can now be fully integrated. Only the absence of a cash dispenser keeps such kiosks from being ATMs.

As with ATMs, the situation in the developing world is crucial to the growth in kiosk installations. Only around 25% of the world's population has access in one form or another to a PC. Careful deployment of kiosks can open up the potential of new technology, particularly the Internet and e-commerce applications, to a far larger proportion, maybe as high as 95%.

What is absolutely critical, of course, is the ability of kiosks to deliver the systems required by users throughout the world. Historically, hardware vendors have taken a proprietary approach, with products and protocols designed purely for their own machines. This has promulgated all the usual problems of closed systems: loss of hardware independence, inability to have a mixed vendor implementation, high cost of change, etc. Now, industry-wide standards are being introduced — a move which is creating an open environment and which will have wide-ranging ramifications for the self-service industry.

Most prominent amongst these standards is WOSA, which has been developed by Microsoft® with design participation from the Banking Solutions Vendor Council (BSVC), comprising many of the main integrators and hardware vendors. They have taken Microsoft's <u>W</u>indows <u>O</u>pen <u>S</u>ervice <u>A</u>rchitecture and added Extensions for Financial Services (the XFS part) in order "to meet the special requirements of financial applications for access to services and devices."

The essence of WOSA is that it allows the seamless integration of Windows® applications with the services and enterprise capabilities needed by users and developers. It is a family of interfaces which shield users and developers from system complexities and which offer, for instance, standard database access (ODBC), standard access to messaging services and communications support, including SNA, RPC, and Sockets. Each of the elements of WOSA includes a set of Application Program Interfaces (APIs) and Service Provider Interfaces (SPIs), with associated supporting software.

The WOSA XFS incorporates the definition of a further group of APIs and a corresponding set of SPIs. The specification defines a standard set of interfaces such that, for example, an application that uses the API set to communicate with a particular service provider can work, without need for enhancement, with another vendor's service provider as long as that vendor is WOSA XFS conformant.

Although the WOSA XFS defines a general architecture for access to service providers from Windows®-based applications, the initial focus has been on providing access to peripheral devices that are unique to financial institutions, such as those which are component parts of ATMs and kiosks. Since these devices are often complex, difficult to manage, and proprietary, the development of a standardized interface to them offers financial institutions immediate gains in productivity and flexibility. This is borne out by Andy Gordon, director of self service at Barclays Bank. Commenting on the bank's decision to run a 10-branch pilot of Siemens Nixdorf self-service terminals, he said "… we are keen to move from our proprietary system to a more flexible approach based on open IT standards." Siemens Nixdorf is to rewrite Barclays' ATM software using a WOSA XFS approach.

The Barclays scenario is likely to be replicated many times over in financial institutions throughout the world. However, self-service applications will still need to communicate with host systems, many of which will still be running on proprietary platforms and in which there has been placed a huge level of investment. The cost of replacing such hosts is likely to be prohibitive, so a framework is essential which standardizes the way in which new technology communicates with legacy systems. Enter, stage left, Bill Gates, founder and CEO of Microsoft.®

In December of 1997, Gates addressed the Retail Delivery Show in New Orleans and announced Windows® Distributed Internet Applications for Financial Services (DNA FS). This multitier architecture, which is based on Microsoft's COM (Component Object Model), separates business logic from both the database and the user interface. This allows a common set of rules to be applied to a variety of user interfaces, including Web browsers. It also allows access to legacy data, irrespective of where they reside. As Alistair Baker, Microsoft's manager in Scotland observes, "This is not the first attempt to define object standards for the industry, but, unlike other approaches, DNA FS makes no attempt to define a high-level system architecture that the entire industry must embrace." Companies using DNA FS, he says, have no need to change or redevelop existing data models and business processes.

Gates' aim with DNA FS is to encourage the development of browser-based applications which would be delivered to the end user via either the Internet or a private intranet. These applications would almost certainly need to access data stored on some form of legacy host. This does not necessarily mean, of course, that all such applications would be intended for use on ATMs or kiosks, though there are many attractions to the Web-enabled route and it seems increasingly clear that the future of self-service systems lies in that direction.

To most people, the Internet is seen largely as a massive pool of information, a vast library of reference information. In reality, that is just one application of the Internet which is, at its very core, a means by which many computers in many locations can all communicate with one another. To create a self-service network, it is a relatively simple matter of hooking all the kiosks and ATMs into the Internet along with the host machine. The Internet takes care of all the communication needs, thereby obviating the need for bespoke or proprietary methods of linking the self-service devices to the host. Moreover, if a second host is required, perhaps in order to deliver an additional self-service application, it is just a matter of coupling that host into the Internet — immediately it is accessible to all the self-service devices. This has a major downward impact on the infrastructure costs.

Some businesses will choose not to use the Internet to carry their self-service traffic, maybe because of security concerns, maybe because they want to have complete control over their own destiny. This does not mean that Web technology cannot be used as a private intranet, accessible only to those users and devices defined by the owner, identical in its topology to the World Wide Web. Intranet applications, like those on the Internet, can run within a browser.

So, the communications medium is readily available and allows standard and broadly used tools to be utilized in the development of applications. What is missing, however, is the means by which such applications can control the devices integral to kiosks and ATMs, like a card reader or statement printer. With the advent of WOSA XFS, all those devices are accessible and controllable in a standard way, but software is still needed to actually do the job. Microsoft's COM architecture is all about objects being created which have specific functionality and which can be integrated in a plug-and-play manner to produce complete applications. What is distinctive about Web-enabled self-service applications is that the integral devices need to be controlled from within a browser, which means the creation of special ActiveX objects which then can be incorporated into the application. Once these objects exist, however, they are readily accessible by tools such as Front Page and languages like C++, Visual Basic, and Java. Suddenly, self-service applications can be created with the toolkit used by countless developers throughout the world, rather than necessarily having to rely on a small, often dwindling, and usually expensive pool of specialists with knowledge of proprietary technology.

This is where third-party products compliant with both WOSA XFS and Windows® DNA FS comes in. These products should contain all the ActiveX objects needed to create hardware-independent applications for ATMs and kiosks.

The presentational quality of what can be achieved is quite breathtaking. Running an application within a browser opens up all the multimedia functionality, such as full motion video, animation, and sound. From a performance perspective, much of the processing is handled locally on the ATM or kiosk, with communication to the host only taking place when necessary. This differs from traditional self-service systems, where everything that is presented to the ATM/kiosk user has been sent down from the host. In this new scenario, if the host is off-line local processing can still be carried out, which is particularly useful if there are informational elements to the application which do not require the link to the host. Concerns about control over what is available at the self-service device are obviated by the use of standard distribution software, such as Marimba's Castanet.

One of the most powerful aspects of this new breed of Web-enabled self-service is that it permits more than one organization to deliver applications through the same device. If, for instance, a hotel chain has a selfservice reservation system, with kiosks located in reception areas, it could also deliver an airline's applications on those same kiosks. Thus, the user can now book a flight and a hotel room at his or her chosen destination. Furthermore, the airline's kiosks can carry the hotel's reservation application. This is all achievable because the two parties' applications are running either in the Internet or, more likely, on private intranets. In this latter case, the intranets are simply combined, by hypertext link, to form an extranet. More companies can join that extranet, thereby increasing both the number of applications available and the number of kiosks over which they are deliverable.

Standardized access methods such as WOSA XFS broaden this potential still further. Both ATMs and kiosks adhere to that standard, which means that whatever applications can be delivered on kiosks, such as the hotel example, can also be made available via an ATM network by a bank which joins the extranet. The bank's applications would also be deliverable on the hotel's kiosks, but it is essential that the kiosk software, specifically the ActiveX controls, can determine, for instance, that a cash dispenser is not enabled and, therefore, cash functions cannot be carried out. All other bank functions, such as balance enquiry and interaccount transfers, would remain operable. The beauty of leaving such device inquiry functions to the ActiveX objects is that the application itself does not need to be altered; it merely needs to test the capabilities of the device, via the object, and then respond appropriately to the information it receives.

So, in many ways the line between ATMs and kiosks is blurring, with identical applications executable on both types of device. The cost of developing those applications and of the communications infrastructure required to deliver them is diminishing, thanks to the use of common, standardized tools and the Internet (or internet-style networks). This is bringing new players into the game — a game traditionally dominated by the banks. All types of organizations are viewing self service as a new channel through which to bring their products and services to market and thereby generate additional revenues. This is coupled with potentially significant cost reduction/containment — no extra staff or premises are required in order to have a promotional and sales facility open 24 hours a day throughout the year. What is more, the self-service applications can often sit in front of existing systems, such as in the hotel reservations example, thus building upon earlier investment rather than negating it.

Pressure is now mounting on the hardware vendors, however, to reduce the price of kiosk equipment to match the reduction in the cost of applications development and delivery. In the same way as a home PC user will not pay $5000 to run a $50 package, kiosk users, now freed from the shackles of proprietary solutions, will not invest large sums in equipment upon which relatively inexpensive applications are to be run. This, along with the predicted volume increases, will inevitably cause prices to continue their recent declines — the average price for a kiosk having been halved since 1993.

Another ingredient in the recipe for change will be the need for kiosks to be smaller, more attractive, and more approachable, especially as they find their way into places such as hotel foyers, tourist information offices, and movie theatres. The design gurus are already working on new shapes, whilst the technicians concern themselves with building and packaging smaller peripheral devices.

From a sprinkling of ATMs 25 years ago, self service has grown into one of the fastest expanding areas of IT. Staggering rates of ATM deployment in the industrialized world (in 1997, NCR installed 3000 units in just 150 days for Ohio-based Banc One) are predicted to be surpassed by implementations in emerging nations, particularly China. In the kiosk arena, one forecast has the number in use in the U.S. alone at around 1 million by the year 2003. Standardized development platforms and communication protocols, most importantly Web browser tools and Internet topology, are underpinning convergence in ATM and kiosk technologies, reducing costs, and bringing new entrants to the self-service arena. Any hardware vendor or integrator attempting to compete must be compliant with industry standards like WOSA XFS, DNA FS, and Microsoft's COM architecture.

One kiosk in a village in a developing country gives everyone in that village access to any number of informational and e-commerce applications. By the same token, that one kiosk makes the provider's products and services available to the whole village — to a whole new and previously untapped market — without the need even for local representation. The shrinking effect caused by advances like intercontinental travel, satellite communications, and the World Wide Web has created what has already been termed a world village. In effect, we are all villagers and we are all developing.

Authors' Bios

Aravinda Korala *is the founder and CEO of KAL, a software company based in Edinburgh, Scotland, which specializes in self-service tools and applications, including Kalypso, a middleware product that Web-enables kiosks and ATMs using open standards. Korala was educated at both London and Edinburgh Universities before working in technical and management consultancy. He established KAL in 1989.*

Philip Basham *has worked in the software industry for 20 years, specializing in financial and banking applications. He assists Korala in KAL's strategic and tactical development.*

Chapter 39

Checking It Twice: Check Imaging System Offers Greater Flexibility and Efficiency

David Ooley

AS FINANCIAL ORGANIZATIONS LOOK TO TECHNOLOGY to increase efficiency, accuracy, and quality of service, many are turning to check imaging and document management systems. Whether these systems are implemented to handle specific requirements of large, commercial clients or simply to track and manage records for primary checking customers, one thing is certain — check processing systems are helping financial institutions streamline their back-office operations and reduce operating expenses.

Today's check processing systems provide an easy, cost-effective way for financial institutions to offer their customers extremely accurate accounts of their deposits and withdrawals. Instead of mailing outrageous amounts of thick envelopes full of processed checks, these institutions have the convenience of sending a couple of sheets of paper containing images of the actual checks. Check imaging systems also allow financial institutions to send large amounts of data on a CD. The institution can include a variety of information on the disk, including records of deposits and withdrawals and bank statements. For the bank, the benefit is that even more money is saved in postage. For the user, the benefit is that financial information is available electronically, and it is accessible using a variety of search criteria. It is also more easily stored, and less likely to be lost in the case of natural disaster.

Before the implementation of check imaging technology, financial institutions provided the actual checks to their customers. Now, with imaging software available, they are able to customize the correspondence depending on their basic goals within the organization. For instance, some customers may want the images to include copies of both the front and back of the check, while others may only want the front. Some customers may be unable to read the small print, which is typical of check imaging, and may want their images to be sent in full size. With image-enabled processing systems, the possibilities are endless. The detail-specific process allows for flexibility and fine tuning to attain and maintain individual customer satisfaction.

As far as search capability is concerned, check imaging solutions allow a variety of search parameters, including "less than" or "equal to" criteria. Users benefit from tremendous flexibility in that there are very few limits on their search criteria.

REAPING THE BENEFITS

Check imaging is rapidly being considered an indispensable aspect of banking. Not only is it more flexible than the methods in past years, but it also benefits financial organizations with regard to cost effectiveness. Since the idea of mailing canceled checks has become obsolete, banks have noticed a substantial cut in the cost of postage.

As it has done in many organizations, technology is limiting the need for larger staffs in the banking industry. Since check imaging solutions allow for computerized storing, there is almost no need for manual organization. There are also benefits enjoyed by both the customers and employees. Now, employees on the bank network can access check images and other account information directly from the server. There is also a virtual elimination of physical check storage, and significant time reductions in statement preparation. The flexibility of the system allows financial institutions to print statements on their own timetable, not on that of a service bureau. As such, the institution has the option of printing the statements at the time that is most compatible with its work flow. This allows banks to shorten their statement cycle time, and again increase their customer service capabilities to meet growing expectations.

Many financial institutions are finding that these check imaging systems are a must for their business operations. The benefits are endless. With the systems, these organizations are crossing new thresholds in customer service efficiency. Instead of having to wait for a statement, customers have the benefit of going to their banks to view the most current information available. Both the institutions and the customers also benefit from the ability to cut and paste reports for their own specific use. They owe it to improving technology.

The systems also enable financial institutions to better serve their larger customers. Previously, some banks found this difficult simply because the massive amount of paper required for statements and checks to maintain their accounts was overwhelming. Now, some leading-edge institutions simply slip a CD into an envelope. On this CD is all of the financial information the customer will need as far as monthly bank records are concerned. This small storage footprint, a significant benefit for all, also allows for very easy and fast retrieval of information. The technology leaves older information storage and management systems in the dust.

STORAGE — YOU HAVE THE IMAGES, HOW DO YOU MANAGE THEM?

Safe and cost-effective storage is one of the most critical components of a company's information access strategy. Not only must organizations evaluate storage alternatives based on access, capacity, and cost, they must also look at the needs of the users. Users that need to access many small-to medium-sized files throughout the day with regular frequency will require a different solution than users running multiple applications wherein the graphics and information need to be processed in real time.

When seeking a storage option for this vital information, there are several aspects to consider. One important consideration is accessibility. There wouldn't be much point in implementing this imaging solution if there was no way to easily access the information. The primary goal is to satisfy the customers, and to make their financial records readily available should they have questions or concerns. By storing the images using CD-ROM or RAID (Redundant Array of Independent Disks) technology, this information is filed, sorted, and protected in such a way that quickly and easily it can be brought to the tip of the customer's finger.

The second consideration is reliability. Much like a network, the information that will be stored is vital. In most cases, it is irreplaceable. Financial institutions will be better served by implementing systems that can be protected in the case of a natural disaster or a system-level failure.

Another aspect is security. Bank records are among the most private and exclusive in the world. The release of this information to unauthorized individuals could prove detrimental to both the customer and the financial institution. So, it is easy for one to understand why it is important to select a storage solution that protects the information.

As in most businesses, financial institutions must consider the legal aspects of their technology decisions. The end user must consider whether the storage media in question will stand up in a court of law. CD technology is one medium that will. In the event of litigation, CDs are considered reliable and accurate information sources.

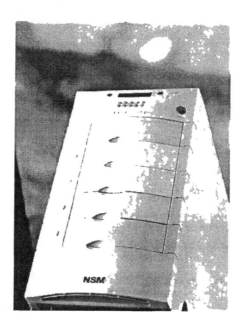

Exhibit 39-1. CD libraries feature storage capacities of up to 150 disks and offer multiple high-speed read/write drives for efficient data delivery across a multi-user network.

RAID technology is a good storage solution for companies that are concerned with speed. RAID is a faster storage medium than CD, but it is not as durable. Many organizations have found that a good balance between the two can be very effective. Storage solutions which include both CD and RAID, as shown in Exhibit 39-1, allow for the flexibility to determine which documents should be stored so that they can be processed quickly, and which should be stored so that they will be available more permanently.

CD technology can be a very effective and reliable route for storage. Many CD storage options may allow for a combination of CD and hard disk technology. Also, each megabyte of CD storage capacity costs only about a penny. CDs provide cost-effective storage of images, graphics, files, video clips and, most importantly, large volumes of paper documents. CD is the only technology that is interchangeable across all hardware platforms and networking protocols. In fact, many financial institutions utilize networked storage systems to manage and maintain their CDs. Storage solutions such as CD libraries provide centralized control, management, and security of financial information while enabling networked data access to the firm's users.

The cost of CD drives has dropped considerably in the last few years. The development and availability of CD-recordable (CD-R) technology are the market drivers. Information can be written to one CD-R disk that is the equivalent of 100,000 paper pages or 20,000 check images. The CD data cannot be altered, and can be read by any CD drive on virtually any computer. CD is the only information storage medium with this platform independence.

Important Considerations for the Storage Solution

- Accessibility and retrieval: a storage solution should be easily accessible. CD libraries allow for easy accessibility and retrieval of documents.
- Security: storage media should be protected with a read-only feature, and should not be accessible to those who do not need to view the information.
- Capacity: users should seek a storage solution with a small storage footprint. With more information on one disk, it is less likely that information will be lost. CD and DVD technology have significant storage capacities.
- Scalability: many storage systems are effective, but when the time comes to upgrade, users find that their systems are not compatible with new technology. It is important to purchase a storage system that is scalable to new media.
- Cost: storage systems can be either very expensive or rather cost-effective. Depending on the organization's needs, plan to spend from $5000 to $13,000 for a storage system.
- Warranty: users should seek a storage system that offers a warranty. In the event of damage, the systems can be very expensive to repair.

SCALABILITY — COMPATIBILITY WITH FUTURE TECHNOLOGY

Though these systems can be an indispensable asset to a financial institution, users should be sure to research how scalable their system will be after the technology is implemented (that is, how easy will it be to migrate through the system according to demand and improvements in technology). It is important to purchase a system that is compatible with the user's current system. Information access solutions should be designed to complement existing technology, not replace it. Rarely in information technology history have legacy systems been completely replaced.

DVD is rapidly emerging as a venue for storage, primarily because it answers the market demand to place more data on less disk space. It is also important to note that the migration path for DVD is much the same as that for CD. As such, financial institutions looking for a scalable CD system might consider whether the solution can be upgraded to handle DVD technology. Many CD libraries incorporate DVD-compatible equipment as a standard part of the product or upgrade path.

Similar to the path of migration from CD to RAID technology, DVD will also be compatible with RAID and other similar storage media. DVD will serve as a cost-effective, portable storage solution. When evaluating DVD scalability or solutions, it is important to note that some DVD-based standards may not yet be resolved, but the market drives and demands for DVD are quickly eradicating such concerns.

WORKING WITH A SPECIALIST VS. IMPLEMENTING AN INTERNAL SOLUTION

Depending on the size and planned use of the system, some financial institutions may opt to implement a solution internally. Others may choose to work with a specialist. One of the deciding factors in this is that managing an internal system can sometimes be more trouble than it's worth.

By working with a company that specializes in check imaging, users gain the benefit of the knowledge of experts in the technology. When there are problems or questions, there is someone to call for answers. On the same note, financial institutions can cut down on training expenses by using an outside source for their inquiries. They can limit their staffing needs in the same respect.

Organizations like Greenway Corporation are meeting their customer's needs efficiently and cost effectively. Greenway, a Georgia-based check imaging company, handles imaging for both large and small financial institutions. Their focus is primarily on strengthening bank profits. They term their technology "reliable and innovative," and insist on detailed analysis of a system before implementing imaging technology.

Greenway's PrimaImage check imaging system allows financial institutions to produce year-end reports detailing all checks in check number order. These institutions notice a significant cost benefit from the system.

With an internal check imaging system, organizations may find that they have a much greater staffing need than they would have if they chose to outsource. With an internal system, there needs to be an expert within the organization that can update, maintain, and troubleshoot the technology. The cost to have this person on board may far outweigh the cost of working with a specialist on an outsourcing basis.

GROWING ERA OF TECHNOLOGY

Especially in recent years, customers have high expectations and multiple options for satisfying their banking needs. They expect to receive detailed information regarding their account activity, and in most cases, they prefer to have access to information in real time. Larger financial institutions are realizing that in order to adequately meet customer expectations they must implement the latest technology available. Since there are other considerations, such as cost, reliability, accessibility, scalability, security etc., it is important to make the right technology decision for both the organization and the customer. By choosing an innovative imaging solution, and using it along with complementary storage technology, many financial institutions will find that the difficult and time-consuming task of handling statements, canceled checks, and other records of account activities will become much easier.

Author Bio

David Ooley is Vice President Sales and Marketing for NSM Jukebox, Deluth, GA, the leader in storage systems for the emerging CD Information Systems market. NSM Jukebox offers a comprehensive suite of CD-based systems that provide growing organizations with a low cost, highly efficient alternative to traditional storage methods. Such solutions increase user productivity and efficiency by maximizing data availability, system scalability and manageability. NSM's CD libraries are deployed worldwide within financial organizations, both within their check imaging systems or as stand-alone networked storage devices. Ooley can be reached at 1-800-238-4676; you can visit the NSM Jukebox Web site at http://www.nsmjukebox.com.

Chapter 40
Internet Banking: Leveling the Playing Field for Community Banks

Kim Humphreys

THE IMPACT OF NON-BANK COMPETITORS entering the financial services industry over the last several years has been significant. As a result, the banking industry has had to reevaluate its role in the payment system and redefine goals in order to retain and grow its customer base. With the objective being to retain current customers and attract new ones, banks are looking to provide improved customer service and convenience. Internet banking offers a viable delivery channel, allowing banks to meet these goals without increasing operating costs. The Internet also presents the opportunity to level the playing field for banks of all sizes, an increasingly significant benefit in view of the trend toward megamergers taking place in the banking industry today.

By the year 2000, home banking and online brokerage will more than double current usage to exceed five million households, predicts Meridien Research of Needham, MA. Every day more than a thousand companies of all types, including financial institutions, go on line. What is happening is a revolution in the way individuals and companies do business. And unlike other technological advancements within the marketplace, the Internet revolution is being driven by the consumer.

It took nearly 30 years for technology like ATMs to be widely accepted by the public, and screen phone technology never really took off. Even the first attempts at direct-dial PC home banking by some of the larger banks in the middle 1980s met with little success. Internet banking is different —

this is the first time customers have led the technology and encouraged banks to move forward, rather than the banks pushing the technology on the customer. Consumers want Internet banking because they have the necessary technology — a computer and Internet access — and they are already using it to conduct electronic transactions.

WHY BANKS SHOULD CONSIDER INTERNET BANKING

Developing an Internet branch demonstrates that the financial institution is responsive to consumer demands. Internet banking also provides community banks with the tools necessary to offer complete customer service and round-the-clock convenience, while streamlining operations and ultimately reducing customer service and operating expenses. In fact, many institutions have found that through the successful implementation and marketing of their Internet branches they have already recouped development costs and are realizing profits through this new delivery channel.

One case in point is First National Bank & Trust of Pipestone, a $147 million institution in rural Minnesota that began offering Internet banking in December 1996. FNB&T Pipestone was able to substantially grow the asset size of the bank without incurring the high cost of building brick and mortar branches. In just over a year, FNB&T Pipestone reported an increase in deposits of more than $5 million through its Web site, with deposits averaging approximately $24,000. The bank's Web site, WWW.FNBPIPE.COM, averages between 2000 and 3000 hits per day, and online product applications and "hot product" pages, used to selectively market the products the bank wishes to promote at any given time, account for the most heavily trafficked areas. Nearly $2 million of FNB&T Pipestone's online deposits were generated near the end of 1997, indicating growing consumer acceptance of the new retail delivery channel.

As previously noted, the Internet offers a real income opportunity and is a long-term strategic necessity for financial institutions. An Internet branch offers financial institutions the ability to grow inside their traditional markets as well as to expand into nearby geographic locations at a much lower cost than building traditional brick and mortar branches.

There is a distinct population of profitable customers who will terminate their current banking relationships and move their money to banks in their areas, offering Internet banking as an alternative delivery channel. They want the convenience of doing their banking online, around their hectic schedules, not just during bankers' hours. These Internet savvy customers are typically better educated, wealthier, and have more need for value-added products and services than the population as a whole.

And although today's users are considered "early adopters," the mass market is quickly following suit. Financial institutions waiting to offer Internet banking should get online soon or they will have missed their best opportunity to offer a service customers are demanding today — meaning lost market share opportunities and an eroding customer base. And this applies at least as much to community banks and credit unions as to large institutions.

Using the Internet as a new delivery channel to market to a highly targeted and profitable segment of consumers, FNB&T Pipestone increased market share outside its traditional market without increasing its marketing budget or staff. And because Internet banking transactions cost far less than those conducted through traditional channels, FNB&T Pipestone was able to lower its operating expenses, while providing customers with personalized service and the ability to bank on their own terms.

INTERNET BANKING RETAINS CUSTOMERS AND BUILDS VALUABLE HISTORY

According to the International Customer Service Association, it costs five times more to acquire a customer than to retain an existing one. The Internet branch plays a valuable role in reducing attrition by providing customers with improved service and convenience and detailed account information collected over the life of the customer relationship. The more transactions customers conduct, the more their account histories grow — account histories that are retrievable online. The older these account histories, the less likely the consumer will go through the trouble of moving to another financial institution, thus losing all of these data. This phenomenon is another reason why it is so crucial for banks to build an Internet branch today. The competitive edge of offering Internet banking capabilities is eroding rapidly. With several more financial institutions offering Web-based banking every week, it will be only a short time before financial institutions without Web banking will be the exception rather than the rule. "If we don't offer this, the customer will find someone else who does," explains Todd Morgan, president of FNB&T Pipestone.

According to a recent Grant Thornton study, more than 90% of community banks cited "employing technology" as the most important factor in their success, with promoting their identity as a community bank a close second. With superior customer service and a more personalized approach to banking being the community bank's appeal, it is imperative that these institutions combine their emphasis on personal attention with their use of technology.

The One-Hour Rule of Internet Marketing

There are no distance limitations on Internet banking. Customers can bank from Boston or Birmingham — or Birmingham, England. Indeed, early marketing efforts yielded customers from all over. This happened primarily when there were only a handful of financial institutions on the Internet, so the consumer had to go to Wells Fargo or Bank of America or another financial institution, often without a local presence, to do their banking online.

But this trend is largely ending as more and more community institutions begin offering products and services online. While most consumers want to conduct the majority of their financial business online, at their convenience, they still take comfort in working with a local institution. The real strength of the Internet branch in expanding the bank's reach is to attract out-of-market customers within an hour's drive of the home community. As a result, an institution can capture a new market without the brick and mortar expense of a physical branch, while still being considered a "local" financial institution.

For example, a financial institution within an hour's drive of a college can capture this Internet-savvy market, as students and faculty alike are using the Internet in their daily lives for research, to sign up for courses, to transmit grades, and more. FNB&T Pipestone followed this philosophy when establishing its Internet branch to attract customers from nearby Sioux Falls, SD and Worthington and Marshall, MN, all of which fall within a 50-mile radius of Pipestone. Shortly after launching the Internet branch in December 1996, FNB&T Pipestone began to draw customers from these previously untapped markets. To date, the bank has acquired more than $6 million in new deposits — three times its initial goal and more than enough to cover start-up, development, and maintenance costs. Additional profits from the Internet branch will further add to the bank's bottom line.

Internet Banking Can Lower Overhead

The Internet is arguably the least expensive retail delivery channel available today, with Internet transactions costing less than one cent apiece. Compare that to $0.27 per ATM transaction, $0.54 and $0.73 per telephone and U.S. mail transactions, respectively, and as much as $1.50 or more for "live" transactions conducted at a brick and mortar branch. Furthermore, an Internet branch can be developed for about the same cost as adding one to two tellers, but without the added expenses associated with payroll — health benefits, FICA, social security, disability, unemployment, etc. And, an Internet branch doesn't get sick nor does it take vacations.

Additionally, savings are realized by the bank when customers use an Internet branch to access account information and to open new accounts, minimizing reliance upon personal bankers and customer service representatives for the most basic transactions. This savings on overhead allows the bank to offer Internet customers preferential rates, helping the bank attract "price shoppers" to add to its market share. Customers know that it costs the bank less to operate an Internet branch than traditional brick and mortar branches, so they want to share in the financial benefit. Therefore, many companies offer customers financial incentives to conduct their banking over the Internet. Both the customer and the bank see this as a win-win situation.

Sometimes Even Break-Even Services Can Be Profitable

The obvious reason for offering Internet banking is to make a profit, and this usually means offering profitable services. For example, bill payment might be a "for profit" service, as customers have shown they are willing to pay for the convenience of electronic bill payment. The exact amount an institution can charge depends largely on market conditions and what competitors offer.

To gain market share, however, a savvy marketing initiative may be to provide bill payment services free of charge for a limited period of time. Even when bill payment is priced at a break-even level, it gives the financial institution another relationship with the customer. Industry studies show that the more relationships an institution has with a customer, the less likely that customer is to go to a competitor. So bill payment can become a tool to build market share.

Cross-Selling with Internet Banking

As Internet transactions become widely available commodities, banks will have to find new ways to differentiate themselves. Meridien Research suggests the evolution of online services will lead to customized financial advice. Using a "fat server" solution, the bank can learn a great deal about a customer's finances and spending habits from the abundance of data collected online. Mining these data, through the system's customer-specific reporting and Internet branch reporting features, the bank can begin targeting select customers for cross-selling opportunities. For example, at its most basic level, the bank may choose to query the database in order to compose a list of all its checking account customers with an average balance of more than $5000. The bank could then alert these customers to attractive CD rates, or money market and savings accounts, by using an automatic e-mail notification system, through statement stuffers, or with telephone solicitations. According to Meridien, only 2% of the world's largest financial institutions currently utilize such programs, giving community banks a possible time-to-market advantage.

The Internet branch also serves as a valuable sales and marketing tool in promoting services offered through the brick and mortar branch. Even though they aren't performed over the Internet today, FNB&T Pipestone prominently advertises its trust services on its Web site. It is important to include this type of information to make customers aware of the availability of these services at the community bank with which they have existing relationships. As a result, they will not feel compelled to take their business to a larger competitor.

HOW TO SPEED PROFITABILITY OF INTERNET BANKING

While there is little question that Internet banking makes sense for the bottom line, one question does remain. When can a bank expect to see a return on its virtual branch investment? As with the construction of a new physical location or the implementation of other types of banking technologies, the costs of building an Internet branch are not justified overnight, but instead are amortized over several years. In the case of an Internet branch, however, the payback will be realized in a much shorter period of time. The financial institution that takes full advantage of this unique delivery channel with effective marketing and cross-selling can make an Internet "branch" profitable in a relatively short time.

To achieve that shorter payback, there are certain strategies the bank should follow:

- Treat the Internet branch as a true branch. "Build it and they will come" might work in *The Field of Dreams,* but it doesn't work with Internet banking. The financial institution that supports the Internet branch just as it would a brick and mortar branch — with advertising, customer service, and other support — will realize profitability sooner.
- Make customer retention and market-share growth the goal, then offer special rates to customers using this less expensive delivery channel, and even give away services to profitable customers. Once customers begin using Internet banking services, they quickly recognize the time and money savings and are willing to pay for the convenience.
- Actively involve bank personnel in the new Internet branch. Employees that use the service and understand first-hand its benefits and ease of use will be better able and more inclined to promote it to existing and potential customers.

Why It Is Important to Act Now

Consumer use of the Internet is growing faster than that of any technology before it — including radio, telephone, and TV. With a mere 3 million people online in 1994, that number jumped to more than 100 million by the end of 1997. And more and more people are logging on every day. Industry

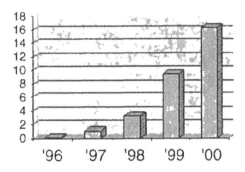

Exhibit 40-1. Projected Internet banking households (in millions), 1996–2000. (Adapted from Booz·Allen & Hamilton, Inc.)

experts suggest that as many as 16 million households, as shown in Exhibit 40-1, will be banking online by the turn of the century. And, as some 1000 companies of all types, including financial services firms, jump on the Internet each day, the bank without an Internet branch will soon become the equivalent of a bank without an ATM.

As long as a bank recognizes the need to offer Internet banking to compete, the most prudent course of action is to be first in the market. This gives the institution the opportunity to build long-term relationships with online customers today, rather than trying to win back those customers after they've gone to a competitor that offers Internet banking. Internet banking has leveled the playing field for community banks and positioned FNB&T Pipestone to compete nationally, regionally, and locally against financial institutions of all sizes.

QUESTIONS TO ASK WHEN EVALUATING AN INTERNET BANKING SOLUTION

Does this solution allow me to collect and store important customer data that can be mined for targeted marketing and cross-selling promotions? The best solution is a "fat server" solution, meaning it is constructed on top of a database that allows the bank to collect and store important customer data, such as spending and saving habits. The bank can then mine these data to segment its customer base and direct specific marketing promotions toward a highly targeted group. For example, the bank can elect to target all customers with checking account balances of more than $5000 to alert them to its savings or money market account offerings.

Can my Internet branch administrator instantly update rate and product information, or must she submit requests and wait for a service bureau to make the changes? The administration interface must allow the Internet branch administrator to update rate and product information at anytime and from anywhere, and not have to rely on a third party to make these important and timely changes. In addition, the changes are written to audit tables in the database that can be used for specific audit procedures in the future.

Can prospective customers submit account applications online or must they print and mail them to my bank? The bank must be able to customize account applications and allow prospective customers to submit applications immediately online.

If the solution offers electronic account submissions, are they secure? Applications should be written directly to a secure database. An e-mail notification is then sent to the designated bank official who opens the application through a secure administration site.

Does this solution provide error checking, or will my customer service staff be required to manually review all incorrect or incomplete applications? The software must automatically check all applications for appropriate and complete information. Applicants should be prompted to correct any errors and complete submissions before they are sent to the bank, thus expediting the process and saving valuable customer service time.

Will my customers be able to pay all of their bills through this solution's electronic bill payment service? A user-friendly interface allows the bank's Internet branch customers to create and edit their own payee menus. Therefore, customers can elect to use electronic bill payment services to pay any business or individual regardless of their ability to accept electronic payments.

Can my customers access the Internet branch using any Internet access device, such as PCs and televisions? The solution of choice must be designed to not only allow a bank's customers to access the Internet branch from anywhere in the world, but also through any secure, Internet-enabled device such as WebTV™.

Can my customers download active statements into personal financial management (PFM) programs such as Microsoft Money™? Most Internet banking solutions allow customers to download account information into their PFMs. The best solution should go a step further by downloading active statements to eliminate redundancies. For example, if a customer enters transaction information into their PFM that is then downloaded from their Internet account, the active statement alerts them to the redundancy. Therefore, a customer will not record the same deposit twice.

Is this solution scalable, and what effect will customer growth have on its performance? The chosen solution must be capable of accommodating any size of customer base, and providing peak downloading performance regardless of a consumer's hardware and software limitations.

How will this solution allow me to track the success of my Internet branch? Perhaps the most valuable tool an Internet banking solution can provide, the reporting feature allows the bank to accurately gauge the success of its Internet branch and determine what modifications can be made to increase that success.

Author Bio

Kim Humphreys *is vice president with nFront, Inc., a leading provider of full-service Internet banking for community banks and winner of Microsoft Corporation's Best Internet Banking Solution Award. With more than 8 years of marketing and public relations experience, Humphreys was instrumental in introducing the world's first Internet bank, Security First Network Bank, in 1995, and for generating public awareness of the ensuing Internet banking industry. In her current role with nFront, and in her previous position as director of public relations for Security First Network Bank and Security First Technologies, Humphreys has contributed to more than 100 publications worldwide on the subject of electronic commerce and Internet banking. She also is a contributing chapter author for* Banking and Finance on the Internet, *Van Nostrand Reinhold, 1997.*

Chapter 41
Straight Talk on SET: Challenges and Opportunities from a Business Perspective

Chris Hamilton

SECURE ELECTRONIC TRANSACTION (SET) PROTOCOL is a secure payment mechanism for network-based payment card transactions, and has been developed jointly by Visa, MasterCard, and other industry participants. SET uses digital IDs (certificates), generated and issued within a hierarchy of trust administered by the Card Brands, to authenticate all parties to a payment card transaction. In parallel, SET's use of industrial strength encryption technology provides confidentiality of the payment information exchanged between parties during the transaction.

By leveraging these two fundamental capabilities, SET delivers its most immediate, tangible value — reduction of fraud while minimizing risk. Since its inception, and in over 100 pilots conducted around the world, SET has established its viability as an agent of change for electronic commerce to fully realize its promise.

WHAT EXACTLY IS SET?

Quite simply, SET is a well-defined, industry-standard, security mechanism that combines data encryption and digital certification for secure, authenticated payment card transactions on the Internet. SET depends on four discrete computer applications to accomplish this. Each of these applications transparently communicate with each other to securely exchange payment instruction and authentication information.

- Certification Authority (CA) — generates and issues digital certificates to the stakeholders in a SET transaction.

- Payment Gateway — conveys SET transactions from the Internet merchant into the traditional payment card processing and network environment.
- Point-Of-Sale (POS) Application — supports the Internet merchant's Web servers and electronic storefront application.
- Electronic Wallet — used by the cardholder's Web browser to make SET purchases by interacting with the merchant's storefront and POS application.

WHAT DOES SET PROVIDE?

SET leverages the existing payment card infrastructure to yield new value. Instead of creating new, unproven payment mechanisms, it extends well-established and proven financial environments to the Internet by delivering the following added value:

- Authentication of all parties to the transaction; cardholder, merchant, financial institution, and certification authority, within a hierarchy of trust.
- Integrity of the payment transaction throughout its entire life cycle.
- Confidentiality of payment instructions for goods and services.
- Interoperability between different vendors' SET products.

Through these fundamental capabilities, SET delivers its most immediate, tangible value proposition to the Internet — reduction of fraud while minimizing risk.

SET'S EXTENDED VALUE

Interchanges between parties within a public, open network environment are anonymous by nature. Put another way, there's no way to tell who the other party actually is. This point is underscored by the now-classic *New Yorker* cartoon quote, "on the Internet, no one knows you're a dog."

SET changes that. Through the use of digital IDs, which are issued by a trusted third party who will vouch for your identity, you can now authoritatively determine not only "that the other party is a dog," but perhaps its pedigree as well.

This resulting, far-reaching benefit strikes at one of the fundamental obstacles that has encumbered the widespread adoption of electronic commerce. Specifically, electronic commerce required a preexisting business relationship in order to exchange business transaction data. Stated succinctly, SET enables financial transactions to take place in a trusted and spontaneous manner over the Internet, even between previously unknown counterparties. More to the point, SET is the first viable payment solution to adequately support the value chain represented by ad hoc electronic commerce.

All of this results in realized value to the market overall, and to the Internet specifically:

- SET opens a new channel of communication between cardholders, merchants, and their respective banks.
- SET leverages the traditional card processing environment by securely extending its capabilities out to the Internet.

FUTURE OF SET

As it is being implemented today, the SET standard supports payment card transactions in a public network environment. But SET is much more than that. Its use of a trust hierarchy represents an archetype for a new model of conducting a wide variety of transactions between stakeholders that extends far beyond consumer purchases. Its architecture can be extended to support not just other financial transactions such as electronic funds transfer (EFT) and micropayments, but also insurance claim/settlement, electronic benefit transfer, government entitlement programs, health care/patient records, and more. Properly utilized, SET represents a powerful agent of change, capable of fundamentally enhancing how we conduct business and the very way we live our lives.

OVERVIEW

Electronic commerce has been in use for decades, but has failed to realize its potential for many reasons:

- Complexity of deployment
- Lack of ubiquitous network access
- Lack of viable, universal standards
- Lack of unified directory services for identifying and contacting potential vendors and trading partners
- Requirement of preexisting business relationships
- No mechanism to authenticate the identity of counterparties
- No way to spontaneously collect payment electronically

The widespread deployment of the Internet and its associated technologies address most, if not all, of these obstacles. The Internet, by definition, provides ubiquitous, affordable access for communicating with vendors, customers, trading partners, and other participants in electronic commerce. The emergence of search engines has certainly facilitated the ability to identify potential sources of supplies and services. The advent of certification authorities and the use of digital certificates for authenticating identities removes the need for preexisting business relationships. Finally, the availability of SET closes the electronic commerce loop by providing a safe and secure method of payment.

633

To reiterate: SET enables financial transactions to take place in a trusted and spontaneous manner over the Internet, even between previously unknown counterparties. This, in itself, is a remarkable accomplishment, as no other purchase mechanism has been capable of providing this same capability before.

WHAT IS SET?

SET is a secure payment mechanism based on a well-defined industry specification. SET was jointly developed by Visa and MasterCard, with participation from leading technology companies.

It utilizes digital certificates, generated and issued within a hierarchy of trust administered by the Card Brands, to authenticate the parties involved in payment card purchases on any type of public network, including the Internet. Through the use of sophisticated cryptographic techniques SET safeguards the confidentiality of payment information, while simultaneously ensuring message integrity. By reducing the potential for fraud and minimizing the risk inherent in any card-not-present transaction, SET can be expected to boost consumer and merchant confidence in electronic commerce.

SET COMPONENTS

SET is based on the four discrete computer applications discussed below. Each of these applications transparently communicates with each other to securely exchange pertinent payment instruction and authentication information.

SET Applications Protocols

Certification Authority (CA). CA generates and issues digital certificates to the stakeholders in a SET transaction. A CA can be privately operated by an Issuing Bank to generate cardholder certificates for its consumers or by an Acquiring Bank to generate merchant certificates on behalf of its merchant base. A direct parallel can be drawn to the physical world of credit cards: plastic cards are issued to customers and merchant accounts can be issued to merchants. In both cases due diligence is performed prior to issuance, and is accompanied by a systematic audit control process.

Similarly, a public service can operate as a CA on behalf of financial institutions, the same way that many banks outsource these parallel processes in the physical world. In either case, the generation and issuance of certificates is performed within the strict guidelines of a hierarchy of trust administered by the Card Brands sponsoring SET as a standard.

Payment Gateway. This application conveys SET transactions from the Internet merchant into the traditional payment card processing and network environment. The SET payment gateway communicates with the merchant POS application using the SET protocol to conduct credit authorization and funds-capture processes. It also scans the cardholder and merchant certificates, checking both their authenticity and their validity, to make sure they haven't been revoked by their respective issuers.

A key function of the gateway is to convert native SET protocol into protocols in common use within the payment card processing environment. This is usually accomplished by interfacing the gateway to an existing payment processing switch, resulting in a seamless integration into the traditional card processing environment.

Point-Of-Sale (POS) Application. POS supports the Internet merchant's Web servers and electronic storefront application. Merchants generally use a specialized storefront application, typically based on a Web server, to present a catalog of goods and/or services for sale on the Internet. The POS extends the functionality of the merchant's storefront application to include payment capabilities.

The POS accomplishes this by bridging the storefront application, the cardholder's electronic wallet, and the payment gateway. It securely conveys pricing and payment instructions between the cardholder and storefront, and credit authorization and funds-capture instructions to the payment gateway. A direct correlation can be made to the credit card swipe box that merchants would use at their countertop. So we can think of the POS as a virtual swipe box.

Electronic Wallet. This is used by the cardholder's Web browser to make SET purchases by interacting with the merchant's storefront and POS application. Electronic wallets directly mirror the functionality of a physical wallet. Just as a physical wallet is used to hold plastic credit cards, electronic wallets store virtual credit cards (cardholder certificates) and provide mechanisms to store receipts and maintain purchase records.

In addition, through SET's security mechanisms, the electronic wallet maintains the confidentiality of purchase instructions submitted by the cardholder to the merchant, and ensures that cardholder information is shielded from unauthorized access.

WHAT IS DRIVING THE NEED FOR SET?

Electronic commerce, as implemented on the Internet, is a natural extension of today's mail order/telephone order (MOTO) market. Simply mirroring existing MOTO business procedures on the Internet is insufficient to create a safe and trusted purchasing environment. Due to the anonymous nature of the Internet, a mechanism was required to cross-authenticate the identity of each party to the transaction, while providing transaction security as well. SET enables that mechanism by using digital certificates to verify each party's identity and industrial-strength encryption to protect transmitted payment information. Beyond that there are additional motivations for SET to be successful, with each market segment representing a different set of needs and dynamics.

Payment card brands need the ability to extend their brand identity into new channels. The Internet is such a channel, and given its characteristics, it represents an ideal environment to accomplish this goal. The obvious result of this brand expansion is to create more opportunities for cardholders to make purchases in a safe and reliable manner. The direct outcome of deploying SET is the reduction of cardholder and merchant fraud and its associated risk and cost.

Banks, likewise, have a need to extend their distribution channels while enhancing the value proposition that their respective brand identities personify. That key value proposition is the financial trust that exists between the bank and its customer. Banks not only want to retain that trust relationship with their customers, but also to reinforce it, regardless of where and how financial transactions take place.

Merchants have a driving need to maintain their competitiveness. That directly translates into understanding and servicing their customer base through the most effective and efficient communications and distribution channels — which in today's world means the Internet. Concurrent with that need is the need to reduce operating costs such as transaction processing fees, while simultaneously reducing associated risk and fraud.

Cardholders, quite simply, need a secure, efficient, and convenient way to shop on the Internet. Even though a consumer's personal credit card liability is limited to $50 in the U.S., there is still a reluctance to use payment cards on the Internet because of the perceived risk. SET provides the basis for establishing cardholder confidence in making Internet purchases. Through the efforts of the card brands and the SET community, the use of SET will eventually become as worry-free and simple as dialing an 800 number to validate a newly received payment card.

Technology vendors are highly motivated to respond to these market demands, realizing that Internet-based payments represent a massive growth market for the technology required to make electronic commerce a reality.

WHAT SET DELIVERS

Since the cardholder is not present while making an Internet-based purchase, SET relies on the use of digital certificates to authenticate the identity of the cardholder to the merchant. The same mechanism assures the cardholder that the merchant is who he claims to be, and not someone else "spoofing" his identity. This bilateral authentication capability augments the traditional credit authorization procedure, which assures the merchant that the cardholder has sufficient available credit to make the purchase.

This capability delivers one of the key values of SET, which is the significant reduction of fraud and its associated risk. In fact, it reduces systemic cardholder fraud and merchant risk so significantly that on January 7, 1998 MasterCard announced that any merchant using SET would be relieved of any risk associated with charge-backs from cardholders claiming they did not make a purchase.

SET'S MAJOR CAPABILITIES

The tangible value proposition that SET delivers — reduction of fraud while minimizing risk — is intrinsically yielded by four key capabilities:

1. **Authentication of the transaction stakeholders.** Each party in a SET transaction is authenticated through the use of their respective digital certificates. These certificates, issued by a neutral, trusted third party known as a Certification Authority, vouches for the identity of the certificate holder. Each digital certificate, which is essentially a long series of numbers similar to an account number, is a unique identifier of the certificate holder. SET certificates actually go beyond simple authentication, by authorizing the certificate holder to participate in a secure payment card transaction on the Internet.
2. **Confidentiality of payment instructions.** Additional security is delivered by ensuring the confidentiality of payment information as it is exchanged between the involved parties. This is accomplished through the use of encryption technology, generally referred to as cryptography. Simply put, encryption scrambles the payment information in a way that is virtually impossible to decode.
3. **Integrity of the payment transaction.** Implementation and deployment of any payment system is not a trivial matter. Today's sophisticated financial environment administers the transfer of monetary value through the transmission of standardized payment instructions. These instructions result in computerized ledger entries governed by banking regulations, which are in turn backed by sovereign governments. SET is intrinsically architected to guarantee that a transaction hasn't been compromised as it changes hands, while simultaneously providing a nonrefutable audit trail.
4. **Interoperability between applications.** Since SET is based on a nonproprietary industry standard associated with a rigorous certification process, users are assured that each SET vendor's various applications will transparently interoperate with each other, regardless of hardware platform, operating system, or telecommunications

protocol. This assurance will facilitate consumer confidence and the widespread industry adoption of SET.

The end result is that SET further extends the global acceptance of payment cards — the most universally accepted form of payment — to the Internet.

SUMMARY

To date, SET has demonstrated its inherent benefits and value in more than 100 pilots conducted worldwide. However, the deployment of SET is still in its early stages, and still has a way to go before it reaches the critical mass required to be universally accepted. Historically, any technology relying on widely deployed infrastructure has faced the same challenges. To draw a direct and relevant corollary, one only has to reflect on the maturity of networked ATM machines in the mid-1980s. The parallels are obvious.

Cardholder Certificates — The Final Catalyst?

One of the key obstacles to the widespread deployment of SET is the issuance of cardholder certificates, which is directly mirrored in the physical world by the issuance, distribution, and management of plastic payment cards. The industry is well on its way to addressing this issue, and there is no doubt that the generation and issuance of cardholder certificates will soon be as straightforward as dialing an 800 number to activate a payment card received in the mail.

Foundation for the Future

SET, as we know it today, is confined to the world of payment card transactions on the Internet. However it is capable of much more than that. SET represents an archetype for a new model of conducting business within a network environment.

Its trust hierarchy and architecture can be extended to support a wide variety of financial transactions, such as checks and EFT, while supporting new financial transactions such as micropayments. Beyond the financial world, SET represents a powerful agent of change, capable of changing how we conduct business in the world of insurance claims and settlements, electronic benefits transfer, government entitlement programs, and the healthcare industry.

For more information about SET see the Visa and MasterCard Web sites: http://www.visa.com and http://www.mastercard.com.

Author Bio

Chris Hamilton *has been active in the field of electronic commerce for over 10 years and in the area of the Internet for over 6, pre-dating the advent of the Web by 2 years.*

Prior to joining GlobeSet, Hamilton was the Director of Marketing at the MCC Research and Development Consortium in Austin, TX for the ElNet project (now a subsidiary of CyberGuard). ElNet was one of the earliest significant efforts to develop and deploy electronic commerce tools on the Internet.

Previously, he held senior positions in Sales Management and Marketing for Sprint's data communications division, where he was responsible for the development of large-scale enterprise networks, specializing in EDI and value-added services.

Chapter 42
Retail Delivery: A Common Strategy Amidst An Uncommon World

Kenneth E. Russell

THE FOLLOWING CHAPTER DESCRIBES THE EVOLUTION in the financial services industry as it relates to the delivery of products and services to customers through the use of technology.

THE "PROBLEM"

One of the major challenges that faces both business and technology managers in the financial services industry today is the absence of a common set of tools to sell, service, and support their customers. Our industry has developed *delivery channels*. These channels are access points with the financial institution's customers, and they are usually supported by various technology solutions to assist in the delivery of products and services.

As the number of access points with customers increases, so does the number of different *delivery systems* to support new channels. In addition, each new delivery channel brings with it a unique set of business requirements that needs to be satisfied. Unfortunately, the existing delivery systems in the industry will not meet these new requirements. From this situation is born a new industry-specific delivery system to address the needs.

While many financial services companies have consolidated and standardized their core processing back-end host systems through mergers and acquisitions, almost every one of these organizations has different delivery channel software solutions — operating under various different

0-8493-9834-7/00/$0 00+$.50
© 2000 by CRC Press LLC

technology environments — to support each of their many points-of-contact with their customers.

I can safely state, from both personal experience and through industry analysis, that nearly every major bank in this country with assets over $50 billion has a different software solution for Teller, for Platform Sales and Service, for Call Center, for Internet Banking, and for ATM and Kiosk Banking.

To further complicate matters, often another business group, such as Marketing, may need to access valuable information from the combination of all these customer delivery channels, which can span every technology platform from DOS, OS/2, Windows NT, UNIX, and even some proprietary operating environments.

This technology boondoggle causes IS managers to cringe when someone from the business side of the organization asks for the addition of a simple customer contact management function that is "just like the one in the Call Center" product, to be added to the Platform Sales and Service system. Unfortunately, what may be a simple function in one delivery system may be very difficult task in another.

It can also create costly replication in the branches. When a branch manager wants to open a new in-store branch location to primarily perform transaction-based Teller functions with some Sales and Service capabilities, the branch administration group may have to install two different PC-servers, operating systems, and workstations, because the Teller system operates on one type of platform and operating system and the Platform Sales and Service product operates on another.

CASE STUDY

If you're still confused about the real issue or if you don't really care what aggravation business and technology managers face, let's take a look at this problem from a customer's perspective.

The following is a real-life example of how *"uncommon delivery channel technology"* can make for an *"unpleasant customer experience."*

In January 1999, my wife and I discovered that someone had obtained her Visa debit card number and was using it around town to make unauthorized purchases. Since the culprits did not have the actual card, they were making phone purchases and either picking up the merchandise or having it shipped to their address. Fortunately, one of the merchants called our bank to verify our address before shipping and discovered that the shipping address was different from our billing address. The merchant then called us, and we immediately took action.

Since our bank is one of the nation's largest banking institutions, I first checked its Internet Banking software *(software product #1, Windows NT based)*. Sure enough, I identified several fraudulent transactions on our account.

I needed to cancel my wife's debit card before additional unauthorized transactions took place, so I called the 800 number noted on the back of the card and spoke to a representative in the ATM/Card Management area. After my protracted explanation, the rep deactivated my debit card *(software product #2, proprietary operating system based)*. I then asked him to reverse the fraudulent charges on our account. His system could not perform those types of transactions, so he directed me to call the general customer service number.

I dialed that 800 number and after another pleasant little trip through IVR land, I found myself explaining my situation at length for the second time. The customer service rep asked me if I had deactivated my card because, remember, customer service doesn't have access to the same systems as the ATM/Debit card management. After I confirmed that I had deactivated my card, the rep then asked which transactions on my account were unauthorized. To determine that, I had to go back online and check the Internet Banking product and tell the customer service rep which transactions to reverse. She reversed the transactions *(software product #3, Windows NT based)* and gave me a provisional credit. I was then told that I would need to obtain an affidavit of fraud form from a local bank branch office, and complete and sign it.

My next call *(third call or fifth if you count the two Internet connections)* was to my personal banker, and yes, you guessed it, I had to explain myself for the third time. I was getting pretty good at this point and didn't even have to look at my notes. My personal banker needed to pull up my account to print some information for the affidavit, so she assessed the Platform Sales and Service system *(software product #4, IBM OS/2 based)* to obtain the information.

Now, all of this may sound like something you'd only read in a white paper on Enterprise Retail Delivery, but in reality this happens every day in almost every major financial services organization. In fact, many of you were probably nodding your head in agreement as you read the above story because it has recently happened to you or someone you know.

THE SOLUTION

In analyzing the above case study, you see that the aggravation and inconvenience to the customer and the duplication of rep services were created because four different software products were involved to satisfy my customer request. Each solution was designed for its own specific function, purpose, and customer delivery channel use, and none of them could totally service the customer.

The simple solution to this problem is to remove the current restraints of *delivery channel*-based solutions and allow all customer points of contact to have access to all of the business functions that are required to service a customer.

This requires a basic design principal of *"one technology for all delivery channels."* Then, on top of a common technology platform, you need an application architecture that is customer-centric, allowing all functions to be driven through a "customer relationship management" model to track and control all access to customers, regardless of how they come into contact with the organization (walk-in branch, phone, Internet, ATM, etc.).

A LOOK BACK — WHERE DID WE COME FROM?

To accurately evaluate where we are currently in this evolution of *delivery channel*-based solutions and what challenges and opportunities lie ahead for the future, sometimes it helps to take a brief look back and follow our steps to better understand how we got where we are today.

Nobody started out years ago with the intention of developing and implementing different software solutions under different operating systems for each of their customer delivery channels. It happened as a result of business needs that had to be addressed at the time. Each independent solution could be fully cost-justified individually in relation to its specific purpose. However, when you now look back and evaluate the cost of ownership, inconsistent customer support, time to market new products, and the overall costs associated with maintaining this type of channel-specific environment, the strategy is hard to support as a long-term solution.

It All Started in the Branch ...

Exhibit 42-1 depicts the early banking model. It was very simple and straightforward. You had a data center with a mainframe-based core-processing solution. A large BackOffice staff, that was usually located in close proximity to the data center, handled all of the transaction proofing, new accounts setup, and maintenance-type functions directly into the core processing software products. The branches took in paper-based transactions, new account forms, and maintenance sheets and passed them to the BackOffice for actual processing.

With the decentralization that took place in the late 1970s and early 1980s, many financial services companies began automating their branches. They focused on high-volume, Teller-based functions, and with that came proprietary-based, distributed processing systems that could provide distributed-level processing in the branch environment.

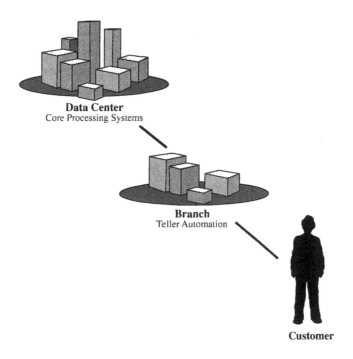

Data Center
Core Processing Systems

Branch
Teller Automation

Customer

Exhibit 42-1. Distributing processing to branches.

The Branch Decentralization Continued ...

Later in the 1980s, decentralization continued with the automation of customer service-type functions, commonly known as Platform Sales and Service. To meet the business needs of this new customer delivery *channel*, additional functionality was needed in the branches. The existing branch Teller systems did not support sales and service based functionality, and because of their proprietary nature, it would have been very difficult and costly to expand this functionality into these existing systems. During this same period, financial PCs were growing popular, and new industry standard operating systems were being released that made developing Platform Sales and Services systems in these new technology platforms more practical that using existing proprietary platforms.

Alternative Delivery Channels Emerge

As new alternative delivery channels emerged (Exhibit 42-2) and customer-based functions began to take place outside traditional brick-and-mortar branches, we saw the need for systems to handle automated teller transactions (ATM), bank by phone (Call Center and IVR), and, in the last

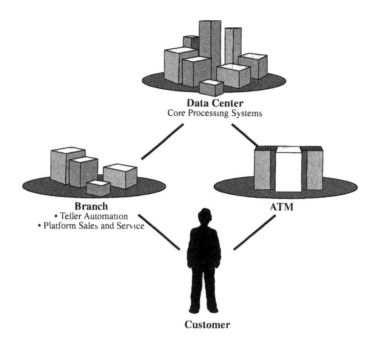

Exhibit 42-2. Alternative delivery channels.

few years, PC and Internet banking. Each of these new channels, as illustrated in Exhibits 42-3 and 42-4, presented its own unique set of business requirements that could not be satisfied by the existing delivery systems.

With this evolution we have seen each of these channels develop and mature a set of products that address only their specific channel requirements.

Where Are We Today?

In the past few years, we have witnessed major changes in the financial services industry. Traditional customer delivery channel lines of Teller, Platform Sales and Service, Call Center, ATM, and Marketing have all been blurred.

What institutions need now is a *channel* that integrates some Teller-based functions, some Sales-based functions, and other customer functions that no single solution today addresses.

Rigid and inflexible, current systems and technologies prevent the bank from responding as the industry continues to evolve and change, as new customer channels emerge, and as new technologies enable organizations to leverage themselves across every point of contact with their customers.

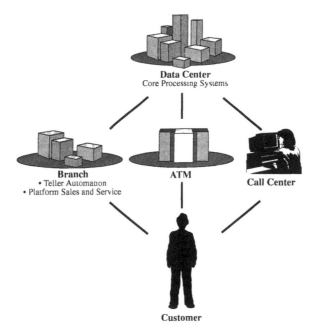

Exhibit 42-3. New sets of channel specific products.

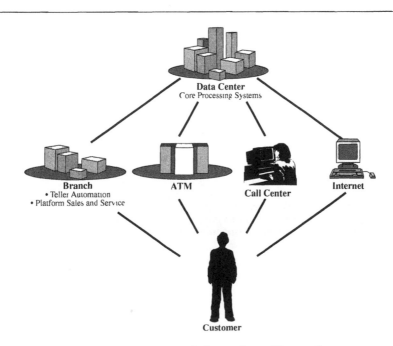

Exhibit 42-4. New sets of channel specific products.

Unfortunately, many delivery channels today operate on the limitations of their existing technology solutions, as noted in my real-life case study above. Instead of technology adapting to the business of the organization, the business responds and adapts to the limitations of the technology.

SUMMARY

As previously stated, "*one technology for all delivery channels*" is the simple answer.

To prepare an organization for this strategy requires an *evolution*, not a *revolution*. No bank is going to rip out its delivery systems and replace them with one common solution in a single project. Here's what needs to be done. The next delivery solution to be implemented must span the organization, providing an enterprise-wide solution with a tactical migration strategy.

For example, if a financial services organization plans to refresh a Call Center channel with new technology, that technology should enable Call Center business functions to be reused across the entire organization. Using this strategy, a *delivery channel* is any set of business functions that an organization needs to offer to a customer access point.

Some financial institutions are now addressing this problem by using middleware-type solutions. The problem with middleware? It simply provides a common front-end to the same old technology issues. Middleware solutions are technology band-aids that stop the bleeding but don't heal the underlying problems.

Author Bio

Kenneth E. Russell, *Vice President of North American Operations for Network Controls International, Inc. (NCI), has significant financial technology experience with banks of all sizes — from NationsBank (now Bank of America), Manufacturers Hanover, and Fleet Bank, to midsize and small Midwestern community banks. With 15 years of experience in banking technology, operations, outsourcing, and project management, Russell has seen enormous changes and challenges in the financial services industry.*

As an engagement manager with Atlantic Data Services, Inc., in Quincy, MA., Russell led the company's development of a Year 2000 practice and held management responsibility for highly integrated and extremely complex consulting engagements with large financial institutions across the country. Prior to that, Russell served as a program manager with Alltel Information Services. He began his career as a programmer, responsible for managing the information systems needs of a small community bank.

Chapter 43
Growing Your Virtual Branch: Strategies for Successful Internet Banking

Jackie Cuevas

WHILE NO ONE CAN PREDICT WITH CERTAINTY HOW THE TECHNOLOGIES OF TODAY WILL AFFECT THE FUTURE, ONE THING IS CLEAR: THE INTERNET IS HERE TO STAY. Financial institutions must move quickly to be a part of the Internet revolution or risk obsolescence. At this point, banks should no longer be asking themselves whether or not they should be online; they should be seeking ways of expanding, enhancing, and improving the services they offer through their virtual branches on the Internet.

The strategic growth of your online branch is essential to keeping it alive and producing optimum results. In this chapter, we will take a look at how to do just that. While this brief chapter is not intended to cover the entire gamut of possibilities for your virtual branch, it will pinpoint some important ways that you can exploit the potential of the Internet to bring you more satisfied customers and increased revenues.

WHAT EXACTLY IS A VIRTUAL BRANCH?

A virtual branch is the Web site of a financial institution that provides online transactional capabilities to customers via the Internet. According to the FDIC, approximately 250 U.S. banks have virtual branches. These virtual branches allow online customers to access account data securely, pay bills, transfer funds, order checks, and perform a variety of transactions via the Internet. Although a virtual branch may share many of the same functions from one institution to another, there are ways that you can make your virtual branch stand out on the World Wide Web.

0-8493-9834-7/00/$0.00+$.50
© 2000 by CRC Press LLC

BRAND YOUR ONLINE SERVICE

It may seem like obvious advice; however, many banks currently online do not have an online brand name that they can develop. Most banks today have effective identities for their checking accounts, their credit cards, and their other products; why not their online products? While advertising your Web site address is a good start, it may not be enough. You may need to do more to create an identity for your virtual branch that truly links it to your entire institution. Consumers are more likely to remember a product name that they associate with your overall brand, such as FirstBankOnline, than just a Web site address. After all, you do not want them just going to your Web site; you want them actually banking there, over and over again.

MAKE YOUR WEBSITE EASY TO FIND

Only the Web's search engines themselves have control over whether your site ever gets listed, but there are a few steps you can take to make this more likely. First, make sure your Web site designer has inserted an appropriate and extensive list of keywords in the HTML (hypertext mark-up language) coding of your site. These keywords, known as a type of meta-tags in HTML, provide information about your site to search engines and Web crawlers that comb the Web in search of data to store for end users.

The next step is to have your Web site address and description listed in major online directories, such as Yahoo!. Then, make sure your Web site also gets listed in more specialized directories, such as Online Banking Report, located at www.onlinebankingreport.com. In addition, many regional and local sites provide low-cost options for promoting your site. Check the Web sites of your local Chamber of Commerce or Visitors' Bureau for possibilities.

PROVIDE PROMOTIONS AND INCENTIVES

When you open the doors of your virtual branch, make it a major affair, just as you would if opening another physical branch. Hold a grand opening event. Send out invitations to your Web site. Offer free online banking or free Internet access via an Internet Service Provider (ISP) for a specific period of time. Give away promotional items with your Web site address on them. Concentrate on freebies that encourage more visits to your online bank, such as mousepads with login instructions for your Internet banking product. Post "virtual coupons" that customers can click on for savings at local retail stores or discounted products from your bank. And for eager but less technically savvy customers, give away computer training, or even computers, from local computer stores.

LINK YOUR ONLINE PRODUCTS TO YOUR OTHER PRODUCTS AND SERVICES

Can your customers on the Internet also access their accounts via your voice response unit and vice versa? If you are promoting a new type of checking account or a new credit card, increase its perceived value by letting customers know that they can access that new account online. If you offer specialized services for senior citizens, more and more of whom are getting wired to the Internet, consider offering online services for seniors and Web site content that seniors will especially enjoy. Do you offer a competitive auto or college loan program that could be accessed on your Web site? Consider which products you can tie to your online branch to enhance the attractiveness of your virtual banking center.

ANALYZE VISITOR TRAFFIC

Where are they clicking? What pages are they hitting — or not hitting? Assessing your customers' online behavior patterns will do a great deal toward helping you know what to do next. Many Internet banking providers or Internet Service Providers can help you monitor what features of your Internet branch are popular. Analytical Web tools can tell you when people visit your site, where they are, what pages they enter your site from, what pages they exit from, and what they click on the most.

You can also use the data mining tools provided by your Internet banking provider. Most Internet banking systems have data mining functions that capture and analyze characteristics of your online customers. Use these tools to target your market segments and cross-sell them on other products and services. For example, you might use data mining to send a customized e-mail message promoting small business loans to your commercial account holders with a checking balance of over a specified amount. Or, you may discover in your data mining that many of your online customers are home owners. A direct mail campaign about home improvement loans might be your next step.

Online surveys provide another way to monitor customer perceptions about your site. Many corporate sites on the Internet have a method for collecting user input from Web site visitors. Some sites use an e-mail link that allows customers to send messages to a general e-mailbox at the bank. Others provide online feedback forms with specific and open-ended questions about the consumer's experience while visiting the site. A feedback form may help you obtain more useful data; keep in mind that the more successful online feedback surveys tend to be brief. Some even offer free promotional items (t-shirts, toasters, etc.) or other incentives to solicit customer feedback.

651

ADD VALUE TO THE PRODUCT

Internet consumers seek content-rich, feature-rich online experiences. To satisfy these consumers, continue to add features to your online branch. The more that your virtual branch develops into a one-stop services center on the Internet, the more your customers will visit your branch. Many online features or products can be easily added to your online repertoire at little cost. Examples include financial calculators, currency converters, online brokerage, stock quotes, insurance quotes, and savings bonds. Many of these will be of such low cost to your organization that you may want to consider packaging them as value-added services for your existing virtual branch.

An important point to consider here is pricing the services you offer at your virtual branch. As online banking competition thickens, pricing may become a key decision-making factor for online consumers. If customers feel bombarded with heavy transaction fees at your Internet branch, they may seek out a better deal for a better price somewhere else.

You can increase the value of your virtual branch for customers by offering useful, up-to-date content. Some banks currently on the Web have community information, links to local events, Wall Street news, and other convenient content. Such content-rich elements bring visitors back to your virtual branch on a regular basis.

EXPLORE ONLINE MARKETING POSSIBILITIES

Opening a virtual bank branch is not just a matter of converting things you do in a physical branch to the Internet. The Internet opens up a new realm of possibilities for financial service organizations. Do not let your imagination be limited to banner ads. Consider directory listings, online seminars for potential customers, chat forums, multimedia branch tours, electronic newsletters, etc. Exchange links with your business partners and customers. For example, if one of your best commercial customers is a car dealership, offer them a link to their Web site from yours in exchange for promoting your bank as a financing option on their Web site. Your Internet banking provider or marketing agency can be a good source of ideas for effectively marketing your virtual branch.

MAXIMIZE CROSS-SELLING OPPORTUNITIES

Each page housed within your virtual branch is a chance to get your customers' attention. In addition, each interaction via other touch-points, such as ATMs, drive-through banks, and lobby visits, is another opportunity to lead customers to your virtual branch. Plug your Internet branch every chance you get, on every marketing piece, every advertisement, every in-person interaction with customers and potential customers. Within your Web site, cross-sell the products your financial institution has to offer. Advertise your certificates of deposit on your savings account page and plug your savings bonds on your seniors' checking account page.

PROVIDE EFFECTIVE ONLINE CUSTOMER SERVICE

The most important factor to consider here is making sure that your online banking product is user-friendly for your customers. Your Web site should be easy to navigate for end users with any level of Web experience. The product should be self-explanatory, with hints and help buttons readily accessible. This will make newer Web users more comfortable with your site.

More seasoned online consumers enjoy the self-service advantages of the Internet. They will arrive at any time, day or night, and make their own decisions and transactions at their own pace. Because the Web is an instant gratification environment, online customers expect instant customer service when they have a problem.

Quality Internet banking products have online help information built in for easy access at any time. Some financial institutions also offer online FAQ's (Frequently Asked Questions), which are documents with questions and answers that allow end users to search for answers themselves before resorting to calling the bank. Some online banks also offer a toll-free support line for technical questions from online customers. Such services can usually be arranged through your Internet banking provider. Of course, customer service basics still apply online. A quick response to an e-mailed message is as important as the prompt handling of a customer's request in your brick and mortar branches. You can also minimize customer service calls by notifying customers of any changes to the Web site or online banking product.

The Internet is a way to share information with your customers. Thus, you should provide your online customers with as much information as they might need while visiting your virtual branch. While you do not want to overwhelm them with lengthy, text-heavy pages, you should give them all the tools they need to get their banking done. Many online banks have account applications and other frequently used forms available through their Web sites. You can allow customers to submit these applications securely on the Web or provide them for easy printing. Your Web site is also a good place to make important announcements, such as holiday closures or the new phone number to your voice response unit. Remember, the more information and tools you provide through your Web site, the more secure your online customers will be in your virtual branch.

You can link the customer service solutions you offer Internet customers with your existing customer service operations by integrating your online products with your call center. This would allow your customers to e-mail or click to request an immediate call back from a live customer service representative. Your customers may be online, but you can still provide the high-touch service they expect from within your high-tech branch.

This chapter has mapped out a strategy for Internet banking that includes promoting your virtual branch, making creative use of the marketing and sales potential of the Internet, and carrying a customer service philosophy over into the realm of new technologies. If you incorporate these tactics into the development of your online banking services, the growth of your virtual branch can significantly impact the healthy growth of your financial institution in the next millennium.

WEBSITES TO WATCH

To keep up with the trends and developments in Internet banking, here are a few key sites to visit on the Web:

American Banker ... www.americanbanker.com
Bank Technology News ... www.banktechnews.faulknergray.com
Bank Info ... www.bankinfo.com
Gomez Advisors ... www.gomez.com
Online Banking Report ... www.onlinebankingreport.com
Secure Community Bank ... www.secure-banking.com

Author Bio

Jackie Cuevas joined Q-UP Systems as the Director of Marketing in April 1998. She works closely with the sales and technology teams to develop marketing and advertising strategies to help ensure Q-UP as a leader in the Internet banking marketplace. Prior to Q-UP, Cuevas served as the Director of Marketing for a New York-based imaging division of Ikon Office Solutions. She has also taught writing courses and authored various articles, including a special report on Internet banking published by Sheshunoff Information Services. Cuevas holds a Master's degree from Texas A & M University, Corpus Christi.

Chapter 44

Selecting and Implementing a Treasury Workstation: The Amway Experience

Kimberly Bethke
James Suttie

WITH CONSTANT ECONOMIC CHANGE AND CONTINUED VOLATILITY IN THE MARKETS, it is imperative for organizations to have the right tools to manage their treasury operations. The treasury function can have a significant impact on the financial health of a company. Minimizing interest expense, mitigating the risk of exposure, and maximizing investment returns are critical. Competition and increasing pressure on margins are forcing these organizations to do a better job in managing cash and other assets. A treasury department's ability to perform depends heavily on the effectiveness of its information systems.

This chapter describes the many benefits of automating the treasury function and describe how Amway Corporation, a leader in the global direct selling industry, selected and implemented its system.

LEGACY SYSTEMS — MULTIPLE, SEGREGATED FILES

Most treasury organizations manage their key information in a pattern similar to Exhibit 44-1. It is not uncommon to see a legacy mainframe system managing long-term debt or a minicomputer tracking investments. To analyze this information, you extract copies of the data and create new spreadsheets. In the absence of a better solution, spreadsheets provide

0-8493-9834-7/00/$0 00+$.50
© 2000 by CRC Press LLC

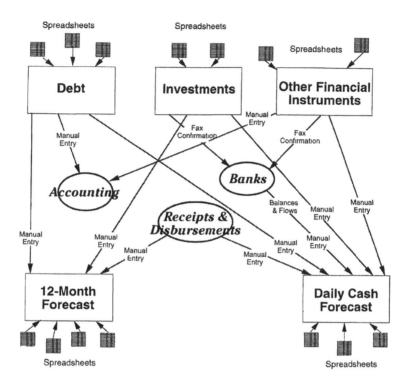

Exhibit 44-1. Legacy systems.

tools to manipulate the data. However, they are not a panacea, for several reasons.

First, staff must re-key the same information into several systems, duplicating effort, wasting time, and introducing the possibility of errors. For example, data for a new investment is entered into the investment spreadsheets. This generates the ticket to be faxed to your bank. The next step is to enter the settlement and maturity cash flows for the investment in the cash flow spreadsheets. After all of this, you must then check the spreadsheets for accuracy.

With long-term debt or derivatives, the cash flows and accounting entries will be more complicated and will occur over longer periods. Managing these types of information flows represents more of a challenge. Due to the technology employed, changes to your debt or investment portfolio may not be reflected in your cash flow projections. The analyst responsible must communicate any new investing or borrowing activity, and, in the rush of the day, this may be missed. As a result, it is not difficult to see why many organizations spend more time on the mechanics of recordkeeping than on assessing their positions and analyzing their alternatives.

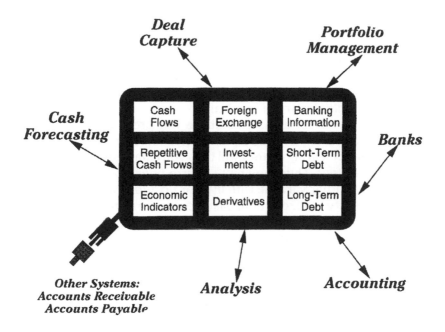

Exhibit 44-2. Single integrated database.

With these unconnected systems, access to relevant data can be slow and cumbersome. For example, a thorough analysis of the last 6 months of investing activities can become a significant drain on your time if you do not have the requisite data in one spreadsheet.

IDEAL SYSTEM — A SINGLE INTEGRATED DATABASE

Conversely, Exhibit 44-2 depicts an ideal system toward which many organizations are striving. At its heart is a database of treasury information that is accessible to all authorized management and staff. In this system, there is only one copy of each piece of information.

In addition, Exhibit 44-2 shows automatic links to internal (accounts payable, billing) and external (banking) systems. The extent of these links depends on the needs of your organization and the value of the information that may be contained in these other systems. Bank links are used to retrieve balance and transaction data, typically before you arrive in the morning. Links to payables or other disbursement data help you to reconcile and predict future cash flows. Accounting data can automatically update your general ledger.

The advantages of a centralized database of treasury information are significant. They include:

- Reduced key entry. Data will be entered only once, and all other uses are performed automatically by the system or by a report. In the case of investments, the confirmation to your bank, the updating of your cash forecast, and the generation of the accounting entries are all created by the initial entry of the deal.
- Enhanced historical data. A database will provide information that may not have been available previously. For example, knowledge of vendor check clearing history will help you establish future cash flows more accurately. Thus, you can analyze your portfolios by broker, term, or any other variable with little or no additional effort. You now have the ability to take action, based on performance.
- Increased productivity. One of the more obvious benefits of a treasury workstation is improved productivity. With an integrated system you can dramatically reduce clerical effort, often in the range of 25 to 50 percent.
- Improved accuracy. An integrated database also provides more control and rigor. All information entered is compared to pre-established values and verified for accuracy. Systems provide drop-down lists for brokers, portfolios, instrument type, and other common fields This minimizes keying and reduces the potential for mistakes. With accurate information you definitely will increase credibility with management.
- Better investment and borrowing decisions. The database environment also allows you to get into the market earlier in the morning to secure a better rate for investing. A treasury workstation will give you more time for planning strategies and assessing alternatives that should result in better investment or borrowing decisions. Furthermore, reducing the average daily cash variance can generate significant savings by allowing you to invest additional funds or reduce overdrafts.
- Greater flexibility. The treasury workstation also integrates several systems into one seamless solution. You do not need to be concerned with the physical location of data. All the information is stored in one place and is immediately available for viewing and analysis. The consistency of the tools that manipulate the information gives them the same look and feel, thus making it much easier to act on behalf of another analyst who may be on vacation.
- Enriched job functions. The improved analytical capability inherent in the database environment often leads to enriched job functions and employee satisfaction. People are attracted to treasury because of the excitement of the function and the fact that they can influence the organization. Eliminating manual activities and providing solid

analytical tools on which to base decisions will make the treasury role more rewarding.

THE AMWAY EXPERIENCE

To create such an atmosphere in its treasury department, Ada, MI-based Amway Corporation selected and implemented the Selkirk Financial Technologies, Inc. Treasury Manager™ workstation to integrate its systems.

One of the world's largest direct selling companies, Amway consists of Amway Corporation, which is privately held by the DeVos and Van Andel families; and Amway Japan Limited and Amway Asia Pacific Limited, which are publicly traded sister companies of Amway Corporation.

Amway reported global estimated retail sales of $7 billion in fiscal year 1997, with the majority of Amway's business outside of North America. More than 3 million independent distributors in 50 affiliate markets are supported by Amway. The company employs more than 14,000 people, with about 5000 located at its global headquarters in Ada. Most of Amway's products are manufactured in Ada or at the company's Nutrilite facilities in California.

Amway's treasury functions are globally decentralized, with the various affiliates managing their own cash positions. The exception is Amway of Canada, Ltd., which has its cash management handled by Amway's Corporate Treasury department. Corporate Treasury assists and advises the affiliates in setting up bank accounts, generating and maintaining banking relationships, credit facilities, and foreign exchange strategies. While Amway's affiliates are managed locally, there remain many intercompany transactions that flow through the corporation. These transactions include payments for product, dividends, and royalties.

Corporate Treasury uses one main concentration bank and five relationship banks for various U.S. operation functions, such as controlled disbursements, foreign vendor payments, foreign subsidiary and affiliate accounts, and foreign exchange transactions. For the Canadian affiliate's cash management, one main bank is used for virtually all cash management functions, accounts payable, bonus, payroll, refunds, and receipts, with accounts in both U.S. and Canadian dollars. Exhibit 44-3 shows the general operations format of Corporate Treasury.

TIME FOR CHANGE

Before Treasury Manager became a part of Amway's treasury operations, the corporation used a combination of manual and electronic systems. Reconciliation of bank balances and transactions, for both prior and current day, involved retrieving the bank reports from a manual dial up,

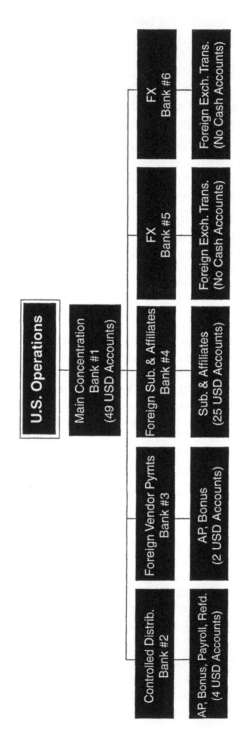

Exhibit 44-3. Amway's corporate treasury.

printing the reports, keying the data into the cash management spreadsheet and other databases as necessary, hard copy storage, and reconciliation. Wire transfers and investment portfolios were tracked using FoxPro databases in which the transactions were keyed, and then the information was re-keyed one to two more times into various other systems, depending upon the transactions to track, account, and transact. Check clearing, incoming funds, and float calculations were handled by pulling paper reports, keying into spreadsheets, and running macros to process the information, then re-keying into the cash management spreadsheet.

Amway used a computerized foreign exchange system for tracking its foreign exchange exposure. This meant that they keyed into the system, printed reports for settlements, and keyed those settlements into the cash management spreadsheet, wire database and bank wire transfer systems. General ledger entries were entered manually by its Corporate Financial Accounting department from wire database, reports and photocopies of bank reports, such as controlled disbursement reports.

The key issues and problems with Amway's methods included extensive duplication of effort, errors in predicting cash flows, and a loss of operational efficiency. The duplication of effort involved in re-keying transactions into multiple spreadsheets and systems was very inefficient and created more opportunity for key errors and omissions. The errors in predicting cashflows arose from the lack of easily accessible historic data to create benchmark forecasts and the inability to determine Canadian check clearing dates automatically and accurately.

Amway management felt that operational efficiency could be increased greatly by integrating and automating several separate manual systems and processes within Corporate Treasury and Corporate Financial Accounting. This would include bank dialups for downloading transactions and balances, generation of reports, generation of journal entries, and integrated investment and forecasting systems that could automatically post information to cash position. Through these improvements and efficiencies, Amway would be able to eliminate the need for additional staffing.

Amway completed an in-depth review of Corporate Treasury processes and functions through a massive corporate-wide process mapping and documentation drive. This allowed it to identify problem areas and ways to improve. They determined that a treasury workstation could help to accomplish Amway's goals.

VENDOR SELECTION PROCESS

In November 1996, Amway began its research at the Treasury Management Association Annual Conference in Atlanta, GA. Materials were gathered on treasury products on the market and contacts were cultivated to facilitate further research. Through this process, Amway was able to identify a wish list of features it felt would be most beneficial to the corporation. A Request for Proposal (RFP) was developed for review by Treasury staff, managers, and Information Systems and then sent to six vendors that were seen to best meet Amway's needs.

Of the six proposals received, three of the vendors were invited to perform in-house presentations. Each vendor received a 2-hour time slot to present their product and to address Amway's specific list of concerns and features. From these presentations, the search was narrowed down to the two most promising, intuitive products.

At this point, Corporate Treasury felt that site visits of companies using these products would be helpful in its decision. The vendors made these arrangements, and the resulting visits provided additional insights toward a final decision. To ensure an objective decision was made, a rating grid was generated to rate the features of the products and the companies involved on the basis of importance and satisfaction. Upon completion of this final step, a formal proposal was submitted with the recommendation to use Treasury Manager. The proposal included a benefit analysis and capital project request.

In making the decision, key problems and possible Treasury Manager solutions were examined. As earlier outlined, one of the most prominent problems was the duplication of effort involved in re-keying data multiple times. Treasury Manager could integrate all of the cash management systems, allowing data to be keyed a single time and significantly reducing the possibility of errors. Cash flow prediction errors in both daily and short- to long-term cash flows could be reduced by using the combined database format of the system to query historical cash flows quickly, accurately, easily, and in a very flexible manner. This enhanced the ability to analyze and predict cash flow patterns and changes occurring in these patterns.

Treasury Manager also had the ability to track check clearing history patterns. While controlled disbursement accounts were used for Amway's domestic treasury functions, Corporate Treasury still tracked large checks that were issued, allowing predictions of controlled disbursement needs before they occurred. The Canadian cash management was different in that no controlled disbursement accounts were used, which meant that accurate check clearing forecasting was that much more important for these accounts. Treasury Manager tracks checks issued by the payee in order to generate a clearing history. This clearing history is used by the system to predict the date a check will clear the bank account.

Operational efficiencies Amway felt would be useful included:

- Automatic bank dialups and download of BAI format information on prior and current day transactions and balances
- Automated, scheduled processes to run reporting and other intraday tasks
- Automatic reconciliation of transactions
- Ability to access all cash management data in one system
- Ability to cross reference actual vs. predicted transactions and facilitate exception reporting

This increase in operational efficiency was able to free up Corporate Treasury personnel to work on more analytical tasks, such as finding ways to earn higher interest on investments or analyzing current market conditions to better manage foreign exchange exposures.

CRITICAL SUCCESS FACTORS

Amway identified several Critical Success Factors (CSF) for the implementation of the new system. The first was that there would be a smooth transition from the old systems to Treasury Manager. This included not adding a great deal of work and interruptions in essential processes, downloading existing information into the system, and the ease of use of the system. The second CSF was that the cash position database would maintain the integrity of Amway's information. Complete, accurate banking information for both current and prior day was essential. Integration with the foreign exchange system was another important factor, as was integration with the general ledger and wire systems. This required that the system be versatile in both upload and download capabilities.

The replacement of Amway's investment databases was critical, as the vendor no longer was supporting the systems in use, and they would need to be rewritten or replaced soon. The final CSF was the integration of systems. Creating one database and one system for all of Treasury activities was the goal. This included daily cash management, electronic payments, investments and borrowings, cash planning (short-term), and cash forecasting (long-term). This would simplify operations and allow access to information more quickly, produce more useful reporting, facilitate analysis of interrelated transactions, and produce more accurate forecasts.

THE IMPLEMENTATION PROCESS

Amway began the implementation of Treasury Manager in December 1997. It was decided that the Cash Forecasting, Short-Term Investments, and Electronic Payments modules would best serve Amway's needs. A technical service representative came to Amway for a week of training and installation of 10 workstations, along with customization as needed. One workstation was set up with a dedicated analog line for daily bank dial-ups, and the remainder would use modem phones. Four workstations were set up with PCAnywhere for support and assistance, and one was set up with a back-up server for disaster recovery purposes. The database and common reports are stored on the network server with shared access, and individual setups are stored on individual drives.

Amway was able to pull up bank reports immediately and began to run the cash position sheet in parallel the first week. After 2 weeks they went live with the Canadian cash position and investments, and went live after 1 month for domestic operations. Report design and modification occurred throughout the process, and Amway has continued to find new uses for the system and its reporting capabilities. Amway has completed work to download files from its accounts payables system and is running parallel with its general ledger interface. The general ledger interface will begin running after Amway's year-end close is complete. Amway has completed internal set up of the wire transfer module but has not begun setting up the actual connection with the bank system. This is on hold, pending the release of a new wire platform from its main relationship bank.

Future tasks for Amway include setting up a download from its foreign exchange system and potentially downloading EFTPS tax payments into Treasury Manager. The corporation also may look into the ability to import account analysis information in electronic format and utilize Treasury Manager to check the legitimacy of charges.

BENEFITS OF THE NEW SYSTEM

Benefits currently realized include the elimination of the need for additional staffing, reduction of morning prior day reconciliation process time by nearly 2 hours, reduction of current day bank polling tasks by an hour, and monthly reporting by at least 11 hours. These numbers include automated bank dialups, downloading information into relevant systems, and automated processes and reports that run throughout the day. Amway has eliminated the need to rewrite three database systems, saving its Information Systems department approximately 640 hours of work. In addition, it has minimized excess cash and short-term borrowings, consolidated and simplified systems, reduced the chance of key errors, and developed a greater ease of use.

Of the critical success factors Amway identified, the majority have been accomplished, and work toward completion of the remaining factors is in process. Amway experienced a very smooth transition into the new system, including complete, accurate banking information, while maintaining the integrity of data as desired. Amway was able to use the automated report generation feature of the system beyond original expectations. Investment systems were replaced and will not need to be rewritten. Key

Treasury systems were integrated, minimizing the duplication of effort and errors in predicting cash flows by utilizing the system to evaluate patterns for deposits, check clearings, and other items on a simpler, more frequent basis. Corporate Treasury has been able to interface with Amway's accounts payable system to download check issues and is in the process of interfacing with the general ledger system.

PITFALLS TO AVOID

Among the pitfalls any project manager should watch for and try to avoid in the process of implementing a workstation is expecting it to meet all needs completely. While a treasury workstation is a useful tool, it cannot run a treasury operation without good, dedicated people. It is critical to obtain complete cooperation from the Information Systems department, as they will be instrumental in installing and providing support for the system. Finally, the project manager must set deadlines for the replacement of old processes and enforce those objectives.

WORDS OF WISDOM

For those looking into a new treasury workstation, it is a good idea to limit the length of vendor presentations and provide to them in advance a list of desired features and concerns that need to be addressed. Customer site visits will allow you to see the system in use and interview its operators to determine their satisfaction with the product. When choosing a product, it is important to consider customer service, program features, future enhancements and development plans.

During implementation of the workstation, it is important to keep an open mind, as flexibility and adaptation are key to the success of the transition to a new system. During and after implementation it is imperative to keep the momentum going. Once momentum ceases, the project has a tendency to become stagnant. After implementation, it remains important to continually review the company's needs and the products and services available.

Authors' Bios

Kimberly Bethke *is a Treasury Analyst at Amway Corporation. Her main responsibilities include North American cash management, global credit facilities, foreign exchange advisory team member, funds transfer systems administrator, and project manager and administrator of Amway's treasury workstation implementation project.*

James Suttie *is President and CEO of Selkirk Financial Technologies Inc. His firm develops and markets Treasury Manager™, a leading Windows-based treasury workstation. Prior to founding his firm in 1988, he held senior positions at Gulf Canada, Noranda Mines, and IBM Canada.*

Section III
Securities Trends in Technology

WHEN I FIRST STARTED AT THE NEW YORK STOCK EXCHANGE, my initial project was to build a system that monitored registered representatives. Called REGIS (okay, so that name wasn't very clever), it used the then state-of-the-art Dialog Management System from IBM to deliver an online interface to end users. Later REGIS was expanded into EAGLE (yes, there were jokes about bird droppings), which encompassed the breadth of the Exchange's regulatory functions such as complaint processing and enforcement actions.

If only today's technology had been available yesterday! What was painstaking yesterday is fairly easy today. The EAGLE developers even built their own e-mail system. Everything, and I mean everything, had to be jury-rigged because the technology just wasn't there. Today's technology consists of visual development systems, program generators, groupware, and Internet-based technologies — replete with add-ins and Java applets.

Just 2 decades ago the pace of technological change was very slow indeed. Today it is so rapid that those on the vendor side of the community consider 3 months to be equivalent to a full year!

A proliferation of consumer-level investment sites has sprung up on the Web. The most popular, with more than 1.6 million visitors checking in regularly, Microsoft Investor features a highly detailed portfolio manager, a "strategy lab" feature where experts go over their investment strategies with readers, mutual fund information, and advisor alerts.

In this section we discuss some of the fundamental technologies within the securities industry such as a Portfolio Management System for the Twenty-First Century and Straight Through Processing. We'll discuss the fine aspects of Logging and Monitoring and delve into the proper way to design Investment Performance Systems.

Like banking and insurance, the securities industry has been forever altered by the advent of the Internet. We can expect more Internet-based investment services, touching the areas of risk management and performance monitoring. The profits of many of the brokerage firms will rise astronomically as attendant costs decrease due to the proliferation of individual investors rushing to the Internet to do online trading. Of course, a large and sustained downturn in the current Bull market could very well do away with that.

But even if there is a downturn in the market, the technological boom is here to stay.

Jessica Keyes

Chapter 45
The Future of the Securities Industry: Convergence of Trust and Brokerage

John Buckner

THE CONTINUED RELAXATION OF *GLASS-STEAGALL,* the reduction in January 1997 of the ineligible revenue rule for the securities subsidiaries of banks, and a 7-year bull market have fueled unprecedented M&A activity in financial services over the last several years. In 1997 we saw a number of banks acquire broker/dealers. Bank of America acquired Robertson Stephens, NationsBank bought Montgomery Securities, and Fleet Financial bought Quick & Reilly.

At the same time, driven primarily by the relaxation of *Glass-Steagall,* banks and insurance companies have formed their own brokerage units, some from scratch, others engendered from traditional bank capital markets operations which have often become Section 20 companies. Moreover, the consolidation trend, with a possible year 2000 hiatus, appears likely to continue well into the future.

John Wimsatt, an analyst at Friedman Billings Ramsey who follows the financial services industry, agrees. "When compared to the international financial services paradigm, such as the European community, financial services consolidation in the United States has much further to go." The Year 2000 problem may delay some merger activities due to the inability of IT departments to integrate systems while undergoing Year 2000 development efforts, but financial services consolidations are likely to resume in earnest well into the first decade of the next millennium.

During this same period, brokerage firms have been quietly establishing broker-affiliated trust companies for their high-net-worth customers and to

0-8493-9834 7/00/$0 00+$ 50

support pension plans. Just a few of the major brokerage firms with trust company subsidiaries include: Alex Brown, Merrill Lynch, Charles Schwab, Legg Mason, Raymond James, Hilliard Lyons, American Express Financial Advisors, Southwest Securities, and Piper Jaffrey.

THE OPPORTUNITY

The new environment therefore results in trust and brokerage entities operating within the same holding company — be it a broker, a bank, or an insurance company. Indeed, mergers and acquisitions at some of the larger banks have resulted in the accumulation of a variety of similar securities processing operations. Operational consolidation efforts notwithstanding, it would not be unusual for a money center bank today to have separate platforms for the following businesses:

Retail brokerage
Institutional brokerage
Bank capital markets
Private banking
Personal trust
Institutional trust
Retirement services
Corporate trust
Custody/global custody
Other (derivatives, risk management,
 foreign exchange, investment portfolio)

With redundant securities processing technology and operations expertise at work across these units, executives at many firms are wondering if there may be opportunities to further collapse securities processing operations. Others are focusing on what may be more significant — opportunities to attract and retain customers by offering a wider range of products and services at substantially lower costs by leveraging the strengths of the technology across the different industry segments.

Regulations, in many cases, limit the extent to which these businesses can be integrated. But regulations continue to change and continue to be relaxed, so let's explore not the regulatory possibilities but rather the technological and operational implications these opportunities present.

FORCES OF CHANGE

While the M&A activities represent one force of change, there are several other catalysts for seeking out operational and technological synergy across these industries. Below is a list of some of these factors and how they might influence both industries separately and financial services generally.

Customer Awareness

The popularity of mutual funds, 401(k) and IRA plans, the explosive growth of the Internet in general and Internet trading specifically, and the longest bull market in history have resulted in a population of Americans who are much more aware of the securities industry than ever before. It is not surprising then, that according to a Tower Group research report, mutual fund investments in this country have grown from approximately $500 million in 1985 to more than $2.5 trillion in 1996.

These new investors are generally unaware of the regulatory or traditional boundaries which have always separated brokerage and trust. A young trust beneficiary who 20 years ago might have left her trust assets in the trust department without question, may now demand Internet account access and discount brokerage commission rates from her trust bank. The same investor, however, accustomed to highly automated tax reporting, might also demand tax-lot accounting from her discount broker. To this new class of investor, the distinctions between trust and brokerage are irrelevant. What is relevant is service, product, convenience, and price.

In tacit acknowledgment that their customers fail to discern these traditional distinctions and are demanding more meaningful and comprehensive products and services, the private banking groups of some major money center banks (e.g., Banker's Trust, Bank of America, and Chase) now offer customers consolidated accounts. While each of these products differ, all of them attempt to combine customer data on statements from as many areas of the institution as possible, regardless of industry segment, including traditional banking (DDA, CD, credit, etc.), trust, and retail brokerage. Some even permit customers to trade securities within trust or brokerage through a link to the DDA system. Today's savvy investor will continue to pressure players in both industries to offer more valuable services and products regardless of industry segmentation. This trend will force financial services firms to develop the same features repeatedly across industry platforms, link platforms together, or integrate the businesses entirely.

Pricing Pressure

Price consciousness among today's investors accompanies this newfound awareness of service and product opportunity. According to many trust company managers who declined to be interviewed for this analysis, personal trust departments are witnessing a runoff in trust accounts to discount brokers due to improved custodial and execution services and lower or nonexistent custodial fees.

At the Private Asset Management department of Montgomery Asset Management L.L.C., Manager Karyn Rozenoff recalls how "just last year we witnessed a significant runoff of high-net-worth personal trust customers to discount brokers offering essentially identical services at substantially lower fees." Trust accounts are legally permitted to choose their custodian, and, after considering their options, many are unwilling to pay a trust company its custodial fees in addition to pass-through brokerage commissions. Choosing a discount broker over a trust company can eliminate an unnecessary layer and additional costs.

On the institutional side, the capture by brokerage firms of a portion of the custodial services offered by banks and global custodians through the introduction of "prime brokerage" clearly underscores the importance that price has already had on that industry segment. At the same time, customers are demanding higher quality service and a wider range of products from their prime broker, sometimes demanding services and products that brokerage systems are unaccustomed to providing. This pressure on price as well as functionality will likely lead to more creative technological solutions to the data processing paradigm in both industries, possibly resulting in a hybrid solution. Moreover, pressure on prices will lead to pressure on cost reduction within operations, which may lead firms to further reconstruct the technical paradigm.

Entry of New Players

Regulations overseas are of course different. While Asian markets tend to more clearly differentiate trust and brokerage services, the recent collapse of these markets has already resulted in relaxation of cross-industry ownership and operation of securities businesses there. In Europe, however, there is little distinction between trust, brokerage, and insurance, with the same firm seamlessly offering all types of services. Doug Dannemiller of the Tower group notes that "these full-service foreign financial services companies tend to view the securities industry less myopically and have entered the U.S. markets with a different perspective toward the business and the customer." In fact, with the availability of 128-bit encryption in the last year, both UBS and Credit Suisse now "lead the way with integrated trust and brokerage services," continues Doug, "by offering U.S. customers Web-based securities trading for private banking customers."

While foreign firms making U.S. acquisitions must adhere to the same regulatory restrictions as U.S.-based firms, they may be more likely to challenge them. Moreover, the large insurance company, a dominant player in Europe, has been until recently a sleeping giant here in the U.S. Already, Travelers has made a significant play to fully integrate financial services and stretch the limits of the regulations by leaping into brokerage with the acquisitions of Smith Barney and Salomon and then merging with Citibank to form the largest domestic financial services company offering an unprecedented array of products and services. Other insurance companies, many of whom possess a large capital base, have made or are planning to make brokerage acquisitions or are in the process of building their own brokerage subsidiaries. These firms come into the securities industry with no preconceived notions regarding boundaries between trust and brokerage systems and services and are likely to lead the challenges to these ideological boundaries.

Over time, the entry of these new players — insurance companies, foreign financial services firms, and mutual fund companies — will force the entire financial services industry to look at securities processing less ideologically and may lead the way to fundamental change in the technical paradigm.

Shear Size

Currently, the largest packaged-software applications for the trust industry can support somewhere in the vicinity of 150,000 to 250,000 accounts. Packaged software for brokerage can support more than a million accounts and tens of thousands of trades per day. The account base of the largest trust banks is approximately 100,000 accounts. One more mega-merger among the largest banks or a series of smaller acquisitions by one of the larger trust banks will encumber system and operations integration efforts on these platforms.

As a result, CIOs of some large firms are already exploring alternatives, including brokerage applications. Undoubtedly, trust industry executives pleased by the capacity of brokerage systems may be disappointed by the lack of certain trust functionality. Could these searches, however, lead to some sort of hybrid solution whereby generic, high-volume processes are handled by the brokerage systems, leaving the trust systems to perform trust-specific functions? Continued consolidation coupled with trust system volume constraints may push some of the largest money center banks to look at cross-industry alternatives to securities processing.

SIMILARITIES AND DIFFERENCES

While an exhaustive list of the similarities of the brokerage and trust industries from a functionality standpoint would be prohibitively long, there are several key areas of similarity that are worth noting:

- Street-side interfaces
- Trade execution and clearance
- Order routing and execution
- Security master information
- "Stock record" processing (dividends, interest, maturity, corporate actions)

The similarities tend to be in the most generic functions of the business and in those functions which are closest to the "street." As we move away from the street and toward the customer or the legal entity of the business, we begin to see differences:

- Regulatory reporting/compliance
- Accounting for the firm
- Accounting for the customer
- Customer reporting

DIFFERENCES NARROWING

Traditionally, not only did customers consider trust and brokerage services as ideologically distinct, but the types of features and functions offered were substantially different and priced accordingly. Trust systems traditionally offered more robust functionality, such as tax-lot accounting, accrual accounting, and common trust fund processing, and charged more for these services in addition to charging for the fiduciary responsibility for the account. Over time, however, these differences have narrowed as rules have changed, systems have been enhanced, and services have been unbundled.

The conversion of common trust funds to mutual funds beginning in August of 1996, for example, meant that a host of investment management expertise previously only accessible to trust customers was suddenly available to trust and brokerage customers alike. Since the broker/dealers had developed more efficient processing engines and industry links (NSCC networking and fund/serve, for example), they could, ironically, deliver these trust products (the converted common trust funds) more cheaply than could the trust companies from which they originated.

Nor have the brokers been sitting by idly from a technology standpoint. Both vendor-supplied and in-house brokerage applications over the last several years have begun to unveil a host of traditional trust system features. Below is a list of just some of these new enhancements to brokerage applications:

- Average cost accounting (for customers in addition to inventory)
- Tax-lot accounting (for customers)
- Portfolio modeling (asset allocation/wrap fee)
- Cash and accrual basis reporting
- Multicurrency accounting (not just dual currency)
- Systematic (periodic) purchases and redemptions
- Customer performance measurement

Meanwhile, trust companies have borrowed some brokerage system efficiencies. Below is a list of just some of the functionality trust systems they have either recently developed or are in the process of developing which have been part of most brokerage application for years:

- ACATS
- Fund/Serve
- Networking
- Margins

CUSTOMER FOCUS

David Pottruck, president and CEO of Charles Schwab & Co. noted at a recent San Francisco Operations Association meeting that one of the key factors for the success of Schwab over the years has to do with the company's focus on the customer:

> All the movement at our company ... all the innovation and change ... is driven by the customer's experience. It is the premier benchmark against which we evaluate every service we provide, every change in pricing, every internal realignment. We look for the product and the delivery system the customer will think is best.

Successful financial services firms of the future will focus on the customer's needs rather than industry tradition and deliver products and services the customer demands in the manner the customer demands them.

One example of this in the brokerage industry is the proliferation of numerous delivery channels for securities products in order to allow the customer the convenience of choice. At many firms, customers can conduct securities transactions through any number of the following delivery channels:

- Touch-tone
- Internet
- Branch-office
- Call center
- Registered representative

UNBUNDLING THE COMPONENTS

Regulatory boundaries aside, brokers might add "trust administration" or "private banker" to the list of available delivery channels. What would stop a brokerage firm from adding trust industry functionality to its brokerage system and running its "trust department" from the same platform? Could the brokerage firm simply provide "fiduciary" services for an additional fee through its trust department?

> According to H. David Johnson, COO of BancAmerica Robertson Stephens Inc., ... if we unbundle trust services, we find four basic functions: custody, transaction execution, asset management, and fiduciary administration. Brokerage firms already perform custodial and transaction execution services in competition with banks and custodians; registered investment advisors as part of any financial services company

can perform the asset management function; and broker affiliated trust companies can (and do) clearly provide fiduciary administration. The real question is how to best deliver these services to customers in the most cost-effective manner.

PUSHING THE LIMITS

Customer focus will force brokerage firms to determine how to leverage trust system features and functions without increasing costs, while it will force trust companies to figure out how to provide traditional trust features at brokerage prices. Over the last several years, Will Derby, senior vice president and CIO of the Asset Management group for NationsBank in Dallas, has evaluated proposals to develop a common securities processing platform.

> In the future, a single base processing platform for all securities subsidiaries will not only provide financial services companies additional processing efficiency but will enable these firms to better serve their customers through consolidated reporting, data warehousing, and client credit risk management.

From a technological and operational standpoint, personal trust and retail brokerage may have more in common than retail and institutional brokerage. If we can get past this paradox and look beyond our ideological tendency toward viewing the industries as inherently different, then we are left with the problem of building the most cost-effective solution. What might this efficient, high-capacity and generic securities processing platform of the future look like?

SINGLE STREET-SIDE PLATFORM

At both Charles Schwab & Co. and Raymond James, some mutual fund trades for the trust company are executed through the brokerage systems to take advantage of more efficient brokerage system processing of mutual fund transactions. The 1998 plans at several money center banks also call for the brokerage units to clear mutual fund trades for the trust department in order to leverage brokerage system capacity and fully operable NSCC fund/serve and networking features which might take months to develop and test in the trust system. SEI Investments now offers its customer a "no transaction fee" or NTF arrangement for processing mutual funds on its Trust3000 system through an omnibus account at the brokerage firm of Jack White & Co.

In essence, these companies are leveraging the strength of the brokerage platform on the back end (high volume capacity, better efficiency) without compromising the uniqueness of the customer requirements best served by the trust platform on the front-end. By linking different front-end systems to a common, generic securities processing platform or back-end system, the differences across industry segments in terms of customer needs and "firm" needs can be addressed without having to tax the more volume-sensitive systems with the overhead of street-side processing.

This model is not very unusual. Many brokerage firms have different front-office systems feeding a common back-office system. The needs of trading and sales staff who are very customer or firm focused are often best served by state-of-the-art front-office systems, while generic clearing and stock record functions are best performed by large-scale back-office legacy applications. The trust industry also supports this model, with workstations for investment management, trade/order entry, custody, and cash management feeding traditional back-office trust accounting systems. According to the Tower Group, 50% of the large account-based assets under management that changed custodians in 1996 went to the 10% of the service providers that have a full suite of workstation-based applications.

If implemented properly, the customer benefits from access to the functionality of all the systems across all industry groups and legal entities while the firm benefits from the cost savings associated with less redundancy in operations and more fully leveraging efficient technology. "The convergence of advanced technology and the evolving diversified financial services industry will dramatically alter our systems and support architectures," explains Hank Alexander, president and COO of BA Investment Services, Inc., a BankAmerica company. "Facing the customer, we will look across products and legal entities; support organizations will consist of a blend of product specific factories and generic shared utilities." While building a single system capable of supporting both industry lines is not unimaginable and would clearly offer the most efficient solution, the front-end/back-end system configuration is much more readily implementable and more fully appreciates the differences which do exist in the businesses.

MODULAR SOLUTIONS

With the proliferation of front-office technology for investment management, trading, and trust administration, the trend toward modular, component-based technology solutions continues in the securities industry. As the technology continues to be based on more and more "open" standards, deployment of "best-of-breed" applications becomes more and more readily achievable. The future may find financial services companies meeting securities industry operations requirements by patching together software applications in a best-of-breed solution which spans industries. For example, it seems conceivable today that a trust company could connect a fund/serve application sold by a brokerage system vendor to its trust system.

Ten years ago few predicted the significant relaxation of *Glass-Steagall* that has occurred over the last several years and the subsequent entry of banks into brokerage and investment banking and insurance companies into brokerage and banking. Ten years from now how far will those boundaries have fallen and what will the technology that supports these new financial services conglomerates look like? If the customer matters, they may be one and the same.

Author Bio

John Buckner is President and CEO of IMIS Inc., a financial services IT consulting company that specializes in the implementation of technology in the securities industry. Founded by Buckner in 1992, IMIS has since grown to more than 100 consultants nationwide by building a reputation as a cost-effective alternative to traditional "Big 6" consulting. Buckner began his career in financial services technology in 1983 as a part-time employee of a software company while attending Princeton University, where he graduated in 1985.

Chapter 46
A Portfolio Management System for the Twenty-First Century

Tim Scatliff

MANY FIRMS HAVE FAILED TO INSTALL AN ENTERPRISE-WIDE PORTFOLIO MANAGEMENT SYSTEM because of the flaws in the plan, not flaws in the product. Attempting to exceed the capabilities of the installation team, trying to build a product that will be all things to all clients, and failing to understand the data model have all been major contributors to extended and failed plans. But the single most important obstacle has been in the delivery. Poorly constructed plans, vendors inexperienced in enterprise-wide solutions, and most importantly, product platforms that are insufficient to support the firms' current and future needs all contribute to a disappointing result.

Investment advisors and clients are consistently demanding contact and portfolio management features as a part of the services offered by their clearing organization. National firms have implemented proprietary portfolio systems at immense expense and resources, while balancing priorities within their organizations. They have had to develop the initial design for these products, build platforms compatible with their technological foundation, and implement this service across a diverse set of investment advisors and clients. The solutions have taken assorted forms, but the key element to success has always been a smooth, timely implementation.

The ability to construct and execute a proven implementation methodology will quickly increase the credibility of the Information Systems (IS) department and the installation team. The product will gain wide acceptance within the firm with a successful plan completion.

0-8493-9834-7/00/$0.00+$.50
© 2000 by CRC Press LLC

This chapter will define a blueprint for a successful enterprise-wide portfolio management solution. The chapter begins with the evolution and rationale behind these systems over the past 10 years. Then follows the functionality that customers have begun to expect in these systems. Finally, this chapter discusses the single, most effective differentiator in this market: an architecture that encompasses all portfolio management functionality and enables easy additions to these services. The architecture must allow a flexible, generic approach to building portfolio systems within an enterprise. This will allow new applications to be built, leveraging the database and overall architecture.

EVOLUTION AND RATIONALE

- Institutional firms have used professional portfolio management systems for decades.
- Managed money has gained wide acceptance and with it the need for professional portfolio reporting.
- Private label funds spring up almost daily, again requiring accurate, automated reporting.
- A bull market increases the acceptance of performance measurement as investment advisors have positive results for their clients.
- Hundreds of financial planning firms are started by professional investment advisors to provide a new niche with more personal investment strategies. Their investment results are now expected to be presented professionally.
- Client statements showing only positions, balances, and check and credit card transactions are no longer sufficient. Clients are demanding current portfolio returns, comparable indices performances, risk analyses, and future life-style needs. They must be easy to use and integrate with other systems.
- Today's investment advisors demand applications that operate seamlessly with other applications on their desktop. Keystrokes to re-enter customer names, account numbers, cusips, etc. are no longer acceptable. The desktop is increasingly required to run the investment advisor's day. These requirements demand a portable, reliable solution that will meet the industry's needs into the next millennium.
- Internal solutions are too difficult to maintain to remain competitive. Professional firms specializing in this niche industry continually "raise the bar" in features, service, support, and technology.

An enterprise-wide object-oriented portfolio solution has now become the industry standard. All wire houses have built or purchased solutions. Correspondent clearing firms have solutions, in-house and "bolt-ons." Many regionals have built solutions with outside vendors that appear seamless. Some discounters and smaller boutiques are offering portfolio solutions. All private money managers have portfolio and performance so-lutions, although not always automated.

Recruiting clients and investment advisors has become difficult without a proven portfolio solution. Investment advisors cannot merely promise these features; they must be immediately deliverable. Delivery must be au-tomated, seamless, scalable, reliable, and vendor neutral. The technology teams in the firm cannot be required to support another database, a new platform, or additional TP monitors.

Contact management and client information systems also have become the norm. Most high producers use manual contact management systems, not linked to the back office. This increases the duplication of data, adds problems of data integrity, "many people touching data," and multiple sources of data. Clients receive multiple mailings for the same product. Ad-dress changes take months as old databases with nonreplicated data con-tinue to mail information to the client, causing the aggravation level to rise.

Solutions exist, but few offer an automated, technically sound, integrat-ed answer. An effective portfolio solution requires an innovative, well-planned architecture. An effective architecture permits a successful imple-mentation. An effective solution requires a flexible, scalable architecture.

There are many contact management, time management, and prospect management products on the market today. They are designed to automate an investment advisor's schedule, keep track of client's call-back objec-tives, various accounts, and even assets not held in the investment ac-count. Competitive pressures have created a proliferation of portfolio management tools for the retail broker.

The financial services industry has escalated the baseline for services to include portfolio management services and reporting. Real-time market data was once a luxury. Debit and credit card services linked to the broker-age account were once only for the large investor. These and many other services have become part of the basic package required to attract clients and new investment advisors. Now clients expect portfolio management services as a part of the financial services offering.

The challenge is to differentiate the solutions that are appropriate for single investment advisors, small independents, and large, enterprise-wide portfolios.

WHAT A GOOD PORTFOLIO MANAGEMENT SYSTEM MUST HAVE

- Integrated contact/client management — investment advisors must be able to use client and portfolio information interactively. There can be only a single source for customer data.

- Automated back-office download — back-office trade and client data must be integrated with the books and records of the firm. This process must be stable, well tested, and relatively seamless.
- Strong reconciliation processes — keeping the back-office data, positions, and balances synchronized with the portfolio product is imperative to building the confidence of the sales force.
- Portfolio management and reporting — clients' view of the product is in the reporting. Strong basic online inquiries and hard-copy reporting are important to the investment advisor and is the primary view of the product from the clients' perspective.
- Market data interface — real-time market data, quotes, research, and news add to the investment advisor's interactive use of the system.
- Capital adjustments (corporate actions, splits, etc.) — corporate actions and reorganizations happen on a daily basis. The sales force must have an automated process to insure that positions are maintained correctly. Particular attention must be paid to the maintenance of a cost basis for each lot.
- Graphics interface — color graphs, charts, and reports are expected in today's environment.
- Word processing interface — lead-generating letters, prospecting letters, seminar invitations, and client follow-ups are also expected in today's automated office environment.

A few of the leading-edge systems offer a wider range of features. More robust features include:

- Financial risk analyses — how does a client's risk profile match the current portfolio?
- Financial planning model — clients today want to know "What if ... ?" in their financial planning strategies. New products present new opportunities and clients can receive assurance that their investments are meeting their goals or can simulate the results of various investment strategies.
- Automated account rebalancing — how would the assets be changed to meet the client's profile?
- Straight through trading — an investment advisor and/or client (based on the firm's practices) must have the ability to electronically facilitate the order entry, processing, and management processes. This should be applicable to order entry through to the affirm and confirmation process.
- Flexible report writer — many systems have robust reporting capabilities, but the appetite for new reports and inquiries is infinite. An easy-to-use report writer also needs advanced database interfaces.
- Multicurrency capabilities — an international capability is in most firms' business plan.

- Multilingual — an international language capability will allow future growth and acquisition opportunities.
- Lot management — the ability to define separate lots for each transaction will provide unlimited future flexibility in client reporting and accounting.
- Outside assets — asset gathering is facilitated by offering portfolio reporting to the client on assets not held in the firm. Products integrating these asset types provide a more complete view of the client's risk, return, and future strategies.
- Interactive computer-based training — the geographic diversity of most firms today requires alternatives to on-site sessions and train-the-trainer methodologies.
- Internet capabilities — this facility must be a part of the design and architecture of the product from its inception. A character or Windows-based product requires extensive redesign and re-engineering to operate effectively on the WWW.
- Intranet capabilities — similar to Internet services, the product must be engineered to run on the firm's intranet, not simply moved to the investment advisor's workstation.
- Remote access support — investment advisors and clients are demanding portable systems, accessible from clients' homes, home offices, and travel locations.
- Client/server compatible — again, systems must be engineered to take advantage of client/server technologies. Choices of objects, database elements, and network variables can all have dramatic effects on the performance and reliability of the product. Products engineered for client/server usage are far more effective than retrofitted products.
- Real-time updates — the proliferation of instant market data access for quotes, prices, research, and news has caused investment advisors to expect similar service levels from their portfolio systems. Most single-user systems require daily manual input of all changes. Some enterprise-wide solutions have built daily "download" solutions, but these are always yesterday's news. Today's systems are building dynamic interfaces to keep the client's assets synchronized with instantaneous changes in positions, balances, and prices.
- Strong service and support organization — customer service, quality assurance, experienced implementation teams, and strong senior management commitment to customer service are key to a successful implementation of these products. Smaller, more marketing-oriented firms will often cut corners in these areas when pursuing new sales.

THE SELECTION PROCESS

The product must be flexible, portable, and scalable. The architecture should support the capability to add new applications without changing the database structure or access, the network qualities, and the message layer. A technologically advanced structure supports:

- Object-Oriented Design.
- Layered Application Design.
- Three-Tier Client/Server with Transaction Processing.
- Platform Adaptable/Portable.
- Database Adaptable/Portable.
- Thin Client.

There are a variety of products that can provide investment advisors with basic features and services. A few can support some of the myriad advanced needs of the market place. Fewer still can complete this on an architectural platform that meets the needs of clients, investment advisors, and operational and technical personnel. Add to this the requirement of protecting the firm from massive future redesigns, and there are few solutions indeed.

That selection process must start with a review of the features listed on preceding pages, rated in accordance with the specific firm's immediate and anticipated requirements. Implementation of a single-user product is simplistic. Implementation of an enterprise-wide solution requires all and more of the listed features, as well as a clearly defined plan.

An experienced vendor will have a process that is adaptable to each client's environment. The resulting process should identify all requirements necessary to guide the client from contract commitment to a complete roll-out of an enterprise solution. Teams will be assembled, responsibilities assigned, milestones set, and communication established to all levels of the overall plan.

The implementation process will include several phases. In the Exploratory Phase the vendor and client review the general applicability of the product and architecture within the client's environment. The client will learn the advantages of the product and architecture. The significant issues will be discovered and mapped into the project plan.

Points covered are

- Review architecture of the system (technical and application).
- Review the functionality of the product for the client.
- Verify the technology in the client's current environment.
- Discussions on the relational database, use of a transaction processor monitor, etc.
- Review the logical data model.
- Estimate the time and costs for the Detailed Design and Specification Phase.

- Estimate the implementation time frame, strategy, and training requirements.
- Estimate initial and ongoing costs.

After the Exploratory Phase, the plan will evolve into a detailed plan fitting the client's specific needs. The blueprint is completed with details of file definitions, milestones, teams, etc.

Steps included are

- Defines customer and vendor teams.
- Details design, testing, implementation plan.
- Defines hardware and communications requirements.
- Details file descriptions.
- Approximates project schedule.
- Defines key milestones.
- Defines testing and rollout phases.
- Integrates spiral model techniques.
- Defines training needs.
- Defines subsequent release schedules, testing methodologies, implementation.
- Defines travel schedule, support requirements.
- Initiates and trains on project planning tools.
- Initiates issue management systems.
- Defines data conversion requirements.
- Defines testing methodologies.
- Sets performance and scalability requirements.
- Obtains sign-offs from both client and vendor.
- Review and define implementation and conversion strategies.

An effective development methodology is the Spiral Model, detailed later in this chapter. The vendor should have a development life cycle that encompasses the following:

- Proof of concept experience.
- Design specifications processes.
- Benchmarking, simulating, and modeling procedures.
- Strong quality assurance team.
- Strong system and user documentation.
- Proven pilot-testing program methodology.
- Reliable rollout program.
- Experienced training team.

Portfolio systems require effective integration with back- and front-office providers, including:

- Back-office data.
- Front-office systems data.

- Trust systems data.
- Market data input.
- Research input.

A vendor that can bring wide experience in these installations, with the depth of features as defined above, is required in order to meet the needs of an enterprise solution. This type of methodology combined with an expandable and adaptable architecture is mandatory.

TECHNICAL ARCHITECTURE

The technical architecture is the foundation on which any application can be built. Whether it be a financial system, a manufacturing application, or a healthcare system, it is the infrastructure that can really make the difference.

Similar to a vast highway system and intercontinental transportation network, it is the infrastructure that ties all the business logic together with all of the various technologies and resources, wherever they may be deployed. It allows users anywhere in the enterprise to connect to application logic on local or remote servers. It allows centralized administrative staff to manage this process, along with the data and information it transports to serve the end user. In its purest form, it is the infrastructure that glues the application logic together with the various operating systems (e.g., Windows NT™, Unix, etc.) and resource managers (e.g., database managers, etc.).

The following is a prime example of this type of architecture. A system should be built with a three-tiered client/server infrastructure designed to support a variety of enterprise solutions. It must be scalable, flexible, and vendor neutral; an object-oriented approach that integrates the power of products like BEA's Tuxedo, and traditional relational database managers such as Sybase and Oracle. The end result is a fully three-tiered client/server infrastructure that makes it possible to be vendor neutral in the ever-changing world of technology.

This same infrastructure can be scaled down to achieve the implementation of the application on a single PC or notebook. The architecture of the infrastructure allows for disconnected computing, where the end-user may occasionally use the application off-site, disconnected from their regular server.

Add-ons can be designed that allow sophisticated developers to leverage a very comprehensive data model designed for the financial industry. These models support global markets, multicurrency, multilingual, performance reporting, accruals, contact management, and client reporting. An application framework or "cookie cutter" can be leveraged by large organizations to integrate new applications into their mission-critical systems.

The system should be based on an object-oriented, three-tiered client/server infrastructure developed entirely in C++ and designed to give the client the best of all worlds. The architecture can include a fully complied C++ thin client, minimizing its use of PC and Windows™ resources.

With a large number of workstations, as is characteristic of an enterprise-wide system, organizations must minimize the maintenance requirements on a per user basis. This is one of many reasons why it is important to keep the business code of the application on one or more distributed servers and not on the workstation itself. In this framework, only the user interface has to reside on the client's computer — all of the business logic is designed to be implemented on branch, regional, and/or central servers. These servers can be managed centrally by the organization's network management and administrative teams.

An open systems environment means you have a choice in the technology you use internally and the systems you interoperate with. It means being vendor neutral and highly portable. It means investing in software that is adaptable and maintainable. It means a living infrastructure that can constantly evolve to take advantage of new technologies or business opportunities.

Reliability and integrity are fundamental to the transaction processing model. Transactions can be defined at a logical level, involving several sequential or nested procedures, instead of being limited to the scope of a single, stored procedure. They can be implemented as real-time and/or batch systems. This is the same technology used by the largest banks and the largest airline reservation systems to handle hundreds of thousands of mission-critical transactions per day across wide geographic regions.

Performance and scalability are inherent to the infrastructure, yet the developer is insulated from the complexities of the environment. Each developer uses a "cookie cutter" to add new transactions. The result is a transaction that inherits all of these features through the application framework.

All objects should be standard C++ objects. They can be transported across the network and be recreated on virtually any server. The industrial strength of C++ and its acceptance as the language of choice for the creation of operating systems and large-scale applications give it the durability and performance that a true enterprise system requires.

The server waits for client-initiated requests. It must be capable of handling a large number of requests simultaneously. It must prioritize its work, handling the most important requests first. It must alert the caretakers when exceptions occur or high-water marks are reached. To be effective, it must initiate and run background task activities. It must always keep running. As the load increases, it needs to be able to scale up and spawn new

687

processes on either the same or alternate servers — it needs to be able to load-balance.

The server cannot be limited to a family of processors that top out early. This is where the portability of the business code is so important. To provide a wide range of server capacities, it should run on both Windows NT™ and Unix operating systems.

The server and its network should support a single login, a standard clock for network time, network monitoring, systems management, a database, transaction services, and object-oriented services.

In summary, the technical architecture is the infrastructure that will support current and future applications. It must be portable, scalable, flexible, and compatible with a variety of operating platforms that it will meet.

FIVE-LAYER DESIGN

The architecture is based on a five-layer design that isolates the various areas of concerns with respect to portability and interoperability. The business code resides within the middle layer and is separated from the user interface via a messaging layer. The database layer is where the physical data model is implemented using either Sybase or Oracle. The database access layer separates the physical data model from the logical view that all application code shares. It is in this layer that the native database drivers are implemented for maximum throughput.

The layers give the architecture the flexibility that enterprise software needs. For example, the message layer that connects the thin client user interface to the business code could be implemented as a WAN or as an Internet connection. The business code can remain virtually unaltered.

The database access layer can use native drivers for Oracle in one implementation and native drivers for Sybase in another.

An object-oriented framework is provided to allow entire applications to be built as a collection of logical units of work — objects that encapsulate the work to be done (e.g., inquiry or update). By using this framework, the developer focuses on the business logic and the resulting code automatically inherits and encapsulates the three-tiered client/server features.

The framework includes a referential integrity engine, a replication engine, an exception-handling engine, and a reporting engine and all the features of a sophisticated TP monitor and relational database manager. To implement the resulting application on a single stand-alone notebook, for example, the message layer is flattened out at the infrastructure level. A new build is done, and all the business code inherits the new environment.

THE SPIRAL MODEL THEORY

Another key to a successful project is the project development techniques used. An object-oriented design should be built on the Spiral Model Theory of system development as described by Boehm. System development goes through the life cycle of requirement specifications, analysis, design, implementation and unit testing, integration, and implementation. This allows a product to develop incrementally over time, and incorporates maintenance into the normal development life of a product. Using this methodology in the design enables more complete functionality, but more importantly it allows a smoother, more predictable implementation plan. It enables products to grow without major redesign, incorporates new database and TP processes more easily, and concentrates the firm's resources on the business logic and rules.

We are living in a world where there are new technologies evolving on a continuous basis. Often, they represent opportunities that influence the area. For a system to last for years and decades, it must be designed to evolve.

An enterprise system has to adapt to many platforms and to varied technological requirements. The business code has to be portable to other systems that are designed to handle different loads. The number of online users may be measured in the thousands or more. Because of the large number of users utilizing a common integrated system at the same time, reliability, integrity, and scalability must be inherent in the infrastructure. Central management tools must exist to manage and report on the system and on its performance. A single system password should be supported.

To maintain the performance, the servers must be able to spawn additional processes or level the load between a number of servers. Because of the potentially vast number of users, the state of the user has to be carried primarily in the client PC and passed to the server only when required. Servers cannot possibly maintain the state of each user in the system and still have resources left to process the work. It must act as a funnel to seriously reduce the number of communications sessions, memory allocations, file allocations, database connections, and other resources.

It cannot use "chatty" protocols to connect the thin client with the server and the server with the database or other resource managers. Ideally, it has to support mainstream technologies from multiple vendors and yet be vendor neutral, allowing a choice for the user when establishing new systems and permitting integration and interoperability with existing systems.

It must be positioned to handle new requirements, many of which are unknown at the time of the initial implementation. It must evolve naturally as the opportunities arise. It must be designed for modularity and change.

For example, there may be a future requirement to address disconnected computing (e.g., an end-user working at home, without a network) and interoperability with the Internet and the WWW. It has to support many user interfaces or views, including issues concerning the presentation, availability, and security of the data.

Not all firms have the time or skill sets required to customize or integrate new systems in the timeframes required by the market. But all firms require office, front office, product mix, investment advisor needs, database, client/server environment, etc. A product with the above design criteria allows these differences to become opportunities to improve the firm's processing capabilities and introduce efficiencies, rather than becoming obstacles. Customization becomes focused on the business rules and investment advisor's needs rather than on the technology platform.

The decision to add contact and portfolio management capabilities to an enterprise's suite of products has progressed beyond the point of "should we?" to the point of "which one?" Firms cannot remain competitive without these services being offered to their investment advisors and clients. Top-producing investment advisors have long since offered portfolio summary information to their best clients as a value-added service. They have accomplished this at great personal and operational expense without the benefit of extensive automation.

New products proliferate; back-office operations areas strive to maintain reporting methods that are discrepant. This has resulted in an inconsistent offering to their client base and a geometric increase in problems. For compliance, legal, and purely professional reasons, firms today need to present a consistent, reliable image to their clients. Investment decisions should be presented professionally with a minimal level of manual intervention. Investment advisors and their support staff need to have a confidence level in these products that mirrors the quality of the data from their back office.

To achieve this, three main decisions must be reached. What level of functionality do I need now and for the future? What architecture will support my current and future Information Systems needs? And which firm has the implementation plan that can be executed confidently within my organization?

This chapter outlined many of the decisions that need to be made to achieve these answers. It can be used as a blueprint to evaluate the market alternatives and to examine the available competitors. No single product fulfills all needs for all firms. No single product can be implemented without some degree of modification, adaptation, and customization. The goal is to select a vendor that can deliver an architecture that supplies the greatest level of flexibility in design, implementation, and future versatility. Limited platforms, limited database structures, limited interface capabilities, and limited experience in completing enterprise solutions will all inhibit the opportunity for a successful installation.

Autho Bio

Tim Scatliff is the Senior Vice President of Technology for Rescom Ventures, Inc. Prior to joining Rescom, Tim spent 21 years in Information Technology with Richardson Greenshields of Canada — the largest privately-owned retail brokerage firm in Canada.

Chapter 47

Logging Monitoring in the Financial Services Industry

Knox Henderson

This can — and does — really happen:

Broker: "Buy fifty thousand shares of XYX Corp. (fictitious name) at fifteen and one half."

Trader: (verifying the request): "OK, buy fifteen thousand shares of XYZ at fifteen and one half."

Broker: "Right."

Trader: (later, after the stock's price has moved up) "Bought fifteen thousand shares of XYZ at fifteen and one half."

Broker: "I said buy fifty thousand shares."

Trader: "You confirmed fifteen thousand at fifteen and one half."

Anyone involved in the securities industry knows these kinds of discrepancies do occur and thousands of dollars can end up going in the wrong direction. Sometimes it works in the trader's or broker's favor, more often it does not. If the customer, through his broker, ordered 50,000 shares at fifteen and one half and the trader purchases only 15,000 — when the stock price moves up, the broker must purchase the additional 35,000 at the higher price and guarantee the customer the fifteen and one half price.

Here is solid justification for recording transactions in the securities industry. In this case, the trader is probably off the hook, because the onus is on the broker to confirm the order when the trader repeats it. But the only way to confirm who said what to whom is to go back to the original transaction.

There are a variety of reasons for recording telephone conversations or capturing computer screen activity in a bank, a securities firm, or an insurance agency. Some reasons are obvious, while others are not. Generally,

0-8493-9834-7/00/$0.00+$.50
© 2000 by CRC Press LLC

requirements for logging and monitoring can be placed into three categories: Compliance, Performance measurement, and Risk management — or CPR.

COMPLIANCE

In many cases there are legislative requirements for recording certain securities or financial transactions. For the most part, financial organizations and insurance companies use recordings to settle disputes or to protect themselves against liability.

In 1996 the SEC issued its 21A Report on the improper activities of numerous NASDAQ market makers involving their colluding to fix price spreads. The tactic: ensure that price spreads were quoted only in $1/4$-point segments rather than $1/8$-point spreads. Twenty-four market-making firms were named in a Department of Justice (DOJ) antitrust case, each of whom was requested to comply to new guidelines set by the DOJ. These guidelines outline recording and monitoring procedures, including how many and how often traders would be monitored, and that the recordings would be monitored without their knowledge. All recordings are to be kept available for 30 days in the firms' compliance departments. The DOJ can come into an office at any time, without notice, and check recordings for antitrust violations.

In addition to voice transactions, the securities industry also relies heavily on written documents such as transaction instructions, recommendations, company prospectuses, etc. These are often sent by fax because of the timeliness of fax transmissions. Here, rules set by the National Association of Securities Dealers (NASD) require supervision and review of the communications between a firm's registered representatives and the public. For outgoing communications, compliance officers must create review procedures and demonstrate reasonable sampling techniques. Member firms must also retain all incoming and outgoing communications for at least 3 years. Proper disclaimers must also accompany any written information regarding securities and other financial instruments.

Fax transmissions can also be stored and archived using advanced fax logging and management technologies. By integrating all of an enterprise's fax machines and fax servers, all incoming and outgoing faxes can be tracked, routed, and permanently stored on a hard drive or DAT (digital audio tape) cassettes to meet a variety of compliance issues. Fax logging also provides a record of fax traffic: where it was sent from and to whom, when it was sent or rerouted and who it was reviewed by. With this new fax logging technology, the chance of losing or misplacing critical and compliant-sensitive fax transmissions is virtually eliminated.

Because banks and insurance companies are heavily involved in investment, they are subject to many of the same compliance issues as the securities industry. In banking, there are requirements for recording wire service transactions, where large sums of money are often transferred between two parties at distant points through verbal instructions. Similar regulations apply to trust account management and well as money market and foreign exchange transactions. Financial institution must maintain archives of voice transactions for at least six months. They also must be able to provide a mechanism for disaster recovery, which requires off-site redundant data.

Insurance companies which provide variable or self-directed policies for their client's assets must also comply with SEC regulations.

PERFORMANCE

The fastest-growing market segment for voice and data monitoring technologies is the call center. Bank-by-phone and insure-by-phone services are becoming the mainstay for financial organizations looking to provide faster and more convenient services. Computer telephony integrated (CTI) technologies have automated many of the telephone functions that have in the past required human intervention. These include call routing, call-holding procedures, and providing screen pops for agents. A screen pop uses the calling-line ID to access data associated with the caller and automatically "pops" the account or customer information in front of the agent while the call is being received.

While banks, investment service providers, and insurance companies are tripping over each other in order to obtain these "have to have" technologies, there will always remain a need for human, voice-to-voice contact in these industries. In fact, the deciding factor for gaining and retaining customers is not the technology, it is still — and always will be — quality of customer service.

Enter the age of performance monitoring. "Your call may be recorded for quality purposes" is becoming a phrase more and more commonplace over the phone. Right off the top, most financial and insurance organizations considering call-monitoring technologies want to explore the legalities around it. Without going into a lot of legalese, the requirements are as follows.

Currently, all but nine states require what is known as one-party consent. That means that at least one person — and this can include the agent — must be aware that the conversation is being recorded. Call centers comply to this requirement by having their agents sign a waiver, stating that they understand and approve of their conversations being recorded. The remaining states require two-party consent, where both parties agree prior to recording the conversation. In these states, callers may hear a message at the beginning of the call: "If you do not wish this call to be recorded, press one," or the system may offer some other method of opting out of the recording. The two-party-consent states include: California, Delaware, Florida, Illinois, Maryland, Massachusetts, Michigan, Pennsylvania, and Washington.

So what is the justification for call monitoring and performance measurement? First you must consider that the most significant cost in your call center is the cost of human resources. This typically accounts for about 70% of your investment in the call center. As a rule of thumb, only 15% goes towards technology and another 15% goes towards paying the phone bill. Quality monitoring ensures that you are getting the best return on investment for the human resources in the call center.

In the 1980s, as call centers began to emerge, agents were monitored using a "silent observation" method, where the reviewer sits side-by-side with the agent and listens in on the conversation. Another method was to record the conversation on reel-to-reel tape recorders. The drawbacks of these methods soon became apparent: supervisors had to spend peak call-center time reviewing agent calls and locating calls on a endless stream of reel-to-reel tape was cumbersome and time-consuming. Besides, there was typically no streamlined process of evaluation providing feedback to the agents. Further, reel-to-reel devices allow only one individual to listen to the calls at a given time.

Today, computer telephony integrated (CTI) quality measurement solutions provide an effective means of gathering a relative sample of calls and provide an arsenal of applications for efficiently and objectively evaluating agent performance levels. These systems interface directly with the PBX/ACD, convert calls into digital format, and store them in a centralized database for easy retrieval. Any number of agents, even in a free-seating environment, can be recorded on a specified schedule (e.g., all agents recorded three times per month). During convenient times, the supervisor can search the database, retrieve calls, and score them using online grading templates. These templates provide data reports that are generated to compare the agent's performance vs. his peers, compare reviewer scores to ensure consistency, and to provide overall call-center productivity reports. Details of the technology are provided later in this chapter. This translates into superior customer service, higher customer retention, lower turnover, a decrease in training time, and a more knowledgeable staff who, in turn, sell more securities and insurance policies, etc.

It doesn't stop there! The latest rave in the industry is a new technology known as screen capture. Call centers can not only capture the original conversation, but can also recreate the computer screen activity that the agent sees during the conversations. This provides insight into how the agent is using the technology available to him or her, or whether the customer interaction system (CIS) itself is effective. Screen capture technology is available for both IBM mainframe systems as well as the PC.

Integrated screen capture and voice monitoring products allow both the voice and the screen activity to be played back simultaneously, exactly as the agent would have seen and heard it.

RISK MANAGEMENT

Imagine you are a registered nurse offering over-the-phone insurance services. A few months ago you had underwritten a health insurance policy for a client. Along with the policy you provided written documentation which included detailed information regarding the scope of the policy. Because this information may have been too technical and complex for your client to fully understand, you describe for the client in full detail what is covered and what is not. Now you receive a call from a physician who is about to perform a procedure on the client. After discussion, you determine that the procedure falls outside the scope of the policy. Later, you receive another call from the irate client who was convinced he had the appropriate coverage, and that you had assured him that he did.

Whether the end result falls into your favor or not, recreating the original transaction brings immediate resolution as to what transpired between the two parties. Bitter arguments that cost valued customers, lengthy legal disputes, and conflicts that negatively affect employee relations and morale, can all be avoided. As one mortgage provider puts put it: "[Call recording] is saving us over a million dollars a year in just settling rate disputes."

This mortgage company and other financial industry executives are finding that recording calls leaves no room for misinterpretation, and that logging and monitoring technologies today can be considered absolutely reliable and fail-safe.

Outside of compliance issues, recording is a must for brokers and dealers who want to address risk management issues such as:

- Transaction verification.
- Prevention against liability posed by lost or misinterpreted voice communications.
- Reconfirmation of major orders.
- Dispute resolution in the event of client complaints.
- Reduced liability insurance costs.

METHODS OF LOGGING AND MONITORING

Now that we have explored some of the whys of logging and monitoring let's look at the hows. As mentioned before, there are a variety of recording requirements — all which fall under the general heading of compliance, performance measurement, and risk management. As we look closer at the actual technology, meeting these requirements is achieved through the following methods of recording:

1. Full-time logging (total recording) — this is required for validating transactions or legal notifications over the telephone typically are required by health, financial, insurance, and investment institutions or by law and government offices to meet legal or legislative requirements.
2. Scheduled recording — the most basic of recording solutions for call centers. Call recordings are automated by time, by agent, or by groups of agents.
3. Selective recording — here is where CTI applications are particularly valuable. Recordings can be initiated via IVR, DNIS, ANI, and CLID and can be organized in databases for ease of analysis for marketing and quality assurance purposes.
4. Event-driven recording — a term often used in the same context as selective recording. However, "selective" recording typically refers to "telephony" occurrences, while event-driven can be seen as computer application-driven. For example, when an agent types in any amount more than $1000 in a particular field, a recording is initiated. Later, those recording can be easily retrieved using the same criteria.
5. Record-on-demand (controlled by the agent) — the agent can press a "Start Record" button on his/her workstation. This is valuable where third-party verification is required or when a call is transferred to a supervisor, who is typically not being monitored.
6. Quality measurement — any of the above recording methods can be used to gather calls to evaluate quality. However, the most effective way to gather a consistent and relevant sample of agent calls is to use a scheduler to collect a percentage of agent calls (e.g., one call per agent per week between 8:00 a.m. and 11:00 a.m.).

TYPES OF RECORDING SOLUTIONS AVAILABLE

Here is an overview of the configurations and interfaces used for computer telephony integrated logging and monitoring technologies.

Trading Turrets

On floors of the world's stock exchange, and in the trading rooms of stock brokers, banks, institutional investors, and other financial organizations, stocks, commodities, money market funds, and debt issues are primarily traded on turrets. The major difference between a turret and a PBX is that a PBX switches a fixed number of lines to a telephone at a given time. A turret switches all of the lines to all of the extensions (turrets). Everyone has access to everyone and several people or locations can be on many lines at the same time. This allows the broker or trader to listen in or talk to groups, obtain prices, and conduct trades.

On the trader's desk, the turret is referred to as the "dealer board" which includes phone lines, speaker lines, and line indicators telling the trader who is on the line. The "back-office" component of the turret, where the switching takes place, takes incoming lines that may or may not be connected to the central PBX/ACD. This is because there can also be lines that run directly to branch locations or other key offices.

The voice logger is directly connected to the turret and records all calls that come through it, inbound, outbound, and internal. Therefore, private lines that the company does not want recorded bypass the turret and are channeled directly to the PBX.

Turrets come with two handsets and typically one or more speakers. The speakers are used to monitor other exchanges, news or wire services in real time, or other exchanges. It is not uncommon for a foreign exchange trader to have up to 30 speakers. For monitoring purposes, each handset and speaker requires its own channel for recording. Sometimes, however, these two handset channels are "summed" together for economy. The drawback of summing is that when the call is played back, the company may not want the conversation with the other party heard by any party reviewing the call. Exhibit 47-1 shows a generic configuration of a trading turret.

Switches — PBX/ACD

A typical telecommunications environment uses a PBX (private branch exchange) and an ACD (automatic call distributor). Some switches such as Lucent's Definity have the ACD capabilities built in. Other vendors, such as Aspect, manufacture ACDs that interface with other PBXs.

There are two key interfaces to a computer telephony integrated recording. First, there is the audio interface, where the actual conversation is recorded. Secondly, there is the call detail interface where call details are sent from the switch, via the CDR (call detail report) port or CTI link. This provides information as to time, date, trunk, extension, and duration of call.

The CTI link, which is the integration between the telephone switch and the computer network, adds further intelligence to the call traffic in the financial or insurance call center. CTI logging means that other call center applications and telephony events can help to tag and identify specific calls, trigger recordings, and narrow search criteria.

For example, a common CTI identifier is DNIS (dialed number identification service). DNIS tells you what number the customer dialed (typically a 1-800 number) The DNIS number is provided in a number of ways — inband or out of band, through a ISDN line, or by a separate data channel. The DNIS number can be used by the CTI monitoring system to trigger a call recording. For example, this means that all banking customers who call

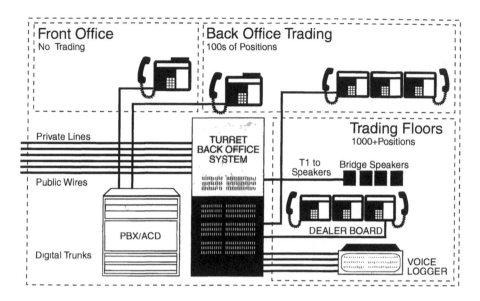

Exhibit 47-1. Telephone anatomy of a trading firm.

1-800-OUR-RRSP will have their calls recorded to verify transactions in a self-directed RRSP.

Similarly, ANI (automatic number identification) or CLID (calling line identification) can also recognize the caller ID and, through the CTI interface, trigger calls "from" a specified area code or a direct line from suppliers, clients, service providers, etc.

Recording technologies today provide a variety of options as to exactly where the recording takes place, as shown in Exhibit 47-2. There are advantages and disadvantages to each configuration. The three key recording interfaces are as follows.

Trunk-Side Recording

Here the logger is directly connected to the incoming trunks (24 channels per trunk) before they are terminated at the switch (PBX/ACD).

Advantages. Trunk-side recording allows you to record all segments. Everything the incoming caller hears and says is recorded, including the touch tones entered into the IVR, the voice recordings from the messaging system, or conversation held with other outside parties conferenced in on the call. Trunk-side recording supports selective recording, used with a call detail logging system, and provides the best audio quality.

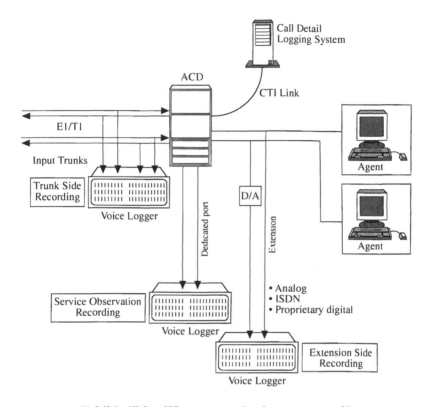

Exhibit 47-2. Where can voice loggers record?

Disadvantages. With trunk-side recording, all channels need to be recorded to ensure no calls are missed. You need to use a call detail logging system to map the appropriate channels and extensions for retrieving the call and it does not record internal calls.

Uses. Consequently, trunk-side recording is best used for full-time recording to meet compliance requirements and provides the safest solution for risk management. It is not a cost-effective solution for measuring quality.

Station-Side Recording

This takes place after the switch, on the line leading to the agents' extensions. These extensions can either be digital or analog. Because digital lines use a proprietary protocol, the voice must be converted to analog to allow the logger to accept the audio and then converted back to digital in the logger's proprietary format.

701

Advantages. Station-side recording requires fewer channels to record because no matter which trunk channel is used, the calls are routed to a set number of predetermined extensions. A call detail logging system is not required to locate the extension/agent to retrieve the call.

Disadvantages. Station-side recording requires more cabling because an independent line is needed for each extension. Proprietary digital protocols require D/A (digital to analog) conversion, and the agents themselves can void the recording.

Uses. It is an economical means of recording full-time in smaller call centers and permits record-on-demand where seating is assigned.

Dedicated Port

Today's PBX/ACDs are built with a "service observation" port that allow supervisor to conference in on another call between two parties and monitor the call as it occurs. Typically, this permits the supervisor to listen only, although some systems also provide access for the supervisor to join in on the conversation.

Manufacturers of recording and logging products have designed interfaces that allow their technology to utilize the service observation feature of the switch for recording calls.

Advantages. Dedicated port recording, or service observation, requires limited cabling, and is the best solution for selective recording and quality monitoring.

Disadvantages. Service observation is not the best solution for full-time recording because it is dependent on the limitations of the service observation port on the PBX/ACD.

Uses. Service observation is used for "selective recording" where you only want to record specific extensions/agents or groups of agents such as money market traders, wire transfer services, self-directed RRSP services, etc. Service observation is also the best means for obtaining quality monitoring where call recordings are initiated on a predetermined schedule. For example, if an insurance call center wants to record each agent three times per month, the logger continues to record those agents until the schedule is satisfied.

FINAL NOTE

Methods of recording and storage for voice logging systems vary, but digital recording technology ensures reliable, high-quality recording with high storage capacity. Systems today can provide thousands of hours of online storage and unlimited storage on DAT tape (and other media). CTI capabilities in today's digital loggers allow the user to quickly search and retrieve calls from yesterday, last month, or last year using a variety of criteria. It is these capabilities that permit end users to address all of their compliance, performance, and risk management needs.

Author Bio

__Knox Henderson__ researches and documents the use of computer telephony integrated (CTI) logging and monitoring technologies. A former securities trader, he has written a variety of articles on the implementation of technologies in the financial, securities, and insurance sectors. NICE Systems is a leading global provider of CTI logging, performance measurement, and workflow solutions for voice, fax, and data. The company provides reliable and secure systems for managing communications transactions in organizations.

Chapter 48
Straight Through Processing
Jim Douthitt

ASK FIVE PEOPLE WHAT STRAIGHT THROUGH PROCESSING (STP) MEANS and you're likely to receive five different answers. More and more, STP is coming to represent a continually evolving set of aspirations rather than an existing reality. The early use of the term referred to automation of all processes involved in the purchase and sale of securities. More recently, STP has been taken to mean complete automation of all aspects of investment operations. As more goals of STP are realized, additional goals are introduced. The scope and aspirations of STP will probably continue to expand for quite some time.

Achieving STP can have vastly different requirements for different entities. For example, the processes to be automated will be different for a brokerage firm than for a stock exchange, which has different requirements than a buy-side financial institution. And, while the focus of STP is frequently on the buy side, the term still applies to virtually all parties involved in executing, clearing, and settling securities transactions.

Analyses of the state of STP often focus on the various entities which contribute to the automation of securities trading, such as FIX, SWIFT, DTC, ISITC, and others. However, the roles that these standards and entities play is constantly changing; generally toward expanding their scope of work in advancing STP. This trend has led to competition among standards and may ultimately lead to the emergence of a single set of standards and clearly defined roles for the remaining players.

History is yet another variable complicating the analysis of STP. The infrastructure which manages investment operations today is a result of evolution, not engineering. For instance, the SEC has long advocated the concept of a single national stock exchange. Yet regulation continues to support a multiple exchange system. Regulation itself has been a result of evolution. With the advent of financial futures, the SEC and the CFTC (Commodity Futures Trading Commission) have, at times, been in conflict. They divide, between them, regulation of financial instruments, each of

0 8493 9834 7/00/$0 00+$ 50

which can impact the value of those regulated by the other. Furthermore, these entities have had to work out disagreements as to their regulatory jurisdictions.

It is easy to see that the scope of what is commonly referred to as STP is very broad; encompassing the universe of investment operations topics. In this analysis, we will focus more on the end objectives of STP and less on the current players and their near-term approaches to the issue. We will focus on the buy-side financial institutions using the broader definition of STP which has more recently become accepted. STP, therefore, is taken to mean complete automation of all aspects of investment operations. Against this backdrop, the analysis of STP will focus on the following:

1. The elements required for buy-side financial institutions to achieve STP.
2. Required elements in the flow of a securities transaction.
3. How various entities add value to securities transactions.
4. How investment systems achieve automation of securities operations in areas other than trading.

ACHIEVING STP ON THE BUY SIDE

Nothing puts the objectives of STP in better perspective than simply stepping back and examining what it is that a financial institution is attempting to accomplish. A buy-side institution is attempting to meet or exceed established investment objectives as efficiently as possible with the best possible customer service. If the institution has achieved STP, trade modeling would be comprehensive enough to automatically adjust the portfolio to better meet objectives within compliance limits and seamlessly result in trade orders. The trade order management system would easily leverage all available venues for execution. Finally, executed orders would automatically result in accounting, performance, analytical and historical data facilitating investment monitoring, analysis, and reporting to management, regulators, and clients.

An STP environment should see a higher portion of labor devoted to portfolio management, analysis, and trade modeling. Less labor would go toward trade affirmation, settlement, custodial reconciliation, front- to back-office system reconciliation, report production, and trade entry. The use of real-time information for flexible trade modeling and trade management would also result in more efficient use of cash. In short, STP would result in reduced overhead and better execution of portfolio management strategies.

Steps in Buy-Side Operations

1. **Perform analysis to determine how best to meet investment objectives** — This includes economic, industry sector, and security-specific

analysis. Such analysis is performed to achieve established investment objectives which may be dictated simply by the liabilities offsetting the assets or by an investment policy. These functions lead to a dynamic model portfolio which may require additional adjustments for specific client criteria. The more efficiently this process is achieved, the more effective the firm will be in meeting client objectives.

2. **Model trades** — Trade modeling includes all the functions involved in determining how to adjust portfolio holdings to better meet the objectives. This can be the purchase of a stock identified, through analysis as cheap, or simply adjusting the duration and/or convexity of the portfolio to better match the attributes of offsetting liabilities. This process is frequently stymied by a variety of factors which may include:

- *Inability to identify favorable trade opportunities.* This is as much a function of investment analysis as it is a function of trade modeling. If data cannot be sorted and analyzed on a timely basis against existing holdings, opportunities will be missed.
- *Inadequate trade modeling facilities.* Oftentimes, the rebalancing criteria can be complicated by special requirements for specific portfolios or by requirements for maintaining sector weights across portfolios with vastly different total holdings. These complications can delay or possibly prevent the timely rebalancing of portfolios and again result in missed opportunities.
- *Inadequate ability to manage the effects of trading.* Purchasing securities requires either the use of idle cash, borrowing, or the selling of another security. Active managers historically have required additional cash balances, and this is at least in part attributable to the shortcomings of their systems. Trade modeling is often not reflective of real-time positions and, frequently, is entirely separate from trade order management. Comprehensive trade modeling needs to consider, and model for, the effects of trading on the remaining portfolio on a real-time basis.

Overcoming system shortcomings often means adopting a simpler, but perhaps less effective, portfolio management strategy.

3. **Manage the trade orders** — Since trades cannot always be executed at one time and, instead, must be executed in separate fills, adequate trade order facilities must be available. Step-outs are sometimes required and additional rebalancing may dictate new trades before a given order is completely filled. Allocations of trades may need to follow different scenarios under different circumstances. Trade order management was once considered the point of initial entry. Now, some systems can take the results of trade modeling and create orders automatically. Automated links for electronically executing trades with counterpartys also improves the trade order management process. The ability to manage all these functions

efficiently has a tremendous bearing on the effectiveness of the firm in meeting its investment objectives.

4. **Monitor and analyze holdings against market conditions, liabilities, investment objectives, and restrictions** — For each of Steps 4 and 5, a tight integration of front-office trade management, modeling, and analysis systems with the back-office is critical to achieving STP. Timely review of current positions requires a reliable portfolio accounting system. Such a system must have facilities for timely, automated reconciliation of holdings, trade affirmation, and settlement. Tight integration of front- and back-office systems improves execution of investment strategies and reduces overhead. It is with Steps 3 and 4 that we see the traditional focus of STP on automating trades. Trade automation reduces trade risk and also reduces middle- and back-office overhead. Trade automation will be examined in detail in the next two sections.

5. **Provide reporting to management, regulators, and clients** — To effectively provide all the reporting and analysis, the portfolio accounting system must take minimal transactional data from the trading system, automatically pull data from external sources, and compute accounting, performance, compliance, and other data as well as automatically generate custom reports using either electronic or paper form. The last section of this chapter will explore the elements of automation necessary to accomplish this aspect of straight through processing.

Having established the objectives of the buy side, it is now appropriate to take a closer look at the minimum required elements of a trade. Automating these elements help to achieve Steps 3 and 4 which, in turn, reduces risk and overhead.

MINIMUM ELEMENTS OF A TRADE

Trading of securities is a regulated process. The process can be different depending on the type of security being traded. The vast majority of SEC-regulated securities are traded on one of the major exchanges and clear through the DTC and the NSCC. For purposes of simplifying this discussion, we will focus on transactions of stocks and bonds clearing through the DTC.

Parties Involved

- Buy-Side Institution: places order with a broker-dealer to execute the transaction; the institution is the initiator of the process.
- Broker-Dealers: brings buyers and sellers together.
- Stock Exchange/NASDAQ/Order Crossing Systems: all of these different entities represent venues for finding an appropriate market price.

- Depository Trust Company (DTC): functions as the clearing house and repository where stock and bond certificates are exchanged. It is a member of the Federal Reserve and is owned by most of the brokerage houses on Wall Street and the NYSE.
- National Securities Clearing Corporation (NSCC): nets the securities and cash transacted by the major counterparties on a daily basis.
- Safekeeping Agent: holds securities on behalf of the owner (i.e., either the buy-side institution or its client). A safekeeping agent can be a custodian bank or a broker-dealer.

Steps in the Process

1. The institution indicates interest in a securities transaction with one or more broker-dealers.
2. The broker-dealers provide offers.
3. The institution places the order with a given broker-dealer.
4. The broker-dealer must then provide a confirmation (a legal requirement) of the trade to the institution.
5. The institution acknowledges the confirmation and submits to the DTC.
6. The DTC affirms the trade upon receipt of acknowledged confirmation from the institution. Affirmation binds the parties to the trade. The affirmation notice must go to the institution, the broker-dealer, and the custodian.
7. Custodians can receive notice either from the institution or from the DTC, depending on the arrangement.
8. Upon the settlement date, securities and cash change hands between the safekeeping agent and broker-dealer, as facilitated by the DTC.

While this basic process can be complicated by block allocations and step-out broker arrangements, the above represents the minimum required steps to complete a simple securities transaction. Each required element adds to the administrative burden and can create delays which would be unacceptable should settlements move from the current T+3 to T+1, as expected sometime in the next few years.

Value for the Buy Side is in Automation

1. Means of signaling intent and agreeing on terms.
2. Trade confirmation.
3. Trade affirmation.
4. Notification of the safekeeping agent.

The next section will cover some of the entities working to make the process more efficient and discuss the products and services they offer.

ENTITIES AND PROTOCOLS AUTOMATING THE SECURITIES TRADING PROCESS

In addition to acting as the repository for most SEC-regulated securities transactions, the DTC offers a number of products which facilitate various aspects of the trading process:

- Institutional Delivery (ID) System is used to coordinate the confirmation, affirmation, and settlement processes for the institutions, broker-dealers, and custodians. Until a recent SEC ruling, it was the only system for accomplishing the affirmation function. ID is capable of accepting SWIFT messages and is expected to soon incorporate FIX message formats as well.
- Institutional Instructions (II) allows an institution to electronically communicate allocations to an executing broker-dealer. It also provides facilities for managing step-outs. II messages can also include matching instructions read by the ID system.
- Notice of Order Execution (NOE) System allows brokers to send order fill details to institutions.
- Standing Instructions Database (SID), like ALERT, is a data warehouse of settlement instructions.

Financial Information Exchange (FIX) Protocol is a standard for sending and receiving messages regarding indications of interest, orders and order acknowledgments, fills, account allocations, news and other administrative messages. It was started by some of the largest buy-side and sell-side institutions in the U.S.

Industry Standardization for Institutional Trade Communication (ISITC) started as an effort to improve trade notification to custodians. The scope of its work has expanded and the organization now has messages for many aspects of the trade process. There are several affiliate ISITC organizations around the globe.

Society for Worldwide Interbank Financial Telecommunications (SWIFT) is a bank-owned consortium which was founded to create settlement messages. It too has expanded its role to include messages to facilitate other aspects of trading. SWIFT creates protocols and manages a telecommunications network.

In one way or another, all these formats and systems (and many others not mentioned here) represent different ways of accomplishing trades electronically. Different providers specialize in different aspects of the transaction sequence. It is unknown which standards, if any, will ever emerge as dominant. In fact, it is more likely that no standard will emerge anytime soon. Complicating the issue is the fact that standards vary from country to country. The long-run objective, however, is to have an environment where the buy side and sell side can use a single set of standards, one for each message type or step in the trade process, regardless of the security type or country in which it's traded. Therefore, the next trend for STP will likely be in the areas of communications protocol conversion and message format translation services. The DTC, for one, already sees itself fulfilling this role.

Automating the Front and Back Office

As stated before, the benefits of STP come from:

- Improving the execution of investment strategies.
- Reducing risk.
- Reducing overhead.

While this can be realized through automation of trade communications, of equal importance is the automation of the front and back office. Below, some of the key points of front- to back-office automation are outlined. Automating these areas of investment operations can have at least as much impact on achieving STP as efforts to improve the efficiency of trade execution.

Portfolio Modeling. Modeling includes all of the processes traders use to determine what positions to open and close. Most front-office trading systems include rebalancing, trade allocation, and trade order management functions. Unfortunately, such systems do not always incorporate the modeling facilities that actually result in trades. To the extent that some modeling capabilities are included in trade order management systems, they tend to be inflexible in their methods. Conversely, traders tend to develop their own modeling techniques. As a result, much modeling takes place outside the trading system on spreadsheets and elsewhere. Historically, custom-tailored modeling techniques have not been easy to incorporate in trading systems in ways that allowed data to flow directly from models to trade orders.

Trade Order Management. Trading systems often present users with interesting compromises. Complex systems can handle a wider variety of trading scenarios but generally carry with them greater overhead in the form of additional required labor. That overhead can carry through even to simple trading scenarios. If a system does not have the ability to handle complex trades involving many steps, manual processes must be used to work around the system limitations. Conversely, if the trade is simple but the trading system is complex, there can be additional overhead associated with one-step trades. A trading system that allows traders to go through only those steps that are necessary to enter the trade is ideal. For instance, if the trade order will be filled over several executions with several broker step-outs, the system should account for each step of the process and allocate across accounts at any point. If, however, the trade is executed all at once through a single broker, the trade system should act as a simple trade capture system, requiring minimal data entry to record all levels of trade information.

Custodial Reconciliation. Reconciliation to custodian records is facilitated by a strong portfolio accounting engine. Many systems can only reconcile holdings, purchases, and sales because the accounting facilities are inadequate to do more. Without greater depth of accounting facilities, income and MBS principal payments must be reconciled manually at greater labor expense and, practically speaking, at the cost of longer delay in identifying custodian error. Ideally, a system would be used that gives complete and accurate cash projections across all security types, thus accomplishing complete and accurate custodian reconciliation automatically across all major custodian banks and many smaller ones.

Securities Accounting. Required depth of accounting functionality is a function of the security types managed, transactions performed, and client needs. Even if broad requirements are not currently present, having the extra accounting capability can provide comfort that new strategic directions will not require significant operational and systems overhauls. Furthermore, securities accounting facilities and extensive relational data storage are critical to automating custodial reconciliation and back-end reporting. In ensuring that the capability currently needed, or possibly needed in the future, is present, some key attributes must be evaluated. These requirements include:

1. Does the system have a verifiable ability to add new security types drawing on a comprehensive set of security attributes? This ability should extend to all types of instruments including derivatives, asset-backed securities, and various foreign instruments.
2. Does the system have all functionality to properly account for multiple currencies? This is not always an easy question to answer. Not only must the system account for a base and local currency, it must also account for the settlement schedules of each country. The system vendor must also have demonstrated a commitment to developing Euro functionality once the rules for this new currency become fixed. Finally, the multicurrency functions must extend to every other aspect of the system, from custodial reconciliation to general ledger entries.
3. Does the system include comprehensive accounting alternatives? These would include a full complement of yield, amortization, and tax lot/average cost accounting methods. Also of value are the abilities to maintain multiple accounting methods for the same holdings and track tax information, such as original issue discounts.
4. Can the system manage corporate actions?

5. Does the system provide enough additional data elements so securities data can be segmented to meet a variety of back-end reporting requirements?

A system meeting all of these requirements is critical to automating custodial reconciliation and producing management and client reports.

Management Reporting and Ad Hoc Query. Management reporting serves a variety of functions. It supports the process of generating client reports. It supports the portfolio and trade modeling functions. And it supports audit and verification processes. Ad hoc queries also support these functions but in a less formalized way. Management inquiries can often generate long cycles of report generation followed by additional queries. Ending such cycles depends on the ability of analysts to provide insightful analysis that gets at the issues management may currently be pursuing. However, such analysis can only be provided if the data needed are both within the scope of system functions and accessible by the analyst.

If reporting facilities are inadequate, the back-office staff can, at times, become entirely consumed attempting to meet new reporting requirements. This type of inefficiency is typically caused by:

1. Inadequate reporting tools. Reporting applications do not have adequate depth to access and manipulate the needed data.
2. Inadequate data. The back-office system does not store the data required.
3. A lack of distributed systems. Management staff does not have adequate desktop tools to query the data on the fly. For such tools to truly save labor, they must be easy to use for non-users.

A portfolio accounting system overcomes all these problems and allows users to realize enormous labor savings if it stores the majority of calculated data. Modern report writing applications are so versatile, they allow reports to be formatted in any way that a spreadsheet can. The calculation and logic functions allow unlimited data analysis. Special custom queries need only be written once. Thereafter, the same query or report can be used again and again. All this is possible if the accounting system stores the majority of data and is ODBC compliant.

Client Reporting. Investment systems often limit the extent of client reporting. Even in this age of considerable computerized modernization, client report packages from sophisticated asset managers are printed and mailed out today with limited, text-based reports of transactions, holdings, and other investment data. Such reports, while providing information, generally do not become an integral part of client operations. Most asset management firms supplement these reports with additional reports providing greater depth of analysis, which are created manually using spreadsheet software. Custom reporting is a service of considerable value which can help to retain clients, especially when clients rely on such reports as integral parts of their own operations. When such services are provided, clients value investment managers, not only for their investment performance and adherence to style, but also for the support they provide to client operations. Custom client reporting is an important means for asset managers to provide additional value-added services and improve client retention.

Managers agree there is tremendous value in providing custom reporting for clients. However, custom reports are not always done to a great extent because they must be generated manually each reporting period. The cost becomes excessive and the process is impractical. If, however, an ODBC-compliant database which stores the majority of calculated data is used, reports, once designed, can be queued to run at appropriate intervals and be sorted and collated with the appropriate number of copies. And with a modern reporting application, the process can go one step further. Reports can be e-mailed to clients or placed on a secure web page in HTML format for them to pick up. Because customization is a one-time labor effort and reports can be batched to run in a production environment, a high level of client customization is economically feasible.

Compliance. Compliance is unusual in that it fits into two parts of the investment operation continuum. At the front end, trades are (ideally) tested for compliance in advance of execution. Since many trade operations are modeling in separate systems, placing orders by phone and *then* entering trades in the trading system, automation can do little to prevent a compliance violation. In the absence of automated compliance testing, traders may rely on lists generated by the back office, showing positions near the limits of compliance rules. Obviously, such methods are less reliable when the array of rules is complex.

Whereas front-end compliance is a preventive function, back-end compliance is a function of verification. Regardless of the degree of automation achieved, both front- and back-end compliance functions must be maintained. In attempting to automate compliance, the most difficult issue is that the same rules must be applied to both the front-office and back-office systems. This either requires the maintenance of rules in two systems or using a single module that is mapped to both systems.

Performance Measurement. The requirements of a quality performance measurement system are often overlooked. Data should be stored to the security identifier level. Without this detailed level of storage, the ability to segment performance results will run into limitations that may be material in some circumstances. Aggregated performance should also be stored at appropriate levels to facilitate ease of reporting. The ability to build composites and run performance from and to any user-defined points in time is also important to automating performance. Finally, the performance system should have adequate facilities to account for late adjustments and complex cash flow and prepayment patterns.

CONCLUSION

STP now represents a set of continually increasing standards to which the investment community aspires. Efforts to improve trade execution are moving faster and will likely focus on the need for translation facilities to accommodate the multitude of disparate message protocols. This focus is likely to remain until T+1 is finally realized. From the operational perspective, efforts to improve STP will continue to focus on the integration of the front and back office and the automation and distribution of reporting and query functions.

Author Bio

Jim Douthitt is the Director of Product Marketing for SS&C Technologies, Inc.'s flagship product, CAMRA and suite of products. Interacting heavily with staff, client support, customers, and prospects, he is responsible for market validation of new development efforts and identifying product enhancements that extend the CAMRA product. His responsibilities also include the design and creation of technical product literature used in various aspects of consultative sales.

Previously Douthitt worked with the Regence Group (formerly King County Medical), the largest Blue Cross Blue Shield plan in the Pacific Northwest. There he directed a staff of over 30 and was responsible for treasury and investments, financial aspects of strategic acquisitions, corporate tax, financial reporting, and other financial activities. Prior to that he was in the audit group with Deloitte and Touche focusing on financial institutions and high technology companies.

Douthitt is a Chartered Financial Analyst and a Certified Public Accountant.

Chapter 49
Designing and Evaluating Investment Performance Systems
Timothy Peterson

PERFORMANCE MEASUREMENT HAS GAINED GROWING ATTENTION in the investment industry. Industry's *de facto* adoption of the Association of Investment Management and Research Performance Presentation Standards™ has raised as many questions as it has attempted to answer, as firms struggle to understand and comply with the rules. Expansion of institutional investing into overseas markets and derivative securities is dating existing investment systems and forcing systems vendors to accommodate new industry needs with respect to performance measurement calculations and international presentation standards.[1] Technological advances, too, are having their effect. Lower data storage costs and greater interconnectivity are fostering the expectation of timely yet detailed investment performance information. Yet the technological aspects of system development are probably simple when compared to the functional requirements in such a dynamic and demanding industry.

Therefore, the focus of this chapter is on identifying the most important issues in the development of software that measures investment portfolio performance. Current and anticipated trends in the financial services and technology industries are also considered. Technical design is not emphasized, though some techniques for implementing functional features are presented. Firms wishing to assess the adequacy of a performance measurement system can readily look for the design characteristics outlined

0-8493-9834-7/00/$0.00+$.50
© 2000 by CRC Press LLC

herein to assist in their evaluation. Unfortunately, the practice of performance measurement is too broad a topic to discuss in detail. To simultaneously relate these practices to the specific development issues described would be a tremendous task, so this chapter assumes much about the reader's knowledge of accounting, investment management, and performance measurement. However, some background information will provide perspective for those unfamiliar with performance measurement practices.[2]

PERFORMANCE MEASUREMENT AND THE PORTFOLIO MANAGEMENT PROCESS

Though some perceive performance measurement at "the end" of the investment management process, it is really just one step in a cycle, as shown in Exhibit 49-1. But its position in the cycle is unique. Not only does performance measurement relate information about past investment strategies, it provides guidance for future strategies. Understanding this link between past and future actions can have considerable implications for performance systems design. This is especially true in integrated investment systems: in many cases the performance system functions as a "data bridge" between back-office accounting and analysis and front-office trading operations.

Performance measurement has three primary functions: to evaluate the ability of a portfolio manager to meet quantifiable objectives, to determine

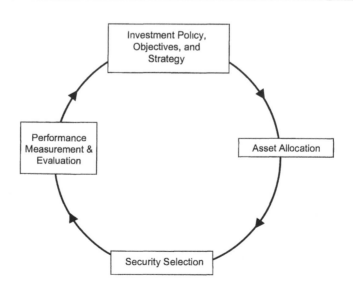

Exhibit 49-1. The portfolio management process.

the effectiveness of an investment strategy, and to measure wealth creation through investing. Institutions will use the former while individual investors are more concerned with the latter. In practice, the statistical techniques used in performance measurement can identify whether returns were earned through skill vs. luck, and even identify specific aspects of an investment strategy that contributed to the overall rate of return earned.

Nevertheless, performance measurement remains a dark horse, even within the financial services industry itself. Information is used internally for management and externally for marketing and client service. Its functions are sometimes located in the accounting department, sometimes in the analysis department, and sometimes absent altogether. Everyone knows what the performance department does, but few outside the process can articulate the work required to produce performance reports. This is because, in part, performance is a relatively new profession. As such, it is growing in complexity year by year. With this in mind, it is not surprising that performance measurement is often overlooked in the software development process. More frequently, performance functionality is typically designed as an "add-on" to the core investment and accounting system, once demand justifies the development (or marketing needs a new product to tout). Such approaches often result in inadequate performance systems, not because of a lack of domain knowledge, but because of the development constraints imposed by the core accounting or investment system.

Performance analysis is typically performed at four major levels, referred to as "performance levels." In order of decreasing data granularity they are

- Security lot (transaction): the lot or transaction level specifies performance for an individual security in a portfolio.
- Asset class: a group of like securities, such as stocks, bonds, and cash. It is a mutually exclusive aggregate of securities.
- Portfolio: sometimes called an account, the portfolio level is usually specified based on investment objective.
- Composite: used primarily for reporting purposes, the composite level is an aggregate of asset classes, portfolios, or both.

In addition, performance measurement has three general areas:

Absolute performance comparison — Comparative performance involves calculating rates of returns for each lot, asset class, portfolio, and composite. The rates of return are then evaluating against a predetermined benchmark. It is a first approximation of whether investment objectives are being met.

Risk-adjusted or relative performance evaluation — Risk-adjusted performance involves evaluating a historical return against the volatility (variance or standard deviations) of those returns. This is a measure of performance stability and consistency. Benchmarks are also used in this process. This is the most valuable type of performance measurement and analysis to the client or prospect of an investment manager.

Performance attribution analysis — Performance attribution involves using statistical techniques to allocate a historical return to specific, pre-defined security characteristics such as duration, convexity, yield curve, credit risk, and market capitalization. It is also used to determine if rates of return were gained via security selection, market timing, or foreign currency return. With this information, managers can more precisely evaluate their investment strategies and decisions.

When implementing a large-scope performance system, it makes sense to do so in phases. However, design considerations for each area specified above must be addressed at the outset, even if certain functionality will be deferred to a later development effort. However, prior to designing system architecture, the data elements, business rules, and functional requirements must first be specified.

FUNCTIONALITY REQUIRED IN A COMPREHENSIVE SYSTEM

Ultimately, good performance software design is about flexible design and building high user confidence. While the information needs and requirements for firms within the financial services industry may be similar, the way firms acquire, process, and distribute that information can vary widely. Stated differently, user-specific requirements can be addressed either during the design of the product or when the package is integrated into the firm's operations. Selecting the latter approach is akin to asserting that the product's design and technical implementation are well suited to such a migration. For mass-produced software packages, this is a bit unrealistic. And when money is involved, users must be able to trust the systems on which their firm or its clients depend.

In truth, the purpose of investing is to earn a rate of return. From this admittedly simple perspective, performance takes on added importance, and ideally should not be worked in on top of existing systems. Integrating performance measurement functionality with the rest of the development process will at least identify, if not alleviate, the constraints imposed by the core investment accounting system. When this approach is not practical, there are features which can increase the versatility of the performance system without risking data integrity and disrupting process flow. With this in mind, the following list proposes several key functional requirements, in descending order of importance:

User-defined reporting — In particular, the ability to create reports that will assist in the reconciliation of a calculated and reported value to its components is paramount. Typically, "canned" reports are sufficient to provide commonly used information. However, report writer capability at the user's fingertips serves to integrate an otherwise "off-the-shelf" package into the operating procedures of the company using the software. Ideally, the firm should be able to report from an ODBC-compliant database.

Adequate validation tools — The ability to quickly identify accounts with abnormal values is essential. This can be done by setting variance tolerances at the system or account level, and by reporting portfolios, asset classes, or securities with returns that lie outside a specified standard deviation from the mean. Robust systems will identify when and which individual components of the return formula exceed user-specified parameters.

Ability to monitor changes to the components of current and historical performance values via an audit trail — This requirement is an acknowledgment that systems break, people make mistakes, and incorrect information finds its way into an otherwise clean process. Changes to historical information will occur and will affect performance. The volume of data and reporting time pressures necessitate an automated mechanism to detect such corrections *at the time of occurrence.* If the performance system cannot automatically post updates resulting from such corrections, then the appropriate level of maintenance is a record of the change that was made along with affected values and processes. This is necessary not only for changes to the accounting data, but for changes to the performance data if direct edits to those data are permissible.

Performance comparison, risk-adjusted analysis, and attribution at the security lot, asset class, portfolio, and composite level, for any time period — Regardless of the performance formula used, the user should be able to get the return for any given measurement period and granularity. The implication is that the components to calculate returns exist in the performance database, and that the user may choose the desired processing and reporting frequency without being limited by the database architecture.

User-defined performance classifications — Asset class categories in portfolio management are primarily based on common security characteristics. The degree of detail for each classification or subclassification is a function of the portfolio manager's judgment, strategy, and style. Consequently, proper evaluation of portfolio performance requires that the end user define the individual categories within the asset class level of performance. Lack of flexibility in this respect provides only marginally beneficial information for the end user. Another related requirement involves the ability to blend individual market indices into a benchmark that will match the portfolio's investment objective.

Flexible data delivery — Paper presentation is becoming archaic. The Internet is becoming the Gutenberg printing press of the twentieth century, and the trend for "information at your fingertips" will find its way into the realm of performance measurement. In addition to the traditional paper and direct connect data delivery methods, database architecture should accommodate FTP, web server, and e-mail delivery. Web-based delivery will likely dominate the market. Initially, firms will post performance results for distribution via the Internet or intranet for consumption by their clients or investment management departments. This method, as with other on-line presentations, should permit "drill down" capability through the performance levels, and temporal drill-down evaluation within each performance level.

Though the technology industry is quick to implement these methods of information transfer, their acceptance by the financial services industry will be slow. Conversions, upgrades, and systems migrations are lengthy processes in large firms. Smaller firms face budget constraints that typically result in acquiring new software only when technology or growth demands it. Even so, firms need only an e-mail connection and a simple, customized, browser package to take advantage of a hypertext file sent via e-mail to simulate push technology. The most sophisticated vendors of performance data will utilize true push and pull technology, with the latter being used for firms with highly specialized data acquisition and performance reporting needs.

Technological advances in information storage and delivery will place the practice of performance measurement into a conflict between sound investment policy and client expectations. Modern Portfolio Theory asserts that performance measurement is a long-term process.[3] Despite that, the combined effect of reduced processing time, cheap data storage, and information-on-demand will be that investors will be able to view returns at will, evaluate their performance, and then examine several different proposed investment scenarios in reaction to their current position and prespecified market assumptions. Though such actions are regarded as inappropriate in many academic circles, performance software vendors should prepare to face this demand, particularly in the individual investor market.

Import/export utility — Few accounting, performance, and investment systems are able to seamlessly interface with other software packages. Yet data will inevitably need to be ported from place to place when an integrated system is not employed, or when stand-alone systems lack interoperability. The ability for the user (with technical assistance) to define single and multiline record formats for data import and export alleviates this persistent problem. Also, such a utility facilitates the conversion from one performance system to another. The ability to easily transfer historically reported data from a legacy system can be a major selling point for newer systems.

Likewise, universe comparison data (such as benchmark indices) are often provided by numerous vendors. These data must be stored uniformly within the performance system database architecture, and a customized field mapping import facility makes this routine function less burdensome for the user.

A third application is the importing of return data for asset classes that are absent from the security models used by the accounting application. In the process of portfolio management, it is important to evaluate the performance of *all* assets under management, not just the traditional securities in your investment accounting systems. Direct population of performance tables through the import of such data ensures that performance reporting is comprehensive.

Customized calculations using stored component information — Each firm's techniques for financial management will vary, and certain additional calculations may be required to accommodate their operations. This is particularly important when internal performance metrics are dependent on the choice of accounting basis (calculation of "book yield" for example).

DATA CONSIDERATIONS

To begin, the basic components of the return formula must be identified. There are numerous formulas for calculating and analyzing rates of return. However, they all use the same components:

- Realized and unrealized capital gains and losses.
- Income accrued and received.
- Buy and sell transactions.
- Transfers, contributions, and withdrawals.
- Market index values or rates of return.
- The associated dates for each data element.

Porting these data to the performance system will largely be a function of the accounting database architecture, or the data file supplied by an external accounting system. Beginning and ending period balances are often used, though this is primarily a function of the return formula chosen. Also, classification of each security's reporting asset class through the security master table is necessary in order to construct meaningful performance reports. The basic performance flows typically come from three sources: the security master file, the accounting transaction database, and the market price history database.

There are several additional reporting requirements: portfolio returns may be reported without a cash component or with a cash component. This is not as simple as it sounds, because the industry definition of "with cash returns" is counterintuitive: cash returns are not reported separately, but are allocated to those of other existing asset classes. AIMR's Performance Presentation Standards identify at least two algorithms for allocating cash returns to those of other asset classes.[4]

There are at least four other additional variations to standard rate of return calculation and reporting:

- Inclusion or exclusion of management fees.
- Inclusion or exclusion of tax effects.
- Inclusion of derivatives and leverage on a hedged and cash basis.
- Inclusion or exclusion of the effects of foreign exchange.

Once the lot performance table has been generated, additional functionality is relatively simple. The lot data can be summarized in asset class and portfolio tables, and these in turn can be summarized into a composite table. Risk-adjusted and attribution performance functionality can be implemented relatively easily with only minor modifications to the existing data tables to create the necessary additional links and associations, though the complexity of the attribution model may necessitate a few additional tables.

In packaged software products, it's important to keep the product functionally scaleable. Not all users will require attribution. Some may require tax performance analysis but not foreign currency performance analysis. "Add-in" functionality, commonly found in spreadsheet programs, is an effective means of marketing a single, modular product to firms with varying degrees of sophistication.

Database Structure and Required Data Tables

Performance database structure is fundamentally a function of the accounting system design. Typical tables include the Security Master, Lot Holdings Master, Accounting Basis Master (if tax information is required), Transaction History, Market History, and Foreign Currency Table, as shown in Exhibit 49-2.

The data from these tables are used to create the "performance flows" and populate the performance tables at each level of granularity. Separately, index and universe comparison data are stored. In some designs it will be possible to store the index data with the market price history data. The four performance data tables, in conjunction with the index and benchmark tables, represent the source for the creation of a data dictionary from which nearly all necessary reports can be generated.

Return Formula Selection

There are several formulas used by industry to calculate a rate of return.[4] When performance measurement systems began to be developed in earnest in the early 1990s, many designers chose to implement the Modified Dietze

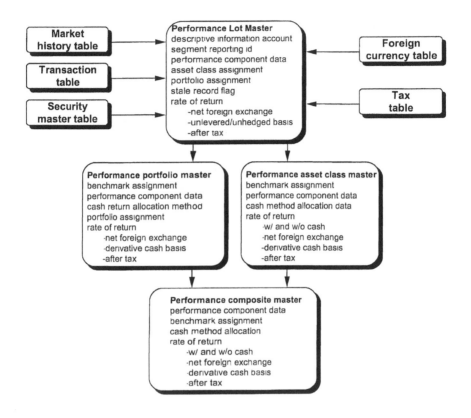

Exhibit 49-2.   A typical accounting system design.

method and formula for "total time-weighted estimates of return" calculations. The rationale, presumably, was that this formula was the most suitable to the nature of software and database design. The formula required predefined measurement periods and so was suited to monthly or quarterly returns generation. The Modified BAI method is similar in its component requirements, but requires an iterative solution, making it unattractive from a hardware performance standpoint, especially when transactions volume is large. The Modified Dietze method, however, offered reduced computation time and data storage requirements because it meant that there was only one record per security per measurement period.

Unfortunately, the Modified Dietze and Modified BAI methods both have certain mathematical limitations that can complicate processing requirements,[5] and neither formula is simple to reconcile or explain to clients. Recently, the industry has begun to move to a daily pricing standard, making the Modified Dietze and Modified BAI formulas obsolete. Yet there is little reason to fear that newer systems will have difficulty adhering to this standard. The components of return for the daily valuation formula are essentially the same for each of the time-weighted estimate formulas, making a database conversion more manageable. Additionally, faster processing speeds and cheaper data storage will mitigate the technological constraints that drove earlier designs.

Storing Return Data: Bane or Blessing?

Unlike most other aspects of the financial management process, performance measurement requires an ever-growing store of historical data. As stated earlier, when the investment accounting data change, performance reports are affected. Many systems will not store rates of return for this reason. The argument is that by calculating returns "on the fly" any performance return reported will always be up-to-date, and that storage space can be reduced. This is predominant in large systems that handle volume transactions. The trade-off is that reporting becomes a more time-consuming process.

There are several reasons why rate of return data should be stored:

1. Reporting a return is done far more frequently than calculating it (theoretically, the return is calculated only once). Thus it would make sense to store the calculated value, increasing processing time up front but reducing it for the more commonly used retrieval procedures.
2. The rate of return is a summary of the underlying transaction information, which admittedly is subject to change. But storing performance returns along with the associated performance components facilitates external reconciliation and validation of the formulas and methodologies used by the system. This, in turn, serves to bolster user confidence in the system's internal calculation and processing methods.
3. Data storage is cheap and storage processes can be batch-processed in time of low-volume data traffic.
4. Data delivery options cannot be limited to paper output. Warehousing return data expands data delivery options to numerous online and web-based applications. Over time, it also provides an in-house data mine for analytic investment research.

There is of course a drawback to comprehensive data warehousing, since performance data are as much a function of time as are the underlying accounting and performance flows. If returns are stored, then changes to historical flow data must trigger recalculation of all subsequent return information, as shown in Exhibit 49-3.

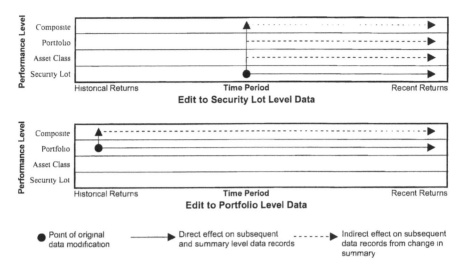

Edits to detail data records will affect higher level summary records All edits will affect return records subsequent to the effective date of the edit

Exhibit 49-3. Effect of historical changes on existing data records.

There are at least two possible methods for handling this difficulty. The first is to identify a materiality threshold. An example is by comparing the dollar amount of the change of the flow to its beginning value. User-specified *de minimus* exceptions will filter out trivial but common corrections to account transactions.

An additional approach is to build a "performance wall," behind which data cannot be modified, as shown in Exhibit 49-4. The term "wall" is a misnomer. In fact, historical data are deleted because they are included in the summary-level calculations and records. Records at the lot level are short lived. But in some cases, corrections to transactions may occur up to a year later, so these records will persist for some time. A satisfactory lot-level performance wall is 6 to 24 months. Performance walls for summary-level data are longer. Composite records, and arguably portfolio and asset class records, can be kept indefinitely, since these records will represent a small fraction of the entire database.

Similar data management techniques can and should be used for market price history and index data. However, the summation level is temporal: after the data has aged for a period of 6 months, daily records are discarded and only monthly records are retained.

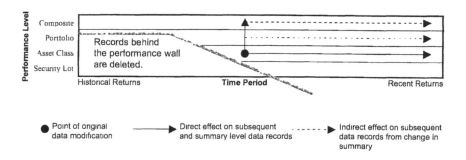

Data records "behind" the performance wall are eliminated This serves to (1) reduce storage space and (2) reduce processing time when historical edits are required

---
Exhibit 49-4. Managing database changes with a performance wall.

COMPLIANCE ISSUES

The financial services industry is heavily regulated. In addition to the Securities and Exchange Commission and state regulatory agencies, the industry is rife with self-regulating organizations such as AIMR, the National Association of Securities Dealers, and the Investment Management Consultants' Association. And there are myriad regulations from foreign jurisdictions that are probably unknown to most U.S. software developers. As investing practices continue to expand globally, firms will find themselves subject to even more constraints, particularly when it comes to reporting achieved investment results in overseas markets.

Determining the appropriate level of rule validation is a dilemma for any software package intended for use in a regulated industry. The assumption by developers is that regulation within an industry is uniform. In fact, it is not, particularly when a firm falls under a regulator's remedial action plan. Regulatory considerations that are "hard coded" into software can cause more headaches than benefits. Inevitably there are always a handful of users who, for whatever reason, require the system's functionality but do not need to comply with the regulatory rules, or have had additional rules imposed upon them by enforcement agencies.

It is important to emphasize that software does not and can not comply with such regulations. Performance rules, in particular, set standards for firms and individuals, not software. But complete understanding of these relatively new rules is not yet widespread, and the tendency for firms to market their performance software as "in compliance" with a set of standards (particularly the AIMR Performance Presentation Standards™) is great.

There are several risks when aligning a system with a set of industry regulations or the standards of a rule-making body:

1. The rules may be interpreted or enforced differently by different firms or agencies (as is the case in the insurance industry).
2. The validations implemented to enforce the rules may be inadequate or incorrect.
3. The functionality implemented to enforce the rules may be a hindrance to those users not subject to the rules, or to those who wish to obtain performance metrics for internal purposes.
4. Rules change, and developers are committed to accommodating these changes in the software.
5. Embedded regulatory functionality requires added education and support for users who are unfamiliar with such compliance standards.

For these reasons, firms acquiring performance software should be wary of claims of software compliance with specific industry standards. Typically, the database structure at initial implementation was not designed around multiple compliance issues, and thus the required data simply have not been recorded. Again, design limitations of the associated investment accounting system make it unlikely that any performance package is the perfect regulatory solution. Software is a tool, and as such, the emphasis and evaluation of a system should be made as to its *ability to assist* the firm in meeting its compliance obligations.

CONCLUSION

Designing an investment performance application involves much more than calculating rates of return. It is about understanding information flow and use in a dynamic process. Performance measurement data are consumed internally and externally: as a quantitative measure in the investment analysis and policy setting process, as a product to clients, as marketing material to prospects, and in some cases as a remuneration tool where performance-based compensation is used.

Identifying how the information will be applied will guide users and developers in prioritizing the functional requirements suggested above, with the result being a system that will be adaptable to the most common business and technological needs.

In the financial services industry, there is a well-known saying, "Some people work for their money, others have their money work for them." If you replace the word "money" with the word "technology," the goal of competitive and efficient performance systems design becomes clear.

SECURITIES TRENDS IN TECHNOLOGY

Notes

1. Simpson, J. D., European economic and monetary union, its impact on portfolio management and performance measurement systems, *J. Perform. Meas.,* 2(1), 5, 1997.
2. For an overview of the performance measurement process and calculations, see Spalding, D., *Measuring Investment Performance,* McGraw-Hill, New York, 1997.
3. Ellis, C. D., *Investment Policy,* 2nd ed., Irwin, Chicago, 1993, pp. 64–70.
4. See *AIMR Performance Presentation Standards Handbook,* 2nd ed., Association for Investment Management and Research, Charlottesville, VA. 1007; *Performance Reporting for Investment Managers.*
5. Revaluation at a performance period mid-point and subsequent recalculations is one such consideration.

Author Bio

Timothy Peterson *is the Associate Director, Performance Measurement with Portfolio Management Consultants, Inc. Prior to joining PMC, he was the Senior Research & Design Analyst with SunGard Insurance Systems, and a Risk Analyst with RiskCap, an insurance risk management consulting firm. Timothy holds a Bachelor's degree in economics and a Master of Science degree in finance with a concentration in information systems from the University of Colorado.*

Chapter 50
Building an Internet Strategy for Full-Service Brokers

Jeanne Chinchar

IN JUST A FEW SHORT YEARS, the Internet has engendered a profound change in the financial services industry. Online investing is growing at breakneck speed, and this boom presents the brokerage industry with new challenges in providing the services and research that investors want. The phenomenal growth of online trading is creating a whole new client base and exerting a significant influence on the stock market as a whole. Full-service brokers are losing market share to discount brokers who challenge the full-service business model.

Full-service brokers are beginning to step into the Internet arena but have yet to forge a compelling presence on the Web that does not conflict with their commission-led, core business structure. By leveraging the power of the Internet, full-service brokers can connect with their existing clients, cultivate new ones, and build their brand identity. They can take their core strengths and combine them with the interactive capabilities of the Web to create a new identity as an online full-service broker.

DEFINING THE PLAYING FIELD

Discount brokers are pure trading operations that provide a simple service; they buy and sell securities at low commission rates. Some leading examples are Datek, Suretrade, and Ameritrade. The Internet has helped spawn a new entity, the full-service discount broker; they offer phone access to brokers, some advice and some additional planning services, in addition to low-cost trades. Leaders in this field include Charles Schwab, Fidelity, E*Trade, and Quick & Reilly.

Full service brokers, such as Merrill Lynch, Salomon Smith Barney, and PaineWebber, to name just a few, provide a wide range of services. They offer advice on which stocks, bonds, commodities, and mutual funds to buy or sell; they offer advice on asset management, financial planning, tax shelters, income limited partnerships, and new issues of stock. Full-service brokerages charge higher transaction commissions and asset management fees because of the depth and breadth of the services they offer, the research staffs they maintain, and the overhead costs of their "bricks and mortar," their physical offices.

THE CHANGING LANDSCAPE

Discount brokers and full-service discount brokers compete with higher-priced full-service brokers by gutting commissions and fostering a research-it-yourself environment for individual investors. They used to compete with each other by slashing prices lower and lower — sometimes offering free trades to lure customers. Now the discounters look to compete by offering other benefits: they are trying to improve customer service, make their sites as easy to use as possible, and add new products and research. However, they lack the high-quality research available only through full-service brokers. And today's online investor is not particularly brand loyal. They are quite willing to "shop elsewhere" and often have accounts with more than one online broker.

There has been a radical change in the flow of investment information due to the commercial growth of the Internet. In the past, brokers gave information about companies to individual clients. Now, individuals search for company information on their own. They look to their brokers for customized advice and analysis, not news.

Today's stereotypical online investor is a transaction-hungry day trader with significant market experience. However, they represent a small portion, approximately 10 percent, of the entire investor universe. According to a Jupiter Communications 1998 online investing report, there are about 2.2 million of these active day traders. There are approximately 20 million advice-hungry investors — high-net-worth individuals who are more concerned about products and services and less interested in cheap trade access. And there are 25 million information-hungry investors, those who may have varying degrees of market experience but are primarily concerned with quality analytical information.

The Internet excels in bringing together instantaneous information and millions of people around the world in an interactive environment. Online investing has grown from 3.6 million accounts in 1997 to 7.3 million in 1998. The number of accounts is projected to reach 9.2 million this year and 15.2 million by 2002.[1]

Full-service brokers have concluded that they need to be online. They believe the numbers and recognize the opportunity presented by Internet access. The valuations of online discount brokers have finally convinced them of the necessity of establishing a presence online. At the end of December 1998, Schwab's market capitalization exceeded Merrill Lynch's valuation by over $400 million. And E*Trade recently topped PaineWebber in its valuation. The message has been received: investors value the online trading option, and selling the vision of consumer empowerment and continuous availability of investing products pays off.[2]

In the real world, full-service brokers set up offices in upscale neighborhoods and wait for clients to come and find them. And that physical presence, especially for regional brokers, is an important ingredient to brand identity. However, on the Internet, it can be difficult to translate that physical presence — that unique personality — into an instantly recognizable online identity. Where full-service brokers so often fail is in not presenting their unique assets in a compelling online format.

For example, a regional broker's major assets may include its physical presence, its special knowledge about local companies, and unique product offerings. Its people are closely connected to the region's people. Thus, the regional brokerage may have the inside track on some unique products, such as local municipal bonds. They may also have more complete knowledge about local companies. The regional analysts establish relationships with local company executives and local individual investors.

So how does a regional broker translate these assets to an online environment? By utilizing the interactivity of the Internet. If a regional brokerage's people are one of its assets, publishing their reports online and fostering dialog and discussion through online forums and e-mail can highlight their importance and build new and stronger relationships. An online site that is as attractive as the bricks-and-mortar office can communicate elegance, stability, and richness. And for those firms that specialize in particular segments of an industry, that unique or top-quality research ought to be promoted and readily accessible.

THE SOLUTION: A SUCCESSFUL ONLINE STRATEGY

Now is the time for full-service firms to capitalize on the rise of online investing. The full-service brokers' core strengths, especially their research and their brand identity of trust and service, can be integrated with the Internet's connectivity to build a new and even stronger identity. The full-service brokerage firm can become a reintermediator between the firm and the individual investor and develop a vibrant, innovative communication channel. The brokerage thereby outdistances the discounters and goes far beyond being just a cheap trade-processing pipeline.

Full-service brokers need to find an aggregator that can leverage their research as a lure. In this way, they can turn the Internet from a threat into a powerful tool. The Internet can be used as a way to reintermediate between

733

their firm and the individual, without running afoul of compliance standards or cutting into full-service brokers' commission rates. They can connect with the millions of information- and advice-hungry investors who want and need the research and services only full-service brokers can provide.

RECENT EXAMPLES

Most full-service brokers do not have an online strategy, but they all agree they need one. Merrill Lynch has taken a brave step forward into the arena, with the launch of AskMerrill.com. By offering free access to top-flight broker research, Merrill has acknowledged the power of the medium and leads the field by example. Merrill's Vice Chairman John L. Steffens has said that the best strategy is "to take advantage of what is scarce online." What is already plentiful — real-time quotes, online trading, etc. — is already a commodity. Identifying what is scarce and supplying it should be the smart online brokerage strategy. Merrill looks at it as getting "wired for wisdom," i.e., synthesizing the vast amounts of information available online into good, actionable investing.

Merrill Lynch launched its free Web site in conjunction with Multex.com in November 1998. Merrill Lynch's Frank Zammataro, Vice President and Director of Strategic Research, explained that Multex.com was chosen in part because the company was already distributing Merrill's research to institutional clients. The research feeds were already set up, so there was no need for Merrill to build the site from scratch.[3]

Merrill expects to build upon the customer value of trust by being able to satisfy different investors with different products and services. They are even experimenting with offering online trading to high-level customers. And the firm recognizes the competition for mind share in the vast Internet universe. They recognize the need to be plugged into an established broker research aggregator so as to extend their identity beyond the borders of their own Web site, in the same way they extend their identity beyond the walls of their offices in the physical world.

Salomon Smith Barney has also partnered with Multex.com in establishing its own online identity. The smithbarney.com Web site furnishes investors with Internet access to portfolio management, investment ideas, and financial planning tools. Online users can monitor their portfolios, select a watch list of securities, and get performance charts, research, and Dow Jones News related to their holdings. Market overviews, individual company analysis, and timely articles on investing are provided, as are calculators and planning tools to help the online users define their investment goals. The site also offers in-depth explanations of all the products and services available to individuals, corporations, and institutional investors.

In addition to their own carefully planned and managed Web sites, full-service brokers need an online network that can help them compete. Full-service brokers can use the research aggregator to:

1. Create a compelling Web offering using broker research, which has historically only been available to clients and institutions, and use it to generate leads by distributing it selectively over the Internet.
2. Use Web tracking capabilities to collect demographics and other key data. Compile this knowledge and then apply it to create better quality service and build solid relationships.
3. Take advantage of personalization techniques available through the Internet to improve relationships even further.
4. Use the Web site to build and sustain brand identity.
5. Use the medium to drive traffic, through key sponsorships and advertising.

A well-established online financial network, dedicated to full-service brokerages, can enhance the ability to serve existing retail accounts and to develop relationships with millions of new investors. Connection with a branded investment Web site for serious investors can boost both visibility and access to a full-service brokerages' high-value content, services, and staff and facilitate the development of new products and services for new and existing clients.

A fully integrated Web site, where no online discount brokers participate and which offers access to research to hundreds of thousands of online investors, serves as a conduit that connects the investor and the brokerage firm. The investor finds the firm's research and grasps the firm's identity in a meaningful context, at the moment when interest is most avid. As the investor gets to know the firm, the firm gets to know the investor, learning more about what types of products and services are needed.

CONCLUSION

Leveraging the interactivity of the Internet is key to all E-commerce. For full-service brokers, interactivity with analysts can be made robust and valuable when presented in the proper form and place. As technology and deregulation alter the landscape of the brokerage industry, full-service brokers can assume a leadership position and maintain a solid foothold in the electronic environment through strategic placement of their quality research, superior services, and overall value.

Notes

1. Franco, S. C. and Klein, T. M., Jupiter Communications, Piper Jaffray Equity Research, "Online Brokerages 1998," February 5, 1999.
2. Gomez, J., "Online Brokers Earn Market Respect," *GomezWire*, (www.gomez.com) December 31, 1998.

3. "Multex.com's site will be the first pay-per-report site aimed at opening up brokerage research to investors," Dow Jones News Service, January 27, 1999.

Author Bio

Jeanne Chinchar is the Executive Editor of Multex.com, Inc. and currently manages the corporate Web site. She is a writer and editor who joined Multex.com as Associate Editor of the online publication, MX Magazine, *and became Senior Editor of the magazine, now renamed* The Ink Well. *In addition to writing and editing the home pages for Multex.com and the Multex Investor Network, Chinchar has published numerous articles for the online magazine, including the weekly, biweekly, and monthly columns, New Buys, Mutual Fund Snapshots, and CountryWatch.*

Prior to joining Multex, Chinchar established her own creative services company, A Perfect World. She has been a writer, editor, and arts administrator for many years and was a senior program director for a nonprofit literary organization for 5 years. Chinchar holds a Master of Arts degree in Media Studies and a Bachelor of Arts degree in Communications.

Chapter 51
Middleware Standards in Capital Markets

Gabriel Bousbib

DESPITE MASSIVE TECHNOLOGY INVESTMENTS OVER THE LAST 2 DE-
CADES, financial institutions remain fairly paper-intensive businesses.
Throughout the entire trading process, from the origination of the order to
the settlement of the trade, paper tickets, paper confirmations, faxes, and
the like clog the desks of traders, sales staff, and operations personnel.
"Reconciliations" between different computer systems, multiple system interfaces laboriously developed, double trade entries, correction of errors,
etc. remain commonplace in many firms, including the most sophisticated.
In brief, despite some improvements such as the move to D+3 in the settlement area, the paperless trading environment is not yet here.

A number of industry experts have been advocating the development of
"data warehouses," i.e., a central data depository that would integrate the
entire transaction universe of the firm, from existing legacy systems, mostly front-office trading applications. A number of "engines," ranging from
risk engines to accounting and settlement applications, could then be applied onto the data warehouse, thus facilitating the true support of the entire trade chain and providing a paperless trading environment. However,
the diversity of transaction types and of the functions applied to these
transactions makes it difficult if not impossible to develop a single database design, valid for all transactions and all functions. For example, spot
foreign exchange trades and structured derivative transactions present
very different characteristics in terms of data requirements. Spot trades
are composed of a small, well-defined number of data elements. Spot trading operations are usually high-volume operations, and as a result, spot
trades will require a product-driven database, specialized by product type,
which allows for high throughput. On the other hand, structured derivative
trades are composed of multiple components, not always known in advance, and trading volumes are usually very low. An efficient database for

such products would need to be component driven, allowing for the easy definition of new transaction types. As this database would not be product driven, it would not usually offer any acceptable scalability for high-volume trading environments.

In our opinion, a more efficient way to address the challenge of a paperless trading environment would be by the development of a common guaranteed delivery transaction protocol, which would allow disparate systems to "talk" to each other. A transaction entered into a front-office system in, say, Tokyo, would be transmitted via the common transaction protocol to the relevant back-office, accounting, risk systems, etc. with the corresponding events (e.g., generate confirmations, payment instructions, recalculate Value-At-Risk, etc.).

More generally, a homogeneous financial protocol can be developed by the software industry to completely interconnect financial systems around the planet. With this protocol in place, the ease of connectivity will increase secure participation in the financial markets. *This will stimulate growth by increasing the capital available to any economic entity by orders of magnitude.* The key is the development of a universal financial computer transaction protocol, which is not yet developed. The costs of maintaining and developing proprietary financial transaction interfaces for large financial institutions is encouraging cooperation with software vendors to cut multimillion dollar software bills. The result is a common protocol allowing transaction data interchange between financial systems. Such a transaction protocol would then have the potential to be as successful as the TCP/IP communications protocol for data transmission, or the Reuters' SSL protocol for real-time market data distribution.

Financial transaction protocols are not new; they have been around for about 25 years, and there are hundreds of them. Object-oriented software technology was not available when most of these protocols were developed. With the recent advent of object-oriented software technology, it is now possible to put advanced functionality into a protocol and make the protocol object available as the protocol specification. To date, a Universal Financial Protocol has not been achieved, partly for cost, lack of cooperation in a cold-war society, and lack of vision on the part of architects in the industry. Each of these factors has improved in recent years, leaving open the possibility of actualizing such a protocol.

1. S.W.I.F.T. — Society for World Interbank Financial Transfers (spot currency)
2. CIRRUS — Cash machine network (spot currency)
3. ADP PSIPT — Back Office Submission
4. CMS — Electronic trading protocol on the New York Stock Exchange
5. CHIPS, FEDWIRE — Central bank wire transfers

6. Reuters SSL — Trading and disseminating prices
7. DTC Protocol — Depository Trust Corporation (securities depository transactions)
8. STAMP — Toronto Exchange interface protocol

The bandwidth of each of these protocols constrains the range of possible business that can be done with them. For example, the CMS protocol is a way to trade on the New York Stock Exchange. Software to send electronic orders has been developed by every member firm of the exchange for doing electronic trading. This software represents millions of dollars in investment and will need to be redeveloped to work in other environments. This unnecessary effort is partly due to intellectual property concerns as the protocol is owned by NYSE and therefore not an open standard. Due to the localization of expertise to each regional exchange, country, and regional electronic protocol, few developers have sought to create a super protocol because it was too great an amount of knowledge to accumulate and consider for development. With the advent of the Internet bulletin board, this is no longer an impediment.

A Universal Financial Protocol would replace all the protocols listed above with a single open standard. Firms would be drawn to it just as the computer industry was drawn to the open standard of UNIX to avoid proprietary operating systems in the middle 1980s and is now being drawn toward the Windows environment. Until recently, UNIX was the de facto standard of the financial world largely because it is an open standard. By fostering the development of standard tools using the Windows environment, Microsoft has successfully established the Windows operating systems as a serious contender for the leading spot in the financial services industry.

A business system supports certain applications that all interact via financial transaction protocols. By unifying the basis of these transaction protocols, and as illustrated in Exhibit 51-1, a Universal Financial Protocol will enable these business systems automatically to be capable of intercommunicating.

Financial information technology will become more available with the advent of a Universal Financial Protocol. Current systems are large and often proprietary, with custom protocol interfaces to other systems within an organization. Installations take years, and software systems are expensive as vendors are recovering profit from the slim margins of consulting to install their products. The next generation of financial transaction servers will come from the database manufacturer with a pre-existing data model to support the Universal Financial Protocol interface. Products that currently require custom development will be available as packages from vendors. Improved interconnectivity between IT systems will lead to wider sharing of business intelligence inside the organization with reduced costs.

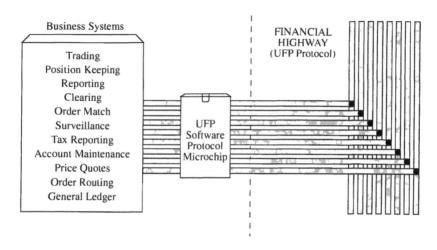

Exhibit 51-1. Universal Financial Protocol.

The protocol must support the following business:

1. *Trading of all traded financial products including derivatives* — The protocol would have a way of describing any traded financial product using data fields in a message. For exotic derivatives, a parsed language field would be used.
2. *Settlement and clearing of the same* — Every trading environment must have a mechanism to transmit the completed transactions to another system, reporting such information as the time, price, location, and reporting authority for the transaction.
3. *International standards for trading of these instruments* — Each country and exchange has some variations in how they trade and settle financial transactions. These issues would be considered in the protocol.
4. *Corporate actions* — The protocol would have a mechanism for requesting and receiving information regarding stock splits, dividends, new listings, and a variety of other operations that affect holdings in these instruments. In the message specification, this is considered as asset redefinition.
5. *Depository transfers* — The protocol would have the extensions to report trading activity to the depository authority responsible for reporting. International variations on this will all be managed as part of the protocol as the transaction is little different than that of an execution report.
6. *Quote request and quote* — To support trading, the protocol must provide a mechanism to request a quote and to receive a quote.

This should even extend to the ability to quote a market such as the open order book for a stock. There is a fine line here between market data required to trade in a transaction format and the broadcast of market data which is not transaction related. This paper considers only the former but leaves open how to draw this line. The Toronto Stock Exchange STAMP specification should be considered regarding this area, as it is a recent protocol specifically designed to cover this area.

7. *Tax transfers* — These transactions are wire transfers to a tax authority. On tax reporting, it is possible that the protocol supports a tax message type which could transfer an entire tax return by using a variety of fields. Tax protocol objects can be designed and published by the tax authority which "plug" into the protocol definition to support their standard for those who use it.

8. *Wire transfers, virtual cash, payments* — Cash payments are the discounted sales of currency which clear immediately. These are already executed regularly in world banking, but the standard is slow, unavailable, and proprietary.

9. *Position transfer and reporting* — For reporting and consolidation purposes, a mechanism must be included to inquire for and transmit a position. This provides for global position consolidation and reporting of profit and loss.

10. *Risk management* — Risk management requires the availability of certain data which is not commonly used in moment-to-moment trading. These data would be available in the Quote transmission portion of the protocol.

11. *Account maintenance and margin functions* — To support remote trading operations and a highly variable customer trading business, the protocol would have the extensions to create and maintain accounts and to manage business related to accounts, such as margin calls.

12. *User maintenance functions* — Combined with accounts, certain trading permissions are often allotted to restrict access or allow access to trading accounts or share limits. These extensions are essential for network-administered trading.

13. *List maintenance facilities* — This is really a special hybrid e-mail message type, which would allow a system to transmit a new composition of a certain list used in list trading. This permits central administration of arbitrage baskets in a network environment.

14. *Binary code transmission* — A binary pricing model should also be transmittable. This would allow a firm to develop a new derivative instrument, transmit a pricing model to another location, and begin trading the instrument immediately by pricing it in all locations. The binary module could be platform specific or in a language like JAVA. Like an extended *file transfer protocol (ftp)*, this extension

would allow a firm to update the trading software environment on each of its client sites.

15. *Credit card transactions* — In the interests of thoroughness, credit card transactions should be included in the protocol, though they may be rarely used in wholesale finance.

The applications of such a Universal Financial Protocol would be multiple, as illustrated below:

- A new regional electronic exchange is set up in Nagasaki, Japan. The exchange purchases a computer and a database software package with an order match system. They connect this system to the secure Internet and because the database server has UFP compliance, they are ready to do electronic business with any registered institution in the world. Not only are orders and reports processed, but clearing records, Quote data and Corporate Actions are also managed by the protocol.

- The same regional exchange purchases a UFP-compliant market surveillance system, which they plug in and install with their order match system. This comes online in less than 1 week from the purchase date.

- A new listing is to occur on this exchange. The institution makes its balance sheet and other such information available to the world financial community via the UFP protocol. The IPO time is reduced by 4 months.

- A foreign exchange dealer in St. Petersburg buys a UFP compliant FOREX dealing system and plugs it in. After configuring their server, they are able to participate fully in their business virtually overnight.

- A brokerage house in Chicago wishes to change back office/clearing partners due to excessive charges. They simply change their UFP compliant interfaces to point to another clearing firm, and they are online in less than 2 days.

- A bank in Paris has 20 offices in various cities in the world. They pay a huge cost for telecommunications to maintain a private secure network for order/report transactions when some offices are submitting as few as two futures orders per day. The bank puts these smaller offices on the Internet using a secure UFP-compliant trading system and reduces their network overhead by 50 percent.

- A Chinese development bank in Hong Kong wants to find a market for an exotic interest rate derivative. They put out indications of interest on their UFP-compliant database server and receive interest from firms in Madrid and in Sao Paulo.

- A small financial engineering company in London develops a pricing model for a digital option. They make the model UFP compliant and are able to guarantee its operation in any world financial center without localization for pricing bus or the local trading system.

- A respected London bank receives the daily transaction activity of its Singapore and Osaka offices via UFP into a UFP-compliant risk management system. Using this, they detect some dangerous trading activity and stop a potentially embarrassing event.

While the Internet was the result of a governmental initiative, it is likely that the development of a Universal Financial Protocol will be the result of the action of industry groups. A recent industry initiative, led by some of the largest American buy and sell-side firms, has led to the definition of standard protocol for indication of interest on equity orders, as well as order routing and execution. The resulting protocol, called FIX for Financial Information eXchange, is attempting to be to order routing what TCP/IP is to the Internet. It does, however, have the potential to being expanded in order to serve the very purpose of a Universal Financial Protocol. The recent initiative of the Chicago futures exchanges regarding the extension of FIX into FIX++ should further accelerate this trend. FIX aspires to be universal; it will require significant involvement from the financial community, including sell-side firms, institutional investors, as well as technology firms and data vendors, with the right vision to accomplish such an ambitious objective. As the largest information vendor in the world, Reuters is committed to further accelerating market transparency by the development of common communication protocols. Reuters has a number of ongoing initiatives in this area, including in particular the development of guarantee-delivery messaging applications (e.g., ETX, ORKA), as well as the incorporation of standard protocols (e.g., FIX, STAMP) into its existing order routing and order management applications.

Author Bio

Gabriel Bousbib *is currently Senior Vice President and Chief Operating Officer, Risk Management Division, Reuters America Holdings. He has overall operational responsibility for Reuters' risk management activities in the Americas, including sales and marketing, technical and application support, as well as development and financial engineering. Reuters' current risk management product line offers a comprehensive range of risk management capabilities, which include order routing and order management, trade capture, position keeping, valuation, tactical as well as strategic risk management.*

 Prior to joining Reuters, Bousbib was a Managing Director and principal of the CBM Group, Inc., a management consulting firm specializing in financial services and risk management. He was formerly the founder of MYCA Inc., a software company developing risk management systems for derivatives dealers. Bousbib previously worked for Merrill Lynch Capital Markets as a risk manager in the derivatives area. He holds an M.B.A. from Columbia University Graduate School of Business and is a graduate from Ecole Polytechnique in Paris.

Chapter 52
The Broker Desktop: The Future of Trading Has Arrived

John McLeod

A BROKER'S DESKTOP COMPUTER USED TO BE JUST A "DUMB" TERMINAL linked to a mainframe computer. It issued quotes and offered limited information about a client's account. Actual trades were done by filling out a paper form and forwarding it to the wireroom, where it was manually inputted and executed.

This typical blend of old and new world technology has clouded the perceptions of the trading services that can be offered by software solutions on the broker's desktop computer. Today, though, a brokerage firm relying on that business model for information delivery and trading will soon find itself going the way of the dinosaur. The wireroom is obsolete, and new technology is opening the door for real-time broker desktop trading and information retrieval.

Personal computers (PCs), along with advances in networking and Internet technology, are turning the broker's desktop into a wealth management machine that gives instant access to information needed to manage accounts and keep clients abreast of changes in fast-paced capital markets.

At the root of it all are powerful software tools delivering everything from quotes and news to financial planning and portfolio management. With the click of a mouse, brokers can access everything about a client and his or her portfolio using innovative integrated software packages that cross the barriers between a brokerage firm's back and front office systems.

Only in the past few years have software developers been able to break through the typical office technology hurdles and deliver enterprise-wide solutions that provide brokers with a detailed, electronic snapshot of their clients' positions.

Everyone will benefit from these advances in broker desktop solutions. For brokers, an integrated system means more timely information and ease of use, which allows them to service more accounts. For their firms, it means greater efficiencies and streamlined operations. For clients, it means better service and, ultimately, savings on trades.

OVERCOMING HURDLES

The chief challenge in developing integrated desktop systems is not creating the software or hardware products themselves. What has been holding back full-scale adoption of these systems is that brokerage firms are only now starting to understand that they can outsource such activity to third parties. Largely, though, brokerage firms remain tied to legacy systems and service bureaus. Even when they update their technology, there is still a belief they must have proprietary systems rather than products developed by outside vendors.

That is changing, driven in large part by the rapid emergence of online and Internet-based brokers who use World Wide Web browser software to deliver integrated trading and portfolio management tools over the Internet. With a PC and online access, clients now have a wealth of information at their fingertips and on their screen, ranging from industry research to real-time quotes to direct trading capabilities. In some cases, a sophisticated client has more firepower in his personal PC than his broker.

The biggest brokerage firms are moving to meet this threat by giving their brokers better research and investment tools on their desktop. Merrill Lynch, for example, will spend $250 million developing its own broker workstation, according to the Tower Group. Smith Barney is expected to spend $250 million developing its stations, Prudential and PaineWebber have each budgeted $150 million, and Dean Witter is spending $125 million. In total, these five firms alone will spend almost $1 billion on broker desktop development.

Why are these costs so high? One reason is that the older transaction-based software on brokers' desktops must give way to new software that encourages "consultative" relationships in which a broker provides value-added, wealth management advice.

To create an effective integrated desktop, brokerage firms must link a variety of stand-alone software solutions or create their own omnibus tools to accomplish different tasks. Many firms have legacy transaction processing and back-office systems for each line of business, such as mutual funds, fixed income, or equities. The problem with this approach is that the systems cannot always talk to each other.

That creates headaches for brokers, who must manage and learn several software applications. Rather than have all the information on one screen, a broker has to toggle back and forth between programs to conduct trades in various financial products. Not only that, but the software packages may not share information and require inputting of the same data over and over, threatening the integrity of client records and increasing the likelihood of errors.

Integrated software programs free the broker from being a data entry clerk. An integrated system also acts as an "umbrella" application, covering all aspects of the organization and allowing information to flow seamlessly. Still, an integrated desktop solution has many other requirements to meet.

THE MODEL INTEGRATED DESKTOP

We don't live in a one-size-fits-all universe. The needs of each brokerage firm can differ greatly. For example, firms providing "customer-direct" services have different needs than those firms offering full-service capabilities.

In customer-direct firms, trade execution services rank first. These firms need to be confident that when a customer pushes an execution button, the trade takes place in a timely fashion. Portfolio analysis is not high on their client's list, though that may change in the future.

For full-service firms, functionality and performance remain key for the broker. They need tools to service their customers better. That means creating simpler user interfaces and developing more sophisticated analytical tools. One hurdle a firm of this type faces in implementing an integrated system is that it may need to distribute software and information updates on a regular basis to desktops, which can lead to business disruption if the software is poorly designed.

Newer players on the wealth management block, such as insurers, who are creating wealth management and brokerage divisions, have other obstacles. They often have little control over the location of the sales force or the individual broker's desktop, which may be in a home office or be an older PC. Insurers must have the capability to use low-cost Web browser services so the sales force can get client information from remote and off-site destinations using the Internet.

With all this in mind, a company looking for the model integrated desktop solution for brokers would have a comprehensive shopping list.

Contact Management

The ideal system covers both prospect management and existing client management. The system must help brokers convert prospects into customers. It must capture demographic information about clients and prospects. It must help brokers identify suitable products and services needed by both existing and potential clients. This means ensuring that the system allows brokers to analyze data and create reports for both prospects and clients. It must permit a broker to create a database of customers and prospects that contains individual, personalized information, such as investment objectives. It should help a broker manage client contact activities, such as "ticklers" for phone calls, and provide a way to follow up contacts and support targeted marketing campaigns.

Seamless Service

For a busy broker to accept a new technology on the desktop, it must be easy to use and not slow him or her down. The system must present the information in a simple, cohesive fashion. It must allow a broker to maneuver quickly between applications or tools. That requires a seamless interface between systems with the mere click of a mouse. The key lies in building a better link between the desktop and the legacy system, and a successful installation depends on the planning and foresight during the system's integration process.

Scalability

A few years ago, a bond trading system was expected to be able to manage and support upwards of 1000 inventory lines and execute a hundred trades an hour. Today, software must support 10,000 different products and thousands of trades per hour. Product offerings will continue to grow, and model systems must have the capability to accommodate updates. For example, a brokerage firm should be able to add new applications that use the underlying database structure or don't require re-entering client data.

Reliability

Without a reliable system, the desktop means nothing. If a broker cannot access information when he needs it, then business is lost and client service suffers.

Vendor Neutrality

While Windows NT and Windows 2000 are the industry standard for broker desktops, UNIX and legacy mainframes still play a vital role in the back office of most firms and will likely continue to do so in the near future. An integrated system must provide straight-through processing from front to back offices. By limiting the need for multiple data entries, a firm will reduce its error and rejection rates. That allows back office staff to focus their efforts on failed executions, rather than concerning themselves with all trades.

Compliance

An integrated system should enhance the compliance function within a firm. It should support "know-your-client" rules and offer brokers an immediate assessment of how a trade fits into a client's profile in relation to his or her investment objectives. It should assist firms in managing their risk and exposure and help them avoid stock market calamities that could hurt profitability and tarnish their reputation.

Asset Management

Asset allocation is critical to successful investing. A good integrated software system will provide brokers with an indication of the client's current asset breakdown, as well as the investor's goal or objectives. This allows the broker to easily monitor a client's account and suggest necessary changes as the market shifts. For example, if a client wants only 10 percent of assets in speculative Internet stocks, the portfolio can quickly become overweighted, given the explosive growth in this sector. By monitoring asset allocations, a broker can quickly lock in gains and restore portfolios to their investment objectives. Desktop automation allows brokers to service more accounts at less cost. WRAP accounts are also growing in popularity. Integrated software packages must be able to manage and implement complex asset allocation models that feature automatic buy and sell triggers. Technology already allows brokers to create "miniwraps" based on regional factors important to a broker's clients in his or her own community.

Real-Time Information

A broker's ability to service clients relies on timely market information. Data must be constantly updated without the need for brokers to continually refresh their screens. In networked systems, online updates are already a reality, but browser-based systems still require brokers to refresh their screen for real-time quotes. The model integrated system must have a capability to receive feeds and updates from external systems and link to operations like quote vendors, exchanges, and newswire services through systems, such as ADP/DNS, Davidge HPNS, ISM/OMS. But that is only half of the equation. The system must then be able to take real-time information and allow brokers to automatically push relevant information to clients and prospects and incorporate alerts so the client is serviced and kept abreast of market changes and knows when to buy or sell.

Single Log-In

For broker ease-of-use, the ideal system must provide single log-in capabilities from one screen so the broker does not have to sign-on as he or she accesses different software applications or tools.

Commonality

An integrated broker desktop must provide screens that are consistent in appearance, logic, and navigation techniques. Brokers should be able to view information, such as trade orders, on a single, consolidated screen to quickly ascertain the status of a client's account.

Inventory Management

When trading, brokers must be able to quickly find products. For example, if a client wants to add a bond to his or her portfolio, the system should provide brokers with search tools allowing them to identify products based on investment criteria, such as a 10-year bond yielding 4 percent. By allowing brokers to plug in their criteria, an integrated software application can shave vital minutes off the time required to develop a client strategy.

Multicurrencies

Integrated systems should be able to juggle different currencies and account for them. It must be able to provide reports in multiple currencies, covering everything from Euros to the yen to dollars.

Multilanguage

In order to serve a global marketplace, integrated systems must also take into consideration different cultures and be able to operate and report in languages other than English.

Settlement

The model solution will provide straight-through processing for all transactions directly to the appropriate settlement and clearing system. In automating these transactions, a firm eliminates the need for wirerooms and manual inputting of information. By capturing the order at the point of sale and driving it straight through, error rates and failed executions are reduced.

Automated Data Transfer

To save time and reduce the likelihood of errors, a model integrated system should have the capability to transfer and share redundant data, such as the customer name and account number, to various applications.

Wealth Management

A 1998 J.D. Power & Associates survey, conducted for Dow Jones, found the primary driver in satisfying investment clients was not low fees. It was the amount of information and education that clients received from financial advisers. The survey of 1200 investors with portfolios exceeding $100,000 found respondents were more satisfied with a financial planner or national brokerage firm than they were a discount broker. That means most clients are looking for wealth management advice, rather than buy and sell services. At a minimum, an integrated system should provide brokers with calculators and tools for creating what-if analysis and future projections.

Reports

The model system should provide comprehensive reports that follow industry standards and highlight items as the adjusted cost base of an investment, needed for income tax reporting. In order to accomplish this, the broker must be able to draw information from a number of different sources, including trade executions and accounting. The system must be adaptable to different levels of client sophistication and allow the broker to prepare reports for everyone from a novice investor to a sophisticated player who knows and understands instruments like options and futures.

Web Access

A recent report by Forrester Research describes the impact the Internet will have on financial transactions, estimating the number of U.S. households conducting online financial transactions will increase from 3.3 million in 1998 to 15.7 million by 2003. Indeed, the steep growth curve that discount brokers are currently experiencing indicates the Web is a force that can no longer be ignored by the full-service brokerage community.

It is important to remember that the Web community is not homogeneous, but serves a variety of different clients, from consumer direct relationships to full-service firms to roving brokers or planners. Web access will be standard fare in most brokerage firms to provide brokers with the ability to maintain regular and, in some cases, instantaneous contact with clients. The model integrated system must not only provide Internet access but must also be able to operate on an intranet or internal brokerage network. By allowing brokers to access portfolio management software through browser-enabled systems, a firm can maintain the software on a single server. This "thin client" software approach serves two functions. It eliminates the need for costly and time-consuming upgrades at the broker's workstation and ends concern over hardware and operating system compatibility since browser software is platform independent. That said, the firm may sacrifice speed and functionality vs. a Wide Area Network (WAN) or a Local Area Network (LAN).

THE INTEGRATED DESKTOP: BUILD OR OUTSOURCE?

With so many different requirements for an integrated solution, should a brokerage firm build its own proprietary system (with its financial and time demands) or take advantage of the economies of scale an outside software vendor can bring to the table?

Retail brokers expect and demand high quality technology. For organizations that want to reduce risk and grow their revenue, outsourcing to a vendor is likely the best alternative. A vendor can factor in the cost of research and development for upgrades and functionality across its total client base, making new tools and applications more affordable than if done in-house.

Everything from software development to infrastructure and network management can be outsourced to qualified and competent organizations. This frees up the brokerage firm's time and effort to focus on differentiating themselves from their competitors by enhancing personnel, training, marketing initiatives, and client development and building leading edge investment products and services.

That said, a firm must assess the vendor's capabilities in these key outsourcing areas:

1. *Vendor Support.* This is critical to the success of any software undertaking. For example, who will provide "help desk" support for the software and for how long?
2. *Upgrades.* The days of buying a software package and not touching it until the next release a few years down the road are gone. A good vendor is constantly looking to upgrade its product — introducing new tools and upgrades to provide brokers with more functionality. Ask whether the vendor offers periodic major and minor releases. A vendor who is constantly upgrading its product is spending money on research and development and reinvesting in its product.
3. *User Groups.* Does the vendor have a user group? A vendor that has feedback from 10 brokerage firms as opposed to one or two is in a better position to address concerns and develop new tools and applications.
4. *Broker Friendly.* Ensure your vendor takes into consideration the end user, which in most instances is the broker and even the client. If the system is not designed with the broker in mind, it will fail. Brokers are not administrators. They do not want to spend their finite time inputting data. Their time is best spent managing client assets, and if the software makes that difficult, they will not use it.

WHY ADOPT AN INTEGRATED SOLUTION?

Adopting an integrated solution offers a number of benefits to a brokerage firm.

Cost Savings. An integrated solution can help firms streamline their operations and turn paper processes into electronic transactions. By providing straight-through processing, a firm can confine order processing — whether for mutual funds, fixed income, or equities — to one department. A hundred processing clerks pushing reams of paper and inputting data can be slashed to 50 focusing on problem trades.

That is particularly important as the cost of trade execution drops and revenues from that activity decline.

Better Client Management. Before the technological revolution swept through brokerage firms, an advisor would hit a wall at 600 to 700 clients. Automation has changed that. Brokers can now manage more clients and sophisticated accounts. Moreover, by providing brokers with the tools to better manage their accounts, a firm cuts down on compliance issues and helps a broker build his book with sought-after wealth management advice.

Recruitment. While competition for clients among brokerage firms is tough, the competition for qualified staff is equally challenging. The broker with the best technological support is the one providing the best service. Superior technology can be a recruiting tool and can differentiate your firm in the marketplace.

WHAT LIES AHEAD FOR THE BROKER'S DESKTOP?

The broker's desktop has come a long way from the dumb terminal. The model integrated desktop described in this chapter is already available today and will set the standard in the new millennium.

The biggest obstacle to putting these cost-effective and comprehensive integrated solutions on brokers' desktops is the investment community's lack of awareness and understanding of their full capabilities.

By working together with qualified and experienced vendors, this obstacle can be quickly overcome, and integrated desktop solutions can begin to help build strong and long-lasting broker–client relationships.

Author Bio

John McLeod has served as president and CEO of Spectra Securities Software since founding the company in 1989. Well-respected within both the financial and technology industries, McLeod has more than 20 years experience in this combined field. Prior to establishing Spectra Securities Software, he served on the board of directors at the Canadian brokerage firm Burns Fry Limited, where he was responsible for the firm's global technology requirements and the implementation of a digital trading floor system. Previously, McLeod held a variety of technical and managerial positions at Peat Marwick Mitchell & Co. and Wood Gundy Ltd. McLeod earned his B. Math degree in Computer Science from the University of Waterloo and was designated a chartered accountant by the Institute of Chartered Accountants of Ontario.

Section IV
Insurance Trends in Technology

YOU'LL BE HAPPY TO KNOW THAT I NEVER HELD A JOB IN AN INSURANCE FIRM, so I can't really reminisce over the "way it used to be" in setting up my discussion about what it's like today. My very first job as a programmer, however, was with a financial firm that did issue credit life insurance. Of course, we're really going back in time now. Way back to 1975. This was the era of the keypunch machine and the IBM 360. Paper ruled the day then.

Paper still rules today. But we're making inroads as, again, the headlines tell us.

The life insurance industry is flocking to the Web with products such as annuities. According to some, the potential for annuities sales over the Web may be even greater than personal lines.

www.quotesmith.com of Darien, IL has expanded its instant insurance price comparison service to include instant quotes for final expense whole life insurance on the Internet. The quotes are for policy face amounts of $2000 to $100,000.

For some, the Insurance Information Exchange (www.iix.com) is a launching pad of information on the Web for interesting things in the insurance community in the same way folks use Digital's Alta Vista to find general information.

Along with inevitable push to all things automated, the insurance as well as the banking industry has shifted its focus to the customer. As Don Chase puts it in his chapter, New Business Model for Insurance Industry Demands New Automation Model, all processes must be designed to satisfy customer needs, rather than the company's needs. The new model is also decentralized, with more responsibility and power given to the people who are on the front lines with the customers, whether they are independent agents, captive agents, or company employees.

Again, the primary focus of this new model for most firms is the ubiquitous Internet — although the internal form of the Internet is considered as well (e.g., intranet, extranet). As Richard DuBois, who contributed the chapter on The Internet and Evolving Technology, explains, the Internet is spawning an unbelievable growth of vendors that have and are continuing to develop solutions for commercial insurance activity on the Internet. Unlike most other technologies that have been presented to the insurance industry, the Internet is a fully operational, fully proven, total communications and data exchange environment, available today for use by the world-wide business community. It cannot be viewed as just another technology that's there for you to use if you want to; it will be the medium by which we will all conduct business in the future. In order to exploit the opportunities of the Internet, a company must shift its strategic approach accordingly.

The Internet is essentially just a network of interconnected computers that contain vast information sources. In order to provide any real value, it must partner with other technologies that make this information accessible and useful.

Although companies such as Yahoo, Excite, and InfoSeek garner lots of headlines and even more investor dollars, they are representative of the biggest of Internet flaws. There is no good way to easily pinpoint the specific Web sites of interest to you without first having to go through pages and pages of irrelevant information. Irrelevancy, then, is the biggest Internet bug.

The advent of Intelligent agents will go a long way toward solving this problem in real-time. But even when it is solved, when you combine information you lift from the Internet with information from in-house and purchased databases, you have a real information explosion on your hands.

This is where Business Intelligence comes in. It provides a framework with which you can use technology to sift through the gigabytes of raw data to turn it into useful knowledge. The chapter on Understanding and Implementing Business Intelligence Solutions in the Insurance Industry explains the process by which a company can utilize this most useful of new technologies.

All-in-all, insurance firms are facing an upheaval in the manner in which they do business. There isn't a facet of the business that isn't, or won't soon be, automated.

Jessica Keyes

Chapter 53
Outsourcing Business Communications in the Insurance Industry

Kim Herren

TODAY, THE IMPORTANCE OF BUSINESS COMMUNICATIONS is unquestioned: transaction-based documents are the lifeblood of every business, including insurance providers. Through business documents, insurance companies acquire and retain customers, communicate important information, issue policies and invoices, and generate cash flow. However, if firms are producing and distributing documents in-house, the process could be costing substantially more than it should.

Surprisingly, many senior managers are unaware of what it actually costs to run an in-house document production and distribution operation, and how outsourcing can be used to their benefit. For example, by outsourcing the printing and mailing of insurance documents, it is common for providers to realize overall cost savings of 20 to 25 percent. The benefits are even more compelling when providers also realize improved document quality and turnaround, and the increased freedom to focus on their core business.

IN-HOUSE PRINTING VS. OUTSOURCING

Recent research from CAP Ventures[1] indicates that document-intensive companies may spend as much as 15 percent of their annual revenues on business communications. That finding is significant; it suggests

0-8493-9834-7/00/$0.00+$.50
© 2000 by CRC Press LLC

that companies place more emphasis on producing and distributing high-quality communications.

In many cases, companies that produce and distribute their communications in-house might do better by outsourcing their business communications function to a strategic ally that has the experience, physical capacity, and commitment to utilizing the latest and best technologies on the market. In today's highly competitive environment, it's vital that executives analyze their options carefully and make the correct choice.

A study summarized in the March 1996 issue of *Mail: The Journal of Communication Distribution* found that "companies report on average a 9 percent reduction in cost and more than a 15 percent increase in capacity and quality with outsourcing." The study of 30 firms ranging in size from less than $1 million to more than $2.5 billion in annual revenue was conducted by The Outsourcing Institute, based in New York City, an international professional association offering objective, independent information on the strategic use of outside resources.

With those kinds of cost savings, more and more executives are focusing intently on the cost-effectiveness of in-house print-mail operations. As a result, many companies are taking a serious look at outsourcing as a cost-effective option.

WHY OUTSOURCE?

As summarized in the November 1997 issue of *Mail: The Journal of Communication Distribution,* a recent outsourcing study commissioned by Pitney Bowes Management Services found that 330 executives gave the following reasons for outsourcing internal functions at their organizations:

- Specialized/core competency issues 59%
- Cost 53%
- Technology changing too fast 45%
- Substitute operating expenses for capital investment 37%
- Move functions off-site to free space 31%

Additionally, a recent DataQuest survey[2] of 250 information systems executives found companies turn to outsourcing for the following reasons:

- Acquire technology skills 49%
- Gain industry expertise 48%
- Increase application expertise 38%
- Add flexibility/reliability 25%
- Improve IT performance 22%
- Link IT and business strategy 12%
- Share risk 10%
- Reduce costs 10%

The decision to outsource the production of communications is one that each company must make after a careful consideration of all the issues. The issues impact all areas of business, from marketing to operations.

On the other hand, insurance companies that choose to produce communications in-house make a long-term commitment to keep up with the rapid advances in technology. Liabilities come along with that commitment, including purchases in sophisticated electronic printing, lettershop and presort hardware and software, regular system upgrades and maintenance, retention and training of both highly skilled and unskilled labor, as well as other operations overhead.

KEY PROCESS ATTRIBUTES

Outsourcing companies that specialize in the production and delivery of business communications provide a broad, sophisticated range of capabilities as part of their output solution. The attributes described below provide insurance companies with greater control over their customer communications process.

Document personalization — Studies have shown communications that are highly personalized and targeted to the end recipient are more likely to be noticed and acted upon. Insurance customers want to be treated as individuals, not account numbers. The latest, flexible communications software used in the production of documents for print-mail, CD-ROM, and other media, permits a greater inclusion of personal data and eliminates irrelevant fields of information.

Document customization — Communications that are tailored from a local or highly recognizable source also make documents more important to recipients. Variable messaging on documents and the inclusion of selective inserts in mailpieces make this possible. For example, when customers receive communications with the address and phone number of their local agent or dedicated customer service representative, or with a custom message or insert offering a service that is targeted to their needs, they are more inclined to value — and act upon — the communication.

Document design — To maximize the effectiveness of communications, and ensure their greatest efficiency and economy in production, proper document design is a must. In a high-volume, print-mail environment, that begins with selecting the correct document base stocks. Experienced and skilled designers, who understand the true limits of communications production and distribution, can balance the aesthetics and functionality of documents.

Enhanced document features — Document formatting software allows for the use of variable fonts, graphics (logos, icons, and other art), bar graphs, pie charts, and highlight color printing on documents. Such enhancements help make documents meaningful and enhance their overall value. Customer communications can be further enhanced by including only relevant information; oftentimes this eliminates the need for customers to call with questions.

Process efficiencies — Specialized high-volume business communications companies can provide numerous process efficiencies. These result in faster production turnaround times and cost savings.

Combined multiple mailings — "Householding" the content of multiple documents being distributed to individuals or consenting family members into single communications means reduced material/service costs and more convenience for customers. For example, in the printing and mailing of healthcare insurance documents, it is common for providers to realize as much as a 30 to 40 percent reduction in annual postage costs using this approach.

Combined data from multiple sources — Data from different products — and different sources — can be combined or "consolidated" onto one document as an added service to customers.

Reduced distribution costs — Large business communications companies can qualify mail for the best postal rates and fastest delivery through the United States Postal Service (USPS). They also can provide economies through other forms of distribution (Internet, fax, CD-ROM, etc.).

Improved document content — Because these companies are accustomed to handling vast quantities of information and documents, they are proficient in maximizing document content. For example, mailed documents are qualified by weight; by balancing messages and inserts to the weight scale, providers can optimize mailpiece content.

Improved quality assurance — Sophisticated firms provide absolute data-to-output quality assurance through advanced process control systems.

Enhanced communications — Through the use of advanced coding (bar codes, DataGlyphs, and other unique identifiers and symbologies), additional information can be included on remittance and response vehicles for added value and increased process efficiencies.

Print-on-demand — Along with the advancements of electronic printing technology for mission-critical documents, on-demand printing has opened a whole new output strategy for the production of mass-customized documents. For provider companies, this technique has revolutionized the production of traditional business documents, as well as communications such as product summaries, enrollment, and marketing kits. Among the benefits: elimination of material waste and reduction of warehousing and inventory functions.

Distributive printing — Speed of delivery is often a factor in the distribution of critical documents going to a national audience. Through distributive printing, communications are printed and mailed from locations offering the fastest delivery through the USPS mailstream. This process shaves days of delivery time from traditional single-site or regional operations. This method is also used to balance production volume over multiple locations.

INDUSTRY APPLICATIONS

While today the insurance industry's communications needs are principally served via paper, tomorrow's communications will require additional distribution methods such as CD-ROM, e-mail, and the Internet. Here are just a few of the applications business communications companies should support.

Policies — Traditional policies may be taken to the next step by consolidating information into attractive, easy-to-read formats. Each policy should be unique and personalized to the individual, with the integration of critical data in reader-friendly text, table, and high-impact graph (bar and pie chart) formats.

Policyholder communications — Highly customized periodic invoices and statements, endorsements, and pending and renewal notices may be consolidated (integrating data from multiple information streams into one document) or combined (collating multiple documents going to a single recipient into one envelope) for optimal processing efficiencies and postal savings.

Personalized booklets and cards — Integrated documents that are produced in a booklet format and uniquely prepared for each policyholder may contain program specifics, preprinted forms, identifications cards or even personalized locator information for nearest service providers within a specified radius of the customer's home address.

Checks — Using today's high-speed MICR printing technology, checks can be customized and printed on generic stock, eliminating the preprinting, inventorying, and warehousing of special stocks.

Reports — Policyholder data can be combined into concise reports keyed to product, provider, branch, and region or correspondent activity. Print-on-demand technology makes it possible to turn these reports out in days.

Marketing and correspondent mailings — Flexible document formats help providers better communicate with their customers, including targeted mailings for up-selling and cross-selling.

SUMMARY

It is incumbent on every insurance provider to produce the most effective business documents in the most efficient way. For many providers, outsourcing the function to companies specializing in those services may be the best solution.

Notes

1. CAP Ventures, Norwell, MA, 1997.
2. DataQuest, San Jose, CA, 1996.

Author Bio

Kim Herren is responsible for strategic marketing direction and support for Output Technologies' corporate-wide initiatives, including communications (public relations, advertising, collateral), sales support, product development, and marketing support systems. She joined Output Technologies in 1982, and has held numerous positions with increased responsibility, including sales representative, product manager, and vice president electronic printing and publishing. Herren holds membership in the Investment Companies Institute (ICI), XPLOR International, and the National Investment Companies Service Association (NICSA).

Headquartered in Kansas City, MO, with 16 locations in North America, Output Technologies is a leading provider of business communications solutions. The company is a subsidiary of DST Systems Inc., also in Kansas City, a leading provider of sophisticated information processing and computer software services and products, primarily to mutual fund, insurance providers, banks, and other financial service organizations.

Chapter 54

New Business Model for the Insurance Industry Demands a New Automation Model*

Don Chase

THE INSURANCE INDUSTRY HAS EMBARKED ON A REVOLUTION in the way it does business. A new business model is emerging, and it demands a new automation model.

What is the new business model? Primarily, it is customer-oriented. That is, all processes are designed to satisfy customer needs, rather than the company's needs. The new model is also decentralized, with more responsibility and power given to the people who are on the front lines with the customers — whether they are independent agents, captive agents, or company employees.

Giving those people the automated tools they need to handle all customer requests, often in a single session, lets insurers satisfy customer needs faster and better. As a result, the new business model is flexible, responsive, and cost-efficient.

Many established companies, especially those with a keen eye on the strategic advantages of leading-edge automation, have already adopted the new business model either comprehensively or in specific niches, such as a specialty line or a residual market. And forward-thinking start-ups are

*"New Business Model for the Insurance Industry Demands a New Automation Model" © Stimpson Communications. Reprinted with permission from *The National Underwriter,* April 28, 1997.

now running their entire company on the new business model and powering it with a network of personal computers.

AUTOMATION AND THE OLD BUSINESS MODEL

In the precomputer days, agencies handled almost all customer service. Though manual, this system was efficient in that there was no duplication of processes by agencies and insurers. The insurer's main role was to provide financial backing and keep statistical information.

The advent of computers in the 1950s allowed insurers to change their business model. As mainframes became entrenched, more functions flowed back to the home office. Agencies did less, and big bureaucracies in both home and branch offices became necessary to run the company's business.

Built around centralized control and a large bureaucracy at the home office, the old business model customarily relies on a mainframe computer system. This technology foundation offers centralized processing power and huge data storage capacity.

However, under the old model, customer support for billing, claims, and policy servicing are often split between the agent and the company, and then often handled by different company departments. Customers with multiple concerns are bounced from agent to company and from department to department, introducing many opportunities to commit errors. That often results in a dissatisfied customer and high service costs that are difficult to manage.

Under the old model, a cadre of highly trained and expensive programmers are needed to maintain the mainframe. Users, such as marketing staff and underwriters, must make a written request to the Information Systems (IS) department, which then puts the request in its queue. The order may take weeks, months, or years to fulfill. The first attempt is often sent back for fine tuning because of communication gaps between the business unit and the IS department and time lags between needs definition and programmed resolution.

Today, the mainframe is still an industry workhorse. But insurers are recognizing that it is a millstone because the environment is so inflexible. Changing any business process is time-consuming and requires expensive programming, and even then the results may not be optimal. The enormous cost and anxiety spurred by Year 2000 compliance issues provides an extreme example. That's why many insurers are no longer putting new lines of business on their mainframes, turning instead to client/server systems that offer a superior, user-friendly development environment centered around service fulfillment at the point of sale.

HALLMARKS OF THE NEW AUTOMATION MODEL

Client/Server Technology

This is the technology footing that powers the new business model. It is the engine of change that is breaking the stranglehold of the mainframe model.

Client/server is a system in which most of the active computing, or processing, can be done on "clients" — inexpensive but powerful personal computer workstations. Meanwhile, the server stores a central database. Servers can be linked to clients by a local area network, a wide area network using dedicated lines, or even ordinary dial-up lines. Ultimately, the link can be the Internet or company intranets.

Today's servers are powerful, fast, and reliable. Many have multiple processors and hard disks that allow scalability and automatic backups in the form of data redundancy (RAID). The clients and the server combine to become a virtual supercomputer with enormous processing power. A client/server system thus can support a sizable insurance company's processing environment.

Computing Power at the Point of Sale or Service

To be effective, automation must be available anywhere it is needed, with consistent results. Under the new business model, the service representative or agent can take care of all the customer's requirements in one transaction. The client/server system puts processing power where's it's needed — on the company service representative's or agent's desktop, or even on a laptop the agent can take to a meeting at the client's home or place of business. (Surely, the Internet will one day become an important point of sale and service as well.) An integrated client/server system can provide the user with proper processing rules at the desktop, resulting in consistent enterprise-wide processing. This offers many advantages, including quotes that match the actual premium.

Flexibility

In today's competitive environment, insurers don't have the luxury of time. They must respond quickly to take advantage of market opportunities. Software that powers the new automation model is tool-based. Instead of having to rely on programming, the user/analyst simply selects a "tool" to quickly change a rate, add a field, or modify an endorsement. In business terms, insurers get a much more cost-effective and timely way to address new or changing market conditions.

Scalability

New-style automation can be used anywhere because it is scalable. The full version of a processing system is used for company-wide functions.

The same software can be "scaled down" to fit on a laptop. This means lower costs, flexibility, more focused access to information, and improved service across the insurer's organization.

ADVANTAGES OF THE NEW AUTOMATION MODEL

First, costs are lower. In part, this stems from lower hardware costs; for example, disk storage on a personal computer is about one-twentieth the cost of the same amount of mainframe storage. A powerful Pentium® PC client now costs the same as a dumb terminal once did.

More importantly, hardware savings are ultimately dwarfed by personnel savings and increased business opportunities. Since users are empowered, programmers and system analysts can be freed from maintenance and development and redirected toward providing more immediate business services to the consumers and the company.

Extendibility is another key advantage of the new automation model. Creating a new product or revising an existing one is not as monumental a task as it is with the old automation model. Insurers can easily adjust both their business tactics and strategies. They can test new marketplaces quickly and inexpensively. If a specific plan doesn't work out, they haven't lost months of time and hundreds of thousands of dollars in programming and management expense.

The Internet along with the company- or industry-specific intranets will ultimately put significant insurance information directly in the hands of the consumer at a reasonable cost. Customers will be able to inquire about their policies and coverages, make changes, and get quotes — all from the convenience of their home computer.

Better access to critical information is another benefit of the new automation model. Integrated new-model systems put information about losses, expenses, market penetration, and agencies at management's fingertips instantaneously. With vastly superior data, company executives can take steps to lower operating costs with more confidence and craft better short- and long-term strategies.

Finally, the new automation model also lets insurers give better, more focused service to the insureds and its agents. With an integrated system, service representatives can answer almost any question posed by a policyholder or agent. They can readily go into the system and prepare a quote, find the cost of a policy change, or check the status of a claim payment.

Since processing is more efficient and more work can be done with fewer employees, progressive companies have begun to feel the positive impact of the new business and automation models. Using a Windows-based client/server system, Philadelphia Insurance Companies of Bala Cynwyd, PA doubled its writings of a specialty line while cutting its staff by 20%.

The Windows-based system in use by Philadelphia lets the staff rate, quote, issue, print, and mail a policy in a matter of minutes. Using similar technology, Colonial Indemnity in Kingston, NY boosted its writings by 50% with half as many employees as it had a few years ago. Since it is Windows based, the new automation model also saves considerably on training.

"One-and-done" may be a catchy phrase, but it does underscore an important message. It means that one employee can take care of most requests from start to finish in one transaction. "One-and-done" also reiterates a key concept expressed earlier in this chapter; by virtue of being customer-centered, the combination of a new business model and new automation provides much greater scope to increase business, lower costs, and offer better service.

For decades, the insurance industry's old model of automation has been both a hindrance and a help in enabling companies to achieve business goals. With a new model of automation supporting today's revolutionary insurance distribution conditions, technology has again become the industry's servant, instead of its master.

Author Bio

Don Chase *is senior vice-president of Allenbrook, Inc. in Portland, ME, provider of a complete Windows-based policy management system for insurers. He can be reached through hillma@ allenbrook.iix.com.*

Chapter 55
The Internet and Evolving Technology: Changing How Insurance Companies Service and Operate

Richard H. DuBois

THE INTERNET IS THE MOST UBIQUITOUS, COMPUTER-BASED TECHNOLOGY ever presented to the human race. Do you agree with this? It would be very surprising if you did not, since the facts and figures totally support this statement. Compared to the Internet, personal computers are a slow-paced technology that still has not reached its full market potential. The Internet user community is growing at a rate that is literally incalculable and unpredictable, and has surpassed even the most aggressive projections for growth.

So what does this have to do with the insurance industry? It's simple when you think about it from an elementary standpoint — market distribution and customer service. The insurance industry — life, health, and property and casualty — markets to both the individual and corporate consumer. In the past, various media and technologies have been used to accomplish the marketing and servicing of their products:

- Marketing: mailings, television, agents, billboards, radio, kiosks, and publications.
- Servicing: service representatives either in person or through the telephone and the mail; or bypassing the service representative by using telephone voice response systems (VRU).

So where does the Internet fit? What's the impact? For the first time ever, the insurance industry, and all other industries as well, have at their disposal a complete, worldwide communications infrastructure ready to use: without concern for the kind of computer or communications technology that has to be used in order to access and utilize the medium. As long as a person, agent, or company has access to the Internet via a personal computer, they can be sold to and serviced.

Is it that simple? No, but compared to what it took in the past to implement technology to provide a business solution, for example, the telephone voice response systems, it's as simple as turning on a light switch. But as with any technology, it is the impact on a company's current processes and procedures that causes the most consternation and challenge. How do you go from a human service representative answering the phone to having your agent or policyholder get needed information and making needed changes to their policies directly through a computer connection? It's called empowerment, which can be perceived to mean loss of control, losing the personal touch, security risks, etc. And how do you know that your product marketing is going to reach your targeted audience? What percentage of your audience uses the Internet in such a way that you can reasonably predict reaching them with your message?

The Internet is slowly, but surely, being embraced by insurance companies and the vendors that provide them systems and services. Look at any insurance publication, i.e., *LOMA Resource, Insurance & Technology, Best's, National Underwriter,* etc. and you see a plethora of articles on using and adapting the Internet to insurance business processing and marketing. The message is clear: the Internet is a tremendous business tool — use it! The banking and brokerage industries have embraced its use dramatically, the insurance industry continues to lag behind in its adaptation and use. This is not lost on those in the industry who see a strong and undeniable push into the insurance industry by banking organizations.

Embracing a new technology has always been a challenge for the insurance industry. The Internet, and its unlimited potential, is by far the most imposing and challenging technology that this industry has ever faced, but it also offers potential rewards that substantially exceed any other new technology.

The Internet presents the insurance company with two challenges: What can we do with the Internet? How do we make it happen? The former is by far the most imposing. How does a company determine what business opportunities are available using the Internet? They can only go by that which has already been implemented, and that which is being postured by a wide variety of vendors and organizations. Insurance Internet commerce is too new to be able to select one or more opportunities that have proven themselves successful in use by other companies.

The Internet is spawning an unbelievable growth of vendors that have and are continuing to develop solutions for commercial insurance activity on the Internet. Unlike most other technologies that have been presented to the insurance industry, the Internet is a fully operational, fully proven, total communications and data exchange environment available today for use by the worldwide business community. It can not be viewed as just another technology that's there for you to use if you want to; it will be the medium by which we will all conduct business in the future. In order to exploit the opportunities of the Internet, a company must shift its strategic approach accordingly.

The challenge is clear: define your business opportunity on the Internet, then find the technical solution to realize that opportunity. The Internet is much too big and much too diverse for any one insurance company to try to create and maintain their own technical solution. Keep in mind that the Internet is both a gateway and a highway to dynamic multi-user information access and exchange. Making this medium a viable and profitable tool to expand and improve your business requires the use of innovative software and hardware products, from web browsers to Intranet servers.

As the insurance industries begin to exploit the Internet and associated technologies, they will continue to redefine their marketing, service, and processing paradigms. The policyholder's service agent of 1997 may well become an interactive web page in 1999. The insurance agent of today could well become a selection on an Internet-based interactive insurance marketplace in the year 2000. The policyholder filing a claim for automobile damage today will probably be able to send a digital camera picture of the damage to the insurance company with immediate payment turnaround — perhaps even a cybercash deposit to the nearest collision repair shop. The list of technology impacts on this industry, borne out of the growth of the Internet, is almost limitless in scope. Digital equipment, advanced software, and the Internet will definitely shape the future of insurance industry marketing and processing. The new millennium will not be kind to technological dissenters or naysayers; technological adaptation to business processes must take place.

Author Bio

Richard H. DuBois has been marketing innovative software systems to the insurance and banking industries for over 15 years. He has held the position of Senior Sales and Marketing Executive for several software firms, has also been Chief Executive Officer for two of these companies. DuBois brings with him a track record of considerable accomplishments in the sales and marketing of software systems to the insurance industry. As Executive Vice President and COO of The Leverage Group, he was behind the development and introduction of the Life Insurance Industry's first, total, Internet business solution, PolicyNet.

DuBois has been published in a number of insurance industry publications as well as having authored his own book, The Complete Guide to High-Yield Power Selling. *He has also been the featured speaker at insurance and financial venues.*

Chapter 56

Producer Management Systems: The Need for Automation and Integration

Scott L. Price

TODAY'S LIFE INSURANCE AGENTS FACE A VARIETY OF CHALLENGES in the marketplace. Increased information volume, sophisticated clients, increased competition, and the need for integrated systems has altered the way agents do business. There are more clients, more life and financial products to sell, and more agents competing for business. To stay ahead of the competition and remain profitable, agents need an integrated, automated business solution that will allow them to organize and maintain their current business and acquire new leads. The business solution needs to be equipped with a wide array of functionality, thus helping agents improve efficiency, profitability, and customer relations. It needs to be user-friendly, with screens that contain fields for pertinent information and are easy to navigate through. That business solution is a client management application that functions as a contact management system as well.

A contact management system is designed to help agents build relationships by supporting all the data they gather about contacts, such as notes they have taken and sales materials sent. Contact management systems help agents build their client base by nurturing and building relationships with prospects. But what happens after a sale is completed? Will agents want to transfer all of their data into a standard client management system to handle annual review follow-ups, In-Force policy management, investment portfolio management, and high-quality presentations?

0-8493-9834-7/00/$0 00+$.50
© 2000 by CRC Press LLC

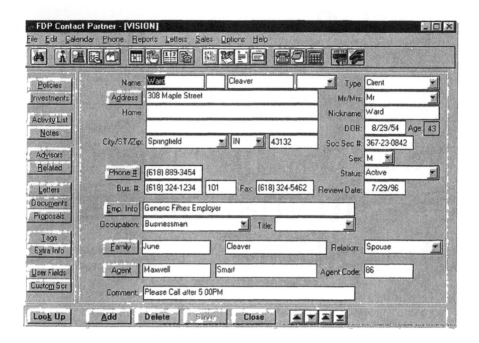

Exhibit 56-1. Client profile screens contain the key information agents need about their clients and prospects, and allow quick access to policy, investment, and proposal screens.

Clients also are prospects for future business. Because clients and prospects are not completely separate, life insurance software applications should not be either. Imagine agents having to transfer all their data from a contact manager to a client manager once a sale is made and then inputting client information back into the contact manager when attempting to sell additional coverage! Agents are more efficient and productive when their client manager combines two applications into one — an effective selling and management tool as shown in Exhibit 56-1.

KEY FEATURES FOR EFFECTIVE PROSPECTING

When beginning the prospecting process, agents first need to populate their database with personal contacts and purchased lists. Client management systems are better selling tools if they can import and convert data from various sources, creating endless opportunities to enhance prospecting lists. The key advantage of utilizing import utilities is that they provide an automated way to get information that in the past was mailed or only accessible online. Agents do not have to manually input this information into their databases if they have access to an import utility.

Once agents have their list of qualified leads, they may want to perform a target market search. For example, an agent many want to search his or her database to find only the individuals that are married, have children, work in either the legal or medical fields, and have a net worth of at least $800,000. This type of target search would be useful if the agent is planning to conduct a seminar on estate planning and wants to target high-net-worth individuals. The agent's ability to search the database for individuals with certain characteristics avoids the inconvenience of going through the list manually and selecting each individual.

Client management systems with the ability to search the database for specific criteria do so via filters. Filters allow agents to choose specific individuals from their database and imported lists quickly and easily, separating out those that meet the requirements set by the agent. After the list of select prospects is created, the agent can save it for future use. When it is time to follow up on the seminar invitations sent, or send out other invitations for a similar event, the agent will have the invitee list on file. In the future, if other prospects that meet the established specific criteria are added to the database, they will automatically be added to the previously saved list. An agent's saved groups are minidatabases in the client management system, which can be deleted at any time.

Prospecting efforts can be automated even further if the client management system is equipped with a report and letter generator, especially one that links with Microsoft® Word™ and Excel™. Agents can have the ability to generate letters and reports from some of the most powerful programs on the market. Formatting, printing, and editing will be made easier for agents if they are using competent systems that are familiar to them such as Microsoft Word and Excel. A report and letter generator provides many advantages such as the opportunity to create invitations and labels for events agents will host, implement a targeted mail campaign, and generate financial reports to indicate a prospect's need for life insurance.

If agents decide to conduct a seminar, they may find it easier and more cost-effective to create the invitations and labels themselves. A report and letter generator can write an invitation for the event and, using the list of names previously saved and a merge feature, address a letter to each of the individuals and produce corresponding labels. Quality client management systems will then create a history that the invitations were sent, attaching a copy of it automatically to each prospect's file. The convenience of a report and letter generator is that any document it created can be saved for future use or deleted at any time, as shown in Exhibit 56-2.

A report and letter generator is also a great tool to use when implementing a targeted mail campaign. Agents may want to set up a process where they mail new prospects an introductory letter, send a second letter 3

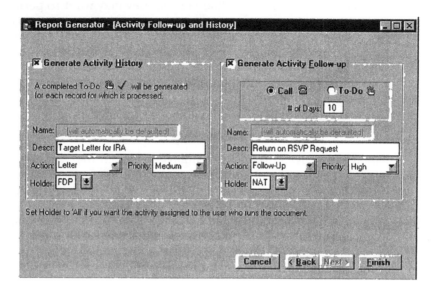

Exhibit 56-2. Report and letter generators also have the ability to generate activity histories and follow-ups.

weeks later, a third letter 2 weeks after that, and conclude with a follow-up call 2 weeks after the last letter was mailed. With a report and letter generator, they can write each of the letters and save them. With the target search capability, agents can select the prospects they want on the campaign and save their names in a separate database. They can then merge the selected individuals with the introductory letter and completely automate the mailing process. Once the campaign is complete, agents can use the saved letters for future mailings.

Another essential element in automating prospecting efforts, shown in Exhibit 56-3, is to have a client management system with an integrated calendar, which gives agents the power to pull up their daily agenda, auto-dial the names of the people they need to call, take notes during a conversation that will immediately get attached to the appropriate prospect file, and generate other follow-up calls or meetings simultaneously.

Calling prospects once in a long while will not cause them to think very highly of an agent's customer service. It takes numerous interactions with a prospect before an agent can satisfy his or her needs and make a sale. Frequency is the key, but it's hard to remember everyone who needs to be called and what was discussed during the last conversation. Imagine if agents had to keep hard-copy documentation of every conversation they had: when the time came to speak with a prospect again, it would take them forever to find all of the individual's paperwork. The ability to attach notes

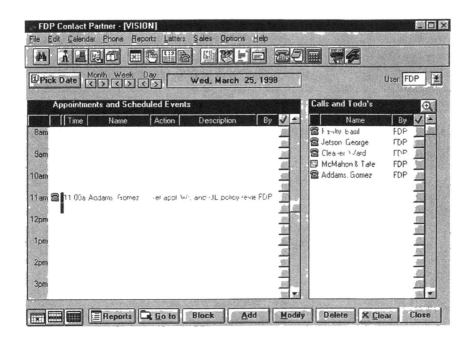

Exhibit 56-3. Integrated calendars allow agents to view and schedule their appointments, calls, and to-do's easily. Clicking on the telephone icon at the top of the screen enables agents to auto-dial the individuals they need to contact.

to individual files saves time, guarantees accuracy, and brings agents one step closer to operating in a paperless office. When trying to set up a meeting with a prospect, agents can easily click on their mouse and get a quick listing of all their upcoming activities and establish a day and hour when they are free to set up an appointment. This allows the agent to assist the prospect quickly and get to the next phone call sooner.

An integrated calendar is helpful when setting up a seminar and the time comes to follow up with invitees. After the invitations are sent out, agents can create a follow-up in 2 weeks to call the individuals that have not responded yet. As individuals confirm their attendance, agents can easily take them off the "call" list and automate the process of tracking RSVPs. If a targeted mail campaign is begun, an integrated calendar will allow agents to generate follow-ups to send the second and third letters and make the phone calls at the end of the campaign cycle.

Contact management, sales illustration, and financial and estate analysis systems require manual entry of the same data, which can increase the risk of data mismanagement. The best way for agents to manage multiple client records is to have a client management system that provides the opportunity to integrate with other insurance-related systems and share the same information. That will enable agents to create colorful charts and graphs that will illustrate the need for life coverage in a manner that is easy for their prospects to understand, while saving time and maintaining accurate information.

A final feature client management systems should have is the ability to save scanned documents. Saving the notes taken and letters sent in prospect files is very important when trying to generate new business because it helps build relationships. However, equally as important are the documents that prospects send to the agent. The best place to store those is right in the database, because agents will have all their prospect information in one place and unnecessary paperwork will be eliminated. This feature enables agents to keep their prospect files more complete and up-to-date.

KEY FEATURES FOR EFFECTIVE CLIENT MANAGEMENT

Quality client management systems are equipped with a wide array of functionality that help agents improve efficiency, profitability, and customer relations. Many of the features used for prospecting are also used for client management. For example, an integrated calendar, the ability to import data, a report and letter generator, and the ability to perform a target market search are all tools used in prospecting that must be utilized for effective client management.

An integrated calendar is necessary for client management because it helps keep activities on schedule and in order of priority. Agents need to make sure they don't forget to follow up with clients — or worse, schedule two appointments at the same time. With an integrated calendar, agents can keep track of their prospecting and client management activities.

Import utilities provide many benefits to agents in addition to creating a faster method to populate prospect lists. The ability to import data also allows agents to download investment transactions from various data repositories and policy information from home offices. The advantage of having an import utility is that agents will be able to obtain real-time client information. Today, life insurance home offices are facing the reality that they have to offer agents policy information via downloads. Captive agents are a thing of the past. Because every individual's need is different, agents can offer clients the policy that best meets the need. That means agents are selling policies from a variety of home offices. To remain profitable in today's evolving industry, home offices need to offer policy information to agents in a manner that is fast, accurate, and easily obtained. This industry trend not only increases the need for home office downloads, it also increases an agent's need to have a client management system equipped with an import utility.

The ability to perform a target market search can also enhance the agents' client-servicing capabilities. An agent may want to perform a target market search of all the clients that live in a certain zip code area, or perhaps spend a day or two in a certain neighborhood and wants to set up appointments with clients to explore the opportunity of selling additional coverage. After the agent creates a list with clients that live in the specific neighborhood, it can be saved for future use. So the next time he or she is in that same area, there is already available a list of contacts to visit. And if some clients move out of that particular zone, or new ones move in, they will automatically be added or deleted from the previously saved list.

Tracking pending policies up until the time they become In-Force is crucial to an agent's business. Agents should be able to monitor underwriting requirements, who the underwriters are, estimated commissions, when the home office received the policy, and any necessary data that prevent the policy from becoming In-Force, such as blood work or an attending physician's statement. This will enable them to monitor the status of the application every step of the way and follow up on any procedures that are taking too long. If clients call to check on the status of their policy, a new business tracking feature will allow agents to pull up the client file and give them precise information.

Once the policy is approved and placed In-Force, the client management system should generate specialized policy reports to show clients the status of their portfolio, track policy renewal dates, generate reminder letters, and show the amount of cash value and death benefit. A policy management feature provides agents, as shown in Exhibit 56-4, with the ability to automatically track conversion dates and the opportunity to sell additional coverage to clients.

Agents should also have information on the average face value and premiums of the policies they manage. This will enable them to determine if they are reaching their target profit goal and can be an indicator that there is a need to focus on more high-end clients. For added flexibility, the system should be able to manage and display screens for all policy types, such as term, whole life, universal life, disability, annuity, health and variable universal life, and annuities. Having all this information at their fingertips will keep agents from endless trips to the file cabinet.

The ability to manage and track investments is critical in today's evolving life insurance industry. Agents are broadening their products and services and offering investment management to their clients. Many agents now refer to themselves as "financial planners" or "asset managers." Clients are trying to consolidate all of their financial planning under one umbrella and want

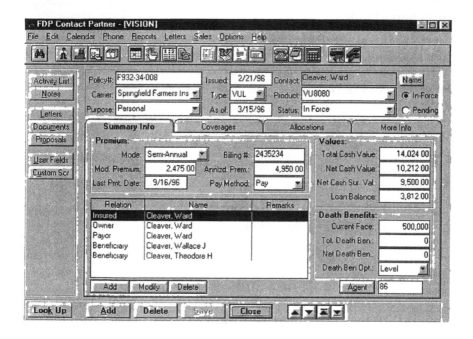

Exhibit 56-4. Agents can track policies quickly with screens that offer a variety of information including policy status, cash value, and death benefit amounts. Agents can effortlessly generate letters, documents, proposals, and custom screens directly from the policy screen.

one-stop shopping for all their life insurance and investment needs. To remain competitive and in business, agents need to be able to offer these products and services to their clients, as shown in Exhibit 56-5. The client management system's ability to import data will be especially important because investment information can be accessed in seconds.

Besides simply tracking client investments, the system should output high-quality investment reports such as Investment Portfolio Summaries, Rate of Return reports, Daily Blotter reports, and even Asset Allocation analyses so clients have a clear understanding of the status of their financial portfolio. Monthly statements with investment holdings and transaction information should also be available from the client management system.

An agent's job is only partially complete once the data and business are organized with a client management system. Agents must have the capability to track their hard work — their commissions — as shown in Exhibits 6 and 7. It may not be that difficult for someone to track first-year commissions. But as years go by, how will they track their commissions from

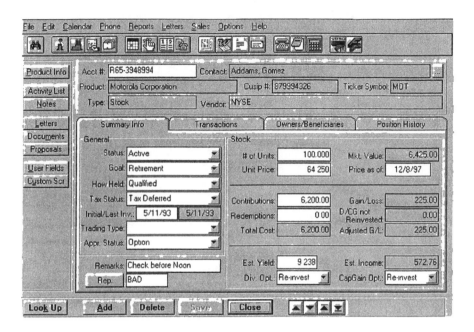

Exhibit 56-5. Agents can increase their efficiency and marketability by using a client management system that enables them to track and manage investments.

countless policy renewals? There is a pretty good chance they cannot track all their commissions manually. That translates into lost money! Agents need to make sure they receive everything that is owed to them. The simplest, fastest and most effective way to do that is with a full-featured commission tracking module that links with their client management system.

The commission tracking module should be able to identify agent splits, reconcile by agent, agency, policy, carrier or line of business, and monitor agent productivity. Client management systems that do not support commission tracking are only doing part of the job.

Today, industries worldwide are taking a trip on the information superhighway. They are trying to find ways to utilize the technology to make their businesses more efficient, productive, and profitable. The life insurance industry is no different, experiencing an increased need for integrated and automated client management systems. These systems are designed to handle the multiple tasks life insurance agents are responsible for. Client management systems give agents a competitive advantage by providing them with a tool that will manage their business in a manner that is efficient

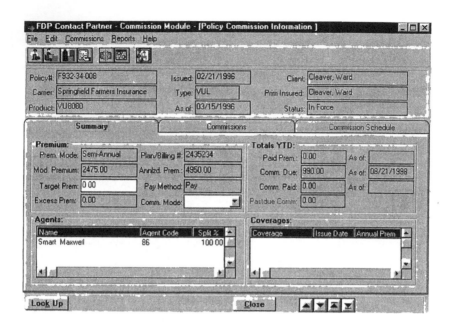

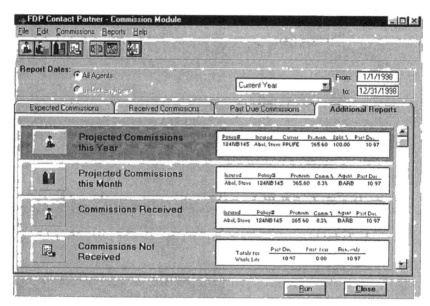

Exhibits 56-6 and 56-7. Commission-tracking modules perform a wide variety of tasks including identifying commissions due and agent splits; reconciling by agent, agency, policy, carrier, or line of business; and generating reports such as "Received Commissions" and "Projected Commissions this Year."

and accurate. They allow agents to dedicate more time to selling and offer clients personal customer service.

Any well-designed client management system should be able to perform the functions discussed in this chapter. It needs to be an automated sales, management, and prospecting tool, not just a computerized office assistant to print labels and envelopes. Agents thinking about buying a system should look into various vendors before making a final purchase. They should order free demos and tutorials to get a better idea of the system's look, feel, and functionality. And, of course, they should talk to their peers. Hearing what fellow agents have to say about the systems they use and getting a demonstration can make the buying process easier. Once agents purchase the client management system that is right for them, increased profits won't be far away.

Author Bio

Scott L. Price is Senior Vice President of Agency Systems and Corporate Officer at FDP Corp., a developer of integrated software for the life insurance, employee benefit, and financial planning industries. Price is responsible for overseeing the Advanced Underwriting, Contact Partner, and Pension Partner product divisions, working with the Vision Team to have all FDP Corp. systems integrated under the Windows 95, Windows NT, and UNIX operating environments, and providing operations support. He has been providing comprehensive software solutions to the life insurance and employee benefit industries for over 20 years. He can be reached at 800-NOW-FDPC or via email at scottp@fdpcorp.com.

Chapter 57

Understanding and Implementing Business Intelligence Solutions in the Insurance Industry

Thomas Chesbrough

CHANGES WITHIN THE TECHNOLOGY SECTOR OF THE INSURANCE INDUS-TRY are occurring with unprecedented speed, traveling farther, and impacting companies more fully than ever expected. Key business drivers are leading insurers to look for technologies and business processes that are significantly different from anything they have used before. Driving forces such as market globalization, increasing merger and acquisition activity, and the critical need to adopt market segmentation strategies are forcing companies to move from the automation age to the information age at an unprecedented pace. Those unwilling to make the move risk being left behind with unsatisfactory business levels, declining profits, and, ultimately, the inability to survive. Leading-edge insurance companies are increasingly looking to data warehousing and business intelligence technology to unlock the vital information stored in corporate databases in order to bring confidence to the management process in this chaotic and rapidly changing environment.

WHAT IS BUSINESS INTELLIGENCE?

Business Intelligence (BI) is more than decision support tools or data warehouses. BI involves all the systems processes, applications, and information structures necessary to have an effective information management environment and support the analytical process of the entire organization.

The BI arena has been an area of confusion for the business executive as well as the technology manager. Each week new tools and buzzwords are created that lead to additional confusion about BI options and their effectiveness. For example, many believe data mining and data warehousing are synonymous. This chapter will attempt to resolve the confusion over business intelligence.

KEY STEPS IN BUILDING A BUSINESS INTELLIGENCE ENVIRONMENT

The key to successfully leveraging your business intelligence (BI) environment is to create a robust framework to store the information. Business intelligence is the process of assembling diverse data, transforming it to a consistent state for business decision making, and providing users with access to this information in multiple views. The following are recommended steps in building a comprehensive business intelligence system. While these steps do not attempt to cover every aspect of BI system development, they do provide a thorough guideline for BI project leaders.

Selecting the BI Team

Perhaps the most important step is selection of the BI team. Developing the BI environment is a corporate function, not solely an IS function. The technical members of the team may build the system, but it is the end users that must determine the data necessary to support business decisions and relay this information to the technical members of the team.

It is critical to identify a project sponsor from the company's business community that will not only fund the project but enthusiastically help define the company's BI needs and promote the use of the BI environment by all staff. After a project sponsor has been chosen, it is important to select a project team that includes knowledgeable individuals from both the technical and business perspective (see Exhibit 57-1). Some of those members may include:

Technical
- Database administrator
- Data architect
- Programmers/analysts

Business
- Business analysts
- End users
- Management
- Training

Define Business and Technical Requirements

The first major step is to define the requirements of the BI system. This can be done most effectively through interviews of essential decision-

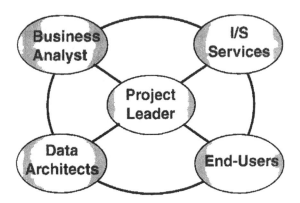

Exhibit 57-1. The BI project team.

makers and stakeholders. It is important to interview the executive staff first in order to determine the company's strategies and objectives. Once corporate strategies and objectives are understood, interviews of other essential decision-makers and stakeholders can be completed to determine their information needs as related to management processes. The BI team should receive input from the following end-user departments:

- Underwriting
- Finance
- Marketing/Sales
- Claims
- Actuary
- Field staff
- Loss prevention, credit and collections, and other key areas should also be interviewed depending upon the organizational structure and corporate objectives for the system

To ensure the success of the BI system, the end user should bring to the interview all reports used to make departmental decisions. Only by understanding the reports currently being used and how they were obtained can an accurate assessment of the end user's information needs be made. In addition to current reports, it is important to discuss information needs that haven't been met with the current system. It is vital to determine this need in the early stages of development. End users often do not realize the decision support options that will be available to them and don't look past the information available in current systems and reports. The interviewer must be aware of the options that are available in the new system so they can ask probing questions of the end user.

The technical side of the organization must also be interviewed. At the technical interviews, it is necessary to obtain copybooks for candidate legacy systems and source databases, as well as descriptions of current tables and fields. It is also suggested that scores of production data be examined in order to identify data quality issues and values contained in fields. This information will help the team understand what user-requested data elements reside in the current system and what additional information needs to be captured (internally and externally) for the new decision support system.

An interview summary should be developed that identifies the appropriate operational data sources for all fields, along with rules regarding format, content, and use of the information once it reaches the data warehouse. This summary will assist the data architect in developing a sound data model.

Results from these interviews will determine the data volumes, hardware and software requirements, delivery timeframes, and implementation costs associated with this project. This information will help establish the priorities for the implementation effort.

Define Project Scope

Each phase of a BI project is an important building block for the next step in the process. Therefore, it is important to establish a project plan that defines all tasks, resources, timeframes, and deliverables. An overview of the project should be developed first, followed by the partitioning of the project into manageable sections. It is critical to keep the project scope manageable, preferably less than 1 year. Remember that a BI system is never complete. It is a continuous process of updating and improving based on changing technological and business conditions.

The project plan will keep all parties abreast of the project status and help avoid obstacles that can result from poor planning. This is not to say that the plan will not change during the project, but the project plan will give management and each team member a guideline for the direction and timing of the project.

Data Model Development

After the interview findings and project plans have been approved, the project can begin. Once the data analyst understands the end-user's business needs as it relates to the data, the data model can be developed. The data model will serve as a map of the data and the relationships between the pieces of data stored in the warehouse. This model should include diagrams of the facts, dimensions, relationships, and keys that will support the information requirements. Exhibit 57-2 illustrates an example of a multiple custom schema for heterogeneous products in insurance.

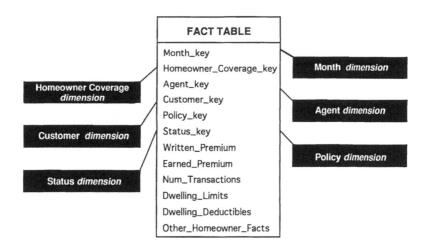

Exhibit 57-2. A multiple custom schema for heterogeneous products in insurance.

The mapping process is one of the most vital parts in developing a data warehouse. It is also the most difficult and time-consuming step. The goal of the model is to structure the data in a format that will deliver business information at the user's request. If the model is not strategically aligned toward the user's type of business, it will almost always lead to failure of the final BI system.

It is important to remember that the goal of the data model is to meet the strategic needs of the company. Many insurers who have developed a data model from scratch have experienced failure in their first several attempts, but you can't model forever. At some point the data model must be considered finished. The key is to develop the best model possible at a particular point in time. Minor adjustments can be made as the project progresses.

Database Design and Development

After the data model is developed, the DBA staff should be able to perform the following tasks:

- Choose the database platform
- Create the physical database schema, including:
  - Fact tables
  - Description tables
  - Relationship tables
  - Denormalize the data
- Create methods of unique identification and interdata referencing
- Create indexes to speed response time

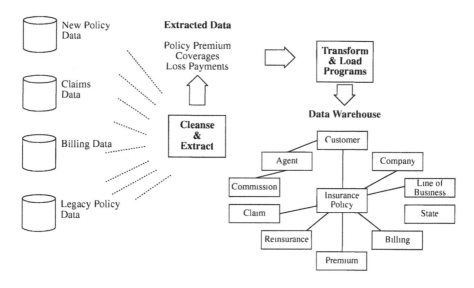

Exhibit 57-3. Loading the transformed data.

Data Extraction and Cleansing

In most organizations, source databases often lack standards that are consistent across all databases. Different formats, structures, attributes, and code sets, all within fields with the same meta-labels, will likely exist. For example, the policy database may identify the customer by last name, while the claims database identifies by social security number, and the billing database by account number. As a result, the data must be reconciled before it arrives in the data warehouse. Data transformation can be accomplished through manual efforts, homegrown or vendor transformation tools. This step, although time consuming, will reap optimal returns for your BI environment.

Loading the Data Warehouse

After the data are scrubbed and cleansed, the data can be loaded into the target database, as shown in Exhibit 57-3. Transformation tools, whether homegrown or vendor-provided, can be used to accomplish this task. This step should be closely monitored to ensure a successful and expedient completion. During this step, the team should also develop a schedule to automate the extraction and data load process.

Data Validation

This step, usually performed by business analysts, verifies processing results by balancing the data to existing reports. The calculations on existing reports should be mirrored to help the balancing effort. Verification can be done manually, or a program can be developed or purchased to automate the process.

It is almost inevitable that there will be some type of error in the initial balancing of the system. Time should be allotted in the project plan to account for modifications to the mapping, transformation, and loading process, thereby allowing the implementation team time to correct errors before roll-out to the entire organization.

Training and Rollout of BI System

In this final stage, end users will be trained in the features and functionality of the data warehouse and front-end BI tools. This will allow them to access the data and perform intelligent queries to support decision making. During the rollout stage, business analysts may prepare predefined queries and reports for management and inexperienced users. Power users will delve into the more complex BI tools to extract strategic information from the new, powerful decision support system.

BOTTOM-UP VS. TOP-DOWN WAREHOUSE DEVELOPMENT

Bottom-up vs. top-down warehouse development continues to be debated. Exhibit 57-4 is a brief overview of the pros and cons of each development method.

Bottom-Up Approach

Data is brought together into a tactical data mart structure, designed to answer specific business questions. The long-term approach is to integrate the data marts into a data warehousing environment.

Exhibit 57-4. An Overview of Warehouse Development Methods

	Bottom-Up Approach Datamarts	Top-Down Approach Data Warehouse
Scope	Tactical	Enterprise-wide
	Multiple databases	Architected
	Application-specific	Application-neutral
Subject	Departmental	Entire organization
	Subject-specific	
Data	Summarized	Atomic Level
	Few data sources	Many data sources
	Redundant data	One source of data
	Lack of standardization	Consistent data
Implementation	90–180 days	7 months–3 years
Characteristics	Restrictive	Flexible
	Short-term strategy	Long-term strategy

Pros. This approach has been highly favored because of the speed of implementation. Typically a data mart can be completed in 90 to 180 days — much faster than an enterprise warehouse. Project complexity is reduced since less data and fewer data sources are used. As a result, man-hours and required resources are reduced.

In addition the costs are smaller and, on the surface, the risk associated with the project is reduced. The cost of data storage, memory requirements, and staff is greatly reduced compared to a larger data warehousing initiative.

This approach is meant to deliver the data to the business units faster than with a data warehouse, and in the short run it may be an effective solution. The user has access to data and query results in a shorter timeframe. As a result, some of the pressure typically applied to IS is reduced compared to the development of a multiyear, million-dollar plan to build an enterprise warehouse from scratch.

Cons. Theoretically, you can build tactical data marts one at a time and eventually have an enterprise information environment. However, actual results show something different. The problems may not appear when building the first data mart, or even the second, but will eventually surface. Often, there will be a redundancy of data. Each data mart is pulling information from a variety of source systems, each with its own interface program. The end result will be a lack of consistency among the data marts. Data marts A, B, and C may show different revenue and loss ratio results based on the source's specific calculation needs. This lack of standardization will always lead to a suboptimal decision, erasing the perceived benefit of lowered risk as discussed in the "Pros" section above.

Even if it were possible to build data marts that were successfully integrated, there is still a fundamental difference between an enterprise-wide data warehouse and data marts. Data marts have a different level of granularity than enterprise-wide data warehouses. Data marts are designed to be at a highly summarized level to meet specific departmental needs. Power users will demand drill down capability to the most detailed level. That functionality is not available in an individual tactical data mart approach.

Top-Down Approach

This approach builds an enterprise-wide data warehouse and develops subject-area data marts that sit on top of the warehouse.

Pros. With the foundation of an information system built on an enterprise-wide data model, a higher level of integrity and consistency will be present in the data, leading to better, more informed decisions. The top-down approach provides a standard and consistent basis for decision making. This approach has also been found to be the most cost effective in the long-run. Many of the problems associated with nonstandard data definitions, as well as problems balancing the same data from different sources, are avoided. In the top-down approach, one source, the data warehouse, serves as the data origin for the subject-area data marts. This ensures that all information is pulled from one single source of accurate data.

Just as often as technology changes, business needs change, too. An enterprise data warehouse can adjust right along with the business changes without having to pull and cleanse new data from operational systems and rebuild data marts.

Cons. Studies have shown that building a data warehouse from scratch can take from 18 months to 3 years to complete. Larger data warehousing initiatives do carry a higher price tag and associated risks. However, steps have been taken to reduce the time, costs, and risks. Prebuilt templates and data models designed for the insurance industry have allowed insurers to pursue an enterprise-wide solution. With this new hybrid approach, insurers can customize the data model for their needs and not spend an enormous amount of time developing them from scratch.

BI TOOLS

Once the data has been loaded into the warehouse and data marts, the next challenge is choosing the appropriate technology to retrieve the data and transform it into useful information for users. There is a multitude of decision support tools available. Looking at the types of end users will assist the team in determining the best tool for the company's users.

A typical insurance organization has four types of end users based upon their data analysis style:

- *Senior management.* They demand BI tools, such as EIS, that notify them of problems when they occur.
- *Midmanagement.* They primarily use structured queries to analyze data and trends specific to their department.
- *Technical.* This group depends upon the BI tools to test the accuracy of their data and will typically write ad hoc queries. They are familiar with the structure of the database.
- *Power Users.* They perform in-depth analysis of the data-through-data mining techniques to look for patterns and trends.

In most cases a single tool will not meet the needs of all users. As a result there are many classes of tools designed to meet the specific needs and preferences of each user group, as illustrated in Exhibit 57-5. These tools can be broken out into four main categories:

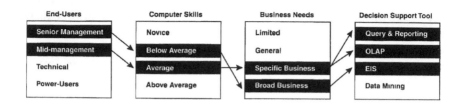

Exhibit 57-5. Different classes of users and their requirements.

- Query and reporting tools
- OLAP
- Executive information systems
- Data mining

QUERY AND REPORTING TOOLS

These tools provide answers to predefined questions. They are very useful for simple, two-dimensional query and reporting purposes. For example, the tool gives users the capability to quickly analyze the current month's written premium compared to the same month the previous year. The tool will retrieve the data, allow limited manipulation, and format the results to the user's liking. The midmanagement, technical, and senior management user groups commonly use this tool.

The reporting tool allows users to document the status of the company at a point in time. For example, insurers typically pay insurance assessment charges based on the insurer's adjusted gross direct written premium for a calendar year. As required, the insurer can produce a report documenting the premium by calendar year.

The following are some typical reports than insurers could retrieve from query and reporting tools:

- Agency listing
- Direct written premium by line of business, state, territory, or agent
- Loss reserves by accident year
- Listing of open claims for an adjuster
- Inforce policy lists by agent, state, or line of business
- Loss ratios by line of business

OLAP TOOLS

OLAP tools were designed for users who need advanced manipulation capabilities with fast results. More powerful than query and reporting tools, OLAP allows the user to view the data across multiple business dimensions

Exhibit 57-6. A Typical Report:
Smith Insurance Company
Direct Written Premium — Last 6 Months

Territory	Worker Comp.	Home-owners	Auto	Inland Marine	Board Owners	Total
Northeast	1,281,283	500,438	838,228	303,474	434,738	3,358,161
Midwest	1,748,383	1,483,347	928,347	483,742	347,384	4,991,203
South	4,383,473	2,348,737	2,587,437	583,743	438,181	10,341,571
Northwest	2,347,387	1,439,847	783,838	492,888	411,483	5,475,443
Total Premium	9,760,526	5,772,269	5,137,850	1,863,847	1,631,786	24,166,378

on very large data sets found in the warehouse. Midmanagement and power users typically use this type of tool as it allows them to drill down, drill up, and drill across the data.

Drill-Down

Drilling-down allows the user to request more detail of a data set. Most OLAP applications give users the functionality to double-click on a specific row to find more detail.

For example, Exhibit 57-6 shows a typical report for Smith Insurance Company. If the end user saw a noticeable increase in written premiums in the South, they could double-click on that row to see the breakout by state, as seen in Exhibit 57-7.

Drill-Up

The drill-up functionality is just the opposite of drill-down. For example, within a time dimension, the user can roll up from months to quarters to years. This functionality allows the users to collapse the detail.

Drill-Across

The drill-across functionality allows the user to view information on a horizontal level. Suppose the user was analyzing number of claims by adjusters at the end of a specified time frame. By double-clicking on claims, more detail can be found on the number of open, reopened, and closed claims during the specified time period. This information is helpful in determining the workload and efficiency of the claims adjuster.

EXECUTIVE INFORMATION SYSTEMS (EIS)

EIS systems have been in use since the mid-1980s. These tools, though overshadowed in the past, have reemerged as high-powered tools for those who do not have time to perform in-depth, daily analysis. EIS is built

Exhibit 57-7.   Drilling Down on a Report:
Smith Insurance Company
Direct Written Premium — Last 6 Months

Territory	Worker Comp.	Home-owners	Auto	Inland Marine	Board Owners	Total
Northeast	1,281,283	500,438	838,228	303,474	434,738	3,358,161
Midwest	1,748,383	1,483,347	928,347	483,742	347,384	4,991,203
South	4,383,473	2,348,737	2,587,437	583,743	438,181	10,341,571
Florida	1,483,743	561,562	486,248	159,781	123,054	2,814,388
Alabama	483,747	258,312	186,478	84,660	58,381	1,071,578
Louisiana	839,487	659,487	578,921	84,321	69,421	2,231,637
Texas	1,576,496	869,376	1,335,790	254,981	187,325	4,223,968
Northwest	2,347,387	1,439,847	783,838	492,888	411,483	5,475,443
Total Premium	**9,760,526**	**5,772,269**	**5,137,850**	**1,863,847**	**1,631,786**	**24,166,38**

around the concept of software agents, who are sent into the warehouse to monitor specific data for changes defined by the user and notify the user when those conditions are met.

Following are examples of software agents that an executive may define through an EIS.

New Business by Agent by Line of Business

Provide notification when the New Business Written Premium for each Agent by Line of Business increases by 20 percent over the previous month.

Incurred Losses by Line of Business

Provide notification when the Direct Incurred Losses with Expense by Line of Business increase by 25 percent or decrease by 10 percent compared to the previous month, as shown in Exhibit 57-8.

As soon as the software agent is sent to the insurance warehouse, it will search for any exceptions in the monitored data. If an EIS application finds an exception, it will alert the EIS user right away, as seen in Exhibit 57-9. With a click of the mouse, the executive can see the exception in the data. Some EIS applications do provide an additional level of detail, allowing the end user to see data that was close to the software agent's conditions but didn't exceed the condition and trigger notification.

EIS tools have empowered end users who previously had not had the time to query the insurance warehouse. Often these types of end users only have a handful of situations they would like to monitor. EIS provides the luxury of easily monitoring key business areas while still performing their other responsibilities.

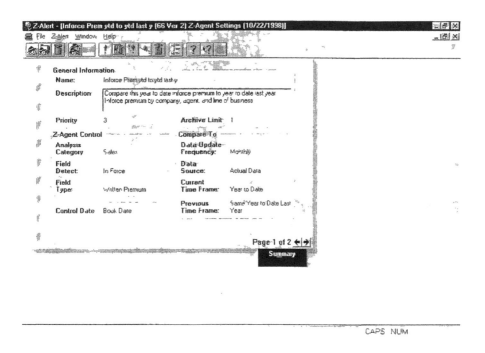

Exhibit 57-8. Reporting on incurred losses.

EIS applications have been designed to be used by novices to power users. Easy-to-use graphical interfaces lead the end users through the simple steps of designing a software agent. In less than 5 minutes, end-users can define a condition and then wait for the software agent to alert them to a change. Results are often displayed visually, such as charts or graphs. Being informed of the change allows the user to quickly isolate and correct any problems that are occurring and to take advantage of potential business opportunities that arise.

DATA MINING

Data mining is one of the newest entries in the business intelligence arena. Insurance companies are just beginning to adopt this method of decision making. The philosophy of data mining is to extract previously unknown patterns and trends in the data. While it may initially sound like OLAP technology, there is a significant difference in how the query is initiated. OLAP is user-initiated, while data mining is initiated by the data. With OLAP technology, the end user has a hunch on what information and relationships are affecting the possible trend and writes a query that pulls information based upon the hunch. Data mining, using a series of

Z-Alert - [04/28/1997 [43] Results for Incurred Losses by LOB]

File   Z-Alert   Window   Help

Line of Business	Current Incurred with Expense	Previous Incurred with Expense	Difference	Variance
Inland Marine, Commercial	3,762.68	4,322 14	-559 46	-12 94
Boatowners	57,435 12	89,788 95	-32,353 83	-36 03
Boiler and Machinery	15,623.25	16,491 10	-867 85	-5 26
Burglary/Theft	17,340.00	14,520.90	2,819.10	19 41
Business Owners	267,382 49	185,612.96	81,769.54	44.05
Commercial Fire	24,985 12	24,910.34	-25.22	-0 10
Commercial Fleet, Voluntary	247,746 30	199,681.28	48,065.02	24 07
Commercial Nonfleet, Voluntary	183,923.97	210,000 00	-26,076.03	-12 42
Commercial Package Policy	88,435 18	109,788.96	-21,364.77	-19 45
Dwelling Fire	-768.26	-734 87	-33 39	4 54
General Liability	28,258 43	30,741.10	-2,484 67	-8 09
Glass	5 100 00	4,900 00	200 00	4 08
Homeowners	163,631 01	142,310.65	21,320 36	14 98
Inland Marine, Personal	12,549.30	19,672.30	-7 123 00	-36 21
Private Passenger, Texas, Assigned Risk	102,558 63	241,915 62	-139,356 99	-57 61
Private Passenger Texas, Voluntary	521,552 99	689,751 64	-188,198 65	-24 39
Private Passenger, Voluntary	12,581 62	11,469 20	1,112 42	9 70
Special Automobile Policy	268,635 91	144,716.20	123,919 71	85 63
Texas Fire	10,715 76	38,495 19	-27,779 43	-72 16
Texas Homeowners	192,774 15	261,465.32	-68,691 17	-26 27
Workers' Compensation	1,895,996 5	1,524,652 6	371,345 87	24 36

Listing of Z-Alert results

Exhibit 57-9. An EIS can show exception data.

advanced statistical techniques, automatically examines all relationships between fields to discover significant relationships or patterns within the data, uncovering correlations between data sets.

Data mining has been used by insurers to:

• Identify fraudulent claim activity
• Forecast the success of marketing efforts
• Analyze customer life cycle
• Profile customer base
• Predict the customer buying patterns
• Increase overall productivity of operations

Data mining tools use a variety of statistical methods to automatically examine the data, such as neural or polynomial networks and symbolic classifiers. These tools actively seek out trends in the entire database, without human intervention and preconceived notions of relationships, and tell the end users what may happen based on the information found. Data mining is a discovery process. The end user may not know what they

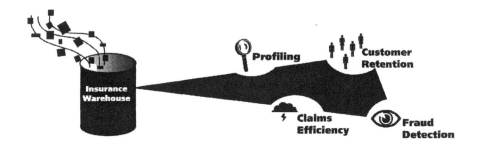

Exhibit 57-10. The verticalization of insurance-specific analytic applications

are looking for, but the tool will surely give them insight on what was once hidden. Data mining does require the user to understand the data and basic statistical concepts in order to use the tools effectively.

INSURANCE SPECIFIC APPLICATIONS

The worldwide analytic application software market is growing at a fast pace — targeted to reach $3.6 billion by 2002, as recently reported by International Data Corporation. The verticalization of insurance-specific analytic applications is in high demand due to strong mandates to improve efficiency and reduce costs, as shown in Exhibit 57-10.

Analytic applications differ from general information access tools in that they are specialized to optimize a specific business operation. They are designed to manage the business function rather than simply measure the performance. The following are just a few examples of insurance-specific analytic applications on the market today:

- Fraud detection
- Customer relationship management (CRM)
- Claims efficiency
- Profiling
- Risk management
- Campaign management

These applications provide additional value to the organization over and above generic decision support tools because they are structured to deliver actionable information that can be related directly to the business function. For example, data mining tools can assist insurers in detecting fraudulent claims. But to search for fraudulent behaviors and anomalies, the end user must know the "rules" of fraud detection, determine the best statistical method to search by, and have the technical expertise to understand the results. Fraud detection applications already have the "rules" in the infrastructure, allowing insurers to question transactions in an automated way.

BI: INTERNET, INTRANET, EXTRANET

The World Wide Web is one of the most powerful distribution channels for information today. Combining the internet and business intelligence has created a technological synergy that will surely maximize a BI investment.

Web-enabled business intelligence tools provide access to the decision support system via browsers, such as Netscape Navigator and Microsoft Internet Explorer. Most often used by mobile users or agents, end users would access the internet through an ISP, log-on to the corporate data warehouse via a Web server, and have instant access to company information as shown in Exhibit 57-11. The field staff would have the same capability as the corporate office to monitor loss ratios, policy counts, sales, sales goals, cancellation information, etc.

Instead of deploying BI tools on all home office PCs, insurers are beginning to implement intranets, a more cost-effective approach, whereby home office end users access the corporate data warehouse via browsers. This approach reduces the licensing costs and compatibility problems that may be encountered with implementing BI on all PCs.

Some insurers have gone one step farther and implemented an extranet — access to the company's intranet by third party users, such as independent agents. Independent agents can connect through third party ISP providers, like IBM or AT&T Network, to look at their policyholders, experience information in the company's agency data mart, and additionally obtain leads.

The biggest concern insurers have regarding the access to company-specific information via the Internet is security. Most Web-enabled applications take advantage of data encryption technology, such as secure electronic transmission (SET) and secure sockets layer (SSL). Web-based BI tools typically have user authentication features that prompt for the user ID and password. In addition, Web administrators can set levels of security based on the user's information needs. As the development of Web-based tools accelerate, security issues will continue to be a top priority for the vendor and the customer.

BUY VS. BUILD

Insurers that have recognized the need for a business intelligence solution have a difficult decision to make. The question of buy vs. build must be closely examined. It was formerly unheard of to buy any type of IT solution. In the late 1970s, insurers were building claims and policy administration systems

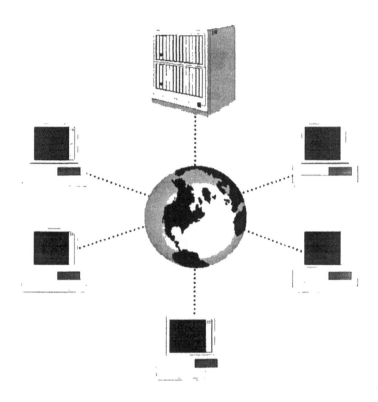

Exhibit 57-11. End users can log on to the corporate data warehouse via a Web server and have instant access to company information.

from scratch. It was not until the early to mid-1980s that companies, such as Policy Management Systems Corporation (PMSC), started to revolutionize the policy systems market by developing package solutions that fulfilled the administration requirements of insurers. It is now much more likely for an insurer to purchase a policy and claims system. Insurers have steered away from building a system from scratch, given the high-level of risk and costs, as well as the uncertainty connected to a project of this size.

The same trend is emerging in the business intelligence market. In the early 1990s, companies saw the information potential of building a decision support system, but the cost of a 3 to 4 year project to develop the system ranged from $5 to $15 million.

Building a data warehouse has become more efficient in the latter half of the 1990s. Reduced hardware costs and tool solutions, such data extraction and transformation tools, have made development more cost effective.

However, risks and uncertainty still exist. Before initiating a project from scratch, the following should be considered:

- Resources — Do the resources on staff exist to develop and complete a project of this size and complexity? Do not underestimate the effort involved in BI projects.
- Time — Are sponsors of the BI system willing to wait for a completed system? Developing this type of solution from scratch typically takes at least 2 full years to complete. Business environments can change in that time frame. Will the outcome meet the needs of the business at the completion of the project?
- Cost — Is the company willing to support the cost of a system from scratch, keeping in mind that a majority of those who develop their own system typically have to scrap the project once or twice during the development phase?

While it is not unheard of to find a company that has been successful in developing its own system, it is much more common to hear of expensive and disappointing failures. One such company spent more than $5 million dollars on a business intelligence environment to cross-sell their products. However, the system was based on the wrong architecture. The IT staff developed a solution they thought would help the marketing staff, but the data model did not produce the correct results. Another company spent $2 million building a BI system. This system, although technically correct, did not involve the end users in the initial requirement assessment, resulting in use of the system by only a handful of users.

The business intelligence market is going through an evolutionary stage. Package BI solutions have been developed to meet the information needs of the company. Additionally, some vendors are developing solutions that will meet the needs of specific industries. These vendors, known as vertical solution providers, are offering prebuilt, insurance-specific data models and templates that link to many policy and claim systems. They also offer insurance applications that assist in pricing, risk analysis, new business acquisition, and retention.

"Buying" these solutions can reduce the implementation time and costs dramatically. The resources required to build the BI system internally can now be used on other IT projects. By using a solution that has been proven at other insurance companies, the risks and uncertainty, not to mention cost associated with "building," can be avoided or significantly reduced.

CRITICAL BI SUCCESS FACTORS

Developing a business intelligence solution is more than an IT objective, it's a business objective. The following eight factors will lead to a successful BI implementation:

1. Involve end users. The end users need to be involved in the entire BI project. Understanding the needs of all end users will ensure the best results possible.
2. Obtain high-level business sponsors. It is critical to have support (financial and nonfinancial) from the business side of the organization during development and implementation. If their money is at stake, they will surely keep the project a priority and stress the usage of the system to their staff.
3. Develop a clear project plan and scope. Think globally, act locally. Model the enterprise and implement it in manageable chunks. This is a journey, not a destination. Implement tested components as the system is built. Establish parameters, milestones, and deliverables up front to prevent misunderstandings regarding the project.
4. Obtain knowledgeable staff. Employing highly knowledgeable staff, whether from inside the organization or external vendors or consultants, will ensure a well-executed implementation.
5. Insurance-specific data model. A strategically aligned, insurance-specific data model will guarantee your BI system meets current and long-term needs.
6. Buy BI tools that best match the user's needs. As stated before, different users need different BI tools. Keep their requirements in mind when choosing the front-end tools.
7. Training. Educate the end users on the available information and use of the tools so they can extract strategic value from the system.
8. Promote the BI system. It is as important to market the BI system as it is to market your products. Show the end users what type of results can be derived from the system. Communicate stories of better results faster than ever before. Offer incentives for those who use the system effectively to resolve a problem or find a new business opportunity.

BUSINESS IMPACT OF IMPLEMENTING A BI SOLUTION

A common concern when confronted with the decision to build a data warehouse, especially in a climate of tight profits and increasing costs, is that of the return on the investment in a BI project. While a return cannot be guaranteed, business intelligence systems allow insurers to reap the following benefits, increasing the likelihood of experiencing a tremendous rate of return.

- Increased productivity — faster access to business information
- Integration of data — one version of truth
- Standardized data across all business units
- Ability to monitor patterns, trends, and exceptions in your data
- A complete picture of your customer

- Improved customer satisfaction
- Improved cross-selling activities
- Market segmentation activity
- Ability to create more profitable and targeted products
- Ability to identify potentially fraudulent claims
- Expense reduction
- Ability to review costs of sales by distribution channel, state, and line of business, reducing cost of policy acquisition

Insurance companies are successfully justifying their BI investment in terms of increased productivity and lower costs. But it is the strategic benefits — the ability to analyze pricing structures, identify new markets and customer needs, and provide customized and value-added services — that are delivering returns of 1000 percent or more on the investment to those that have implemented business intelligence and successfully use the information. Although the returns are impressive, you won't hear much about them. Few in the insurance industry want to reveal their strategic weapons. One fact, however, has become clear: business intelligence is no longer a competitive advantage, it's a necessity for survival.

Author Bio

Thomas Chesbrough, CPCU, is President & CEO of Kapstone Systems, Inc., a Kansas City-based business intelligence company providing information products and services to the insurance industry. He has over 15 years of experience in the insurance industry implementing information management solutions for several insurance organizations and leading the effort to build and implement one of the first comprehensive data warehouses in the insurance industry. He has spoken at numerous insurance and data warehousing symposiums and forums and serves on several insurance technology advisory councils. Chesbrough graduated from Northern Illinois University in 1982 with a B.S. degree in Computer Science, Business Management, and Economics. He received his Master of Business Administration from Northern Illinois in 1987 and his Chartered Property and Casualty Underwriter designation in 1998.*

Section V
Appendix

NO HANDBOOK IS COMPLETE WITHOUT A LIST of products and services. This list represents the product sets and services of the many companies who contributed to this book. It makes a handy reference list for products that will be of interest to you.

Products covered include:

Appendix A
Selected Product Briefs

ASSET ALLOCATION

Portfolio Management Consultants, Inc.

Address: 555 17th Street, 14th Floor, Denver, CO 80202
Phone: (303) 292-1177
(800) 852-1177
Fax: (303) 292-0330
Web Site: http://www.pmcdenver.com
Sales Contact Name: Raquel Hinman, Scott Wilkinson

■ Product: Allocation Manager ®

Version Number: 4.0

Description Summary: Allocation Manager creates an effective bridge between your customers and their asset allocation, mutual fund selection, ongoing management, and reporting needs. Working from a graphic user interface, Allocation Manager assists the sales representative in taking the customer through an extensive, yet efficient, electronic profiling questionnaire. Based on the customer's specific investment goals, the program assigns a risk profile ranking.

A "what if" function allows for a variety of potential scenarios and investment strategy options to be explored. Once the customer profile and investment objectives are finalized, Allocation Manager provides a preliminary asset allocation recommendation, with mutual funds appropriately allocated. A customized proposal can be printed for client presentation and consideration.

Product Feature List:
- Built-in help
- Educational tutorials
- In-depth customer profile

- Asset allocation and portfolio modeling
- Fund selection
- Contract preparation and printing
- Investment policy preparation and printing
- Performance reporting

Pricing: Free
Hardware requirements: IBM-compatible PC with 486 chip or better; 8 MB RAM; 50MB disk space; Microsoft Windows NT workstation or Microsoft Windows 95 or greater
Software requirements: N/A

ATMS AND KIOSKS

KAL

Address: John Cotton Building, Sunnyside, Edinburgh, EH7 5RA
Phone: +44 (0) 131 659 4900
Fax: +44 (0) 131 652 1193
E-Mail: info@kal.com
Web Site: www.kal.com
Sales Contact Name: Philip Basham

■ Product: Kalypso

Description Summary: Kalypso brings web-enabled applications to self service devices, such as kiosks and ATMs (Automated Teller Machines). It is compliant with Microsoft's DNA FS framework and uses industry standard ActiveX components. It allows applications to run under Windows NT within a browser, such as Microsoft's Internet Explorer, thereby delivering the user-friendly benefits of multimedia browser technology to self service.

Kalypso allows hardware independent kiosk/ATM applications to be written usingan open WOSA XFS approach and with web tools, like Front Page, and languages such as C++, Visual Basic and Java.

Product Feature List:: Compliant with WOSA XFS, DNA FS
Pricing: On application
Hardware Requirement: Hardware independent
Software Requirements: Windows NT

BANK MARKETING

Medici Technology, Inc.

Address: P.O. Box 8, Hanover, NH 03755
Phone: (603) 643-9575
(800) 479-0495
Fax: (603) 298-8560
E-mail: Info@medici.com
Web Site: www.medici.com
Sales Contact Name: Harry "Brud" Deas

■ Product: Medici Mosaic

Description Summary: Medici Mosaic is an easy-to-use action-oriented strategic marketing product designed for use by the CEO or Marketing Manager of a small bank. Medici processes account records for a bank and creates a customized CD/ROM containing software, processed bank records, household and commercial prospects, digital map files, and help and tutorial facilities. The CD/ROM contains everything the bank needs to take strategic marketing action; no additional purchases are required.

Medici Mosaic is organized to look like a handbook of strategic marketing tailored for the bank. Chapters cover subjects including customer retention, prospecting, site and competitive analysis. Users can buy household and commercial prospects directly off the CD/ROM through a metering system with no delays for order fulfillment. Medici also offers training and consulting service for implementing strategic marketing initiatives.

Pricing: $10,000 to $20,000 depending on size of bank
Hardware requirements: Windows 95 or NT

BANKING SYSTEMS

Ionic Systems International Limited

Address: PO Box 246, Kelly Street, Rhinecliff, NY 12574
Phone: (914) 976-3007
Fax: (914) 876-7479
E-Mail: bernardlunn@hotmail.com
Web Site: www.ionicbankware.com
Sales Contact Name: Bernard Lunn

APPENDIX

■ Product: The Banking Engine

Version Number: 1.1

Description Summary: The Banking Engine is a multicurrency, multi-branch core banking system that supports Retail and Trade Finance operations. The Banking Engine uses a three-tier messaging architecture with a thin client Presentation Layer running on Windows 95, an Application Layer running on NT or UNIX, and a Database Layer that can use SQL Server, Oracle, Sybase or DB2.

The layered, messaging architecture is particularly suited to the integration of multiple delivery channels such as Internet, ATM, voice response, and SWIFT.

Product Feature List:: Core Financial Accounting, MIS, Retail Banking, Trade Finance
Pricing: Price on application

Network Controls International, Inc.

Address: Nine Woodlawn Green, Suite 120, Charlotte, NC, 28217
Phone: (704) 527-4357
Fax: (704) 523-3502
E-Mail: nci@nci-inc.com
Web Site: www.nci-inc.com
Sales Contact Name: Ken Russell

■ Product: NCI Business Centre™

Description Summary: An enterprise-wide solution designed for the financial services industry, NCI Business Centre uses a single technology to provide banking automation for all delivery channels: marketing, teller, call center, platform, and virtual banking. The Virtual Banking channel of NCI Business Centre enables your bank to offer Internet banking to their customers.

NCI Business Centre brings together the most powerful network and database technology available to:

- Offer Internet banking to their customers
- Improve all aspects of your bank's day-to-day operations
- Ensure that you'll be ready to make full use of new and emerging technologies

- Collect, consolidate and complement all your bank's data so you can easily access and analyze critical information to make better-informed decisions
- Enhance your customer relationships at all points of contact
- Reduce the total cost of running your bank

Product Feature List:: A single technology provides banking automation for these delivery channels:

Call Center

- Improves productivity
- Increases sales
- Provides computer telephony integration
- Gives you telemarketing capabilities
- Eases navigation
- Offers call wrap-up and work flow management
- Reduces training
- Improves customer contact statistics

Virtual Banking

- Enables your customers to obtain your services over the Internet, using Microsoft Internet Explorer bundled with any Windows 95 or NT operating system
- Permits more than 100 million Internet users to become your potential customers
- No special software is required by your customers or prospective customers for installation
- Provides support for other emerging technologies

Platform

- Expedites all traditional functions
- Gives CSR sales scripts and product suggestions
- Performs customer needs analysis
- Models financial scenarios
- Streamlines account-opening and staging process through easy-to-use Wizards
- Accesses and prints rules, rates and other disclosures
- Checks account applicants against an OFAC database
- Tracks and reports performance by CSR, branch, region, and enterprise

Teller

- Offers the speediest teller services possible
- Shortens training curve for new employees
- Provides a complete package of transactions

- Includes innovative product enhancements, such as customer mini-profile, integrated signature verification, several types of EJ searching, cross-sell prompts, and referrals

Marketing

- Develops and delivers data-driven relationship marketing campaigns
- Analyzes customer portfolios
- Runs customer profitability analysis
- Lowers the costs of acquiring and retaining customers
- Analyzes the consequences of product pricing changes
- Trims unprofitable customers from product mailings
- Helps you market nontraditional banking products

Pricing: Varies, depending upon institution size and number of branches

Hardware requirements:
Server Processor: Pentium Pro, II, or Xeon; 200Mhz or faster; Multiple processors are encouraged for large-scale enterprise installation.
RAM: 256Mb minimum
Free Disk Space: 2Gb minimum
Monitor: VGA supporting 800 x 600 resolution
Network Interface Card: 10Mbps/100Mbps with RJ-45 jack

Workstation(s):
Processor: Pentium II, 266Mhz or faster
Operating System: Windows 95/98/NT Workstation 4.0
RAM: 64Mb minimum
Free Disk Space: 100Mb
Monitor: VGA supporting 800 x 600 resolution
Network Interface Card: 10Mbps/100Mbps with RJ-45 jack

Network Infrastructure Equipment:
10/100Mbps Ethernet hub(s), Cisco 2524 (or better) Ethernet Router with integrated CSU/DSU, 10/100Mbps Patch Panel(s)

Operating System Requirements:
Windows NT Server 4.0 with Service Pack 4 installed

Software requirements:
Server: Microsoft Internet Information Server 4.0, Microsoft Internet Explorer 4.0 (128-bit encryption US, 40-bit encryption Int'l), Microsoft SQL Server 7.0 or Oracle Version 8.0, Microsoft SNA Server, Microsoft Message Queue Server, Microsoft Transaction Server

Q-UP Systems

Address: 8303 N. Mopac, B450, Austin, TX 78759
Phone: (512) 342-9910
(800) 500-3002
Fax: (512) 342-9921
E-Mail: info@qup.com
Web Site: www.qup.com
Sales Contact Name: Wade Sanders, Director of Sales

■ Product: Voice Banking System (VBS)

Description Summary: VBS provides 24-hour telephone access to all accounts and the ability to inquire into the following information: DDA Accounts—balance inquiry, NSF and unpaid notification, transaction history, last five deposits, inquiry by check number, and current and previous YTD interest; Savings Accounts—balance inquiry, transaction history, current and previous YTD interest, and last deposit; Time Deposit Accounts—balance inquiry, maturity date, accrued interest, last interest paid, current and previous YTD interest; Loan Accounts—balance inquiry, regular payment amount, next payment due date, payoff amount and date, and current and previous YTD interest; Funds Transfer—DDA or SAV to DDA or SAV, and DDA or SAV to loan payment; Rates and Product information; Usage Reports and System Monitoring; Bank Information Options; Additional Options: Spanish instructions, history fax, and memo post updates.

The Y2K Voice Banking System is NT-based and can reside on the same server as the Internet Banking System. This allows for one interface and saves on additional hardware costs. The system was introduced in 1997.

Product Feature List: See above
Pricing: Contact Wade Sanders for pricing
Hardware requirements: Windows PC (can run on the same server as the Internet Banking System)
Software Requirement: NT 4.0 or higher, IIS 3.0 or higher

■ Product: Web Site Design

Description Summary: This product offers customized pages of site design, which includes logo and animated graphics, bank-branding, and Interactive tools. The Interactive Tools with the Web site Design product are Stock Quotes, Daily Investment Summaries, Financial Calculators, Currency Converter, and Insurance Quotes. Q-UP also offers the optional services of Web site hosting, secure online applications, and support and maintenance (Changeit - bank makes its own changes to the Web site, maintenance programs — annual support or contract changes as needed).

Web Site Design was introduced in 1996 and has been targeted at community financial institutions.

Product Feature List: See above
Pricing: Contact . Wade Sanders for pricing
Hardware requirements: N/A

Wilco Systems Inc.

Address: 17 State Street, New York, NY 10004
Phone: (212) 269-3970
Fax: (212) 269-3925
E-Mail: info@wilco-int.com
Web Site: www.wilco-int.com
Sales Contact Name: Bob Santangelo

■ Product: STB2

Version Number: 2.40

Description Summary: An integrated, real-time front and back office order processing and information system for private banking that can operate for multiple currencies, sites and languages. STB2 covers cash and securities operations, customer valuations, and performance calculations, and general and analytical accounting. It also serves as a data repository for MIS and regulatory reporting.

Pricing: Not disclosed

BUSINESS INTELLIGENCE

Thazar Solutions Corporation

Address: 9201 State Line Road, Kansas City, MO 64114
Phone: (816) 760-5000
(888) 527-7866
Fax: (816) 760-5060
E-Mail: slrutherford@thazar.com
Web Site: http://www.thazar.com
Sales Contact Name: Sandra Rutherford

■ Product: Thazar Business Intelligence Suite™

Description Summary: Thazar Solutions Corporation provides Thazar Business Intelligence Suite™, a comprehensive data warehousing and decision support suite designed exclusively for the insurance industry. A combination of software and analytical services, Thazar includes a robust Insurance Warehouse, subject-specific data marts, and a full spectrum of insurance-specific applications. Thazar Solutions provides the insurance industry with the data analysis capacity to monitor overall business performance, develop pricing strategies, locate profitable business segments, reduce claim reserves, improve customer retention, and to see the business in a perspective previously not available.

Product Feature List

Thazar was developed solely for the insurance industry; therefore, Thazar Solutions consultants can discuss and analyze business strategies specific to the competitive pressures in the insurance environment. Thazar includes an insurance-specific, enterprise-wide data model and templates, reducing the time and cost of bringing a robust business intelligence system on-line. Thazar is completely customizable and works with major policy issuance, administration, claim, and billing systems, as well as in-house developed systems. Thazar includes data marts that are tuned to support the decision-making needs of specific business functions, such as sales, retention, claim, exposure, and experience. Thazar Solutions decision support tools allows the end-user to track, monitor, and analyze insurance data from a simplified to a complex analysis level. Thazar Solutions knowledge of the insurance industry is broad and deep and offers a variety of business intelligence consulting offerings.

Pricing: Tier-based

Rule Machines Corporation

Address:134 Fifth Avenue, Suite 205, Indialantic, FL 32903
Phone: (407) 984-4402
Fax: (407) 984-3774
E-Mail: Info@RuleMachines.com
Web Site: www.RuleMachines.com
Sales Contact Name: Robert Zimmer

■ Product: Visual Rule Studio

Version Number: 2.0

Description Summary: Visual Rule Studio enables you to efficiently develop Business Rule applications that are truly robust and sophisticated. Visual Rule Studio leverages the capabilities of the two leaders in separate industries by uniting the powerful Inference Engines of Rule Machines Corporation with the proven Rapid Application Development capabilities of Microsoft Visual Basic 5.0. Visual Rule Studio provides the powerful inferencing strategies needed to solve today's complex business issues.

The Visual Rule Studio Inference Engines and Production Rule Language (PRL) are internationally recognized as the best in the industry. PRL is devoted to pure rules, demons, and knowledge. This purity combined with its clear, English-like syntax enables almost anyone to learn PRL quickly and easily. This proven technology was first developed in 1984. Today, every industrialized country in the world, 91 of the Fortune 100 corporations, and all major U.S. government agencies use Visual Rule Studio technology.

Product Feature List

- Backward chaining
- Forward chaining
- Hybrid chaining
- Fuzzy logic reasoning
- Business rule isolation
- Business rule abstraction
- Business rule integration
- Production rule language
- COM interoperability
- Native visual basic installation

Pricing: $995 – $6995
Hardware requirements: Computer/Processor: PC with a 486DX/66 or higher (Pentium or higher recommended)
Memory: 12 MB RAM for Windows 95 or NT 4.0 (recommended: 16 MB or more for 95, 32 MB or more for NT)
Hard Disk: 10 MB
Drive: CD-ROM
Display: VGA or higher
Peripherals: Microsoft Mouse or compatible
Software requirements: Operating System: Windows 95 or higher, Windows NT 4.0 or higher (Service Pack 2 recommended with NT 4.0) (Intel)
Software: Visual Basic 5.0 Professional or Enterprise (Service Pack 2 recommended)

CALL MONITORING

NICE Systems

Address: 180 6651 Fraserwood Place, Richmond, BC, V6W 1J3 Canada
Phone: (604) 207-0600
(800) 663-5601
Fax: (604) 207-0607
E-Mail: na_sales@nice.com
Web Site: www.nice.com
Sales Contact Name: Inside Sales

■ Product: NiceLog*

Version Number: 7.5

Description Summary: NiceLog is the most advanced and scalable CTI voice logging system on the market, providing continuous, high-quality digital recording and archiving of telephone conversations. Designed with an open system architecture, NiceLog fully integrates with leading ACD, Turret systems, PBX and CTI components, and can be controlled, accessed and maintained locally via LAN, or remotely via WAN/modem.

Product Feature List:

- Up to 192 recording channels per unit
- ACA, NICE's proprietary Advanced Compression Algorithm, enabling up to 8760 channel hours of recordings online
- DDS-3 6 DAT tape stores up to 21,000 hours of audio
- Ability to record both analog and digital inputs in a single NiceLog
- Supports up to 20 output channels
- DAT Library for locating archived calls, with multisite DAT Library support (centralized DAT library for multiside logging system)
- Optional disk/DAT mirroring
- Optional hot standby

■ Product: NiceCLS*

Version Number: 4.2

Description Summary: NiceCLS stores all incoming and outgoing call information in a comprehensive database. NiceCLS enables users to conveniently locate, access (and playback) voice recordings based on call details, such as the date, time, and duration of the call, extension number, calling or called number, agent/dealer ID, transaction ID, customer ID, and business data.

Product Feature List

- Easy-to-use GUI
- SQL,ODBC-compliant, multiuser client-server
- LAN: Ethernet, Token Ring
- Protocols: TCP/IP, Novell IPX
- Remote access via modem
- Remote diagnostics
- Access/security control

■ Product: NiceUniverse*

Version Number: 3.1

Description Summary: NiceUniverse is a comprehensive quality measurement solution that automates call center agent monitoring and screen capture. The system provides objective evaluation tools and helps identify training requirements for call center agents. NiceUniverse uses a switch-independent CTI interface that integrates with leading ACDs and PC networks.

Product Feature List

- Flexible scheduling
- Synchronized voice and screen capture and playback
- Acceleration/deceleration of playback
- Quiet period indication
- Annotations
- Custom surveys
- Folder-based searching capabilities (ANI, DNIS)
- Custom report generator
- Security (seven levels)
- Automatic database management
- Import/export data
- Conversion of voice files to .WAV files

CASH MANAGEMENT

ARKSYS

Address: 17500 Chenal Parkway, Little Rock, AR 72211-9138
Phone: (501) 218-7226
Fax: (501) 218-7302

E-Mail: mail@arksys.com
Web Site: www.arksys.com
Sales Contact Name: Scott Zust

■ **Product: Commercial-ACCESS and Personal-ACCESS**

Version Number:1

Description Summary: Commercial-ACCESS, a cash management system, designed for the Internet, but ready for use as a secure proprietary on-line system. Commercial-ACCESS can be used as an intranet product, allowing you full control over all of your cash management requirements.

Personal-ACCESS is a PC-based home banking solution that enables financial institutions to offer either a proprietary or private interface or a nonproprietary or network (Internet) interface. Personal-ACCESS provides financial institutions with the ability to author and brand its own system.

Pricing: Contact vendor
Hardware requirements: IBM AS/400
Software requirements: OS/400, Windows NT server

Q-UP Systems

Address: 8303 N. Mopac, B450, Austin, TX 78759
Phone: (512) 342-9910
(800) 500-3002
Fax: (512) 342-9921
E-Mail: info@qup.com
Web Site: www.qup.com
Sales Contact Name: Wade Sanders, Director of Sales

■ **Product: Cash Management**

Version Number: 3.11

Description Summary: Allows commercial customers 24-hour access to manage funds in all of their accounts. The Cash Management product provides commercial customers with the following capabilities, Wire Transfers, EFTPS Tax Payments, Payroll/Direct Deposit, ACH Origination, Universal Bill Payment, and Stop Payment. In addition, commercial customers can view summary and details, check ledger balances, float balances, hold amounts, view history, view postings, manage other accounts, and export data in ASCII format to accounting software.

APPENDIX

The product, introduced in 1996, is designed for any size financial institution to offer all businesses the ability to manage accounts and finances. The Q-UP product offers a simplified, full-service approach to cash management. The designers have taken the difficult to understand ACH terminology and clarified the meaning of debits and credits by making the buttons on the Cash Management Menu read ACH Payments/Debits and ACH Receipts/Credits.

Product Feature List: See above
Pricing: Contact Wade Sanders for pricing
Hardware requirements: Server Grade machine
Software Requirement: NT 4.0 or higher, IIS 3.0 or higher

Superior Software, Inc.

Address: 16055 Ventura Boulevard, Suite 650, Encino, CA 91436-2609
Phone: (818) 990-1135
(800) 421-3264
Fax: (818) 783-5846
E-Mail: nrimer@ix.netcom.com
Web Site: http://www.superior-software.com
Sales Contract Name: Sheri or Alys

■ Product: CF: Cash Flow Analysis

Version Number: 4.0

Description Summary: Cash Flow (CF) Analysis offers the user a complete business analysis for business plans, substantiating bank loans or for efficient management. It is a menu-driven, stand-alone program designed to do business analysis and cash flow projections without the use of spreadsheets.

CF gives you up to a 5-year projection with easy data input. You can view or print up to 13 reports for each year including Line of Credit, Net Income, Cash Flow, Working Capital, Sales, Gross Profit, G&A Expense, A/R, A/P, Accrued Expense, Ending Balance Sheet, Ratio Analysis, and Data Input Summary. The program automatically amortizes debt payments and calculates taxes and depreciation. It provides full formula traceback with one keystroke, and gives you a consolidation of divisions.

Product Feature List

Creates up to 5 years of cash flow projections without the use of cryptic spreadsheet-type formulas for companies that do not want to expend the time and money necessary to build financial information internally in the form of spreadsheets. CF allows businesses to plan for their future cash needs in an affordable manner. The user can make cash flow projections for each division or subsidiary of a company and then consolidate those into one master projection. It allows the user to enter an opening balance sheet (for existing companies) to create a more accurate or realistic projection. CF allows the user to enter numbers or "create" numbers by itemization or by the use of simple to use, menu-driven formulas creating relationships between categories and subschedules. The itemization function of CF can be used as a calculator and in making notes for itemization of an entry.

Other menu driven features include:

- Six methods of depreciation are available for acquired capital assets
- Automatic amortization of debt
- Federal income taxes automatically calculated on the annualization of income approach
- CF allows the user to provide investors as well as financial institutions with complete information for bank loans and venture capital, including ratio analysis providing liquidity, leverage, profitability, activity, and growth ratios
- Detailed month-by-month yearly reports include: Line of Credit Analysis, Net Income, Cash Flow Working Capital, Sales, Gross Profit, G & A Expense, Accounts Receivable, Accounts Payable, Accrued Expense, Ending Balance Sheet, Summary of Data Input

Pricing:
Single user license — $495
Limited site license — $645 (in company's name for up to five users)
Unlimited site license — $995 (in company's name for over five users)
Extended memory version — $795, $1045, and $1395 respectively
Hardware requirements: PC or compatible
Software requirements: None — CF is an application program that works independently

---

CHAT

Acuity Corporation

Address: 11100 Metric Blvd, #725, Austin, TX 78758
Phone: (512) 425-2200
(888) 242-8669
Fax: (512) 719-8225
E-Mail: info@acuity.com
Web Site: http://www.acuity.com

APPENDIX

Sales Contact Name: Mark Roycroft

■ Product: ichat ROOMS

Version Number: 4.0

Product Feature List

- Event moderation — Advanced event moderation features simplify the management of large, live discussions that can involve thousands of simultaneous users
- Numerous client options — Java, Netscape Plug-in, ActiveX control, and HTML client interfaces provide numerous options for Windows, Macintosh, and UNIX users
- Intuitive user interface — Visitors enter a conversation simply by typing
- Private messaging — Support for public and private messages offers users one-to-one and one-to-many communications channels
- Multimedia support — ROOMS is multimedia-ready, supporting sound, video, and VRML
- File transfer — A convenient client-to-client file transfer capability increases desktop productivity, allowing users to instantly share files
- HTML embedding — Messages may have embedded hyperlinks and HTML formatting; important notices or comments can appear in bold text, or a URL can be conveniently displayed as a clickable link
- Collaborative browsing — ichat ROOMS' support for collaborative site navigation enhances customer service and group interaction
- Robust administration — Administrators have easy access to detailed conversation and server status logs and configuration settings, which can be modified remotely via a simple HTML interface
- API — C++ extensions (servelets) enable administrators to add new and unique features to ROOMS
- Seamless product integration — With shared authentication functions, ROOMS functions as part of the ichat real-time enterprise architecture

Pricing: Concurrent user pricing, starting at $595

Hardware requirements: Depending on your system, approximately 32 MB of available memory and a minimum of 20 MB disk space is required

Software requirements: Available for Windows NT 4.0 and Solaris 2.5.1; works with Microsoft IIS and Netscape Enterprise Web Servers

■ Product: ichat Message Boards

Version Number: 2.0

Description Summary: Message boards is a client-server software system that allows users to search for information and post questions and answers in a threaded, hierarchical format. Since Message Boards uses standard HTML and users access discussion forums right from their browser, no additional client software is needed. Server setup and configuration is conducted through an HTML interface, enabling robust forum management and remote administration.

Product Feature List

- Browser based — Employees or customers can instantly access online discussion groups from within their favorite Web browser; no additional software is required
- Highly configurable interface — A configurable HTML interface allows site administrators to easily create unique, branded user experiences; iHTML, ichat's interactive extension to the HTML standard, allows developers to embed ichat Message Boards functionality within their Web site or intranet
- NNTP client support — NNTP (Network News Transfer Protocol) client support allows network news users to connect and participate in discussion forums
- Organized discussions — ichat Message Boards discussion groups are displayed hierarchically, allowing users to easily follow conversation "threads"
- Moderated topics. — The moderation option allows administrators to effectively organize and lead discussions; question and answer message areas can be regulated so that only approved responses are visible to regular users; similarly, a moderated company information area can contain postings that are prescreened by site administrators
- Versatile administration — Message Boards permits administrators to delegate message management to topic owners and forum moderators; an HTML interface enables quick and easy remote administration, with new topics and moderated threads established with the click of a mouse; content filtering can also be controlled at the topic group level
- Text searching — Message subject and topic key word search support enables ichat Message Boards to serve as a document and information archive; frequently asked questions can be quickly sorted or all messages referring to a particular project name can easily be found

Pricing: Message Boards starts at $2995 for 50 concurrent users
Hardware requirements: Intel-based Windows NT 4.0 or Sun Solaris 2.5.1; 32 MB RAM and 20 MB disk space (minimums)
Software requirements: Major Web server (Netscape Enterprise Server or Microsoft IIS)

APPENDIX

■ Product: ichat Paging System

Version Number: 1.1

Description Summary: The ichat Paging System™ delivers critical new real-time communications capabilities to the desktop. Users can instantly send high-priority messages or determine whether a colleague is online. With a clean, professional interface that displays messages on top of open windows, the Paging System enables individuals to exchange information with new levels of immediacy.

When phone calls are routed to voice mail and e-mails are lost in heavy traffic, ichat Pager users benefit from real-time, impossible to miss desktop communication. Additionally, by adding contacts to their list of associates, users can see when others are available for instant messaging, invitations to Netscape Conferences and Microsoft NetMeetings, or Quick Chat™ text conferencing.

Product Feature List: Server features

- Global messaging — Connected to the ichat Global Message Router, individuals, and groups can send and receive messages from users of remote Paging Systems; messages sent to offline users are stored for later delivery
- Scalability — Add multiple Paging Servers to your Web site or intranet to support tens of thousands of simultaneous users
- Notify your users — With the ichat Paging Server's flexible administrative tools you can easily communicate with your users by sending instant messages, URL's, or links to live audio streams; tools are provided to send messages to multiple user categories including all online users, users in specific interest groups, or to individual users
- Display advertising/informational banners — With an external ad server you can insert images into all user messages; graphic image size is variable; you can include any size image and the client application will size to accommodate it; using an intelligent background file caching scheme, client response is not slowed by the addition of banner graphics to instant messages
- Customizable Interface — Administrators can customize the Pager client interface to contain customer logos, links to Web sites, links to ROOMS chat or Message Board discussions, or lists of other users
- Server Logging and Monitoring — Monitoring server events, system messages, and server uptime through the HTML interface is straight forward; you can also track user activity, server load and usage, and message delivery systems

Administrative Controls

The ichat Paging System is easily administered via an HTML interface. Administrative functions include:

- System security: Encrypted passwords, IP restrictions
- Text filtering: Eliminate specified text or regular expression matches from message content
- User management
- Client configuration tools
- Message gateway application
- Client features
- Instant Messaging — Send and receive instant messages from other users
- Quick Chat™ — Easily initiate a real-time chat session with one or more users
- Privacy — Optionally hide your user profile information, receive pages only from certain users, or ignore individual users
- User status information — Indicates when other users are online, idle, or away from their computer
- Interest categories — Sign up for server-defined interest categories to easily find users

Pricing: The Paging System starts at $1595 for 100 concurrent users
Hardware requirements: Intel-based Windows NT 4.0 or Sun Solaris 2.5.1; 48 MB RAM and 64 MB disk space (minimums)

CONSULTING

Computer Science Innovations, Inc.

Address: 1235 Evans Road, Melbourne, FL 32904-2314
Phone: (407) 676-2923
(800) 289-2923
Fax: (407) 676-2355
E-Mail: info@csihq.com
Web Site: http://www.csihq.com
Sales Contact Name: Rudy Hallenbeck (extension 218), Vice President, Sales & Marketing

■ Product: Software Engineering Services (Object-Oriented, Web-Based or Analytical System Development)

Description Summary: CSI has developed numerous application systems that encapsulate the decision-making process of an expert. These systems often rely on a central information repository. CSI has recently developed custom application systems that make the central repository and the decision process available on a network via browser technology, thus both preserving expertise and enhancing the capabilities of junior personnel. CSI engineers are experienced with a variety of architectures, and utilize a broad range of development platforms, languages and tools, to meet the needs of our customer base, including Oracle, Informix, Sybase, and SQL Server.

CSI employs its Cognitive Engineering Methodology (CEM) in developing various types of systems including decision support, pattern recognition, simulation, and predictive applications.

IMIS Inc.

Address: 712 Sansome Street, Second Floor, San Francisco, CA 94111
Phone: (415) 543-2939
Fax: (415) 391-4985
E-Mail: imis@imisinc.com
Web Site: www.imisinc.com
Sales Contact Name: James Balbo

Description Summary: IMIS Inc. is a financial services consulting company specializing in the implementation of technology in the securities industry. We offer consulting services on a time and materials basis and provide trust companies, brokerage firms, banks, mutual fund companies, and insurance firms a cost-effective alternative to traditional "Big 6" consulting. Our 100 consultants average more than 13 years of securities industry experience and currently manage technology projects across the country and internationally for more than 40 financial services companies. Unlike "body shops" who merely process resumes, all IMIS employees are fully salaried and are provided significant benefits and incentive packages which enables us to attract and retain the industry's very best professionals.

Our RFPDB software application was unveiled at the ABA's NFSOC trade conference in March of 1998 and provides IMIS the opportunity to compete effectively against the larger consulting firms in the system search market. Our proprietary database application, RFPDB, comes preloaded with business requirements for each business segment (brokerage, trust, investment management, etc.) and serves to automate electronically the entire Request for Proposal process from requirements gathering and weighting to vendor response compilation and comparison. By pairing our software application with an IMIS industry expert and project manager, IMIS can compete head-to-head against the much larger consulting firms with a superior product offering and lower prices.

Output Technologies

Address: 2534 Madison Ave., Kansas City, MO 64108
Phone: (816) 221-1234
(800) 252-4541
Fax: (816) 843-6579
E-Mail: info@output.net
Web Site: www.output.net
Sales Contact Name: Kathi Naughton

■ Product: Business Communication Solutions

Version Number: Solutions are customized to each client/business

Description Summary: Output Technologies is uniquely suited to help insurance organizations "mass customize" communications that are personalized to individual customers and customized to groups. Through value-added communications, Output Technologies helps organizations achieve increased customer loyalty, improved communication comprehension, increased revenue generation, improved cash flow, improved customer care, and an increased competitive advantage.

Output Technologies' system focuses on leveraging two major resources: information and design. Output Technologies refers to its sophisticated and innovative ability to marry communication "form and function." As digital technologies continue to advance, businesses need highly specialized and refined methods to deliver communications; in some instances, they need to employ multiple means to connect with their customer. Today, Output Technologies' primary distribution options include: electronic printing and mailing, telemarketing and fulfillment, lithography, CD-ROM, computer output microfilm (COM), and the Internet. To help ensure the integrity of business communications, Output Technologies employs the highest quality control and quality assurance methodology to communication generation, production, and distribution.

Sealund & Associates Corporation

Address: 3001 Executive Dr., Suite 200, Clearwater, FL 33762
Phone: (813) 572-1800

APPENDIX

(800) 434-8000
Fax: (813) 572-9993
E-mail: info@sealund.com
Web Site: www.sealund.com

Description Summary: Sealund & Associates Corporation provides full service custom training solutions for Fortune 500 and 1000 companies such as Chase Manhattan, Lehman, Citibank, IBM, and AT&T. S&A is the country's leading training development company utilizing multimedia and Web-based technologies. S&A is currently developing several online banking training applications for large international banks. These applications function using the latest Internet-based technologies such as Java, Javascripts, and Quick Time. S&A has produced award-winning multimedia titles such as *The Basic Enforcement Academy Training (BEAT)*. Created in conjunction with the St. Petersburg Junior College and the Florida Department of Law Enforcement this project won the Technology Research Award by the Tampa Bay Regional Planning Council. As well this project is featured in *The Ultimate Multimedia Handbook* (Revised, McGraw-Hill 1997). Sealund & Associates has also received an award from IBM for the delivery of "The Americans with Disabilities Act Compliance Training" using OS/2 and CD-ROM. During the mid-80s, the company began designing and building computer-based training (CBT) for mainframe systems such as Hogan, M+I, and IBA. Working with national companies such as Michigan National Bank and CNA, S&A developed comprehensive training design and development methodologies that are now used in corporations around the world. Sealund & Associates professionals are top instructional designers, software and system engineers, multimedia specialist, and graphic artists. Founded in 1985 by Barbara Sealund, the company recognizes the need for corporations to move toward more technologically based training solutions to better serve their employees and customers worldwide.

Services offered:

- Training
  - System conversions
  - Application training
  - Sales training
  - Online help systems
- Multimedia
  - Multimedia-based training
  - Sales presentations
- Internet/Intranet
  - Web-based training
  - Documentation conversions
  - Systems training

- Site development
- Documentation
  - User guides
  - Reference manuals

CONTACT MANAGEMENT

FDP Corp.

(800) FDP-CORP
Fax: (305) 854-6305

E-Mail: todds@fdpcorp.com
Web Site: www.fdpcorp.com
Sales Contact Name: Todd Sears

◼ Product: Contact Partner™

Version Number: 2.5

Description Summary: Full–featured client and contact management system designed to help agents increase sales, streamline client service operations, and maximize office efficiency. Functions as an integrated marketing/ management tool to completely automate the tasks of prospecting, lead follow-up, new application tracking through underwriting, and in-force policy servicing.

Product Features List

Client Service/Information Management
- Individual information
- Business information
- Employee census data
- Complete policy information
- Basic investment information
- Advisor information
- New business tracking
- Underwriting requirement tracking
- Client/Policy service tracking
- Birthday/Anniversary date tracking
- Integrated notepad
- Mass modify and delete
- Custom screen creation
- Data import/export
- Date Compliance with the year 2000

- Sales illustration storage

Sales and Marketing
- Sales tracking module
- Call-backs and follow-ups
- Appointments
- Agent production tracking
- Groups and filters wizard
- List views with saved groups and filters
- Reports using saved groups and filters

Activity/Time Management
- Complete interactive calendar
- Monthly/weekly/daily views
- Appointment scheduling and tracking for multiple agents
- Call scheduling and tracking
- To-do lists
- Calendar reports
- Executive day planner report formats
- Fax template
- Auto dialer

Basic Investment Tracking (tracks the following types of investments)
- CD
- Mutual fund
- Stock
- Variable annuity
- GIC
- Limited partnership
- Bond
- Segregated fund
- Liability
- Tracks owners and beneficiaries
- Tracks position history
- Investment product prices are tracked through price history table
- Security price update
- Fee adjustments
- Reconciliation available for both position and transaction amounts
- Stock dividends and splits
- Distribution adjustments

Investment Reports
- Investment portfolio summaries including variable life and annuity packages
- Investment performance reports with IRR calculations
- Daily blotter reports
- Bank balance sheets

Investment Transaction Downloads
• DST faunal

Office Automation and Management
• Report generator with preformatted reports
• Link with MSWord
• Label and envelope printing
• Mass mailings/mailing lists
• Production reports
• Customizable field help

Pricing: Call for quote; available on a site license and individual basis

Hardware requirements:
Processor: Pentium 150 MHz and above
RAM: 32 Mb
Hard Disk Storage: 70 Mb
Display Adapter: VGA (color monitor)
Mouse: Windows compatible
Operating System: Windows 3.1, Windows 95, or Windows NT

DATA VISUALIZATION

Computer Science Innovations, Inc.

Address: 1235 Evans Road, Melbourne, FL 32904-2314
Phone: (407) 676-2923
 (800) 289-2923
Fax: (407) 676-2355
E-mail: info@csihq.com
Web Site: http://www.csihq.com
Sales Contact Name: Rhonda Delmater (ext. 213), Program Manager

■ **Product: Visualizer Workstation**

Version Number: 1.1

Description Summary: CSI's Visualizer Workstation enables users to virtually "fly" around and even through their data, viewing it from various perspectives. Analysts can rapidly identify visual trends and correlations within their data, and then apply powerful statistical and knowledge engineering tools to refine their hypotheses. The n-dimensional viewing capability aids analysts in discovering new insights about prospects, customers, patients, or other populations of interest. Users can view, manipulate, and analyze sets of discrete data points in up to 10 dimensions, simultaneously. Nearness, occlusion, and perspective are preserved. Visualizer Workstation provides a user-friendly front-end for a combination of several CSI data mining software functions including Select, Autocluster, Statistics, and Knowledge-Based Trainer.

Data is prepared for visualization through enhancement, by applying tools that find and emphasize information-bearing aspects. Data enhancement tools allow users to determine which data items are "most significant," can rank-order data items by predictive power (salience), and can apply transforms which concentrate information into the smallest number of features.

Product Feature List

- Data Preparation Tools: registration, normalization, and feature extraction
- SELECT provides a menu interface to create a subset of the population for analysis
- The ACL tool (Automatic Clusterer) performs unsupervised data clustering
- ND GRAPHICS, the n-dimensional graphics engine, is used to depict feature vectors
- DKBT (descriptive knowledge-based trainer) collects descriptive statistics about aggregations within a dataset and displays them in sentence form
- STATISTICS shows histograms by feature by aggregate
- REPORTS provide statistical information in tabular format

Pricing: Starts at $495 per seat for an individual analyst license. Complementary Advisor tools also are available in configurations to meet the requirements of a large enterprise.

Hardware requirements: 200MHz, 64MB ram, 1GB available disk space, 1024 x 768 resolution, 1152 x 864 or higher recommended

Software requirements: Microsoft Windows NT Workstation (includes Open GL)

DATA MINING/WAREHOUSE

Angoss Software Corporation

Address: Suite 200, 34 St. Patrick Street, Toronto, Canada
Phone: (416) 593 5122

Fax: (416) 593 5077
E-Mail: info@angoss.com

Web Site: www.angoss.com
Sales Contact Name: sales@angoss.com

■ Products: KnowledgeSEEKER and KnowledgeSTUDIO

Version Number: SEEKER (4.4) / STUDIO (2.0)

Description Summary: KnowledgeSEEKER — the industry-leading decision tree data mining solution for quantitative experts and business analysts. Available in client and server configurations, it quickly and efficiently explores, identifies, and displays, in easy to understand visualizations, patterns and relationships in large volumes of data. KnowledgeSEEKER is used by Global 2000 businesses in the financial services, telecom, healthcare, and retail sectors to derive actionable business information from their data assets for competitive advantage. Unique selling features are ease of use, high performance, and affordability.

KnowledgeSTUDIO — a new generation of data mining technology from ANGOSS. Supporting all major data mining techniques through a "project/workbench" user interface that has a true Office '97 look and feel, and with a unique three-tiered client server and "in place (at the warehouse/mart) mining" architecture, KnowledgeSTUDIO provides exceptional performance, high scalability, and easy customizability at an affordable price. KnowledgeSTUDIO is a powerful and flexible environment for professional analysts and business users to quickly explore, reveal, and understand relationships in large volumes of data and to generate predictive models. All of KnowledgeSTUDIO's views are ActiveX controls and as such can be embedded into Visual Basic applications.

Product Feature List

Profiling, Interactive Visual Decision Trees, Neural Nets and Automatic Cluster Detection. Reads from and writes to all major data formats (including SAS and SPSS) and generates "rules reports" in English and major programming languages for easy implementation of predictive models in operational systems.

Pricing: Leads the industry, contact ANGOSS.

Hardware requirements:
KnowledgeSEEKER: Processor: 486 or higher, Memory: 4MB of free memory minimum, Disk space: 3MB of free disk space
KnowledgeSTUDIO: Processor: Pentium or higher, Memory: 64MB of memory, Disk space: 50MB for installation plus additional for client data analysis

Software/Systems requirements:

KnowledgeSEEKER: UNIX: AIX (IBM), HP-UX (HP), IRIX (SGI), Digital Alpha (COMPAQ), Sinux (SIEMENS), Solaris (SUN), SCO, Linux. Microsoft® Windows: 3.1, 95, 98, NT

KnowledgeSTUDIO: Client: Microsoft® Windows: 95, 98, NT

Server: Microsoft® Windows: NT Server, N Workstation

UNIX: Solaris (SUN) under development for 2.0 release

In Place Mining Drivers: SQL Server 7, COMPAQ Info Charger, COMPAQ / Tandem MX (certification in progress), Sybase IQ (certification in progress)

Under development / evaluation: DB2 (IBM), Teradata (NCR)

Database formats supported:

KnowledgeSEEKER: Access, dBase II, III and IV, Excel, Gauss, Lotus, KnowledgeSEEKER, ODBC, Paradox, Quattro Pro, SAS - Transport, SAS v6.0x and Transport, SAS v6.11 and v6.12, Sawtooth, Smartware, Splus, SPSS native format, SPSS (Por), Stata, Systat, SQL*Net (Oracle)

KnowledgeSTUDIO: Access, dBase II, II and IV, Excel, Gauss, Lotus, KnowledgeSEEKER, ODBC, Paradox, Quattro Pro, SAS - Transport, SAS v6.0x and Transport, SAS v6.11 and v6.12, Splus, SPSS native format, SPSS (Por), Stata, Systat

---

Inventure America

Address: 30 Broad Street, New York, NY 10004
Phone: (212) 208-0604
Fax: (212) 825-1040
E-Mail: jmcgann@inven.com
Web Site: http://www.inven.com – www.rangersoftware.com
Sales Contact Name: Jim McGann

■ Product: Ranger

Description Summary: RANGER is an innovative new solution for the Distributed Integration of data and analytics. Distributed Integration is a new way to integrate global financial data, analytics, and applications for rapid distribution to a large community of users. Unlike most traditional data warehousing solutions, Distributed Integration does not require that all data be co-located in a single corporate database. Instead, the Distributed Integration architecture relies on Internet technologies to create a virtual data warehouse that is optimized for scalability and cost-effective delivery of critical data to large user communities. For more information, contact the Inventure Web site at www.rangersoftware.com.

Firstlogic, Inc.

Address: 100 Harborview Plaza, La Crosse, WI 54601-4071
Phone: (608) 782-5000
(888) 215-6442
Fax: (608) 788-1188
E-mail: information@firstlogic.com
Web Site: www.firstlogic.com
Sales Contact: Information Center

Company Description: Firstlogic's i.d.Centric data quality suite provides proven software technologies and services that cleanse, enhance, and match data to make customer-focused database information more reliable and accurate. i.d.Centric offers several sophisticated solutions to help users build data quality into their data warehouse, data mart, and database marketing applications. The software intelligently parses (identifies) individual components of customer data; standardizes, corrects, and enhances it using empirical data sources; locates matches within and across databases; and consolidates matching data.

■ Product: Address Correction and Encoding (ACE)

Description Summary: Address Correction and Encoding (ACE) is a data warehousing product that parses (identifies), corrects, and verifies street and city names, ZIP+4 codes, delivery-point barcodes, and county codes. The software can parse completely unfielded address data and provide address correction and standardization at the street level. ACE is certified for accuracy.

Product Feature List

1. Parses (identifies) individual address components.
2. Standardizes address information.
3. Corrects and enhances addresses using empirical data sources.
4. Verifies and corrects addresses online during data entry.
5. Ensures data quality for data warehousing and database marketing applications.
6. Offers an international solution for the global marketplace.
7. Increases the value of addresses.

Pricing: Call vendor for pricing information.

APPENDIX

■ Product: Match/Consolidation

Description Summary: Match/Consolidation is a data warehousing product that provides data matching and reporting capabilities. It significantly improves accuracy and performance in matching and consolidating customer data and identifies customer relationships. The software also includes full business-to-business parsing and multipass processing.

Product Feature List

1. Locates matches within and across databases.
2. Allows user to define multiple sets of business rules.
3. Ensures data quality for data warehousing and database marketing applications.

Pricing: Call vendor for pricing information.

■ Product: TrueName

Description Summary: TrueName improves the quality of name information in databases. The software identifies name, company name, and title components even when the information has been entered inconsistently. TrueName intelligently parses (identifies) all elements of name data and standardizes them for greater accuracy in matching records. It is an integratible tool that also locates and identifies business and financial data, such as Trustee, ITF, wros, etc. TrueName provides standard representations of individual and business elements to improve matching and provide a more complete base of customer knowledge.

Product Feature List

1. Parses (identifies) name, business, and title information, and provides match standards (such as James for Jim).
2. Creates name- and gender-appropriate greetings (precise genderization).
3. Ensures data quality for data warehousing and database marketing applications.

Pricing: Call vendor for pricing information.

■ Product: Clear ID

Description Summary: Clear ID is the next generation in data quality tools to help companies better understand their individual customers by correcting, verifying, and enhancing their customer data. It is the only product of its kind that combines high-performance data quality processing with a data overlay from an industry-leading data provider. Clear ID provides advanced data correction and verification as well as extended data enhancement and move updating.

Product Feature List
1. Verifies the accuracy of existing customer information.
2. Updates the addresses and phone numbers of customers who have moved.
3. Helps identify relationships between customers.
4. Ensures data quality for data warehousing and database marketing applications.

Pricing: Call vendor for pricing information.

■ **Product: Fusion**

Description Summary: Fusion intelligently consolidates the "best" elements from all available data sources to provide users with a complete customer view. It is the only product of its kind with the built-in logic to help users selectively choose fields and build a "best" consolidated record.

Product Feature List

1. Supports priorities on a field-by-field basis.
2. Complete set of tie-breaker logic.
3. Builds a consolidated or "best" record.
4. Not restricted to just name and address information
5. Ensures data quality for data warehousing and database marketing applications.

Pricing: Call vendor for pricing information.

E-COMMERCE

CyberCash, Inc.

Address: 2100 Reston Parkway, Suite 430, Reston, VA 22091
Phone: (703) 620-4200
Fax: (703) 620-4215
E-Mail: info@cybercash.com
Web Site: www.cybercash.com
Sales Contact Name: Richard K. Crone

■ **Product: Electronic Cash Register for Internet payments: credit card, electronic check, and electronic cash**

Version Number: 3.0

APPENDIX

Description Summary: CyberCash is introducing a new Internet payment architecture for our CashRegister that will make it easier to integrate store-fronts, operate payment services, and enjoy upgrades to new services, standards, and options as they become available. With the CR3 Series, We lower the technical and financial hurdles to secure Internet payments. The CyberCash CashRegister connects a storefront or Web site to the Cyber-Cash payment services, enabling businesses to accept secure, real-time payments at their Web site.

Product Feature List

1. Secure credit card transactions (including both SSL and SET).
2. CyberCoin service, for cash payments from $0.25 to $10.
3. PayNow electronic check service, for interactive billing applications.

Pricing: N/A
Hardware requirements: all platforms
Software requirements: all platforms

GlobeSet

Address: 1250 Capital of Texas Hwy. So., Building One, Suite 300, Austin, TX 78746
Phone: (512) 427-5100
Fax: (512) 427-5101
E-Mail: info@globeset.com
Web Site: www.globeset.com
Sales Contact Name: Michael Prentice

■ Product: GlobeSet Payment System

Description Summary: Our GlobeSet Payment System™ includes:
- GlobeSet Wallet™, a cardholder application that stores a buyer's account information and communicates with merchants via the SET protocol
- GlobeSet POS™ ,a software point-of-sale device that connects the merchant to the buyer's electronic wallet and to the financial payment gateways
- GlobeSet Gateway™, a payment gateway application connecting the merchant to the payment processor's legacy systems for payment authorization
- GlobeSet CA™, a digital certificate application that generates and manages the digital identification certificates supporting SET-based, public-key encryption

Product Feature List: Products support SET transactions over the Internet.

Pricing: Sold through OEM channels

Hardware requirements: NT or UNIX servers, PC

Software requirements: NT or UNIX operating systems

Acuity Corporation

Address: 11100 Metric Blvd, #725, Austin, TX 78758

Phone: (512) 425-2200

(888) 242-8669

Fax: (512) 719-8225

E-Mail: info@acuity.com

Web Site: http://www.acuity.com

Sales Contact Name: Mark Roycroft

■ Product: WebCenter

Version Number: 2.0

Description Summary: Acuity WebCenter™ 2.0 is an enterprise-class, Web-centric solution for e-commerce and online support. Unlike single-purpose customer interaction tools, WebCenter integrates interactive self-service, automated e-mail response, Web-based question queuing and routing, and live interaction through multiple channels, including live text communications, browser screen synchronization, CTI callback, and voice/video conferencing. WebCenter's highly scalable communications capabilities enable major corporations to deploy Internet-based call centers, driving what Forrester Research estimates will be a 43 percent reduction in cost per contact vs. traditional call centers, and increasing e-commerce margins by 15 to 25 percent.

Product Feature List: WebCenter consists of three core components: the Web Response Unit, the WebACD, and the Communication Interface Unit. Features include:

Web Response Unit (WRU)

- Authentication Mechanism. The WRU includes an authentication mechanism that allows verified login of registered users; anonymous login with optional data collection; or verification through external authentication mechanisms such as SQL databases, LDAP directory servers, or third-party customer interaction packages.
- FAQ Database. The WRU maintains a database of frequently asked questions (FAQs) stored in a format that allows easy import/export and full-text searching of all data.

- User Response Function. All search returns (including natural language queries) allow customers to extend their search or get additional offline help through email, fax, or a telephone call.
- Integration With External Knowledge Bases. The WRU leverages the in-place data infrastructure by aggregating search results from multiple databases — presenting the customer with a user-friendly interface to information from existing data repositories.
- WebLink™ Module. The WRU includes WebLink, a package of NSAPI and ISAPI interfaces to Netscape Enterprise Server and Microsoft Internet Information Server, allowing easy integration with existing Internet infrastructures.

WebACD (Web Automated Call Distribution)

- Agent Queue Management. The WebACD maintains a queue of available agents, with real-time updates on activity.
- Active Task Queue Management. The active queue contains unresolved tasks. The queue reflects information such as waiting time, number in queue, and priority.
- Integration with Existing Systems. WebCenter can integrate existing customer care systems, ACD systems, and ticket tracking systems.
- E-mail Routing and Automated Response. WebCenter incorporates robust e-mail management capabilities, providing automatic responses to common questions and queuing of other e-mail messages for agent review.
- Real-Time and Historical Reports. Managers and supervisors can run detailed, up-to-the-minute reports on agents or groups.

Communications Interface Unit (CIU)

- Data Wake. To provide session context and aid in problem resolution, agents can view the customer's original question, all attempted knowledge base searches, and the URL of the button used to initiate the session.
- Screen Synchronization. With WebCenter's CIU, agents can push URLs directly to the customer's screen, including links to specific FAQ entries contained in the WRU FAQ database.
- Text Conferencing. Text conferencing offers easy-to-integrate and deploy, real-time communications for customer/agent interaction. All interactions are logged and can be maintained over secure (SSL) connections.
- CTI Callback. Computer Telephony Integration provides a mechanism for customer callback queuing in traditional ACD systems, allowing the customer to specify a telephone number and preferred time for a return call. This process integrates with the existing ACD or PBX system.

- H.323 to PBX Telephony Linkage. An H.323 to PBX gateway allows agents to establish voice conferences with a customer who is using an Internet phone (H.323-compatible) interface.

Core Features

- Standards-Based System. WebCenter embraces industry standards wherever relevant, including (but not limited to) RVP, X509v3, SSL, HTTP, HTTPS, and XML.
- Proven Technology Foundation. WebCenter leverages the ichat Real-Time Enterprise platform to provide a proven, stable Web-based infrastructure that is currently deployed at over 1100 customer sites and has demonstrated real-world scalability of 20,000+ simultaneous users.

- API Interfaces. Components are accessible via API interfaces, allowing customization of system functionality and integration of third-party applications without modifications to the core applications.
- HTML-Based System Management. WebCenter is easily managed via an HTML-based interface. Agents, managers, and administrators have full control of the system from anywhere in the enterprise.
- Web Security. Secure Sockets Layer (SSL) security is provided for all WebCenter communications through the HTTPS protocol.

Pricing: Traffic-based model starting at $125,000
Hardware requirements: Varies by deployment
Software requirements: Intel Windows NT 4.0, Web server (Microsoft IIS or Netscape Enterprise server supported)

ICentral, Inc.

Address: 225 N. University Ave., Provo, UT 84601
Phone: (801) 373-4347
(888) 373-4347
Fax: (801) 373-7211
E-Mail: info@icentral.com
Web Site: www.shopsite.com
Sales Contact Name: Jan Johnson, VP marketing

■ Product: ShopSite Pro

Version Number: v3.3

Description Summary: ShopSite Pro is a secure, online store creation and management application designed to meet the needs of site developers and merchants who are seeking to build a professional, yet affordable storefront. In addition to its site creation and management tools and secure shopping basket, ShopSite Pro includes real-time credit card authorization, a site search engine and an Associates Tracking program.

Product Feature List

- Ported to several UNIX OS and NT
- Client-side, any platform that supports a standard browser
- Foreign language support
- Unlimited simultaneous shoppers
- Online help
- Payment information encryption
- E-mail notification of orders
- Auto shipping and tax calculation
- First virtual payment system
- Customizable order system
- Easily indexed by search engines
- Sales stats
- Traffic stats
- Page creation/site management tools
- Direct media upload
- Media library manager
- Database upload
- Order database download
- Credit card authorization
- Stats plus
- Associates tracking
- Site search
- Large database handling tools
- Interface to other applications
- SmartTags
- Discount calculation
- Automatic product upsell
- Global database editing

Pricing: $1295 (MSRP)

Hardware/Software requirements: These system requirements are for the average functional store

Web Server: Operating systems — OpenLinux, Linux, Free BSD, or BSDI on Intel

- Solaris on SPARC shipping; Solaris on Intel coming soon
- NT and IRIX coming soon
- 16MB RAM
- 10 MB hard drive space (up to 25 MB may be required for install only)

Hardware platforms must be running: Stronghold, Netscape, or any NCSA-compatible, secure web server software, PERL 5.003 or greater Sendmail

Client-side (Web Site Developer or Merchant): Requires Netscape browsers or Microsoft Internet Explorer, Versions 3.0 or later, running on the user's system of choice (PC, Mac, or UNIX)

Client-side (Shopper): Browser of choice

■ **Product: ShopSite Manager**

Version Number: v3.3

Description Summary: ShopSite Manager is for the small- to medium-sized business manager who wants to begin marketing and selling products on the Internet, or who currently has a Web site, but wants to take the next step of selling products online.

For Web site designers, it reduces the many tedious tasks involved in maintaining a Web site, allowing them to concentrate on pure design. It empowers merchants, not only allowing them to make day-to-day merchandising changes without impacting the site designer. For the do-it-yourself merchant, this person can use ShopSite Manager and build an entire site without knowing HTML.

Product Feature List

- Ported to several UNIX OS and NT
- Client-side, any platform that supports a standard browser
- Foreign language support
- Unlimited simultaneous shoppers
- Online help
- Payment information encryption
- E-mail notification of orders
- Auto shipping and tax calculation
- First Virtual payment system
- Customizable order system
- Easily indexed by search engines
- Sales stats
- Traffic stats
- Page creation/site management tools
- Direct media upload
- Media library manager
- Database upload
- Order database download
- Credit card authorization

Pricing: $495 (MSRP)

APPENDIX

Hardware/Software requirements: These system requirements are for the average functional store

Web Server: Operating systems:

- OpenLinux, Linux, Free BSD, or BSDI on Intel
- Solaris on SPARC shipping; Solaris on Intel coming soon
- NT and IRIX coming soon
- 16MB RAM
- 10 MB hard drive space (up to 25 MB may be required for install only)

Hardware platforms must be running: Stronghold, Netscape, or any NCSA-compatible, secure Web server software, PERL 5.003 or greater Sendmail

Client-side (Web Site Developer or Merchant): Requires Netscape browsers or Microsoft Internet Explorer, Versions 3.0 or later, running on the user's system of choice (PC, Mac, or UNIX)

Client-side (Shopper): Browser of choice

■ Product: ShopSite Express

Version Number: v3.3

Description Summary: ShopSite Express is a shopping basket software application that allows a site developer to build a site using his or her HTML tool of choice, then quickly and easily add "order" and "checkout" buttons to the Web site. Shoppers can click on these buttons and place an order in the secure shopping basket.

ShopSite Express offers a simple point-and-click, fill-in-the-blanks interface. Enter product information (name, price, ordering options) into ShopSite Express through the browser interface. After configuring tax and shipping (so it will be calculated automatically for shoppers), click on the "Create Links" button and ShopSite will automatically generate "order" and "checkout" buttons for each product in the ShopSite database. These buttons can drag-and-dropped onto the HTML editing window.

Product Feature List

- 25-product limit (no real-time credit card handling capabilities, but can capture and store credit card information securely in the orders database for manual processing later)
- Ported to several UNIX OS and NT
- Client-side, any platform that supports a standard browser
- Foreign language support
- Unlimited simultaneous shoppers
- Online help
- Payment information encryption
- E-mail notification of orders

- Auto shipping and tax calculation
- First virtual payment system
- Customizable order system
- Easily indexed by search engines
- Basic sales stats

Pricing: N/A (sold only through certified hosting partners, no MSRP available)

Hardware/Software requirements: These system requirements are for the average functional store

Web Server: Operating systems: OpenLinux, Linux, Free BSD, or BSDI on Intel

- Solaris on SPARC shipping; Solaris on Intel coming soon
- NT and IRIX coming soon
- 16MB RAM
- 10 MB hard drive space (up to 25 MB may be required for install only)

Hardware platforms must be running: Stronghold, Netscape, or any NCSA-compatible, secure Web server software, PERL 5.003 or greater Sendmail

Client-side (Web Site Developer or Merchant): Requires Netscape browsers or Microsoft Internet Explorer, Versions 3.0 or later, running on the user's system of choice (PC, Mac, or UNIX)

Client-side (Shopper): Browser of choice

ENTERPRISE APPLICATION INTEGRATION

MINT Communication Systems, Inc.

Address: 650 Fifth Avenue (12th Floor), New York, NY, 10019
Phone: (212) 977-7366
Fax: (212) 977-7399
E-Mail: ziv@mintco.com
Web Site: www.mintech.com
Sales Contact Name: Ziv Lotenberg

■ Product Name: MINT

Version Number: 5.2

Description Summary: MINT is a global provider of Enterprise Application Integration (EAI) solutions for the financial services market. MINT's unique approach to EAI empowers business users in financial institutions to drive the application integration processes. The MINT suite of products enables seamless integration of disparate applications and networks. This is accomplished through dynamic routing and transformation for inter-application messages based on their content and user-defined business rules. MINT's products enable business users, rather than IT professionals, to define rules using business terminology and MINT's financial knowledge base. MINT's products facilitate cost-effective and rapid integration of heterogeneous networks, operating systems and applications, rapid deployment of new best-of-breed applications while preserving legacy systems, easy access to timely information and simplified process control.

Product Feature List

- Comprehensive message broker platform for fast and cost-effective EAI
- Intelligent, rule-based middleware with robust message manipulation capabilities
- Guaranteed delivery of messages and files
- High availability module for continuous operations in case of failure
- Easy-to-use graphical user interface
- Communication with external networks and standards, including SWIFT, ISITC, CREST, FIX, CHAPS, SIC, SECOM, and others
- Easy-to-use uniform connectivity APIs to many platforms, including Windows, UNIX, and IBM mainframes, as well as various legacy systems interoperability with IBM's MQSeries, Tibco's TIB, BEA's Tuxedo/M3 middleware pipelines, and various CORBA-based ORB environments
- Runs on a variety of industry standard UNIX systems from leading hardware vendors in various configurations

Pricing: Depending on configuration
Hardware requirements: SUN, HP, and RS/6000 for MINT server. Windows NT/95 for MINT clients
Software requirements: Solaris, HP-UX, or AIX operating systems and Oracle/Sybase database

---

EXTRANETS

Aventail Corporation

Address: 808 Howell Street, 2nd Floor, Seattle, WA 98101
Phone: (206) 215-1111
(877) 283-6824
Fax: (206) 215-1120
E-Mail: info@aventail.com
Web Site: www.aventail.com

Sales Contact Name: Chris Kenworthy, VP of Sales

■ Product: Aventail ExtraNet Center

Version Number: 3.0

Description Summary: Aventail ExtraNet Center (AEC) is the most comprehensive, flexible, and easy-to-use solution for securing and managing extranet communication. It provides comprehensive access control and tools to make it easy for companies to define how, when, and what resources are accessed by key individuals outside the physical walls of the corporation. It includes a suite of services beyond basic encryption, including rules-based access control, user-based authentication, key/certificate management and distribution, active content filtering, intelligent logging and reporting, and the ability to secure Java, ActiveX, legacy host, and custom corporate applications. Aventail ExtraNet Center is the only product on today's market that is specifically focused on delivering the necessary security, management, and application and network integration for building a sophisticated, flexible, easy-to-use extranet.

Product Feature List

The latest features include:

- Sophisticated Security and Authorization — Aventail ExtraNet Center not only provides strong encryption and authentication, but also granular authorization that enables administrators to define user privileges based on a broad range of parameters.
- Ability to Cross Firewall Boundaries Securely — Aventail ExtraNet Center can traverse any firewall. In addition, the new MultiProxy™ feature allows the client to optionally use an HTTP proxy to cross firewall boundaries securely without requiring any reconfiguration of the firewall.
- Application Independent — Aventail ExtraNet Center supports all IP-based applications including legac host, Web, JAVA, ActiveX, CORBA, DCOM+, custom corporate, and client/server applications.
- Simple Policy-Based Management — The Aventail Policy Console, a single intuitive interface, allows administrators to easily create, delete, or modify extranet users' profiles. Using the Aventail Management Server, managing multiple ExtraNet Center servers can also be done securely from any remote or local workstation.
- Infrastructure Independent — Aventail ExtraNet Center runs on most operating systems and works with any encryption and authentication method.
- Transparent Client — Aventail Connect(tm), the client component of Aventail ExtraNet Center, is completely transparent to the end user. It is designed for nontechnical users, can be installed in minutes, and

makes no technical modifications to the desktop. Aventail Connect includes Secure Extranet Explorers, a revolutionary application that enables users to browse selected 32-bit Windows-based file systems.

- Automated Client Configuration and Distribution — Network administrators can create up to tens of thousands of custom Aventail Extranet clients in one easy step with the Aventail Customizer™. With this tool, network administrators can easily distribute clients and make them available in a central, networked directory for easy access, download, and installation.

Pricing: Bundled pricing starts at $7995

Hardware requirements: Product can run on the following:

Server: Processors: Sparc, x86, Power 2, PowerPC, hppa, and Alpha Operating Systems — Windows NT 3.51 and 4.0, Solaris 2.5, AIX 4.2, Linux 2.x, Red Hat Linux 5.2, HP-UX 10.x, and Digital UNIX. Memory Requirements — 32 MB recommended

Client: CPU — 486/50 IBM PC or compatible

Processors — Sparc, x86, Alpha, and PowerPC; Operating Systems — Windows 3.x, Windows for Workgroups 3.11, Windows 95, Windows NT 3.51 and 4.0; Memory Requirements: 16 MB recommended; Software requirements: Aventail ExtraNet Center client/server software

---

FAX MANAGEMENT

Teubner & Associates, Inc.

Address: 623 S. Main Street, Stillwater, OK 74074
Phone: (405) 624-8000
(800) 343-7070
E-Mail: faxgate.sales@teubner.com
Web site: www.teubner.com
Sales Contact Name: Ed Graves

■ Product: Faxgate®

Version Number: 4.5

Description Summary: Faxgate is an inbound and outbound fax gateway or host and LAN computing environments that offers an integrated hardware/software solution for electronically sending and receiving facsimiles on an enterprise-wide scale. Faxgate makes your business more profitable and gives you a competitive advantage by delivering documents faster, more efficiently, and for less money. Faxgate integrates like no other product, delivering true enterprise fax automation in a unique combination of depth of function, breadth of connectivity, and the strength of production fax. Supporting a multitude of applications, including SAP and extensive messaging and e-mail integration, Faxgate seamlessly enables your day-to-day business operations.

Pricing: Varies based on configuration, starts at $2500
Operating environment: Windows for NT server

FINANCIAL APPLICATION DEVELOPMENT

The MathWorks, Inc.

Address: 24 Prime Park Way, Natick, MA 01760
Phone: (508) 647-7000
Fax: (508) 647-7012
E-Mail: finance@mathworks.com
Web Site: www.mathworks.com/finprod
Sales Contact Name: Cathy DeYoung

■ Product: MathWorks Financial Engineering Workshop

Description Summary: The MathWorks Financial Engineering Workshop integrates analysis tools, model design, simulation, and code generation into a single, interactive environment. Based on MATLAB, the Workshop provides a common development platform for research, system design, and rapid prototyping of financial applications. The Workshop provides, in a single, integrated and affordable package, all the tools you need to explore, simulate, prototype, and validate financial models and applications. The components of the Financial Engineering Workshop are MATLAB, Excel Link, and the Financial, Otimization, and Statistics Toolboxes. Optional components include the C/C++ Compiler and C/C++ Math Libraries.

Product Feature List

- Over 500 math functions
- Numerical computation and simulation
- Data analysis and visualization
- GUI building tools
- Multidimensional arrays
- Interactive code profiling and debugging
- Fixed income pricing, yield, and sensitivity analysis
- Portfolio analysis and optimzation
- Derivative pricing and analysis
- Calendar functions

- Linear and quadratic programming tools
- Direct access from all MATLAB functions from Excel spreadsheet
- Probability distributions and random number generators
- Multivariate analysis
- Parameter estimation and fitting

Pricing: Please call

Hardware requirements: PC, UNIX, Mac compatible; specific hardware requirements are available on our Web site

Software requirements: PC, UNIX, Mac compatibl; specific software requirements are available on our Web site

---

GIS

Geographic Data Technology, Inc

Address: 11 Lafayette St, Lebanon, NH 03766
Phone: (603) 643-0330
(800) 331-7811
Fas: (603) 643-6808
E-mail: info@gdt1.com
Web site: www.geographic.com
Sales contact name: Steve Morse

■ Product: Dynamap/2000

Description Summary: Dynamap/2000 is the premier street and boundary database for business geographics applications in the U.S. GDT has over 50 people dedicated to adding new streets and addresses, keeping up with postal changes and improving quality and accuracy. Dynamap is available in many formats, compatible with all commonly used GIS desktop mapping and geocoding packages.

Pricing: Call

Hardware and Software requirements: The Dynamap database is used on all current Platforms and software including mainframes, workstations, and PCs.

INSURANCE RATING SOFTWARE

Computer Science Innovations, Inc.

Address: 1235 Evans Road, Melbourne, FL 32904-2314
Phone: (407) 676-2923
(888) 823-2923
Fax: (407) 676-2355
E-Mail:poolplus@csihq.com
Web Site: http://www.csihq.com/poolplus/
Sales Contact Name: Judy Kennedy (ext. 231), Product Manager

■ **Product: PoolPlus for Windows (Insurance Rating Software for Florida)**

Version Number: 1.0

Description Summary: PoolPlus is the most complete and accurate rating program for Florida Independent Insurance Agents.

Product Feature List

- Simultaneously rates wind premiums with homeowners or commercial property
- Imports saved quotes to expedite rating for the wind and flood modules
- Generates and prints customer copy of quotes
- Generates and prints rating worksheets
- Prints plain paper applications

Pricing: $120 per copy for each Florida rating module or any three modules for $299, $30 annual update subscription
Hardware requirements:
Intel microprocessor
Random access memory (RAM) 8 MB (16 MB under Windows 95)
Hard disk space available: 15 MB
Mouse or track ball recommended
VGA or SVGA Monitor
Software requirements: MS Windows® Version 3.1 or Windows 95® (recommended)

■ **Product: PoolPlus for Windows (National Insurance Rating Software)**
Version Number: 1.0

APPENDIX

Description Summary: PoolPlus National Flood Rating software provides flood insurance ratings for the entire U.S.

Product Feature List

- Provides ratings for standard, residential, condominium association, preferred risk, mortgage portfolio, and provisional policies
- Minimizes data entry requirements
- Automatically determines Pre or Post FIRM status
- Automatically calculates CRS discounts and community probation surcharges
- Saves, quotes, worksheets, and applications
- Generates and prints customer copy of quotes
- Generates and prints rating worksheets
- Provides ability to fax or e-mail quotes, worksheets, and applications

Pricing: $279 per seat, $50 annual subscription
Hardware requirements:
Intel microprocessor
Random access memory (RAM) 16 MB minimum (32 MB recommended)
Hard disk space available: 15 MB
Mouse or track ball recommended
VGA or SVGA monitor
CD ROM
Software requirements: MS Windows® 95 or Windows NT

INTERNET ACCESS

Resonate

Address: 465 Fairchild Drive, Suite 115, Mountain View, CA 94043
Phone: (650) 967-6500
Fax: (650) 967-6561
E-Mail: info@Resonate.com
Web Site: www.Resonate.com
Sales Contact Name: Cameron Lorentz

■ Product: Global Dispatch, Central Dispatch, and Application Dispatch

Description Summary: The Resonate Dispatch Family of products enables the fastest and most reliable Internet access through a system of integrated products that intelligently select, schedule, and route requests to the optimal network resource or service.

Central Dispatch: Provides superior control and distribution of Web traffic and allows CIOs, network managers, and system administrators to quickly and efficiently implement scalable, reliable, enterprise-wide, multiserver Web sites.

Global Dispatch: Enables excellent performance from your existing resources by intelligently determining the optimal POP locations for maximized resource availability. Global Dispatch seamlessly integrates with server-level scheduling and load-balancing solutions to provide enterprise-wide availability and performance.

Application Dispatch: Provides dependable access to application services by scheduling requests to the least-loaded, most-available application server. You can also set service level priorities that allow more critical application requests to be scheduled according to level of importance.

Product Feature List

Global Dispatch:

- Latency-based scheduling
- High availability for mission critical applications
- Reliability
- Simple set-up

Central Dispatch:

- Resource-based scheduling
- High availability
- Scalability
- High performance
- Heterogeneous support

Application Dispatch:

- High availability
- Service level priorities
- Superior application performance
- Many-to-many mapping

Pricing: Introductory pricing at $10,000.
Hardware requirements: Platforms supported — Sun SPARCservers, Pentium, and Pentium Pro, IBM/AIX servers
Software requirements: Supports all commercially available Web server software

---

INTERNET BANKING

Corillian Corporation

Address: 3601 SW Murray Blvd., Suite 300, Beaverton, OR 97005
Phone: (503) 627-0729
(800) 863-6445
Fax: (503) 641-5575
E-Mail: info@corillian.com, sales@corillian.com
Web Site: www.corillian.com
Sales Contact Name: Peter Ghavami, VP of Sales

■ Products: Voyager server; MoneyPAD Personal Financial Appliance

Version Number: Voyager v2.0; MoneyPAD v1.5

Description Summary: The Voyager platform is a high performance middleware server built on the Windows NT operating system that is designed to handle Internet delivered core banking and bill payment transactions. The Voyager platform provides a link between financial institution legacy host systems and customers using OFX-enabled personal financial management software and browser-based (HTML) financial interfaces.

Voyager Server Applications enable financial institutions to provide their consumers and small business clients with access to a variety of services, including banking, bill payment, brokerage and point-of-sale transaction initiation. Corillian's Client Applications are customizable browser-based user interfaces based on de facto standards such as HTML, JAVA, and Active X. The Browser Banker is a customizable HTML-based user interface. MoneyPAD is the Personal Financial Appliance that performs transactions over the Internet, while providing the financial institution's customer a unique, branded service environment.

Product Feature List

Voyager Platform

- Supports secure real-time banking, bill payment, and brokerage
- Supports FULL synchronization and file recovery
- Built on MS Windows NT operating system
- Uses a three-tier architecture to manage transactions without duplicating existing data/processes
- Integrates legacy financial data
- Incorporates JAVA script technologies
- Uses MS communications technology, distributed COM

- Open system, supporting current and anticipated OFX/GOLD specifications
- Scaleable using Intel-based servers
- Stringent Internet security

MoneyPAD:

- ActiveX-based software client
- MoneyPAD Banker provides real-time banking, bill payment, and brokerage
- MoneyPAD Designer provides tools for designing, branding, and personalizing

Pricing: Varies; based on number of "user licenses" and professional services requirements.

Hardware requirements: Firewall Server hardware; HP Server P6200 Model D4346N; Traffic Cop/Auto IP Switch; Cisco Router; 3Com SuperStack; APC; WAN monitor; hardware-based disk redundancy

Software requirements: Win NT Server 4.0; MS SQL Server 6.5; MS IIS 3.0; NT Service Pack #3; PC Anywhere 8.0; Crystal Reports 6.0; Voyager; Digital Certificate

---

Goldleaf Technologies, an Equifax Company

Address: 103 Commerce Street, Suite 120, Lake Mary, FL
Phone: (407) 829-4445
(888) 453-5323
Fax: (407) 829-4452
E-Mail: sales@goldleaf-tech.com
Web Site: www.goldleaf-tech.com
Sales Contact Name: Christine Bauer, Vice President of Sales and Marketing

■ Product: ACH Origination, Corporate Cash Management, Home Banking, Telephone Banking, and Internet Banking

Description Summary: Goldleaf markets and supports the Customer-Link™ suite of electronic banking software solutions. These state-of-the-art products include ACH origination and cash management for the financial institution's corporate clients and telephone, home, and Internet banking for the retail client. Feature-rich CustomerLink products are unique in their market. CustomerLink solutions allow independent financial institutions the opportunity to offer affordable, technologically advanced services to clients in a continuously evolving marketplace.

APPENDIX

Goldleaf now serves over 1400 successful financial institutions with more than 8000 products installed. With the help of Goldleaf's products, these customers generate additional revenue, increase/retain market share, and decrease operating expenses. Today's financial marketplace is extremely competitive for independent banks, savings banks, and credit unions, and Goldleaf is committed to strengthening the customers' relationships with their financial institution.

Product Feature List
Contact Goldleaf for more information.

Pricing: $10,000 – $50,000
Hardware requirements: Call for configuration
Software requirements: Call for configuration

---

nFront, Inc.

Address: 1551 Jennings Mill Road, Suite 800A, Bogart, GA 30622
Phone: (706) 369-3779
Fax: (706) 369-8611
E-Mail: apowell@banking.com
Web Site: www.banking.com/www.nfront.com
Sales Contact Name: Alan Powell

■ Product: nHome™

Description Summary: nHome, the company's Microsoft NT-based Internet banking application, enables banking customers to open new accounts, apply for loans, view account balances and histories, pay bills, transfer funds, download images of cleared checks, customize reports, and download active statements into personal financial management packages at anytime, from any location, using any secure, browser-enabled device such as personal computers and televisions. From the bank's perspective, nHome allows the financial institution to expand its reach to a broader market, primarily composed of the most profitable banking customers, while taking advantage of the least expensive delivery channel available today. Because customers are afforded greater access to and control over their account information, the bank's customer service overhead ultimately can be reduced. And, perhaps most importantly, through the collection of data captured online in this fat server solution, the bank can target specific customers for more efficient and effective cross-selling and marketing campaigns.

Product Feature List

- Secure account and credit applications
- Account summaries and histories
- DDAs
- Savings
- CDs
- IRAs
- Mortgages
- Loans
- Equity lines of credit
- Funds transfer
- Bill payment
- Immediate and future transfers and payments
- One-time and recurring transfers and payments
- Custom reports
- PFM downloads
- Account type
- Date
- Check number
- Quicken™
- Transaction amount, transaction type
- Microsoft Money™
- Interactive calculators
- Personal information manager
- Retirement planning, college planning
- PIN management
- Mortgage estimating
- Loan estimating
- Change of address, etc.
- Check imaging
- Administrative interface
- Internet branch reporting
- Data mining/cross-selling
- Update rates and product information
- Customer specific reporting
- Download secure online applications
- Automatic sales message delivery
- View audit tables and customer stats
- E-mail notification system
- Online help
- Branded online demo

Pricing: Based on asset size of institution.

APPENDIX

Hardware requirements:
- Pentium 75 Processor or greater PC
- 16 MB RAM or greater
- 28.8 BPS Asynch modem or greater
- CD ROM drive
- Monitor
- Keyboard
- Mouse
- Dedicated analog telephone line for dialup connectivity
- PC must be housed in a secure area of the bank and be available to receive daily ACH files and transmit nightly balance files (basically, a PC running Windows 95 with 16 MB RAM and an Asynch modem)

Software requirements:
- Microsoft Windows 95, Version 4.00.950 B or greater on CD ROM
- Microsoft Plus!

Q-UP Systems

Address: 8303 N. Mopac, B450, Austin, TX 78759
Phone: (512) 342-9910
(800) 500-3002
Fax: (512) 342-9921
E-Mail: info@qup.com
Web Site: www.qup.com
Sales Contact Name: Wade Sanders, Director of Sales

■ Product: Internet Banking System (IBS)

Version Number: 3.11

Description Summary: The Internet Banking System provides 24-hour access to accounts and financial services. The system allows bank customer to view all account balances, view history of all accounts, search history, export history to personal finance software, transfer funds between accounts, establish "deposit only accounts," pay all bills, control personal payee database, change address, re-order checks, stop payments, purchase savings bonds, and set up Q-cards (automatic e-mail reminders). In addition, Q-UP has set up IBS as a modular system, which means the bank can opt to add the following modules to the basic platform: View Statements, Memo Posting, Check Imaging, Check Re-Ordering, Credit Card, and Real-Time.

The product was introduced in 1996 and went live in January 1997. The product is designed for any size financial institution and the primary niche has been the community bank market. Q-UP offers flexible system architecture, which means the financial institution has the option of housing the turnkey system on-site or having Q-UP host the system at their Cyber Service Center.

Product Feature List
See above

Pricing: Contact Wade Sanders for pricing
Hardware requirements: Server grade machine
Software Requirement: NT 4.0 or higher, IIS 3.0 or higher

INVESTMENT

Multex.com, Inc.

Address: 33 Maiden Lane, 5th floor, New York, NY 10038
Phone: (212) 859-9800
(888) 2MULTEX
Fax: (212) 859-9810
E-Mail: multex@multex.com; feedback.min@multexsys.com
Web Site: multexinvestor.com
Sales Contact Name: Scott Meyer, Director of Business Development

■ Product: The Multex Investor Network

Description Summary: The Multex Investor Network is the online site where serious investors can read and discuss investment research and make smarter investment decisions. It is the only interactive Internet community providing access to more than 250,000 investment research reports from more than 250 brokerage firms, investment banks, and independent research providers worldwide. This is the real research, containing advanced, quantitative analysis written by top analysts whose opinions move markets. Membership in the Multex Investor Network is free and includes: participation in engaging discussion groups; insightful, though-provoking articles; advanced searching capabilities; ability to track favorite companies; ability to locate and download reports for free and for purchase in real time.

Product Feature List

- Access to more than 250,000 investment research reports from more than 250 prestigious research providers from around the world
- Discussion forums
- Original content

Pricing: Membership is free, and includes free reports: Multex Stock Snapshots, Multex ACE Consensus Estimates and others; free original content; free access to discussion forums and free personalization capabilities. Pricing on individual reports from research providers varies, usually based on length of report, starting at $4. Reports are sold in their entirety and in original format.

Hardware requirements: Macintosh or PC/486 or better

Software requirements: Web browser (Netscape 3.0 or greater, Internet Explorer 3.0 or greater, or America Online 3.0 or greater; Adobe Acrobat Reader 3.0 or greater

---

LIFE INSURANCE AND ANNUITY ADMINISTRATION

The Leverage Group, Inc.

Address: 68 National Drive, Glastonbury, CT 06033
(800) 892-3334
Fax: (860) 657-1256
E-Mail: market@levgrp.com
Web Site: www.levgrp.com
Sales Contact Name: Sales Department

■ Product: PolicyLink

Version: 4.0

Description Summary: The Leverage Group is a leading ind pendent software and services company that develops and markets advanced client/server based system solutions to the life insurance and annuity industry. Founded in 1984 and based in Glastonbury, CT, The Leverage Group is one of the largest software vendors in the insurance industry with over 100 clients. The Leverage Group provides PolicyLink — the year 2000 life insurance and annuity administration system that offers many integrated features and major technological achievements for the optimum processing solution: client/server technology, complete policy administration, commission processing and payout processing, 100 percent graphical user interface design, rapid product development, multiproduct support, complete variable processing, RDBMS query and reporting, icon controlled integrated functionality, and it's 100 percent Web enabled. It's the life insurance and annuity administration system you can depend on for the year 2000 and beyond.

Product Features List

• Production proven life insurance and annuity administration system

- Year 2000 compliant
- Client/server technology
- 100 percent graphical user interface
- Windows and UNIX
- Unlimited life insurance and annuity policy/product volume
- 100 percent Web enabled
- Complete legacy replacement system
- Multiproduct support
- Advanced, rapid product development platform
- RDBMS query and reporting
- Icon controlled, integrated functionality

Pricing: Call

MULTICASTING

StarBurst Communications Corporation

Address: 150 Baker Ave., Concord, MA 01742
Phone: (978) 287-5560
(800) 585-3889
Fax: (978) 287-5561
E-Mail: info@starburstcom.com
Web Site: www.starburstcom.com
Sales Contact Name: Bill Andrews

■ Product: StarBurst OmniCast

Version Number: 1.0

Description Summary: StarBurst OmniCast offers a revolutionary information delivery system that couples extensive file management and multicast group management capabilities with StarBurst's industry-leading Multicast File Transfer Protocol (MFTP) file delivery solution. OmniCast provides reliable, efficient, and simultaneous transfer of data "packages" from a single site to many, even thousands, of recipient sites. It is ideal for software distribution, enterprise-wide business data delivery, Intranet information "push," multimedia file distribution, Web-site content replication, database replication, and other file transfer applications.

Product Feature List

- Intuitive graphical user interface to rapidly define and manage target receiver groups packaging tools for organizing, bundling, and managing files and directory structures

- File and package compression utility for greater network efficiency
- Flexible scheduler for defining future and regular jobs
- Administrator and user modes
- Real-time job monitoring
- Historical transaction and error reporting
- DNS and DHCP support

Platforms: Windows NT and Windows 95. Sun Solaris planned for release in 1998. t 3.x clients.

■ Product: StarBurst Multicast

Version Number: 3.04

Description Summary: StarBurst Multicast provides group management and reliable, efficient, and simultaneous transfer of data files from a single site to many, even thousands, of recipient sites. It is an ideal solution for software distribution, enterprise-wide business date delivery, Internet/Intranet information "push," multimedia file distribution, web site content replication, database replication, and other one-to-many file transfer applications. StarBurst Multicast offers significantly faster file delivery, reduced network traffic, and reduced server resource usage when compared to traditional point-to-point file transfer methods such as TCP-based File Transfer Protocol (FTP).

Product Feature List

- Intuitive graphical user interface
- Extensible command line interface for scripted operations
- Unattended installation and operation at remote sites
- Real-time transfer status monitoring
- Extensive sender and receiver logging
- Settable transfer rate allows file transfers to occur simultaneously with other network applications
- Powerful "resume" feature allows stoppage of transfer for resumption later
- Interoperable among diverse client/server platforms

Platforms: Server and Client: Sun Solaris, DEC Alpha UNIX, Windows NT, Silicon Graphics IRIX, IBM AIX 3.2.5, and 4.2

Client only: Windows 95, OS/2, SCO UNIXWare, SCO OpenServer 3.2 & 5.0, IBM 4690, Sun Interactive UNIX

■ Product:StarBurst Multicast Sender for SMS

Version Number: 1.4

Description Summary: StarBurst Multicast Sender for SMS is an SMS add-on that significantly reduces network and system costs associated with software management of networked PCs. StarBurst Multicast Sender improves the software distribution capabilities of Microsoft® System Management Server (SMS) by reducing network traffic, decreasing the load on sending servers, and minimizing software transfer times.

Product Feature List

- Brings MFTP benefits to Microsoft SMS
- Intuitive SMS-consistent GUI minimizes learning curve
- Unattended installation simplifies deployment
- Runs as integral Windows NT service
- Extensive sender logging
- Detailed receiver logging to the Windows NT Event Log.

Platforms: Microsoft SMS

■ Product: StarBurst Multicast SDK

Version Number: 1.04

Description Summary: StarBurst Multicast SDK is a rich software development environment for authoring custom applications based on StarBurst's Multicast File Transfer Protocol (MFTP™). End-users, systems integrators, and other developers can utilize StarBurst Multicast SDK to dramatically improve the file transfer efficiency and group management of their own applications. StarBurst MFTP supports the reliable, efficient, and simultaneous transfer of data files from a single site to many, even thousands, recipient sites. Potential applications for MFTP technology include electronic software distribution, database updates, point-of-sale data distribution, and multimedia content delivery. Applications based on MFTP offer faster file delivery, reduced network traffic, and reduced server resource usage when compared to applications based on traditional point-to-point file transfer methods.

Product Feature List

- Extensive API based on Berkeley sockets exposes all MFTP capabilities
- Common API for Windows 95, Windows NT, plus a variety of UNIX platforms simplifies porting
- Cross-platform support allows interoperability between diverse client/server platforms
- Includes software, sample programs, documentation, and telephone support

APPENDIX

Platforms: Sun Solaris, DEC Alpha UNIX, Windows NT, Silicon Graphics IRIX, IBM AIX 3.2.5 and 4.2, Windows 95, SCO OpenServer 3.2 and 5.0, OS/2, IBM 4690, SCO UNIXWare, Sun Interactive UNIX

MULTIMEDIA

See CONSULTING

NETWORKING

Litton Network Access Systems

Address: 3353 Orange Ave., Roanoke, VA 24012
Phone: (540) 342-6700
(800) 537-6801
Fax: (540) 342-5961
E-mail: info@netaccsys.com
Web site: www.netaccsys.com
Sales Contact Name: Tom Paredes

■ **Products: Litton Network Access Systems Family of ATM Access Products including CAM 7665 Communications Access Multiplexer, CAM 7640 ATM Multiservice Multiplexer, and the ATM Circuit Emulation (ACE) Card for IBM Nways ATM Workgroup Switches and Hubs**

Description Summary: The CAM family of ATM Access products offer network consolidation of circuit-based and constant-bit rate traffic over an ATM network, including voice over ATM. Designed for any platform density (from 1 to 80 T1s), the CAM products can deliver leased line savings in less than 12 months. The ACE card provides the same T1/E1 circuit emulation service as the CAM 7665 and 7640, but is designed as an add-in module for IBM Nways ATM Workgroup Switches.

Pricing: Pricing for the CAM 7640/7650 starts at $15,000. The CAM 7665 basic configurations begin at less than $30,000. The ACE card is offered at approximately $11,000 for four ports, $15,000 for eight ports. For additional features and hardware/software requirements, please visit our Web site.

OPTICAL STORAGE

NSM Jukebox

Address: 2405 Commerce Ave., Bldg 2000, Duluth, GA 30096
(800) 238-4676
E-mail:info@nsmjukebox.com
Sales Contact Name: David Ooley, Vice President, Sales and Marketing

■ Products: Mercury, CDR100, and Satellite.

Description Summary: The Mercury family is designed for the most demanding multiuser networks. All Mercury products hold up to 150 CDs, all are network enabled, and the Mercury 40 has four high-speed, read-only drives for optimal performance. The Mercury 40 NET has an embedded controller to ensure plug-and-play support for Novell networks. The Mercury 31's concurrent read–write capability enables accurate disc mastering while supporting multiuser read access. The Mercury family is capable of managing both RS232 and SCSI implementations. **Pricing:** Starting at $13,000

The CDR 100 family of jukeboxes is an ideal, low-cost solution for all kinds of data management challenges. For users who require read-write capabilities, the CDR 100 Recordable is bundled with mastering software for automatic, unattended production of hundreds of CDs per day. For users who require read-only access to a prerecorded archive of 100 CDs, the CDR 100 XA features compact efficiency and high-speed robotics for information on demand. **Pricing:** Starting at $5000

The Satellite family offers the most compact and flexible jukeboxes available. Managing 60 to 135 CDs, the Satellite can be custom fit to meet both the capacity and access needs of the most demanding applications. Up to three read–write drives support automated CD production. If user access has top priority, five read-only drives (a 12:1 disc-to-drive ratio) can deliver data at breakthrough speeds. Only the Satellite can change dynamically in accordance with specific application requirements. **Pricing:** Starting at $10,000

OPTIMIZATION/RISK SYSTEMS FOR PORTFOLIOS

Financiometrics Inc.

Address: 208 Moraga Way, Orinda, CA 94563
Phone: (925) 254-9338
Fax: (925) 254-2932
e-mail: jkale@financiometrics.com
Web Site: www.financiometrics.com
Sales Contact Name: Jivendra Kale

■ Product: QOS-MAX

Version Number: 9.2

Description Summary: QOS-MAX is an exceptionally fast quadratic optimization system, designed for security level optimization of stock and bond portfolios with several thousand assets. It uses the Best-Kale QP algorithm, which is an enhanced active set analysis technique for large-scale portfolio optimization. Quadratic optimization is the preferred technique for portfolio construction when the asset return distributions are approximately normal, which is true for portfolios of stocks and bonds where risk and return are measured relative to a benchmark index. QOS-MAX is a subroutine library with functions for optimization with a full asset covariance matrix, optimization using a factor model, and matrix checking for ensuring that covariance matrices are positive semidefinite.

Product Feature List

1. Specify a risk-return tradeoff for the optimal portfolio.
2. Minimize variance for a given expected return.
3. Maximize expected return for a given variance.
4. Maximize the Sharpe ratio.
5. Find the highest threshold return for a given Sharpe ratio.
6. Separate variable transactions costs for each asset, where transactions costs increase with trade size.
7. Separate upper and lower bounds for each asset.
8. Linear equality and inequality constraints on portfolio attributes, factor loadings, and asset groups.
9. Turnover constraint.
10. Separate target values and penalty coefficients for each asset.
11. Target values and penalty coefficients for portfolio attributes and factor loadings.
12. Limit on number of assets in the portfolio.
13. Interface to in-house or vendor supplied factor model.

14. Allows risk-free asset.
15. Allows forward positions.
16. Does linear optimization as a special case.
17. Does domestic and international asset allocation.
18. Tracks a market index.
19. Creates market-neutral portfolios.
20. Immunizes bond portfolios.
21. Thread-safe for intranet and Internet applications.
22. Optimizes portfolios with as many assets and other parameters as the hardware and operating system can handle.

Pricing: N/A

Hardware requirements: PC, SUN, or any other hardware.

Software requirements: NT, Windows 98, OS/2, Solaris, intranet or Internet, or any other operating system. QOS-MAX is available as either a C or Fortran object code library. Source code is also available.

■ Product: Growth Optimization System

Version Number: 9.2

Description Summary: The Growth Optimization System constructs portfolios for high long-term growth with downside protection. A "Growth Optimal" portfolio can be constructed to maximize long-term growth and downside protection can be added to the growth optimal portfolio to the extent desired by the investor. The amount of downside protection added corresponds to the Degree of Loss Aversion specified by the investor. This system is designed for investors and institutions with long horizons, such as pension funds and endowments. It is used for asset allocation and security level optimization, and is particularly effective when asset return distributions are skewed or fat-tailed. It uses the Best-Kale NLP algorithm for portfolio construction. The Growth Optimization System is a subroutine library with functions for optimizing portfolios given the joint distribution of asset returns and the Degree of Loss Aversion for the investor.

Product Feature List

1. Maximize long-term growth by setting the Degree of Loss Aversion to zero to construct the growth optimal portfolio.
2. Add downside protection to the growth optimal portfolio by specifying a positive value for the Degree of Loss Aversion; the larger the value for the Degree of Loss Aversion, the greater the amount of downside protection added to the growth optimal portfolio.
3. Generates portfolios with positively skewed return distributions.
4. Uses the entire joint distribution of asset returns, which allows investor preferences for higher expected returns, lower standard deviations of return, higher positive skewness (magnitude of losses is

smaller than magnitude of gains), to be taken into account in portfolio construction.

5. Separate upper and lower bounds for each asset.
6. Linear equality and inequality constraints on portfolio attributes such as regional exposure, sector exposure, beta, yield, duration, etc.
7. Allows risk-free asset.
8. Does domestic, international, and emerging markets asset allocation.
9. Does manager allocation for multiple manager applications.
10. Thread-safe for intranet and Internet applications.
11. Optimizes portfolios with as many assets and other parameters as the hardware and operating system can handle.

Pricing: N/A
Hardware requirements: PC, or SUN
Software requirements: NT, Windows 98, OS/2, Solaris, Intranet or Internet. The Growth Optimization System is available as either a C or Fortran object code library.

■ Product: Equity System

Version Number: 3.30
Description Summary: The Equity System is a comprehensive system for risk attribution, performance attribution and evaluation, index tracking, active portfolio optimization, normal portfolio construction, and back-testing for equity portfolios. It is based on a fundamental factor model with 76 factors, where the factors are associated with the fundamental attributes of firms, such as industry exposure, company size, book/price ratio, earnings/price ratio, growth, dividend yield, systematic and residual risk. An added feature of the model is that it is an "Industry Kernel Model," where the industry factors are treated as primary factors and the other factors are orthogonal to the industry factors. This type of model has better risk and return attribution properties than the typical multifactor model. The model is based on more than a decade of data without survival bias, and using only the latest available data as of each date in the data history.

Product Feature List

1. 76-factor model with 67 industry groups and 9 other fundamental factors.
2. Model is updated monthly.
3. Industry exposure for each company is for up to 10 different industry groups.
4. Covers approximately 10,000 companies traded in the U.S.
5. Risk prediction based on the factor model.
6. Attributes risk to market exposure, fundamental factors, and company specific factors.

7. Measures risk relative to a benchmark index.
8. Attributes performance to market exposure, fundamental factors, and company specific factors.
9. Evaluates performance relative to a benchmark index.
10. Tracks the performance of individual stocks relative to the benchmark for evaluating stock picks.
11. Attributes performance to a user-specified industry grouping in addition to the 67 industry groups specified in the factor model.
12. Screening capability.
13. Back-testing capability.
14. Optimizes active return and risk using Financiometrics Inc.'s Quadratic Optimization System.

Pricing: N/A
Hardware requirements: PC
Software requirements: Windows 98

■ **Product: Performance Attribution and Evaluation Service**

Description Summary: The Performance Attribution and Evaluation Service provides performance and risk attribution reports for equity portfolios based on the history of month-end portfolio holdings supplied by money managers, consultants, and sponsors. It uses Financiometrics Inc.'s Equity System for generating the reports. The attribution is done using the 76-factor fundamental factor model used in the Equity System. A report that tracks the performance of each stock pick relative to the benchmark is also included. Portfolio holdings are sent to Financiometrics Inc. over the Internet in Excel or ASCII files, and the reports are returned over the Internet also.

PAGING

Absolutely Software Inc.

Address: 1515 North Federal Highway, Suite 300, Boca Raton, FL 33432-1994
Phone: (561) 852-0681
(888) 922-7638 (888-Y-ABSOFT)
Fax: (561) 852-2669
E-Mail: kathy.krebs@absoft.net
Web Site: www.absoft.net
Sales Contact: Name: Eric Brill

APPENDIX

■ **Product: Air Apparent for Windows NT**

Version Number: 1.2

Description Summary: Air Apparent for Windows NT is the most popular suite of paging products for the Windows NT operating system. Air Apparent is an end-to-end paging solution, integrating into virtually every legacy application and diverse computing environment. It provides reliability, fault-tolerance, and supports environments with high volumes of paging traffic. Best of all, it was built around the Internet (TCP/IP) protocol as an internal networking backbone. The server page enables e-mail, help desk, monitoring, and network management software into one centralized paging server. Air Apparent works with all major carriers and was built on open-standard protocols only.

Product Feature List

- Benchmarked at 10,000 pages per hour
- Communicate with on-site terminals, local and nationwide wireless carriers
- Compatible with alphanumeric pagers, iDEN and PCS phones
- Delivers multiple messages per dial-up, increasing throughput
- Detailed audit trails for all communications port activities
- Explorer-like interface
- Maintenance of transaction and error logs
- Maintenance of users, groups, services, and port configuration
- Message log that tracks activity of pages dispatched

Pricing: From $799 – $6125

Hardware System Requirements: An Intel 486 or Pentium microprocessor, 32 MB of memory minimum, one 3.5" high-density drive, CD-ROM drive, VGA, Super VGA, or higher-resolution video graphics adapter, Network adapter card, Modem(s), TCP/IP stack

Software System Requirements: Microsoft Windows NT V3.51 or higher operating system

---

PORTFOLIO ANALYSIS/MANAGEMENT

Portfolio Management Consultants, Inc.

Address: 555 17th Street, 14th Floor Denver, CO 80202
Phone: (303) 292-1177
(800) 852-1177
Fax: (303) 292-0330
Web Site: http://www.pmcdenver.com
Sales Contact Names: Raquel Hinman, Scott Wilkinson

■ **Product: ADAM**

Version Number: 5.2

Description Summary: ADAM is a comprehensive analytical portfolio analysis program. ADAM offers portfolio analysis, a portfolio optimizer, investment policy preparation, risk tolerance questionnaire, database with over 10,000 mutual funds and 250 indices and managers, the ability to analyze mutual funds with a factor analyzer, historical performance calculation and presentation, hypothetical spending scenarios and analyses. Adam also permits you to develop customized slide-show presentations detailing the results of your analysis.

Product Feature List

- Built-in help
- Educational tutorials
- In-depth customer profile
- Asset allocation and portfolio modeling
- Fund selection
- Contract preparation and printing
- Investment policy preparation and printing
- Performance reporting

Pricing: Free
Hardware requirements: IBM-compatible PC with 486 chip or better, 8 MB RAM, 50 MB disk space, Microsoft Windows 95 or greater
Software requirements: N/A

Rescom, Inc.

Address: 1150 Waverley Street, Winnipeg R3T 0P4 Canada
Phone: (204) 284-2100
Fax: (204) 284-3838
Sales Contact Name: Doug Mann

■ **Product: MarketMate Enterprise**

Description Summary: Object-oriented, three-tiered client service portfolio management system, multilingual, multicurrency, AIMR compliant. Rescom's newest portfolio management offerings utilize leading edge technologies that are designed to evolve as the needs of the user change. RES is the term used to describe Rescom's Enterprise Solutions. RES is the architecture infrastructure on which application functionality resides. The first application to reside on RES is MME, or MarketMate Enterprise.

RES is an Open Systems Architecture that is vendor neutral and supports enterprise wide systems. RES architecture can be two tier or three tier. In a two-tier client/server configuration, the application logic is either buried inside the user interface on the client (workstation) or within the database (the server), or both. In a three-tier client/server system, the application logic resides in the middle tier, separated from the data and the user interface. This provides substantial cost savings, greater scalability, and is more robust and flexible. Data can be distributed to multiple servers, allows dynamic load balancing and provides dynamic reporting and controls. RES is architecture driven, utilizes Object Oriented Programming and C++, and was implemented using Relational Database Technology. The development of RES has been separated into five encapsulated layers to provide a very flexible system that offers greater portability to different user interfaces (browsers), TP monitors, and RDBMS's.

RES is industry-independent and can satisfy the needs for thousands of users in one or many locations or one or two users operating disconnected from the servers. MME provides comprehensive browse lists for securities, clients, accounts, portfolios, transactions, and memos. Standard reports within MME can be customized easily by the user selecting and arranging the colums and/or headings from a predefined list. MME can prepare valuations in any currency. Book costs are available in up to four currencies. MME maintains book cost using Average Cost, LIFO, FIFO, and Specific Match accounting. MME supports all AIMR performance presentation standards. The flexibility to calculate performance gross or net of fees with or without cash allocation is included. Performance can be calculated at the holding level or the portfolio level and can be presented by Asset Type, security Type, Industry Category, Currency, and Country. The MarketMate Enterprise Solution is designed to evolve as the needs or the user change. It should be thoroughly considered before any new portfolio management solutions are implemented.

Product Feature List

MME presents a whole new level of performance and productivity capabilities. The MME extensive data model supports a large number of key functions including:

- Portfolio management
- Contact management
- Portfolio reporting
- AIMR compliant performance reporting
- Accrual calculations
- Graphics
- Real-time market-to-market and portfolio valuation
- New account opening and maintenance

- Risk profiling
- Portfolio asset allocation and rebalancing
- Full multicurrency
- Multilingual
- Financial planning
- Electronic order entry

Hardware requirements: HP-UX server, Windows NT client
Software requirements: Tuxedo, Sybase, Oracle, Informix

SS&C Technologies, Inc.

Address: 80 Lamberton Road, Windsor, CT 06095
Phone: (860) 298-4500
(800) 234-0556
Fax: (860) 298-4900
E-Mail: SOLUTION@sscinc.com
Web Site: http://www.ssctech.com
Sales Contact Name: Julie Donaldson

■ Product: CAMRA 2000

Version Number: Version 2

Description Summary: CAMRA 2000 offers global investment profession-als the power and flexibility to manage the entire investment process effi-ciently and seamlessly. The core inventory manager delivers a single, consolidated "book of record" which is accessible across your entire enter-prise — from front and back office.

By accessing detailed information in real-time, CAMRA 2000 facilitates de-cision-making trading, compliance monitoring, and portfolio management. The result: you focus on your core business-managing investments.

Product Feature List

- Online pre- and post-trade compliance
- Online trading room
- Automated Bloomberg data exchange
- Multicurrency processing
- Four accounting bases supported: GAAP, STAT, Management, and Tax
- U.S. and Canadian regulatory reporting
- Performance measurement (consistent with AIMR standards)
- Extensive online market analytics database
- Mutual fund accounting including NAV
- Money market processing

- Automated TBA/dollar roll processing
- Optimized MBS pool allocation with EPN E-Z Link
- Custodian, pricing, corporate action, factor, F/X, G/L, DTC, and NAIC interfaces
- Integrated SQL report writer with ODBC for ready access to all stored data
- 32-bit operating environment for improved reliability, memory utilization, and performance
- Supports both Windows '95 (and Windows NT) operating systems on the desktop

Pricing: N/A
Network Information: Windows NT, Novell, Banyan
PC Hardware requirements: Intel X86 based (P90 recommended)
PC Operating System: Windows 95, Windows NT
PC Memory Requirements: 24 MB (minimum Windows 95), 32 MB (minimum Windows NT)

PROPERTY/CASUALTY POLICY ADMINISTRATION

Allenbrook, Inc.

Address: 900 Chelmsford Street, Cross Point, Tower 1, Lowell, MA 01851
Phone: (978) 937-2980
Fax: (978) 937-5464
E-mail: marketing@allenbrook.iix.com
Web Site: www.allenbrook.com
Sales Contact: Robert Dolan, VP Sales and Marketing (ext. 136)

■ Product: Phoenix Enterprise Insurance Solution

Description Summary: Phoenix from Allenbrook, Inc. is a comprehensive Windows-based property and casualty policy administration and management system that can boost insurance company profitability. Phoenix, a client/server solution, combines fully integrated personal and commercial lines policy, accounting, and claims management modules. Phoenix lets insurers manage flexible plans of insurance and develop new products quickly to reach additional market niches. Year 2000 compliance is included in the design. Allenbrook delivers enterprise-wide automation benefits and provides expert insurance/technology support to some of the most successful insurance companies in North America.

Product Feature List

- Policy administration

- Rate quote
- Underwriting
- Billing and collections
- Claims administration
- Bureau feporting
- Reinsurance interface
- Conversion support

Hardware/Software Requirement: Client/Server, PC-based enterprise insurance application using Novell or NT Server, and SQL Base, Oracle, SQL Server or DB2/400; 32 MB RAM; Pentium processor; 400 MB hard drive (minimum for client level Phoenix components); Windows 95/NT

RE-ENGINEERING

Hamilton Technologies, Inc.

Address: 17 Inman Street Cambridge, MA 02139
Phone: (617) 492-0058
Fax: (617) 492-1727
E-Mail: sales@htius.com
Web Site: http://world.std.com/~hti
Sales Contact Name: Hannah Gold

■ Product: 001 (pronounced "double oh one")

Version Number: 3.2.8

Pricing: Seat and component based
Hardware requirements: UNIX (HP, Sun, RS6000, Alpha), Windows (NT).
Software requirements: Developer Package for hardware environment of choice which includes C compiler and GUI environment (Motif or Windows)

Description Summary: Hamilton Technologies, Inc. (HTI) was founded in 1986 to provide products and services to modernize the system engineering and software development process in order to maximize reliability, lower cost, and accelerate time to market. HTI's flagship product, 001, is based on HTI's Development Before The Fact (DBTF) formal systems theory used to develop systems in terms of System Oriented Objects (SOO's). This paradigm integrates systems and software engineering disciplines and transforms the software development process away from an inefficient and expensive curative process to a preventative, more productive, reliable process. 001 is a completely integrated systems engineering and software development environment. It can be used to define, analyze, and automatically generate complete, integrated, and fully production-ready code for any kind of software application with significantly lower error rate and high reusability. Since 001 has an open architecture it can be configured to generate (or interface to) systems at all levels including for hardware platforms, software platforms, programming languages, databases, operating systems, Internet systems, embedded systems, communication protocols, GUIs and legacy code of choice.

Here are some of the set of properties and features that make the 001 tool suite environment unique:

- Always No. 1 when put to the test
- Formal, but friendly, systems language based on Development Before the Fact (DBTF)
- All 001 systems are system oriented objects (SOOs): integration of object-oriented and function-oriented parts of a system, lending itself to component based development; objects are systems and systems are objects
- All objects under control and traceable
- Inherent reuse and resource allocation
- Same language for all phases, systems, and viewpoints
- No interface errors
- Integrated seamless design and development environment: systems to software, requirements to design to code to tests to other requirements and back again; level to level and layer to layer
- Executable specification simulation
- Integrated metrics for predictive systems with a mechanism to trace from requirements to code and back again
- 100 percent automatic code generation for any kind of software application
- Open architecture: 001's generator can be configured for any kind of architecture including language, operating system, database, communications protocol, Internet and legacy environment of choice; once configured, 001 will automatically regenerate the new system to reside on that architecture
- Maintenance performed at the blueprint level; a change to the application is made to the specification, not to the code; a change to go to a new architecture is made to the architecture configuration of the component, not to the code
- GUI environment tightly integrated with the development of an application
- Automated testing
- Automated documentation

- 001's systems have built-in quality, built-in productivity, and built-in control
- 001 was completely defined and generated with itself

New Art Technologies, Inc.

Address: 514 Portside Drive, Edgewater NJ 07020
Phone: (201) 941-6226
(800) 276-1118
Fax: (201) 313-5286
E-Mail:info@newarttech.com
Web Site: www.newarttech.com
Sales Contact Name: Rebecca Lakser

■ **Product: NA2000 SCAN**

Version: 5.0

Description Summary: NA2000 SCAN is an easy-to-use, reliable programming language-independent utility that first finds all of your source program files on standalone PCs or LAN networks and then scans them for specified references. NA2000 provides a detailed analysis report that programmers can use to make their changes as well as a management report that managers can use to estimate job size and cost. NA2000 SCAN cuts your analytical time down from months to mere hours.

NA2000 SCAN provides several hundred Y2K "seeds" which you may modify, add to, or exclude from the scanning process. You may also elect to ignore or exclude any text strings from the scanning process. Any programming language source code file may be analyzed including COBOL, C, HTML, JAVA, FORTRAN, BASIC, VISUAL BASIC. Output analyst reports pinpoint matches per program showing actual lines of code and why that line of code was reported upon as well as a cross-reference report which is sorted alpha via variable. All output may be exported to your favorite spreadsheet and/or database program.

Product Feature List

- It can process over 500 programs at a time on a Windows PC
- Over 450 specific "intelligent" selection criteria find date-related variables
- Optional user input file permits you to enter up to 499 data names specific to your particular company or industry
- Optional user "exclude" file permits you to enter up to 50 data names that you wish to exclude from the scan; you may exclude from any-

877

where in the line of code or specify to exclude if variable is at start of line of code only

- Optional "ignore" file lets you bypass particular words in a line of code to be scanned
- NAXREF is an included cross reference facility that lets you see exactly where each variable or routine name is used
- It can process any language as long as the file is in an ASCII format
- An included file locator finds files on drives you specify — even your network drive
- It processes file extensions you specify (e.g., .cbl, .cob, .cpy, .for, .bas, C, etc.)
- Scan processing report details specific program and line number of date related "hits"
- Alternate "short report" limits the number of "redundant hits"
- Export results to spreadsheet or database
- Management report details number of lines of code requiring modifications
- Management report details number of hours/man years required to perform this job and total estimated cost of job
- Excellent tool for auditing the work of consultants and outsourcers

Hardware/Software requirements: Windows 3.1, 95, or NT

■ Product: NAIMPACT

Version: 3.0

Description Summary: NAIMPACT is a Windows-based, interactive analytical tool that provides developers the ability to assess the extent of programming change when they are handed a set of requirements from end-users. NAIMPACT provides a complete programming language-independent impact analysis workbench. With the click of a mouse the programmer analyst can select one or more files to scan and then review and edit those results right online. He or she can even export the results to a favorite database and/or spreadsheet program right from NAIMPACT. Either NAIMPACT's Y2K seeds can be used or the programmer analyst can edit the list of seeds right online. Boolean operatives such as AND, OR, and NOT can be used to make NAIMPACT's scanning process extremely flexible. Additionally the programmer analyst can specify that NAIMPACT constrain its search to either match the search term exactly or "fuzzy" in on a match at a specified percentage level (i.e., 25 percent, 50 percent, 75 percent)

Product Feature List

- Windows-based, completely interactive; developers can iteratively assess the impact of making changes to one or multiple programs at a time

- Programming language independent; can process any language including Cobol, Fortran, Assembler, C, etc.
- Default search criteria file contains over 200 year 2000 date-related criteria; developers can choose to use or not use this file
- Developers can enter up to 499 of their own search criteria
- Boolean search criteria (consisting of AND, OR, NOT) can be utilized (e.g., STAT AND WORKING OR ACCOUNTS)
- Constrained and nonconstrained searches (constrained search means that there must be a 100 percent match between the search criteria and the code; unconstrained search means that there doesn't have to be a perfect match
- Fuzzy search capabilities — ability to match at 75 percent, 50 percent, and 25 percent levels between search criteria and code
- Impact analysis report details number of hours/man years required to perform this job and total estimated cost of job. Developer has ability to modify default criteria and iteratively run the impact analysis
- Scan processing report details specific program and line number of related "hits"
- File viewer permits developer to click on "hit" and see associated program code. You can open your code editor from within NAIMPACT; stores and recalls your favorite editor name/location
- Cross reference report provides alpha listing by "hit" in a spreadsheet-type format
- Export results to favorite database and/or spreadsheet

Hardware/Software requirements: Windows 3.1, 95, or NT

■ Product: NATRACE

Description Summary: NATRACE for COBOL and NATRACE for C are Windows-based, interactive analytical tools that provide developers the ability to "explode" the impact of a single variable throughout a given COBOL or C program down to a depth of 1000 nodes. Particularly useful for year 2000 analysis, NATRACE, which contains language parsers for C and COBOL, easily pinpoints nonobvious impacted related variables. For example, in a given COBOL program you might have a variable called WS-DATE which is an obvious date reference. But as we "explode" WS-DATE, we find that it impacts some nonobvious date references, as shown below:

```
MOVE WS-DATE TO WS-D-AREA.
COMPUTE WS-D-AREA = 7 * NUMS.
ADD WS-D-AREA TO WS-TOTAL.
ADD WS-DATE TO B-VAR GIVING C-VAR
```

So we find that WS-DATE impacts both WS-D-AREA, WS-TOTAL, and C_VAR, all nonobvious date-related references. NATRACE will trace and report on all impacted variables.

Product Feature List

- Windows-based, completely interactive
- NATRACE handles C comments even when the comment spans multiple lines; it also understands bitwise, logical, and shorthand operators
- Because C may or may not be CASE dependent, NATRACE for C permits you to select whether or not the scan is CASE dependent
- NATRACE for C also permits you to decide whether to perform a search where the structure and the member are joined (e.g., rec.name) or not joined (e.g., name)
- NATRACE for C can trace searched for variables within a structure
- NATRACE for C provides a listing of traced variables found used by functions
- NATRACE for COBOL handles redefines as well as variables within group levels
- Handles COBOL and C programs where a command spans multiple lines; pre-processor "collects" all related code and spans it across one single record for analysis purposes; will not lose sight of code where the target is separated by multiple lines from the source
- Explodes a tree structure of affected variables; each, in turn, becoming a branch of the same tree spawning new branches
- File viewer permits developer to click on "hit" and see associated program code
- All report results can be printed as well as stored in a text file

Hardware/Software requirements: Windows 3.1, 95, or NT

■ Product Name: NAEXCEL FOR SPREADSHEETS

Version: 3.0

Description Summary: NA-Excel, a Windows-based interactive utility, solves the problem of what to do with those millions of spreadsheets written by both programmers and end-users. With NA-Excel even an end-user can quickly spot date-related references and change them on the spot. It's a must-have for all corporations. While organizations are busy assessing the impact of the millennium date change on their stock of programmer written systems, a much larger threat looms on the horizon. Much of today's decision support analyses are performed by end-users who use computer-based spreadsheets such as Microsoft Excel and Lotus 1-2-3 to make billion-dollar decisions.

Product Feature List

- Can be used for Excel, Lotus 1-2-3, and Quattro Pro spreadsheets
- Uses Microsoft Excel as an automation server
- Completely visual
- Processes a complete workbook within seconds
- Processes worksheets, macros, as well as modules
- Can process from one to an infinite number of spreadsheets at one time
- Full reporting capability lets you see an online report as well as print to paper and to a file for later processing
- Optional "cell highlighting" in interactive mode colors the "found" cells in red for easy spotting and modification
- Over 100 date-related references included as a starter "search table". The search table may be modified to add additional date variables OR to totally change the criteria. For example, NAEXCEL can be used to search for Eurodollar dependencies just by changing the search table. The starter date-related references include all Excel date and time functions such as NETWORKDAYS, YEARFRAC, TIMEVALUE, etc.
- Wildcard searching capability
- Runs under Windows 95/NT

Hardware/Software requirements: Windows 95, or NT

■ Product Name: NAWORD for document search, replace, and comparison

Version: 1.0

Description Summary: NA-Word speedily searches your documents to locate, compare, or replace strings of text you specify. Since Microsoft Word is used as an automation server, NA-Word can process, other than text and MS-Word formats: WordPerfect, Microsoft Works, HTML, all programming language code, Microsoft Write — essentially anything that Microsoft Word supports. NA-Word can search your entire local/LAN drive finding files that you specify (of course, you can use wildcard searches) then it can "find" (wildcard capability) or even "find and replace" strings that you specify. But it can even do more! Programmers often need to compare two files to one another. NA-Word provides a host of comparative options — on a binary basis or on a document basis — highlighting what's different. You can even perform a compare where you specify the starting and ending record and column numbers for the two comparison files.

Product Feature List

- Useful for all documents; can also be used for programming languages (e.g., Java, C, and HTML)
- Can process from 1 to n files at a time matching up to 1000 variables at a time

- Has a file finder which can find files anywhere on your local/network drive
- Capable of wildcard matching; "sounds like" matching; case sensitive/insensitive; whole word matching; all variation matching
- Option for "coloring" found matches red; ability to "unclear" red highlighting
- Can save changed document right online
- Capable of replacing found text automatically with a replacement term
- Can scan macros/modules within document
- File comparison function enables binary compare, document compare, and line-by-line compare
- Percentage matching shows ratio of matching one document to another; ability to specify starting/ending line numbers and starting/ending column numbers
- Runs under Windows 95/NT workstation

Hardware/Software requirements: Windows 95 or NT

RELATIONSHIP MANAGEMENT

Baker Hill Corporation

Address: 655 West Carmel Drive, Suite 100, Carmel, IN 46032-2500
Phone: (317) 571-2000
(800) 821-8664
Fax: (317) 571-5125
E-mail: marketing@bakerhill.com
Web site: www.bakerhill.com
Sales Contacts: Laura Kunkel, Patrick Spencer

■ Product: OnePoint®

Version: 6.3

Description Summary: OnePoint is a Windows-based Relationship Management Solution. OnePoint offers seamless integration from the desktop with Fair, Isaac's SBSS-CreditDesk™ and Dun & Bradstreet data. Its four integrated modules include:

- Sales management/business development
- Underwriting/credit analysis
- Pricing and profitability
- Portfolio management/exception tracking

Pricing: Varies depending on your needs; call for more information

Hardware: Novell Netware or Windows NT Server
Software: Windows 3.1, 95, or NT

SECURITIES BACK-OFFICE SYSTEMS

Comprehensive Software Systems, Ltd.

Address: 25178 Genesee Trail Road, Golden, CO 80401
Phone: (303) 526-5515
Fax: (303) 526-9362
E-Mail: outreach@cssltd.com
Web Site: www.sni.net/cssltd
Sales Contact Name: Jon Farinholt

■ Product: Comprehensive Software Systems

Version Number: n/a

Description Summary: CSS is a complete, front to back office, modular financial services software solution for the securities industry. CSS has committed to develop browser-based applications, leveraging the burgeoning power of the Internet and placing CSS at the forefront of emerging technologies. The system encompasses several distinct products — including BrokerView™, Order Management System (OMS) and the Message Switch, Business Process Support, back-office modules, and the database — that can be used as a complete system or can be selected individually and implemented with existing systems. A brokerage firm can run its entire business using solely CSS products, or a firm can select particular products that will most benefit the firm and interface them with any custom or third-party applications. CSS is flexible enough that the products and support offered can easily be tailored to suit the needs of a business of any size, even extending beyond the brokerage industry and into other branches of financial services.

BrokerView is the primary tool that a broker or trader would use, giving access to all of the functionality that a broker or trader would need to place and maintain orders, manage his portfolio and clients' assets, and keep abreast of the market. A set of Profile modules forms the basis of the system, storing necessary data on the firm and its subsidiaries, employees and associated personnel, and all of the firm's products. The CSS Entitlements module regulates, based on the firm's settings, which of the functionality is available to which employees, based on logon. OMS and the Message Switch deliver outstanding speed and reliability for processing orders, and a separate Mutual Funds module means firms can place orders of any type. Business Process Support is a set of modules (Imaging, Workflow, Document Production, and Archiving) that automate business processes and eliminate a firm's reliance on and maintenance of paper documents. CSS has also developed a unique database that is powerful and flexible enough to be a separate product, one with potential applications in other areas of financial services.

Product Feature List

- Scalability and extensibility (to fit any size and to grow with the firm)
- Speed, reliability, and accuracy
- Stand-alone or interfaced with legacy system
- Designed for the complete integration of firm needs
- Browser-based, which provides all functionality from remote locations
- Customizable
- Ease of implementation
- Low-cost hardware requirements
- Year 2000 and OATS compliant

Pricing: Custom, based on user requirements.

Hardware requirements:

CSS Client:

Pentium 200 MHz with 256 KB cache
64 MB RAM
1.6 gB Drive
Video Card with 2MB
10/100BaseT NIC

Web Server:

Pentium II 333 MHz or dual processor with 512 KB cache
256 MB RAM
2 gB system drive
2 gB drive
100BaseT NIC

Application Server:

Dual processor Pentium Pro
200 MHz or 333 MHz with 512 KB L2 cache
256 MB RAM
2 gB system drive
4 gB application drive
100BaseT NIC
Internal CD-ROM drive

Message Switch Server:

Pentium Pro 200 MHz with 512 KB L2 cache
256 MB RAM
2 gB system drive
2 gB application drive
100BaseT NIC

Database Server:

Dual or Quad processor Pentium Pro
200 MHz with 512 KB L2 cache
512 MB or 1024 MB RAM
2 gB system drive
Disk space dependent on database size
100BaseT NIC
Internal CD-ROM drive

Software requirements: Microsoft Windows 95 or Windows 98, Microsoft Windows NT Workstation and Windows NT Server, Microsoft SQL Server 6.5, Microsoft Office 97, Internet Explorer 4.01, Internet Information Server 4.0 (including Microsoft Transaction Server)

SYSTEM MONITORING

Computer Science Innovations, Inc.

Address: 1235 Evans Road, Melbourne, FL 32904-2314
Phone: (407) 676-2923
(888) 823-2923
Fax: (407) 676-2355
E-Mail: poolplus@csihq.com
Web Site: http://www.csihq.com/lookout
Sales Contact Name: Rudy Hallenbeck (ext. 218), Vice President, Sales and Marketing

■ Product: LookOut

Version Number: 2.0

Description Summary: Lookout is a task management utility for Windows 95 or Windows NT that initiates the execution of application software, tracks active tasks, and notifies the system operator when the task ends or problems occur. Lookout provides invaluable assistance to system administrators by automatically performing several activities that otherwise require manual intervention. Windows Magazine rated Lookout Version 1 as

APPENDIX

Superior Shareware in May 1997. Lookout is a simple, yet very powerful utility that significantly enhances the productivity of system administrators. Lookout eliminates the mundane task of monitoring application software programs and waiting for tasks to complete. For example, an application may require considerable time to finish processing or an application may be executing which is never supposed to stop. Lookout recognizes when a task ends and can notify the system operator via a traditional message box, a sound file or audible beep, electronic mail, event log (Windows NT only), voice telephone, pager, or fax. Lookout can even automatically restart the application, if desired.

Product Feature List

- Lookout offers a variety of job scheduling options
- Applications can be scheduled to start at a specific time, execute until a specific time, execute at specific time intervals, or execute for a specified duration of time
- Lookout itself can be initiated at system startup and subsequently execute applications in accordance with a predefined schedule of events completely without human intervention
- Lookout can be setup to monitor task execution via process status, processor utilization, and now in Version 2, the Windows NT event log

Monitored Activities

- Task startup
- Task shutdown
- Task CPU usage
- Windows NT event log notification methods
- E-mail
- Sound file
- Message box
- Event log (NT only)
- Modem/beeper
- FAX

Pricing: A single license is $89 and can be obtained via the Internet at http://www.csihq.com/lookout. A demonstration copy with a 30-day trial period is also available at the same site.

Hardware requirements: N/A

Software requirements: Windows 95 or Windows NT

TRADING

Reuters America, Inc.

Address: 1700 Broadway, 2nd Floor, New York, NY 10019
Phone: (212) 603-3300
Fax: (212) 603-3671
E-mail: info.risk@reuters.com
Web site: www.risk.reuters.com
Sales Contacts: Rosanne Donahue or Ulises Calatayud

■ PRODUCT: Kondor+

Version: v.1.8

Product Summary: Kondor+ is an integrated trading application providing deal capture, position keeping, portfolio valuation, realized and unrealized P&L analyses, and tactical risk management capabilities. Kondor+ tracks credit risk, counterparty risk, settlement risk, asset/liability management, interest rate exposure, VaR (Delta/Gamma approach), scenario analysis as well as sensitivity ladders, simulations, and hedge recommendations. Kondor+ calculates sensitivities including duration, convexity, delta, and gamma. Real-time hedge equivalent ratios are calculated for equities and fixed income instruments. Gap and hedging reports can also be run on demand. Kondor+ is designed to handle the widest range of financial instruments, including money market, fixed income securities, foreign exchange transactions, equities, exchange traded, and over-the-counter derivatives.

Pricing: Kondor+ installation begins at $300,000, scaleable depending on nature of assets chosen and number of traders supported
Hardware requirements: Solaris 2.5.1, Windows NT 4.0, AIX 4.1, or HP-UX 10.20

Wilco Systems Inc.

Address: 17 State Street, New York, N.Y. 10004
Phone: (212) 269-3970
Fax: (212) 269-3925
E-Mail: info@wilco-int.com
Web Site: www.wilco-int.com
Sales Contact Name: Bob Santangelo

APPENDIX

■ Product: Gloss

Version: 2.6

Description Summary: An integrated system for the trade processing, clearing, settlement, and accounting of a wide range of instruments including international debt, equities, treasury and repo. Gloss provides a highly efficient STP environment with an extensive range of functionality for international, domestic, and emerging markets. It is a proven product with a large user base that spans the world's major time zones — an impressive list of international clients includes Nomura, Merrill Lynch, Goldman Sachs, Bear Stearns, and others. Many of these have chosen Gloss as an integral part of their global strategy.

Pricing: Not disclosed
Hardware requirements: UNIX server with UNIX NT or Windows clients
Software requirements: UNIX operating system and Sybase database

■ Product: GlossTRADER

Version: 1.70

Description Summary: A real-time trading and decision support system for fixed income trading, sales, and repo desks. The system integrates the major tasks faced by a modern trading desk, offering deal capture, position keeping, and pricing functionality.

Pricing: Not disclosed
Hardware requirements: Pentium PC or NT workstation
Software requirements: Windows NT operating system and MS SQL Server database

■ Product: Gloss STP Explorer

Version: 1.3

Description Summary: Gloss STP Explorer is a unique, proactive exception-handling facility that has recently been added to further enhance the Gloss system's ability to reduce operational risk. Both business and systems processing exceptions are now routed dynamically to the relevant users' desktops the instant that the exception occurs. Users can then analyze, repair, and resubmit using an easy-to-use graphical application. This means that exposure to unsettled trades, regulatory reporting delays, and reduced system performance is kept to an absolute minimum.

Pricing: Not disclosed
Hardware requirements: UNIX server with UNIX NT or Windows clients
Software requirements: UNIX operating system and Sybase database

■ **Product: GlossHUB**

Version: 2.6

Description Summary: A transaction-oriented middleware product that provides guaranteed end-to-end messaging between two or more separate systems. GlossHUB handles message format transformation and routing between systems using different formats and different communications protocols. GlossHUB systems can easily be linked to build a network of message routing systems.

Pricing: Not disclosed
Hardware requirements: UNIX server with UNIX NT or Windows clients
Software requirements: UNIX operating system and Sybase database

■ **Product: GlossLINK**

Version: 3.4

Description Summary: Comprises a range of software modules which provide links to major international exchanges, clearing centers, global custodians, and other system. These include Euroclear, Cedel, Trax, ISMA price reporting, Bloomberg trade feed, interface to ADP's Brokerage Processing System (US), Crest (London Stock Exchange), SEGA (Zurich Stock Exchange), DTC (US), DWZ (Germany), CGO (Central Gilts Office, UK), SEQUAL, telex, and many others.

Pricing: Not disclosed
Hardware requirements: UNIX server with UNIX NT or Windows clients
Software requirements: UNIX operating system and Sybase database

---

TREASURY MANAGEMENT

Selkirk Financial Technologies, Inc.

Address: Suite 430 - 475 West Georgia Street, Vancouver V6B4M9 BC, Canada
Phone: (604) 682-2862
(888) 682-2862
Fax: (604) 682-1059
E-Mail: evangelista@selkirkfinancial.com
Web Site: www.selkirkfinancial.com
Sales Contact Name: Geoff Bullen

APPENDIX

■ **Product: Treasury Manager**

Version Number: 4.2

Description Summary: Treasury Manager™ is a fully-integrated Microsoft Windows-based treasury management system. Its cash, portfolio, and risk management capabilities are designed to help corporations make better informed treasury decisions while introducing the structure and controls required in today's treasury world. The system's suite of applications allows treasury staff to share information and collaborate on important projects while forecasting cash and managing foreign exchange, debt, investment, and derivative portfolios. Customers can expect a payback of less than 1 year.

TRANSACTIONAL APPLICATION SERVICES

Persistence Software

Address: 1720 South Amphlett Blvd., Suite 300, San Mateo, CA 94402
Phone: (650) 372-3600
(800) 803-8491
Fax: (650) 341-8432
E-Mail: info@persistence.com
Web Site: www.persistence.com
Sales Contact Name: Al Cohen, VP of Worldwide Sales Operations, (650) 372-3668, alcohen@persistence.com

■ **Product: PowerTier for C++ and PowerTier for Enterprise JavaBeans**

Version Number: 4.4

Description Summary: Persistence Software is a leading provider of Transactional Application Servers for developing, deploying, and managing enterprise applications. Persistence PowerTier for Enterprise Java-Beans (EJB) dramatically reduces development time with container-managed persistent objects, and optimizes performance with shared transactional caching. PowerTier integrates with leading component modeling and development tools, delivering an open solution for Server-based Rapid Application Development (S-RAD). Over 200 Global-1000 companies have accelerated the delivery of applications and ensured scalability using PowerTier's patented object-relational technology.

Persistence PowerTier provides the industry leading implementation of the Enterprise JavaBeans 1.0 specification, with full support for Entity Beans and container-managed persistent objects. This enables developers to work with relational data as a set of objects, and eliminates 90 percent of the SQL data access, JDBC connection and transaction management code within an application while simplifying issues such as object mapping, identity, caching, and concurrency.

Product Feature List

- Fully compliant with the Enterprise JavaBeans 1.0 specification
- Full support for the both Session Beans and Entity Beans
- Automatic generation of Container Managed Persistent Objects
- Automatic creation of deployment classes and interfaces
- Embedded object-relational mapping
- Shared transactional object cache
- Multi-threaded server
- Java Transaction Service (JTS) support
- RMI and CORBA integration

Pricing: Please contact Persistence Sales at (800) 803-8491

Hardware & Software requirements

Windows NT: Pentium PC or better, 20 MB of free disk space, a minimum of 64 MB of RAM, installed client-side RDBMS libraries, and verification that you can connect to your RDBMS from the PC. Windows NT 4.0 Service pack 3, Sybase 11.x ctlib, Oracle 7.3.4 and 8.0.4 servers with 7.3.4 clients. Oracle 8 servers with Oracle 9 clients, Informix 7.X and 9.X servers. 7.X servers are supported with 9.X clients only. Microsoft SQL Server 6.5

UNIX: Solaris 2.5.1+, 20 MB of free disk space, a minimum of 64 MB of RAM, Sybase 11.x ctlib, Oracle 7.3.4 and 8.0.4 servers with 7.3.4 clients. Oracle 8 servers with Oracle 9 clients. Informix 7.X and 9.X servers. 7.X servers are supported with 9.X clients only

Java Compilers: Sun JDK 1.1.6 (or higher), 1.1.6 is recommended, Symantec Visual Cafe 2.5+

VIRUS PROTECTION/SECURITY

Finjan Inc.

Address: 2860 Zanker Road, Suite 201, San Jose, CA 95134-2120
Phone: (408) 324-0228
(888) FINJAN-8
Fax: (408) 324-0229
E-Mail: info@finjan.com

APPENDIX

Web Site: www.finjan.com
Sales Contact Name: Robert Tas, Vice President of Sales

■ Product: Finjan SurfinGate

Version Number: 4.03

Description Summary: Finjan SurfinGate is the industry's first gateway-level mobile code security solution, enabling protection of corporate networks from hostile or unintentional damage caused by Internet mobile code technologies such as Java, ActiveX, JavaScript, and Visual Basic Script. SurfinGate 4.03™ is an essential mobile code security tool for any business using the Internet, extranets, or intranets for business transactions. With its unique patent-pending, content-inspection technology, SurfinGate helps protect businesses from the many forms industrial espionage, data modification, data deletion, and e-mail fraud caused by hackers using Internet mobile code technologies. SurfinGate inspects Java, HTML, JavaScript, and ActiveX mobile code content at the gateway level, away from critical resources, and assigns a unique ID and applet profile to incoming code, noting any possible security breaches. A SurfinGate server can be positioned after a corporate firewall and any other existing proxies, and also acts as an HTTP server. This architecture allows mobile code traffic to be stopped and inspected before attacks can happen.

Product Feature List

- Provides complete, centralized control over Java, JavaScript, ActiveX, and other mobile code activity in the corporation
- Helps prevent undetected, costly mobile code attacks such as political hack attacks, corporate netspionage attempts and Web graffiti damage
- Provides detailed logs and mobile code reports that help prove "minimum level of care" security often legally required in public companies
- Enables safe Internet/intranet/extranet surfing while taking full advantage of Java, JavaScript, and ActiveX technologies
- OPSEC™ CVP API Protocol Compliance: SurfinGate 4.03 supports the open platform for Secure Enterprise Connectivity (OPSEC™), which allows it to be deployed seamlessly within any OPSEC-certified enterprise-wide security framework

Pricing: $1250 (10 users) to $18,500 (unlimited)
Hardware requirements: 233 MHz Pentium and above, Sun Sparc Ultra 10, 128 to 256 MB RAM, 20 MB disk space
Software requirements: Windows NT 4.0 or Solaris 2.5.1 and 2.6

■ Product: Finjan SurfinShield Corporate

Version Number: 4.0

Description Summary: Finjan SurfinShield Corporate is the first mobile code security solution that offers centralized security management for enterprise desktops, allowing IT managers to set corporate-wide security policies from a central console. SurfinShield Corporate keeps an eye on all the Java and ActiveX elements running on each individual desktop, continually monitoring mobile code behavior during run-time. Depending on the security level selection, SurfinShield Corporate automatically kills any Java or ActiveX element that tries to breach the security rules before the code is allowed to do damage.

With SurfinShield Corporate, companies can manage Internet mobile code security on thousands of individual desktops from one central console. It can be integrated seamlessly into a corporate network configuration, interoperating with other security devices including firewalls and other corporate software distribution products. This added layer of protection helps to secure against mobile code that is encrypted or compressed and not inspected at the firewall. It also protects employees working at home or on the road with laptop PCs.

Product Feature List

- Centralized security policy management and administration
- Includes X-Box™, Finjan's proprietary sandbox for Java and ActiveX, and the Finjan DMZ, which runs ActiveX controls in an isolated environment
- Automatic or Manual Kill (stop running) of applets and controls
- Centralized suspicious applets and controls database provides a list of suspicious applets and controls, which is updated in real-time and shared by all SurfinShield clients
- Centralized installation allows a pre-configured (by the System Administrator) SurfinShield client application in a public server for easy distribution
- Java Demilitarized Zone (DMZ) adds an extra layer of security to the Java Security Manager by extending the security options that the JSM provides
- A monitor bar allows the user to view and control each Java applet and ActiveX control that is running
- Full Security Configuration, including File Access Permissions, that allow users to benefit from the advantages of Java applets and ActiveX controls without compromising internal security

Pricing: $165 per seat, with price reductions based on quantity
Hardware requirements: 10 MB disk space, 16 MB RAM
Software requirements: Windows 95, Windows NT

Trend Micro, Inc.

Address: 10101 N. De Anza Blvd. 4th Floor, Cupertino, CA 95014
Phone: (408) 257-1500
(800) 228-5651
Fax: (408) 863-6362
E-Mail: sales@trendmicro.com
Web Site: www.antivirus.com
Sales Contact Name: Jim Leonard

■ Product: InterScan VirusWall

Version: 2.52

Description Summary: InterScan VirusWall is a high-performance three-in-one product suite that provides comprehensive virus protection at the Internet gateway. Each product component can be installed and managed independently or in concert, allowing great flexibility and scalability for small to large networks. Real-time scanning stops viruses and other malicious code from using the gateway as an access point to internal networks. Detects viruses and blocks Java and ActiveX malicious code hidden in SMTP mail, HTTP, and FTP traffic. Server-based, Internet-enabled management tools give administrators maximum control over virus protection throughout the enterprise. Available for Windows NT (Intel and DEC Alpha), Solaris, and HP-UX.

Product Feature List

- Scans and cleans inbound and outbound SMTP mail and attachments in real time
- Optionally blocks Java applets, ActiveX objects, and unsigned or non-commercial software (NT version only)
- Detects and removes known and unknown macro viruses on the fly
- Sends customizable warnings messages to sender, recipients, and administrator
- Lets you preschedule pattern file updates for automatic download from the Web
- Includes viewing utility for real-time performance monitoring
- Tracks infections through detailed activity log
- Includes Windows GUI and ISAPI/CGI Web browser configuration interfaces
- Available for Windows NT, Solaris and HP-UX; DEC UNIX and AIX implementations coming soon

Pricing: Up to 25 users, $950

System Requirements:

Windows NT version: Windows NT 3.51 or above, PC with Pentium processor, 16 MB RAM, 12 MB disk space (at installation)

Solaris version: Solaris 2.5 or above, 32 MB RAM, 150 MB swap space, 15 MB disk space (at installation)

HP-UX version: HP-UX 10.x, 64 MB RAM, 100 MB swap space, 100 MB disk space (at installation)

■ **Product: OfficeScan for Small Business Server**

Version: 2.0

Description Summary: OfficeScan for Microsoft Small Business Server (SBS) provides around-the-clock real-time protection against viruses from any source to all desktops on SBS networks. Deploys centrally from an internal Web server, using ActiveX components or log-in scripts to deliver client antivirus software. Desktop configurations, including scanning and cleaning, are centrally controlled through a single management console. OfficeScan for SBS installs directly to the Internet Information Server and integrates automatically as a separate module into the SBS interface. An HTTP agent at the desktop listens for upgrade, update, and configuration messages from the server and downloads the needed components from the server. Virus activity is reported to the server in real time by the client component.

Product Feature List

- Deploys from the server, using ActiveX components
- Centrally controls desktop configuration
- HTTP agent at the desktop listens for update messages from the server
- Reports virus activities in real time
- Includes real-time scanning of Exchange mailboxes
- Detects and removes known and unknown viruses, including macro viruses

Pricing: Up to 50 users, $450

System Requirements:
Server: Microsoft Small Business Server (Windows NT)
Client: Microsoft Windows 95

■ **Product: ScanMail for Lotus Notes**

Version: 1.4

Description Summary: ScanMail® for Lotus Notes and Domino detects and removes viruses hidden in databases, as well as e-mail attachments, before infections can spread to the desktop. Scans and cleans e-mail attachments in real time at the router; also scans and cleans databases and modified data during replication in real time. Scans existing message attachments in mailboxes to root out old infections. On-demand database scanning cleans existing infections. ScanMail provides frequent automatic Web-based virus pattern updates and maintains a comprehensive activity log. Its configuration interface is fully integrated with the Lotus Notes user interface. Available for Windows NT and Solaris.

Product Feature List

- Scans and cleans mail and attachments in real time at the mail router
- Scans and cleans databases in real time
- On demand database scanning to clean existing infections
- Scans and cleans all modified data in real time during replication
- Detects and removes known and unknown macro viruses on the fly
- Functions as a native Notes server task
- Scans Web traffic on Domino servers
- Updates virus pattern files automatically
- Sends customizable warning messages to sender, recipient, and administrator
- Remote management from any Notes workstation
- Tracks infections through detailed Notes-format activity log

Pricing: Up to 25 users, $750
System Requirements: Windows NT 4.0 or above with Lotus Notes Server 4.0 or above, or Sun Workstation running Solaris 2.5 and Lotus Notes Server 4.0 or above

■ Product: ScanMail for Microsoft Exchange

Version: 1.53

Description Summary: ScanMail® for Microsoft Exchange Server detects and removes viruses hidden in e-mail attachments and public folders in real time before infections can spread to the desktop. Scans manually or at prescheduled intervals. Automatic updates can be configured at prescheduled intervals or accessed manually and are distributed to all connected post offices. ScanMail's virus scanning is transparent unless a virus is detected, when customizable warning messages are sent to administrator, sender, and recipients. ScanMail's powerful scanning engine uses rule-based and pattern recognition technology and includes Trend Micro's MacroTrap, which detects and removes known and unknown macro viruses. Available for Windows NT (Intel and DEC Alpha).

Product Feature List

- Scans and cleans files attached to Exchange mail messages in real time
- Scans and cleans shared files in real time
- Scans and cleans public folders in real time
- Detects and removes known and unknown macro viruses on the fly
- Includes custom solutions to new virus problems through Trend's Virtual Virus Hospital
- Sends customizable warning messages to sender, recipients, and administrator
- Enhanced performance mode for large installations
- Installs and updates at the Exchange Server automatically
- Lets you preschedule update deliveries for automatic download from the web
- Tracks infections through detailed activity log
- Available for Intel and DEC Alpha platforms

Pricing: . Up to 25 users, $750
System Requirements: Windows NT 4.0 or above with Microsoft Exchange Server 4.0 or later

■ Product: ServerProtect

Version: 4.52

Description Summary: ServerProtect efficiently safeguards multiple servers and domains from virus attack with next-generation antivirus software that can be installed and managed from a single console. All servers within one domain can be automatically configured and installed concurrently, using native NT or NetWare tools for secure remote management.

ServerProtect automatically downloads new virus patterns and distributes them to all servers in the same domain. Provides comprehensive logging and reporting capabilities that take in all desktops in every domain on the network and is available for Windows NT and NetWare.

Product Feature List

- Provides centralized multiple domain installation and management
- Offers secure remote management
- Lets you preschedule automatic scans and update deliveries
- Tracks infections through detailed activity log
- Detects and removes known and unknown macro viruses
- Integrates with and manages Trend's desktop protection software
- Updates and distributes virus patterns with a single click and supports proxy server
- Scans for malicious Java and ActiveX code (NT version)

- Available for Windows NT and NetWare

Pricing: Up to 25 users, $600

System Requirements: Windows NT: NT Server 3.51 or later, Intel PC with Pentium processor or better or DEC Alpha, 32MB RAM, and 8MB free disk space. NetWare: NetWare 3.11 or later, Intel 386 PC or better, 8 MB RAM, and 8 MB free disk space

■ Product: ScanMail Lotus for cc:Mail

Version: 1.62

Description Summary: ScanMail® for Lotus cc:Mail scans traffic passing through the cc:Mail server, stopping viruses from using the network as a distribution mechanism. Scans and cleans files attached to e-mail messages in real time, as well as existing message attachments in mailboxes to root out old infections. ScanMail detects and removes known and unknown macro viruses on the fly, using Trend's powerful virus scanning engine. Includes batch scanning capability for multiple remote post offices. Supports multiple users logging into a single PC and scans manually or at prescheduled intervals. Provides frequent automatic Web-based virus pattern updates. Available for all major cc:Mail platforms.

Product Feature List

- Scans and cleans files attached to mail messages in real time
- Detects and removes known and unknown macro viruses on the fly
- Protects both LAN and Remote cc:Mail users
- Batch scanning capability for multiple remote post offices
- Supports up to 512 Post Offices on one LAN
- Sends customizable warning emssages to sender, recipients, and administrator
- Installs and updates at the mail server automatically
- Tracks infections through detailed activity log
- Includes automatic deployment of software from server to workstations
- Provides centralized console administration
- Automatic pattern updates via Internet or BBS, with support for proxy server

Pricing: Up to 25 users, $750

System Requirements:

Server: Novell Netware 3.x or above or Windows NT Server 3.51 or above. Banyan, LANtastic, and DEC Pathworks networks are also supported, client piece installation cannot be automated in these environments

Client: Windows 3.x, Windows 95, or Windows NT Workstation 3.51 or above

cc:Mail: Lotus cc:Mail LAN and Remote 2.x through 8.x:DB6 and DB8databases supported

■ Product: Microsoft Mail

Version: 1.0

Description Summary: ScanMai[®] for Microsoft Mail scans and cleans files attached to e-mail messages in real time, before infections can spread to the desktop. Installs and updates at the mail server automatically and deploys software from the server to workstations. Provides frequent automatic Web-based virus pattern updates. ScanMail's virus scanning is transparent unless a virus is detected, when customizable warning messages are sent to administrator, sender, and recipients. ScanMail's powerful scanning engine uses rule-based and pattern recognition technology including Trend Micro's MacroTrap, which detects and removes known and unknown macro viruses. Available for Windows and Windows NT with Microsoft Mail.

Product Feature List

- Scans and cleans files attached to e-mail messages in real time
- Detects and removes known and unknown macro viruses on the fly
- Sends customizable warnings of virus infections to sender, recipients, and administrator
- Installs and updates at the mail server automatically
- Includes automatic deployment of software from server to workstations
- Tracks infections through a detailed activity log
- Includes custom solutions to new virus problems through Trend's Virtual Virus Hospital
- Provides centralized console administration
- Includes automatic, prescheduled virus pattern updates via Internet or BBS

Pricing: Up to 25 users, $750

System Requirements:

Server: Windows NT 3.51 or above, Windows 95 or above, PC with 486 processor, 8 MB of RAM, 4 MB of disk space

Client: Windows NT 3.51 or above, Windows 3.1 or above, PC with 386 processor or above, 4 MB of RAM, mapped drive for M:\ for post office

About the Editor

JESSICA KEYES is president of New Art Technologies, Inc., a high-technology software development firm. Prior to New Art Technologies, she was Managing Director of R&D for the New York Stock Exchange and has been an officer with the Swiss Bank Company and Banker's Trust, both in New York City.

Keyes has a Master's Degree from New York University where she did research in the area of artificial intelligence. She has given seminars at universities such as Carnegie Mellon, Boston University, the University of Illinois, James Madison University, and San Francisco State University. She is a frequent keynote speaker on the topics of competitive strategy using information technology and marketing on the information highway, and is an advisor for DataPro, McGraw-Hill's computer research arm, as well as a member of the Sprint Business Council. She also is a founding Board of Director member of the New York Software Industry Association and has recently completed a 2-year term on the Mayor of New York City's Small Business Advisory Council.

A noted columnist and correspondent with over 150 articles published, Keyes is a publisher of the *Small Business Journal* and several other computer-related publications. She also has authored and/or edited 12 books.

The New Intelligence: AI in Financial Services, HarperBusiness, 1990

The Handbook of Expert Systems in Manufacturing, McGraw-Hill, 1991

Infotrends: The Competitive Use of Information, McGraw-Hill, 1992

The Software Engineering Productivity Handbook, McGraw-Hill, 1993

The Handbook of Multimedia, McGraw-Hill, 1994

The Productivity Paradox, McGraw-Hill, 1994

Technology Trendlines, Van Nostrand Reinhold, 1995

How to be a Successful Internet Consultant, McGraw-Hill, 1997

Webcasting: Broadcast to your Customers over the Net, McGraw-Hill, 1997

Datacasting, McGraw-Hill, 1997

Handbook of Technology in Financial Services, Auerbach, 1999

Internet Management, Auerbach, 2000

Infotrends was selected as one of the best business books of 1992 by the *Library Journal*. *The Software Engineering Productivity Handbook* was the main selection for the Newbridge book club for computer professionals.

The *McGraw-Hill Multimedia Handbook* is now in its second reprint and was translated into Chinese and Japanese during 1995. *How to be a Successful Internet Consultant, Webcasting*, and *Datacasting* have recently been translated into Japanese.

Index

Milton Keynes UK
Ingram Content Group UK Ltd.
UKHW031536071024
449327UK00023B/1842